RESOURCES
OF THE
EARTH
∎

RESOURCES OF THE EARTH

■

JAMES R. CRAIG
Virginia Polytechnic Institute and State University

DAVID J. VAUGHAN
The University of Manchester

BRIAN J. SKINNER
Yale University

PRENTICE HALL
Englewood Cliffs, New Jersey 07632

Library of Congress Cataloging-in-Publication Data

Craig, James R., (date)
  Resources of the earth / James R. Craig, David J. Vaughan, Brian
J. Skinner.
      p. cm.
  Bibliography: p.
  includes index.
  ISBN 0-13-774423-4
    1. Natural resources.   2. Environmental policy.   I. Vaughan,
David J., (date).   II. Skinner, Brian J., (date).   III. Title.
HC21.C72 1988
333.7—dc19   87-29502
                                                           CIP

Editorial/production supervision: *Maria McColligan*
Chapter openings and cover design: *Lorraine Mullaney*
Manufacturing buyer: *Paula Massenaro*

© 1988 by Prentice-Hall, Inc.
A Division of Simon & Schuster
Englewood Cliffs, New Jersey 07632

ISBN 0-13-774423-4

Printed in the United States of America
10 9 8 7 6 5 4 3 2 1

Prentice-Hall International (UK) Limited, *London*
Prentice-Hall of Australia Pty. Limited, *Sydney*
Prentice-Hall Canada Inc., *Toronto*
Prentice-Hall Hispanoamericana, S.A., *Mexico*
Prentice-Hall of India Private Limited, *New Delhi*
Prentice-Hall of Japan, Inc., *Tokyo*
Simon & Schuster Asia Pte, Ltd., *Singapore*
Editora Prentice-Hall do Brasil, Ltda., *Rio de Janeiro*

Our entire society rests upon—and is dependent upon—our water, our land, our forests, and our minerals. How we use these resources influences our health, security, economy and well being.

John F. Kennedy
February 23, 1961

CONTENTS

4

ENERGY FROM FOSSIL FUELS

71

5

ENERGY FOR THE FUTURE—
NUCLEAR POWER AND OTHER POSSIBLE ALTERNATIVES

123

6

ABUNDANT METALS

165

7

THE GEOCHEMICALLY SCARCE METALS

197

8

FERTILIZER AND CHEMICAL MINERALS

245

9
BUILDING MATERIALS AND OTHER INDUSTRIAL MINERALS
269

10
WATER RESOURCES
299

11
SOIL AS A RESOURCE
339

12
FUTURE RESOURCES
358

PREFACE

*"There is a mine for silver
and a place where gold is refined.
Iron is taken from the earth,
and copper is smelted from ore.
Man puts an end to the darkness;
he searches the farthest recesses
for ore in the blackest darkness.
Far from where people dwell he cuts shafts
in places forgotten by the foot of man;
far from men he dangles and sways.
The earth, from which food comes,
is transformed below as by fire;
Sapphires come from its rocks,
and its dust contains nuggets of gold. . . .
Man's hand assaults the flinty rock
and lays bare the roots of the mountains.
He tunnels through the rock;
his eyes see all its treasures.
He searches the sources of the rivers
and brings hidden things to light.
But where can wisdom be found?"*

(Job 28:1-6, 9-12 RSV)

We live in an age of rapidly increasing world population and rapid technological advance. The burden of feeding and providing for this population is ever-growing and is coupled with increasing demands for improvements in the material quality of life. Yet, the Earth has only limited resources and exploiting these resources may itself lead to damage or destruction of a part of the living world. The issues that concern the resources of the Earth are of vital importance to each and every one of us, yet few people have a sound knowledge of exactly what the Earth's resources are, and how they are located, exploited, and utilized. The irregular distribution of resources leads to the complex inter-relationships that are expressed in the patterns of world trade. These complexities and the impact that resource exploitation and utilization have on the environment in which we live are also understood by relatively few people.

This book, *Resources of the Earth,* has been written in the hope of increasing the general level of knowledge and understanding in these truly vital areas. It is aimed chiefly at the college or university student, although we hope it will also find readers amongst those who have long since left their college days. No doubt, some of the students who read this text will go on to study the Earth, mineral, environmental, or related sciences at the higher level, but it is hoped that many whose major interest lie outside these areas will find it of value. It is written at a level that presupposes some background in science, although not necessarily above that found in senior science classes in high schools in the U.S.A. or "sixth forms" in Great Britain. There is an extensive glossary and appendices to help those unfamiliar with the terminology and some of the concepts used. In this text, the term "resources" is used to mean those chiefly inorganic material resources that are traditionally part of the disciplines of geology, mineralogy, and soil science. Thus, metals, industrial rocks and minerals, chemical minerals, water, and soils are all discussed at length. Major sections are devoted to fossil fuels such as coal and oil (which are, of course, organic in origin) and to nuclear power and alternative energy sources (solar, wind, wave, geothermal, etc.). There are also chapters dealing with the sources, exploitation, and utilization of these particular resources and chapters dealing with more general questions concerning historical and environmental aspects of Earth resources and with the question of resources for the future.

Perhaps our major objective in writing this book is best summed up in a quotation from our friend Dr. Paul Barton, Jr. of the United States Geological Survey. In his Presidential Address to the Society of Economic Geologists (Nov. 7, 1979), he said, "It is as important for the future voter to appreciate the realities of our resource-environment situation as it is to be able to read the ballot. I believe that our principal hope is in education. . . ."

ACKNOWLEDGMENTS

The authors are indebted to a great many individuals whose various ideas, comments, questions, and criticisms have contributed to the final text. Countless former students and professional colleagues have stimulated us and either provoked us with questions or educated us with answers. We are especially grateful to those who critically reviewed the manuscript at various stages—Dr. J. Donald Rimstidt, Polytechnic Institute and State Univ.; Dr. Half Zantop, Dartmouth Univ.; Dr. John E. Callahan, Appalachian State Univ.; Dr. Barbara Dexter, SUNY at Purchase; Dr. George McCormick, Univ. of Iowa; Dr. Lawrence D. Meinert, Washington State Univ. at Pullman; and Dr. Udo Fehn, Univ. of Rochester. In the preparation of the manuscript we wish to thank Peggy Keating, Christine Gee, and especially Margie Sentelle for the countless hours of typing and retyping. We are grateful to the many companies and individuals who contributed illustrations and to Llyn Sharp who helped in the preparation of so many photographs.

We dedicate this book to our wives and children, Lois, Nancie, and James; Heather and Emlyn; Catherine, Adrienne, Stephanie, and Thalassa.

James R. Craig
David J. Vaughan
Brian J. Skinner

RESOURCES
OF THE
EARTH

1

The world is constantly in a state of change. In order to meet the needs of a growing population, we must employ old and new techniques. The new technologies are more productive but require the use of greater amounts of resources. (Punjab, India; courtesy of the United Nations. Photograph by J. P. Laffonte.)

MINERALS:
THE FOUNDATIONS
OF SOCIETY

THE COMPLEX NETWORK

All the materials needed for health and prosperity in our complex society come from the earth. Food and water, clothes and dwellings, automobiles, trains, radios, and even the paper on which these words are printed all contain one or more materials drawn from the earth. How straightforward it would be if we could consider uses and needs of each material irrespective of the others. However, that is not possible because the way we use materials involves a network of complex dependencies by which use of each material contributes directly or indirectly to the use of every other material.

Consider bread, an everyday commodity most of us take for granted. Bread is made from the flour of cereal grains such as wheat and rye. The flour-making process employs grinding wheels made of steel alloys, and the grinder is driven by motors powered by electricity derived by burning oil, natural gas, or coal. The flour-making process therefore depends on supplies of fuel drawn from the earth and supplies of iron to make steel. When we take a step back in the bread-making process and consider the production of a grain such as wheat, a still wider pattern of dependency can be discerned. Wheat requires a fertile soil for growth and an adequate supply of water; both soil and water are important resources. The farmer who grows the grain uses a tractor to till the soil. The metals in the tractor and the

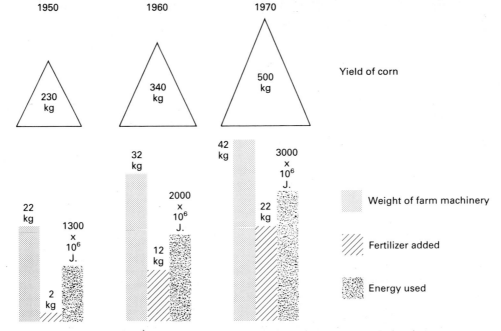

FIGURE 1-1. The relationship between production of food and consumption of mineral resources. To increase the yield of corn the farmer has to apply more fertilizer and till the land more intensively, thereby employing more and heavier farm machinery. The energy figures take into account such factors as the energy used to make tractors and prepare fertilizers. (After Pimental et al., *Science*, vol. 182 (1973) p. 443.) The graphs were drawn from data compiled in 1973; since that time the upward trends have continued. By 1980, the average amount of fertilizer added in the United States was more than double the 1970 figure, while in Japan and some countries in Europe it had reached levels twice as high as those in the United States.

fuel to power it all come from the earth. To reap the maximum harvest the farmer must add fertilizer and any chemical constituents, such as nitrogen, phosphorous, and potassium, that the growing wheat may need but are not supplied in sufficient quantities by the soil. The source of these chemicals is once again the earth. Bread-making and modern bread-distributing processes are actually a good deal more complex than the picture just presented because they also involve such things as baking ovens, storage systems for the grain, transportation systems for the bread, and chains of stores through which it is sold. The point is that material production and the use of natural resources are interdependent, whether the resources are renewable plants, trees, and cereal grains, or nonrenewable mineral resources such as oil and steel. A less obvious point, but one that is equally important, is that supplies of food, metals, fer-

tilizers, fuels, and innumerable other resources come from widespread geographic areas. No country is completely self-sufficient. Therefore, efficient and effective use of resources requires an efficient and effective trading system.

An impressive demonstration of the way that use-rates of resources are interrelated is shown in Fig. 1.1. This figure records the relationship between the amount of corn (a renewable resource) produced per hectare, and three kinds of nonrenewable resources—the machinery used by the farmer, fertilizer added to the soil, and energy used to power the machinery and process the fertilizer chemicals. Food yields depend directly on the amounts of each of the nonrenewable resources.

The interrelationships between our uses of the earth's materials grows ever more complex. As new technologies are developed and as larger and more complex social structures emerge, we tend to use materials in larger quantities and in ever more diverse ways. As a consequence, humans are also building an increasing dependence on supplies of those same materials. Just as the yield of corn depends on the use of fuel, fertilizer, and machinery, so does the size of another renewable crop, the human population, depend on supplies of food and water, and therefore on supplies of fuels, metals, and other materials won from the earth. The world's population has reached its present size of more than 5 billion because there is a complicated network that manages to supply us with the food we need. Terrible scenes of the famines in Africa, caused by disruptions in food supplies, are all too common in the newspapers and on television (Fig. 1.2). Such local famines, whatever their cause, are small examples of what would happen on a much larger scale if the global food network were disrupted. Because adequate food production now requires adequate mineral and energy production, minerals and energy have also become parts of the foundation of all societies. If some of the important minerals and energy sources should run out, or for some reason be denied us, social chaos could ensue, and the eventual but inevitable result would be a drastic reduction of the world's population.

POPULATION GROWTH: THE FORCE THAT DRIVES RESOURCE CONSUMPTION

Many millenia ago our ancestors were hunters and gatherers for whom nature's random production of grains, fruits, and animals provided a bountiful sufficiency. When local population needs began to exceed the natural yield of materials, farming was developed out of the necessity to control, and thereby to increase, the production of fruits, grains, and meats. Archeologists suggest that farming commenced in the Middle East about 10,000 years ago. From that time on, the world's popu-

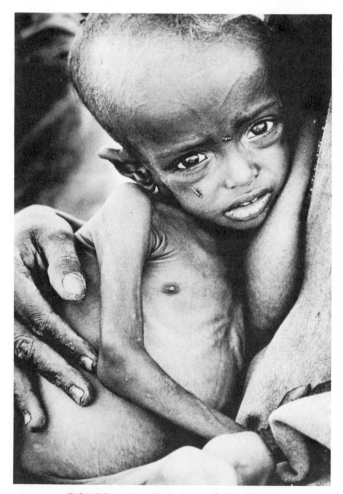

FIGURE 1-2. The dreadful evidence of starvation. This Ethiopian child of the Sahel region of Africa has suffered such severe malnutrition he cannot recover to a normal life. (Photograph courtesy of the Catholic Relief Services.)

lation has not only grown larger, it has grown ever more dependent on the controlled production of food and clothing and thereby on all the other materials we draw from the earth. So far as historians and archeologists have been able to decipher, world population grew slowly but more or less steadily through to the end of the sixteenth century A.D. (Fig. 1.3), interrupted only by occasional outbreaks of plagues, pestilences, and famines. One of the worst epidemics started in Europe when crusaders, in 1348, inadvertently brought back rats bearing plague-carrying fleas from Asia Minor. Starting in Italy, bubonic plague swept through Europe over a period of 2 years. Between a third and a quarter of the entire population died, and the populations of some cities were reduced by half. Small wonder that that particular outbreak was known as the Black Death.

At about the end of the sixteenth century, the world population began to grow more rapidly. The initial causes for the increase in rate seem to have been primarily due to advances in medical care and in hygiene in the cities, but a marked improvement in the diets of Europeans also occurred when potatoes and maize were introduced from the Americas. World population reached 1 billion by about 1800 A.D. One hundred and thirty years later, by 1930, the population reached 2 billion (Fig. 1.3). A scant 45 years was all the time it took before the population doubled again to reach 4 billion in 1975. During the 1970s the world population grew at a rate of about 2.2 percent a year. However, by 1983 the overall growth rate had declined to about 1.7 percent, although some regions still had much higher growth rates. Despite a slowing of the overall growth rate, the world population will probably number nearly 7 billion

by 2000 A.D. This stupendous number, which almost defies imagination, means that humankind has a task of herculean proportions ahead if all the new members of the human race are to be well fed and given the chance to enjoy a decent life. Many of the problems will be social and political in nature, but underlying everything will be the needed scientific and engineering expertise to exploit the earth's resources. Not only must the supplies be fairly divided, but exploitation must be carried out in such a way that the environment is not so fouled and irretrievably spoiled that we ruin the planet on which we live.

Neither the density of population nor growth rates of populations are uniform around the world. The most populous countries today are China, with about 1 billion people, and India with 7 hundred million. These two countries plus the United States, the Soviet Union, and Indonesia account for more than half of the present world population. The situation is changing rapidly, however. The rates of population growth in different countries seem to vary inversely with the extent of industrial development and standard of living. As a result, the technologically advanced countries tend to have both low birth rates and populations that have reached or are now approaching a stable size. In such countries it is not necessary for people to have large families to support them in their old age. Less-developed countries, on the other hand, tend to have higher birth rates and populations that are still expanding rapidly. Such countries tend to have agriculturally based economies, and large families are a way to provide the needed manual labor in order to assure security in old age. The difference between these two societies can be seen in the **age-sex**

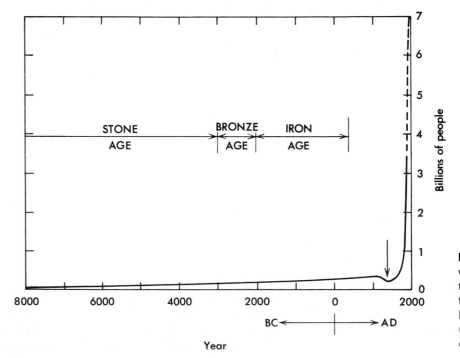

FIGURE 1-3. Growth of the world's population through history. Notice the arrow marking the sharp drop due to the Black Death that struck Europe in 1348. (Data from the Population Reference Bureau.)

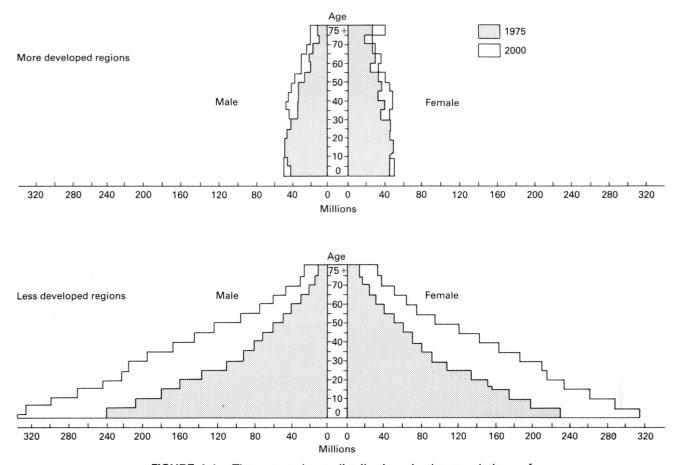

FIGURE 1-4. The age and sex distributions in the populations of the more developed countries differs dramatically from those of the less developed countries. In the more developed countries, where sizes of populations are approaching stability, the number of young people below 25 years of age is approximately the same as the number older than 25 years. This means that adults producing children are doing so at a rate that is approaching the one-for-one replacement rate. By contrast, the child-bearing adults in less developed countries tend to produce many more children than are needed for replacement, so that populations grow larger and the age-pyramid grows broader. (From the Global 2000 Report for the President of the United States, 1980.)

pyramids shown in Fig. 1.4. The near stability of the more developed regions is reflected in the fact that the number of people below child-bearing years is nearly identical to the number of adults producing children. Hence, there is an approximate one-for-one replacement. By contrast, adults in less-developed regions of the world are bearing many more children than are needed to replace themselves. As long as such a trend continues, the pyramid will get broader and the population of such a region will grow ever larger. Even if the adults in these populous regions started today to have just enough children to ensure a one-for-one replacement, the populations of these regions would continue to grow for at least two generations because of the present ratio of children to adults.

What will the ultimate size of the world's population be? Obviously, the population cannot continue to grow unchecked forever. This is true if for no other reason than the fact that in a continually growing population a point must be reached when there is no longer enough room for everyone to stand up. A recent study by a member of the Population Council (Demeny, 1984) used data and projections from the World Bank and the United Nations and drew conclusions that are not exactly comforting but that are more optimistic than the picture of an ever-increasing population. Demeny's encouraging conclusion is that population growth patterns in all countries of the world will follow a similar pattern (Fig. 1.5). Some countries are further advanced in the pattern than others. Demeny suggests that the populations of to-

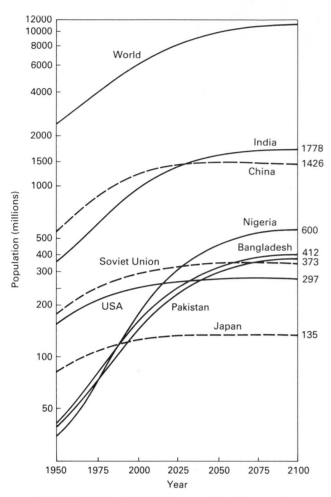

FIGURE 1-5. Projected growth of populations in several large countries, and for the world as a whole, to the year 2100. Demographers suggest that by 2100 A.D., the world will have attained a constant sized population. (From Demeny, *Population and Development Review*, vol. 10, no. 1 (1984) p. 103.)

day's less-developed countries will eventually level off despite the present high birth rates. The indication is that rates of population growth for all countries will decline and approach zero sometime during the next 120 years. Projecting demographic trends far into the future is an uncertain process at best. Nevertheless, present trends suggest that by the year 2100 A.D. the world's population will have levelled off to a number between 11 and 12 billion people. The seven most populous countries in decreasing order of size, in the year 2100 A.D. are predicted to be: India, China, Nigeria, Bangladesh, Pakistan, Indonesia, and the Soviet Union. These seven countries will account for approximately 50 percent of the world's population. The times in the future when the populations of different countries level out will vary from country to country, but all will have reached a stable figure by about 2100 A.D.

Can the earth supply the material needed for 11 billion people to enjoy a reasonable life? Some experts believe that 11 billion is far too large for a continuous and healthy balance to be attained in food and other material supplies. Others are convinced that economic and technological growth will help us find ways to meet the challenge, and that the world's population can safely grow to an even larger size than 11 billion. Possibly both sets of experts are too extreme in their conclusions, but the final answer lies in the future. Despite uncertainties, many of the problems that must be faced are already apparent—problems such as a disparity in living standards between regions that are industrially advanced but poor in mineral resources, as opposed to regions that are rich in resources but little developed industrially. The forces that drive resource consumption are human needs and desires. The controls underlying resource availability and use, however, are often geological and environmental. The interplay between availability and need is probably the most difficult problem the human race has to face, and it is one of the basic issues that must be confronted in trying to end such a continuing scourge as war.

This book addresses the environmental and geological questions involved with resource use. However, we must remember that use and production of resources are inevitably intertwined with, and immensely complicated by, social, political, and strategic issues.

MATERIALS WE USE

No classification of natural resources is completely satisfactory, but one convenient way to start the classification is to separate resources into two broad groups—renewable resources and nonrenewable resources. **Renewable resources** are those materials that are replenished on short time scales of a few months or years. Examples are the growing plants and animals from which we get our food, the energy we draw from the wind, flowing water, and the sun's heat. Use of renewable resources raises questions concerning rates of use rather than the ultimate total quantity of a given resource that shall ever be available. Given an infinite amount of time, it would be possible to grow infinitely large amounts of food and draw infinitely large amounts of water from a flowing stream. However, we cannot eat food faster than it can be grown, nor can we draw water from a flowing stream at a rate faster than a limit imposed by the volume of the water flowing in the stream.

Nonrenewable resources are those materials of which the earth contains a fixed quantity and which are not replenished by natural processes operating on short time scales. Examples are oil, natural gas, coal, copper, and the myriad other mineral products we dig and pump from the earth. Notice that the definition includes a

qualification concerning replenishment on short time scales. This is needed because new oil, gas, and certain other resources are continually being formed in the earth, but the formative processes are so slow that sizeable accumulations only develop over tens of millions of years—vastly slower than the rates at which we mine materials. The substances we dig from the earth's crust today are the products that have accumulated over the past 4 billion years. The rates of replenishment of fuels derived from fossil organic matter, and of metals distilled from the earth's mantle and core, are so exceedingly slow that the crop we are mining today is the only crop we will ever have—hence, the term nonrenewable resources. Questions surrounding nonrenewable resources are therefore questions of total supply and how fast we are consuming that total supply. The total amount ever to be available to us in the future is identical to that which is available today.

Most nonrenewable resources are also **mineral re-** **sources,** by which we mean they are nonliving, naturally occurring substances that are useful to us, whether they are organic or inorganic in origin. We use this broad definition in order to include all natural solids, plus liquids such as petroleum and water, and gases such as natural gas and the gases of the atmosphere. A possible confusion in terminology becomes apparent when one considers a resource such as water. Water in a flowing stream is a renewable resource because it is replenished on a short time scale by rainfall. By contrast, water in a deep aquifer in a desert area, as in Israel or central Australia, is a nonrenewable resource because it is only replenished over time scales of thousands or tens of thousands of years.

To reduce the confusion arising from terminology, we have classified and discussed the mineral and energy resources covered in this book by the manner in which they are used. The general classification, as demonstrated in Fig. 1.6, divides resources into three major

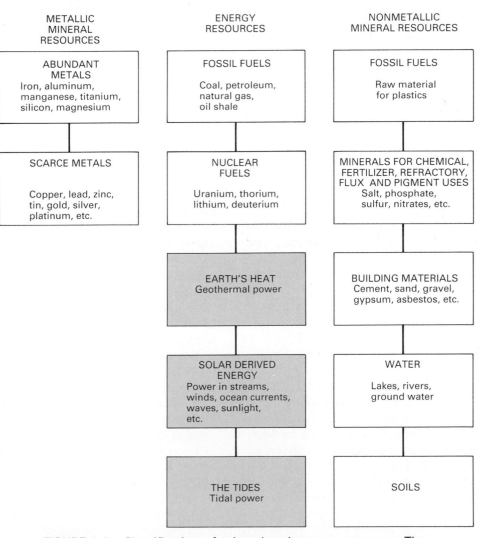

FIGURE 1-6. Classification of mineral and energy resources. The shaded boxes indicate those energy resources that are not mineral resources.

use groups. First, there are **metals,** which are a group of chemical elements that either singly or in combination have those special properties such as malleability, ductility, fusibility, high thermal conductivity, and electrical conductivity that allow them to be used in a wide range of technical applications. Metals have been the key materials through which humans have developed the remarkably diversified society we now enjoy and by which we have managed to proceed from the primitive societies of antiquity to the present. It is not surprising that the metal-winning and metal-working skills of ancient communities have been used as a measure of societal development and hence that terms such as *Bronze Age* and *Iron Age* have come into common parlance. Metals can be divided into two classes on the basis of their occurrence in the earth's crust. The geochemically **abundant metals** are those that individually constitute 0.1 percent or more of the earth's crust by weight. They are iron, aluminum, silicon, manganese, magnesium, and titanium. The term *abundant* is used for two reasons. First, because these metals occur in so many diverse ways in the earth that reserves of rich mineable ores are truly enormous and, even though rich deposits are not uniformly distributed around the world, the question of sufficiency for future generations is not in doubt. Second, the geochemically abundant metals form most of the common minerals, and as a consequence they influence many of the geologic processes that shape the earth. Geochemically **scarce metals,** by contrast, are those that individually constitute less than 0.1 percent by weight of the earth's crust. They are metals such as copper, lead, zinc, molybdenum, mercury, silver, and gold. The scarce metals are present in such tiny concentrations in the earth that they play very minor roles in geological processes, and very special (even rare) circumstances are needed in order for local concentrations to form. Unlike the abundant metals, therefore, mineable deposits of scarce metals tend to be smaller and less common. As a consequence, the question of sufficiency for future generations is a more important one where scarce metals are concerned.

The second major group in the resource classification presented in Fig. 1.6 includes those substances and sources from which we now, or in the future, might draw energy. Some of the resources, such as the fossil fuels and uranium, are nonrenewable resources. Other energy resources, such as running water and solar heat, are renewable. The importance of the energy resources, which are now recognized as being vital to the operation of modern society, was first brought into focus by the so-called energy crisis of 1973 when Middle Eastern oil was withheld from Europe and the United States. Subsequently, worldwide attention has been focussed on the cost and sufficiency of energy resources for the future.

The third group of resources includes all those material substances used in one way or another for reasons other than their metallic properties, or their energy content. Such resources include the minerals used as sources of chemicals—minerals such as halite ($NaCl$) and borax ($Na_2B_4O_7 \cdot 10H_2O$)—plus minerals used as the raw materials for fertilizers. This group also includes the water and soils vital to the production of foodstuffs. Also falling into this category are the wide range of industrial minerals that are used in everything from smelting metals to drilling for oil and in such diverse products as paints, fillers, and abrasives. The construction and building industries employ large volumes of many different materials drawn from the earth, for example, crushed stone, sand, gravel, and the raw materials for cement and concrete.

CONSEQUENCES OF RESOURCE EXPLOITATION

The earth can be envisioned as a huge machine with two sources of energy. The first source is the sun's heat. This is responsible for the turbulence in the atmosphere that we call wind, for the temperature variations across the face of the earth that makes equatorial regions warm and polar regions cold, for ocean currents, for evaporation of the water that forms clouds and leads to rain, and for most of the other phenomena, including growth of plants, that happen at the earth's surface. Flowing water, moving ice, blowing wind, and the downhill sliding of water-weakened rocks and mud are the main agents of erosion and transportation by which materials are moved as solids, liquids, and gases around the globe. If the sun were the only source of energy, the earth would by now be a nearly smooth globe devoid of mountains. The reason that the earth is not a smooth globe is that the second major energy source, the earth's internal heat, causes slow horizontal and vertical movements in the seeming solid rocks of the mantle and crust. These slow movements produce the crumplings and bucklings of the surface that thrust up mountains, split continents apart to form new ocean basins, and cause continents to collide and destroy old ocean basins.

The two systems of forces—those driven by the sun's external heat energy and those driven by earth's internal heat energy—maintain a dynamic balance. The balance involves myriad natural transfers of material through streams, oceans, atmosphere, soils, sediments, and rocks. As new mountains like the Alps are thrust up, erosion slowly wears them down. If a balance were not maintained, not only would the face of the earth be smooth, but the compositions of the ocean and atmosphere would be different. The movement of materials from rocks to soils to streams to oceans and back to rocks is called **geochemical cycling,** and the dynamic balance that results is called the **geochemical balance.**

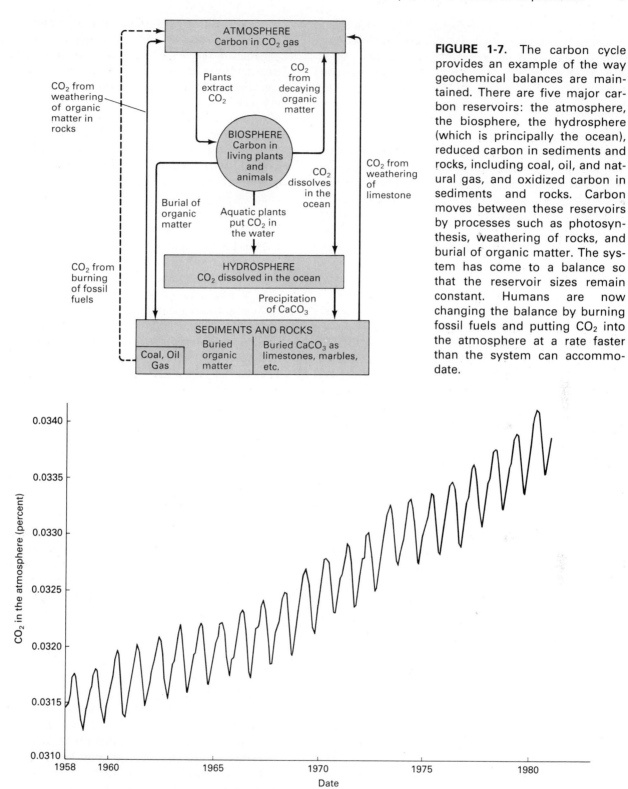

FIGURE 1-7. The carbon cycle provides an example of the way geochemical balances are maintained. There are five major carbon reservoirs: the atmosphere, the biosphere, the hydrosphere (which is principally the ocean), reduced carbon in sediments and rocks, including coal, oil, and natural gas, and oxidized carbon in sediments and rocks. Carbon moves between these reservoirs by processes such as photosynthesis, weathering of rocks, and burial of organic matter. The system has come to a balance so that the reservoir sizes remain constant. Humans are now changing the balance by burning fossil fuels and putting CO_2 into the atmosphere at a rate faster than the system can accommodate.

FIGURE 1-8. Carbon dioxide buildup in the atmosphere as measured at the observatory on Mauna Loa, an extinct volcano in Hawaii. The yearly oscillation is due to the control exerted by the seasons on the cycle of plant growth and respiration in the northern hemisphere. (Data from Geophysical Monitoring for Climate Change, published by the National Oceanic and Atmospheric Administration, U.S. Government.)

One of the major consequences of our exploitation of natural resources is that we humans are interfering with the balances of natural geochemical cycles. An example is shown in Fig. 1.7 where the major reservoirs and flow paths for carbon at the earth's surface are shown. There are five main reservoirs of carbon compounds: (1) carbon dioxide (CO_2) in the atmosphere; (2) carbon tied up in the cells of living plants and animals (the biomass); (3) organic matter buried in sediments and sedimentary rocks which includes oil, natural gas, and coal as well as the small percentage of carbon compounds found in all sediments and sedimentary rocks; (4) carbon dioxide dissolved in the oceans; and (5) carbon tied up in shells, limestones, and marbles as calcium carbonate ($CaCO_3$). The fluxes of carbon between the five major reservoirs are nicely controlled, so that on time scales of thousands of years, the system remains in balance.

Human involvement with the geochemical cycling of carbon involves the rapid removal of organic carbon (in the form of fossil fuels) from sedimentary rocks, and the conversion of that carbon to CO_2 through burning. Eventually, as burning is continued, the other reservoirs and fluxes must readjust, and the system will tend toward a new dynamic balance. The rate of readjustment is slow, however, when considered in terms of a human life span. Seen from our perspective, the CO_2 content of the atmosphere is slowly but steadily increasing (Fig. 1.8). Because CO_2 plays a major role in the thermal properties of the atmosphere, a change in the CO_2 content of the atmosphere may cause slow changes in other geochemical cycles. For example, rainfall patterns will change and, in turn, alter the availability of water. Changes in the water supply could affect the use of soils and the supply of crops.

The production and use of every natural resource, from the clearing of forests and the tilling of fields, to the mining of copper and the burning of coal, causes changes in the natural geochemical cycles. The changes may be large or small, local or global, pleasant or unpleasant. They may be given names such as pollution and environmental degradation, or may even be called disasters, but they are all consequences of the exploitation of natural resources. Among the topics addressed in this book, therefore, are some of the environmental consequences of the increasing exploitation of natural resources.

RESOURCES, RESERVES, AND ORES

Few things seem to cause more confusion than the words **resource, reserve,** and **ore** as they are applied to mineral deposits. Indeed, it is not uncommon to find the words used interchangeably, as if they meant the same thing. The meanings are actually very different. In part,

the confusion arises because *resource* and *reserve* are common words and each has a range of meanings depending on the materials being discussed. To a greater extent, however, the confusion arises for another reason. Even though mineral commodities are used in every aspect of our daily lives, few among us have actually seen a mineral deposit and thereby developed an understanding of how big they are, how they vary in richness, and what difficulties are involved in producing mineral raw materials. Further confusion results from the misuse of the words by those seeking to make financial investments in mineral resources. The terminology given below is that adopted by the U.S. Geological Survey, the U.S. Bureau of Mines, and most other responsible geological organizations.

The use of standard and exact terms as shown in Fig. 1.9 is necessary for valid estimates and comparisons of resources worldwide, and for long-term public and commercial planning. In order to serve these purposes, the classification scheme is based on both: (1) geological characteristics—such as grade, tonnage, thickness, and depth of a deposit; and (2) profitability assessments dependent on extraction costs and market values.

A mineral resource is defined as "a concentration of naturally occurring solid, liquid, or gaseous material, in or on the earth's crust, in such form and amount that economic extraction of a commodity from the concentration is currently or potentially feasible." In the geological sense, the resources are subdivided into those which have been identified and those as yet undiscovered. Depending on the degree of certainty, the identified resources fall into the categories of measured (where volumes and tonnages are well established), indicated (where volume and tonnage estimates are based on less precise data), and inferred (where deposits are assumed to extend between or beyond known resources.) In terms of profitability, resources are classed according to their current economic status as shown at the left-hand side of Fig. 1.9.

When referring to metal-bearing materials, reserves or ores are "that part of the resources that can be economically and legally extracted at a given time." These are the materials that are mined or otherwise extracted and processed to meet the everyday needs of society. It is important to note that the legal as well as the economic constraints must be considered because issues such as land ownership, the discharge of mining wastes, potential carcinogenic effects of products, or the incorporation of lands into national parks or wilderness areas may exclude otherwise mineable resources from reserve status. In such cases, those materials would continue to be considered as resources. Their potential for extraction would be high, but they would not become reserves unless laws or other restrictions were changed.

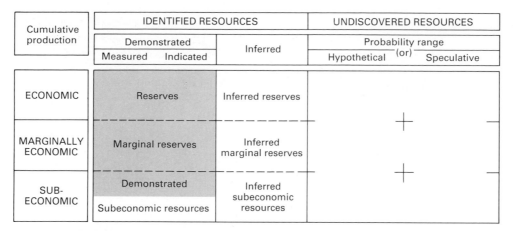

Cumulative production	IDENTIFIED RESOURCES			UNDISCOVERED RESOURCES	
	Demonstrated		Inferred	Probability range	
	Measured	Indicated		Hypothetical (or)	Speculative
ECONOMIC	Reserves		Inferred reserves		
MARGINALLY ECONOMIC	Marginal reserves		Inferred marginal reserves		
SUB-ECONOMIC	Demonstrated		Inferred subeconomic resources		
	Subeconomic resources				

FIGURE 1-9. Resources are classified according to geological understanding (increasing from right to left) and economic viability (increasing from bottom to top). The best known and most profitable of the resources fall into the category of reserves (commonly called *ores* when referring to metal-bearing deposits) and constitute our present source of mineral commodities. The shaded portion of the diagram illustrates which materials are included in **reserve base**, a term that is now being widely used. (Diagram from U.S. Bureau of Mines, Mineral Commodity Summaries, 1986.)

The quantities of reserves at any time are well defined but change constantly. They decrease as ores are mined out but increase as new discoveries are made or as technological advances occur. Also, they rise as the market value of mineral products rise, and they decrease when the market value falls.

There are many historical examples of resources becoming ores. A famous one occurred about the beginning of the present century when two young mining engineers, D. C. Jackling and R. C. Gemmell, discovered that copper deposits previously ignored because of their very low grades, could be worked at a profit by using new bulk-mining processes. A second famous example occurred soon after the end of the Second World War, as the richest portion of the iron ores of the Great Lakes region were running out. New mining and processing technologies allowed the leaner and formerly unworkable low-grade deposits called **taconites** to be worked. Taconites are now highly desirable ores and supply most of the iron used in the United States.

Also, there are many examples of ores becoming too expensive to be mined and thereby slipping back again to resources. A very recent example of backward slipping concerns numerous gold mines around the world. When gold was selling for close to $800 an ounce in 1980, it was possible to work very low-grade ore. Some grades were so low, in fact, that it cost upward of $700 per ounce to recover the gold. The reserves of all gold mines were expanded as a result of the high price. When the price of gold retreated below $400 an ounce in the mid-1980s, reserves declined again as the previously low-grade ores once again became resources.

In recent years, a broad term called the **reserve base** has been introduced to include the previous **reserves, marginal reserves,** and a portion of **subeconomic reserves.** It thus encompasses not only the reserves but also the "parts of the resources that have a reasonable potential for becoming economically available within planning horizons beyond those that assume proven technology and current economics." Although this is a less well-defined quantity, it does take into account the resources that, although not now mineable, will likely be available for our use.

It is all too easy to overlook the fact that quite large concentrations of materials can, for one reason or another, be too expensive to exploit. We must always keep in mind the fact that while mineral resources are the products of processes operating in the past, they become ores only if we are clever enough to discover the deposits and then find ways to exploit them profitably. As we shall see in the next chapter, the history of our use of resources is a record of a steady increase in both the range of natural materials we have learned to use and the diverse ways in which we use them.

2

Hadrian's wall, built between 122 and 136 A.D., was a Roman defensive barrier guarding the northern frontier of the Province of Britain until the end of the fourth century. It extended 118 kilometers (73 miles) across the narrowest portion of Britain and was for most of its length 6 meters (20 feet) high and 2 to 3 meters thick. (Photograph courtesy of the British Tourist Authority.)

EARTH RESOURCES THROUGH HISTORY

When man rose above the brutish individualism of his primordial state, he turned to the soil, to win food for his family; he paused in his migration; the soil held him; it gave root to the primitive community . . . . But the nomadic habit lingered . . . . The hills beckoned, the sea called, the more venturesome left . . . in search of materials wherewith to fashion their implements. They sought gold for ornament, copper for tools, iron for weapons and . . . they became miners . . . . Civilization developed on . . . a basis of . . . metals. The need of them . . . induced enterprising men to probe the hills and scour the deserts in search of the mineral deposits that are distributed with such perplexing diversity in the outer crust of the earth . . . . The miner . . . advanced far across the world, ever pioneering the advance . . . He was not only the pioneer, but he left marks to show the way; he blazed the trail for civilization. He has done it with geographic exurberance and equatorial amplitude . . . . Trade follows the flag, but the flag follows the pick.

T. A. RICKARD, EPILOGUE OF MAN AND METALS, 1932

INTRODUCTION

The earth's natural resources are the raw materials from which, directly or indirectly, all products used in our society are made. The utilization of earth resources either in their natural or processed form dates from our early ancestors' dependence on drinking water and salt in their diets, on their shaping of stone tools, and on their use of natural pigments for decoration and illustration. From such simple and individual needs, mineral resources have acquired national and international importance as they have become materials of trade and the basis for profit and power. This is perhaps best demonstrated by petroleum which is the most valuable and most vital of mineral commodities being exchanged between nations today.

The quantities of various mineral resources used by particular societies vary widely but generally correspond on a per capita basis with the degree of the development and standard of living. Figure 2.1 illustrates the annual per capita consumption of a variety of mineral resources in the United States. The quantities would be similar for other highly industrialized countries such as Canada, Britain, Germany, France, Sweden, or Australia. Individually, of course, very few, if any, of us use 3600 kilograms (7900 pounds) of stone or 165 kilograms (360 pounds) of salt, but for our society to provide the vast array of products and services we enjoy, these quantities are used by various industries on behalf of each of us.

The international importance of mineral resources is evidenced by the fact that the value of world crude mineral production exceeds $200,000,000,000 (£150,000,000,000) annually; that processing raises the value of these commodities to more than $500,000,000,000 (£360,000,000,000) annually, and they account for about 30 percent of the total of all traded materials. This chapter summarizes the changing and growing uses of mineral resources through history as well as some of the influences they now have on the political and economic aspects of modern society.

RESOURCES OF ANTIQUITY

The beginnings of our use of earth resources are lost in antiquity, but it seems likely that our ancestors' earliest concerns were water and salt for their diets and suitably shaped rocks to aid in hunting. The constant need for water was a dominant factor in a person's choice of a dwelling site and determined early migration routes. Some things never seem to change, for in spite of our technological advances, water remains a key factor in the location of major population centers. Salt was originally provided by meat-rich diets, but the development of societies with cereal-based diets required the acquisition of salt to use as a food additive. Beyond being a necessary dietary component, the addition of salt was also the cheapest and easiest way to preserve food and to enhance its taste. Consequently, salt became a commodity of exchange before recorded history and salt routes crisscrossed the globe long before the birth of Christ. Salt (in Latin, *sal*) was a good antiseptic, hence Salus

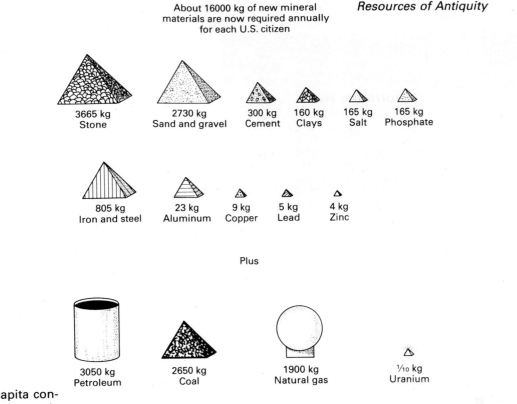

FIGURE 2-1. The per capita consumption of mineral resources is both varied and large. (From the U.S. Bureau of Mines.)

U.S. Total use of new mineral supplies in 1984 was about 3840 million metric tons

was the Roman goddess of health. A Roman soldier's pay, consisting in part of salt, was known as *salarium,* from which we derive the word *salary*. From this, and the payment of salt for slaves, came the expression of a worthless individual being "not worth his salt."

The use of rocks as tools extends back at least 1 million years. At first, they were crudely chipped into useful shapes, but subsequently, numerous prehistoric peoples developed techniques to shape **flint, obsidian,** and other tough rocks with uniform properties into delicate implements and tools (Fig. 2.2). A major advance occurred prior to 9000 B.C. when our ancestors began to fire clay to make pottery. The pottery, which represented the first synthesis of materials from minerals, provided a better means for storage and transport of food and water, thus helping in the struggle for survival. This led to the development of the ceramic arts of brick making, glazing, the making of mineral pigmented paints, and even glass making by about 3500 B.C.

The first metals were utilized by humans before 15,000 B.C. They were gold and copper because these are the two metals that most commonly occur in the metallic, or native, state. No doubt, the first finds were treated as curiosities because the metals felt, looked, and behaved differently from brittle rocks. However,

the ability to shape the metals into useful and desirable forms developed rapidly (Fig. 2.3). Before 4000 B.C., our ancestors had learned that copper could also be extracted from certain kinds of rocks by primitive smelting techniques in which charcoal, no doubt, supplied the heat and means of reducing copper ores to free copper metal. Within a thousand or so years, silver, tin, lead, zinc, and other metals were also being extracted and ultimately combined to form alloys such as brass (copper and zinc), bronze (copper and tin), and pewter (tin and other metals such as lead, copper, or antimony).

Iron, though much more abundant in the earth's crust than most other metals, is more difficult to extract and hence its use came somewhat later. It is believed that the first iron utilized came from meteorites. It is easy to imagine that the iron, especially if a meteorite were seen to fall to earth, must have evoked much wonder. The strength and hardness of the iron made it superior for weapons and led to its widespread use and apparently generated numerous myths concerning its magical powers when shaped into weapons. Pliny, a Roman writer of the first century, described iron as the "most useful and most fatal instrument in the hand of man," but perhaps its usefulness is best summarized by the lines of Rudyard Kipling's "Cold Iron":

FIGURE 2-2. Tools shaped by the chipping and working of flint and obsidian were among humans' earliest uses of mineral resources. The spear point shown here is from the Neolithic period in Egypt. (Photograph courtesy of Department of Anthropology, Smithsonian Institution.) (catalog no. 467794)

Gold is for the mistress - silver for the maid -
Copper for the craftsman cunning at his trade.
Good! said the Baron, sitting in his hall,
But iron - Cold Iron - is master of them all.

Although we commonly center our attention upon particular metals by using terms such as **Bronze Age** or **Iron Age,** our ancestors were using an increasingly broad range of mineral resources as the ages passed. Simple crudely shaped rock fragments were replaced by carefully shaped knives and arrow and spear points. The use of animal hides for storage gradually gave way to pottery and ceramics; shelters of plant materials and skins gave way to more permanent and protective bricks and mortars.

The development of first the Greek and then the Roman empires saw the extensive development of mining and stone-working industries to provide the building materials for their great palaces, stadiums, theaters, temples, roads, and aqueducts (Fig. 2.4). These cultures not only used much greater volumes of mineral resources but also vastly expanded the varieties. They also began to use large quantities of processed resources such as cements and plaster to supplement and bond the cut stone. The Greeks developed domestic metal mines and used silver mined near Athens to finance the fleet that defeated the Persians at Salamis in 480 B.C. They also used gold from Northern Greece to support the activities of Alexander the Great in about 330 B.C. As the Romans expanded their control throughout the Mediterranean and beyond, they extracted metals first by plunder, then by tribute, and finally by mining. Examples include the mercury from Spain, copper from Cyprus, and tin from the British Isles.

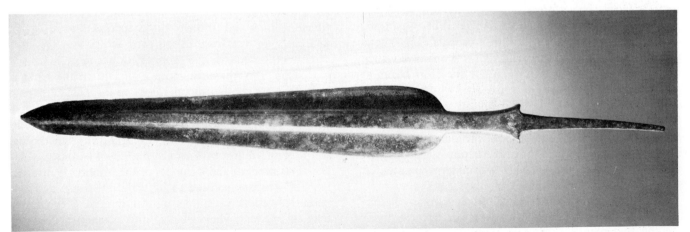

FIGURE 2-3. Early metal tools were found to be superior to stone tools. Hence, the use of metal tools spread rapidly, first involving the use of single metals and then as alloys. The bronze spear point shown here is from Luristan in the highlands of Iran. (Photograph courtesy of Department of Anthropology, Smithsonian Institution.) (catalog no. 328574)

FIGURE 2-4. The Romans were masters of construction as evidenced by the carefully cut and fitted limestone blocks of the Coliseum in Rome. (Photograph courtesy of Istituto Italiano di Cultura, New York.)

FROM ROME TO THE RENAISSANCE

The gradual collapse of the Roman Empire resulted in a breakdown of its organized society including the production, transportation, and marketing of mineral resources. The onset of the Dark Ages in Europe saw trade decline, mines close, and most people turning to subsistence agriculture. Mineral resource needs were met primarily by reusing the materials at hand and mining was confined to exploitation of salt needed for food, some alluvial gold recovery, and mining for other metals at a few centers such as Cornwall, Devonshire, and Derbyshire in England, and Saxony in the Erzgebirge in Germany.

The first emergences of Europe from the Dark Ages began after 800 A.D. and coincided with the discovery and development of mineral deposits in southern Germany. These and other reopened deposits provided metals, especially silver and gold, to trade for spices, gems, and silks from China and India. The overland trade routes through Assyria and Persia dating from Ancient days were replaced by new routes through Egypt, down the Red Sea, and across the Indian Ocean. The flow of metals from northern and central Europe southward raised Mediterranean ports, such as Venice, from small fishing villages to major trade centers.

Spain and Portugal rose to new importance as Christopher Columbus opened the seas westward to the New World in 1492 and as Vasco da Gama found the eastward sea route around the Cape of Good Hope to India. This shifted the trade centers for metals as well as other commodities from Venice to the Iberian Peninsula. Spain's fortune grew rapidly as significant quantities of gold and silver from the New World flowed into her coffers. Spanish treasury reports confirm that at least 181 metric tons (5,800,000 troy ounces) of gold and 16,887 metric tons (540,000,000 troy ounces) of silver were brought to Spain between 1503 and 1660. This treasure in no small way helped finance the Renaissance that was developing in Europe as well as Spain's participation in several wars at this time (Fig. 2.5).

The discovery of new lands and precious metals stimulated other European countries—England, France, the Netherlands—to also look westward. After the division of South America between Spain and Portugal by the Pope's decree of the Treaty of Tordesilla (also known as the Line of Demarkation), England, France, and the Netherlands searched the coastal areas of North America. Although the impacts of their explorations have subsequently proved great, their initial ventures were disappointing because the native peoples they encountered were hunters with no gold and generally no metals at all. The British and French did, of course, partially compensate themselves for this disparity of

(a)

(b)

FIGURE 2-5. (a) Spain's recovery of large amounts of gold and silver from the lands she had claimed in the Americas resulted in growing animosity between Spain and England, because the English desired a share of the wealth. In the hope of ending English raids on Spanish ships and ports, Philip II of Spain assembled the Spanish Armada, a fleet of 130 ships that sailed for England on May 20, 1588. The defeat by the English on July 29 was a great blow to the prestige of the Spanish and reduced the influence of Spain on the high seas. (Courtesy of the Beverly R. Robinson Collection of the U.S. Naval Academy Museum.) (b) The silver eight real coin, commonly called a "pieces of eight", was used throughout the Spanish-speaking world. These fragments show how the coins were commonly chisled into smaller denominations called "bits". The most popular bit was a quarter of a coin and led to the slang term "two bits" for the American quarter. (Courtesy of the Colonial Williamsburg Foundation.)

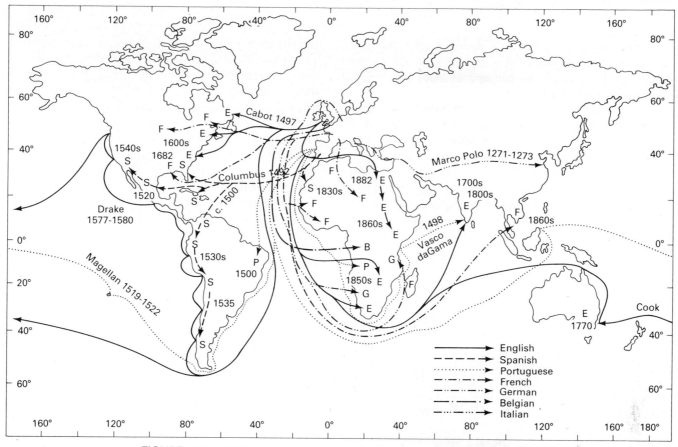

FIGURE 2-6. Major colonial routes and the extension of the influences of the major European powers from the late 1400s through the late 1800s. There has been no attempt to include all European excursions nor to represent multiple, often successive, colonial influxes.

gold distribution through the use of pirates who were only too happy to relieve Spanish galleons of their cargo.

GLOBAL EXPLORATION AND COLONIALISM

Humankind's curiosity and sense of adventure combined with a desire for riches and a need for resources have made us explorers since before recorded history. The Phoenicians, who sailed throughout the then known world of the Mediterranean, and the Romans, whose empire extended from Britain to the Orient, were among the first great explorers and colonizers to exploit resources from very wide areas. It was, however, the explorations of the Europeans from the fifteenth until the nineteenth centuries (Fig. 2.6) that left their mark on the ownership and exploitation of mineral resources in the twentieth century. Portugal and Spain became the first of the modern European countries to send out explorers in search of sea routes to India and the Far East in the 1400s. The discovery of new lands and new trade routes by Columbus and Vasco da Gama were encouraging, but the finding of gold in the hands of natives of

Africa and the West Indies provided a strong incentive to explore further. On his return Columbus reportedly said, "The gate to the gold and pearls is now open, and precious stones, spices, and a thousand other things may surely be expected."

Conflict between the two major Catholic sea powers, Spain and Portugal, over rights to explore and claim the New World seemed inevitable, so the Pope intervened in 1494 and drew a north-south boundary 100 leagues (later moved to 360 leagues) west of the Cape Verde Islands. Portugal was granted the rights to lands east of this line and Spain the lands to the west. The long-term consequence has been that the bulge of South America projecting east of this line is now Brazil, where Portuguese is spoken. In contrast, nearly all other countries of South and Central America speak Spanish. The discovery of gold proved to be a powerful incentive to the Spanish whose conquistadors under Pizarro and Cortez rapidly subdued the large indigenous empires centered in Peru and Mexico and plundered their gold and silver. King Ferdinand, in a letter to Pizarro wrote, "Get gold, humanely if you can, but get gold." Cortez said, "I came to get gold, not to till the soil like a peas-

ant." The King's and Cortez's desires were richly met as the Spanish galleons carried an estimated 181 metric tons of gold and 16,887 metric tons of silver back to Europe between 1500 and 1660.

The exploration of eastern North America was carried out by the British, Dutch, and French who hoped to find gold and silver just as the Spanish had in South America. They, of course, encountered only forest-dwelling Indians who used little or no metal and who knew nothing of gold. As a result, the exploration and colonization of North America proceeded much more slowly than that of Central America and western South America where mining of gold and silver spurred on the Spanish conquests through the early years of the sixteenth century.

While the Spanish made great inroads in South America, other European countries explored and established colonies in the coastal regions of Africa. However, it was not until the 1800s, with the Industrial Revolution in full swing, that the great interior of Africa was opened to colonialism. Then, driven by the desire to take possession of all available lands that could provide raw materials and potential markets, the European countries divided the rights of exploitation of all Africa and parts of Southeast Asia among themselves. Since the middle of the twentieth century, and as a result of concerns for human rights, decline of power by the European countries, and the rise of nationalistic feelings, the colonies have, one-by-one, gained independence.

THE INDUSTRIAL REVOLUTION

The Industrial Revolution, which spread across Europe in the 1700s and 1800s, was made possible by the development of the coal and iron industries, and in turn stimulated a vast increase in the consumption of these and other mineral resources. The Industrial Revolution converted the Western world from a basically rural and agricultural society, in which people raised most of their own food and made their own material goods, into a largely urban and industrial society. Two events occurring near the beginning of the eighteenth century in Great Britain played major roles at the onset of the Industrial Revolution. The first was the production of the first commercial steam engine in 1698 by Thomas Savery, a Cornish army officer. In 1712, Thomas Newcomen, a Devonshire blacksmith, improved on Savery's engine and built the steam engine that provided a previously unimagined power to remove water from coal mines and from the copper and tin mines of Cornwall in Southwest England. The Newcomen engines, although widely used for more than 50 years, were inefficient, es-

pecially in the loss of steam, because there existed no way to bore the 40- to 100-inch diameter cylinders truly round. This problem was finally solved by James Watt, a Scottish engineer, and John Wilkinson, a Staffordshire ironmaker, who developed and first sold a new and more efficient steam engine in 1776. The importance of the Newcomen and Watt engines to early British mining is demonstrated by the presence of more than a thousand abandoned engine houses that still dot the Cornish landscape (Fig. 2.7).

The building of massive steam engines for use in mines and factories required a second major development—the use of coal to make iron and to fuel the steam engines. From earliest times through the 1600s, Great Britain's hardwood forests had provided the fuel (as charcoal) for the early iron making as well as for manufacturing processes, construction, and home heating. By 1700 the British faced a fuel crisis because so much of the forest had been cut. Although coal had been used locally as fuel, its use had not become widespread.

FIGURE 2-7. Wheal (mine) houses that contained the steam engines used to drive machinery and to pump water from the tin mines in southwest England in the 1700s and 1800s still dot the Cornish countryside. This restored structure and beam engine is near Camborne. (Photography by J. R. Craig.)

FIGURE 2-8. The English canal system, here shown at Paddington Junction where the Grand Union Canal joins the Regents Canal was developed to transport coal, iron ore, and finished products in the early 1800s. (This reproduction drawn by Thomas Shepherd between 1820 and 1830; courtesy of the British Waterways Museum.)

Not only was wood in short supply, but it also lacked sufficient heating capacity to drive some of the new steam engines. Coal proved to be an abundant substitute for wood, and coal generated more heat than an equal volume of wood. Furthermore, iron makers discovered that coal could be converted to coke and proved to be better than the charcoal that had been used for the smelting of iron. The use of coal and coke, combined with new smelting and iron-rolling techniques, vastly expanded the British capability to produce more iron to make more machines that, in turn, used more coal as a fuel.

The onset of the Industrial Revolution necessitated the development of transportation systems to move the coal, iron ore, and other freight. Until the early 1800s waterways were the only inexpensive and efficient means of moving large quantities of materials. The British widened rivers and streams and built an impressive system of canals linking large cities with coal fields and major rivers (Fig. 2.8). In the early 1800s the steam engine was modified to drive land vehicles and locomotives, and the great era of railroad transportation began.

Although it took some time for the products and the ideas of the Industrial Revolution to reach the Americas and other parts of the world, when the ideas did arrive the impact was always dramatic and invariably produced major changes in life style, such as migration of populations to the cities, vast expansion in the mining of coal and iron ore, and the development of much more effective transportation systems.

HUMANS AND METALS

The developing complexity of society linked to an increasing dependence on a variety of resources is nowhere better illustrated than in the use of increasing numbers and quantities of metals through time. Archeological records indicate that primitive or **Stone Age** peoples relied only on implements that were broken or shaped from stone. The earliest records of metal usage are lost in antiquity but certainly date from before 15,000 B.C. Native copper and gold were the first metals used in virtually all cultures, because they were the only metals available. These metals were used in the production of ornaments, amulets, tools, and weapons because they could be pounded or carved, and even melted and cast, into many shapes (Fig. 2.3).

By 4000 B.C., copper was being smelted from sulfide ores in Egypt and Mesopotamia. The steps leading to the origins of smelting, the intentional extraction of a metal from its ores, are unknown, but they probably began before 4000 B.C. with the accidental melting of metallic copper from copper-bearing sulfide, oxide, or carbonate minerals in a hearth, camp fire, or pottery kiln. Once the association of the ore (many copper-

bearing minerals such as malachite and azurite are brightly colored and hence easily recognized) with the metal was noted, it was recognized over long periods of time that the presence of charcoal in the fire both heated and reduced the metal to allow its extraction. Either through rapid communication of the techniques or many separate discoveries, copper smelting was practiced throughout southwest Europe, the Middle East, and as far as India by shortly after 3000 B.C. The earliest smelted coppers were often impure because of the presence of small amounts of arsenic and antimony minerals that occur with the copper sulfides. Thus the smelting created unintentional, but nevertheless useful alloys that were much superior to pure copper in terms of hardness. These alloys were further improved when work hardened by pounding, a process which removed the brittleness associated with cast objects. Beneficial as the arsenic and antimony were, it was the impurity of tin, either from tin sulfide (**stannite**) or the oxide (**cassiterite**) that effectively ended the Copper Age and ushered in the Bronze Age.

The addition of tin confers on cast copper objects considerable strength in the as-cast state, without the need for **cold-working.** This discovery, first documented in Iran between 3900 and 2900 B.C., spread rapidly throughout southeast Europe, the Mediterranean area, and India and resulted in the development of the tin trade. The first significant sources of tin were probably in Italy, Bohemia, Saxony, and possibly even Nigeria, and marked the first instance of foreign dependency on natural resources for many nations. The usefulness of bronze led to a large increase in the scale of metallurgical operations so that ingots of bronze weighing more than 30 kilograms were being produced in the Mediterranean area by about 1600 B.C. The zenith of the Bronze Age was reached in the period 900–750 B.C.

Throughout the Copper and Bronze ages, gold was gathered from placer deposits and extracted from lode (vein-type) deposits in the Middle East. Because most naturally occuring gold is relatively pure (less than 20 percent impurity contents of silver and copper) and occurs as the native metal, the production of gold was primarily a question of human physical strength rather than smelting techniques. Silver occurs in the native state, but it is probable that silver bars found with lead bars at Troy (2500 B.C.) were extraced from natural gold-silver alloys by a refining process known as **cupellation.** This process, still used today, employs lead, which is relatively easily smelted from the lead sulfide galena, to extract the silver from the gold. This silver was formed into a variety of ornaments but lead was not widely used until the Romans found it useful in making pipes to transport water.

The earliest archeological iron implements were from meteoritic iron that can be identified by its characteristic nickel contents. These have been found from the Middle East, the Americas, and even Greenland. The rarity and uniqueness of iron led to its being highly prized; indeed, the knife that lay on Tutankhamun's mummy within its sarcophagus was made of wrought iron.

The first working of terrestrial iron began about 1300 B.C. in Asia Minor and may well have resulted from the accidental building of a fire on iron-oxide rich rocks or even the unanticipated extraction of iron from rocks while trying to refine copper. The early production of iron was made by heating the iron ore in a hot charcoal fire. The iron was slowly reduced by the carbon reacting with it and removing the oxygen as carbon dioxide. The fires were not hot enough to melt the iron but did soften it so that it could be pounded or forged into wrought iron. The scale of iron production gradually increased from initial production of only small items of jewelry to large-scale production of weapons by about 1200–1000 B.C. Knowledge of iron working spread from Turkey and Iran to areas around the Mediterranean by about 900 B.C. to coastal Africa and Great Britain by about 500 B.C., and to India and possibly China by 400 B.C. By the early days of the Roman Empire, iron was being used for nails, hinges, bolts, keys, chains, and weapons. The small foundries that dotted the empire persisted until the Romans withdrew, after which time iron making, like other forms of industry, was much reduced. In spite of iron's usefulness, the difficulty of producing large quantities kept the supply limited until about 1340 A.D. when the invention of the blast furnace permitted iron workers to obtain temperatures high enough to make molten iron. This technological breakthrough has had a profound and lasting effect on civilization because it made iron, and subsequently steel, cheap and available on the large scale that would be necessary for the Industrial Revolution.

The molten metal could be easily fabricated into useful cast iron objects using preformed molds. This practice became widespread, but the iron was relatively brittle and soft due to the impurities of carbon and other elements. Nevertheless, as noted earlier, there was a rapidly growing demand for the iron and consequently a seemingly insatiable appetite for the forests to provide charcoal fuel. The British admiralty became alarmed about the supplies of timber for ships and royal edicts were issued in the 1530s and 1550s forbidding the use of certain forests for manufacturing charcoal. The demand for hardwood to make charcoal devastated forests in Europe, especially in England, and led to an energy crisis. The shortage of charcoal put some iron makers out of work and led others to seek alternative energy sources such as coal. It took many failures and more than 100 years, but finally in the early 1700s, iron was successfully smelted in England using coke produced from coal. The use of the coke opened up England's ample coal resources, led to the development of her

mining industry, and placed her at the forefront of the Industrial Revolution.

There was yet, however, one more major breakthrough to come—steel. The iron was strong and useful, but it had little flexibility and the castings were brittle. The desire to improve the properties of iron led to the discovery of steel. The first type formed, and still the most widely used today, is carbon steel. It is formed by blowing enough air through the molten iron to lower the carbon content to less than 1 percent. The result is a harder, stronger, more workable and flexible metal that has found thousands of uses. The date of the first steel making is not known because no doubt some was accidentally synthesized from time to time in the normal melting and forging processes. The birth of the modern steel industry is usually dated at 1740 when a process was devised to produce a uniform quality carbon steel.

Mining of the ores from which metals are extracted has been an extremely laborious task throughout most of human history. The earliest methods of employing the hammer and chisel were supplanted by a fire-setting technique in which the rocks were heated in the workings by fire and then cracked by throwing cold water on them. Between firings the loosened fragments were chiseled out and removed. Finally, in 1627, some 1400 years after its development by the Chinese, gunpowder was introduced into mines in Germany. Its use spread throughout Europe and the world during the next 200 years. Explosives marked a major step forward in the exploitation of resources because they greatly increased our capacity to mine ores by allowing the focusing of large amounts of energy for the first time.

Although there were many developments in mining and smelting techniques, it was not until the Industrial Revolution in the eighteenth and nineteenth centuries that scientists and metallurgists discovered large numbers of new metals (Fig. 2.9). Many of these metals were at first novelties with little practical use. For example, nickel was discovered in 1751 and several grains were isolated in 1804, but it remained a scientific curiosity and found no major usage until nickel steels were developed in 1889. Similarly, aluminum was first discovered in 1827, but because of the difficulty of extraction it was one of the most expensive of metals. Consequently, Napoleon III had aluminum forks and spoons for himself and honored guests while lesser guests ate with gold utensils. Only after the development of efficient electrical extraction techniques did the price of aluminum drop from more than £130 per kilogram to less than £0.5 per kilogram and the metal begin to find significant use.

The Industrial Revolution brought iron and carbon steel into a new prominence both in terms of variety of uses and in the volume of metals consumed. They were used both in the machines of industry and many of their products. The first iron-based alloys were carbon steels

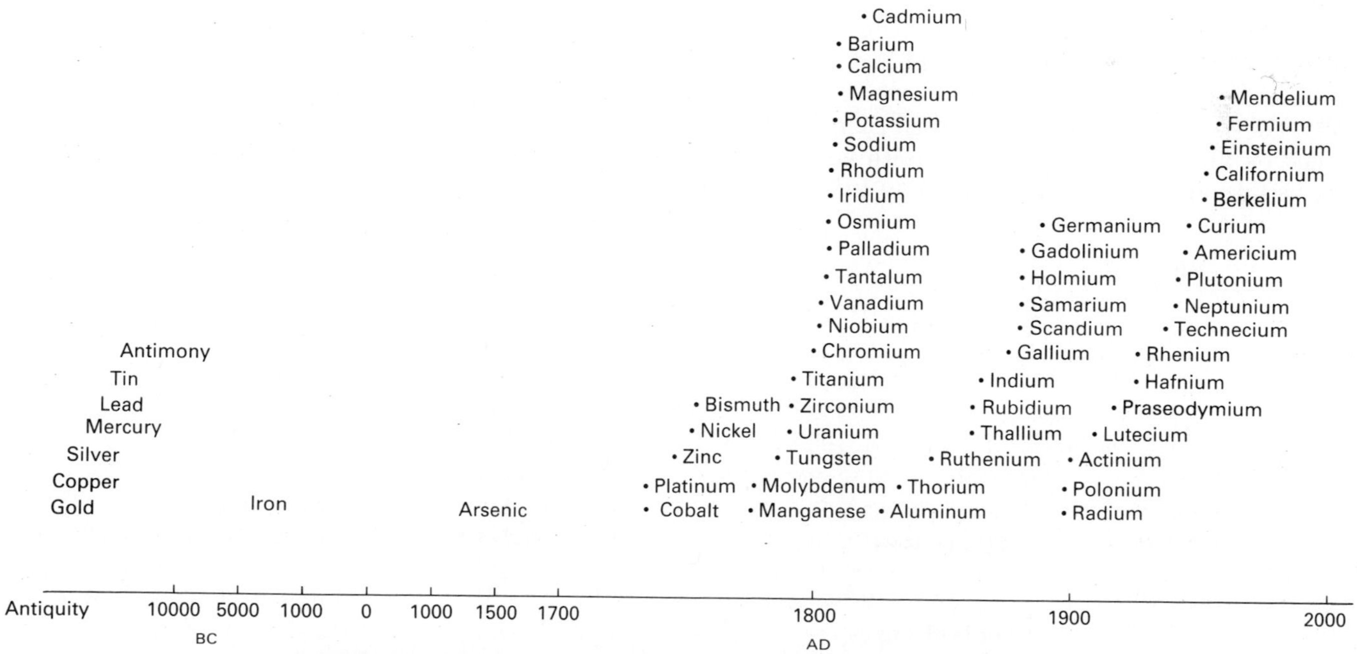

FIGURE 2-9. The discovery of various types of metals throughout history. Note that the time scale is not linear but is expanded after 1700 when the growth of modern chemistry and the onset of the Industrial Revolution led to the discovery of a large number of metals.

that resulted from the dissolution of carbon in the iron during smelting. In the latter part of the nineteenth century, recognition of the superior properties of this steel relative to iron prompted the search for other useful alloys based on the newly discovered metals. Consequently, many new varieties of steel incorporating nickel, cobalt, titanium, niobium, and molybdenum were developed. Such work was accelerated by the development of the internal combustion engine, aircraft, and weaponry during the twentieth century.

The advent of aircraft spurred the development of new lightweight metals, especially aluminum and titanium. When the jet engine replaced the piston engine, new high-temperature alloys were needed, and more emphasis was placed on metals such as cobalt, vanadium, and titanium. With the dawn of the nuclear age in 1945, much of the world's attention turned toward two long known but little used metals, uranium and thorium. In recent years, there have been some remarkable advances in the utilization of metals in the field of medicine (e.g., barium dyes for X-ray diagnostic work and synthetic radioactive isotopes for cancer treatment), electronics (e.g., the use of gallium and germanium in transducers and the rare earth elements in color TV phosphors), and energy production (e.g., platinum group metals as catalysts in gasoline production). Our progression from the use of simple native metals to accidentally discovered alloys, to engineered compounds, to exotic rare metals, and even to artificial elements, is a measure of our technological advancement. At the same time, it is necessary to recognize that our dependence on virtually all naturally occurring metals (and, indeed, all elements) results in a vast and complicated worldwide supply network. We also know that there are no new naturally occurring metallic elements to be found on the earth. Thus, we must learn how to make the best use of those now available.

MODERN TRENDS IN RESOURCE USAGE

The modern era of resource extraction and usage began with the Industrial Revolution. In practical terms, the amount of nearly any resource used before that time is negligible in comparison to today's consumption. The onset of the Industrial Revolution brought about the need for more coal, iron, and other metals to build and fuel the new machines, to supply the factories, and to develop the cities. The demands required larger and more efficient mining methods and more efficient transportation systems to move the products. The continued growth of industry, fed both by a growing world population and rising standards of living, has resulted in ever greater demands for the earth's resources to feed, warm, house, and accommodate humankind. W. C. J. van Rensberg, a noted resource analyst, pointed out that in the period from 1770 until 1900, when world population approximately doubled, mineral production grew tenfold. From 1900 until 1970, when world population increased about 2.3 times, mineral production increased twelvefold. From 1970 until 2000, when population will have about doubled, mineral production will probably have tripled.

This worldwide trend is especially pronounced in the more developed countries such as the United States as shown by the comparison of the increases in population and increases in the production and usage of some important mineral commodities in Table 2.1. This table reveals two very important points about the production and use of mineral resources by industrialized nations in general, and by the United States in particular:

1. The rate of mineral resource usage has risen much more rapidly than has population growth.

TABLE 2-1

Comparison of the United States production and usage of some important metals and of population in 1875 and 1985

	1875 (× 1000 mt) Produced and Used	1985 (× 1000 mt) Produced	Used	Increase in Production	Used
Aluminum	not used	4350	5174	—	—
Copper	18.3	1510	2170	82.5×	119×
Lead	53.2	350	1140	6.6×	21.4×
Pig Iron	2,057	45,350	46,620	22.0×	22.7×
Zinc	15.2	227	1022	14.9×	67.2×
Silver (million troy oz)	24.5	39.4	160	1.6×	6.5×
Gold (million troy oz)	1.6	2.5	3.3	1.6×	2.1×
Population (millions)	45.1	237		5.25×	

(Data from U.S. Bureau of Mines.)

*Approximately 90 percent of the bauxite from which the aluminum was produced was imported.

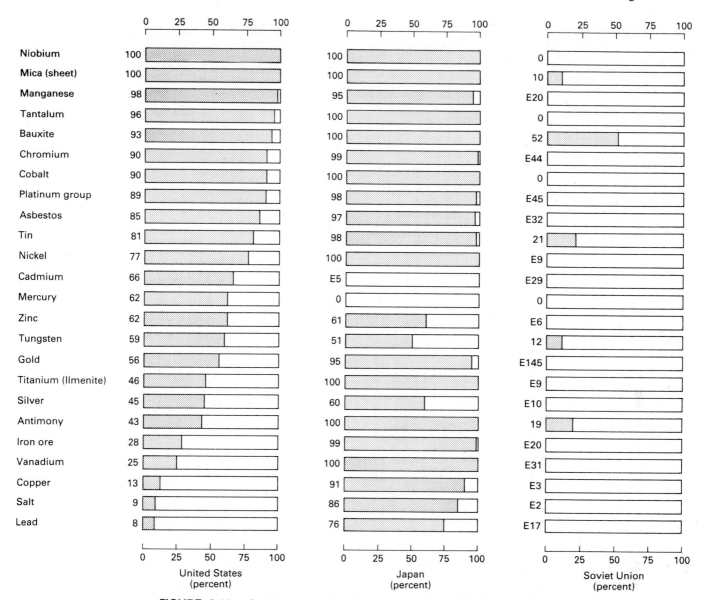

FIGURE 2-10. Comparison of the import reliance of the United States, Japan, and the Soviet Union in the early 1980s for several types of mineral resources as shown by the shaded bars. Notice the variable but generally higher degree of import reliance of the United States and Japan. E indicates that a resource is exported. (From the U.S. Bureau of Mines.)

2. The percentage of mineral resources being supplied domestically has decreased; conversely the percentage of imported resources has increased.

The first point results from the rise in the standard of living, and the expansion of industry that relies on the mineral raw materials. To a lesser degree it also reflects the increased size of the population. It is important to note that the United States, with approximately 6 percent of the world population, uses approximately 30 percent of the mineral resources and that the per capita use of nearly every commodity in America dwarfs that of people in the developing countries. To bring all peoples up to the American level of mineral resource consumption would require a 700 percent annual increase in the production of each commodity. To do this in the year 2020 when world population is projected to have doubled, it would be necessary for annual production to increase 1400 percent.

The second point illustrated by the figures in Table 2.1 is that the United States (and many other highly developed countries) which was essentially self-sufficient

in its production of most metals in 1875 now relies heavily on imports and accumulated stocks. This lack of self-reliance is, in some cases, due to economics (i.e., U.S. mines cannot produce the material as cheaply as foreign sources because their labor is cheaper or because their governments subsidize mining), but in many cases it is also the result of the depletion of the richest ores. Increasing foreign dependence creates a drain on capital, a loss of jobs, and a loss of security over the supply of strategic materials. The degree of dependence of the United States on foreign sources for nonfuel commodities is illustrated in Fig. 2.10, that shows some of the broad range of imported materials and the highly variable degree of import dependence. The United States is not alone in its dependence on foreign suppliers. This is apparent from the comparison of the import reliance of Japan that is shown in the center column in Fig. 2.10. The position of the Soviet Union as shown in the right-hand column stands in stark constrast to that of the United States or Japan. The high level of Soviet self-sufficiency results both from the domestic availability of mineral resources, subsidization of industry, and the relatively more limited availability of consumer goods (e.g. cars, appliances) that are made from the resources.

The general trends in the changing number of working mines, amounts of domestically produced metals, and the amounts of imported metals were outlined for industrialized nations as early as 1929 by Hewett, an American mining geologist, as shown in Fig. 2.11. The curve defining the amount of metal produced annually starts at zero when mining first commences in a country and ends again at zero when all ore deposits have been worked out. The area under the curve is a measure of the total amount of metal produced in the useful lifetime of the mines. The curve defining the number of mines is a measure of the rate of extraction of the metal. Many small easily extracted ore-bodies are mined early in a country's development, but the bulk of the metal comes from larger, longer-lived mines. Ultimately, the mines become exhausted and domestic metal production drops. As this occurs the country becomes increasingly dependent on imports from foreign sources. The relative positions of the United States, Britain, and the Soviet Union are shown in terms of the three curves. It is fair to note that these curves are generalizations and do not fit all countries. Indeed, there are industrialized countries like Japan that have never had a strong mineral base and many less developed countries like Bolivia that have not developed major industrialization.

The aging and depletion of mines in the major developed countries, coupled with their high labor costs and discovery and development of mines in other parts of the world, has resulted in a dramatic decrease in the developed countries' share of world metal production as

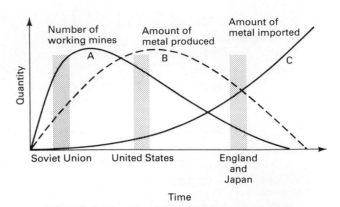

FIGURE 2-11. Traditional stages in mine development, metal production, and imports in industrial countries. Curve A, representing the number of working mines, rises rapidly as a new country is prospected, but it declines when the rate of mine exhaustion exceeds the discovery rate. Curve B, representing metals produced, also rises and falls as mines are worked and eventually exhausted. Curve C, representing metals imported, rises exponentially and expresses the increasing inability of a country to meet its own needs. The approximate present positions for three industrial countries are indicated. With traditional development, each country moves along the time axis from left to right. For example, England was in about the position of the United States in the late nineteenth century, at which time the United States was at about the same stage of development as the Soviet Union is today. Consequently, the Soviet Union is self-sufficient in most metals, the United States in a declining number, and England and Japan in very few.

shown for several metals in the United States in Table 2.2. This trend means that most of the jobs in the mining industries and most of the profits from the export of mineral commodities have shifted from the United States and the other major developed countries to the developing countries. Another consequence, discussed in a later section, is the increasing dependence of the

TABLE 2-2

The changing proportion of the United States' production of some important metallic resources

Mineral Resource	United States Share of World Production (%)			
	1955	1965	1975	1985
Copper	37.3	25.4	18.4	13.5
Lead	14.0	10.1	16.4	11.9
Zinc	16.3	12.9	7.6	3.7
Silver	19.7	15.5	11.8	10.9
Iron ore	28.2	13.4	9.0	6.0

(Data from U.S. Bureau of Mines.)

major developed countries on foreign sources for strategic mineral commodities.

In terms of impact on life styles and revenues generated, the most important modern trend in resource usage has been the rapid rise in the use of petroleum throughout the twentieth century. In the early 1900s, oil yielded the gasoline to power the growing number of automobiles, but coal continued to be the major energy source for industry. The depression years of the 1930s saw only a slow growth in oil demand because of the difficult economic times, and the World War II years saw only controlled growth because of wartime restraints. However, after World War II, the rapid expansion of the world economy, the shift of industry from coal to oil as an energy source, the growth of the automobile industry, and the ready availability of cheap oil from the then recently opened very rich Middle Eastern oil fields, led to a very rapid rise in the demand for oil. This has led to an unprecedented dependence of much of the world on one small geographic area for its major energy supplies and a high rate of flow of the world's money to the Middle Eastern countries in order to buy the oil.

GLOBAL DISTRIBUTION AND THE INTERNATIONAL FLOW OF RESOURCES

The Irregular Distribution of Resources

It is important to realize that mineral resources in general, and the scarce metals in particular, are not evenly distributed within the earth's crust. Furthermore, only 0.01–0.0001 percent of the total amount of any metal has been significantly concentrated into economic deposits and is ever likely to be extracted and utilized. Because the geologic processes which have concentrated the minerals and metals have not been random, the distribution of the resources and the reserves is also not random. The geographic irregularity of resources, like the number and size of deposits (Fig. 2.12) is, in general, a function of the abundance of the resource. The geographic distribution will also be a function of the variety of processes by which a resource may be generated. Thus iron ores, composed of the most abundant metal oxides and generated by a variety of **sedimentary, igneous,** and **metamorphic** processes, are widely distributed. Even though aluminum is more abundant than iron in the earth's crust, the most desirable ore of aluminum, bauxite is only concentrated into potentially economic deposits by one process—tropical weathering—and bauxite aluminum ore is therefore less available than iron ores and is much more limited in its geologic and geographic distribution. The base metals, copper, lead, and zinc, are nearly three orders of magnitude [Fig. 2.12(a)] less abundant than iron and aluminum. However, their ores may form by several geologic processes and so their deposits are relatively widely spread in terms of geology and geography. Metals such as platinum, gold and mercury which have a very low crustal abundance and are concentrated only by a limited number of geologic processes are very irregularly distributed.

Our estimation of the mineral resources available in any area is dependent on our understanding of the geology of that area and the degree to which exploration has been carried out. Thus, it is not too surprising to discover that a few of the larger major industrial countries where there has been more detailed geologic exploration are the sites of many mineral resources and reserves and that areas, such as Antarctica, which have been little explored, have fewer known resources. It is reasonable to expect that intensive exploration of poorly known remote areas in the future will add to the quantity of mineral resources and reserves.

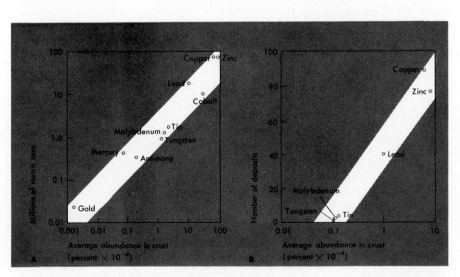

FIGURE 2-12. Number (a) and size (b) of ore deposits of many types of metals as a function of general crustal geochemical abundance. It is apparent that the number and size of the deposits of a metal are larger for metals of greater abundance. (From B. J. Skinner, *Earth Resources*, 3rd ed., Prentice Hall.)

Even taking into account the disparities in the degree of our geological knowledge of different areas of the earth's crust, it is apparent that the various mineral resources display great geographical irregularities in distribution and abundance. These irregularities result from the nonuniform distribution of the geological processes that formed them and give particular economic and political significance to many types of resources. Nowhere is this more vividly seen than in the Middle East where the large reserves of petroleum have led to an enormous influx of the world's wealth and a constant vying between the world's powers for political favor.

The irregularity of geographic distribution of mineral resources is exemplified in Table 2.3. It is apparent that five of the major industrial nations—the United States, Canada, South Africa, Australia, and the Soviet Union and which constitute 34 percent of the world's land area—possess a disproportionate amount of many of the world's important mineral resources. Other prime examples include the Middle East holding more than 50 percent of the world's known oil reserves, Brazil holding 69 percent of the world's titanium reserves, China holding 47 percent of the world's tungsten reserves, and Zaire holding 50 percent of the world's cobalt reserves.

The existence of mineral reserves within a country's borders has historically been a requirement for a minerals industry, although Japan has demonstrated an ability to develop such an industry on the basis of imported raw materials. However, the existence of mineral deposits alone is not sufficient to ensure a viable mineral industry because other factors such as high labor costs or low productivity (tin in England), environmental restrictions (coal in the United States), absence of transport systems (Brazil), availability of cheap imports (oil in the United States in the 1960s), high transportation costs (fluorspar in the United States), and political instability (many developing countries) may deter development.

Even if resources were uniformly distributed and developed, the differences in population and, more importantly, the differences in demand would still result in resources having great political and economic significance. Unfortunately, political and economic aspects have commonly dominated the other more utilitarian and humanitarian aspects of resources exploitation and probably will continue to do so in the future.

The International Trade of Resources

The irregular distribution of mineral resources and the tendency for the industrialized nations to use much larger quantities of resources than they produce, result in the massive movement of mineral commodities along the world's trade routes. In 1981 the value of mineral resources in world trade exceeded $500 billion. By far, the most valuable traded commodity was petroleum; its value alone exceeded $400 billion. The importance of mineral products to the economies of some developing countries is evidenced by noting that they account for about 70 percent of Bolivia's foreign exchange earnings, about 70 percent of Chile's total exports, and about 60 percent of Zaire's foreign exchange. Even industrialized countries such as Australia and South Africa rely on the export of mineral resources for about 40 and 50 percent of their total export values, respectively. Not surprisingly, several of the Middle Eastern oil countries derive nearly all of their export earnings from oil. The United States, like many other industrialized nations, imports large quantities of many raw and processed mineral commodities. Much of this, however, is subsequently exported as finished products.

Although most of us are aware that countries like the United States import many commodities, we tend to overlook the fact that the same commodities may also be exported. Thus, the United States imports and exports coal, oil, and numerous other mineral goods. This at

TABLE 2-3

Percentages of known world reserves of some important mineral commodities possessed by the five major industrial mining countries

	United States	Canada	South Africa	Australia	Soviet Union	Total
% of world land area	6.4	6.7	0.8	5.2	15.0	34.0
Platinum	1.3	0.8	80.8	—	16.7	99
Gold	11	6	47	4	21	89
Vanadium	3.8	—	19.8	0.7	60.3	84.6
Molybdenum	54.4	6.5	—	—	4.6	65.5
Potash	0.5	73.7	—	—	15.8	90.0
Chromium	—	—	67.6	—	0.5	68.1
Manganese	—	—	40.7	5.6	44.4	90.7
Zinc	8.3	15.5	7.1	12.5	6.5	49.9
Silver	24.8	11.6	—	3.3	26.2	65.9

(Data from the U.S. Bureau of Mines.)

first seems peculiar, but it commonly results from the differences of ship versus overland transportation rates. Thus the city of Boston has at times found ship-transported coal from Europe cheaper than rail-transported coal from the nearer domestic Appalachian fields of Kentucky and West Virginia. Another cause for the importing and exporting of the same commoditites is the **spot market.** Most large corporations require a stable long-term supply of raw materials and therefore often enter into multiyear contracts with suppliers at pre-agreed prices. When these companies or smaller non-contract companies need extra amounts of raw materials, they bid for them on an open or spot market in which prices may be higher or lower than long-term contract prices. These prices may also fluctuate rapidly, whereas contract prices are stable. The materials available on the spot market vary in quantity, quality, and place of origin from one day to another.

The increasing dependence of the industrialized nations such as the United States on other nations for resource materials clearly emphasizes the need for international cooperation and highlights the impossibility of becoming isolationist.

The Control of Resources: Corporations, Governments and Cartels

Corporations. Private companies and corporations have long been the traditional means of ownership of the mineral industries in capitalist societies. Most began either through single individuals or through small groups who put together venture capital to finance the extraction and processing of minerals. The more successful prospered, often expanding into large corporations, whereas the less successful went out of business or were bought up by the larger corporations. Today there remain many small mining, drilling, and processing operations but the overwhelming bulk of mineral commodities are produced by a relatively small number of large corporations. Most mineral companies began with a single product, but in recent years there has been a tendency to expand into multiple mineral commodities in order to have greater flexibility in changing markets. Typical examples are the large oil companies, many of whom expanded into coal and metal mining. However, as a result of the downturn in metal mining in the 1980s, many of these companies have closed their metal mining divisions.

Throughout the first half of the twentieth century, many American, European, Canadian, Australian, and South African corporations expanded into the developing, often still colonial, countries in Africa, South America, and Southeast Asia. Subsequently, especially in the 1960s and 1970s, the desire for independence and control of their own resources has led many former

colonies to alter the original terms of mineral exploitation agreements. Hence, either through nationalization (acquiring more than 50 percent control) or through expropriation, the ownership of the mines and oil fields of many of the developing countries has been assumed by the host countries. This has not only weakened the dominance of some of the large mineral companies but has also given greater political significance to the mineral commodities.

The first major act of nationalization to affect American companies and supplies occurred in 1938 when the Mexican government nationalized its oil industry and formed Petroleos Mexicanos (PEMEX), the state-run petroleum company. Nationalization of American oil interests also occurred in Peru but was a more gradual process beginning in the early 1960s. More recently, a wave of nationalization has affected the world's copper industries. This began in 1967 when Chile announced plans to gradually nationalize the copper mines developed by major American companies; expropriation was finally announced in 1973. Between 1970–1975 the Zambian government assumed complete ownership of its major mines, and in 1973–1974 Peru nationalized its major producers.

Although nationalization and expropriation have commonly been justified by the host countries on the grounds that foreign companies have been improperly exploiting the local resources, the actions have often backfired because the threat of future repetition limits the willingness of foreign companies to participate further in the development of a country's resources. Without the expertise and venture capital of the major companies, developing countries commonly do not have the capability to discover and exploit the resources for themselves.

Governments. The degree of control over mineral resources exercised by governments varies widely from one nation to another and within individual nations, depending on the philosophy of the rulers or ruling party. Traditionally, the governments of capitalist countries have regulated mining methods and imposed taxes on earnings or profits but have left the extraction of minerals and fuels to private corporations. In contrast, socialist and communist societies have tended to have state operated or quasi-governmental companies. In a capitalist society, a company must mine at a profit or go out of business. Reductions in demand for a domestically produced mineral commodity, resulting from economic recession, importation of lower-priced foreign materials, or other circumstances usually causes cutbacks in production, and manpower, and, if too severe, closure of the operation. In socialist or communist societies, mining at a profit is desirable but not essential to survival. Thus, state-run mines often continue

to produce large amounts of mineral commodities even at a loss because the government always provides employment for all workers, and the government needs the mineral commodities for foreign trade.

In countries such as Norway, unprofitable mines are frequently subsidized by the government because such expenditure is cheaper than the welfare which would be required for the unemployed if the mines were closed, and because many northern and interior parts of the country would depopulate if the mines did not provide jobs. Other governments, such as those of the Irish Republic and some Canadian provinces, have provided cash subsidies, tax relief, or low interest loans to companies in order to start mining or continue operation of unprofitable mines and to maintain jobs.

It is apparent that the governments of the developing countries now realize the importance of their mineral resources to the developed countries and to their own development. They need foreign capital to develop their resources but are no longer willing to give up control to foreign companies. Accordingly, as the United States and the countries of Western Europe become more dependent on these countries for resources, the negotiation of mining rights, production quotas, taxes and royalties, and the prices of the minerals will become ever more delicate issues.

Cartels and Syndicates.   Cartels and syndicates are groups of companies or individuals who join together to control or finance the production of some commodity. Their primary aims are usually to control the availability of their commodity and to maximize the income from its sale. Numerous cartels, syndicates, and trade organizations (less formal groups) exist in the mineral industries but most remain relatively inconspicuous and little known to the general public. The one obvious exception in recent years is the Organization of Petroleum Exporting Countries (OPEC), which after achieving the dominant position in oil production, shocked the world by announcing an embargo on shipments to the United States and several European countries in 1973. Ever since, most other cartels have wanted to control the prices of their commodities as well as OPEC controlled world oil prices through the 1970s. A less conspicuous, much longer-lived and even more successful organization is the DeBeers syndicate which has controlled the distribution and pricing of the world's gem diamond supply for nearly a century.

Some of the major mineral commodity organizations are listed in Table 2-4. No others have had the success of OPEC or DeBeers because they have not controlled so important a commodity nor have they controlled it so dominantly. The increasing number of developing countries participating in cartels and other trade organizations suggest that such groups may play a

TABLE 2-4

The major mineral cartels, syndicates, and trade groups

Name	Commodity	Membership
Organization of Petroleum Exporting Countries (OPEC)	Petroleum	Algeria, Ecuador, Gabon, Indonesia, Iran, Iraq, Kuwait, Libya, Nigeria, Qatar, Saudi Arabia, United Arab Emirates, Venezuela
DeBeers	Diamonds	Operates in several countries but does not have members
Intergovernmental Council of Copper Exporting Countries (CIPEC)	Copper	Chile, Peru, Zambia, Zaire
International Bauxite Association	Bauxite	Australia, Guinea, Guyana, Jamaica, Sierra Leone, Surinam, Yugoslavia
Tungsten Producing Nations	Tungsten	Australia, Brazil, Bolivia, Canada, China, France, Peru, Portugal, S. Korea, Thailand, Zaire
Association of Tin Producing Countries (ATPC)	Tin	Australia, Bolivia, Indonesia, Malaysia, Nigeria, Thailand, Zaire
International Tin Committee	Tin	All major producers and consumers

more important role in the future availability of mineral resources. In order to better understand cartels and syndicates, we shall briefly examine the development of the two most important ones—OPEC and DeBeers.

OPEC and Middle Eastern Oil: OPEC has become a familiar word worldwide as this oil cartel has achieved international importance. The birth and development of OPEC are rooted in the early discoveries and subsequent partitioning of oil rights in the Middle East. The control of the oil resources of the Middle East did not become an important concern of Western nations until World War I because the energy needs of the industrial economies of Europe had been met by coal, and the United States had sufficient domestic oil. However in 1901, a far-sighted British engineer, William D'Arcy, was granted the exclusive privilege to "search for, obtain, exploit, develop, render suitable for trade, carry away, and sell natural gas, petroleum, [and] asphalt . . . throughout the whole extent of the Persian Empire" (modern Iran) for £20,000 cash, £20,000 stock, 16 percent of annual net profits, and a rent of £1800 per year. After near bankruptcy, oil was finally discovered in 1908 and in 1911 the British Admiralty,

under Winston Churchill, signed a 20-year supply contract. The coup by the Reza Shah in 1921 required new agreements that provided new income but at the same time extended D'Arcy's company exclusive rights until the year 1993.

American interests entered the scene in the 1920s when British and American companies merged. The United States believed that it had an "energy crisis" and sought more foreign oil to supply its growing needs. The American involvement came through the purchase of oil rights throughout the Middle East, especially the Arabian peninsula, by the famed "seven sisters"—Standard Oil of New Jersey (Exxon), Texaco, Gulf, Mobil, Standard Oil of California (SOCAL or Chevron), Anglo-Persian, and Royal Dutch/Shell. Gulf bought up Saudi Arabian leases which had originally been granted to a Major Holmes for £2000 a year; but Holmes found no oil. SOCAL obtained concessions in Saudi Arabia in 1933 for 60 years for £5000 per year, a £150,000 loan, and a royalty of 4 shillings per ton *for all time* and a promise of *no taxes*. Finally, in 1938, after much searching and drilling, the first of the large oil fields was discovered. The German threat to overrun North Africa and the Middle East in the early years of World War II ended with their defeat at El-Alamein in 1942. In spite of consolidation of a patchwork of regional governments and some new negotiation of concessions, the seven sisters increased their control during and after World War II and began major oil exports to the nations that were rebuilding in Europe and to Japan. By 1949 they controlled 65 percent of the world's oil reserves and 92 percent of reserves outside the United States, Mexico, and the Soviet Union.

The 1950s was a bonanza period for the international oil companies in the Middle East as production and profits rose to a total of nearly $15 billion. Production of this low-cost oil led to a surplus of crude oil and increased imports into U.S. markets. Import quotas, that protected those markets for higher-priced U.S. domestic oil, increased the supply of crude oil which was now forced to seek European markets. This led the international companies, without consultation with the producer governments, to reduce posted oil prices by about $7\frac{1}{2}$ percent to about $1.80 per barrel; actual oil prices dropped as low as $1.30 by the mid-1960s. This brought about a significant and unanticipated drop in the revenues to the Arab countries that were enraged by such unilateral action. In September 1959, the oil ministers of Saudi Arabia, Kuwait, Iran, and Iraq were joined by the minister from Venezuela in Baghdad and formed the Organization of Petroleum Exporting Countries which set as its objective the maintenance of stable oil prices at a restored pre-1959 level. OPEC failed to restore prices but did succeed in preventing further cuts and gradually increased the proportions of the countries

TABLE 2-5

Membership of the Organization of Petroleum Exporting Countries

Algeria	Saudi Arabia*
Ecuador	United Arab Emirates
Gabon	Abu Dhabi
Indonesia	Fujairah
Iran*	Sharjah
Iraq*	Dubai
Kuwait*	Ras al Khaimah
Libya	Ajman
Nigeria	Umm al Qaiwain
Qatar	Venezuela*

*Organizing members in 1960.

to the companies profits from 50:50 to more than 85:15. As shown in Table 2-5, three more major producers joined OPEC within 3 years and, ultimately, the membership grew to 13 nations.

During the 1960s, political and economic divisions within OPEC and the availability of excess production capacity worldwide prevented OPEC from increasing oil prices. The OPEC countries relied on the increase in oil produced (from 8.7 to 23.2 million barrels per day in 1960 and 1970 respectively) to provide more oil revenues ($2.5 billion in 1960 to $7.8 billion in 1970). By about 1970, the oil scene was changing as the world's (and especially the United States') cushion of spare crude oil output capacity was dropping. The Suez Canal remained closed as an aftermath of the 1967 Israeli-Egyptian War. The 500,000 barrel per day Trans-Arabian pipeline (Tapline) which transported Saudi Arabian crude oil to Syrian ports was ruptured, and the Middle Eastern Arab world grew hostile toward the West in general, and toward oil companies in particular. In 1971, OPEC began to form a united front and even threatened an embargo. Consequently it won price concessions which raised the price to about $3.00 per barrel. Arab frustration over the stalemated Arab-Israeli conflict and over the reluctance of oil companies to raise prices grew until late in 1973.

On October 6, 1973, Egypt and Syria moved militarily to dislodge Israel from land it had held since 1967. As a result, the atmosphere at the OPEC meeting that began in Vienna 2 days later was electric. OPEC moved swiftly in rejecting company proposals to raise oil prices by 8–15 percent and countered with a staggering 100 percent increase proposal. On October 16, the price was finally pegged at a 70 percent increase ($5.12 per barrel) and on October 17, OPEC pronounced that oil-consuming countries were divided into four categories with the United States among the "embargoed." The communique said that the Arab oil cutback would let the United States know "the heavy price which the big industrial countries are having to

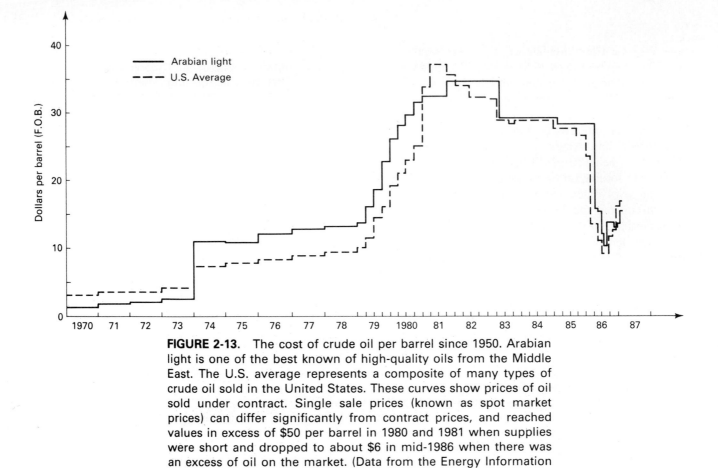

FIGURE 2-13. The cost of crude oil per barrel since 1950. Arabian light is one of the best known of high-quality oils from the Middle East. The U.S. average represents a composite of many types of crude oil sold in the United States. These curves show prices of oil sold under contract. Single sale prices (known as spot market prices) can differ significantly from contract prices, and reached values in excess of $50 per barrel in 1980 and 1981 when supplies were short and dropped to about $6 in mid-1986 when there was an excess of oil on the market. (Data from the Energy Information Agency.)

pay as a result of America's blind and unlimited support for Israel."

Panic struck the oil industry and the western world in general as suddenly the principal energy source of the industrialized nations, previously always assumed to be cheap and available, was suddenly scarce and expensive. By January 1979, OPEC raised oil prices to $11.65, and the energy crisis led to lines of customers at gasoline stations and limited allocation schemes. OPEC had become a household word.

Although there have been no more embargoes, OPEC was very effective in raising the price of world oil (Fig. 2.13) and did occasionally threaten to withhold oil. The rapid rise in the price of oil, especially between 1979–1981, stimulated the exploration for new oil fields, substitution of other fuels, and conservation.

The success of the new exploration was coupled with a price that was high enough to make previously known, but uneconomic, oil profitable and resulted in a significant increase in the world's oil supply. England, Norway, Mexico, and many other countries became major exporters of oil, thus providing a competition for OPEC. This resulted in a gradual slide in the price of oil after the peak of about $35 in 1980 and 1981. The culmination came at the end of 1985 when both OPEC and non-OPEC suppliers began undercutting prices in order

to maintain or secure larger portions of the oil markets. Oil markets had a flood of excess oil, and prices tumbled with that for Arab Light crude (a premium grade oil from Saudi Arabia) selling for $6.08 in late July 1986. OPEC oil ministers had agreed since December 1985 that they should cut production in order to dry up the excess of oil on the market and drive prices higher, but they had been unable to agree on how much each country's production quota should be reduced. Economic considerations were constantly influenced by the on-going Iran-Iraq War and the reluctance of either of these OPEC members to see the other benefit from added oil revenues. Furthermore, Saudi Arabia, the dominant OPEC producer, was upset by the failure of the other members to follow its lead or recommendations on quotas.

It is difficult to predict the future of OPEC oil production and the price of oil, but, as discussed in Chapter 4, the OPEC members control the bulk of the world's known oil reserves, and, if they can again agree on policies and quotas, they will play a very significant role in world energy matters and politics in the decades to come. It is also apparent that future OPEC efforts to dramatically raise the price of oil will likely increase production from non-OPEC crude oil sources as it did in the early 1980s, result in increased conservation, and

stimulate interest in competing forms of energy. Consequently, many analysts believe that the world may see future tightening of oil availability, but that "crises" of the type seen in 1973 and 1979 are unlikely.

Diamonds and the DeBeers Sydnicate: The earliest known accounts of **diamonds** are of Indian stones being transported to Greece in about 480 B.C. Throughout most of subsequent history, diamonds have been among the most valuable of mineral commodities per unit weight or size. They were mostly found in alluvial deposits in river beds in India and Brazil and rarely in various other parts of the world and hence remained relatively scarce and valuable until late in the nineteenth century. This situation changed dramatically after a South African Boer farmer's children found a "pretty pebble" in the sandy bed of the Vaal River in 1866. By the 1870s prospectors had located rich alluvial deposits

and diamond pipes in South Africa. The deep weathering allowed the rock to be easily removed by steam shovels just like loose gravel. The sudden influx of millions of **carats** (the standard measure for diamonds, equal to 1/5 gram) of diamonds onto a relatively small world market resulted in a price collapse which saw the value drop to less than 1 dollar a carat and the abandonment of many mines which were no longer profitable.

Cecil John Rhodes, famed British colonial statesman, founder of Rhodesia (now Zimbabwe), and sponsor of the Rhodes scholarships at Oxford University, moved to South Africa at the age of 17 in 1870 and became a supervisor at his brother's diamond mine the following year. Over the next 15 years he gradually gained control over several additional mines and in 1888 formed the DeBeers Consolidated Mines, Ltd. This consortium was established to control the production and sale of the world's diamonds, nearly all of which now came from Rhodes' mines (Fig. 2.14). The basic opera-

FIGURE 2-14. The "Big Hole" at Kimberley in South Africa was one of the early rich diamond mines brought into the DeBeers Syndicate by Cecil John Rhodes. The hole is 495 meters deep and is now partially filled with water. In its short life, it produced more than 14 million carats of diamonds. (Photograph courtesy of DeBeers Consolidated Mines Ltd.)

tion was simple and exceedingly successful—the mines would release only the number of gem diamonds to meet the demand, largely stones for the rings of American brides.

DeBeers' continued to control the total world market, even as new mines outside of South Africa were opened, by contracting to buy all gem quality stones from the new operations. When the demand for diamonds dropped during the depression years of the 1930s, DeBeers merely cut back on production and stockpiled stones. Subsequently, the American and European markets grew and stabilized through the 1960s. DeBeers then turned their attention to the nearly untapped market in Japan where diamonds were not traditionally prized. As a result of the trend toward westernization and agressive advertizing, the Japanese market rapidly expanded. In the 10 years from 1967–1977, the percentage of Japanese brides receiving diamonds rose from 5 to more than 60 percent.

Over the years, numerous individuals have pointed out that the perceived value of diamonds, like that of gold, has been purely arbitrary and bears no relationship to their intrinsic value. It has generally been believed that DeBeers created and maintained an illusion through advertising that "diamonds are forever," that they are the best symbol of love, and that they have a market value far greater than nearly any other substance. The major diamond producers have cooperated with DeBeers in maintaining a limited availability of diamonds, because it is the only way that prices could be held high. If an open market for diamonds were to develop, the price would probably drop drastically and fluctuate widely. Since the late 1970s, the world's diamond market has lacked some of the traditional stability that the DeBeers syndicate had provided and this has resulted in considerable uncertainty regarding the future value of diamonds.

The decline in value of the American dollar in the late 1970s led to much speculation in diamonds as investments and a rapid rise in their value. This trend was reversed in the early 1980s when high interest rates drew investment money out of diamonds and resulted in the dumping of many diamonds onto the world market. The availability of these stones and the flow of new diamonds from recently opened mines in the Soviet Union, Africa, and Australia reduced DeBeers' influence over the world market and stretched their financial resources as they tried to continue buying up gem quality stones. It is not clear whether or not DeBeers will be able to continue to maintain prices and its control of the world's diamond markets in view of the increasing numbers of gem stones. The future of the diamond market is further clouded by the potential production of synthetic diamonds of gem quality. Previously only industrial stones have been produced synthetically.

Resources in World Politics

Strategic Resources. The term strategic has been applied to a variety of mineral resources, especially metals, which have become important to certain key industries. There is no absolute definition of what is a strategic mineral, but the term is most often employed today in referring to metals used in military defense and in energy programs such as chromium, cobalt, niobium, nickel, platinum, and tantalum. To this group are often added titanium, manganese, aluminum, and up to 10 or more other mineral commodities depending on who compiles the list. Furthermore, we have come to recognize the vital importance of chemical minerals and fuels to feed and drive our industries and fertilizers to grow our foods.

What constitutes a strategic resource has changed throughout time. For earliest humans, the only strategic mineral materials were water and salt. In the Bronze Age copper and tin assumed vital roles as the principal metals for tools and weapons. The Romans are said to have required three basic metals for their society: iron for weapons, gold to pay the soldiers, and lead to make the pipes to transport water. The vast complexity of modern technology has expanded the list of important, if not always vital, minerals on which we depend for our life styles.

The primary concern of many governments now, as in the past, is that there should exist a reliable and adequate supply of the strategic materials. The United States, Great Britain, Japan, and most of the other major industrialized nations do not have adequate domestic supplies of many of the mineral commodities they consider strategic. Figure 2.10 shows the high degree of American and Japanese dependence on foreign supplies for many important mineral commodities in comparison with the Soviet Union which is much more self-sufficient. The need to ensure the availability of strategic materials in times when political, economic, social, and military factors can disrupt the flow of foreign supplies affects governmental and industrial policies. Major mining and manufacturing companies in industrialized countries will often participate in joint ventures in foreign countries, especially in the developing areas of Africa, Latin America, and Southeast Asia but only if they feel that their investments are safe. Consequently, American governmental policies in trade, assistance, and even military presence are directly affected by the nation's needs for mineral resources and, to some extent, by the foreign investment of American companies. This has been especially evident in dealings with the oil-rich countries of the Middle East because of the dependence of the United States and its allies on oil.

In order to prevent disruptions in supplies, espe-

cially from foreign sources, and from halting necessary industries, many governments have developed stockpiles. The concept of the stockpile as applied to food stuffs, as well as mineral commodities, is as old as recorded history. The Biblical story in Genesis 41 relates how the stockpiling of grain during 7 years of plenty permitted Egypt to survive the ensuing 7 years of famine. Nations today have responded not so much to prophecy, as did Egypt, but to actual or imminent shortages. Now nearly all major industrialized countries have stores of important materials. The modern American stockpile of strategic mineral commodities was conceived during World War I when the United States found itself cut off from supplies of several minerals that had been imported from Germany. The first substantive action, however, was taken in 1938 when Congress, fearing the likelihood of another war, appropriated funds to initiate the procurement of materials. This was followed by the passage of the Strategic Materials Act of 1939 and the purchase of materials such as tin, quartz crystals, and chromite. At the end of World War II, the surplus government stocks of minerals were transferred to the Strategic Stockpile, and Congress enacted the Strategic and Critical Materials Stock Piling Act of 1946. This act, which is the basis of the present stockpile, reads in part, "The purpose of this act . . . is to . . . decrease and prevent wherever possible a dangerous and costly dependence of the United States upon foreign nations for supplies of . . . materials in times of national emergency." The paramount importance of strategic minerals for economic prosperity and for waging war was recognized by both Germany and Japan during the 1930s and both countries acquired stocks of the mineral commodities they deemed necessary for their aggressive plans. (Additional details are given in the section on "Resources and International Conflict.")

Although the United States' military establishment has maintained specific reserves of petroleum (such as the Naval Arctic Petroleum Reserve which covers vast areas southwest of the North Slope oil fields in Alaska), the oil embargo of 1973 raised great concern regarding the nation's petroleum reserve status. Accordingly, the government authorized the development of a Strategic Oil Reserve of 1 billion barrels of oil and subsequently began to acquire oil and store it in large caverns carved into salt domes in Louisiana and Texas. Despite episodic development and the opposition of OPEC, which preferred not to have such stores which could be used to lessen the control of their policies on world oil supply, the oil reserve had risen to more than 500 million barrels by mid-1986. Although the goal of 1 billion barrels is significant, it represents only about 60-days supply of American oil needs!

There can be little doubt that the strategic impor-

tance of mineral resources will increase in the years ahead as the industrialized nations increasingly turn to the developing countries for more resources. At the same time, the increasing populations of the developing countries and the increase in their own needs will stretch their abilities to provide the resources. This will be tempered by the needs of the developing countries for foreign revenues, generated largely through the export of mineral resources. It is clear, however, that the international flow of strategic minerals and fuels will continue to play a major role in the world's political and economic activities in the future.

Resources and International Conflict. Mineral resources are the raw materials and fuels by which modern industrialized societies function. To be deprived of them would rapidly lead to a collapse of a nation's economy and industry. So vital are these resources that countries have before, and may again, fight for them.

The primary mineral resource today is oil and the world's principal reserves lie in the Middle East. Accordingly, there has been considerable speculation that a future world-wide conflict could well begin over control of the Middle East because whoever controls that oil has a powerful edge in any conflict. The importance of oil and other minerals has been apparent in earlier times of conflict. Thus, prior to World War II, both Japan and Germany considered their needs for oil, steel, and other minerals before beginning aggressive actions.

In the 1920s and 1930s, Germany was rebuilding from the defeat in World War I and clearly recognized the need for resources to run any future war machine. In 1936 Hitler ordered that Germany should be 100 percent self-sufficient in terms of the raw materials—oil, steel, iron ore, synthetic rubber, and aluminum—in the event of war. Because of the shortage of crude oil, Germany constructed synthetic oil plants which produced petroleum from coal. Once war had begun, Germany found that her iron ores were insufficient, so ores were imported from Sweden and the occupied areas of Austria, Czechoslavakia, and the Alsace-Lorraine area of France. Alloying metals were in short supply, but the occupied countries often provided the sources: Norway, nickel; Ukraine, manganese; and Balkans, chrome. Germany's copper, lead, and tin reserves were limited, but the seizure of stocks of these metals in occupied countries and energetic salvage drives provided what was needed.

Japan, which had been bogged down in a semi-colonial war in China, waged in large part for control of the coal and oil there and for several years used the distraction of the German defeat of France and Holland to move into the rice fields of Indo-China, the rubber plantations of Malaysia, and the oil fields of the Netherlands

East Indies to obtain the resources needed for the war being planned. President Roosevelt reacted to this action by placing an embargo on the top grades of scrap iron and oil sales to Japan from the United States in July 1940. Relations between the two countries deteriorated for a year until the United States broke off negotiations in July 1941, and Japan found itself in a total embargo of all strategic materials. The greatest concern was for oil: The navy had only an 18-month supply and the army had only a 12-month supply. The military leaders argued vehemently for war as they saw their fuel supplies growing ever smaller. They believed that a swift attack to incapacitate the American Pacific Fleet would leave Japan free to exploit and import the oil she needed from Southeast Asia. Hence, Japan attacked Pearl Harbor on December 7, 1941.

The wartime shortages emphasized the critical importance of many mineral resources, especially oil. Consequently, all the major industrial nations have become more concerned about having stockpiles of strategic materials and maintaining access to the major supplies. Developing and future technologies may redefine which mineral resources are vital but will not lessen our future dependence on resources in general.

FURTHER READINGS

BUTOW, R.J.C., *Tojo and the Coming of the War*. Stanford, California: Stanford University Press, 1969, 584 p.

FLAWN, P.T., *Mineral Resources*. New York: John Wiley and Sons, 1966, 406 p.

NEWBY, G., *The World Atlas of Exploration*, New York: Crescent Books, 1985.

RICKARD, T.A., *Man and Metals*. New York: Arno Press, 1974, 1068 p.

SCHROEDER, P.W., *The Axis Alliance and Japanese American Relations 1941*. Ithaca, New York: Cornell University Press, 1958, 245 p.

SEYMOUR, I., *OPEC: Instrument of Change*. New York: St. Martin's Press, 1981, 306 p.

TYLECOTE, R.F., *A History of Metallurgy*. London: The Metals Society, 1976, 182 p.

WARREN, K., *Mineral Resources*. New York: John Wiley and Sons, 1973, 272 p.

3

The giant smelter at Morenci, Arizona, is one of the world's largest copper-producing complexes and demonstrates the impact of mining, smelting, and waste disposal on the environment. Ore from an open pit mine just out of view at the left is brought by truck to the mill and smelter which make up the complex of buildings surrounding the two smokestacks. There the valuable copper minerals are separated from the containing rock, and the copper-rich concentrate is smelted down to copper metal. (Photograph by B. J. Skinner.)

IMPACT ON THE ENVIRONMENT OF RESOURCE EXPLOITATION AND USE

During the period roughly up to 1975, governments were concerned primarily with setting up institutions and adopting new laws and regulations to abate and control environmental pollution. Today a second generation of environmental policies is emerging. In addition to the abatement of gross pollution there is a growing commitment to the wise husbandry of all natural resources and to the improvement of the quality of life.

FROM A REPORT ON THE STATE OF THE ENVIRONMENT
IN OECD[1] MEMBER COUNTRIES

INTRODUCTION

The second half of the twentieth century has seen a very rapid growth in awareness of the importance and complexity of environmental problems by scientists, political leaders, and the public. This has led to much more research on environmental problems, the teaching of courses on environmental science at colleges and universities, the formation of campaigning groups or even political parties united by environmentalist causes, and, ultimately, legislation to help prevent deterioration of the natural environment through human activities. This rising tide of activity has resulted both from public awareness of our cumulative abuses of the environment through past centuries and from the rapidly increasing levels of resource exploitation and utilization linked to population growth and growing rates of material consumption in many countries.

This volume is not a text on environmental sciences, but it would be misleading to discuss the resources of the earth (fuels and other energy sources, metals, industrial rocks and minerals, fertilizers, water, and soils) without considering the impact that their exploitation and use has on the world in which we live. These are matters that rightly concern every one of us and that carry very serious implications for future generations. In this chapter, we first examine the ways in which exploitation of resources directly affects the environment: the effects of mining, quarrying, dredging, well drilling and production, and also the effects of processing and smelting of ores. Next, we examine the ways in which using these resources affects the environment: the burning of fossil fuels, the burning of nuclear fuels and the disposal of the hazardous wastes that this creates, and the problems of **pollution** caused by other industrial processes. Finally, we examine the problems involved in disposal (or, where possible, of recycling) of

wastes that are produced in vast amounts, not only by manufacturing industries but by each one of us in our everyday lives.

HOW EXPLOITING RESOURCES AFFECTS THE ENVIRONMENT

Many of the most obvious, and some of the most severe disruptions of the natural environment come from the exploitation of resources. Mining, quarrying, dredging, the drilling and extraction from wells, are activities that have marked impacts on the landscape and environment. Directly linked to these activities are problems concerned with the disposal of the waste products that are often produced by them. Further environmental problems may be caused at the site of exploitation when various extraction or concentration processes are employed. For example, most metal mines remove from the ground an ore that contains only a very small proportion (commonly less than 10 percent) of the metal being extracted. In order to extract that metal, the ore must first be subjected to a broad range of physical and chemical processes. Thus, for the example of metal extraction, there are at least three aspects of the process that create potential environmental problems: the mining operation, the disposal of very large quantities of waste rock, and the smelting and refining of the ore.

Mining and Quarrying—The Methods

The method used to extract metallic, industrial or chemical minerals, building materials, or solid fuels such as coal or uranium, depends on the nature and location of the deposit. Depending on the deposit size, shape, depth beneath surface, and **grade** (percentage of valuable material or quality and purity), either a surface mining or underground mining technique is employed.

Surface mining, which accounts for about two-thirds of world solid mineral production, especially that involving sand and gravel, stone, phosphates, coal, cop-

[1]The Organization for Economic Cooperation and Development that includes the United States, Australia, Japan, United Kingdom, Canada, New Zealand, and 18 other, chiefly European, countries.

per, iron, and aluminum, generally involves **open pit mining** or a form of **strip mining.** Open pits are an economical method of extraction where large tonnages of reserves are involved, high rates of production are desirable, and where the waste material overlying the deposit (**overburden**) is thin enough to be removed without making the operation uneconomic. The term **quarry** generally refers to an open pit mine from which building stone or gravel is extracted. Many of the largest open pit mines, such as those in the southwest United States from which copper is won (Fig. 3.1), are developed as conical chasms with terraced benches that spiral downward to the bottom of the pit. These benches serve as haulage roads and working platforms on the steep, often 45°, sloping sides of the pit. Extraction proceeds by drilling, blasting, and loading material into large trucks that haul rock and ore out of the pit. The depth and diameter of the pit increase as mining takes place, in some cases reaching diameters of more than 2 kilometers and depths of several hundred meters.

The world's largest open pit mine at Bingham Canyon, Utah, has involved cutting away an entire mountain to form a pit roughly 3.5 by 2.5 kilometers and 1 kilometer deep. At the height of production, more than 100,000 metric tons of ore grading from approximately 0.3 percent copper were being produced per day. With a waste to ore stripping ratio of 3:1, this involved drilling, blasting, and removing an average of 400,000 metric tons of material per day using power shovels of 5–20 cubic meter capacity, rail cars of up to 80 metric tons capacity, and diesel trucks capable of handling up to 140 metric tons per load.

Strip mining is employed when the material to be extracted forms a flat-lying layer just beneath the surface. Many coal seams are exploited in this manner, but the method is also widely used in mining tar sands, phosphates, clays, and certain kinds of iron and uranium ores. These are all materials that can occur as thin, near-horizontal layers, often underlying enormous areas of country. The mining method involves removal of the overburden to expose the coal or other resource that is then scooped up and loaded into trucks or trains. The waste rock is dumped to the rear, and the mining continues along a strip that extends as far as practical. A new strip is then started parallel to the first, and waste from this strip is dumped on the preceding strip (Fig. 3.2). Large mechanical shovels and drag lines are used in removing overburden and the material being mined. Clearly, the ratio of overburden to material being mined is a crucial factor in this type of operation.

Underground mining, involving a system of subsurface workings, is used to extract any solid mineral resource that cannot be worked at the surface. Most mines consist of one or more means of access via vertical **shafts**, horizontal **adits**, or inclined roadways (**inclines**) as shown in Fig. 3.3. These provide transport of men, machinery, materials, and the extracted ore and wastes. They also form part of the systems for ventilation and

FIGURE 3-1. The huge open pit mine at Bingham Canyon, Utah, is more than 3 kilometers across and illustrates the magnitude of the environmental impact of the modern mining operations needed to supply our resources. Not visible are the large areas required to place the waste rock from the mine. (Courtesy of Kennecott Corporation.)

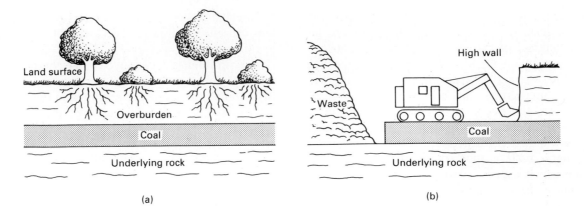

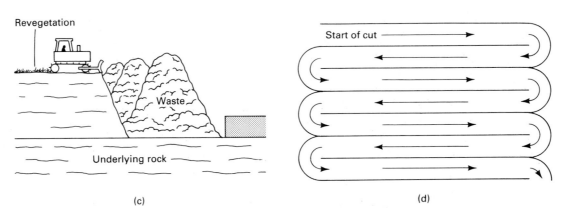

FIGURE 3-2. The sequence of steps involved in strip mining. (a) profile before mining; (b) profile during mining; (c) profile as land surface restoration begins; (d) plan view of mining sequence.

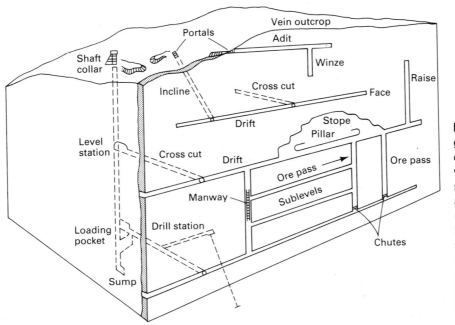

FIGURE 3-3. A schematic diagram of an underground mining operation. The roomlike areas where ore is removed is called a stope. The drifts and crosscuts are the tunnels leading to the mine entrance. Most deep mines have vertical entrances called shafts, but many near-surface mines have inclined or horizontal entrances termed inclines or adits. (After W. C. Peters, *Exploration and Mining Geology*, New York: John Wiley & Sons, 1978.)

the control of underground water that are essential to mining operations. Indeed, in many underground mines, substantial amounts of energy are expended in pumping air and water to keep the working areas dry and well ventilated. This is particularly the case where mining takes place in an extremely hostile environment. For example, the zinc mine that operated for many years at Friedensville, Pennsylvania, was in a karst terrain where water had to be pumped out routinely at rates at around 95,000 liters (25,000 gallons) per minute to prevent

flooding of the workings. When heavy rains fell on the mine area in February 1976, the pumping rate was raised to a peak of 227,000 liters (60,000 gallons) per minute to keep the mine from flooding. At the Konkola Mine in Zambia, possibly the wettest mine operating in the world today, the pumping rate is 280,000 liters (73,000 gallons) per minute. In the deep gold mines of the Witwatersrand, South Africa, mining levels are often more than 3000 meters below the surface, and the rock temperatures are over 32°C. Underground work-

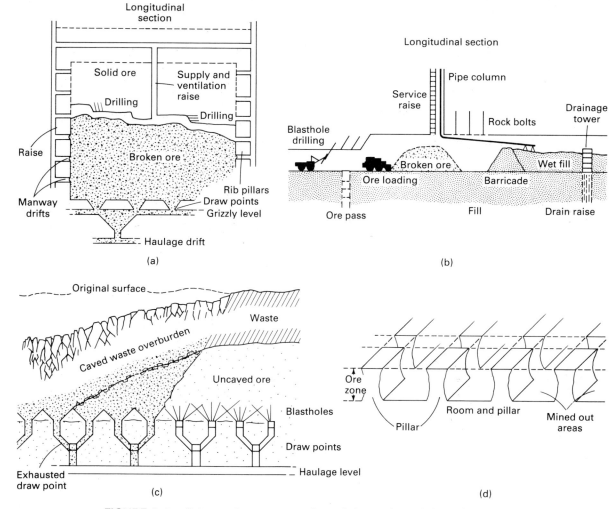

FIGURE 3-4. Schematic representation of the major mining methods. (a) Shrinkage stoping—ore is drilled and blasted from the ceiling (called the "back") and allowed to fall; subsequent drilling and blasting is carried out by working on top of the broken ore. (b) Cut-and-fill stoping—as ore is removed, the open space left is refilled with waste material. This method has the advantage of filling the open mined-out stopes and disposing of the wastes below ground but is very expensive. (c) Block caving—an entire mass of ore is loosened by blasting from below and then is allowed to slowly flow through the draw points. (d) Room and pillar—the ore is mined in a series of rooms, leaving pillars to support the overlying rocks. [(a) (b) (c) After W. C. Peters, *Exploration and Mining Geology*, New York: John Wiley & Sons, 1978.]

ings usually consist of intersecting horizontal tunnels (**drifts** and **crosscuts**) often on several **levels** and joined by further vertical openings (**raises** or **winzes**). The region where ore is extracted in a metalliferous mine is referred to as a **stope**, and the area that is actually drilled and removed is called a **face**. Examples of some of the many underground mining methods are shown in Fig. 3.4. The method employed in any mine will depend on the shape, size, and grade of the ore body or seam that is being worked. This, in turn, will determine the kinds of machinery used to breakup and carry away the ores and waste rocks. In most mines, ore extraction and mine development involve drilling, blasting, and removal with mechanical diggers onto underground railway cars or dump trucks that reach the surface via a shaft, incline or adit. Some coal mines today are only about 1 meter high, just high enough to allow the use of continuous mining machines that cut the coal with rotating teeth and then feed it back to transport cars or conveyor belts. In contrast, some large stopes, such as that shown in Fig. 3.5, that have been excavated in the zinc mines of the Appalachians stand as open galleries more than 70 meters high and 100 meters long. Other factors that will affect the mining methods are related to ground conditions such as the strength of rocks encountered underground, fracturing in these rocks, and the ground water conditions. For example, drifts, crosscuts, and stopes in a tin mine in **granite** may require little or no roof support, whereas in a coal mine in much weaker sedimentary rocks, extensive roof support with timbers or other props may be needed.

A number of more unusual mining methods are used to extract particular resources. **Hydraulic mining** uses high-pressure jets of water to wash soft sediments down an incline toward some form of concentration plant where dense mineral grains (such as gold) are separated. **Solution mining** involves dissolving the ore in water or some other fluid introduced into the ore body and has mostly been used to extract salt or sulfur (Fig. 3.6). An extension of the principles involved in solution mining has been applied to the extraction of metals by **in situ leaching**. The method is being used to recover copper, gold, and uranium from low-grade ores. The value of *in situ* leaching is evidenced by the fact that today it permits the economic extraction of gold ores grading 0.02 troy ounce per metric ton (0.6 parts per million), whereas conventional mining requires a minimum grade of about 0.2 troy ounce per metric ton (6 parts per million). *In Situ* leaching is thought by some to be a mining method likely to have much wider application in the future. Proposals have included the detonation of nuclear blasts at the bottom of a large ore body to cause extensive fracturing, drilling of wells into this mass for injection and recovery of leach liquors such as

FIGURE 3-5. A large hydraulic drill is cutting blast holes in a zinc ore between the pillars that support the overlying rock more than 15 meters above. (Courtesy of ASARCO Incorporated.)

sulfuric acid that will dissolve the valuable metals. It must be stated that there are many problems still remaining with such futuristic mining methods.

Environmental Impact of Mining and Quarrying

Much of the impact of mining and quarrying is obvious: the disruption of land otherwise suitable for agriculture, urban, or recreational use; the deterioration of the immediate environment through noise and airborne dust; the creation of an environment that is among the most dangerous for its workers and is potentially hazardous for the public. These are all environmental problems associated with mining. However, mining is a relatively short-term activity, and much can be done both to limit environmental damage during mining and to restore the land when mining operations are complete. Today, in many countries legislation has been enacted at nearly all levels to ensure that these steps are taken. However, such laws have commonly had adverse effects on the

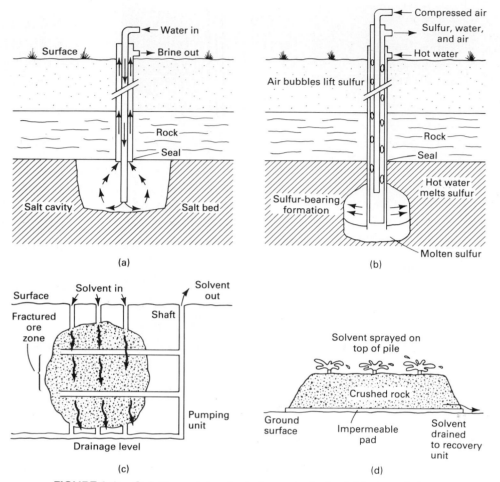

FIGURE 3-6. Solution mining techniques include: (a) bottom injection systems used to dissolve soluble materials such as salt; (b) the Frasch system in which superheated water is pumped down to melt sulfur; the molten sulfur is carried upward in the innermost pipe; (c) *in situ* ore leaching in which a solvent (commonly an acid) is drained downward through a previously fractured ore zone; and (d) heap leaching in which broken rock is placed on an impermeable pad on the ground, and a solvent is sprayed over the rock.

production of mineral resources because the restrictions they impose have made mining uneconomic. Unfortunately, the absence of adequate controls over some mining activities in the past has left numerous scars on the surface of the earth and a resistance among many members of the public toward new mining activities in their localities.

Fortunately, many underground mines leave little evidence of their presence even after the mining operations have ceased. Usually they are filled slowly by percolating ground waters, but the rocks are strong enough to stand solidly in spite of the abandoned mine openings and passageways. Sometimes the old mines can, in fact, be put to very good use. Examples include the storage of an important archive of seeds of the world's major grains in an old coal mine in Spitsbergen, the burial of

nuclear wastes in abandoned salt mines in Germany, and the development of an extensive office and shipping complex in an old limestone mine in Kansas City, Missouri, (Fig. 3.7). In all three of these examples, the old mines are water tight, and the air temperatures and humidities remain nearly constant.

When an open pit mine closes, a large hole remains without any readily available waste rocks to fill it, except at very great cost. The pit slopes are often very steep and cannot be reclaimed by soil coverage and planting. If the ground water table is high enough, the bottom of the pit may be flooded, creating an artificial lake. The very large open pit mines are therefore difficult, if not impossible, to reclaim. Smaller open pit mines and quarries, on the other hand, can often be filled with waste rock or, if the geologic and ground wa-

FIGURE 3-7. The underground openings left after a mining operation has ceased can sometimes be put to good use. This former limestone operation in Kansas City, Missouri, mined using a room and pillar method, has been converted into a large underground storage area. Other parts of the same mine contain a trucking operation, an office complex, and a post office. The addresses are appropriately known as Underground Drive. (Courtesy of Hunt Midwest Real Estate Development Inc.)

ter conditions permit, can be used for the disposal of refuse or other waste materials (see p. 61). Gravel pits or rock quarries can sometimes be filled with water and become recreational lakes.

Active strip mines [Fig. 3.8(a)] often have an exposed face, called the *high wall*, where rock is being mined, an open cut, and piles of recently removed waste material. When merely abandoned these activities leave mounds of waste material too steep to build on or farm, without vegetation and therefore easily eroded, without

fertile soil, and with the ground waters poisoned by the effects of mining. Many thousands of acres of land in coal mining areas of Kentucky, West Virginia, Illinois, and other parts of the United States have been devastated in this way. Nevertheless, reclamation as a part of strip mining can be straightforward. Nearly all modern mining operations are required to include this as a normal final stage of extraction. As shown in Fig. 3.8(b), waste mounds can be smoothed out, topsoil stored and returned, and ground covering plants such as clover

FIGURE 3-8. (a) An operating coal strip mine in eastern West Virginia. In the foreground the overburden has been removed, exposing the coal bed (on which the front end loader is sitting). Once the coal has been removed (as in the background where the pick-up trucks are parked), reclamation will begin. The cliff at the right, known as the "high wall," reveals how much overburden had to be removed to excavate the coal bed. (Photograph by J. R. Craig.) (b) Proper reclamation procedures can restore previously mined areas to productive and attractive landscapes. (Courtesy of Lee Daniels.)

FIGURE 3-8. (cont.)

planted until the soil is sufficiently restored to allow other crops to flourish. In some of the most mountainous areas of West Virginia, the horizontal benches left after reclaiming strip mines are proving useful because they provide the only flat land, with excellent meadows for cattle and wild deer.

Underground mining does not lead to such drastic disruptions of the surface as open pit and strip mining, but a new hazard encountered is **subsidence**. This problem occurs most often where underground mining has approached the land surface or where the rocks are naturally weak or highly fractured. This is commonly seen where mining has been undertaken in soft sedimentary rocks, as in many coal mines, and where a method such as the "room and pillar" (see Fig. 3.4) was used. More

than 8000 square kilometers of land in the United States, for example, has subsided due to underground coal mining, and many more areas are threatened. Solution mining and the pumping of brine or water can also cause local subsidence. Subsidence is usually gradual and causes cracks, surface troughs, depressions, or bulges (Fig. 3.9). Sometimes, however, it is sudden and results in the destruction of houses and other buildings, roads, and farm areas.

An extreme example of this occurred at the zinc mine at Friedensville, Pennsylvania, in 1968. Gradual subsidence, with occasional minor episodic movement had begun to be noticed in 1964. Careful monitoring, including the installation of acoustic **seismographs** (rock movements were often inaudible to the unaided

FIGURE 3-9. The effects of subsidence in an old coal mining area are evident near Sheridan, Wyoming. Mining in the 1920s was carried out using a room and pillar method. Subsequently, there has been collapse of the overlying rocks into many of the rooms. (From C. R. Dunrud, U.S. Geological Survey Professional Paper 1164, 1980.)

ear) allowed the mine geologist to define and isolate the problem area. At 10:41 A.M. on March 27, 1968, a block of rock 225 meters long, by 115 meters wide, and over 180 meters thick dropped catastrophically. The energy released by this 11,000,000-metric ton block was equivalent to an earthquake of magnitude 3 on the **Richter Scale** and was recorded on several seismographs in the area. A vacant house and a portion of a state highway were destroyed, but there were no injuries or lost work time.

In addition to the impact that mining activities may have on the landscape, the environment may be disrupted over a wider area by changes in the distribution and chemistry of surface or ground waters. An example of this is **acid mine drainage** that is produced when the iron sulfide minerals, pyrite and marcasite (both forms of FeS_2), or pyrrhotite ($Fe_{1-x}S$) are exposed to oxidation by moist air to form sulfuric acid (H_2SO_4) plus various other sulfate compounds and iron oxides. Pyrite and marcasite occur as minor minerals in many coals and are important along with pyrrhotite in many metallic mineral deposits. The generation of sulfuric acid can occur when these minerals are exposed to air in underground mines, open pits, or the dumps of waste material left by the mining operations. Water passing through the mines or dumps becomes acidified and then can find its way into rivers and streams or into the ground water system of the area. It has been estimated that up to 10,000 miles of streams have been affected in this way in the United States alone, largely because of the impact of abandoned mine workings. The result is a major pollution problem giving rise to barren soils, and rivers and streams devoid of living things.

Although not so widespread as the problem of acid drainage, other undesirable compounds may also enter streams or ground waters from mines and mineral processing plants. These include arsenic and various compounds of heavy metals such as lead, cadmium, or mercury. The mining of uranium leads to particular problems that are discussed later in this chapter.

Disposal of Mining Wastes

Nearly all mining operations lead to the generation of waste rocks, often in very large amounts. If the method being used is strip mining, then the waste can be used in reclamation, but in underground mining operations and most kinds of open pit mining, an alternative method of disposal has to be found. Usually, this simply involves dumping the wastes in piles at the surface next to the mine workings. More rarely, the waste rock can be put back into the openings created by mining (**backfilled**). However, the cost involved in doing this is commonly

prohibitive, and backfilling may seriously restrict the development of the mine by making large areas no longer accessible.

Piles of waste rock are often unsightly and may be dangerous. Often, these wastes have been through a process of crushing associated with the separation out of the coal, metalliferous or industrial minerals being exploited. This increases the volume of the rock by as much as 40 percent and produces a material that may be unstable when placed in steep piles. A tragic illustration of this occurred in 1966 in the Welsh mining village of Aberfan. There, a 125 meter (400 feet) high pile of rock, which had accumulated on a mountainside during nearly a century of coal mining, slid down and engulfed many houses and a school, killing 144 people. This avalanche was estimated to have been made up of nearly 2 million metric tons of coal-mining waste.

Alternatives to the simple dumping of mining wastes, such as using them for landfill, are likely to be expensive and impractical in most cases. However, waste dumps can certainly be made safe and often can be reclaimed as recreational or agricultural land. Such reclamation may involve lowering the slopes on dumps and encouraging vegetation growth through **hydro-mulching** or **hydro-seeding**. These processes consist of spraying the dumps with a pulp or mulch of organic material such as bark or hay mixed with seeds and a binding substance. The organic substance provides some bed material for germination of the seeds. Once this happens, the roots will hold the mulch in place and form a protective layer of vegetation to minimize water erosion. The lower the slope on the dump, the more likely that revegetation will be successful.

There are numerous examples of successful reclamation of mining waste materials ranging from the planting down of the large piles of tailings outside Johannesburg, South Africa, to the seeding of the white quartz sand waste tips surrounding the china clay pits of Cornwall, England (see Fig. 9.18).

Dredging and Ocean Mining—
Methods and Environmental Impact

Dredging involves removal of unconsolidated material from rivers, streams, lakes, and shallow seas using machines such as the bucket-ladder dredge, dragline dredge, or suction dredge (Fig. 3.10). These methods are used extensively for the recovery of sand, gravel, and minerals such as the oxide ore of tin (cassiterite), gold, and diamonds. The largest and most advanced dredgers are those employed in the tin fields of Southeast Asia, some of which can handle up to 5 million cubic meters per annum and recover material as deep as

FIGURE 3-10. A small dredge operating in Alaska is recovering placer gold from river gravels. The bucket line at the left side cuts into the sediments and carries them into the dredge. The coarse rocks are dumped-off a conveyer belt projecting out on the right side. Gold particles are recovered by sluices and jigs within the dredge, and the fine sediments are pumped back into the river. The dredge moves slowly by digging on one end of its own small lake and dumping waste rock on the other end. (Photograph by Ernie Wolford and Joe Fisher, courtesy of Alaska Division of Mining and Geologic Survey.)

45 meters below the pond surface. In Sierra Leone and Ghana, large-scale diamond mining operations are undertaken using draglines, well suited to the swampy ground.

The oceans have long provided a source of sodium, magnesium, and bromine salts from materials dissolved in seawater. However, with the depletion of more conventional sources of other minerals, increasing attention is being paid to the mineral potential of deeper seas and oceans. Metal-rich sediments are known to occur in the Red Sea and along certain of the ocean ridges, but the main interest centers on **manganese nodules** (see p. 181). These pea- to cobble-sized, roughly spherical nodules cover large areas of the deep-ocean floor in places. As well as large amounts of manganese, they contain substantial nickel, copper, cobalt, and, in lesser amounts, a wide range of other elements. In fact, the total quantities of such metals as copper, nickel, and cobalt in manganese nodules probably equals the total in all known land deposits of these metals. They are very attractive as a resource, but mining the nodules poses technical, legal, and potential environmental problems. Most nodules lie beneath 4000–5000 meters of water, and various dredging or siphoning methods have been proposed for their recovery. Although the technical problems can probably be overcome, indeed some systems have already been tested and proved feasible, rights to mine nodules and the distribution of profits gained in their mining is a matter of continuing international disagreement. This is because the nodules largely lie in international waters, and all nations can claim some right to share their ownership.

Dredging and any form of ocean mining involves significant disruption of the natural systems of river, lake, shore, sea, or ocean and may result in the destruction of biological systems. There may also be long-term effects on river and ocean currents, sedimentation patterns, and patterns of erosion. The severity of the environmental impact of nodule mining is not known, but there are concerns that the disruption and dispersal of the sediment may harm delicate and little-known deep-sea fauna.

Well Drilling and Production— Environmental Impact

The drilling of wells is a method of exploiting liquid and gaseous resources that goes back many centuries, even being mentioned in 1500-year-old Chinese manuscripts as a means of tapping underground strata for brine. Modern drilling methods are used in the exploitation of water and geothermal energy and in the exploration and production stage of the oil and natural gas industries. Apart from the relatively minor disruption of the environment caused in the actual drilling of water or geothermal wells, there is little danger of damage arising from these activities. Drilling for oil and gas, on the other hand, does involve certain risks, although the disruption to the environment is generally much less than in major mining operations.

The technology involved in modern (rotary) drilling to locate and exploit oil and gas is discussed in detail in the chapter on fossil fuels (see p. 95). The greatest hazard that may be encountered during drilling is the

blowout which occurs when a high pressure oil or gas accumulation is unexpectedly encountered, and the column of (heavy) drilling fluid in the hole fails to contain the oil or gas that erupts from the wellhead (Fig. 3.11). The fire hazard is great, and severe pollution of the surrounding area can occur very rapidly. Nowadays, blowouts are comparatively rare because of improved equipment and monitoring of the drilling process. Thus, symptoms such as an increase in drilling rate accompanied by an increase in return flow of the drilling mud indicate that fluid from the hydrocarbon reservoir is entering the wellbore. Valves at the surface known as blowout preventers can then be closed and corrective measures, such as increasing the density of the drilling mud, taken to enable drilling to continue. In spite of these safety measures, major problems still occur. For example, one well blew out and caught fire in the Gulf of Mexico near the Yucatan Peninsula in 1979. It spewed oil for more than 9 months with a loss of oil

estimated at more than 130 million gallons (3.1 million barrels).

Clearly, the dangers to human life and to the environment are greater in the offshore oil fields that have been so extensively exploited over the last two decades. Nevertheless, major accidents have been relatively rare, although risks must increase as fields in deeper offshore waters and even less hospitable seas are developed. Some spillage of oil into the seas seems inevitable at such sites, and, as at all operations, care must be taken to prevent oil and brine seepage at the wellhead.

Processing and Smelting of Ores

The ores of all metals (see Chapters 6 and 7) and most of the industrial minerals (see Chapter 9) require a great deal of processing following their removal from the earth. Such processing is usually done at or near the sites of mining.

The percentage of metal in an as-mined ore ranges from greater than 30 percent in many aluminum and iron ores down to less than 0.0001 percent in the case of gold (Table 3.1). Even in copper mines, the grade in many currently worked deposits averages only 0.1–0.5 percent. In most ores, the metal-bearing minerals (commonly oxides, sulfides, arsenides, or, more rarely, alloys of the metals) are intergrown on a microscopic scale with valueless minerals (termed **gangue**) such as silicates or carbonates of the rocks that act as hosts to the ores (Fig. 3.12). In many operations, the first stage of processing is therefore a size reduction (or **comminution**) of blocks up to a meter across down to particles only a few tenths or hundredths of millimeters in diameter. This is achieved by first **crushing** and then grinding or **milling** the ores, using equipment of the types shown in Fig. 3.13. Whereas crushing is commonly a dry process, milling involves the abrasion of particles suspended in a fluid (usually water) and is therefore a wet process. This makes handling easier and reduces dust problems. The object of comminution is to break down the ore so that the ore mineral particles are freed or **liberated** as much as possible from the gangue. The second stage in ore processing involves separation of the ore and gangue minerals, and this may involve one or more of several methods. These commonly make use of differences in density, magnetic, electrical, or surface properties between the ore and the gangue minerals (Table 3.2).

The end products of such mineral processing operations (often termed **beneficiation**) are a **concentrate** of the ore minerals and a much larger quantity of waste gangue material known as **tailings**. Commonly, the tailings that are in the form of a fine-grained watery mixture, a slurry, are dumped into an artificial pond or lake and the fine particles allowed to settle. The water may

FIGURE 3-11. A blowout such as that shown here is one of the greatest hazards that can be encountered while drilling for oil. Extremely high pressures have forced the drill rods out of the hole and destroyed the drill tower. (Courtesy of Shell International Petroleum Company Limited.)

TABLE 3-1

Concentrations of metals in the earth's crust, their minimum grades to be mined, and the degree of natural concentration required for exploitation

Metal	Crustal Abundance (%)	Approximate Minimum Grade to Be Mined (%)	Approximate Degree of Concentration, Needed To Be Mined
Aluminum	8.2	40	5×
Iron	5.6	25	5
Titanium	0.57	1.5	25
Manganese	0.095	25	260
Vanadium	0.0135	0.5	35
Chromium	0.010	40	4000
Nickel	0.0075	1.0	130
Zinc	0.0070	2.5	350
Copper	0.0055	0.5	90
Cobalt*	0.0025	0.2	80
Lead	0.00125	3	2400
Uranium	0.00027	0.01	40
Tin	0.00020	0.5	250
Molybdenum*	0.00015	0.1	660
Tungsten	0.00015	0.3	2000
Mercury	0.000008	0.1	12,500
Silver*	0.000008	0.005	625
Platinum	0.0000005	0.0002	400
Gold*	0.0000004	0.0001	250

*Much of these metals is recovered as by-products of the mining for other metals.

be recirculated as the quantities used in many operations are very large and laws commonly forbid its reuse for domestic purposes. In the past, tailings dumped in this way were often left as surface scars when mining ceased or were discharged directly into streams. The problems arising from potentially toxic concentrations of certain elements in tailings and in the waters used in processing operations and the harmful effects of these fine particle contaminants on aquatic organisms, have led to laws prohibiting or controlling this type of dumping. The special problems associated with the disposal of uranium mill tailings are discussed later in this chapter.

(a)

(b)

FIGURE 3-12. These photomicrographs of polished surfaces of ore samples are only 0.6 millimeters across and illustrate the very fine-grained nature and intimately intergrown textures of ore minerals. In order to separate the various types of minerals, the ores must be crushed fine enough to free or "liberate" the individual grains. (a) Crystals of pyrite (FeS_2) in a matrix of chalcopyrite ($CuFeS_2$). (b) An intimate mixture of galena (PbS), sphalerite (ZnS). (Samples from Japanese volcanogenic ore; photographs by J. R. Craig).

TABLE 3-2

Mineral processing: Methods of mineral separation

Mineral Property Exploited	Method	Applicable to
High density (S.G.)	Mineral jig	Coarser-grained ores of lead (galena), barytes, etc.
	Shaking tables	Finer-grained ores of tin (cassiterite), gold, etc.
	Heavy media (liquid) separation	Preliminary separation of many denser ore minerals
Magnetism (chiefly ferro- or ferrimagnetism)	Magnetic separator	A small number of ferro- or ferrimagnetic minerals (magnetite, pyrrhotite, etc.) Some more weakly magnetic minerals (wolfram, ilmenite, etc.)
Electrical properties	High tension separation	Dry particulate ores containing metallic conductors (e.g., ilmenite, cassiterite) and insulators (e.g., monazite)
Surface chemical properties	Froth flotation	A very wide range of metal sulfides and oxides as well as nonmetallic minerals

The concentrate usually contains the metal in the form of oxides, sulfides, or related compounds, and the traditional method of recovery of the pure metal is by the pyrometallurgical procedure called **smelting**. The most familiar smelting process is the recovery of iron from its oxide ores that is discussed in detail in Chapter

4. In summary, carbon monoxide, resulting from the incomplete combustion of coke, reacts with iron oxide at high temperatures to form metallic iron and carbon dioxide.

Many other metals are produced by reduction of oxides that are sometimes present as such in the ore and

(b)

(a)

FIGURE 3-13. (a) The fine grinding required to liberate the ore minerals is often accomplished by large ball mills such as these. Coarse fragments of ore and steel balls 3 to 6 centimeters in diameter are fed into the mill that revolves rapidly. The tumbling action of the balls and the ore grinds the ore to a fine powder. Water is added to prevent the generation of dust and to allow the powdered ore to flow out in a slurry. (Courtesy of Cleveland Cliffs, Inc.) (b) After grinding, a process of selective flotation is commonly used to separate the various types of ore minerals. The ore minerals attach themselves to small air bubbles pumped through the pulp. Addition of an organic substance to produce a stable "froth" enables the ore minerals to float-off the tops of the cells at the right side of the photograph. (Photograph by J. R. Craig.)

sometimes formed by **roasting** the ore prior to smelting. Roasting is heating in air without melting to transform sulfide minerals (also metal arsenides, antimonides, etc.) into oxides by driving-off the sulfur as gaseous sulfur oxides. Lead, zinc, copper, and nickel are examples of metals usually found as sulfides and that are roasted before reduction. Copper (and nickel) sulfide ores, instead of being roasted and smelted directly, are often smelted to a **matte** that is a mixture of copper (or nickel) and iron sulfides and then **converted**. This is a process in which air is blown into the molten matte, oxidizing the sulfur to sulfur dioxide and changing the iron to an oxide that combines with a silica flux to form a slag, leaving the copper as impure metallic copper. For metals of a low boiling point, such as zinc, cadmium, and mercury, distillation may be employed in the later stages of extraction.

Smelting and other kinds of **pyrometallurgy** have often been very significant sources of air pollution because substantial amounts of gases such as sulfur dioxide and carbon dioxide, as well as particulate matter, may be emitted into the atmosphere by smelters. There has been much pollution caused by these and other noxious gases, as well as the small quantities of toxic metals such as arsenic, lead, mercury, cadmium, nickel, beryllium, and vanadium that are released. Monitoring of the trace amounts of such metals in air and in rainfall shows that they travel over long distances and in considerable quantities, generally within fine particulates. The long-term effects of pollution from this source on human, animal, and plant life remain poorly understood.

HOW USING RESOURCES AFFECTS THE ENVIRONMENT

Once resources have been extracted from the earth and processed, further disruption of the environment may be caused by their actual use. The principal example is the burning of fossil fuels in power stations, homes, and engines (particularly automobile engines) that result in emission of gases, particles, and, in some cases, excess heat into the environment. The burning of nuclear fuels in power stations generates extremely toxic radioactive waste products that require special means of disposal. The use of oil to manufacture a wide range of petrochemicals, and of metals and minerals to make a wide range of industrial chemicals and products, also generates wastes and pollutants. Some of the effects on the environment of such resource utilization will now be discussed.

Burning of Fossil Fuels

The greatest problem caused by the burning of fossil fuels is air pollution. A good example of this is in urban areas in the United States and Europe (Fig. 3.14) where the pollutants come mainly from motor vehicles and from power plants, with substantial contributions from domestic and industrial heating systems. Industrial processes such as smelting (see p. 48) can make significant contributions locally, and the burning of solid wastes may add further to air pollution.

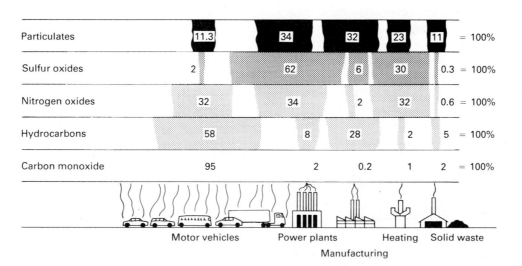

	Motor vehicles	Power plants	Manufacturing	Heating	Solid waste	
Particulates	11.3	34	32	23	11	= 100%
Sulfur oxides	2	62	6	30	0.3	= 100%
Nitrogen oxides	32	34	2	32	0.6	= 100%
Hydrocarbons	58	8	28	2	5	= 100%
Carbon monoxide	95	2	0.2	1	2	= 100%

FIGURE 3-14. Schematic representation of the sources of air pollution. (After diagram by New York State Department of Environmental Conservation.)

The main pollutants from these sources are carbon monoxide, carbon dioxide, hydrocarbon compounds, nitrogen oxides, sulfur oxides, and particulate matter. Complete combustion of fossil fuels yields mainly carbon dioxide (CO_2) and water vapor. These products are not really pollutants, as they are already present in the atmosphere in significant amounts. Nevertheless, the burning of the fossil fuels is leading to a steady increase in the CO_2 content of the atmosphere and consequent changes in other geochemical cycles and in the thermal properties of the atmosphere (see p. 54). The most serious pollution arises from incomplete combustion and from the release of impurities during combustion. For example, carbon monoxide (CO) is a highly toxic gas given off in substantial amounts by incomplete combustion of gasoline in automobiles. Such incomplete combustion also gives rise to fine particle carbon (**soot**). Both oil and coal contain sulfur-bearing compounds as impurities. These give a mixture of oxides, mainly sulfur dioxide (SO_2) and trioxide (SO_3) when burned. Nitrogen compounds are also found in all fossil fuels, and these produce various oxides of nitrogen [mainly nitrogen monoxide (NO) and nitrogen dioxide (NO_2)] on combustion. Coal also contains incombustible fine particles of mineral matter emitted as **fly ash** from chimneys when it is burned. Various hydrocarbon compounds and more complex substances also result from the burning of fossil fuels. Some undergo reactions in the atmosphere, as in the **oxidants** that are produced by reactions involving hydrocarbons and nitrogen oxides in the presence of sunlight. These pollutants produce a **photochemical smog** found in the atmospheres of sunny urban areas with large volumes of automobile traffic (Fig. 3.15). Other pollutants produced in far smaller quantities include various particulate lead compounds from leaded gasoline and a considerable range of (frequently toxic) metals, gases, and complex compounds given off during various industrial processes or in the burning of wastes.

How do these pollutants behave on entering the atmosphere? This depends on the atmospheric conditions at the time and in particular on the temperature of the air at various heights above ground. Under what could be called average conditions, air temperature drops steadily at a rate of about 1°C for every 1000 meters increase in altitude. In this case, there is an equilibrium in which gains and losses of energy in the atmosphere (mainly as heat from the sun or radiated from the earth's surface) are in balance. At any particular time and place, the actual temperatures may be cooler than the equilibrium conditions (Fig. 3.16). If smoke from a chimney enters such an atmosphere, it is warmer than its surroundings and rises, gradually mixing with the air, and being dispersed. It is also possible for the air at some given altitude to be warmer than the equilibrium conditions. Such a warm layer may rest stably over the

cooler and denser air beneath—a condition known as **atmospheric inversion**. These conditions can develop at the end of a sunny day when the ground, and air near the ground, start to lose heat rapidly. This will continue through the night and the following early morning, after which heat from the sun may cause turbulent mixing of the layers of air and a breakup of the inversion. On the other hand, weather conditions may allow the inversion to persist all day or for several days. Exhaust gases from motor vehicles and smoke from chimneys that do not penetrate above the inversion layer will be trapped and may lead to the blanketing of the affected area in a dense smog. Smoke from chimneys that does penetrate this layer (which may extend from tens to hundreds of meters above ground) will be dispersed in the much larger volume of air in the overlying atmosphere. This is a major reason for building tall chimneys, the tallest of which approach 400 meters (~1200 feet) high and rival the world's tallest buildings in height.

What are the harmful effects caused by air pollution, whether from burning of fuels in vehicles and power plants or from other industrial processes? Some of the effects are obvious: the reduction of visibility, soiling of buildings, and creation of an environment which is bad for human health. As well as the possible effects on long-term human health, there have been notorious cases of deaths directly caused by air pollution. For example, in London in 1952, a severe smog lasting several days led to some 4000 more deaths than would have been expected at that time of year. Deaths occurred chiefly amongst those already suffering from respiratory and cardiac disease. Such episodes led to clean air laws that have restricted the burning of certain types of fuels and have greatly reduced the problem in that city.

The question of how the air pollution we create affects climate is more controversial. Dust particles can potentially reflect the sun's rays and cause lower temperatures, but major volcanic eruptions introduce far more dust into the upper atmosphere than people's activities. The effects of even the largest such eruptions have generally been local and short lived. Air pollution promotes fogginess, cloudiness, and possible rainfall on a local scale by providing nuclei for the condensation of drops of moisture. Worldwide effects on precipitation are much more difficult to assess.

The burning of fossil fuels is certainly causing changes in the chemistry of the atmosphere. One such effect already mentioned is the worldwide increase in carbon dioxide (See Fig. 1.8). The importance of this increase arises from the fact that CO_2, along with water and ozone, absorbs and therefore conserves heat given off by the earth. The trapping of heat in this way is called the **greenhouse effect**. Some scientists have estimated that CO_2 concentration will increase enough over

FIGURE 3-15. The effects of atmospheric inversions on atmospheric pollution. These three views of downtown Los Angeles show: top—a clear day; middle—pollution trapped beneath an inversion layer at about 75 meters; bottom—pollution under an inversion layer at about 450 meters. (Photographs courtesy of South Coast Air Quality Management District, from J. N. Birakos, "Profile of Air Pollution Control," County of Los Angeles, 1974.)

the next half century to raise the average surface temperatures by 0.5°C. It is hard to assess the accuracy of such predictions, let alone the effects of such a change on world climate.

There are similar problems regarding the effects of pollution on the upper atmosphere and particularly on the layer of ozone (O_3) that protects the earth from much of the sun's ultraviolet radiation. The exhaust from high-flying supersonic jets could damage the ozone layer, as well as introducing particles, water, CO_2, and nitrogen oxides. Other sources of possible damage to the ozone layer are the compounds called **chlorofluoromethanes** (or freons) such as $CFCl_3$ that are used as propellants in aerosol cans. If these compounds reach the upper atmosphere they can react with and destroy the ozone. Such changes in the chemistry of the upper atmosphere may cause an increase in earth surface temperatures and increases in ultraviolet radiation that could damage and affect human health.

The sulfur dioxide (SO_2) emitted when coal is burned (see Chapter 4), and also by many smelters, is thought to be the cause of one of the most serious forms of pollution—**acid rain.** Sulfuric acid, produced on combination of the SO_2 with rain water, has damaged plants and soils and lowered the **pH** in many streams and lakes throughout the world. Normal rain water has a pH of about 5.7, but much of the rain in Europe and the eastern United States has an average pH of 4.0, and readings as low as 2.1 have been reported. If the pH drops below 5.0, fish usually disappear, and plant life is severely affected. The effects of the sulfur and nitrous oxides released by coal burning has been the subject of much debate, often from very biased viewpoints. In 1983, the U.S. National Academy of Sciences released a report that noted that the burning of fossil fuels, especially coal in power plants, is the principal source of the oxides responsible for the acid rain in the northeastern United States. Furthermore, the report noted a direct correlation of sulfur oxide content in acid rain with the sulfur content in the fuels. Reduction of the sulfur oxide emissions by half, the recommended target, can be achieved by only three methods: (1) a change to another type of fuel—oil, nuclear, etc.; (2) installation of expensive air cleaner systems; and (3) a switch to lower-sulfur coals. Critics of the National Academy's report point out, however, that there was as much coal burned in the United States and Europe in the 1950s as in the 1980s but that there was much less acid rain effects in the 1950s. They suggest that either coal burning is not the culprit or that alkaline emission that previously neutralized the acid is now being cleaned up too thoroughly. Clearly, the problem of acid rain is far from being completely understood or solved. Regardless of the debates, more than 15,000 lakes in Scandinavia and Canada have

been damaged by acid rain, much of which is attributable to emissions in other countries. Acid rain also speeds the decay of buildings, sculptures, and other structures, particularly those made of **limestone** or **marble.**

The control of air pollution involves both legislation to limit emissions and the use of various devices to remove as many of the noxious substances as possible from exhaust gases and power plant or smelter emissions. Because polluted air may travel hundreds of miles, affecting areas far away from the pollution source, the difficulties of introducing adequate legal controls are compounded by the need for international agreements.

A final, and rather ironic form of pollution that results from burning fossil fuels and certain other kinds of

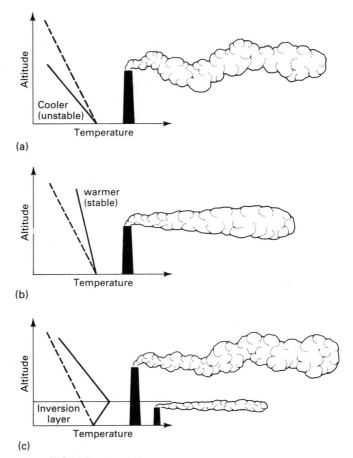

FIGURE 3-16. The effects of air temperature on pollution. The dashed line is the normal temperature gradient; the solid line is the actual gradient in each diagram. (a) Air is cooler than normal creating unstable but smoke-dispersing conditions. (b) Air is warmer than normal creating stable smoke-dispersing conditions. (c) An inversion traps the smoke from the lower stack.

FIGURE 3-16.   (*cont.*) Very tall stacks such as this one 370 meters (1216 feet) at the Homer City Electric Generating Station in Pennsylvania are constructed so that waste gases and particles that escape entrapment in filters are released high enough in the atmosphere to allow for dilution and dispersal to minimize pollution problems. (Photograph courtesy of The Pennsylvania Electric Company, a member of the General Public Utilities System, and New York State Electric and Gas.)

power generation is **thermal pollution**. Commonly, power plants take water from rivers, lakes, and sea coasts, use it for cooling, and then return it at a higher temperature. This affects ecosystems and may cause the death of fish and other aquatic life accustomed to the cooler water conditions. One alternative is to dissipate waste heat into the air via cooling towers, but this can affect the local climate and involves unsightly structures. A much better solution employed in some areas is to make use of such excess heat in nearby homes and factories, thereby also conserving energy.

Disposing of Nuclear Waste Products

The mining and processing of uranium ores, the fabrication of nuclear fuels from these ores, and the burning of the fuels in nuclear power stations generate waste products requiring disposal. The safe disposal of these products of the nuclear fuel cycle (which is discussed in detail in Chapter 5) is understandably a matter of great public concern, particularly as the small amounts of radioactive poisons that can prove lethal cannot normally be detected by the senses. Nuclear weapons manufacture and development also generate significant amounts of highly radioactive waste. The long-term disposal of the most dangerous of radioactive wastes is still an unresolved problem. Before considering the possible answers to this problem, we need to discuss the various kinds of radioactive waste and the quantities in which they are produced.

Categories of Radioactive Waste.   The nature of a radioactive waste material, in addition to whether it is in solid, liquid, or gaseous form, depends on the concentration of radioactive **isotopes** that are present. Although such wastes emit rays or subatomic particles that can damage living tissue, the level of this emission decreases with time. The rate of this **decay** of radioactive isotopes varies widely and is measured in terms of **half-life**, the time taken for the level of radiation emitted by an isotope to be reduced to one-half of its initial value. The nature of the decay process is such that given 1 gram of a substance like the radioactive isotope of iodine, ^{181}I, with a half-life of 8 days, the emitted radiation falls to half of the original after 8 days, one-quarter after 16 days, one-eighth after 24 days, one-sixteenth after 32 days, and so on. Half-lives can range from only fractions of a second to millions of years, so that some materials remain lethal for hundreds or thousands of

years, whereas others become virtually harmless in a matter of days or months. Most radioactive wastes are mixtures of short- and longer-lived isotopes. These isotopes include species produced directly by the burning of the fuel and others produced when the materials in close proximity to the fuel are irradiated. The principal radioisotopes involved, along with information on emitted radiation, half-life, and the units used to measure radioactivity, are given in Table 3.3.

The main subdivision of these materials as far as disposal is concerned is into **low-level, intermediate-level**, and **high-level** wastes. Low-level wastes are generally those in which the maximum level of radioactivity is up to 1000 times that considered acceptable in the environment, intermediate-level wastes have 1000 to 1,000,000 times that considered acceptable, and the high-level wastes have still greater activities. As seen in Table 3.4, the volume of high-level wastes produced is a very small proportion of the total; however, it does account for 95 percent of the total radioactivity of the wastes with which we must deal.

Low-level Wastes and Their Disposal. Large quantities of waste are produced at uranium mines as at other mining operations. Although the mined ores are processed by crushing, grinding, and separation of a concentrate rich in the uranium minerals, the residue (**tailings**) commonly contains much of the total radioactivity originally associated with the ore. This is because it is a far greater volume of material than the concentrate. The disposal of uranium mill tailings can give rise to human exposure at unacceptable levels of radiation, because the material has been finely ground and can be transported by wind and water. Also the radioactive gas radon, which is produced by the decay of uranium, can escape into the atmosphere more easily from this pulverized material. A further point to note is that several of the radioisotopes present in the tailings are very long-lived, such as thorium-230 with a half-life of 77,000 years. This means that the containment of these wastes must be designed to take account of geological processes of erosion and redistribution occurring over very long time periods. In practice, the wastes are usually

TABLE 3-3

Radioactive isotopes occurring in nuclear wastes

Principal Fission Products		Products of Irradiation of Nonfuel Materials	
Isotope	*Half-life*	*Isotope (and Source)*	*Half-life*
krypton-85	<9.4 yr	*From air and water:*	
strontium-89	54 d	tritium, H-3, (^{2}H)	12.3 yr
strontium-90	25 yr	carbon-14 (^{14}N)	5700 yr
zirconium-95	65 d	nitrogen-16 (^{16}O)	7.3 sec
niobium-95	<35 d	nitrogen-17 (^{17}O)	4.1 sec
technetium-99	<5×10^5 yr	oxygen-19 (^{18}O)	30 sec
ruthenium-103	39.8 yr	argon-41 (^{40}A)	1.8 hr
rhodium-103	57 min	*From sodium (coolant):*	
ruthenium-106	1 yr	sodium-24 (^{23}Na)	15 yr
rhodium-106	30 sec	sodium-22 (^{23}Na)	2.6 yr
tellurium-129	<72 min	rubidium-86 (^{85}Rb)	19.5 hr
iodine-129	1.7×10^7 yr	*From metals and alloys:*	
iodine-131	8 d	aluminum-28 (^{27}Al)	2.3 min
xenon-133	<5.3 d	chromium-51 (^{50}Cr)	27 d
cesium-137	33 yr	manganese-56 (^{56}Fe)	2.6 hr
barium-140	12.8 yr	iron-55 (^{54}Fe)	2.9 yr
lanthanum-140	40 hr	iron-59 (^{59}Co)	45 d
cerium-141	32.5 d	copper-64 (^{63}Cu)	12.8 hr
cerium-144	590 d	zinc-65 (^{64}Zn)	250 d
praseodymium-143	13.8 d	tantalum-182 (^{181}Ta)	115 d
praseodymium-144	17 min	tungsten-187 (^{186}W)	24 hr
promethium-147	2.26 yr	cobalt-58 (^{58}Ni)	71 d
		cobalt-60 (^{59}Co)	5.3 yr

Units of Radioactivity
Unit of activity is the Curie (Ci); 1 Ci = 3.7×10^{10} disintegrations/sec
Unit of exposure dose for X-rays and γ-rays = Roentgen (R)
1 R = 87.8 erg/sec (5.49×10^7 MeV/g) in air
Unit of absorbed dose = Rad; 1 rad = 100 erg/g (6.25×10^7 MeV/g) in any material
Unit of dose equivalent (for protection) = Rem (SI unit equivalent = Sievert; 1 rem = 10^{-2} sieverts)
Rems (roentgen equivalents for man) = rads $\times$ QF where QF (quality factor) depends, for example, on type of radiation
(γ-rays QF$\cong$1, thermal neutrons QF$\cong$3, α particles QF$\leqslant$20)

TABLE 3-4
Estimated volumes of solid radioactive waste resulting from the generation of electricity from a 1 megawatt (10^6) nuclear power plant operation for 1 year (including wastes generated at fuel manufacturing and reprocessing plants)

Category of Waste	Volume (M^3)
Low-level wastes (untreated)	2000
Intermediate-level wastes (after treatment)	100
High-level wastes (after solidification)	2

(Data from United Kingdom Atomic Energy Authority, 1982.)

dumped at or near the mine and subsequently stabilized by earth cover and vegetation. It is clearly important that water seeping through the wastes should not enter ground water systems that provide water supplies for human or animal consumption. It is also important that the wastes are kept well away from human activities other than the mining operation. Unfortunately, this has not always been so in the past. For example, at Grand Junction, Colorado, more than 300,000 tons of radioactive tailings were used as fill material for land on which many buildings were later constructed. Some of the waste was even used to make concrete blocks used in the foundations of houses. The recognition of elevated levels of radioactivity in these buildings led to a clean-up program costing many millions of dollars.

One of the principal isotopes monitored is radon (^{86}Rn) because it is a gas and is readily absorbed in the human body where it greatly raises the prospects of cancer. Concern about radon levels in homes, resulting either from radioactive wastes or from natural radioactivity in underlying rocks, increased dramatically in the United States in 1985 when a worker at a nuclear power plant in Pennsylvania set off radiation alarms as he came to work in the morning. Surveys of his home in Colebrookdale, Pennsylvania, revealed that radon gas, seeping from the uranium-bearing rocks beneath his house, was confined and had built up because the house was very tightly insulated. Subsequent surveys in different parts of the United States have revealed that houses in many areas have radon gas levels higher than recommended safe levels. Most problems of this type can be remedied by the installation of ventilation systems, but some require removal of the building materials that contain the radioactive elements.

Large volumes of low-level waste are also produced in nuclear power stations, research laboratories, hospitals, or by various nuclear industries. Typical items are contaminated laboratory equipment or protective clothing and even contaminated animal wastes. The lower activity wastes are usually sealed in drums, commonly after burning in special incinerators to reduce their volume, and buried in shallow trenches beneath a meter or so of soil (Fig. 3.17). The site should be care-

FIGURE 3-17. Low level nuclear waste is packed in drums and is buried in shallow trenches where it is isolated from surface runoff and from ground water. (Courtesy of United States Geological Survey.)

fully chosen as regards geological and geographical setting and radioactivity in the area regularly monitored to ensure that any contamination of plants, soils, and ground water is within accepted limits. The upper limits of radiation exposure or dosage for workers in the nuclear industries and for the general public are commonly governed by legislation based on the recommendations of the International Commission on Radiological Protection (ICRP). The ICRP limit for public exposure is given in Table 3.5 along with doses arising from various sources for the population of Britain.

Low level wastes of somewhat higher activity have often been cast into concrete, enclosed in sealed drums, and dumped on the deep-ocean floor. At an internationally agreed site in the Atlantic Ocean some 800 kilometers from southwest England, tens of thousands of tons of such wastes have been dumped in this way. The sealing in concrete is to enable handling of the material and to ensure it reaches the bottom of the sea intact, where it should remain intact for many years. The safety of this disposal method is based on the vast dilution of the activity as it slowly disperses at the bottom of the ocean some 5 kilometers down.

Low-level liquid wastes arise at nuclear power stations and at plants where nuclear fuel is reprocessed. Such wastes are often treated and then discharged into rivers and into the sea. The levels of radiation in waters and marine life are closely monitored when this is done and kept to acceptable levels. Nevertheless, this is a procedure that has understandably given rise to public concern and pressure from environmentalist groups. Radioactive gases are also given off from power plants in very small amounts.

Intermediate-Level Wastes and Their Disposal. Materials such as certain components from nuclear power plants and the flasks used to transport fuel, as well as various liquids used in the plants, have intermediate levels of activity. At present, these are often stored in tanks or other containers at nuclear plants with a view to eventual disposal by methods similar to those used for the low-level wastes. Another possibility involves treatment to remove long-lived active constituents so that the bulk of the material is discharged or buried as low-level waste.

High-Level Wastes and Their Disposal—A Great Debate?. The high-level wastes from the nuclear power industry account for roughly 95 percent of the radioactivity but only about 0.1 percent of the volume of waste generated. These consist of large quantities of liquid wastes and used fuel rods giving off very high levels of radioactivity and substantial heat. At present, they are stored in stainless steel tanks, similar in design to the one shown in Fig. 3.18, at sites of the fuel reprocessing plants or power plants where they are generated. The problem of their eventual disposal has been the subject of much research, and no one has agreed on a solution yet. Meanwhile, these lethal substances continue to accumulate. One estimate of their toxicity suggests that less than 4 liters of the hundreds of millions of liters held in storage would be enough to bring every person in the world to the danger level for radiation exposure if it were evenly distributed. Although the safety record in the storage of these highly active wastes has been good over the nearly 30 years in which this has been done, leakages from the storage tanks have occurred, resulting in contamination of the ground around them.

Most long-term nuclear waste disposal strategies require that the waste is first solidified. One method of doing this is to incorporate the waste into a glass, a process known as **vitrification**. The French have developed a method for doing this on an industrial scale using a

TABLE 3-5

Radiation doses experienced by average citizens of Great Britain with their sources and the internationally accepted upper dosage limit

Radiation Source	Annual Dose in Microsieverts (μSv)*
ICRP limit (for public citizens)**	5000 (5 rem)
Natural background (average)	1860
Natural background (range)	1500-3000+
Medical diagnosis and treatment (average)	500
Air travel, television watching, nuclear weapons tests, etc.	18
Discharges from the nuclear industry (excluding Chernobyl)	3

*The sievert (Sv) is a unit of radiation that takes into account the biological effectiveness of different types of radiation. There is no evidence of harmful effects from radiation at levels below about 1/100 of a sievert (10,000 μSv).

**ICRP = International Commission for Radiation Protection.
(After United Kingdom Atomic Energy Authority, 1982.)

FIGURE 3-18. Temporary above ground storage of high-level nuclear waste in a mobile canister at the Surry Nuclear Power Plant in Virginia. (Courtesy of Virginia Power.)

glass containing boron and silicon. This process can be designed so that the glasses survive the effects of heating and radiation from the wastes, but there is concern about the ability of such glasses to survive attack by water or brine solutions at elevated temperatures. These are important considerations because the solid wastes are likely to be buried deep in the earth. The alternative to vitrification is to incorporate the waste into ceramics or synthetic minerals; crystalline minerals in which the radioactive elements would be more tightly and stably bound, much as they were before mining. An example of such a material is the mixture of titanium oxide minerals (titanates) developed by an Australian group and known as **SYNROC**. The composition of this material is shown in Table 3.6, and, as the name suggests, it is actually a synthetic rock. Proponents of this method of waste processing point out that the radioactive elements are being returned to the sort of chemical environment in which they are most stable in the earth. Certainly, experiments show that SYNROC remains stable in contact with brine solutions to much higher temperatures than glasses, temperatures in excess of 700°C.

Solidification is only the first step in the ultimate disposal of nuclear wastes. Solidified waste can be stored in vaults or reinforced and shielded buildings above ground, having first been sealed into concrete and stainless steel canisters. Such methods are used in France where the canisters containing vitrified waste are placed in a vault and cooled in a stream of air. Perhaps wastes in such stores could be kept safely for the indefinite future with minimal surveillance and maintenance. However, there are inevitable concerns of the vulnerability of such stores in war, or through acts of terrorism or major disasters.

Various options have been considered for the ultimate disposal of the solidified wastes. The more extreme proposals, such as removal from the earth by rocket or burial in the polar ice caps, have been rejected on technical or safety grounds. The remaining options are disposal on the bed of the ocean, burial in deep-ocean sediments, or deep burial on land. It is possible that larger amounts of higher level wastes could be disposed of in the oceans, either on the ocean bed or

TABLE 3-6

Mineralogical and chemical composition of SYNROC,* the titanate ceramic wasteform designed to incorporate radioactive wastes in a stable form for disposal by burial in the earth

Component (wt %)	Formula	Acts as Primary Host for
Hollandite (33)	$Ba(Al,Ti)Ti_6O_{16}$	Cs, Ba, Rb, K, Cr
Zirconolite (28)	$CaZrTi_2O_7$	Th, U, Pu and tetravalent actinides, Zr
Perovskite (19)	$CaTiO_3$	Sr, Na, trivalent actinides, rare earths
Rutile (15)	TiO_2	
Alloy (5)		Tc, Mo, Ru, Pd, S, Te

(Data are from Ringwood, A.E., *Mineralogical Magazine*, vol. 49, p. 159–176, 1985).
*Actually the commonest of several forms of SYNROC known as SYNROC-C.

buried within deep ocean sediments. There are areas of the ocean floor where sediments have remained undisturbed for millions of years and are likely to remain very stable. Although these appear technically to be a good possibility for disposal sites, there are certain to be major legal problems in obtaining the necessary international agreements. Also, despite several decades of research, more needs to be known about dispersal mechanisms of the wastes before further ocean bed dumping could be considered acceptable. Considerable research has also been done on suitable deep burial sites on land. Clearly, a very stable environment and one relatively impervious to ground water is needed. Some have suggested burial in salt deposits because they deform plastically rather than fracture, and their presence (since they are water soluble) is evidence of a dry environment. However, they are known to contain pods of brine that could prove highly corrosive if brought in contact with

solid wastes. Furthermore, some experiments have suggested that the 1–2 percent of water dispersed in salt beds may actually migrate slowly towards the hot area around the radioactive wastes. Other environments being considered include shales or crystalline rocks such as **basalts** or granites, the sort of rocks within which the uranium minerals would have originally occurred in nature.

Ideally, the geological environment should form a natural barrier to fluids that could attack and disperse the waste or to any other mechanism of dispersal. It should be an environment as free as possible from any risk of earthquake or volcanic activity. As well as natural barriers to the escape of the wastes, there would certainly be artificial or "engineered" barriers. These might include sealing the solid wastes in corrosion-resistant canisters, perhaps of stainless steel, and surrounding it with absorbent materials such as **clays** or **zeolites.** The

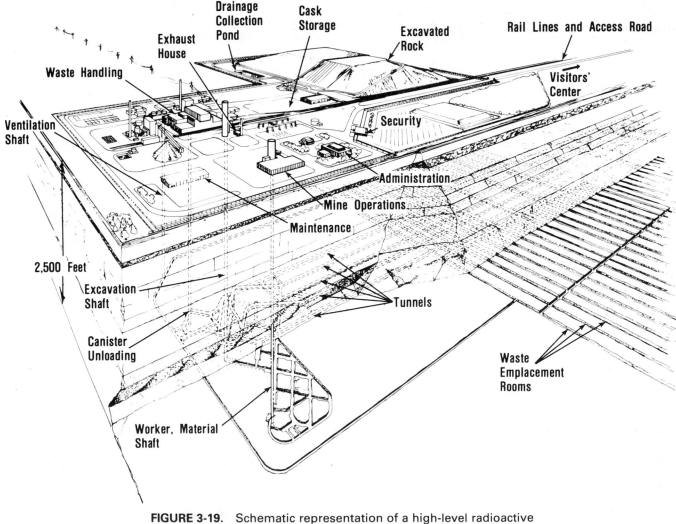

FIGURE 3-19. Schematic representation of a high-level radioactive waste burial site. (Courtesy of Office of Nuclear Waste Isolation, Battelle Project Management Division.)

waste might be deposited in the site simply by drilling large diameter, deep holes as has been suggested for wastes in the form of SYNROC. In this case, it is proposed that 1-meter diameter holes are drilled down to 4 kilometers depth and the bottom 3 kilometers filled with waste in this particularly stable form. Other sites are envisaged as more like mines, with shafts allowing access for people and materials and the wastes stored in galleries (Fig. 3.19). Old mine workings would be evaluated for this purpose, for obvious reasons of savings in costs.

Since the construction of the first nuclear power plants, much effort has been put into the problems of disposing of the very dangerous wastes that they produce. There appear to be technical solutions to this problem that involve only small risks to humans and the rest of the living world, less than the risks involved in current methods of temporary storage. Which of the solutions will be adopted, and when, depends largely on economic and political factors. Governments and companies have to be convinced that levels of spending on the safest options for disposal are justified, and the public has to be convinced that a disposal facility in their area poses negligible risk to them and to future generations.

Other Industrial Processes—Waste Products and Pollution

Many industrial processes based on mineral resources create and discharge substances that can have adverse environmental effects. The releases may be accidental as in the case of oil spills, or they may result from direct application, as in the fertilizers, pesticides, and herbicides used in modern agriculture. Such agricultural pollutants pose particular problems because they are widespread **nonpoint sources** of pollution, unlike the dump, power plant, or factory that emits pollutants from a **point source**, which is a small and exactly defined area.

Although many of the substances that are deliberately released into the environment appear to enter into various chemical and biological cycles without harmful effects, some are causing widespread concern. Certainly our knowledge of the paths followed by many of these substances after their release is inadequate. We know very little of the long-term effects that may result from prolonged buildup of many substances in particular environments. A well-known example of the problem comes from the chemical industry.

A chemical plant that started production in 1932 was emitting mercury-containing waste into Minamata Bay in Japan. This waste included a highly poisonous compound, methyl mercuric chloride, which was not diluted to a harmless level as expected but which prefer-

entially accumulated in fish that constituted a major portion of the diet of the local inhabitants. As a result, more than 1500 people suffered mercury poisoning; 241 died and many others were seriously disabled. Ever since, it has been referred to as Minamata disease. Unfortunately, the disease was not identified until 1956, and although the toxic discharges were stopped in 1960, their effects are still being registered.

DISPOSAL OR RECYCLING OF INDUSTRIAL AND DOMESTIC WASTE PRODUCTS

Archeologists have learned much about past civilizations from studying their waste products. The archeologists of the future will surely have a rich supply of material from our age, because advanced industrial societies produce vast quantities of waste each year in addition to those arising directly from mineral exploitation or the utilization of resources. These include agricultural wastes, domestic or municipal refuse, and the waste products of manufacturing industries. Most of these materials are in the form of solid waste. There are lesser amounts of liquid waste material generated by industry and in the form of sewage.

The disposal or treatment of these wastes are important matters in regard to earth resources because, at least in some cases, they are potential sources of energy or, through recycling, of the raw materials originally obtained from the earth. Their disposal involves another disruption of the environment, whereas their recycling somewhat reduces the need for mining with its environmental disruption as well as the problems associated with disposal. After considering the nature and problems of disposal of both solid and liquid wastes, the question of recycling will be discussed.

Disposing of Solid Wastes

In the United States, over 5000 million tons of solid waste is generated every year, and this is a quantity that continues to increase. Of this solid waste, the majority is agricultural waste, and a substantial amount is mineral waste of the kind already discussed (waste rock, tailings, etc.). Domestic or municipal refuse accounts for less of the bulk but contains within it many valuable raw materials and many potential pollutants(Fig. 20). Manufacturing wastes may also contain valuable metals, fibers, and chemicals, as well as toxic by-products. The relative proportions of these solid wastes are shown in Fig. 3.21. The composition of typical domestic trash in the United States is shown in Fig. 3.21 from which it can be seen that it is made up of roughly 50 percent paper, 12 percent food wastes, 9 percent glass, and the re-

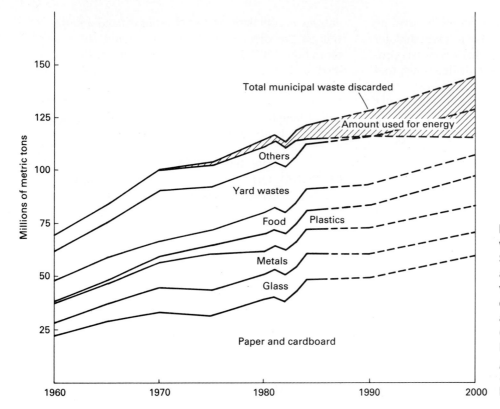

FIGURE 3-20. The municipal waste streams in the United States, 1960–2000. The shaded area indicates the proportion converted into energy production but does not indicate which materials are extracted for this purpose. (Data from Franklin Associates Ltd., *Characterization of Municipal Solid Waste in the United States 1960 to 2000*, Prairie Village, Kansas, 1986.)

mainder of a variety of materials including garden wastes, wood, plastics, cloth, and rubber.

The majority of solid wastes are disposed by open dumping, much less material is incinerated or disposed of in sanitary landfill, and about 10 percent simply discarded. The open dump is the most primitive and most widely used means of solid waste disposal, accounting for disposal of more than half of the waste generated in the United States and the rest of the world. Municipal waste is often compacted after collection, hauled to the dump, and spread on the ground by bulldozers. Although scavenging by junk dealers may recover some materials, especially metals from the dumps, most of the material is left to rot. Although at one time this waste was set on fire to help reduce the total volume,

such open burning is now largely prohibited because of fire hazard and air pollution. The open dumps themselves, as well as being unsightly, are a potential breeding ground for diseases carried by flies and rats and commonly cause contamination of rivers and ground waters by hazardous chemicals or organisms. Many coastal cities, including New York City, dump their municipal wastes in the ocean, barges being used to carry the waste out to sea and discharge it into a natural trench or canyon on the ocean floor. This certainly causes disruption of the marine environment with the destruction of communities of the bottom-dwelling organisms.

The sanitary landfill is a greatly preferable means for disposal of solid domestic trash. In this case, the refuse is deposited at a carefully chosen site where con-

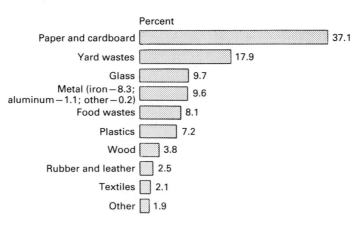

FIGURE 3-21. The percentages of the various materials that comprised municipal waste in the United States in 1984. (Data from Franklin Associates Ltd., *Characterization of Municipal Solid Waste in the United States 1960 to 2000*, Prairie Village, Kansas, 1986.)

tamination of surface water or ground waters will not be a problem or where drainage is controlled. After the waste is brought to a site, it is compacted with bulldozers or other heavy machinery, and each day the waste is covered with a layer of earth 15–30 centimeters thick, to exclude air and vermin. No open burning is permitted at the site which is usually fenced off. Three methods of sanitary landfill are commonly used. In the *area method*, which is well suited to flat ground or broad depressions, wastes are spread on the surface and covered with earth to form a "cell" that usually represents one day's waste (Fig. 3.22). Additional waste cells can be deposited on top of finished cells and then a thick layer of soil to form a capping. In the *trench method*, a broad trench is excavated and filled with compacted refuse. The excavated material provides a soil cover in this method that is well suited to level terrain. The *ramp*

method is well suited to sloping areas. Refuse is spread over the hillside, compacted, and covered with earth that is often excavated from a cut at the base of the slope. Completed landfill sites are usually covered with a layer of soil $\frac{1}{2}$–1 meter thick that may then be seeded and used for park land or recreation areas. In some cases, hills have been constructed for use as ski slopes or other amenities developed. A good example is Mount Trashmore (Fig. 3.23) at the City of Virginia Beach, Virginia, where the shallow depth to the water table would not permit excavation of a pit to use as a waste dump site. There, 1000 tons of garbage per day were dumped, spread, compacted, and covered with earth to build a hill 100 × 260 meters and 22 meters high and containing 580,000 metric tons of solid domestic waste. By the daily compaction of alternating layers of 45 centimeters of waste and 15 centimeters of soil, a structure

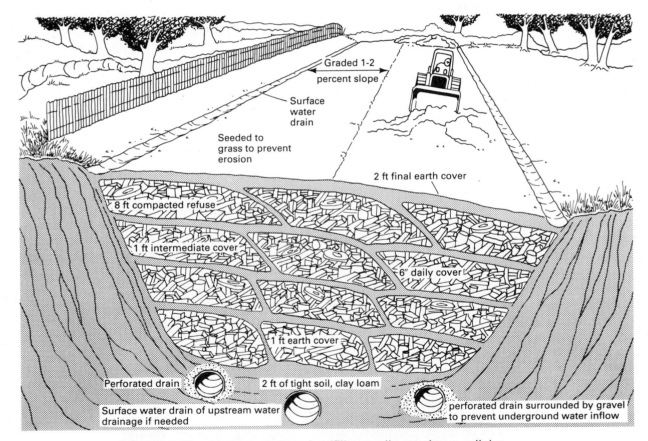

FIGURE 3-22. Modern sanitary landfills usually employ a cellular design such as shown here. After cutting a large trench or pit, the refuse is dumped daily and compacted into lenslike cells, each of which is covered by 0.3 meters (1 foot) or more of soil. The bottom and sides of the landfill are lined with impermeable, usually clay-rich soils, to prevent seepage of leachate into the ground water. When the landfill is closed, a thicker layer of soil is used to seal the upper surface; grass and other vegetation is planted to prevent erosion. (After a diagram of New York State Department of Environment Conservation.)

FIGURE 3-23. Subsurface burial of municipal waste may be impractical in coastal or other areas where the water table is very shallow. Virginia Beach, Virginia, solved the waste disposal problem by building 20 meters high "Mount Trashmore," incorporating more than 575,000 metric tons of solid waste. After final sealing and landscaping, it is now a city recreation area. (Courtesy of The City of Virginia Beach, Virginia.)

was created free from problems of unpleasant odors, fires, vermin, and ground water pollution. This has been used to site a recreational area with a playground, amphitheatre, soapbox derby track, picnic areas, and adjacent to the hill, a freshwater lake. The success of Mount Trashmore has now led to the development of a second similar site. Landfills are generally not suited as sites for buildings because of possible subsidence and escape of gases or contaminated waters. Although the advantages of sanitary landfill over open dumping are obvious, they still present problems in terms of available space. On average, a well-manged landfill operation requires 1 hectare of land each year for 25,000 people. For a city like New York with a population in excess of 12 million people, this could demand 480 hectares of land every year. Also, as the more obvious locations for landfill sites are used up, more distant sites have to be employed, increasing transport costs and disruption of the surrounding countryside.

In many large cities, refuse is not simply dumped, it is incinerated. This reduces the weight and volume of the waste, and the solid that remains is usually inert and can more safely be used as fill material. However, the burning of materials as complex as municipal trash is not simple. Substances that release poisonous gases or particles when burned are often present, so that costly pollution controls are needed to meet modern standards of air cleanliness. The capital cost of building a modern incinerator and the costs of operation are often much greater than those for a landfill operation. In addition to air pollution, certain materials commonly found in refuse produce gases that corrode furnace interiors. For example, polyvinyl chloride (PVC), a plastic widely used in goods such as toys, containers, records, and so on produces highly corrosive hydrogen chloride gas when burned. However, one important factor that helps to compensate for these difficulties is the energy generated by the incineration of wastes. The heat given off by

the process of incineration is increasingly being used for space heating of buildings or for electrical power generations. The increasing problems of refuse disposal, combined with increasing energy costs, has led to many energy-generating plants using solid wastes being constructed throughout the world over the past decade.

The generation of energy in the form of heat by the burning of solid wastes leads to the general question of how energy may be extracted from solid wastes. A number of these alternative energy sources are discussed in Chapter 5 and, in particular, the ways in which organic wastes and plant materials (including manure, sewage, and wastes from crop cultivation) can be used to produce gas (e.g., methane) or liquid fuels. It has also been suggested that methane gas given off by the degradation of material in sanitary landfill sites could be tapped and used for energy generation. This would involve trapping methane below an impermeable (clay, for instance) cover and extracting it from wells drilled into the mass of decaying material. A more direct method of extracting potential fuel materials from wastes is **pyrolysis**, a process that involves heating the wastes in the absence of air to drive off and collect volatile substances. This is further discussed on p. 67. All recycling, in fact, leads to an overall saving in energy and can be regarded as an aspect of energy, as well as material, conservation.

Disposing of Liquid Wastes

Two main kinds of liquid waste are generated by humankind. The first, common to primitive or advanced societies alike, is made up of sewage and domestic waste water. The second is the wastes produced by industrial activity, particularly by such industries as pulp and paper production, food processing, and the manufacture of chemicals.

Sewage and domestic waste water amounts to

enormous volumes: On average, every man, woman, and child in a modern industrial city generates between 75–200 gallons per day (700 liters per day). The most convenient place to discharge these wastes, whether treated or untreated, is a nearby river, watercourse, or directly into the sea. This has been the practice since earliest times and one which has led to countless illnesses and deaths from water-carried diseases when controls have been inadequate. The reasoning behind discharge into marine waters as it is still practiced today is that small volumes of waste do little harm when diluted in the vast oceans. However, mixing is far from complete in coastal waters and even less so in estuaries, and the volumes discharged are substantial. For example, an estimated 3.5 billion gallons of waste water is being discharged into estuaries and coastal waters of the United States per day. The city and county of Los Angeles together discharge 700 million gallons per day. What is the nature of this waste water, and how is it treated?

Municipal sewage is 99.8 percent water. The remaining 0.2 percent, however, may contain a variety of organic compounds in suspension or solution, some of which may be toxic. Many of these are biodegradable but still lead to consumption of oxygen in the environment. Others may serve as nutrients that can promote growth of algae in an environment into which they are discharged. The greatest concerns are over the few toxic substances such as heavy metal compounds and pathogenic organisms that can cause diseases such as typhoid, dysentery, diarrhea, and cholera. A wide variety of mechanical, chemical, and biological methods can be used to clean up sewage water. Some treatment plants remove only the coarsest fraction of the pollution, whereas others may yield outgoing water (effluent) that is of drinkable (**potable**) quality. A typical full-scale treatment plant may involve two or three stages of processing (Fig. 3.24). Primary treatment usually involves screening to remove large objects and a series of settling tanks to remove successively finer suspended solids. Secondary treatment often uses the action of bacteria in the presence of ample oxygen to decompose much of the remaining matter. The sewage may be sprayed over a bed of stones in a trickling filter or, in the activated sludge process, may be mixed into an aerated tank with a bacteria-laden sludge. The sludge residue is usually dried and may be incinerated or disposed of in sanitary landfill. The effluent is still laden with bacteria that are killed by a disinfection process, usually chlorination. In some cases, tertiary or advanced treatment is used to remove specific pollutants such as synthetic chemicals and salts. This may involve the addition of certain chemicals or substances to absorb the pollutants. The ultimate destination of most effluents that have undergone primary and, in some cases, secondary treatment (or even no treatment at all) are the rivers, estuaries, seas, and oceans. However, some sewage wastes are disposed of on land, the nutrient materials present in the treated wastes being used as a fertilizer.

The range of liquid wastes that are generated by industrial processes is considerable. They include many oil-based materials such as spent lubricants and fuel oil residues along with various solvents, paints, and resins. Industry is also the source of much of the hazardous chemical wastes containing toxic heavy metals and dangerous organic chemicals. Some examples of the tragic problems caused by uncontrolled or poorly controlled discharge of such toxins into the seas have already been discussed. Aside from these severe cases, what are the likely consequences of pollution of rivers and seas by waste waters, and what sort of safety standards should be applied?

Although slow filtration of ground water through

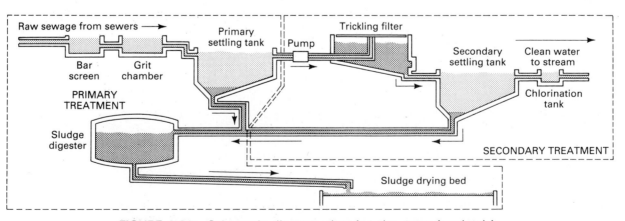

FIGURE 3-24. Schematic diagram showing the steps involved in the treatment of sewage wastes. (From The Living Waters, U.S. Public Health Service Publication No. 382.)

the earth and dilution of wastes by oxygen-rich surface waters can absorb and degrade varying amounts and types of waste, these natural systems of purification are easily overburdened. The consequence of introducing nontoxic organic substances into natural waters is to deplete or consume the oxygen supply in these waters. This is because oxygen is used by microorganisms feeding on the organic pollutants and hence increasing the **Biochemical Oxygen Demand** (BOD). Exhaustion of the oxygen supply kills all the natural organisms, and putrification begins. Another group of harmful although nontoxic pollutants are the phosphates and nitrates. These are often introduced onto the land as fertilizers and then find their way into rivers and lakes where they stimulate excessive growth of algae. They are often not removed by standard treatment plants. This leads to a degrading process known as **eutrophication** in which the water becomes overburdened with dead and dying organisms. This occurs most often in shallow bodies of standing water. In addition to these pollutants are the whole range of toxic substances directly hazardous to humans as well as other forms of life. Ultimately, the levels of all such pollutants can be controlled by appropriate legislation. The U.S. Environmental Protection Agency, for example, requires that most waste water should be treated to the equivalent of secondary treatment involving removal of greater than 85 percent of suspended solids and 5-day BOD. The consequence of inadequate control of pollution caused by liquid wastes

can be seen today in areas such as the coastal waters around New York City and coastal areas of the Mediterranean (Fig. 3.25). In such areas, fish and shellfish harvests are contaminated or destroyed along with the ruination of tourist and recreational facilities.

On the other hand, there are also dangers in unnecessary or overly strict regulation. An example is provided from the Wisconsin lead-zinc district in the United States, a significant region for the production of these metals for the last 150 years. The U.S. Environmental Protection Agency demanded there be no more than 0.5 parts per million of zinc in water effluent from a mine in this district, one-tenth of the 5 parts per million limit set by the Public Health Service as a maximum for this metal in drinking water. In fact, zinc is not toxic to humans even at much higher levels, and this limit was based on taste tests, not possible health hazards, zinc often being considered beneficial. The operating mine's effluent actually contained 2.5 parts per million—fine by Public Health Service standards but five times that demanded by the Environmental Protection Agency. Unable to comply, the mine had to close with the consequent loss of metal production and employment. The reason for setting the limit at 0.5 parts per million was to permit more fish in the streams, but this has not happened since closing the mine because the natural local ground water contains about as much zinc as the mine effluent. An ironic footnote to this story is that the Environmental Protection Agency's offices in Wash-

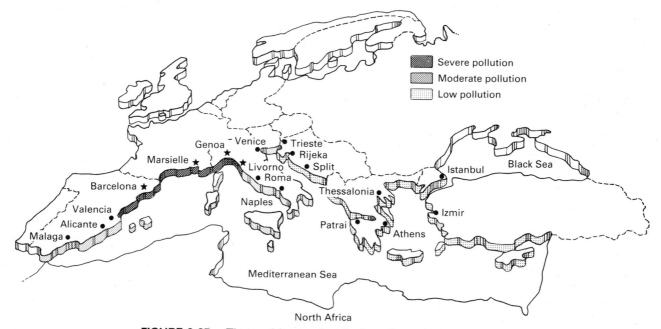

FIGURE 3-25. The problems of pollution along the Mediterranean coastline resulting from domestic sewage, and industrial waste in the mid-1970s is illustrated by the shading along the coastline. The stars indicate the major sources of the pollution.

ington were using drinking water containing 20 parts per million zinc 40 times the level imposed as an acceptable maximum for the Wisconsin mine effluent.

Recycling

Most of the refuse discarded by people in modern industrial societies contains large amounts of material that could be reused or processed to reclaim valuable raw materials. Such **recycling** often conserves not just material resources but fuel as well. For example, nearly 20 times as much energy is required to produce aluminum from bauxite as is required to remelt aluminum scrap, and over twice as much energy is needed to manufacture steel from primary raw materials as from scrap. Recycling operations also generally emit less pollutants than the original process as, for example, in the recycling of metals such as copper because the recycling does not require roasting or smelting.

The recycling of materials ranges from simple reuse or reclamation of an object (e.g., the reuse of bottles for beverages or milk) to complex processes of recovery by physical or chemical means (e.g., the revulcanization of rubber which is discussed below). Certain finished products, parts of products, or raw materials are clearly more easily recycled than others. For example, scrap paper and related materials made up of cellulose fiber can readily be pulped and used again to make paper and cardboard. A junk automobile, however, presents a formidable recycling problem, with its many components made of materials ranging from rubber and plastic to glass and a whole range of metals and alloys.

It is possible to envisage a society in which most durable goods are used for much longer than at present and then broken into their component parts to reclaim raw materials. However, for reasons we shall discuss below, less than 2 percent of the solid wastes generated in the United States, the world's greatest consumer country, are recycled. Before considering these largely social and economic aspects of recycling, we shall consider the technology of recycling.

Except for the larger items of machinery such as automobiles, most of the rubbish of modern society finds its way into municipal trash. There are also the more specialized forms of rubbish generated by agricultural and other industries. Most of this material cannot be reused and must be broken down into raw materials. Examples of the processes by which this is done include the following:

Melting of metals, glass, and some plastics which can then be purified and recast or remolded,
Revulcanizing of rubber which is a material that cannot be simply heated and remolded. It must be shredded, broken down chemically, and then reacted with sulfur compounds,
Pulping to reclaim fiber from waste paper or other natural material containing cellulose fiber such as wood, reeds, and sugar cane stalks. The material is stirred and beaten to form a slurry, inks are dissolved, and the pulp put through the usual papermaking processes;
Pyrolysis is heating materials in the absence of air to about 1650°C so that it decomposes to a range of chemical compounds. There are also the processes by which organic wastes can be broken down such as *composting* to make fertilizers, *rendering* of animal wastes to make such products as soaps and glues, and *fermentation* to make alcohols, gases, and a variety of other products (see also Chapter 5).

Although agricultural and industrial wastes may be fairly homogeneous and simply recycled through one of the above processes, domestic trash is a mixture of many kinds of material. Expecting the householder to separate cans, bottles, paper, organic wastes, and so on for separate collection may be unrealistic, although schemes for the collection of bottles or cans operated successfully during World War II and still do in some areas of the United States and Britain. Furthermore, notable success has been achieved in certain other countries, particularly Japan, where about 10 percent of municipal waste is recycled. In that highly organized industrial country, with very limited natural resources, the necessary incentives have been provided to develop alternatives to the throw-away society. In Hiroshima, for example, disposal of raw refuse has been reduced by 40 percent since 1976 by paying for separated wastes using monies saved in not having to operate landfill sites. Separation at the source is often undertaken by nonprofit groups such as student clubs and parent-teacher associations. A program involving source separation and computerized processing is now enabling 90 percent of the garbage of the Japanese city of Machida to be recycled. Commonly, however, the problem has to be tackled by separation at the disposal facility. Various devices that have been employed include screens, magnets to remove iron, or the use of compressed air to separate light from heavy items. A series of devices of the type shown in the flow diagram of Fig. 3.26 are needed to bring about complete separation. In this system, large items are removed manually and the remaining refuse fed with water into a pulper. The fiber component is pulped, brittle material such as glass is pulverized, but stronger solid objects are not affected. The fiber slurry is drained through a screen (2 centimeters mesh size) and large objects (over 2 centimeters) removed and washed. From

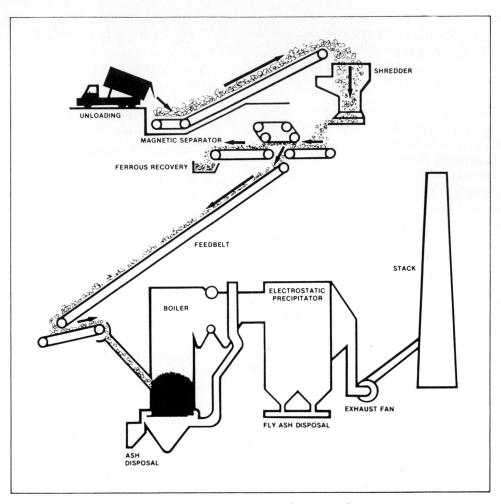

FIGURE 3-26. Schematic diagram showing a modern waste treatment system in which there is the recovery of ferrous scrap and the generation of useable heat by burning most of the other waste. The amount of ash for disposal is only a small fraction of the initial mass of the waste. (From R. Davies and P. Ketchum, "Energy from Waste," *GEOS*, vol. 15, no. 2, p. 18, Energy, Mines, and Resources Canada, 1986. Used with permission.)

this, iron is separated magnetically and other metals manually for sale as scrap. The fiber slurry is pumped to a cyclone that removes pulverized glass, metals, bone, sand particles, and other materials. The remaining slurry is made of paper, food wastes, cloth, plastics, and via further pulping and screening operations, paper fiber is extracted. Organic materials are used as a fuel.

Such schemes for the recycling of domestic waste are unfortunately rare, whereas recycling of metals is much more widespread. Of course, in industries using metals, as in a metal fabricating shop, large quantities of uncontaminated scrap are generated, and this has a ready market. Consequently in the United States, roughly 40 percent of copper and lead, 30 percent of stainless steel, 25 percent of aluminum, and 14 percent

of zinc are recycled along with high percentages of the precious metals. Nevertheless, the quantities of such metals annually discarded in the United States is vast—over 11 million tons of iron and steel, 800,000 tons of aluminum, and 400,000 tons of other metals. As already noted, the savings involved in recycling are not only of the raw materials themselves but also of energy. It has been suggested that recycling of the more than 50 billion steel cans alone that are used annually in the United States would save energy equal to the output of eight 500 megawatt power plants. Furthermore, discarding an aluminum beverage container wastes as much energy as pouring out such a can half-filled with gasoline. It is particularly the two metals, iron and aluminum, for which recycling offers the greatest benefits through sav-

ings not only in raw materials but also in energy and much reduced environmental damage. (Recycling aluminum reduces air emissions associated with its production by 95 percent, for example.) This is because of the vast consumption of these two metals and large amounts of energy used in producing these materials that are essential to modern societies. The one other recyclable material that occupies a special place is wood, since it is a fuel, building material, and raw material for chemical industries and paper manufacture. Paper products use about 35 percent of the world's commercial wood harvest, and recycling half of the paper used in the world today would meet nearly 75 percent of the demand for new paper and free 8 million hectares (20 million acres) of forest from paper production. In spite of the great advantages, however, only about one-quarter of the world's steel, aluminum, and paper is recovered for reuse.

Why then is recycling not undertaken on a much larger scale? The factors that dictate this are not technical, but economic and social. Thus in the field of metals, the ore mining and processing industries are established groups often operating on a large and highly organized scale. Scrap metal operations are often small, labor intensive, and incur heavier transportation costs because of their scale. A domestic refuse reclamation plant is currently more costly than landfill disposal, a cost that will have to be borne by local citizens in their rates and taxes. Some citizens may be prepared to pay the few extra dollars a year to remove the need for unsightly landfill operations and save precious raw materials, but many, not being directly affected, will not make this sacrifice.

Two factors are likely to bring about more widespread recycling in the future. One will be the need to use land area for more valuable purposes than that of a landfill. The other will be the cost of the raw material produced from its primary source that will increase as supplies become scarcer or more expensive to extract. The benefits of recycling, in saving not only precious raw materials but also energy, and in reducing problems of waste disposal and pollution, are very clear. Unfortunately, in most countries, there are not the economic and social incentives needed to set up large-scale recycling operations at the present time.

FURTHER READINGS

COATES, D.R., *Environmental Geology*. New York: John Wiley and Sons, 1981.

DETWYLER, T.R., *Man's Impact on Environment*. New York: McGraw-Hill, 1971.

HOLDGATE, M.W., KASSAG, M., and WHITE, F., editors, *The World Environment 1972–1983. A Report by the United Nations Environment Programme,* Volume 8 in the Natural Resources and Environmental Series. Dublin: Tycooly International Publishing, Ltd.

MACDONALD, E.H., *Alluvial Mining*. London: Chapman and Hall, 1983.

NATIONAL ACADEMY OF SCIENCES, *Mineral Resources and the Environment,* a report prepared by the Committee on Mineral Resources and the Environment, February 1975.

PETERS, W.C., *Exploration and Mining Geology*. New York: John Wiley and Sons, 1978.

WILLS, B.A., *Mineral Processing Technology, 2nd ed.* New York: Pergamon Press, 1981.

4

The rapid expansion of the oil industry in the early part of the twentieth century combined with the views of nearly limitless supplies of oil sometimes led to the intense clustering of oil wells as seen at Signal Hills, California in the 1920s. (Courtesy of Shell Oil Company.)

ENERGY FROM FOSSIL FUELS

It is difficult for people living now, who have become accustomed to the steady exponential growth in the consumption of energy from the fossil fuels, to realize how transitory the fossil-fuel epoch will eventually prove to be when it is viewed over a longer span of human history.

M. KING HUBBERT,
IN SCIENTIFIC AMERICAN (1971)

INTRODUCTION

Every action we take, every procedure we design and even the process of reading these words and thinking about their meaning requires **energy**—the actual or potential ability to do **work.** The primary function of the machines we build is to convert energy into useful work. We ourselves are machines that convert the energy stored in the food we eat into the activities we consider as useful work. Unfortunately, we are not very efficient when judged simply as machines, and even when we are most industrious each of us capable of only doing enough work to keep a 100-watt light bulb burning. Because of our limitations, far back in our history, we found it expedient to turn to supplementary sources to provide energy to do things that we did not want to do or of which we were not physically capable. The first of these supplementary sources were probably other humans (slaves) and animals. Because these sources proved inadequate to meet our needs, we turned to progressively more sophisticated means such as sails for ships, wind mills, water wheels, steam and internal combustion engines, electric motors, and eventually nuclear power plants.

The human appetite for energy to build and maintain modern society has grown so large that the supplemental energy expenditures now far exceed our individual muscle energy in every aspect of life. Whereas our earliest ancestors relied on the energy from their own bodies as "one-manpower," we now augment our own body energy with that from a vast variety of supplemental sources. We can envision this supplemental energy as silent slaves working continuously to feed, clothe, and maintain each and every one of us. The number of these available energy slaves varies widely from one country and culture to another. Hence the supplementary energy used per person is equivalent to 15 energy slaves in India, 30 in South America, 75 in Japan, 120 in the Soviet Union, 150 in England and Europe, and about 300 in the United States and Canada. We see the work in the form of numerous machines that perform various jobs for us, but each of the machines has an earth-supplied energy source such as petroleum, natural gas, coal, running water, or uranium. Just how dependent we have be-

come on these energy slaves can be envisioned by considering the consequences of them going on strike (i.e., if all the earth's energy supplies ran out or were not available). We would be reduced to our own muscle power to supply all our needs. Our technological society would come to an abrupt halt and we would very soon find ourselves unable to feed and maintain the world's population. Muscle power alone could not hold back the inevitable starvation, famine, and pestilence that would rapidly reduce the world's population. The survivors would be forced to live much as our early ancestors did thousands of years ago, prior to the development of the resources that now provide most of our supplemental energy.

ENERGY UNITS

Because energy is the capacity to do work, and there are many types of work—mechanical, electrical, and thermal, for example—there are many different types of units by which energy is measured. The **joule** is the electrical energy needed to maintain a flow of 1 ampere for 1 second at a potential of 1 volt. The **calorie** is the energy needed to raise the temperature of 1 gram of water 1 degree Celsius. The **British thermal unit** (BTU) is the heat energy needed to raise 1 pound of water 1 degree Fahrenheit. The variety and interchangeability of energy units is shown in Table 4.1. In order to be able to compare the stored energy that we might be able to extract from various sources, we shall be using the joule as our standard unit of energy. However, in order to permit us to relate to the normal energy production statistics we hear about on a daily basis, we shall also equate joules with the commonly employed units such as metric tons of coal, barrels of oil, and trillions of cubic feet of gas.

Although the total energy available from any source is important, we must also be concerned about the rate at which energy is used and the maximum rate at which it can be supplied. In the case of a windmill, for example, we cannot use energy faster than is supplied by the wind pushing the blades. We must, therefore, also consider a time-dependent function called **power,** by which we mean the energy used per unit of

TABLE 4-1

Energy equivalences

1 btu	= 252 gram-calories = 1055 joules = 2.93×10^{-4} kwh
1 joule	= 0.239 gram-calorie = 0.00095 btu = 2.78×10^{-7} kwh
1 gram, calorie	= 4.189 joules = 0.00397 btu
1 watt	= 1 joule/sec = 0.239 cal/sec = 0.0569 btu/min = 0.00134 horsepower
1 Quad (btu)	= 10^{15} btu = 1.05×10^{18} joules = 2.93×10^{11} kwh

1 million (10^6) btu equals approximately:

90	pounds of bituminous coal and lignite production (1982)
125	pounds of oven-dried wood
8	gallons of motor gasoline or enough to move the average passenger car about 124 miles (1981 rate)
10	therms of natural gas (dry)
11	gallons of propane
1.2	days of per capita energy consumption in the United States (1982 rate)
2	months of dietary intake of a laborer
20	cases (240 bottles) of table wine

1 million btu of fossil fuels burned at electric utilities can generate about 100 kilowatt-hours of electricity, while about 300 kilowatt-hours of electricity generated at electric utilities can produce about 1 million btu of heat.

1 quadrillion (10^{15}) btu equals approximately:

44	million short tons of bituminous coal and lignite production
63	million short tons of oven-dried wood
1	trillion cubic feet of natural gas (dry)
170	million barrels of crude oil
500	thousand barrels per day of crude oil for 1 year
35	days of petroleum imports into the United States (1982 rate)
30	days of United States motor gasoline usage (1982 rate)

1 barrel of crude oil equals approximately:

5.7	thousand cubic feet of natural gas (dry)
0.26	short tons of bituminous coal and lignite production
1700	killowatt-hours of electricity consumed

1 short ton of bituminous coal and lignite production equals about:

3.9	barrels of crude oil
22	thousand cubic feet of natural gas (dry)
6600	kilowatt-hours of electricity consumed

1 thousand cubic feet of natural gas equals approximately:

0.18	barrels (or 7.5 gallons) of crude oil
0.045	short tons (or 90 pounds) of bituminous coal and lignite production
300	kilowatt-hours of electricity consumed

1 thousand kilowatt-hours of electricity equals approximately:

0.59	barrels of crude oil (although it takes about 1.7 barrels of oil to produce 1000 kWh)
0.15	short tons of bituminous coal and lignite production (although it takes about 0.5 short tons to produce 1000 kWh)
3300	cubic feet of natural gas (dry) (although it takes about 10,000 cubic feet to produce 1000 kWh)
27.2	gallons of gasoline

time. The widely used term **horsepower,** familiar to most people, originated from the use of horse-drawn plows and wagons. It has persisted as a measure of the strength of engines, including those in automobiles, because in 1766, James Watt, a Scottish engineer, measured the power of his steam engine against the power of a horse. In this book, for the sake of consistency, we shall use the power unit **watt** that is defined as the consumption of one joule of electrical energy per second. The watt is commonly used in every day discussion of household appliances and light bulbs and will become even more familiar as we increasingly use energy from renewable sources, such as heat and light from the sun.

As with food and other renewable resources, it is not the total amount of solar energy that has or will reach the earth that is important, but rather the rate at which it continues to reach us.

THE CHANGING USE OF ENERGY

The progression from hunting and gathering to a modern technological society is characterized by both vast increases in the amounts of supplemental energy consumed and marked changes in the sources of that energy. Supplemental energy use remained relatively low

until the industrial revolution swept across Europe and North America in the eighteenth and nineteenth centuries. Prior to that time, our primary sources of supplemental energy were wood, wind, running water, and animals.

The onset of the Industrial Revolution in England required unprecedented amounts of fuel to drive the newly invented engines. It was soon obvious that wood could not supply the needs, and that the entire British Isles were in danger of being deforested. Consequently, the British turned to coal, which proved to be a superior heat source. Coal soon became the fuel for the Industrial Revolution worldwide, and this led simultaneously to two significant changes in the energy-use pattern in the industrialized nations of the world. The total amount of energy used rose dramatically and coal rapidly replaced wood as the major fuel. The scene was similar in each country and is especially well shown for the United States in Fig. 4.1. In 1850, wood constituted approximately 90 percent of the American fuel source; by 1880 this had dropped to 50 percent; and by 1900 to only about 10 percent. Coal remained the dominant energy source, providing nearly 75 percent of the nation's energy in 1920, until the rapid expansion of oil and gas use surpassed it in the 1940s and 1950s. Total energy production in the United States and the world rose dramatically from the 1940s until the 1970s when the 1973 OPEC oil embargo and rapid price increases for the fossil fuels shocked the world. These events led to a slower rate in growth of world energy demand and a slight decrease in energy consumption of some major countries like the United States (Fig. 4.1).

Since about 1880, the fossil fuels—coal, oil, and natural gas—have served as the major sources of energy for the United States and other industrialized nations. It has now become clear that supplies of these fuels, though large, are limited, and that some day other fuels will be needed to replace them. Thus it appears that the period from about 1880 to about 2100 or 2200 A.D. will be known as the "Fossil Fuel Era" to historians in the future. This leads to the important question of what will be the energy sources beyond the fossil fuel era? The relatively rapid rise in nuclear power in the 1960s and 1970s seemed to ensure that the use of nuclear power would ultimately surpass that of fossil fuels. The generation of electricity by nuclear power plants was projected to be safe, efficient, and so cheap that household electric meters would become unnecessary. The enthusiasm of the nuclear power industry was severely dampened, however, when there was a partial meltdown of the reactor at Three Mile Island in Pennsylvania in May 1979. This event, along with huge cost overruns in the construction of power plants, a reduced projection for electricity demand, and the widespread realization that safe

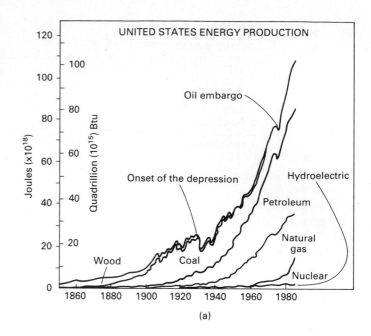

(a)

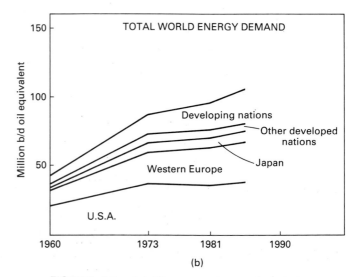

(b)

FIGURE 4-1. (a) The energy requirements for the United States have risen dramatically since the mid-nineteenth century. Note also the progression from wood to coal and then the rapid growth of oil and gas use since the middle of the twentieth century. (Data from U.S. Geological Survey. After D.L. Gibson, Energy Graphics, Prentice Hall, 1983.) (b) World energy demand grew rapidly from 1960 until 1973 when the rates of growth were reduced. The U.S. proportion of total world energy demand has decreased as other economies, especially those in developing nations, have risen. (After International Petroleum Encyclopedia, 1984.)

disposal of nuclear waste is an enormous problem, led to the cancellation of many projected power plants, including many already partially constructed. The magnitude of the nuclear power industry problems in the United States is perhaps best exemplified by the default of the Washington Public Power Supply System (known as WPPSS in Washington or "Woops" on Wall Street) in construction of power plants after the investment of $2.8 billion, much of which was in privately held bonds. All these problems were compounded by the accident at Chernobyl in the Ukraine region of the Soviet Union in April 1986. Accordingly, the ultimate fate of the approximately 100 nuclear power plants operating in the United States is uncertain. Despite the American and Soviet problems, additional nuclear power plants are still being planned and constructed in several European countries and in Japan. These countries, with few fossil fuel resources of their own, see nuclear energy as preferable to increasing cost and potential unreliability of imported fossil fuel supplies.

In any discussion of energy it is important to consider the usage as well as the source. This is well shown in Fig. 4.2, which although drawn for the United States, is representative of most industrialized nations. This diagram illustrates the complex nature of energy genera-

tion and the end distribution of energy in the transportation, industrial, residential, and commercial realms. Unfortunately, the laws of thermodynamics state that we cannot build 100 percent efficient machines. This, combined with our own inefficiencies, results in the loss of approximately 25 percent of the energy in conversion and transmission. The rapid rise of energy costs in the 1970s and early 1980s led to much energy conservation and significant improvements in efficiency, but we shall probably never be able to increase the overall efficiency above about 80 percent. The diagram also demonstrates the very heavy dependence of modern society on the fossil fuels. Consequently, they will be the topics with which we commence our discussion of energy sources.

FOSSIL FUELS

Almost all sedimentary rocks contain organic matter. The amount ranges from only trace quantities in some sandstones to the major constituents in coals and oil shales. All this organic matter, consisting of hydrocarbons in a vast variety of different molecular species, is part of the **carbon cycle** (Fig. 4.3). The carbon cycle is a complex series of chemical reactions by which the car-

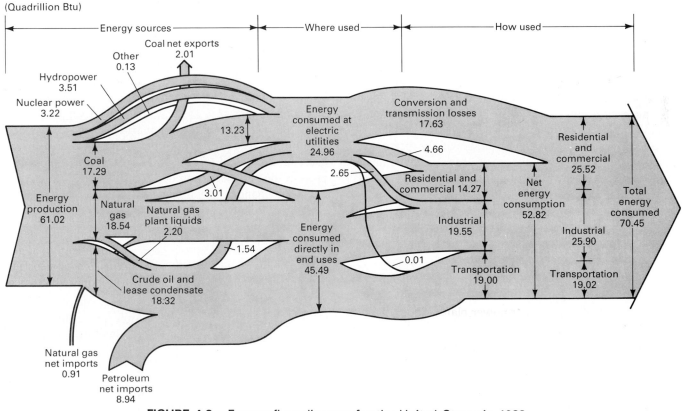

FIGURE 4-2. Energy flow diagram for the United States in 1983. (From U.S. Energy Information Administration, 1983 Annual Energy Review.)

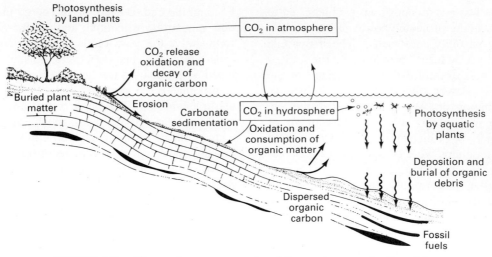

FIGURE 4-3.   The main components of the carbon cycle. Fossil fuels are formed as a result of carbon dioxide from the atmosphere being converted by photosynthesis into organic matter. Subsequently, some of the organic matter has been trapped in the sediments, and a small portion of that is preserved as fossil fuels.

bon may pass back and forth from solid rock to air, to dissolved gases in waters, to plants and organisms. By far, most of the organic matter ever formed in the biological realm has been consumed or destroyed and thus returned to other parts of the carbon cycle. A small fraction of the organic matter, estimated to be no more than 1 percent of the total, has, however, been preserved by being buried in various types of sediments before being eaten, altered, or oxidized away. Of this preserved material, most occurs as minor disseminated components of fine-grained sediments (Fig. 4.4). Lesser amounts are present in carbonate rocks, sandstones, and bituminous (or conspicuously hydrocarbon-containing) rocks. Only a very small percentage of the preserved organic material is present in a form concentrated enough that it can be used as a **fossil fuel.** This term is rather loosely defined but is generally understood to in-

clude the organically derived sedimentary rocks and rock products that can be burned for fuel.

Fossil fuels occur in three forms that are familiar to most people—**coal, petroleum,** and **natural gas.** Less well known, because of only limited and local use, are **oil shales,** tar sands, heavy oils, and **peat.** Although the various fossil fuels are quite different in appearance and are processed and utilized in different ways, they all share a similar origin as trapped organic debris in sedimentary rocks (Fig. 4.5). Their variety results from differences in the types of original organic matter (e.g., leaves and stems in a fresh water swamp versus phytoplanktonic organic matter in a marine basin) and the degree of alteration occurring after trapping as a result of bacterial decay and as a result of rising temperature and pressure due to increasing depth of burial.

The changes which occur in buried organic matter

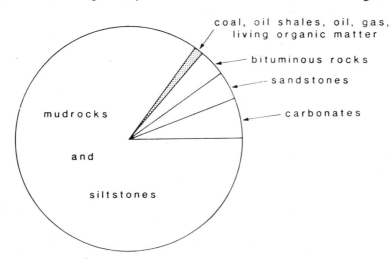

FIGURE 4-4. The distribution of organic matter in sediments in terms of the total mass of organic carbon. The fossil fuels constitute only a very small proportion of all organic carbon. [From M.A. Barnes, W.C. Barnes, and R.M. Bustin, "Diagenesis 8: Chemistry and Evolution of Organic Matter", *Canada Geoscience,* vol. 11 (1984). Used with permission.]

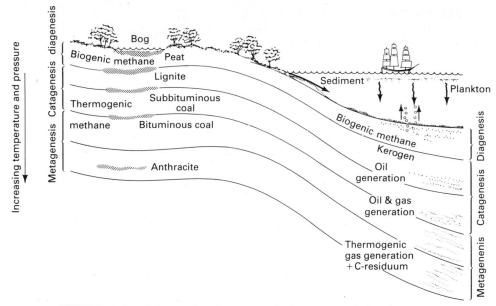

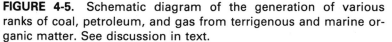

FIGURE 4-5. Schematic diagram of the generation of various ranks of coal, petroleum, and gas from terrigenous and marine organic matter. See discussion in text.

tend to be both progressive and irreversible and are schematically shown in Fig. 4.4. In general, the earliest changes which take place at very shallow burial depths are biochemical, occurring as a result of the metabolism of bacteria, fungi, and other microorganisms. A primary product of this activity, regardless of the type or location of the organic matter, is **methane gas** (CH_4) sometimes known as **swamp** (or **marsh**) **gas.** At greater sediment depths, the microbial activity is slower, but the increased temperature and pressure tend to result in the driving-off of water and the **cracking,** or breakup, of complex hydrocarbon molecules.

The original type of organic matter plays an important role in the generation of fossil fuels. Prior to the Devonian Period there were few land plants; hence photosynthetic marine phytoplankton and bacteria were the principal sources of the organic matter in the sediments. These types of organisms, that still constitute most of the organics in the modern marine sediments, contribute mainly proteins, lipids, and carbohydrates. In terrestrial environments, the higher plants contribute resins, waxes, lignins, and carbohydrates in the form of cellulose. Table 4.2 presents a comparison of some of the major organic constituents in the different types of living matter that serve as precursors to fossil fuels and the carbon, hydrogen, sulfur, nitrogen, and oxygen contents of these constituents and the fossil fuels. In the conversion from organic debris to fossil fuel there is the expulsion of water, a general reduction of oxygen and nitrogen, and a general increase in carbon and hydrogen. As a result of these changes, the fossil fuels are superior heat sources compared to fresh organic matter,

such as wood and leaves. Those organics in the marine realm generally are altered into gas and petroleum, whereas those in the terrestrial rocks may form gas and coal. In some organic-rich shales, such as oil shales, the burial temperatures have never been high enough to completely break down the original organic molecules. Temperatures have only been sufficient enough to alter them to large waxy molecules known as **kerogen.** These can be converted to oil and gas by various refining processes.

Although the fossil fuels represent parts of a broad continuous spectrum, they are discussed individually below. The conventional fossil fuels—coal, petroleum, and natural gas—are discussed first, then oil shales, tar sands, and heavy oils. All the fossil fuels are chemically similar in that they consist primarily of hydrocarbon molecules. The differences in the physical properties—from an invisible gas such as methane, to a yellow to brown syrupy liquid such as petroleum, to a black solid such as anthracite—reflect the vast differences in arrangements and sizes of the hydrocarbon molecules and the differing ratios of hydrogen to carbon contents. During burning, it is the combustion of carbon and hydrogen with atmospheric oxygen that produces nearly all the heat; hence, the higher the contents of these elements, the better is the fuel.

Coal

Introduction. The fossil fuels that bear the greatest witness to the original organic matter from which they were derived are peat and coal. In most

TABLE 4-2

Representative compositions of living matter and fossil fuels

Part A: Living Matter

Substances	Major Constituents (wt%)		
	Lipids	Proteins	Carbohydrates
Green plants	2	7	75
Humus	6	10	77
Phytoplankton	11	15	66
Zooplankton	15	53	5
Bacteria (veg.)	20	60	20
Spores	50	8	42

Part B: Petroleum

Substances	Elemental Composition (wt%)				
	C	H	S	N	O
Lipids	80	10	—	—	10
Proteins	53	7	2	16	22
Carbohydrates	44	6	—	—	50
Lignin	63	5	0.1	0.3	31
Kerogen	79	6	5	2	8
Natural gas	75–80	20–25	trace–0.2	trace–minor	—
Asphalt	81–87	9–11	0.3–6	0.8–2.2	0–4
Petroleum	82–87	12–15	0.1–5	0.1–5	0.1–2

Part C: Coal

Substances	Elemental Composition (wt%)				
	C	H	S	N	O
Peat	21.0	8.3	—	1.1	62.9*
Lignite	42.4	6.6	1.7	0.6	42.1*
Sub-bituminous	76.3	4.7	0.5	1.5	17.0
Bituminous	87.0	5.4	1.0	1.4	5.2
Semianthracite	92.2	3.8	0.6	1.2	2.2
Anthracite	94.4	1.8	1.0	0.7	2.1

*Remainder is ash and moisture.

(Data from Chilingarian and Yen, *Bitumens, Asphalts, and Tar Sands,* and from Books, ed., *Coal Development,* U.S. Bureau of Land Management, 1983.)

forms these substances contain abundant imprints of leaves, stems, seeds, and spores of the plants that were compacted to form the beds we now mine. Because peat is the clear precursor of coal, it is included in the following discussion under the general title "coal." Coal was a very common household fuel in the United States and Europe in the second half of the nineteenth century and first half of the twentieth century. In the second half of the twentieth century its use in homes was largely replaced with oil, gas, or electric heat because these were more readily available and much cleaner to use. Although coal is no longer in use directly in many homes, it is used indirectly because it is the major heat source in the electrical power plants that supply the homes. The cheap and convenient petroleum replaced some coal usage in power plants in the 1950s and 1960s, but there has been a return to increased coal usage since the 1973 OPEC oil embargo caused concern over supplies and brought about sharp rises in the cost of petroleum. There exists today much more fossil fuel energy worldwide as recoverable coal than as recoverable oil; hence, it is clear that we shall rely on coal as an energy source for many years to come.

Coal has been classified in several ways. We shall employ the simple and widely used terms of *peat, lignite, bituminous coal,* and *anthracite.*

History of Coal Use. The origins of coal use are not known, but there is evidence that 3000 to 4000 years ago, Bronze Age tribes in Wales used coal in funeral pyres of their dead. Coal was also probably used by the Chinese as early as 1100 B.C. and by the Greeks in 200 to 300 B.C., but nearly a thousand years passed before coal had any lasting impact on civilization.

The widespread use of coal as a fuel began in the twelfth century A.D. when the inhabitants of the north-

east coast of England found that black rocks weathering out of coastal cliffs would burn hotter than wood which was becoming scarce. The name, in fact, derives from the Ango-Saxon *col* first used to refer to charcoal. This evolved to *cole*, the spelling used until about 300 years ago. Inefficient burning of impure coals released repugnant odors that caused Londoners to complain about air pollution in 1273 and ultimately led to an edict from King Edward I in 1306 banning the use of coal. However, by the onset of the Industrial Revolution in the late 1600s and 1700s, England was facing a crisis as its forests were being depleted to make charcoal and the admiralty feared for sufficient timber to maintain its fleets. The value of coal as a substitute for fuel wood became apparent, but two other developments further brought coal into its own as a fuel. About 1710, Abraham Darby, a Shropshire iron maker, developed a method of using coke, made by heating coal in the absence of air, to smelt iron. The first commercial steam engine, produced in 1698, burned wood or charcoal; however, as these engines were perfected and came into wide usage during the 1700s, coal became the fuel to drive them.

Although the Pueblo Indians of the southwestern United States used coal in pottery making for many years, the first recorded discovery of coal in North America was by a French exploration party in 1679 along the Illinois River about 130 kilometers southwest of Chicago. The first New World mining effort began in 1750 near Richmond, Virginia, where a Huguenot colony worked exposed seams. Coal mining then began in western Pennsylvania in 1759 and soon spread throughout the area of the Appalachian coal fields.

The development of the Industrial Revolution rapidly increased the demand for coal both in Europe and the United States. In England and in several parts of the eastern United States the most efficient way to transport the coal was by canal systems. The development of railroads in the early 1800s supplanted, in part, the canal systems but also provided another major market for the coal. Then in the 1890s, with the development of the steam-driven electric generator, coal became the principal fuel for electric power plants, a position it continues to hold today.

Formation of Coal. Coals of all types are the compacted and variously preserved remains of land plants. Many plant remains such as leaves, stems, and tree trunks are visible to the naked eye and many others such as spores are visible under the microscope. Most of the plant matter today, as in the past, is not preserved but is decomposed nearly immediately where it falls or breaks down during the early stages of burial. Only where plant growth is abundant and the conditions for preservation are optimum can there accumulate thick

masses or organic matter that could ultimately become coals. The higher forms of plants with cellulose-rich stems and leaves that constitute coals did not evolve on the continents until the Devonian. The Paleozoic coal beds of the Carboniferous in Europe and North America were dominated by ferns and scale-tree (Fig. 4.6). In contrast, the Mesozoic and Tertiary swamps consisted of

(a)

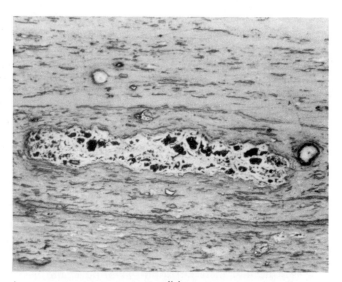

(b)

FIGURE 4-6. (a) Many coal beds contain imprints of the plants from which they were formed. Here the bark of a Cycad tree from a Mississippian (Carboniferous) age coal is visible. (Photograph courtesy of S. Scheckler.) (b) A microscopic view of a Mississippian age coal in which layers of macerals, the organic constituents of coal, are visible.

angiosperm (flowering) plants much like those forming today.

Most of the world's coals are known as **humic coals** and consist of organic debris that has passed through a peat stage. Their major components are lustrous black to dark brown materials known as **macerals** (the organic equivalents of the minerals that constitute a rock) (Fig. 4.7). Much less common, but locally important, is another type of coal known as **sapropelic coal.** The two varieties of sapropelic coals, called **boghead** and **cannel coals,** consist primarily of spores and fine-grained featureless algal debris that collected in oxygen-deficient ponds, lakes, and lagoons. These coals have compositions similar to the kerogen that are precursors to oil; indeed, when subject to higher temperatures and pressures, they yield oil and gas rather than the black vitreous maceral seen in humic coals.

The formation of the major coals (humic types) begins with the accumulation of organic debris in peat swamps where the stagnant waters prevent oxidation and destruction. It has been estimated that under average peat-forming conditions only about 10 percent of the plant production is preserved. The highest rates of plant growth occur in tropical forest swamps, but these are also the sites of the greatest bacterial activity that destroy vegetable matter; hence, few peats develop in the tropics. Today the major peat-forming areas occur in the temperate to cold regions, such as Ireland, Scandinavia,

FIGURE 4-7. The horizontal layering in the coal represents the layering of compacted organic matter; differences in the reflectivity result from differences in the content of the macerals. Pyrite (FeS_2,) although not visible in this sample, occurs locally in coal beds and is the principal contaminant that results in environmental pollution. (Photograph by J.R. Craig.)

Alaska, and Canada, where abundant rainfall promotes rapid plant growth but where the cooler temperatures retard bacterial decay. If the rates of peat accumulation in the past were similar to the 1 millimeter per year we see now, the major coal basins must represent swamps that persisted for tens of thousands of years.

The geologic study of coal-bearing sequences reveals that many formed in areas of successive transgression and regression of shorelines. This is seen in the interbedding of marine sediments with the coals and with lacustrine and terrestrial beds. A common sequence would have been the development of a near-coastal swamp along the margin of a basin with the accumulation of thick masses of peat as the basin slowly subsided. If the rate of subsidence exceeded the slow buildup of peat and sediment, the sea advanced (or transgressed) over the swamp, covering and preserving the peat with sands and muds. Where the seawater was warm and clean, lime muds often accummulated. Frequently, the subsidence was followed by a reemergence of the coastal area (with a retreat or regression of the ocean) and a subsequent reestablishment of a swamp and the deposition of another layer of peat. As a result of such cyclical deposition, many parts of the world's major coal basins contain tens to scores of individual coal beds separated by sandstones, shales, and limestones (Fig. 4.8). The individual coal beds range in thickness from only a few centimeters to tens of meters. The individual coal seams often split into two or more seams indicating that deposition in the peat swamp was continuous in some areas but interrupted in others. This situation is seen today in swamps that lie in major deltas where the distributaries keep changing direction and where there are many differences in the rates of subsidence and sediment accumulation.

Peat formation has taken place continuously since the development of land plants in the Devonian, but the size of the swamps and their degree of preservation has not been uniform. By far, the greatest period of coal swamp formation took place in the last 70 million years or so of the Paleozoic Era (Fig. 4.9). During this time, the great coal beds of Britain and of the eastern United States were laid down. The abundance of the coal in these beds in Britain led to this span of geologic time being named the Carboniferous. Another great period of coal deposition extended from the beginning of the Jurassic until the mid-Tertiary. It was during this period that the major coals of the western United States were deposited. Deposition continues today in localized areas such as the Everglades of Florida, the Dismal Swamp of Virginia and North Carolina in the United States, and in the coastal swamps of Canada, Scandinavia, and Ireland. Although these do not rival the peat swamps of the past, they do give us a first-hand opportunity to under-

FIGURE 4-8. The cyclical development of coal-forming conditions resulted in the deposition of multiple coal beds in many areas as are visible in this roadcut in western Virginia. (Photograph courtesy of Geological Consulting Services, Inc.)

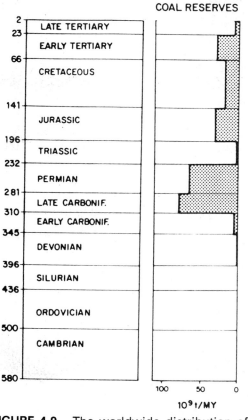

FIGURE 4-9. The worldwide distribution of coal reserves in terms of millions of tons accumulated per million years during geologic time is shown by the graph on the right-hand side of the diagram. The absence of land plants prior to the Devonian precludes earlier coals; the late Carboniferous (Mississippian) and Permian were the periods of most prolific deposition. [Figure after the Demaison (1977) and Bestougeff (1980) and from Bois, Bouch and Pelet, *American Association of Petroleum Geologists Bulletin,* vol. 66 (1982) p. 1264. Used with permission.]

stand the conditions that must be present for peats and coals to form.

Immediately after accumulation of the dead plant remains, compaction occurs and bacterial and fungal attack begins. In the formation of peat, the cellulose and other original plant components are decomposed resulting in the production of biogenic methane gas, carbon dioxide, and some ammonia (NH_3). The remnant is a mass of brown, hydrated gels, rich in large hydrocarbon molecules.

Coalification is the process by which the organic components that survived peat formation undergo further physical and chemical changes as a result of biochemical action and of rising temperature and pressure. As burial depth increases, temperature is by far the most important factor in coalification. The progressive increase in the **rank** of coal is peat, lignite (or brown coal), bituminous (or hard-) coal, and anthracite, as shown in Fig. 4.10. The precise assignment of rank is determined by the carbon content, the calorific value (or heat given off during burning), the moisture content, and volatile matter content. The most significant chemical changes are the progressive decrease in the oxygen and hydrogen contents and the resultant increase in the carbon content, as shown in what is known as a van-Krevelen diagram (Fig. 4.11). As this process proceeds the number of distinguishable plant remains decreases and more and more of the shiny black macerals are formed. There is a progressive decrease in moisture and an increase in density, calorific value (up to anthracite), and the degree of polymerization (coordination of carbon atoms).

The World's Coal Reserves and Coal Production. The coal resources of the earth are large but very irregularly distributed. Of the nearly trillion tons of recoverable coal reserves, two-thirds occur in the United States, the Soviet Union, and China (Table 4.3

Rank stages		Characteristics	H₂O %	Heat content
Brown coal or lignite	Peat	Large pores Details of original plant matter still recognizable Free cellulose	~ 75	3000 kcal/kg (5400 Btu/lb)
	Soft brown coal	No free cellulose		
	Dull brown coal (Hard brown coal)	Marked compaction of plant structures	~35	4000 kcal/kg (7200 Btu/lb)
	Bright brown coal (Hard brown coal)	Plant structures partly recognizable	~25	5500 kcal/kg (9900 Btu/lb)
Hard coal	Bituminous		~10	7000 kcal/kg (12,000 Btu/lb)
	Anthracite	Plant structures no longer recognizable		8650 kcal/kg (15,500 Btu/lb)

(left axis: Rank increasing ↓)

FIGURE 4-10. The ranks of coal, the calorific value, and some important physical characteristics. [Modified from *The International Handbook of Coal Petrography* (1963).]

and Fig. 4.12, 4.13). The other countries with significant reserves include: West Germany, Poland, Australia, and South Africa. On the other hand, coal reserves are virtually absent in the entire continent of South America. The amount of coal production parallels the magnitude of the reserves with the United States, the Soviet Union, and China accounting for nearly 55 percent of the world total.

Within the United States, coal fields are widespread with four major provinces accounting for most of the reserves (Fig. 4.14 and Table 4.4). In general, the Eastern and Interior Provinces contain bituminous coal, whereas the Rocky Mountain and Northern Great Plains Provinces are richest in sub-bituminous coal and lignite. Anthracite occurs locally in all provinces, but the country's major production and reserves lie in eastern Pennsylvania. Alaska contains significant amounts of sub-bituminous coal, but its remoteness leaves these deposits largely as resources rather than as reserves.

The mining of coal, like that of metal ores, began as a very labor intensive industry. The coal beds were easier to follow and mine because many were nearly horizontal and were much easier to break with a pick and shovel than were metal ores. On the other hand, conditions were difficult and dangerous because many coal seams were less than 1 meter in thickness and the mine openings were only as high as the seam was thick. Furthermore, mine fires and explosions resulting from seepage of methane gas into the workings was a common event. In the 1800s, in Britain, the United States, and several other countries, children commonly worked in the coal mines because of their small size and because they could be paid so little. Prior to 1898 the work week in the United States bituminous mines was 60 hours. It was then reduced to 52 hours where it remained until 1917 and finally to 40 hours in 1933. The problems of low pay and long hours led to unionization and brought about the establishment of very strong unions in the

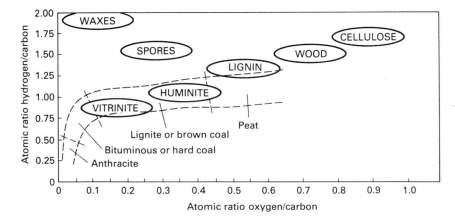

FIGURE 4-11. The van Krevelen diagram illustrating the evolution of the composition of organic matter as it is converted into coal. The carbon content and the calorific value rise as the organic matter progresses to lower H/C and O/C ratios.

TABLE 4-3

Recoverable world coal reserves* ($\times 10^9$ tons)

	Anthracite and Bituminous	Lignite	Total (%)
Americas:			
United States	248.16	35.25	283.41
Canada	4.18	2.33	6.51
Other	19.26	0.02	19.28
Total	271.59	37.61	309.19 (31.3)
Western Europe:			
Germany, West	32.98	38.67	71.65
United Kingdom	5.06	0	5.06
Other	5.22	20.64	25.87
Total	43.26	59.31	102.58 (10.4)
Eastern Europe and U.S.S.R.:			
U.S.S.R.	166.67	98.22	264.89
Poland	30.00	13.20	43.20
Czechoslovakia	3.00	3.15	6.15
Other	0.26	8.39	8.65
Total	199.93	122.96	322.89 (32.7)
Africa			
South Africa	57.04	0	57.04
Other	8.17	0	8.17
Total	65.21	0	65.21 (6.6)
Far East, Oceania, Other:			
China	108.90	0	108.90
Australia	32.52	39.90	72.42
Other	3.02	2.64	5.35
Total	144.44	42.06	186.67 (18.9)
WORLD TOTAL	724.42	262.11	986.54 (100%)

*As of 1980, these data include only coals economically extractable at the time of determination.
(Data from *Annual Energy Review 1984,* Energy Information Administration.)

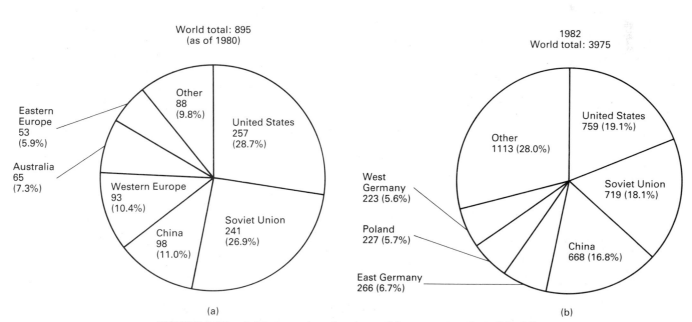

FIGURE 4-12. (a) International recoverable reserves of coal in billions (10^9) of metric tons as of 1980. (b) International coal production in 1982 in millions (10^6) of metric tons. (From U.S. Energy Information Administration, 1983 Annual Energy Review.)

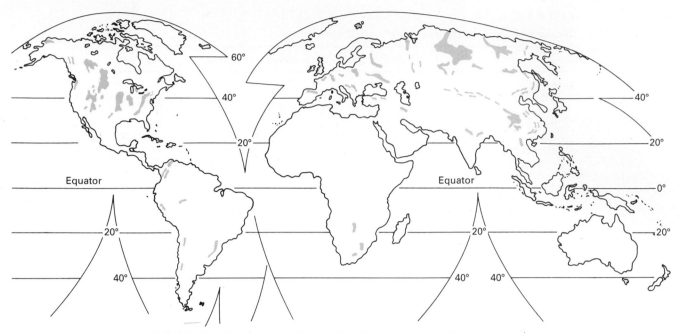

FIGURE 4-13. The geographic distribution of coal fields through-out the world. (After Fettweis, World Coal Resources, Elsevier, Amsterdam, 1979.)

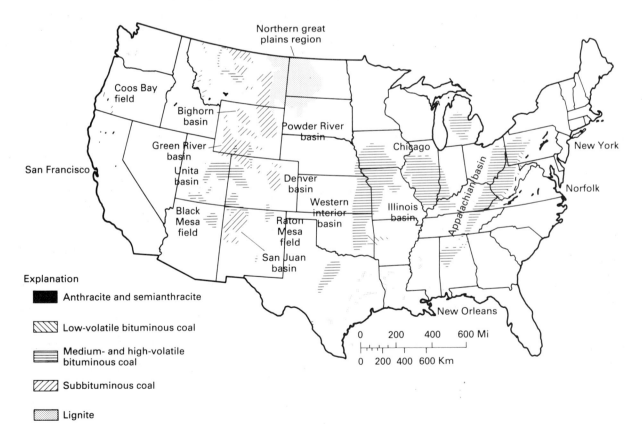

FIGURE 4-14. The major coal fields of the United States. Eastern Pennsylvania contains nearly all of the anthracite. The Eastern and Interior provinces are dominantly bituminous coal, whereas the Rocky Mountain province contains mostly sub-bituminous coal and lignite. (From the United States Department of Energy.)

TABLE 4-4

Demonstrated reserve base* of coal in the United States and 1984 production (million short tons)

Coal Producing Region and State	By Rank					By Potential Mining Method		Production 1984
	Anthracite	Bituminous	Sub-bituminous	Lignite	Total	Underground	Surface	
Appalachian Total:	7204.7	102,875.1	—	1083.0	111,162.7	90,148.2	21,014.5	443.0
Alabama	—	4118.9	—	1083.0	5,201.9	1740.0	3461.9	27.1
Georgia	—	3.6	—	—	3.6	1.9	1.7	0.2
Kentucky, Eastern	—	12,564.8	—	—	12,564.8	8492.7	4072.1	124.8
Maryland	—	809.9	—	—	809.9	706.1	103.8	4.2
North Carolina	—	10.7	—	—	10.7	10.7	—	—
Ohio	—	18,944.8	—	—	18,944.8	13,019.5	5925.3	39.0
Pennsylvania	7079.2	22,926.0	—	—	30,005.2	28,831.6	1173.6	75.1
Tennessee	—	952.8	—	—	952.8	636.7	316.1	7.7
Virginia	125.5	3196.7	—	—	3322.2	2497.8	824.4	35.3
West Virginia	—	39,346.8	—	—	39,346.8	34,211.2	5135.6	129.6
Interior Total:	104.1	121,509.1	—	13,505.9	135,119.2	93,814.8	41,304.4	194.5
Arkansas	104.1	288.4	—	25.7	418.1	272.5	145.6	0.2
Illinois	—	78,769.3	—	—	78,769.3	63,112.2	15,657.1	65.3
Indiana	—	10,510.0	—	—	10,510.0	8934.8	1575.3	36.8
Iowa	—	2195.9	—	—	2195.9	1733.6	462.3	0.5
Kansas	—	990.9	—	—	990.9	—	990.9	0.8
Kentucky, Western	—	20,947.0	—	—	20,947.0	16,921.1	4025.9	40.7
Michigan	—	127.7	—	—	127.7	123.1	4.6	—
Missouri	—	6056.2	—	—	6056.2	1479.1	4577.1	4.7
Oklahoma	—	1623.8	—	—	1623.8	1238.4	385.4	5.3
Texas	—	—	—	13,480.3	13,480.3	—	13,480.3	40.2
Western Total:	27.8	24,740.9	181,652.4	30,251.1	236,672.1	140,954.3	95,717.8	252.6
Alaska	—	697.5	5441.0	14.0	6152.6	5423.0	729.6	0.8
Arizona	—	381.9	—	—	381.9	101.6	280.3	11.7
Colorado	25.5	9044.7	3962.7	4189.9	17,222.8	12,272.0	4950.8	16.7
Idaho	—	4.4	—	—	4.4	4.4	—	—
Montana	—	1385.4	103,198.7	15,764.5	120,348.6	70,958.7	49,389.9	32.8
New Mexico	2.3	2053.1	2647.1	—	4702.5	2129.4	2573.1	24.6
North Dakota	—	—	—	9908.5	9908.5	—	9908.5	20.6
Oregon	—	—	17.5	—	17.5	14.5	2.9	—
South Dakota	—	—	—	366.1	366.1	—	366.1	—
Utah	—	6422.6	1.1	—	6523.7	6155.8	267.9	13.1
Washington	—	303.7	1157.2	8.1	1469.0	1332.3	136.7	3.9
Wyoming	—	4447.5	65,227.1	—	69,674.6	42,562.7	27,122.0	128.4
U.S. TOTAL	7336.6	249,125.0	181,652.4	44,840.0	482,954.0	324,917.3	158,036.6	890.1

*(Data from Energy Information Administration; U.S. Department of Energy, Demonstrated Reserve Base of Coal in the United States. These data include potentially economic coals as of 1982. To convert these values into metric tons, multiply by 0.902.)

early years of the twentieth century. In spite of union efforts to maintain jobs, mechanization has markedly changed coal mining and resulted in a reduction in the number of miners in the United States from more than 700,000 in 1923 (to produce 510 million metric tons) to only about 120,000 in 1984 (to produce 807 million metric tons). Similar trends have been seen in all the major coal-producing countries.

Modern coal mining is accomplished by either the underground (deep-mining) or the surface (stripping or open cast) methods described in Chapter 3. In underground mining, the pick and shovel of the past have been replaced by drills and cutting machines which much more efficiently cut into the coal and dump it onto a conveyor belt for removal to a loading site or to the surface. The most common type of mining removes only about 50 percent of the coal while leaving the rest as pillars to support the overlying rock (Fig. 4.15). The spacing and size of the pillars depends on the depth below surface, thickness of the coal, stability of the roof rock, and number of individual coal seams being mined. After initial mining has been completed, usually at least some of the coal in the pillars is also recovered in a process of "robbing the pillars." This occurs during the retreat or final stages of mining in an area. A newer and more efficient mining method makes use of a continuous mining machine (Fig. 4.16) that moves back and forth and

removes nearly 100 percent of the coal by a rotary cutter. The machine and the conveyor belt that carries out the coal are protected by a steel canopy. The machine, the belt, and the canopy advance together as coal is cut and the overlying rock is allowed to subside in a continuous but controlled manner. The thickness and quality of a coal determine whether a given seam is economic to mine, but generally most beds greater than about 61 centimeters (24 inches) in thickness are mineable. Underground mining is inherently dangerous, and tragically many miners are killed every year by roof falls. Many coals are also gassy and yield large amounts of methane. Despite the former use of canaries and the modern use of air-sensing equipment to test for methane, rapid gas buildups can still result in explosions. Perhaps the magnitude of the safety problem can be appreciated when one realizes that since 1870 more than 120,000 coal miners have been killed in the United States and more than 20,000 in West Virginian mines alone. Even with all the precautions taken today, approximately 100 miners are killed in United States coal mines every year.

Surface mining requires the removal of the overlaying strata to expose the beds of coal; once exposed, they are removed by bulldozers and frontend loaders, power shovels, or large drag lines. In order to rapidly and efficiently remove large tonnages of overburden, the

FIGURE 4-15. Pillars of coal are often left on each side of the area where coal is removed to support the roof as mining progresses. These pillars, which may contain a large proportion of the coal, are commonly removed as miners "retreat" from a mine when its reserves are exhausted. (Photograph courtesy of Bethlehem Steel Company.)

FIGURE 4-16. A continuous mining machine in operation. The coal is cut by the rotating cutting drum at the front and is carried by conveyor belt to the back where it is loaded into rail cars or placed on another belt for removal from the mine. (Photograph courtesy of The A. T. Massey Coal Co., Inc. and Heffner and Cook, Inc.)

equipment has constantly increased in size. The largest power shovel in the United States, the Gem, which operates in Ohio, weighs about 7000 metric tons, is about 60 meters high, has a shovel capacity of 130 metric tons, and is said to be the largest mobile land piece of equipment in the world (Fig. 4.17). Economics generally dictates which coal beds can be extracted through surface techniques. The rule of thumb has been that the surface extraction is economic if the ratio of the depth of overburden to be removed to the coal thickness does not exceed 20 : 1. Where the overlying rock thickness is too great for surface removal, the mining may proceed as an underground mine, or coal may be removed by augering. Augers are drills, up to 1 meter or more in diameter, that can be driven into horizontal or gently dipping coal beds. As the auger turns, it cuts the coal and feeds the broken pieces out just as a hand drill or brace-and-bit feeds out wood chips. Although the augers can remove only about 50 percent of the coal in a seam, it is coal that could not be economically recovered by any other means.

Most coal production in the first half of this century came from underground mines because coals exposed at the surface were too deeply weathered to be useful and because there were no practical means of removing the large quantities of overlying rock to expose deeper coal beds. Most of the beds that were amenable to surface mining such as those in the western United States were so far removed from the markets that transportation was either not available or not economic. The

FIGURE 4-17. The "GEM," or giant earth mover, the largest power shovel in the United States, is shown here mining in Ohio. The shovel, with a capacity of 300–500 metric tons per shovel load, is used to strip off the overburden to expose the underlying coal beds. (Courtesy of Consolidation Coal Company.)

development of very large power shovels and draglines made surface mining of beds as much as 30 meters deep economic. The conversion of an area from underground to surface mining is visible in the Powder River Basin area of Wyoming (Fig. 4.18) where subsidence of early 1900s underground workings occurs adjacent to a modern strip mine removing the same coal bed. The rapid increase in surface mining at the expense of deep mining has occurred worldwide and is especially apparent in the United States where the percentage of surface-mined coal has risen from 25 percent of the total in 1949 to nearly 60 percent in 1984. Other reasons for the increase in surface mining of coal in the United States include: (1) greater demand for the lower-sulfur, near-surface coals that are found in the western states; (2) the development of power plants near the western coals: (3) the increased safety; (4) the greater per person productivity; and (5) the absence of unions in many of the surface mines in the west.

Coal mining and coal use have been the subject of many environmental concerns, especially in recent years. Most of these concerns have centered on the problems of acid mine drainage, acid rain, increased carbon dioxide levels in the atmosphere, and surface mine reclamation. The first two are related to the sulfur which is present in all coals in amounts between 0.2–7.0 percent. Generally, about one-half of the sulfur present is bound within organic macerals; the remaining sulfur occurs principally as the two forms of iron disulfide (FeS_2), pyrite, and marcasite. The sulfur was originally derived from the organic matter and from sulfate in ground water which was reduced by bacterial action. Once the coal is exposed to air and water by mining, the iron sulfide is converted to ferrous sulfate, ($FeSO_4$) and sulfuric acidc (H_2SO_4). The washing of these compounds by rain water into rivers and streams has left thousands of kilometers of waterways devoid of fish and other aquatic fauna and flora. The ferrous iron is readily soluble in the strongly acidic waters washing off exposed coal beds or waste piles but is oxidized to ferric iron as these waters are diluted by stream water. The result is the precipitation of iron hydroxides as gelatinous, reddish-brown coatings on the rocks and plants. Our understanding of the processes involved in stream pollution and the concern that no further abuses occur has led to much more stringent regulations regarding the discharge of mine waters and of the dumping of iron sulfide-rich mining debris.

In spite of cleaning efforts to remove the pyrite from coals before it is burned, some pyrite remains and so does the organic sulfur in the coal. Burning the coal releases some sulfur dioxide which has been considered a significant contributor to acid rain.

On the third issue, there is no question that the burning of coal (or any fossil fuel) raises the CO_2 levels of the atmosphere, but there is a very large question as to the ultimate effects. It is clear that as we have progressed into the fossil fuel era, the atmospheric carbon dioxide level has nearly doubled. Because carbon dioxide is effective in keeping infrared radiation from radiating away from the earth, there are concerns that a general global warming could result. Presently, however, there is a great deal of uncertainty about how high the carbon dioxide levels are likely to rise and what the magnitude of warming is likely to be.

All types of underground mining can lead to problems of subsidence after the mining is finished. An example may be seen in the foreground of Fig. 4.18 which

FIGURE 4-18. In the Powder River basin of Wyoming a modern surface mine lies beyond an area where underground mining in the early 1900s removed coal from the same bed. The holes in the foreground are the result of surface collapse into the old workings. [From U.S. Geological Survey Professional Paper 1164 (1983).]

shows an area in Wyoming where many of the mine openings which were only a few tens of meters below the surface have caved in. Similar closed mines underlie many mined areas in England and the eastern and central United States. More spectacular than the subsidence of old coal mines are underground coal fires. In the United States, where there are an estimated 300 such fires, and in many other parts of the world, coal beds have been accidentally or spontaneously ignited. If there is an adequate oxygen supply, the underground fires can smolder for years and travel for considerable distances. The most famous mine fire was at Centralia, Pennsylvania, where a burning waste dump ignited an exposed coal seam in 1961. The fire, despite the expenditure of millions of dollars trying to smother it by flooding the coal seam with water, continues to burn. The fire has progressed under much of the town, causing local subsidence and giving rise to the sudden appearance of cracks that issue hot and noxious gases. Many residents have left the town, and those who remain usually have household monitors for deadly gases such as carbon monoxide that occasionally seep into homes.

Peat Resources

Peat has been used as a fuel in several European countries for centuries but is little known as an energy source in most of the rest of the world. However, in those other areas, including the United States, peat is widely used for agricultural purposes. Peat is generally considered as a young coal because it consists of plant matter that has been only slightly compacted and decomposed. Peats are classified into three general categories on the basis of biological origin and state of decomposition. Those that are least decomposed and richest in mosses are widely used for horticultural purposes as peat moss but have little fuel value. Those that are more decomposed and compressed have heat values, after air drying, only

about 25 percent lower than lignite and have considerable potential as a fuel. This peat, when air dried to about 35–40 weight percent moisture, contains more nitrogen and less sulfur than higher ranks of coal. Direct combustion is the simplest way to derive heat from peat, but there has been increasing research into the conversion of peat into methane gas by bacterial digestion or by thermal breakdown at 400–500°C.

The world's largest peat producer by far is the Soviet Union where 400 million tons were mined and more than 80 million tons were burned in 1984 in 76 power plants, accounting for 2–3 percent of the nation's electricity generation. Ireland is famous for its peat harvesting, and although its production is very much less than that of the Soviet Union, the 6 million tons burned do account for 25 percent of Ireland's total energy generation.

There is little consensus as to the world's available peat resources, and the values included in Table 4.5 are among the more conservative values. Only a few counties such as the Soviet Union, Finland, and Ireland are now actively exploiting peat as a fuel source, but many other countries such as the United States and Canada are considering the potential of peat. In fact, Minnesota has begun converting some heating plants in public buildings to peat-burning systems, and the United States' first peat-to-energy project was begun in 1984 when special sodding machines began scooping up wet peat and extruding it as log-shaped blocks (Fig. 4.19). The peat occurences of the United States are similar to those in many other parts of the world in that they are concentrated in coastal areas and in glacial terrains. Consequently, much of the American peat lies in environmentally sensitive or restricted zones such as protected wetlands and game refuges. The great peat resources of Canada commonly occur in remote and sometimes arctic regions where their extraction would not be economic. Nevertheless, peat does constitute a

TABLE 4-5

World peat resources and production

	10^6 hectares with >30 cm peat	Reserves (×10^6 m.t.)	Production, 1984, 10^3 tons		
			Fuel	Horticultural	Total
Canada	170	10,000	—	600	600
U.S.S.R.	150	20,000	80,000	320,000	400,000
U.S.A.	40	7000	—	720	720
Finland	10.4	7000	3100	2500	5600
Germany, Fed. Rep.	—	500	—	2400	2400
Ireland	1.2	200	6000	—	6000
Others	49.2	5300	—	1680	—
WORLD TOTAL	420.8	50,000	89,100	327,900	417,000

(Data from Institute of Gas Technology, 1981, and U.S. Bureau of Mines, 1984.)

(a)

(b)

FIGURE 4-19. (a) Mining peat in the traditional manner in Ireland. After digging, the peat is stacked and dried before burning. (Photograph courtesy of Irish Tourist Board.) (b) Logs of compressed peat being extruded as the sodding machine moves across a drained portion of a bog in North Carolina. (Photograph courtesy of First Colony Farms, Inc.)

considerable fossil fuel resource, but its use will probably remain relatively limited and local in the near future.

Petroleum

Petroleum, long scorned by most of society as a sticky, foul-smelling material to be avoided, has now emerged as the principal fossil fuel of our times. In contrast to coal, the physical appearance of petroleum bears no evidence of its origin as marine planktonic materials because of the complete reconstitution that has occurred during subsequent burial. The following discussion will consider the origin, occurrence, extraction, refining, and future potential of petroleum as a fuel.

History of Petroleum Usage. Petroleum, commonly thought of as the most important of the modern fuels, has actually been used in a variety of manners since before recorded history. In the petroleum-rich areas of the Middle East, near the Tigris and the Euphrates, petroleum and **bitumen** occur in numerous natural seeps that have been exploited by many different peoples. The early Mesopotamians did not use oil because they could not handle its flammability, but the later Akkadians, Babylonians, and Assyrians found numerous uses for the sticky bitumen as a glue for arrowheads, setting inlays in tile designs, and as a mortar for holding building bricks together. The famous Tower of Babel, a seven-stage pyramid that reached a height of 90 meters (295 feet) above the roofs of Babylon, consisted of bricks cemented with bitumen. Meanwhile, the peoples living along the rivers found that tar waterproofed their boats. This knowledge is evidenced in two early Biblical narratives that note that Noah, after building an ark of gopher wood, was to "coat it with pitch or tar inside and out" and that Moses' mother got a "papyrus basket for him, and coated it with tar and pitch." Natural floating masses of bitumen were harvested from the Dead Sea; in fact, Mark Anthony included the concession for the gathering of the material as one of his many love tokens given to Cleopatra. The Egyptians also found that the bitumen served very well as a preservative for mummies when they ran short of the resins originally used. In the Americas, the Indians likewise used tar and oil from natural seeps to caulk canoes and to waterproof blankets. They also used tar in medicines, gluing Toltec mosaic tile designs, and probably as a fuel.

The use of bitumen probably changed little from the days of early Babylonia until about 1000 A.D. when Arab scientists discovered distillation. By the twelfth century the Arabs were producing tons of kerosene. Unfortunately, this technological advance was lost with the decline of scientific progress in the Middle East after the twelfth century and was not rediscovered until the nineteenth century.

Through the 1600s and early 1700s most Europeans and early American settlers knew little, if anything, of petroleum. By about 1750, numerous oil seeps had been found in New York, Pennsylvania, and West Virginia, and wells drilled for water and salt often produced small amounts of oil. This oil was generally considered a nuisance because of its smell and tendency to stick to everything. Some uses were discovered, and about 1847 Samuel M. Kier, who operated a salt business in Pittsburgh, began bottling oil to be sold as a side line. Even the famed frontiersman Kit Carson collected oil and sold it as axle grease to pioneers moving west. Until the 1850s the major sources of lubricants and illuminants were vegetable and animal oils, especially whale oil. A major step toward the petroleum industry

occured in 1852 when a Canadian geologist, Abraham Gesner, made the modern discovery that kerosene (called coal oil) for use in lamps could be produced from oil and coal by distillation. The usefulness of oil was rapidly realized in various parts of the world, and in 1857 a Canadian named James M. Wilson dug an oil well and built a refinery to produce lamp oil near Oil Springs, Ontario. In the same year, oil production from hand-dug pits reached 2000 barrels in Rumania.

In spite of these accomplishments, the modern oil industry generally traces its origins to the first American oil well which was drilled by Edwin L. Drake along Oil Creek near Titusville, Pennsylvania in 1859. Prompted by the potentialities of oil as a fuel, lubricant, and illuminant, George H. Bissel, a New Haven, Connecticut businessman, found partners and in 1854 established the Pennsylvania Rock Oil Company to drill for oil near Titusville, Pennsylvania. Their hopes were indeed spurred when Professor Benjamin Silliman of Yale University analyzed a sample of crude oil skimmed from a Pennsylvania spring and reported in 1855, "In conclusion, gentlemen, it appears to me that there is much ground for encouragement in the belief that your company have in their possession a raw material which, by simple and not expensive process, they may manufacture very valuable products." The initial effort failed and ended in bankruptcy, but the investors regrouped under the new name Seneca Oil Company and hired Drake, an unemployed railroad conductor, to direct its operation. Drilling began in June 1859 using a wooden rig and a steam-operated drill [Fig. 4.20(a)]. Because water and cave-ins threatened the well, Drake drove an iron pipe 12 meters (39 feet) into the ground and proceeded to drill inside the pipe. Oil-bearing strata were encountered at a depth of 21.2 meters ($69\frac{1}{2}$ feet) on August 27, 1859. The oil rose to just below the ground surface. Drake mounted a pump on the well and began producing 10–35 barrels per day. The oil was initially sold for $20 a barrel, but the success resulted in the drilling of numerous other wells [Fig. 4.20(b)], and the price of oil dropped to 10 cents a barrel within 3 years. Boom towns of tents and shacks sprang up rapidly, and wagons and river barges carried the oil in wooden barrels to refineries built along the Atlantic Coast. Railroads soon built branch lines to the oil fields, and by 1865 the first oil pipeline was constructed to carry oil 8 kilometers to a railroad loading area. In 1874 a 97 kilometer pipeline was constructed to transport 3500 barrels a day from the oil fields to Pittsburgh. After Drake's success, oil discoveries spread rapidly—West Virginia (1860), Colorado (1862), Texas (1866), and California (1875). In many of these areas, the initial discoveries led to the drilling of numerous very closely spaced wells as is shown in the opening photograph of this chapter. The first of the giant fields in the Gulf Coast area was

(a)

(b)

FIGURE 4-20. (a) Edwin Drake (right) in front of his oil well on the banks of Oil Creek in Titusville, Pennsylvania in 1861. This well represents the beginning of the modern extraction of oil. (b) The success of Drake's first well resulted in the drilling of large numbers of closely-spaced wells as shown here in 1861 on the Benninghoff Farm along Oil Creek. (Photographs courtesy of American Petroleum Institute Photographic and Film Services.)

opened when Spindletop gushed nearly 60 meters into the air on January 10, 1901 (Fig. 4.21) and yielded 100,000 barrels a day.

Meanwhile, commercial oil production also spread rapidly throughout the world. Italy became a small producer in 1860 and was rapidly followed by Canada, the Soviet Union, Poland, Japan, Germany, India, Indonesia, Peru, Mexico, Argentina, and Trinidad. The knowledge that oil and tar seeps had been worked in the Middle East for thousands of years stimulated considerable exploration interest in the region in the late 1800s and early 1900s. Small, but encouraging, discoveries were made in Iran in 1908 and in Iraq in 1927. The true potential of the area finally became apparent when the first of the large fields was discovered in Saudi Arabia in 1938. Subsequent drilling since that time has shown that the Middle East contains more than half of the world's known reserves.

Petroleum exploration after World War II expanded throughout the world from the tropics to the polar regions and led to discoveries on every continent. Although numerous small fields have been found, the

FIGURE 4-21.   Spindletop, in southeast Texas, was one of the most famous gushers. It began flowing on January 10, 1901, at a rate of 100,000 barrels per day in a gusher that reached a height of 60 meters (175 feet). (Photograph courtesy of the American Petroleum Institute.)

two discoveries that have received the greatest publicity in recent years have been those of the North Sea in 1965 and the Alaskan North Slope in 1968 (Fig. 4.22).

The Formation of Petroleum and Natural Gas.   The most important fossil fuel in the modern industrial world is **petroleum,** the base for most lubricants and fuels and for more than 7000 organic compounds. Early discoverers applied the Latin terms *petra,* ("rock") and *oleum* ("oil") because they found it seeping out of the rocks. Petroleum, now commonly called oil, crude oil, or "black gold," has its origin, just as all fossil fuels, in organic matter trapped in sediments.

Petroleum rarely occurs without accompanying natural gas, a mixture of hydrocarbons of light molecular weight that are gaseous under earth surface conditions. In contrast to petroleum, which consists of at least scores of different hydrocarbon compounds, natural gas is dominantly (often 99 percent or more) composed of methane. Minor amounts of the other hydrocarbon gases ethane (C_2H_6), propane (C_3H_8), and butane (C_4H_{10}) may also be present. In addition, there can be admixed and variable amounts of carbon dioxide (CO_2), hydrogen sulfide (H_2S), helium (He), water vapor, and nitrogen gases such as ammonia (NH_3). Petroleum forms almost exclusively from the organic matter in marine sediments, whereas natural gas forms both in marine and terrestrial rocks. As early as 1781, the Abby S. Volta of Northern Italy provided insight into the formation of oil and gas when he noted, "Fermentation of buried animals and plants generates oil, which is transformed into naptha (a term for volatile colorless gasolinelike fluids), by distillation due to the underground heat and in turn is elaborated into vapors."

The Abby's views were quite accurate, for we now know that it is the modification of buried organic matter that leads to the formation of oil and gas. As noted in Fig. 4.4, natural gas forms with both oil and coal and by at least two processes. Most organic matter, even when buried, is totally decomposed by organisms or by oxygen in circulating waters. The portion which survives is still subject to attack in the oxygen-free environment by anaerobic bacteria. The product of the bacterial action which may occur any time from immediate burial to millions of years later is **biogenic gas.** This gas is principally methane, although variable amounts of other gases may also be present, and is constantly rising in small amounts from swamps, soils, and sediments on the sea floor.

In the marine realm, the principal types of organic matter trapped in the sediments are the remains of free-floating planktonic organisms which constantly rain onto the sea floor (Fig. 4.23). This debris is rich in organic matter called **lipids** but also contains significant amounts of protein and carbohydrate. Terrestrial plant

(a)

(b)

FIGURE 4-22. (a) Oil platforms such as these in the North Sea are used to drill for oil and then to pump it via submarine pipes to onshore facilities. The smoke results from the flaring or burning of some excess natural gas. (Photograph courtesy of Shell U.K.) (b) The Alaskan Pipeline, which extends for 960 miles and cost $9.5 billion, transports 1.5 million barrels of oil per day from Prudhoe Bay on the North Slope of Alaska to Valdez where it is loaded onto tankers for transport to refineries. (Photograph courtesy of Sohio Petroleum Company.)

debris is significantly different in containing large amounts of cellulose and lignin that make up woody tissue. The process of oil and gas formation in marine sediments is summarized in Fig. 4.24. The depth scale, which also corresponds to a general increase in time and temperature as well, is only approximate and may vary with the nature of the original organic matter. The depth of burial has been subdivided into three major zones in which the processes of **diagenesis, catagenesis,** and **metagenesis** are active. These processes constitute a continuum of increasing burial temperature and pressure in response to which minerals and organic matter are altered. Diagenesis occurs from the surface of the depositing sediment to depths of a few hundred meters where temperatures are generally less than 50°C. Minerals are dissolved and precipitated by ground waters, and much organic matter is oxidized or consumed by burrowing organisms or by bacteria. Anaerobic methanogenic bacteria are commonly very active in the upper parts of this zone and are responsible for the generation of considerable amounts of biogenic gas. Catagenesis, which occurs in the temperature range of 50° to about 150°C and pressures up to 1500 bars at depths to about 3.5–5 kilometers, brings about compaction of the rock and the expulsion of water. The organic matter is progressively altered to kerogen and produces liquid petroleum. Biogenic gas-producing processes decrease in effectiveness, but thermogenic gas processes become important and result in the formation of gas by thermal cracking of some of the kerogen. As depth continues to increase, petroleum-forming processes give way to **thermogenic gas** production. This gas is commonly referred to as wet gas because the dominant constituent, methane, is accompanied by minor amounts of ethane, propane, and butane which are easily condensed into a fluid phase. Below depths of 3500–4000 meters, where temperatures exceed about 150°C and pressure rises above about 1500 bars, the early stages of metamorphism occur. When dealing with organic matter, this is referred to as metagenesis. At this stage, the remaining organic matter is either converted to dry gas, nearly pure thermogenic methane, or remains as a carbon-rich residue. With deeper burial, metamorphic effects increase and the residue is converted to graphite.

From the previous discussion, it is apparent that rocks containing different types of organic matter or rocks that contain similar organic matter but which have been subjected to different burial depths could yield very different ratios of oil and gas. This is indeed true. Marine sediments with lipid-rich matter tend to yield oil and wet gas when subjected to catagenesis. Terrestrial, cellulose-rich matter yields coal and dry gas when subjected to the same conditions. Organic-rich marine sediments buried to depths of 2000–3000 meters usually

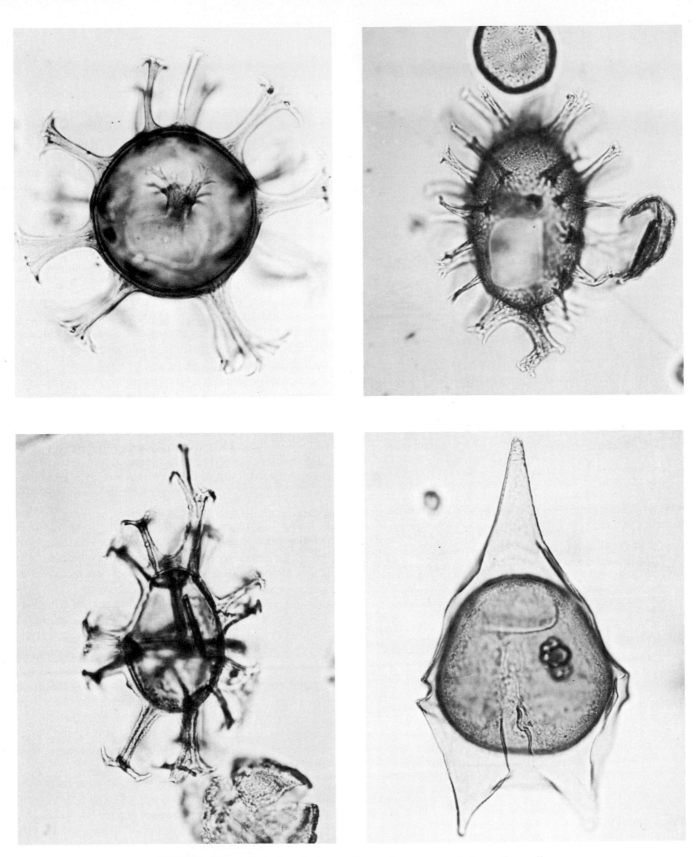

FIGURE 4-23. Petroleum forms from the accumulation of small floating plankton such as these modern dinoflagellates. The hydrocarbons of each of these, which average 0.55 millimeters in diameter, are converted into kerogen and ultimately into oil and gas. (Photograph courtesy of D.M. McLean.)

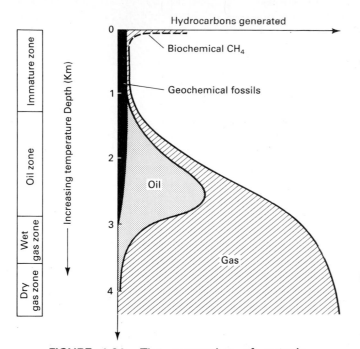

FIGURE 4-24. The conversion of organic matter to kerogen and to oil and gas is shown as a function of the depth of burial (with corresponding increases in temperature and pressure). Biogenic methane is generated by near-surface bacterial activity. The actual depths of the thermogenic generation of oil and gas vary slightly from one area to another depending on rock type, the geothermal gradient, and the nature of the organic matter.

yield considerable oil and gas, but the same sediments, if buried an additional 1000 meters, usually yield much gas but little oil.

The formation of petroleum, including heavy oils, and natural gas has depended on the availability and preservation of marine planktonic organisms. These creatures have been present in the world's oceans since the late Precambrian, but their abundance has generally increased with the progression of time. Not surprisingly, the known reserves of liquid and gaseous hydrocarbons reflect this increase in plankton over time (Fig. 4.25). The increased abundance of hydrocarbons in younger rocks no doubt also evidences the escape from and destruction of some oil and gas in the older rocks as a result of weathering and erosion. Methane gas can form through some types of metamorphic and igneous reactions and is found trapped in tiny inclusions in some minerals. Most petroleum geologists believe, however, that only organically produced gas will ever be found in sufficient quantities to be economically recovered.

The initial amounts of organic matter in nearly all sediments are too low and dispersed to form commercial quantities of oil. Economic accumulations only oc-

cur where the petroleum has migrated from its **source rocks,** where it was generated in small dispersed amounts, into porous and permeable carrier or **reservoir rocks** (usually sandstones or porous limestones). The final requirement for commercial oil and gas accumulations are **traps** (Fig. 4.26), zones in which the migrating hydrocarbons become confined and prevented from further movement by an impermeable seal or cap rock. There are two general types of traps: **structural traps,** formed by folding or faulting and **stratigraphic traps,** created where layers of porous, permeable rocks are sealed off by overlying impermeable beds. In the Gulf Coast region of the United States and a few other geologically similar areas, considerable amounts of petroleum occur in structural traps that have developed adjacent to salt domes which have bowed up and penetrated oil-bearing strata as shown in Fig. 4.26. The migration of water and natural gas along with the oil usually results in a layered configuration in the traps, with the more dense water below and the less dense gas above the oil.

Oil Recovery. The earliest recovery of oil was from natural seeps where oil, and commonly natural gas, has migrated along faults or along bedding planes either to the earth's surface or into zones of moving ground water that then also carry the oil until it surfaces in a spring. At the surface the natural gas dissipates in the air and the light fractions of the oil evaporate, leaving tar or pitch behind. The pitch was gathered from the shores or scooped off the surface as early as thousands of years ago in the Middle East and in the Americas. Although oil still locally seeps out onto the earth's surface, virtually all the oil produced in the world today is recovered through wells employing the primary or secondary methods of extraction described below.

The earliest oil wells were drilled by driving rotating pieces of pipe that had crudely formed cutting teeth into the soil and rock. These simple drills were replaced by **cable-tool drills** that consist of a heavy bit attached to a long steel cable. The cable raises the bit and drops it again and again so that it cuts little by little into the rock. Periodically, the cable and bit are withdrawn from the hole and the loose fragments of rock are flushed out. The cable tool drills, which effectively reached depths of several thousand meters, have now been replaced by **rotary drills** that are more efficient and can operate at depths greater than 10,000 meters. This drill employs a complex bit that has a group of rotating teeth that cut into the rock as the bit rotates (Fig. 4.27). The bit is attached to the base of a series of hollow steel pipes which are rotated by motors on the drill platform. Drilling fluids and muds are pumped down the center of the pipe to cool the bit and to flush the rock chips out of the hole. In order to change drill bits, the drill crew must

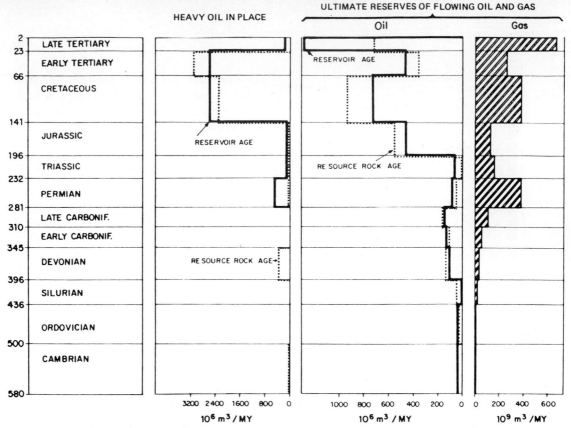

FIGURE 4-25. The distribution of the ultimate reserves of oil and gas and of heavy oil in place in terms of millions of cubic meters per million years as a function of geologic time. [Figure after Demaison (1977) and Bestougeff (1980) and from Bois, Bouch and Pelet, *American Association of Petroleum Geologists Bulletin,* vol. 66 (1982), p. 1264. Used with permission.]

Types of Oil and Gas Accumulations

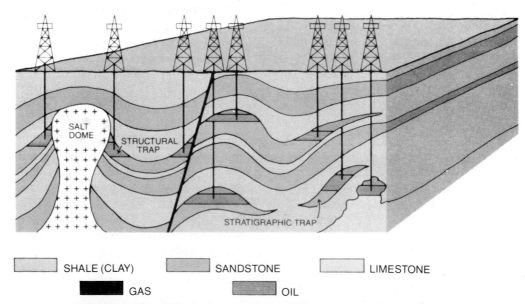

SHALE (CLAY)   SANDSTONE   LIMESTONE

GAS   OIL

FIGURE 4-26. Although caused by different natural phenomena, all types of hydrocarbon traps perform the same role: providing a site for the subsurface accumulation of oil and gas and, thereby, creating the fields that are sought by the drill. This simplified sketch shows examples of major traps. (From *How Much Oil and Gas,* Exxon Background Series; reprinted with permission of Exxon Corporation.)

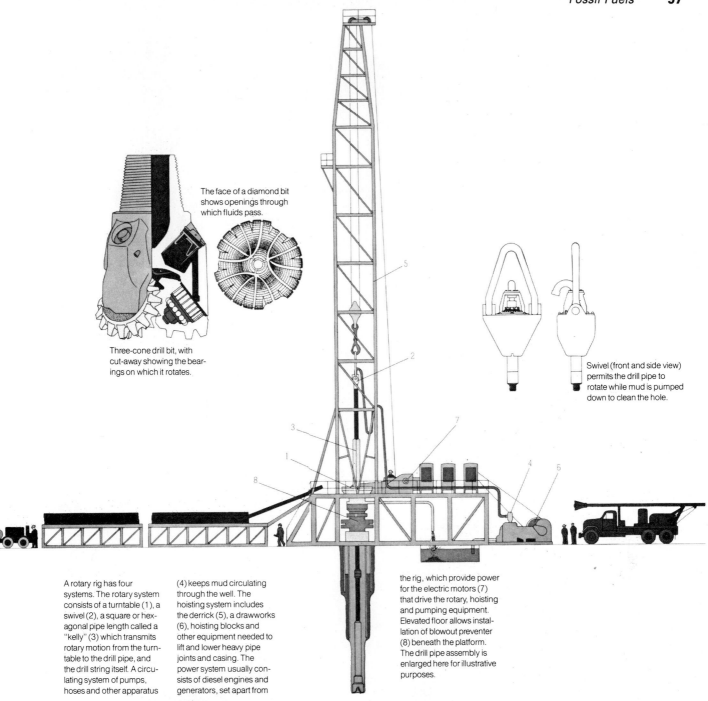

The face of a diamond bit shows openings through which fluids pass.

Three-cone drill bit, with cut-away showing the bearings on which it rotates.

Swivel (front and side view) permits the drill pipe to rotate while mud is pumped down to clean the hole.

A rotary rig has four systems. The rotary system consists of a turntable (1), a swivel (2), a square or hexagonal pipe length called a "kelly" (3) which transmits rotary motion from the turntable to the drill pipe, and the drill string itself. A circulating system of pumps, hoses and other apparatus (4) keeps mud circulating through the well. The hoisting system includes the derrick (5), a drawworks (6), hoisting blocks and other equipment needed to lift and lower heavy pipe joints and casing. The power system usually consists of diesel engines and generators, set apart from the rig, which provide power for the electric motors (7) that drive the rotary, hoisting and pumping equipment. Elevated floor allows installation of blowout preventer (8) beneath the platform. The drill pipe assembly is enlarged here for illustrative purposes.

FIGURE 4-27. Cross section of a typical rotary drill rig used on land in the search for oil and gas. (From *The Upstream,* Exxon Background Series; reprinted with permission of Exxon Corporation.)

raise the entire stem of drill pipes and disconnect them in 10- to 20-meter lengths. Once the bit has been replaced, the entire stem must be reassembled pipe-by-pipe as it is lowered into the hole. On land, drilling is carried out by rigs of the type shown in Fig. 4.25(a). In recent years, much oil well drilling has been carried out on the continental shelves and has employed either floating, stationary, or boat-mounted rotary drills (Fig. 4.28).

Because the petroleum within rocks occurs as small droplets and films between grains, in pores, and along small fractures, its movement is usually very slow. In order to allow the petroleum to flow more readily, it is often necessary to either enlarge the natural

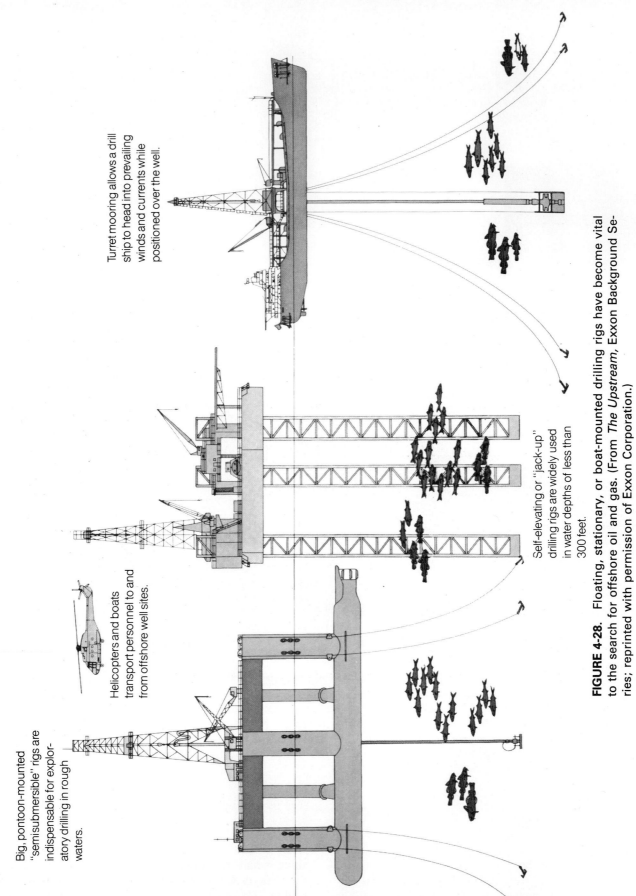

Turret mooring allows a drill ship to head into prevailing winds and currents while positioned over the well.

Self-elevating or "jack-up" drilling rigs are widely used in water depths of less than 300 feet.

Big, pontoon-mounted "semisubmersible" rigs are indispensable for exploratory drilling in rough waters.

Helicopters and boats transport personnel to and from offshore well sites.

FIGURE 4-28. Floating, stationary, or boat-mounted drilling rigs have become vital to the search for offshore oil and gas. (From *The Upstream*, Exxon Background Series; reprinted with permission of Exxon Corporation.)

flow channels in the rock or to make new ones. One common method is the injection of strong acid solutions which dissolve cementing agents that restrict the permeability between pore spaces. In another commonly employed method, water and coarse sand are pumped down the well under pressure high enough to fracture the oil-bearing rock. The sand grains permanently prop open the fractures to allow oil movement. In other areas, high caliber bullets or small explosive charges are used to fracture the rock near the well. All these procedures also increase the amount of total oil recovery because they open new channels and break open tightly constricted pores from which oil would not otherwise have been able to migrate.

Primary recovery is the simplest and least expensive method of recovering oil from wells because it takes advantage of natural pressures within the petroleum reservoir to push the oil to and sometimes up the well. If natural pressures are extreme, the initial drilling into a reservoir can produce a **gusher** (Fig. 4.21), in which the oil is sent spouting out of the top of the hole. Gushers were actually quite rare in the past and are nearly always prevented today by the presence of special valves, which will stop or control the flow of oil if high pressure is present. If the natural pressures are low, the oil must be lifted to the surface by pumps placed at the bottom of the oil well.

The natural pressures that aid in the concentration and extraction of oil are water drive, gas expansion, and the evolution of dissolved gas from the oil [Fig. 4.29(a), (b), (c)]. Most petroleum contains dissolved gases held in solution by pressure, much the same as CO_2 is held in soda water as long as a can or bottle is unopened. When petroleum removal begins, the confining pressure drops and some of the gas comes out of solution. Just as the evolution of CO_2 causes some of the soda to overflow from the can or bottle, the evolution of the natural gases can force some of the oil from the rock into the reservoir and up the well.

In many traps, natural gas either in liquid or gas form lies above the petroleum as shown in Fig. 4.29(b) and exerts considerable pressure from above. As oil is withdrawn up the well, the gas cap expands and thus continues to help push oil toward the well. Water drive [Fig. 4.29(a)], usually the most efficient of the natural processes, occurs when the pressure in the water of the underlying portion of the reservoir is sufficient to push the oil ahead of it as oil is removed.

Although natural processes can help significantly in oil migration and recovery, the primary oil recovery commonly reaches only 20 to 30 percent of the total oil in the reservoir. In order to increase the recovery of the oil, artificial or **secondary recovery** techniques are employed. These procedures most commonly employ wa-

ter, steam, or chemical flooding that displace or dissolve and mobilize the oil [Fig. 4.29(d), (e), (f)]. **Water flooding,** the most common and economical method, involves injection of water down one or more wells at the periphery of the trap or field. The water displaces some of the oil and drives it toward production wells where it is pumped out. **Steam flooding** [Fig. 4.29(e)] is a variant of water flooding in which superheated steam is injected into a well. The heat lowers the viscosity of the oil, and thus, permits it to move more easily. The condensed steam then serves as water flooding. **Chemical flooding** [Fig. 4.29(f)] is similar to water flooding except that it employs either a chemical (such as a light hydrocarbon) which is soluble in the petroleum and reduces its viscosity or a chemical (such as a polymer or a surfactant) which helps reduce the tendency for the petroleum to stick to mineral grains. Generally, chemical solutions are injected into one well and the petroleum is extracted from another.

Sometimes natural gas recovered with oil is separated and reinjected into an expanding gas cap to help maintain reservoir pressure and improve oil recovery. This gas then also represents a potential future resource because much of it can be extracted later if economic conditions are favorable. In spite of expensive secondary recovery procedures, commonly 50 percent or more of the original oil remains in the ground.

In recent years, especially after the rapid rise in oil prices in 1979–1981, there has been considerable speculation about **oil mining.** Interest in such procedures has been fueled by economics, by the declining amounts of proven liquid petroleum reserves, and by the observation of the American Petroleum Institute that the 10 largest oil fields in the United States will still contain 63 percent of their original oil in place after full production. In the United States alone, this amounts to an estimated 300 billion barrels, 10 times the country's known recoverable liquid petroleum reserves. Worldwide, the potentially recoverable original oil is no doubt many times larger than the 2000 billion barrels of oil expected to flow out through wells. This is in addition to oil shales and tar sands discussed later. Oil mining could be carried out: (1) as surface mining, much as low-grade copper ore is extracted in many parts of the world today; (2) as underground mining, using large tonnage extraction procedures as employed in many metal mines; or (3) as underground drainage systems, in which the oil drains into underground cavities in response to gravity. In the first two techniques, the rock, which may contain 0.1–0.5 barrel of oil per ton, is extracted, crushed, and then either treated with steam or chemical solvents to liberate the oil. The underground drainage systems would involve mining tunnels under the oil-bearing horizons and then drilling up into those horizons. The

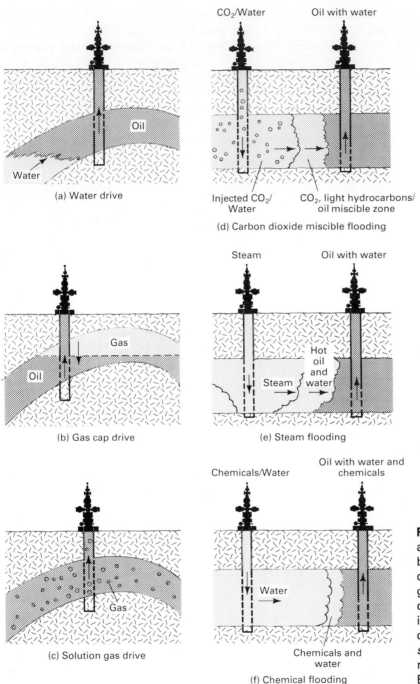

FIGURE 4-29. Recovery of oil and gas from "traps" may be by primary methods—(a) water drive, (b) gas drive, (c) solution gas drive; or by secondary methods—(d) carbon dioxide miscibility flooding (e) steam flooding. (f) chemical flooding. (From *The Upstream,* Exxon Background Series; reprinted with permission of Exxon Corporation.)

rock would be fractured and perhaps treated with steam or chemicals to reduce the viscosity of the oil and its tendency to stick to the sediments. The oil would drain out through the holes into storage chambers, from which it would be pumped to the surface for processing.

Oil mining is by no means a new concept. The digging of surface pits to gather oil occurred in the Baku area of Persia as early as the sixth century B.C., and in 1830 this area was reportedly producing 30,000 barrels of oil per year from pits and springs. Hand-dug shafts

and wells were yielding oil that seeped into them in the sixteenth and seventeenth centuries in areas as diverse as Sumatra, Germany, Cuba, Mexico, and Switzerland. The only serious twentieth century oil mining efforts came about during World War II when Germany and Japan, faced with wartime needs, carried out limited operations and when the need for a special grade of oil spurred an attempt in Pennsylvania. The decline in oil demand and the reduction in price since the late 1970s removed the major incentives for oil mining (as well as

oil shale recovery), and all proposed operations have been postponed or cancelled. They will likely only be revived if the price of oil rises significantly.

Petroleum Refining. Crude oil as extracted from an oil well is a black, sticky fluid with a consistency that varies from watery to syrupy. It often bears little resemblance to the gasoline, kerosene, lubricating oils, chemicals, plastics, and myriad of other petroleum products we use every day. The crude oil actually consists of a mixture of thousands of hydrocarbon compounds which must be separated and isolated before they can be made into the products with which we are familiar. The process by which this is accomplished is called **refining.** A primitive method of refining was developed by Arab scientists in the Middle East in about 1000 A.D. when they boiled bitumen and condensed it on a hide or in a water-cooled glass column. Although these technological innovations were lost with the decline of science through the Middle Ages, they were rediscovered and serve as the basis for modern refineries. [Fig. 4.30(a)]. The first step in refining is the **distillation** or **fractionation** of the crude oil into a series of fractions on the basis of their condensation temperatures. The crude oil is first heated to nearly 500°C and then separated into a large number of different products as shown in Fig. 4.30(b). The lightest of the fractions, light gasoline, rises to the top of the tower; heavier fractions, diesel fuel and heating oil, condense at a lower level. The heaviest residuum, that used for asphalts, is taken out at the base of the tower. The composition of a typical crude oil is given in Table 4.6.

In the early days of the oil industry, distillation was the primary means of separating products. The most useful fractions were kerosene, heating oils, and lubrication oils. Gasoline was too explosive for household use and was commonly discarded. With the age of the automobile, there was an increasing demand for a higher percentage of gasoline. This brought about the development and increasing use of techniques for the conversion of less useful heavier fractions into lighter ones.

TABLE 4-6

Composition of typical crude oil

Components (molecular size)	Volume Percent
Gasoline (C_4 to C_{10})	27
Kerosene (C_{11} to C_{13})	13
Diesel fuel (C_{14} to C_{18})	12
Heavy gas oil (C_{19} to C_{25})	10
Lubricating oil (C_{26} to C_{40})	20
Residuum ($>C_{40}$)	18
TOTAL	100

(Data from Hunt (1979) *Petroleum Geochemistry and Geology*.)

Thermal cracking is the application of heat and pressure to heavy hydrocarbons to crack or break them into lighter ones. **Catalytic cracking** accomplishes the same result through the use of a catalyst, usually a synthetic zeolite mineral that speeds and facilitates the process. The zeolites not only reduce the energy requirements for cracking but have also proven useful in adding hydrogen, through a process called **hydrogenation,** to the hydrocarbons in oil and thereby increasing the production of gasoline. Crude oils range widely in quality in terms of the distillation products and the amounts of contaminants (mostly sulfur but also some metals such as nickel and vanadium), but modern refineries can produce nearly 50 percent gasoline, 30 percent fuel oil, and 7.5 percent jet fuel from the original oil. Separation of the sulfur is necessary to make the use of the fuel products environmentally acceptable and has resulted in petroleum refineries becoming major producers of sulfur. In fact, in the United States petroleum refining now accounts for about 30 percent of domestic sulfur production.

Where is the World's Oil Found? Two of the most important and frequently asked questions regarding the sufficiency of oil are: (1) Where is the oil?, and (2) How much oil is there? Neither question can be answered with complete certainty, but exploraton for more than 100 years and the drilling of millions of wells allows us to make reasonable estimates.

It has now been established that petroleum forms from organic matter buried in sedimentary rocks and that even low-grade metamorphism destroys or converts to graphite any liquid hydrocarbons originally held in sediments. Accordingly, the search for oil is confined to the approximately 600 sedimentary provinces known to exist around the world on the basis of geologic mapping (Fig. 4.31). By the mid-1980s more than 420 of these basins had been tested by at least exploratory drilling. Virtually all these provinces contain some hydrocarbons, and more than 240 have oil or gas that is economically producible. However, the nearly universal occurrence of hydrocarbons should not mislead us from recognizing that significant accumulations of oil or gas are very rare events, geologically and statistically.

After more than 100 years of exploration in greater than 75 percent of the potential oil-bearing sedimentary areas, including all the largest and most accessible ones, we have found only seven provinces that contained more oil than the world used in a single year in the peak consumption years of the 1970s (Table 4.7). Seven provinces (each with at least 25 billion barrels of known recoverable oil) contained more than two-thirds of known world recoverable reserves. The one megaprovince, the Arabian-Iranian, more commonly just re-

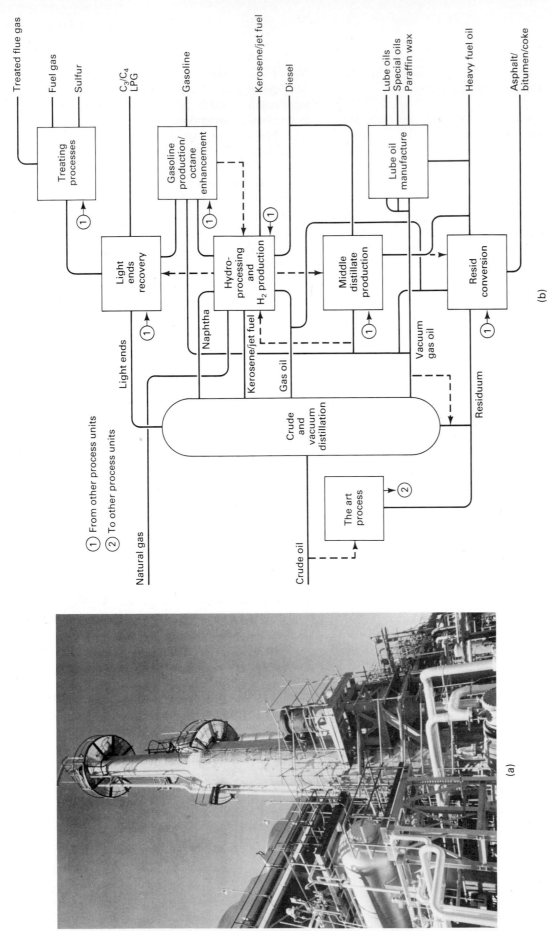

FIGURE 4-30. (a) Crude oil is converted into a wide variety of useable products in a series of complex physical and chemical steps in a refinery such as the one shown. (b) Within the refinery, the crude oil is distilled by heating at temperatures of up to 500°C, and some fractions are reacted with natural gas. The final products include gases, gasoline, jet fuel, diesel fuel, and several types of oil, waxes, and tars. Contaminants such as sulfur and metals are removed. (Photograph courtesy of The M.W. Kellogg Company.)

(b)

(a)

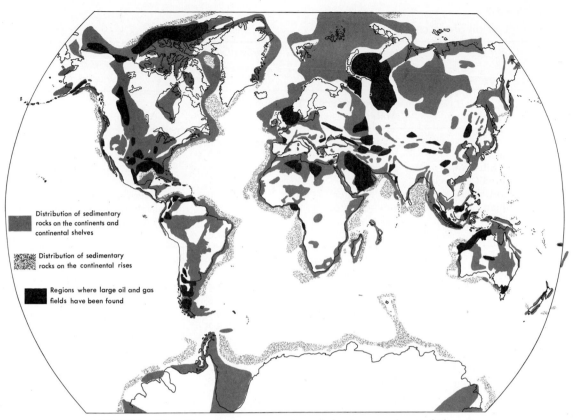

FIGURE 4-31. The major areas of sedimentary rocks and the regions where major occurrences of oil and gas have been found. The largest field, by far, is that which occurs in the vicinity of the Persian Gulf (see Table 4.7). Future discoveries will most likely be made on the deeper portions of continental margins and in areas that are little known, such as the continental shelves around Antarctica. (From B.J. Skinner, *Earth Resources, 3rd ed.,* Englewood Cliffs, N.J.: Prentice Hall, 1986, p. 38.)

Distribution of sedimentary rocks on the continents and continental shelves

Distribution of sedimentary rocks on the continental rises

Regions where large oil and gas fields have been found

ferred to as the Middle East, contained 626 billion barrels, nearly half of the world's presently known resources. The 25 major provinces, those each with at least 7.5 billion barrels of known recovery, contained 1118 billion barrels, or more than 88 percent of the total produced and remaining world oil reserves. This means that only 6 percent of the world's explored sedimentary provinces and 10 percent of those with producible oil contained almost 90 percent of the known recoverable world oil.

We do not know where, when, or how much additional oil will be found. However, the largest and most accessible sedimentary areas have already been extensively explored; hence, future discoveries will most likely be made in smaller and more remote areas where production will be more difficult and costly. Furthermore, the rates of worldwide oil discovery have been decreasing, and some areas such as the North American Atlantic continental shelf, once thought to possess significant oil potential, have failed to yield any recov-

erable oil. Prior to 1935, the worldwide rate of oil discovery (based on 5-year running averages) was never greater then 12 billion barrels per year. From 1935 to 1970 it averaged 25–30 billion barrels per year; and since 1970 it has averaged 15–18 billion barrels, values less than annual production (approximately 20 billion in 1979 and approximately 17.5 billion in 1984).

The geologic and climatic conditions necessary for oil occurrence and preservation have been present in many parts of the world at different times in geologic history. Petroleum formation has been a continuous process since the Precambrian time, but worldwide there were four intervals which seem to have been most productive in terms of oil source sediment generation (see Fig. 4.25): (1) late Devonian (360–340 million years ago); (2) late Pennsylvanian (carboniferous)-early Permian (310–250 million years ago); (3) late Jurassic-late Cretaceous (150–70 million years ago); and (4) Oligocene-middle Miocene (35–12 million years ago). Each of these intervals began with plate tectonic activity

TABLE 4-7

The major oil provinces of the world

Province	Location	Known Recoverable as of 1-1-81 (billion barrels)	Age of Major Source Rock(s)
Megaprovinces (100 billion barrels plus)			
1. Arabian-Iranian	Arabian-Persian Gulf	626.3	Cretaceous, Jurassic
Superprovinces (25–100 billion barrels)			
2. Maracaibo	Venezuela-Colombia	49.0	Cretaceous
3. West Siberian	Soviet Union	45.0	Jurassic, Cretaceous
4. Reforma-Campeche	Mexico	42.2	Jurassic, Cretaceous
5. Volga-Ural	Soviet Union	41.0	Devonian
6. Permian	United States	32.6	Permian, Pennsylvanian
7. Sirte	Libya	28.0	Cretaceous, Paleocene
Superprovinces Subtotal		237.8	
Other Major Provinces (7.5–25 billion barrels)			
8. Mississippi Delta	United States	22.4	Miocene-Oligocene
9. Northern North Sea	UK-Norway-Denmark	22.4	Jurassic
10. Niger Delta	Nigeria-Cameroon	20.8	Oligocene-Miocene
11. Eastern Venezuela	Venezuela-Trinidad	19.5	Cretaceous
12. Texas Gulf Coast-Burgos	United States-Mexico	18.7	Oligocene-Miocene, Eocene
13. Alberta	Canada	17.0	Cretaceous, Devonian
14. East Texas-Arkla	United States	15.2	Cretaceous
15. Triassic	Algeria-Tunisia	13.5	Silurian
16. San Joaquin	United States	13.0	Miocene
17. North Caucasus-Mangyshlak	Soviet Union	12.0	Oligocene-Miocene, Jurassic
18. South Caspian	Soviet Union	12.0	Miocene
19. Anadarko-Amarillo-Ardmore	United States	10.8	Pennsylvanian
20. Tampico-Misantla	Mexico	10.7	Jurassic, Eocene
21. Arctic Slope	United States	10.3	Cretaceous
22. Central Sumatra	Indonesia	10.0	Miocene
23. Los Angeles	United States	8.9	Miocene
24. Chautauqua	United States	8.5	Pennsylvanian
25. Sung-liao	China	8.5	Cretaceous
Other Major Provinces Subtotal		254.2	
All Major Provinces Subtotal		1118.3	
All Other Provinces Subtotal		146.7	
WORLD TOTAL		1265.0	

(Data from R. Nehring (1982) *Annual Reviews of Energy.*)

which created rapidly subsiding basins which filled with organic-rich sediment. Petroleum formation continues today and no doubt will in the future as the same types of geologic processes operate, but the rate of its development is far too slow relative to the rates of consumption for it to be considered as a renewable resource.

International Petroleum Production and Trade. Petroleum has become not only the principal energy source in the world today, it has also become the most important and most valuable commodity of international trade. A complex web of trade routes shown in Fig. 4.32 crisscrosses the world's oceans and continents

linking the politics and economics of countries that would otherwise have little in common. Since the 1940s, international oil trade has more or less followed total world production. After peaking in 1980 when the international flow of oil exceeded 31 million barrels per day, it decreased to approximately 28 million barrels per day in 1984. This represented only about 50 percent of total world production, largely because two of the largest producers, the Soviet Union and the United States, domestically use much of the oil they produce. As might well be expected from the previous discussion, the oil-rich Middle East is now the world's major oil exporter with supplies going mainly to Western Europe,

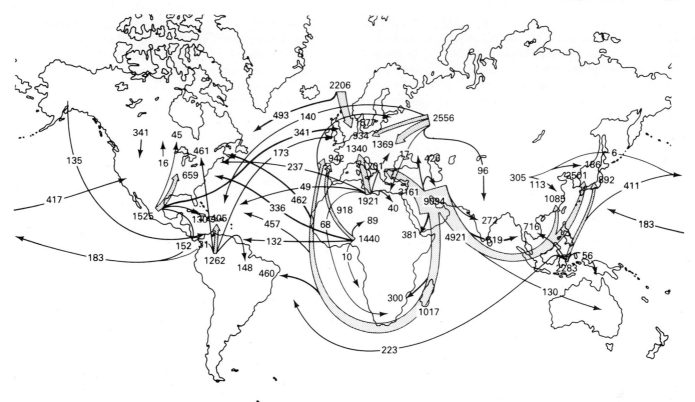

FIGURE 4-32. The complexity of international crude oil trade routes in 1984; all numbers are in thousands of barrels per day. Arrows indicate origins and destinations of the major shipments, but not necessarily specific routes. (From U.S. Energy Information Administration, 1986 Annual Energy Review.)

Japan, and the United States. Western Europe also obtains oil from the North Sea fields and Africa, Japan from Indonesia, and the United States from Mexico, Venezuela, Africa, and the North Sea. In order to meet the large and constant demands for oil and to minimize the transportation costs, the modern oil tankers (Fig. 4.33) are now the biggest ships afloat, with the largest ones reaching lengths of more than 430 meters (1300 feet) and widths of more than 66 meters (206 feet) and carrying more than 3.5 million barrels of oil (500,000 metric tons). Prior to the closing of the Suez Canal in the 1967 Middle East conflict, most tankers carrying Middle Eastern oil to Western Europe or the United States passed through the canal. Now none of the largest tankers will fit through the locks. They must sail around the Cape of Good Hope to deliver their cargo.

The United States was the world's principal petroleum producer from the days of the Drake well in 1859 until the mid-1970s when it was surpassed by Saudi Arabia and the Soviet Union. The Soviet Union has kept most of its oil for domestic use and the supply

FIGURE 4-33. The tanker Batillus (550,000 tons = 499,000 metric tons, 1350 feet = 430 meters long, 206 feet = 66 meters wide), shown here loading oil in the Persian Gulf, is representative of the modern large oil transport ships. (Photograph courtesy of Arabian American Oil Company and American Petroleum Institute Photographic and Film Services.)

of Soviet satellite nations in Eastern Europe. In contrast, Saudi Arabia and the other OPEC members (the history of this organization is discussed in Chapter 2) became the major suppliers for the noncommunist world. The share of world oil produced by OPEC rose from about 41.5 percent in 1960, to more than 55 percent in 1973 and 1974. The subsequent increased production in the Soviet Union and other countries and the reduction in OPEC production after 1979 had reduced the OPEC share to about 33 percent by 1983. Nevertheless, the OPEC members retain about 67 percent of the world's reserves.

The total annual world production of petroleum rose from a few thousand barrels in 1859 to more than 20 billion barrels in 1979. The rise was gradual and irregular through the first half of the twentieth century as wars promoted petroleum use and the depression in the 1930s lessened demand. After World War II, production and demand rose steadily until 1973 when the OPEC oil embargo spread fear of oil shortages. After a slight dip in world production in 1975, production rose again until 1979 when energy conservation, stimulated by a doubling of oil prices, resulted in a reduction of approximately 15 percent by 1983 (Fig. 4.34). This reduction in oil consumption, and especially in dependence on OPEC, is well demonstrated in the case of the United States (Fig. 4.35). The total oil usage by the United States rose from 6.1 million barrels per day in 1949 to 19.2 million barrels per day in 1978, but then dropped to less than 16 million in 1983. The use of imported oil,

and especially that from OPEC nations, followed similar trends. Total imports reached 8.8 million barrels per day (OPEC portion = 6.2 million barrels) in 1977 but were reduced to 5.0 million barrels per day (OPEC portion only 1.8 million barrels) by 1983.

The reduction in world usage of oil that began in about 1980 will extend the life of world oil supplies and has for some time reduced the political and economic impact of OPEC. Nevertheless, it is clear that the approximately two-thirds of known world oil reserves held by OPEC nations will become increasingly important in meeting world needs as other reserves such as those in the United States, the North Sea, and the Soviet Union are depleted.

How Much Oil Is There and How Long Will it Last?   Throughout the first 100 years of the modern petroleum industry, little thought was given to how much extractable oil the earth contained. The exploration of new sedimentary basins and the drilling of new wells on land and on the continental shelves led continuously to the discovery of new fields. World oil reserves rose faster than we could use the oil. The availability, relative cleanliness of use, and low price of oil-based products, especially gasoline, promoted ever-increasing usage. It was not until 1973 when the OPEC embargo cut off a significant proportion of petroleum supplies to Western Europe and the United States, that most of the general public began to realize that there are limits to the world's oil supplies. The shock of the embargo cou-

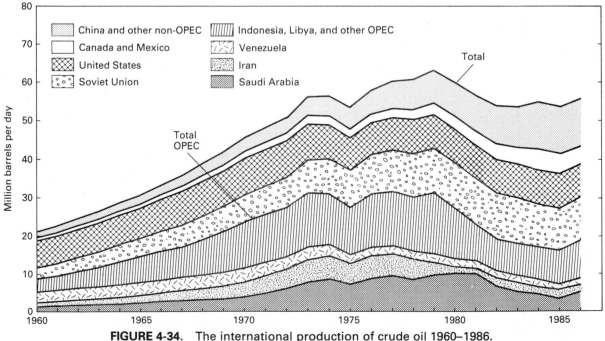

FIGURE 4-34.   The international production of crude oil 1960–1986. (Updated from U.S. Energy Information Administration, 1983 Annual Energy Review.)

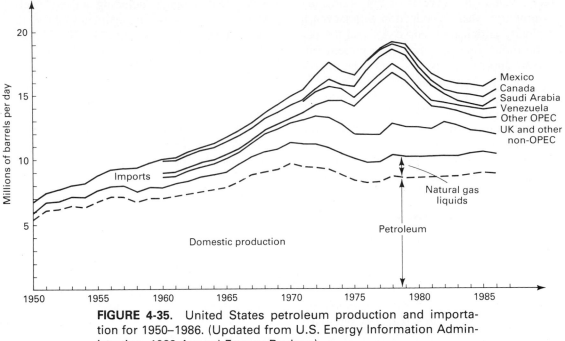

FIGURE 4-35. United States petroleum production and importation for 1950–1986. (Updated from U.S. Energy Information Administration, 1983 Annual Energy Review.)

pled with a subsequent increase in the price of oil (from about $3 to about $10 in 1973–1974 and from about $10 to about $20 in 1979–1980, and ultimately to about $35 in 1981) led to the frequent references to the terms oil *crisis* and *shortage*. These terms may have been overused, but they helped focus attention on the very real fact that the world's oil supplies are indeed limited.

As early as 1948, Dr. M. King Hubbert of the U.S. Geological Survey presented a diagram, similar to that shown in Fig. 4.36, that indicated a severe decline in the world's oil reserves before the year 2000 if the trend in oil production was left unrestricted. His predic-

tion, made at a time when expanding postwar economies of Europe, Japan, and the United States were being fueled by what seemed to be endless supplies of oil, was little noticed by the general public and the oil industry. However, the massive amounts of exploration, drilling, production, and computer modelling of world oil supplies in the intervening years have served to confirm Dr. Hubbert's conclusions. His original curve assumed that unrestricted production would lead to a constant increase in world output until the mid-1990s and then an equally rapid decline (curve A in Fig. 4.34). Since the late 1970s world oil consumption has declined and now

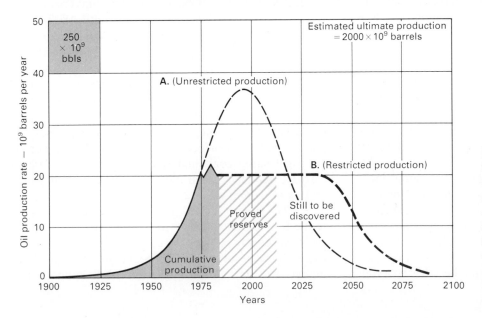

FIGURE 4-36. World oil production as a function of time. The original estimates projected unrestricted production along curve A, but the reductions in usage and the restricted production since 1979 now suggest that the curve will be more like B. (After L.F. Ivanhoe, *Oil and Gas Journal*, December 24, 1984. Used with permission.)

appears to have leveled off (curve B of Fig. 4.34). By curtailing consumption, yearly production will not reach the values originally anticipated (curve A), and the period over which production can remain near present values is extended by approximately 25 years. The important point to note is that regardless of the curve employed, the world production of oil will begin to decline rapidly sometime between 2015–2035.

A most important aspect of the Hubbert-type curves concerns the total amount of petroleum in the earth's crust. No one knows how much petroleum exists, but the expanding knowledge of the world's sedimentary basins and the mechanisms of the oil generation now permit reasonable estimates. There is always the hope that future technological developments will increase oil discoveries or extraction techniques, but for the moment we must consider only the liquid petroleum that is extractable by the conventional primary or secondary recovery procedures described earlier. It is important to bear in mind that the oil recoverable by simple pumping is usually only approximately one-third of the total amount present because most of the crude petroleum remains stuck on mineral surfaces and trapped in small pore spaces and fractures in the rock. The added procedures (water flooding, CO_2 injection, etc.) used to liberate more of the oil generally raise the total to no more than 50 percent.

Accordingly, the two meaningful questions are, How much oil reserve do we have now? and How much liquid petroleum can we ultimately recover? The first question can be quite accurately answered, but the second one can only be estimated. The present oil reserves are very irregularly dispersed geographically, with more than 55 percent of the world total occurring in the Middle East (Table 4.8). Saudi Arabia with 25 percent of the world reserves (169,000 million barrels) dwarfs all other nations; only Kuwait, the Soviet Union, and Iran have more than 50,000 million barrels. The United States which consumes approximately 26.5 percent of world production has only 27,300 million barrels or 4.1 percent of world reserves. At current rates of production, world reserves would last about 35 years; United States reserves would last only 8.6 years.

The question of total oil recovery is subject to estimates of the volumes, ages, and types of sedimentary rocks and the percentages of recovery obtainable. Although all these estimates are subject to potential inaccuracy, there has been a general consensus of opinion among university, oil company, and governmental workers. The range of credible estimates, made since World War II, of total recoverable liquid petroleum is shown in Fig. 4.37. With the exception of two estimates, one at 4000×10^9 barrels and the other covering a very broad range including an extremely optimistic 5600×10^9 barrels, all estimates since 1958 are between 1200×10^9 and 3500×10^9. The average post-1970 estimates of approximately 2000×10^9 barrels suggests that another 750×10^9 barrels remains to be discovered beyond the 590×10^9 barrels already consumed (through 1986) and the approximately 670×10^9 barrels of proven reserves.

It is important to note that there is no proof that any of this additional 750 billion barrels exists, and to note that none of it is of any value or utility until it has been discovered and exploited. Furthermore, it is highly probable that most future oil discoveries will be as small fields which will be harder to find, will occur in deeper rocks or under deeper water, and will reside in more remote and hostile areas of the world. The statistical distribution of known oil fields and the extensive degree to which the world's sedimentary basins have already been explored, strongly suggest that we shall not find any more large oil fields like those listed in Table 4.7.

Natural Gas

The History of Natural Gas Usage. The first recorded use of natural gas was in ancient China where the people had learned to pipe it through bamboo poles so that they could burn it to boil saline brines and obtain the residual salt. By about 600 A.D., temples in what is now the Baku area of the Soviet Union, on the west coast of the Caspian Sea, contained eternal flames fueled with gas piped from fractures in the rocks.

The use of gas as an illuminant in the modern world began with gas distilled, or manufactured, from coal, wood, and peat in Belgium and England in the early 1600s. Although several men experimented with gas lamps in homes, abbeys, and even university classrooms in the late 1700s, it was not until 1802–1804, when William Murdock, a Scottish engineer, installed coal gas lights in cotton mills that the gas industry became industrially important. This led to the establishment of commercial gas light companies in London in 1812 and in Baltimore in 1816. Within a few years, gas lighting had spread throughout Europe, the Americas, and to the Orient. Manufactured gases are still important and are produced by a variety of methods involving heating coals and reacting water with calcium carbide, but their usage has been much overshadowed by that of natural gas.

The modern natural gas industry traces its origins to the United States, where in 1775 French missionaries reported seeing "pillars of fire," seeping gas that had accidentally been set on fire. The same year George Washington saw "burning springs," in which flaming gas rose

TABLE 4-8

International recoverable crude oil reserves as of January 1, 1985

	Reserves (bbls × 10⁹)	Production 1984 (bbls × 10⁹)
North America:		
Mexico	48.6	1.007
United States	27.3	3.197
Canada	7.1	0.515
Total	83.0 (11.9%)	4.719
Central and South America:		
Venezuela*	25.8	0.657
Ecuador*	1.4	0.092
Others	7.5	0.541
Total	34.7 (5.0%)	1.290
Western Europe and U.S.S.R.:		
U.S.S.R.	63.0	4.318
United Kingdom	13.6	0.913
Norway	8.3	0.242
Others	4.5	0.242
Total	89.4 (12.8%)	5.715
Middle East:		
Saudi Arabia*	171.7	1.807
Kuwait*	92.7	0.359
Iran*	48.5	0.799
Iraq*	44.5	0.420
United Arab Emirates*	32.5	0.445
Others	8.5	0.426
Total	398.4 (57.0%)	4.256
Africa:		
Libya*	21.1	0.426
Nigeria*	16.7	0.516
Algeria*	9.0	0.225
Egypt	3.2	0.266
Others	5.5	0.273
Total	55.5 (7.9%)	1.690
Far East and Oceania:		
China	19.1	0.807
Indonesia*	8.7	0.536
Other	9.8	0.595
Total	37.6 (5.4%)	1.938
WORLD TOTAL	698.7 (100%)	19.608
OPEC TOTAL	481.1 (68.9%)	6.373 (32.5%)

*OPEC member

(Data from U.S. Energy Information Administration.)

from the water, near Charleston, West Virginia. In 1821, mysterious bubbles were found rising from a well drilled for water at Fredonia, New York. After the driller abandoned the well, small boys accidentally ignited the escaping natural gas, creating a spectacular sight. Shortly thereafter a gunsmith named William Hart recognized the commercial potential and drilled a gas well 8 meters (27 feet) deep at the same site. The initial wooden pipes (made from hollowed logs) were replaced with lead pipe, and the gas was piped to a local inn where it was used to fuel 66 gas lights. More gas wells were completed, and a natural gas distribution company was formed at Fredonia in 1865.

Natural gas was also found with oil at Titusville, Pennsylvania, in 1859 and in other subsequent oil wells, but there was little market and no pipelines for its distribution; hence, its usage was much overshadowed by manufactured gas which could be produced wherever needed. Long distance pipelines to transport natural gas finally appeared in 1872 when a 40 kilometer (25 mile) wooden pipeline was constructed to supply hundreds of customers in Rochester, New York, and a 9 kilometer (5.5 mile) metal pipeline carried gas to Titusville, Pennsylvania. The fledgling industry was nearly killed when Thomas Edison's electric light bulb appeared in 1879 but grew slowly on the basis of its use as a heating fuel

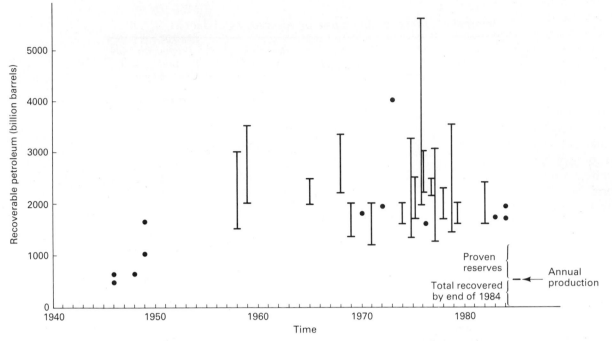

FIGURE 4-37. The estimates of the total conventionally recoverable reserves of liquid petroleum made by governmental, university, and industrial experts between 1946 and 1985 are plotted in terms of the date they were compiled. Dots represent estimates given as a single value; vertical lines represent the ranges of estimates that gave minimum and maximum values. The estimated quantities of ultimately recoverable oil rose from 1946 into the 1960s as worldwide exploration expanded but have generally come into agreement at about 2000 billion barrels since the late 1970s.

rather than as an illuminant. A major impetus came with the discovery of large gas fields in Texas, Oklahoma, and Louisiana. By 1925 there were 3.5 million gas consumers, but all were situated near the gas fields. The great expansion of the gas industry and its growth to the status of a major energy source came about in the late 1920s and 1930s with the introduction of a much stronger seamless, electrically welded pipe that could carry much greater quantities of gas under high pressure. In 1947 two pipelines known as the "Big Inch" and the "Little Inch," originally built during World War II to transport oil from east Texas to Pennsylvania, were converted to carry natural gas. This opened up the United States East Coast and brought about the dominance of natural gas over manufactured gas.

The Modern Natural Gas Industry. Prior to the 1940s growth of the gas industry was slow, and vast quantities of gas that had no market were allowed to escape or were burned off (flared). Seamless pipes that made possible the transmission of natural gas over long distances became available in the 1920s, but it was not until after World War II that the rebuilding of Europe

and the growth of the American suburbs provided large new markets. The gas was found to be especially attractive as a fuel because it requires no refining and only minor processing, is easily handled, burns cleanly, and provides more heat per unit weight than any other fossil fuel. Now it is piped to tens of millions of homes, businesses, institutions, and industries and provides 25 percent of the total energy needs of the United States and Europe. In addition to its common use as a heating fuel, it is widely employed in the manufacture of thousands of chemicals with such diverse uses as plastics, detergents, drugs, and as a major component in the manufacture of fertilizers.

The gas industry is composed of three major sectors—production, transmission, and distribution. The production of the gas is very similar to that of petroleum, but the extraction of the gas is often easier because it moves through pores and cracks in the rock more readily and because it does not stick to the mineral grains. Generally, more than 99 percent of the useful gas consists of methane, but minor amounts of ethane, propane, and butane and some carbon dioxide, hydrogen sulfide, helium, and ammonia may also be present.

Approximately 80 percent of the world's gas reserves is believed to be of thermogenic origin and is recovered from wells that range from only a few hundreds to about 10,000 meters in depth. The 20 percent of the natural gas that was biogenically produced usually is found at relatively shallow depths. More that 95 percent of the gas today has been obtained in its present state. However, locally and for special purposes, gas is manufactured by heating coal, or by reacting steam or hydrogen with coal or heavy oils. Probably the most widely known of the synthetic gases is acetylene (C_2H_2), formed by the reaction of water with calcium carbide or by thermal cracking of methane. Acetylene is used in welding because it produces a hotter flame than other gases.

After extraction from wells, the gas is piped to processing plants where impurities such as water, sulfur, and other impurity gases are removed. At the same time traces of the characteristic coal gas scent are added to enable human detection because natural gas otherwise has no aroma. The gas is then sent through the transmission lines under high pressure (at velocities of about 24 kilometers per hour). Compression stations along the line restore the pressure as it drops due to friction and tapping by communities. Within each community the gas is then sent via the smaller distribution lines to individual homes and businesses. From the original 9 kilometer pipeline used to transport gas near Titusville, Pennsylvania, the pipeline system in the United States has grown to more than 1,800,000 kilometers, not counting the individual service lines to homes. Natural gas consumption for home heating is much greater in the winter months than in the summer months, and the long-range transmission system cannot handle sufficient gas to meet demand on the coldest days. Accordingly, much gas is pumped into underground storage facilities such as caverns and old gas fields along transmission lines during the summer months so that it may be extracted when needed during the winter.

Until recent years it was impractical to bring natural gas from many oil fields scattered around the world to the major industrial consumers, because there was no way to profitably transport it. Now, however, much natural gas from the fields of the Middle East, Africa, and South America that used to be burned off, is liquified and transported in large, liquid natural gas (LNG) transport ships (Fig. 4.38). The gas is cooled and held below $-162°C$ ($-259°F$) where it becomes liquid and occupies only 1/1600 of its gaseous volume. The refrigerated tanks on the ships permit large quantities of the LNG to be economically transported worldwide. On arrival at its destination, the LNG is allowed to warm and return to the gaseous state and is fed into the normal gas transmission lines.

FIGURE 4-38. Liquid natural gas transporting ship. The gas is liquified by cooling, transported, and then allowed to convert back to a gas by warming so that it can be transmitted through pipes for industrial, commercial and domestic use. (Photograph courtesy of American Gas Association.)

International Gas Production and Reserves. The increasing demand for natural gas and its irregular global distribution has led to it becoming a major commodity of international trade (Fig. 4.39). Western Europe is the recipient of piped gas with major supplies coming from the Soviet Union and from the North Sea fields of England, Norway, and the Netherlands. Large amounts of gas are also piped from the fields of western Canada and from Mexico to the United States. Japan, now a major consumer of gas, receives much of her gas via liquid natural gas carriers from southeast Asia and the Middle East. The anomalous situation of the United States being a major gas importer but still sending the gas from Alaska to Japan has developed because the companies can sell that gas for more on the international market than on the regulated domestic market.

International gas reserves and production are given in Table 4.9. The Soviet Union is by far the world's leader in reserves and has, since the mid-1970s, become a major exporter, having built large pipelines to transport the gas to Western Europe. The other European countries with major reserves and production were gas importers until the North Sea oil and gas fields were developed in the 1960s and the 1970s. England, Norway, and the Netherlands are now self-sufficient and are able to supply part of the needs of the rest of Western Europe. Iran is second only to the Soviet Union in gas reserves, but its internal and international political problems, especially its long war with neighboring Iraq, have resulted in little sale of gas in recent years. The United States is well endowed with natural gas, but it is also a very large gas consumer and imports approxi-

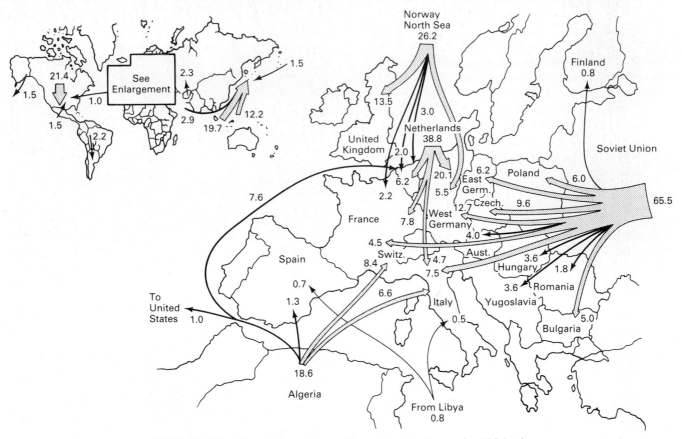

FIGURE 4-39. The international flow of natural gas in 1984; the numbers are in billions (10^9) of cubic meters. Arrows indicate origins and destinations of the major shipments, but not necessarily specific routes. (From U.S. Energy Information Administration, 1986 Annual Energy Review.)

mately one-third of its needs. From 1975–1985 the rate of discovery of new gas was slightly less than the rate of domestic gas consumption; hence, the reserves have declined about 8 percent in that time. This has left the United States with a reserve to production ratio of about 12 years. In contrast, the similar world ratio is approximately 58 years.

The world's ultimate resource potential of natural gas is not known with certainty, but the heat potential for worldwide gas reserves is presently equal to that of petroleum reserves. As with petroleum, most of the major sedimentary basins have been tested, and most of the major gas fields have been found. Future discoveries will be smaller than the large fields found in the past, and their development will be more costly. We are not now in any situation of impending doom with regard to natural gas, but we must recognize that in the foreseeable future reserves will decrease and costs are going to rise.

Heavy Oils and Tar Sands

The early history of petroleum centered on the use of bitumen, black viscous to semisolid hydrocarbon materials that are found where oil has lost its lightweight

volatile components through exposure to air. The modern oil industry concentrates on liquid petroleum which is much more easily extracted and processed. Nevertheless, there remain large quantities of natural bitumen-like hydrocarbons, the heavy oils and tar sands, which will likely serve as important sources of oil in the future. There is no simple single definition for these materials, but all are characterized by being: (1) dark in color; (2) so viscous that they will not flow naturally and respond poorly to primary or secondary recovery techniques; (3) high in sulfur (3–6 percent), nickel and vanadium (up to 500 parts per million); and (4) rich in hydrocarbons known as **asphaltines** (a primary constituent of asphalt). Heavy oils and tar sands occur alone or with liquid petroleum and owe their origin to at least three processes that may have operated singly or jointly on the petroleum. Some have formed, as did most early discovered bitumen, through **oxidation** and the loss of the lightweight volatile fractions, which leaves behind the heavy organic molecules. The two other modes of origin recognized are **thermal maturation,** in which the light fractions have been driven off or converted to gas due to natural heating, and **biodegradation,** in which bacteria consume the lighter fractions leaving heavier components behind.

TABLE 4-9

World natural gas reserves of January 1985 and international production during 1984

	Reserve		Production	
	$(ft^3 \times 10^{12})$	$(m^3 \times 10^{12})$	$(ft^3 \times 10^{12})$	$(m^3 \times 10^{12})$
North America:				
United States	198	5.61	17.7	0.50
Canada	92	2.61	2.4	0.07
Mexico	77	2.18	1.1	0.03
South America:				
Venezuela	55	1.56	0.6	0.02
Argentina	25	0.71	0.4	0.01
Others	28	0.79	0.5	0.01
Europe and U.S.S.R.:				
U.S.S.R.	1450	41.09	17.7	0.50
Norway	89	2.52	0.9	0.03
Netherlands	68	1.93	2.7	0.08
United Kingdom	28	0.79	1.2	0.03
Other	39	1.11	3.6	0.10
Middle East:				
Iran	479	13.57	0.2	0.01
Qatar	150	4.25	—	—
Saudi Arabia	127	3.60	0.2	0.01
Other	113	3.20	0.8	0.02
Africa:				
Algeria	109	3.09	0.9	0.03
Nigeria	36	1.02	—	—
Other	42	1.19	0.2	0.01
Far East and Oceania:				
Malaysia	50	1.42	—	—
Indonesia	40	1.13	0.7	0.02
China	31	0.88	0.4	0.01
Other	76	2.15	1.5	0.04
WORLD TOTAL	3402	96.40	53.7	1.52

(Data from *Annual Energy Review 1984;* Energy Information Administration.)

Heavy oils and tar sands are known from several parts of the world [Fig. 4.40(a)], but they remain relatively little publicized or exploited because their recovery and use is more difficult and expensive than liquid petroleum. The largest deposits occur in Northern Alberta in Canada and in the Orinoco district of Venezuela, but significant resources also exist in the United States, in the Middle East oil fields, and in the Soviet Union. The estimates of the oil in place and recoverable vary widely from one study to another, so the figures given in Table 4.10 should only be viewed as rough estimates.

TABLE 4-10

Heavy oils and tar sands (in millions of barrels)

Country	Oil in Place	Recoverable
Canada	2,950,200	213,340
Venezuela	700,000–3,000,000	500,000
U.S.A.	77,160	30,065
U.S.S.R.	630	30
Middle East	50,000–90,000	4700
TOTAL	3,777,990–6,117,990	748,135

In Canada, two commercial plants have extracted tar sands in the Athabasca area [Fig. 4.40(b)]. These two open pit operations will be able to extract only a few percent of the hundreds of billions of barrels of oil held there in their operating lifetimes of 25 years or so. The tar-rich sands are removed by large rotary bucket wheel excavators or drag lines and then processed with hot water and chemicals to separate the oil from the sand. Once separated, the oil is processed in special refineries to remove sulfur and to produce a variety of useable petroleum products (Fig. 4.41). Canadian pilot plants have also begun to experiment with a variety of *in situ* extraction techniques including the so-called "huff-and-puff" procedure in which superheated steam is injected into an oil zone for about a month to heat and soften the oil. Then the more fluid oil is pumped out for at least a month before the cycle is repeated.

The physical and chemical properties of heavy oils have severely limited their recovery, and countless problems remain. Nevertheless, their ultimate exploitation is certain when reserves of liquid petroleum are reduced. Because the hydrocarbons in these deposits are too viscous to be pumped, the recovery methods needed

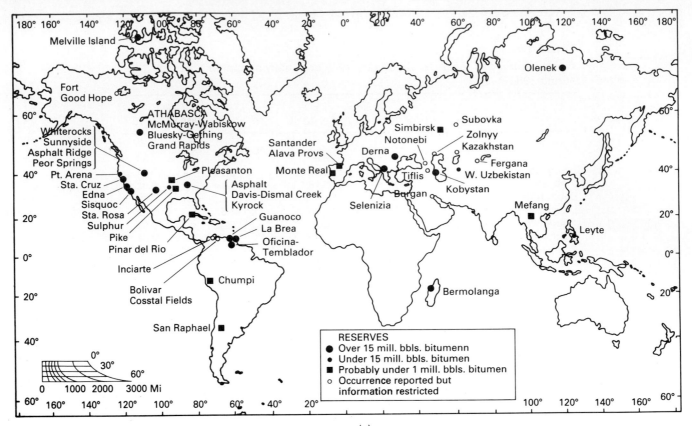

(a)

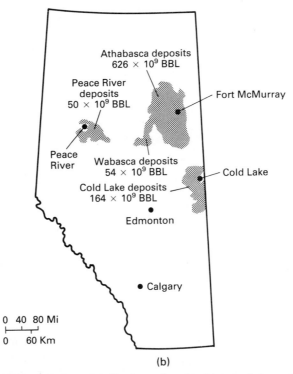

(b)

FIGURE 4-40. (a) The distribution of major tar-sand deposits in the world. (b) The location and size of the heavy oil deposits in Alberta, Canada. [After P.H. Phizackerley and L.O. Scott and from F.K. Spragins, respectively, in G.V. Chilingarian and T.F. Yen, *Bitumens, Asphalts and Tar Sands,* Amsterdam, Elsevier Sci. Pub. Co. (1978) p. 57 and p. 94. Used with permission.]

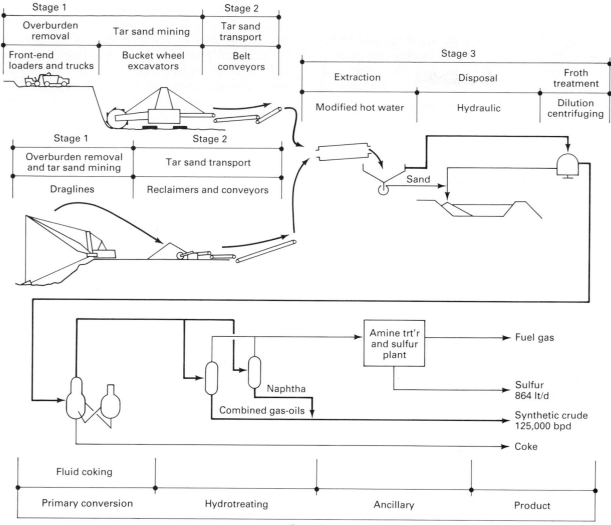

FIGURE 4-41. Diagrammatic outline of the mining and processing of a heavy oil deposit to extract crude oil, gas, sulfur and coke. [After F.K. Spragins in G.V. Chilingarian and T.F. Yen, *Bitumens, Asphalts and Tar Sands,* Amsterdam, Elsevier Sci. Pub. Co. (1978) p. 108-110. Used with permission.]

will employ enhanced recovery techniques or conventional mining of the oil-bearing rock. The most commonly employed enhanced recovery techniques involve softening or liquifying the oil by heating it with injected high pressure steam or by some sort of electrical device lowered down drill holes. Another, at present, experimental technique involves igniting some of the oil underground and then letting the heat generated by the fire melt or fractionate the lighter components so that they can be recovered from pumped wells. Other efforts utilize the injection of natural gas which will dissolve some of the heavy oil and allow it to flow so that it can be pumped out.

Oil Shale

Oil shales are a diverse group of fine-grained rocks which contain significant amounts of the waxy insoluble hydrocarbon known as kerogen. The kerogen is actually a mixture of a large number of complex, high molecular weight hydrocarbons much of which can be converted to oil on heating to temperatures of 500°C or more. The oil shales are part of the spectrum of organic-bearing, fine-grained sediments that range from carbonaceous shales through oil shales to sapropelic coals. The amount of organic matter ranges from as little as about 5 percent to more than 25 percent, and the yield of petroleum during

processing can be as much as 100 gallons per ton of shale.

Although oil shales are generally thought of as fuels of the future, the history of their exploitation extends back at least to 1694 when an English patent was granted for a process to make "oyle out of a kind of stone." Because the richest of oil shales burn much like coal, it is probable that they had been used as solid fuels long before the potential for oil extraction was discovered. During the nineteenth century small-scale oil shale industries developed in Europe, Africa, Asia, Australia, and North America where petroleum was in short supply. A small oil shale industry flourished in France from about 1838 to about 1900, and a few deposits continued to be mined through government subsidized operations until 1957. The largest and best known operations were those in central Scotland where oil shale processing began about 1850 and continued until 1963. The average yields from the earliest Scottish operations were at least 30 gallons per ton. Yields gradually decreased to about 25 gallons per ton, but the total production was about 100 million barrels. Less well documented but probably equally large production has been derived from both the Eastonian region of the Soviet Union and the Fushun area of Manchuria where production continues. Production has also been reported from Spain, Sweden, Italy, Germany, Australia, and Switzerland.

Oil shales form where there is simultaneous deposition of fine-grained mineral debris and organic material in a nonoxidizing environment free of destructive organisms. The fine-grained nature of the sediments indicates that deposition must have occurred in quiet lakes, swamps, or marine basins that were rich in organic matter. No doubt, many types of organic debris have contributed to the formation of the kerogen, but the principal precursor appears to have been the lipid fraction of blue-green algae species that can thrive in both fresh and salt water. Relatively rapid accumulation of the clays and organic debris under stagnant, reducing conditions protected them from destruction. Continued sedimentation of overlying rocks provided the compaction and burial depth so that temperatures probably rose to 100–150°C. This mild heating resulted in the loss of much of the most volatile fractions and left the heavier molecular weight and more refractory organic residue.

Although oil shales have been known and exploited on a small scale for many years, they began to receive a great deal of attention in the mid-1970s when the price of liquid petroleum rose sharply and the world's supply was uncertain. Oil shales are known from all the continents in Lower Paleozoic through Tertiary age rocks. The major oil shale resources are listed by continent in Table 4.11. In the United States the greatest attention has been focused on the Piceance Creek basin in eastern Colorado and the Uinta basin in western Utah (Fig. 4.42) in which the Eocene Green River Formation contains perhaps as much as 2 trillion barrels of oil (Table 4.11). Very large quantities of the hydrocarbon-rich Devonian Chattanooga shale underlie at least 10 states in the eastern United States as shown in Fig. 4.40. Unfortunately, most of this formation and its equivalents will yield only 1–15 gallons of oil per metric ton by the conventional processing techniques discussed below; hence, their extraction for oil is not feasi-

TABLE 4-11

Shale oil resources of the world, in 10^9 barrels in terms of oil content

Continent	Identified Resources		Hypothetical Resources		Speculative Resources	
gallons of oil per tons of shale	25–100	10–25	25–100	10–25	25–100	10–25
North America:						
U.S.—Green River Shale	418	1400	50	600	—	—
U.S.—Chattanooga Shale	—	200	—	800	—	—
U.S.—Alaskan Marine Shale	Small	Small	250	200	—	—
U.S.—other shales		Small	—	—	600	23,000
Canada	Small	Small	50	100	1000	23,000
South America	Small	800	—	3200	2000	36,000
Africa	100	Small	—	—	4000	80,000
Asia	90	14	2	3700	5400	110,000
Europe	70	6	100	200	1200	26,000
Australia and New Zealand	Small	1	—	—	1000	20,000
TOTALS	678	2221	552	8800	15,200	318,000
GRAND TOTAL	345,451					

(Data from U.S. Geological Survey Professional Paper 820.)

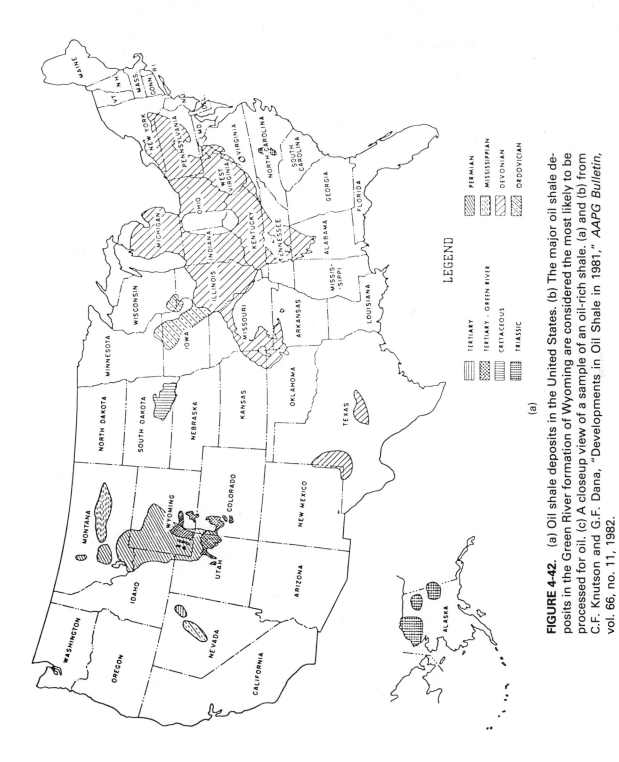

FIGURE 4-42. (a) Oil shale deposits in the United States. (b) The major oil shale deposits in the Green River formation of Wyoming are considered the most likely to be processed for oil. (c) A closeup view of a sample of an oil-rich shale. (a) and (b) from C.F. Knutson and G.F. Dana, "Developments in Oil Shale in 1981," *AAPG Bulletin*, vol. 66, no. 11, 1982.

(a)

LEGEND

TERTIARY	PERMIAN
TERTIARY - GREEN RIVER	MISSISSIPPIAN
CRETACEOUS	DEVONIAN
TRIASSIC	ORDOVICIAN

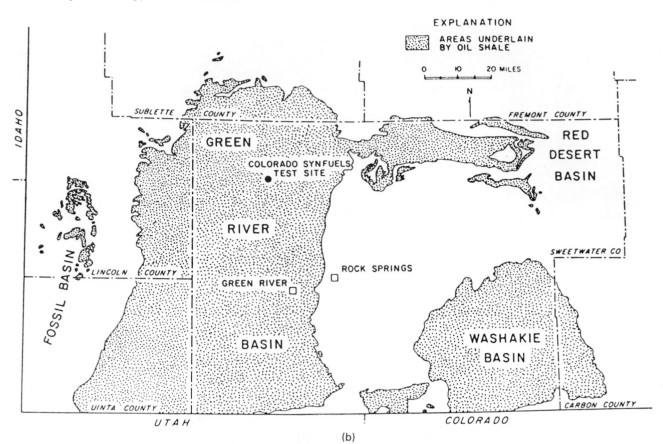

(b)

(c)

FIGURE 4-42.   *(cont.)*

ble in the foreseeable future. Several major projects were initiated in the western United States in the mid-1970s. However, a combination of rising production costs and declining liquid petroleum prices resulted in a suspension of all major operations in the early 1980s. They may yet produce oil, but only after there has been either a considerable rise in the price of oil or the development of a severe shortage.

Several production methods have been proposed for the recovery of the hydrocarbons from oil shales. The two principal ones are surface mining and processing [Fig. 4.43(a)] and *in situ* retorting [Fig. 4.43(b)]. The first method involves open pit mining or bulk underground mining of the shale, grinding it into fine par-

ticles, and heating it to about 500°C in a large pressure cookerlike kiln called a **retort.** The volatilized hydrocarbons are condensed and can then be processed in the same manner as conventionally recovered oil and gas. In order to be viable, the refining process must yield more fuel than it consumes. The mining and processing facilities are very expensive to construct and present environmental problems such as the generation of dust during mining, the need for very large quantities of water during processing, and the generation of very large quantities of waste rock. This last problem results from the expansion, or "popcorn effect," of the shale when it is heated. There is a larger volume of rock waste to be disposed of than there was when mined.

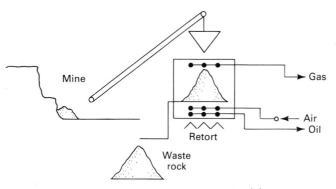

(a)

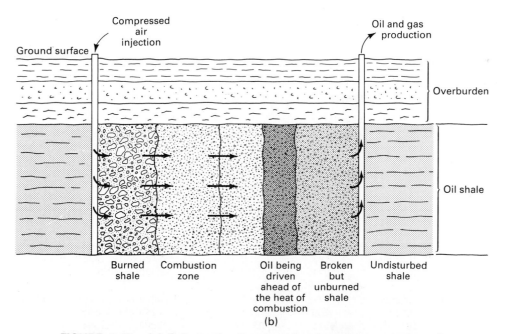

(b)

FIGURE 4-43. (a) Schematic diagram showing the processing of oil shale after mining. The retort would be operated at 400–500°C to release the gas and oil from the crushed shale. (b) The *in situ* oil shale retorting process relies upon the movement of a combustion zone through the shale by injecting air into one well and extracting oil and gas from another well ahead of the combustion zone. The shale is first broken to permit the movement of air and gases.

The second technique, *in situ* retorting, is similar to processes used for enhanced oil and tar sand recovery. It involves the development of underground tunnels known as drifts either above and below, or on both sides of a block of oil shales as much as 10 meters or more on each side. After the tunnels are completed, the rock is shattered by thousands of kilograms of explosives. The broken rock is then ignited and the rate of combustion is controlled by a flow of air, diesel fuel, and steam. As the fire burns downward in a vertical retort or from one side to the other in a horizontal retort, the rock ahead of the combustion zone is heated to approximately 500°C and much of the kerogen is vaporized and driven ahead to be drawn out as oil and gas through wells or drains. The remaining bitumen serves as a fuel for the advancing fire. This method is lower in mining costs, greatly reduces the problem of disposal of processed rock, and requires much less water. The burned shale expands to fill the original chamber and leaves a relatively stable ground surface that reveals little evidence of the activity below. One potential problem, although less so in the arid oil shale-rich areas of the western United States than many other areas, is possible contamination of ground water supplies by waters that leach through the burned out retorts.

The ultimate commercialization of oil shales will depend on the costs of producing the oil; however, there will also be useful by-products such as ammonia and sulfur produced in the processing of the gases. Furthermore, some oil-shale deposits, such as those in the Piceance Creek Basin of Colorado are rich in the minerals halite (NaCl), dawsonite [NaAl(CO$_3$)(OH)$_2$], and nahcolite (NaHCO$_3$) which could be recovered and used as sources of chemicals and aluminum. Estimates have been made that a commercial, above-ground processing plant in the Piceance Creek Basin in Colorado producing 13,000 barrels of oil per day, would also produce 220,000 tons of alumina (Al$_2$O$_3$), 550,000 tons of sodium carbonate (Na$_2$CO$_3$), and 1,600,000 tons of NaHCO$_3$ per year as by-products.

FUTURE FOSSIL FUEL RESOURCES

We now live at the height of the fossil fuel era, and many aspects of our life styles are dependent on a constant supply of fossil fuels. These fuels are not, however, evenly distributed geographically; hence, the fossil fuels have become important in the complex web of international economics and politics.

Table 4.12 lists the present known reserves of fossil fuels along with at least order of magnitude estimates of potentially recoverable resources. It is apparent that the world's present dependence on oil for more than 50 percent of energy supplies cannot continue indefinitely. Far greater energy potential exists in coal and in oil shale, and it is to these fuels that we shall have to turn as the world's oil supplies dwindle. Massive, sudden changes in life styles are unlikely. As oil reserves decrease and oil prices rise in the years ahead, however, it is probable that increasing use will be made of the other fossil fuels and that fuels such as oil shale and some heavy oils, which are not now economic, will become cost competitive.

TABLE 4-12

Energy potential of the world's fossil fuels

Fuel	Reserves* Conventional Units	Reserves* kw hr ($\times 10^{12}$)	Reserves* Joules ($\times 10^{19}$)	Resources** Conventional Units	Resources** kw hr ($\times 10^{12}$)	Resources** Joules ($\times 10^{15}$)
Petroleum	698.7 $\times 10^9$ bbls	1188	428	1420 $\times 10^9$ bbls	2414	869
Natural gas	3402 $\times 10^{12}$ft^3	1021	367	16,000 $\times 10^{12}$ft^3	4800	1728
Heavy oil + tar sands	748 $\times 10^9$ bbls	1272	458	4000 $\times 10^9$ bbls	6800	2448
Peat	50 $\times 10^9$ tons	269	97	240 $\times 10^9$ tons	1289	464
Coal	986.54 $\times 10^9$ tons	6511	2344	7800 $\times 10^9$ tons	51,480	18,533
Shale oil	—	—	—	345 $\times 10^{12}$ bbls	586,500	211,000

U.S. power consumption in 1984 = 73.7 $\times 10^{15}$ btu = 21.6 $\times 10^{12}$ kw hr = 77.7 $\times 10^{18}$ joules
World power consumption in 1983 = 280.1 $\times 10^{15}$btu = 82.1 $\times 10^{12}$ kw hr = 295.2 $\times 10^{18}$ joules

*Basis for calculations of wattage: 1 bbl oil = 1700 kw hr = 6120 $\times 10^6$ joules; 1000 ft^3 gas = 300 kw hr = 1080$\times 10^6$ joules; 1 mt peat = 5370 kw hr = 19,332 $\times 10^6$ joule; 1 ton coal = 0.9078 mt = 6600 kw hr = 23,760 $\times 10^6$ joules.

**Resource estimates vary widely. These values should only be taken as order of magnitude.

FURTHER READINGS

Energy Information Administration, *Energy Annual Review*. Washington, D.C., published annually.

Energy Information Administration, *Monthly Energy Review*. Washington D.C., published monthly.

International Petroleum Encyclopedia. Tulsa, Oklahoma: Pennwell Publishing Co., published annually.

NEHRING, R., Prospects for conventional world oil reserves. *Annual Review of Energy,* vol. 7, p. 175–200, 1982.

PARENT, J. D., *A Survey of United States and Total World Production, Proved Resources, and Remaining Recoverable Re-*sources of Fossil Fuels and Uranium. Chicago, Illinois: Institute of Gas Technology, 1983.

PUNWANI, D. V., ed., *Peat as an Energy Alternative II.* Chicago, Illinois: Institute of Gas Technology, 1982.

SINGER, S. F., "World Demand for Oil." In J. L. Simon and H. Kahn, editors, *The Resourceful Earth.* New York: B. Blackwell Publishers, 1984, p. 339–386.

TISSOT, B. P. and WELTE, D. H., *Petroleum Formation and curence,* 2nd ed. Berlin: Springer-Verlag, 1984, p. 699.

5

Nuclear power plants such as the North Anna Power Station in Virginia are supplying increasing amounts of electrical power in many nations. The reactors are housed in the large dome-shaped concrete buildings. (Courtesy of Virginia Power.)

ENERGY FOR THE FUTURE—NUCLEAR POWER AND OTHER POSSIBLE ALTERNATIVES

> *Energy is the sine qua non of a modern society's ability to do the things it wants to do. Such goals as maintaining the standard of living for a growing population, national security, improved quality of life, increased affluence and increased assistance to less developed societies can only be attained with increasingly large amounts of energy. While lower energy costs allow a society more freedom of action in seeking its goals, the availability of energy is the first requirement of having any freedom of action at all.*
>
> DIXY LEE RAY IN REPORT TO THE PRESIDENT OF THE UNITED STATES,
> DECEMBER 1973

INTRODUCTION

Although we now live in the fossil fuel era, as evidenced by the fact that 95 percent of the energy used by modern society is derived from fossil fuels, it is clear that this heavy dependence on coal, oil, and related fuels cannot continue indefinitely. Accordingly, it is important to consider the nuclear and alternative energy sources that can be used to meet our needs in the years to come.

Energy actually reaches the earth's surface from three sources (Fig. 5.1). The most evident and most important source is the sun. As well as being a direct source of heat, the sun warms the atmosphere and oceans, producing wind, rain, and ocean currents. Eventually, most of the energy from the sun is radiated back into space so that the earth's surface remains in

thermal balance. Humans have long made use of **solar energy** indirectly by harnessing the power of running water and the wind and by burning plant matter that represents energy stored by photosynthesis. Subsequently, we have built our modern society primarily on the fossil solar energy locked in oil, coal, and natural gas. Now we are beginning to harness solar energy more directly through solar collectors and photovoltaic devices. The second source of energy comes from the earth's interior and is derived from the disintegration of radioactive elements such as uranium and thorium. When this process is sped up under artificial conditions, we have nuclear power plants. Such processes occur naturally within the earth and provide a source of heat that can be exploited as **geothermal energy.** The third source of energy comes from the gravitational interac-

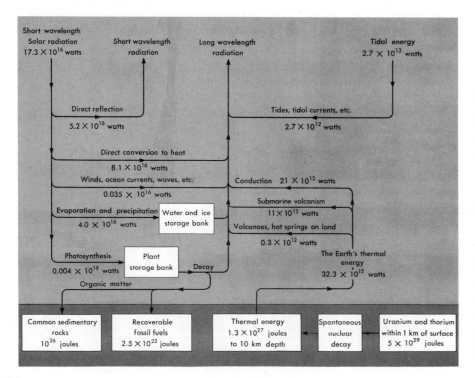

FIGURE 5-1. Energy flow diagram for the surface of the earth. The principal source of energy reaching the surface is short wavelength solar radiation. Additional energy comes from tides and from heat flowing from the earth's interior. The nearly constant average temperature of the earth's surface indicates that the total energy radiated back into space must be just equal to the total energy reaching the surface. (After M.K. Hubbert, Energy Resources, Publication 1000-D, Committee on Natural Resources, National Academy of Sciences—National Research Council, Washington, D.C., 1962.)

tion between the earth and moon that produces the tides. **Tidal energy,** although very small compared to the other sources, is a renewable resource that is being exploited.

The natural disintegration (or **decay**) of radioactive elements takes place very slowly within the earth. However, the breakdown of uranium and thorium can be artificially induced in **nuclear fission,** a process discussed in detail in this chapter. In nuclear fission, the breakdown is very rapid, and it immediately releases very large amounts of energy. Today, the burning of nuclear fuels such as uranium takes place in nuclear power plants. Uranium (and thorium) are, therefore, nonrenewable nuclear fuels mined in much the same ways as other metals. Because nuclear power occupies a special place among the energy sources developed in our own age and has been regarded by many people as the most important energy source for the future, it is discussed first in this chapter. Later sections are devoted to discussing alternative sources such as solar, hydroelectric, wind, wave, ocean, tidal, and geothermal energy and also energy from biological materials and wastes. Finally, we return to a different, and as yet undeveloped, form of nuclear power, that derived from nuclear fusion.

The one thing that is already clear from Fig. 5.1 and will be emphasized in this chapter is that *energy is not in short supply*. The questions are how to use it economically, safely, and responsibly.

NUCLEAR POWER—URANIUM AND NUCLEAR FISSION

The burning of conventional fossil fuels such as coal and oil are *chemical* reactions that proceed with the emission of heat. The energy is released as a result of changes in the bonds between the electron shells of the atoms. Chemical reactions involve only the transfer or sharing of electrons so that the nuclei are unaffected and the chemical elements retain their integrity. In contrast, nuclear energy is generated by changes in the bonding that holds the nucleus together—forces that are roughly a million times greater than the electron energies.

Early chemists believed that the chemical elements could never be created or destroyed (and that the atom could not be split). However, in 1896, the French chemist Becquerel discovered that certain chemical elements (notably uranium) undergo a spontaneous disintegration with the emission of energy in the form of particles or rays, a process that was named **radioactivity.** Subsequently, it was found that all elements with an atomic number greater than 83 are radioactive. In effect, their nuclei are so large as to be unstable, and they breakdown or decay with the emission of energy in the

form of rays or particles. These decays are spontaneous nuclear reactions, the end result of which is the transformation of the element concerned into one or more other elements. There are also a small number of elements of low atomic number, each having one naturally occurring radioisotope (e.g., $^{14}_{12}C$, $^{40}_{19}K$, $^{87}_{37}Rb$). The energy emitted has to do with holding or binding together the nucleus and, as can be seen from Fig. 5.2, the binding energy of a nucleus varies as a function of the total number of protons plus neutrons making up that nucleus (the mass number). The curve of mass number versus binding energy is such that the lightest and heaviest elements have lower nuclear binding energies. The breakdown of a large nucleus like uranium into two smaller nuclei such as barium and krypton is called **nuclear fission.** Another way of releasing energy is by the joining of the nuclei of very light elements, such as hydrogen and lithium, to form heavier elements, a process called **fusion.** In either case, a small amount of matter has been converted directly into a large amount of energy, because whenever a nucleus is formed, its mass is slightly less than the sum of the masses of the individual protons and neutrons that comprise it. For example, helium (He) contains two protons and two neutrons in the nucleus and should weigh 4.03303 atomic mass units. In fact, helium only weighs 4.00260 units. The missing mass was converted into energy when the protons or neutrons joined to form the nucleus (i.e., it is the binding energy). Before this century, it was believed that matter could be neither created nor destroyed, but, in 1905, Einstein postulated the equivalence of matter and energy. His famous equation ($E = Mc^2$ where E = energy, M = mass, and c = velocity of light) related that conversion of a very small amount of matter to the production of very large amounts of energy (since c^2 is a very large number). In chemical reactions, such as those occurring when coal or oil is burned, the conversion of matter into energy is so small as to be undetectable. In nuclear reactions, the energies involved are so much greater that this conversion can be measured.

Nuclear Fission

The decay of natural radioactive materials, such as minerals containing uranium or thorium, takes place very slowly and over a great span of time (millions of years). We cannot slow the natural fission process, but we can accelerate it by bombarding radioactive nuclei with neutrons or by bringing together enough radioactive nuclei that their natural rate of neutron emission is sufficient to cause an increase in the rate of decay. The only naturally occurring atom that is readily fissionable is the isotope of uranium with mass number 235 (^{235}U). Many reactions occur during the fission of ^{235}U. One example is that when this atom is bombarded with neutrons (n), it

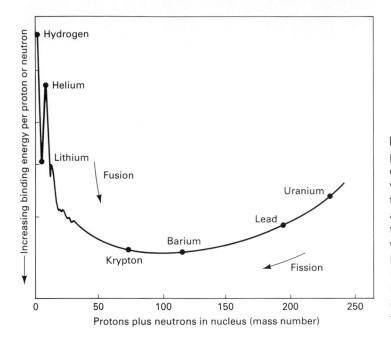

FIGURE 5-2. Binding energy, produced by conversion of some of the mass of an atomic nucleus, varies with the number of protons and neutrons. The higher an atom sits on the curve, the more the energy that will be given off when protons and neutrons combine to form its nucleus. The arrows indicate the directions of movement along the binding energy curve during fusion and fission.

may split into isotopes of barium (^{141}Ba) and krypton (^{92}Kr) with the release of further neutrons and energy:

$$^{235}_{92}\text{U} + \text{n} \longrightarrow \ ^{141}_{56}\text{Ba} + \ ^{92}_{36}\text{Kr} + 3\text{n}$$
$$+ \ \text{energy (200 million electron volts}^1) \qquad (5.1)$$

The released neutrons can penetrate the nuclei of adjacent atoms of ^{235}U so that the reaction can continue, provided enough uranium is present. Thus, a **chain reaction** is created given that a sufficient amount (the **critical mass**) of uranium is present (Fig. 5.3). If this chain reaction is allowed to proceed uncontrolled, then the result is the explosive release of enormous amounts of energy, in other words, an atomic bomb. However, if the fission of uranium proceeds under carefully controlled conditions, the energy released can be extracted and used in power generation. If we consider reaction (5.1) and the emission of 200 million electron volts (or 3.2×10^{-11} joules) per fission event, we can calculate that the 2.56×10^{21} atoms in *every gram* of ^{235}U can release 8.19×10^{10} joules. This is equivalent to the heat of combustion of 2.7 metric tons of coal or 13.7 barrels of crude oil. Obviously, this makes uranium a very attractive fuel to consider for power generation, and the technology necessary to exploit uranium fission has developed rapidly since World War II.

Thorium, which in nature is almost entirely made up of the isotope ^{232}Th, is an alternative source of fissionable material. Although ^{232}Th is not itself capable of sustaining a nuclear chain reaction, it can absorb neutrons from the controlled fission of ^{235}U to eventually become ^{233}U after passing through various fairly short-lived isotopes and emitting β particles:

$$^{232}_{90}\text{Th} + \text{n} \longrightarrow \ ^{233}_{90}\text{Th}; \ ^{233}_{90}\text{Th} - \beta^- \longrightarrow \ ^{233}_{91}\text{Pa};$$
$$^{233}_{91}\text{Pa} - \beta^- \longrightarrow \ ^{233}_{92}\text{U}. \qquad (5.2)$$

The isotope ^{233}U is fissionable and can be made or bred from thorium in a nuclear reactor. However, the vast majority of nuclear power programs are based on uranium as a fuel, so the use of uranium as a source of energy will be emphasized in what follows.

Uranium and How It Is Used— The Nuclear Reactor

The controlled fission of uranium for power generation takes place in a **nuclear reactor**. However, uranium extracted in mining operations is dominantly made up of the ^{238}U isotope (99.3 percent); the fissionable ^{235}U isotope comprises only 0.7 percent of the toal uranium and another isotope, ^{234}U, comprises only 0.005 percent. Although reactors using natural uranium were among the first developed, particularly in England, many modern reactor designs require a fuel with ^{235}U at concentrations much higher than 0.7 percent. This necessitates a costly process of separation and concentration before the mined uranium can be used as a fuel. In fact, uranium differs from fossil fuels in that complex processing operations are often involved both before and after it is burned in the reactor, and these operations form a sequence known as the **nuclear fuel cycle** that we shall discuss before looking at the reactors.

---

^{1} 1 million electron volts $= 1.6 \times 10^{-13}$ joules.

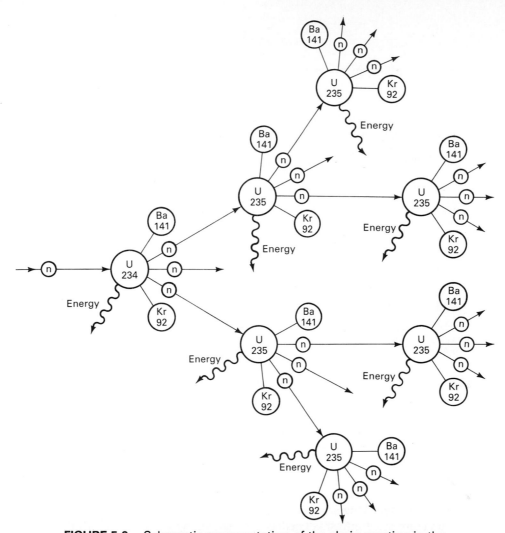

FIGURE 5-3. Schematic representation of the chain reaction in the fission of uranium. When a high energy neutron (n) is absorbed by the nucleus of a uranium atom, it results in nearly spontaneous fission of the uranium nucleus producing ^{141}Ba and ^{92}Kr, more neutrons, and a large release in energy. The released neutrons cause the fission of other uranium nuclei and the reaction proceeds in a rapidly expanding steplike, or chain, reaction.

The Nuclear Fuel Cycle (Fig. 5.4). The mineral deposits of uranium are discussed later in this chapter, but obviously the first stage in the cycle is the mining of these deposits. Mining involves standard open pit and underground operations employing methods similar to those for the mining of other low-grade ores (see p. 39). Because many uranium ores contain an average of much less than 1 percent of U_3O_8 (conventionally, grades and production figures are expressed in terms of this oxide), extensive beneficiation is needed. This involves mechanical concentration of size-reduced ore, perhaps making use of the high specific gravity of uranium minerals, followed by chemical methods such as leaching and solvent extraction to form an end product called **yellowcake,** a crude oxide containing 70–90 percent U_3O_8.

The *enrichment* of uranium to produce a fuel containing more than 0.7 percent ^{235}U is a very difficult and expensive process, as it involves separating two isotopes (^{235}U and ^{238}U) that have essentially no chemical difference and very little mass difference between them.

The most common method used is gaseous diffusion that is based on the fact that a gas diffuses through a porous membrane at a rate inversely proportional to the square root of its mass. The U_3O_8 is converted to gaseous uranium hexafluoride (UF_6) before being passed through thousands of porous barriers to separate $^{235}UF_6$ from $^{238}UF_6$. The enrichment process accounts for

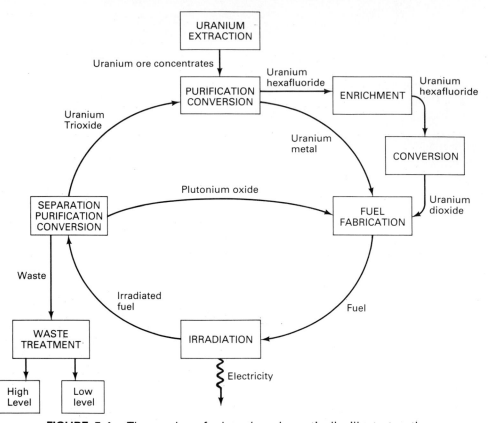

FIGURE 5-4. The nuclear fuel cycle schematically illustrates the steps involved in the conversion of uranium ore into nuclear fuel and ultimately into nuclear waste.

roughly 30 percent of the nuclear fuel costs. Following enrichment, the UF_6 is converted to a ceramic powder such as an oxide (UO_2) and compacted into small pellets that can be loaded into metallic tubes to form **fuel rods** or **fuel elements.**

The fuel elements are loaded into the reactor core and can be burned for power production and typically are irradiated in the core for several years, eventually being removed because the fissionable content has dropped too low to sustain the chain reaction or because the fuel element has been damaged by radiation. This spent fuel is, nevertheless, intensely radioactive as a result of a variety of isotopes produced in the fission process. Commonly, after removal it is stored in water pools for at least several months to allow short-lived fission products to decay. It may then undergo reprocessing to recover significant quantities of uranium (and plutonium created in the reactor) that can be used in new fuel elements and to concentrate the radioactive waste products for eventual disposal. The subject of radioactive waste disposal has already been discussed in Chapter 3.

The Nuclear Reactor. In order to understand the role of nuclear power at present and its future poten-

tial, it is necessary to know something about nuclear reactors. The different types and designs are many and varied, but certain major categories can be defined. The first experimental and commercial reactors employed natural (unenriched) uranium as a fuel.

A substantial fission chain reaction normally cannot be produced in a simple block of natural uranium,[1] because not enough neutrons emitted by the fission process would be captured by the small number of ^{235}U nuclei available. However, these neutrons are travelling at high velocities, and if they can be slowed to very low velocities, then the probability of the collision (more correctly termed **capture**) with further ^{235}U nuclei is greatly increased, and a sustained chain of fission reactions is just possible. The neutrons are slowed by allowing them to collide with nuclei of light elements and transfer some of their energy in the same way as a moving billiard ball does on striking a stationary one. The

[1] A probably unique exception is the "fossil" natural fission reactor described from a uranium mine at Oklo in the Gabon Republic of West Africa (Scientific American, 235, p. 36, 1976). Here, scattered pockets of rich ore achieved the necessary (**critical**) conditions in unusual geologic conditions at a time in earth history (about 2000 million years ago) when the natural relative abundance of ^{235}U was greater (about 3 percent of total uranium).

light elements used in this way are known as **moderators,** and two such elements have been widely used; one is carbon in the form of **graphite,** and the other is **deuterium** (the name given to the isotope of hydrogen with mass number 2) as deuterium oxide or "heavy water." Development of the graphite-moderated natural uranium reactor for power generation was pioneered in Britain where the world's first large-scale nuclear power station at Calder Hall first produced electricity in 1956. From this prototype the first generation of nuclear power stations in Britain was developed on the Magnox reactor (Fig. 5.5). It is important to realize that in a nuclear power station, the reactor simply acts as a source of heat and so replaces the furnace in a conventional power station. Different reactors employ different methods of extracting the heat and, in this case, pressurized carbon dioxide gas is blown through the core and the hot gas then passed through heat exchangers to heat water and produce steam that can drive turbines and generators as in conventional power stations. The reactor must be operated under conditions in which a fission chain reaction can be maintained and at a constant power output—a condition known as **criticality.** In the Magnox reactor, this condition is maintained using boron steel control rods that very strongly absorb slow neutrons and are lowered into the core to slow the fission reaction or raised to increase reactivity and power output. The other type of reactor that has been developed so as to use natural uranium as a fuel is a heavy-water-moderated system pioneered by the Canadians (in the so-called "Candu" program).

If natural uranium can be used as a fuel for power generation, one may ask, why bother with the costly process of fuel enrichment? The answer is that if natural uranium is enriched even to a modest degree by the addition of fissionable isotopes, many of the problems of reactor design found in natural uranium reactors are overcome, and there are important gains in manufacturing and operational efficiency. For example, ordinary water or organic liquids may be used to moderate neutrons, the moderator and fuel may be intimately mixed to form a **homogeneous system** (although serious corrosion problems arise) and with high enrichment, it is even possible to completely dispense with the moderator. Other advantages arise from much greater freedom in the choice of constructional materials so that, for example, maximum operating temperatures can be increased. For reactors using enriched uranium, the number of possible types becomes very large. However, existing and planned types of reactors can be roughly divided into four groups:

1. heterogeneous graphite-moderated, gas-cooled reactors, e.g., the advanced gas-cooled reactor (AGR);

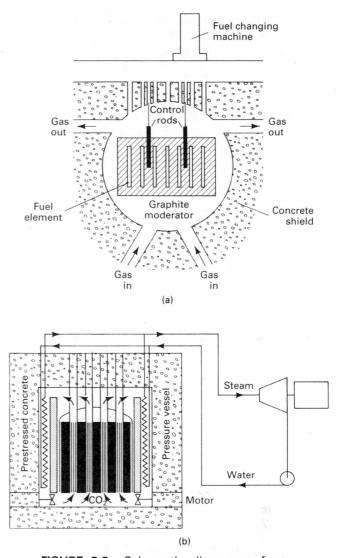

FIGURE 5-5. Schematic diagrams of gas-cooled reactors that use carbon as the moderator. (a) The advanced gas-cooled reactor was an advanced form of a gas-cooled reactor that used more enriched fuel and could operate more efficiently and at much higher temperatures. (b) The Magnox reactor, the first generation of nuclear power plants, employed carbon dioxide as the means of transferring the heat from the reactor core to a heat exchanger where electricity is generated.

2. heterogeneous water-moderated and cooled reactors, e.g., light water reactors such as the boiling water (BWR) and pressurized water (PWR) reactors;

3. homogeneous reactors, e.g., the homogeneous reactor experiment (HRE); and

4. fast (unmoderated) reactors.

The advanced gas-cooled reactor (AGR) is an example of the first type that represents the second generation of reactors in Britain following the Magnox reactors and using fuel with a 2.5 percent fissile material. As Fig. 5.5 shows, graphite is still used as a moderator with carbon dioxide coolant and a system of control rods, but enrichment allows a considerable increase in operating temperature and, consequently, in efficiency.

The second major reactor type uses water instead of a gas as a means of extracting heat from the reactor. Reactors of this type which were developed in the United States require fuel with 2–5 percent fissionable material and include the boiling water reactor (BWR) and the pressurized water reactor (PWR) (Fig. 5.6). In both of these types of reactors water acts as the moderator and coolant. The prototype PWR "Yankee" was built in Massachusetts and became fully operational in 1961, and the prototype BWR "Dresden" was constructed at about the same time in Illinois. The Dresden core consisted of 57.5 tons of uranium oxide enriched to 1.5 percent ^{235}U and produced 200 megawatts of electricity. The water was maintained at a pressure of 70 atmospheres that allowed boiling at 300°C, so that this high-temperature steam could be used to directly drive turbines before being condensed and returned to the reactor vessel.

The use of enriched fuels enables systems to be designed in which the fuel and moderator are intimately mixed. Small experimental **homogeneous reactors** have been developed, such as the homogeneous reactor experiment (HRE) of the Oak Ridge Laboratories in the United States. Systems like this may involve fused salts of the fuel and moderator or a solution of uranium salt in water. They have not been successfully developed on a large scale, partly because of the serious corrosion problems that arise.

The last main category of reactor types are very important for the longer term future of nuclear fission as a source of energy. These are the so-called **fast reactors**. When the uranium fuel is highly enriched, it is possible to maintain the chain reaction using high velocity (fast) neutrons and dispense with the moderators entirely. In such a system, the core can be quite small, and a high proportion of neutrons can be allowed to escape through the surface. If a blanket of the nonfissionable ^{238}U is wrapped around this core, then these emitted neutrons can be used to make or *breed* a fissile isotope of plutonium:

$$^{238}_{92}U + n \longrightarrow {}^{239}_{92}U; \quad {}^{239}_{92}U - \beta^- \longrightarrow {}^{239}_{93}Np;$$
$$^{239}_{93}Np - \beta^- \longrightarrow {}^{239}_{94}Pu. \qquad (5.3)$$

In this way, more fissile material can be made in the blanket than is consumed in the core. Such fast reactors are known as **fast breeder reactors.** The implications

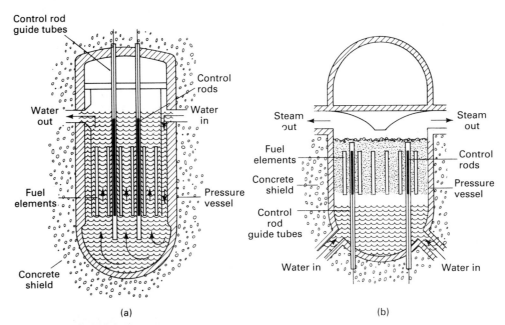

FIGURE 5-6. (a) The pressurized water reactor uses water under high pressure as both the moderator and the means of transferring heat from the reactor core to the electricity generating plant. (b) The boiling water reactor is maintained at a pressure of about 70 atmospheres that allows boiling at about 300°C. The steam thus generated is used to directly drive turbines to generate electricity.

of this development for nuclear power generation are considerable because the reactor is capable of breeding its own fuel by converting the vastly more abundant ^{238}U isotope to a usable isotope.

A prototype fast breeder reactor first became operational at Dounreay, Scotland in 1959 (Fig. 5.7). The central core of 220 kilograms was enriched to 46.5 percent ^{235}U, and the heat output (60 megawatts) of a volume the size of a small garbage can was immense (roughly comparable to that of 600,000 100-watt light bulbs). The coolant used was molten sodium and potassium, a much more efficient coolant than water, or the gases used in other systems. A further 12 megawatts of power is produced from fission processes in the blanket of 20 tons of depleted uranium. The molten metal coolant, in turn, generated steam to drive the turbines and generators. This prototype reactor operated successfully until 1977 when it was replaced by another fast breeder of improved design. The largest fast breeder reactor in the world is the Super Phenix at Creys-Malville

in France, having an output of 1200 megawatts. Other developments in this field include work in the United States on a modified core for the PWR with a breeder blanket and the molten salt breeder reactor (Fig. 5.7) under development at the Oak Ridge National Laboratory. Here, features of the thermal reactor with its moderator are combined with a breeder cycle.

Nuclear Reactor Safety—After Chernobyl. There are few subjects in the whole area of resources and energy that cause greater public concern than the potential for accidents at nuclear power plants. In spite of the very stringent safety precautions that are taken in the design, construction, and operation of nuclear plants, major accidents have occurred in recent years. It is therefore important for us to examine the risks associated with nuclear power as objectively as possible when decisions concerning energy policy have to be made.

In all commercial nuclear reactors, a fission chain reaction is sustained at the level of criticality, which

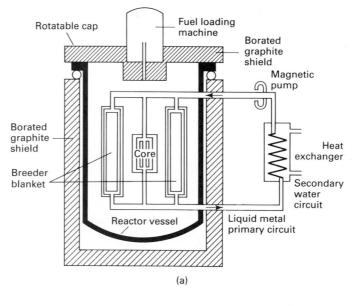

(a)

FIGURE 5-7. Schematic diagrams of fast-breeder nuclear reactors in which a blanket of nonfissionable ^{238}U is placed around the core. The ^{238}U is converted to ^{239}Pu, a fissionable isotope, at a rate faster than the core is consumed. (a) In the loop-type fast-breeder reactor, the heat is carried out of the reactor vessel by a molten metal to a heat exchanger. (b) In the molten salt-breeder reactor, salt transports the heat to a series of heat exchangers so that electricity can be generated.

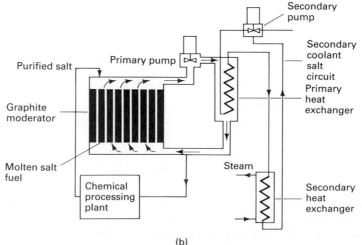

(b)

means constant power output. In order to maintain the balance in most reactor types, rods of material that capture neutrons very strongly and compete with the fission process can be lowered into the reactor core to slow the reaction or raised to speed it. These control rods are usually made of cadmium or boron and are inserted or removed automatically in response to power fluctuations. Clearly, a first hazard is the failure of the system, which would result in continued increase in power output. To guard against this, reactors are equipped with ancillary control rods designed to respond automatically in such a situation (or other dangerous situations) and to bring about a reactor shutdown, or *scram*, as it is commonly called. If these devices fail, the reactor can rise above criticality in a runaway in which the rate of reaction would increase in an unchecked manner. Fortunately, this situation could not produce a nuclear explosion like that of a nuclear weapon, but it could allow the temperature to rise to a level that would melt or even vaporize parts of the reactor. The damage to the reactor would probably render it no longer critical, and power would eventually fall. The greatest hazard would be escape of gaseous radioactive iodine (^{131}I), an isotope (half-life of 8 days) that is readily taken up in the human thyroid gland. Radioactive xenon and krypton gas and solid isotopes of strontium (^{90}Sr) and cesium (^{137}Cs) are lesser dangers. To prevent escape of dangerous fission products into the environment, reactors are enclosed in various steel and concrete vessels.

In the heavy-water-moderated reactors of the Candu program, an additional safety feature is a dump tank into which the moderator can be readily emptied, should all else fail to prevent a runaway. However, in the pressurized-water reactor, the loss of moderator, which also acts as a coolant, is a further hazard. Loss of coolant or coolant flow is probably the most serious hazard in most reactor types, so that coolant flow is always carefully monitored. Fast-breeder reactors present their own safety problems. For example, if the core should melt, it could reform in such a way as to be even more reactive. Diverters positioned beneath the core ensure separation to prevent this if melting should occur. Again, it should be emphasized that a nuclear reactor cannot explode like a nuclear bomb; the danger arises from the escape of highly poisonous or toxic fission products into the environment.

Up until 1979, the nuclear industry worldwide could claim an impressive safety record. The only significant release of radioactive material had been in Britain at Windscale in 1958. It involved a graphite-moderated, air-cooled reactor that was actually shut down at the time. The release, mainly of radioactive iodine (^{131}I), did not endanger life, but milk produced in an area around the reactor of 10 by 30 miles was unusable for a time. Much more recently, two serious accidents that have significantly increased public concern and damaged the image of the industry have been those at Three Mile Island, Pennsylvania, in the United States in March 1979 and Chernobyl in the Ukraine of the Soviet Union in April 1986.

The Three Mile Island facility located on an island in the Susquehanna River near Harrisburg, Pennsylvania, is a pressurized water reactor. Such reactors have both a primary cooling system to carry the fission heat to the steam generator and a secondary cooling system to carry steam from the steam generator to the turbine. Each system has its own pumps (the reactor cooling system pumps and the feed water pumps, respectively). Both systems carry heat from the reactor core to areas outside. At 4:00 A.M. on March 28, 1979, the main feed water pump failed, and three reserve pumps (two electric and one steam driven) went on automatically. However, in the 15 seconds required for these pumps to build to normal pressure, the primary system heated and increased in pressure such that the automatic reactor shutdown procedure went into operation. A pressure relief valve in the primary system also opened to release pressure—all these responses were quite proper and designed to occur. Unfortunately unknown to the operators, valves connected to the reserve pumps, and supposed to be open at all times, were closed so that the steam generators soon boiled dry. In addition to this, the pressure relief valve in the primary system failed to reset properly and was now leaking. In the long, complex series of events that followed, the pump valves were opened and eventually the leaky valve blocked, but the operators were misled into thinking that there was too much water in the primary system instead of too little. As a result, the core lay uncovered for several hours, and substantial damage occurred before the situation was finally brought under control. The factors leading to the Three Mile Island accident involved three main ingredients: a temporary, abnormal situation aggravated by human error, a small loss-of-coolant accident, and the misreading of the situation by the operators. Ultimately, although very costly damage was done to the reactor itself, the dangers to the public were very small. In the early stages of the accident, radioactive xenon (^{133}X) was released. Actual exposure is calculated to have the potential to cause death by cancer of less than one person in the next 30 or 40 years.

Tragically the accident at Chernobyl in April 1986 did result in loss of life and in significant contamination over a very large area. The accident centered around attempts to test a system for providing the necessary cooling water in the event of a reactor shutdown. These tests were to coincide with the actual closing of the reactor for its annual maintenance. In attempting to create the necessary conditions for this poorly planned test, automatic systems for operation of the control rods, emer-

gency core-cooling systems, and various other fail-safe devices were overridden by the operators. When the test began to go wrong, operators tried to save the test and prevent damage to the reactor. Their actions were totally against regulations and led to a complete loss of control. In the words of Soviet Academician Legasov, reporting to an international group of nuclear scientists in Vienna, the reactor was "free to do as it wished." Control rods were leaping up and down and water and steam sloshed around uncontrollably. In less than 1 second, the power surged from 7 percent to several hundred times its normal level. The effect was like setting off half a ton of TNT in the core, and two explosions lifted the roof of the reactor, throwing red-hot lumps of

graphite and pieces of uranium oxide fuel over the immediate area.

Over the next 10 days, while the Soviets struggled to quench the fire, roughly 10 percent of the core material was dispersed into the atmosphere to fallout over the Soviet Union and Europe. Large areas of the Soviet Union, Poland, Sweden, and Finland (Fig. 5.8) were particularly affected, but significant increases in radiation levels were recorded as far away as Norway, Italy, and Britain where fallout from Chernobyl led to restrictions on the sale of crops and livestock. In the immediate area of Chernobyl, one person was apparently killed within the reactor and about 20 severely irradiated (of whom 17 died within 6 weeks), but many thousands

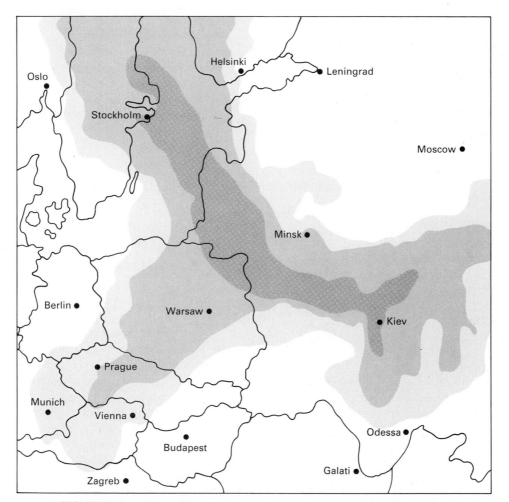

FIGURE 5-8. Map of the area most affected by the accident at the Chernobyl nuclear reactor near Kiev in the Soviet Union in late April 1986. The shading shows simulation of the integrated dose of ^{131}I to adult thyroid glands accumulated from 26 April to 1 May 1986 (based on calculations done at the Lawrence Livermore National Laboratory in California.) The central, darkest area had doses in excess of 1 rem, the intermediate zone had doses between 0.1 and 1 rem, and the outer zone had doses between 0.01 and 0.1 rem. (See Tables 3.3 and 3.5 for information on units of radioactivity and dosages experienced from other sources.)

more face an increased risk of death from cancers associated with the radiation.

What then can we say about the risks associated with nuclear power generation? It is still fair to say that the risk of death or serious injury to a member of the public as a result of a nuclear accident is very small, particularly when compared to many of the risks taken by people in every day life (e.g., compared to the one-in-50 risk of death or serious injury in a motor accident in an average life span, that associated with nuclear power would be one in many thousands). Nevertheless, the lessons of Three Mile Island and Chernobyl must never be forgotten. To quote from the magazine *Nature* (editorial, vol. 323, no. 6083), "The difficulty is that what went wrong at Chernobyl on 26 April could have happened anywhere. That is the plain truth which no amount of technical comparison of different reactor types can possibly conceal. Moreover, there have been several occasions in the recent past when nuclear accidents, luckily smaller in scale, have been brought about, because operators have chosen to disregard the regulations they are supposed to live by, or have been deserted by common sense and elementary caution." It is also important to remember that other aspects of safety and security, such as the hazards associated with nuclear waste disposal and the relationship that may exist between nuclear energy programs and the proliferation of nuclear weapons, must be considered in the overall formulation of policies regarding nuclear power.

Uranium in the Earth

Uranium is a rare element with an average concentration in the earth's crust of only about 2 parts per million. Although it can occur in very trace amounts in a variety of minerals, the large size of the uranium atom tends to exclude it from early crystallizing minerals in magmas. Hence, the uranium is commonly concentrated in the final (residual) melts and fluids and in silica-rich rocks like granites that are rich in alkali elements such as sodium and potassium. In such rocks, uranium concentrations may range up to tens, or even a hundred or more, parts per million. This uranium may be located in certain rare minerals that occur in such rocks as minor components (e.g., zircon, sphene, and apatite), or it may occur as the most important ore mineral of uranium, uraninite (UO_2, also called **pitchblende**). Here, the uranium is in the uranous (U^{4+}) state. Occasionally within or close to such igneous rocks, very high concentrations of uranium minerals may occur either in veins or as more irregularly distributed disseminations. Such deposits were among the first uranium ores to be found and exploited and were the source of much of the uranium used by Pierre and Marie Curie for their pioneering work on radioactivity.

Most of the uranium at the surface of the earth probably formed in association with igneous rocks as described above. However, a very important feature of uranium in the U^{4+} state is that it is readily oxidized to the uranyl (U^{6+}) state. Whereas U^{4+} compounds are highly insoluble, U^{6+} combines with oxygen to form the uranyl ion $(UO_2)^{2+}$ that, in turn, can form soluble complex compounds with species like carbonate, sulfate, and fluoride. Near-surface ground waters are commonly oxidizing in nature and hence provide a ready means of leaching and carrying uranium. Although much of this uranium may then be dispersed, the ground waters carrying the metal may pass into rocks in which reducing substances, commonly decaying organic matter, convert the soluble U^{6+} ion to the insoluble U^{4+} form, thus resulting in its precipitation. Other reactions involve absorption of the uranium by another mineral such as apatite, $(Ca_5(PO_4)_3(OH,F)$ in which U^{4+} replaces some Ca). The leaching, transportation, and precipitation of uranium in this way can lead to the formation of large bodies of rock enriched in the metal, and deposits produced by these second stage processes are the most important sources of uranium.

The most important types of uranium ore deposits are listed with examples in Table 5.1. The igneous deposits include various types of ores disseminated in alkali rocks and granites, although these are not very substantial contributors to world uranium resources. Deposits of the metamorphic group include the concentrations (known as **skarns**) that have formed at the contact between molten igneous rocks and the rocks into which they have been emplaced. Also in this general category are the ores originally formed deeper in the crust when heating has caused some melting and the migration of material.

Some of the most famous and important of all uranium deposits are detrital in origin, e.g., those of the Witwatersrand in South Africa and Elliot Lake (also called the Blind River) in Canada. Characteristically, ores of this type occur in very ancient (Precambrian) rocks made largely of quartz pebbles and regarded as representing former stream channels. The Witwatersrand area is better known as the world's greatest gold-producing region (see Chapter 7), but in recent years about 10 percent of the known world production of uranium has also come from this area. Although the processes by which these ores formed remain controversial, it is widely believed that the gold and uranium were carried along the bottoms of stream channels as detrital grains. These grains would have been washed into the streams from source areas upstream and concentrated by virtue of their high density (in much the same way as gold is concentrated in the prospector's pan). The deposits at Elliot Lake in Ontario, Canada, exhibit all the features shown by the Witwatersrand region, but a

TABLE 5-1

Important types of uranium ore deposits

Deposit Type		Characteristic Elements	Examples
Igneous	In pegmatites, alkali igneous rocks, carbonatites and related rocks (pegmatites)	U, Nb, Th, Cu, P, Ti, Zr, rare earths	Prairie Lake, Ontario, Canada Pocos du Coldas, Brazil Ilimaussaq, S. Greenland Rossing, S.W. Africa
Metamorphic	In contact areas between igneous and host rocks (skarns) or from the partial melting of rocks deep in the earth	U, Th, Mo, rare earths, Nb, Ti	Rossing, S.W. Africa
Detrital	Deposited in the bottoms of ancient rivers, lakes (fossil placers)	U, Th, Ti, rare earths, Au, Zr, Co	Witwatersrand, S. Africa Elliot Lake, Ontario, Canada
Unconformity	Occur close to a conspicuous Mid-Proterozoic unconformity	U, (± Ni, rare earths, Ti, etc.)	N. Saskatchewan, Canada (Rabbit Lake, Key Lake, etc.) Northern Territory, Australia (Jabiluka, Nabarlek, etc.)
Hydrogenic (deposited from fluids and waters)	From high-temperature water or fluids (hydrothermal) forming disseminations or veins (vein type)	U, Th, rare earths, (± Cu, F, Be, Nb, Zr)	Bokan Mt., Alaska, U.S.A. Rexspor, B.C., Canada
	U. deposits formed at the same time as host shales, limestones, phosphate rocks, etc.	U, P, V, Cu, Co, Ni, As, Ag, C	Ronstad, Sweden Kitts, Labrador, Canada
	U. deposited from low-temperature waters introduced into sandstones, conglomerates and forming disseminations or, sometimes, veins (sandstone type)	U, C (± Cu, V, Mo, Ag, Ni, As, Co, Au, Se, Bi)	Colorado Plateau area and Wyoming, U.S.A. Cypress Hills, Saskatchewan, Canada Beaverlodge, Saskatchewan Port Radium, N.W.T., Canada
	As an encircled cap at the surface of other deposits	U, Cu, Ag, Ni, As	Eldorado, Sasketchewan, Canada Rossing, S.W. Africa

marked difference is that, although a major uranium producer, these ores do not contain significant quantities of gold.

The deposits categorized in Table 5.1 as hydrogenic include all those in which the uranium appears to have been deposited from water, either as a high-temperature fluid or a much lower temperature one such as ground water. The boundaries between the different subcategories shown here are not always clear, but at least the divisions indicate the different processes at work. The veins formed by deposition from high-temperature fluids always show a fairly close spatial link with granites or similar rocks from which the fluids could have been derived. Such vein deposits are no longer a major world source of the metal. The richest uranium deposits in the United States are of the type found in Jurassic and Triassic sandstones in the Colorado Plateau area of western Colorado, eastern Utah, northeastern Arizona, and northwestern New Mexico. Similar deposits in younger rocks occur in Wyoming and are forming today in Texas. These deposits, commonly known as roll-front deposits, have formed through the precipitation of uranium from ground waters carrying the metal in solution as uranyl complexes. The precipitation occurs as a result of reduction where the solutions encounter organic matter, as evidenced by the replacement of fossil logs by uranium or where the solution reacts with trapped H_2S. They owe their character-

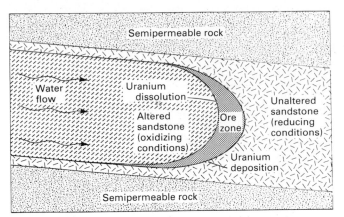

FIGURE 5-9. Many of the uranium deposits in the western United States are of the roll-type as shown in cross section above. Oxidizing ground waters dissolve the low concentrations of uranium and reprecipitate it further down an aquifer where reducing conditions are encountered. This results in a progressive accumulation of uranium and the movement of the arc-shaped deposit along the aquifer.

istic shape, as shown in the cross section in Fig. 5.9, to the movement of fluid through the porous sandstones and the dissolution and reprecipitation of uranium and other metals along a moving front. Uranium is also concentrated in organic-rich black shales (such as the Chattanooga shale of Alabama and Kentucky) but generally at much lower concentration levels.

The Search for Uranium Deposits

Since 1945, uranium has been the subject of the most intense mineral exploration activity ever undertaken for any metal, involving both government agencies and private companies. This search employed all the standard exploration techniques but also made use of the techniques that detect the same radiation that we exploit in nuclear power plants. The emission of the radiation is helpful in locating the uranium, and is detected by means of the following methods.

Gross Count Surveys. The simplest technique, which was widely used in early exploration, is to survey the ground using portable detectors that record total radiation levels without determining anything about the nature of the radiation. Such simple Geiger-Muller and scintillation counters are of low sensitivity but have the advantage of being relatively cheap to setup and operate. They may be handheld, mounted on a vehicle, or may be airborne, in which case they form a useful method of rapid reconnaissance. One problem is that the penetration of Gamma-rays through rocks and soils is limited to a distance of 10–20 centimeters so that thick overburden may obscure the signal.

Gamma-ray Spectrometry. This involves equipment capable of determining the strength of radiation of different energies. In other words, the gamma-rays characteristic of uranium (1.76 million electron volts), thorium (2.61 million electron volts), and potassium-40 (1.46 million electron volts) being emitted over an area can be measured and linked to other geologic information that is available. Again the basic technology can be incorporated into handheld, vehicle-mounted, or airborne systems, with considerable sophistication being possible in airborne systems having on-line computer processing of data. The overall costs of gamma-ray spectrometry may be five to 10 times greater than for gross count surveys, and, like the latter, gamma-ray spectrometry is limited to measuring only surface radiation to a depth of 10–20 centimeters. Water, vegetation, snow cover, and even the air can also absorb and shield gamma-radiation. Hence, airborne surveys need to be flown at low altitude to ensure detection.

Radon Measurement. Radon (^{222}Rn) is a radioactive gas given off by the decay of uranium (^{238}U). It is chemically unreactive, so it remains a gas and tends to move upward through soils above uranium-bearing rocks. As noted in Chapter 3, the accumulation of radon in homes in such areas is a recently recognized health hazard. Various techniques have been developed to sample and measure radon gas in the air and in soils, such as the radon emanometer. Radon also enters stream, lake, and spring water in areas around uranium deposits, and methods of measuring its concentration in natural waters have been devised. Although helpful in exploration, radon is considered a major health hazard, and the discovery that it has built up to significant levels in homes in many areas underlain by uranium-bearing rocks is prompting much concern.

Uranium Reserves and Resources and the Future of the Fission Reactor

Reserves of rich deposits of uranium in the non-Communist world are widespread but not large (see Table 5.2), although the figures are probably conservative because an element of secrecy surrounds the subject of uranium [Fig. 5.10]. Substantial deposits that are economically recoverable now or in the foreseeable future are known on all continents. Assessment of the potential of lower-grade deposits is difficult because the necessary data are not available. Within the United States, the kinds of source materials available have been broadly evaluated, as illustrated in Fig. 5.11. It has recently been argued by geologists in the United States that the distribution of uranium in the earth's crust follows a log-normal abundance curve with a 300-fold increase in recoverable uranium for each 10-fold decrease in ore grade (Fig. 5.12). Such a trend would guarantee an ever

TABLE 5-2

Estimated uranium resources in ores rich enough to be mined for use in uranium-235 power plants, together with estimated rates of production for 1990. Data are reported as the oxide, U_3O_8. No distinctions are drawn between reserves and resources, and no data are reported by the Communist countries

Country	Reasonably Assured Resources (m.t. of U_3O_8)	Estimated Production Rate, 1990* (m.t. of U_3O_8 per yr)
Australia**	1,600,000	9000
U.S.A.**	894,000	6000
Republic of South Africa***	391,000	6000
Canada***	235,000	13,000
Niger***	160,000	?
Namibia***	133,000	4000
France***	55,300	?
Other***	608,000	5000

*Production rate estimate from *Mining Annual Review*, 1983.

**Resource data from *American Association of Petroleum Geologists*, Bulletin v.67, p.1999–2008, 1983.

***Resource data from *Mining Annual Review*, 1980. Much of the large "other" category is in low-grade deposits in Sweden.

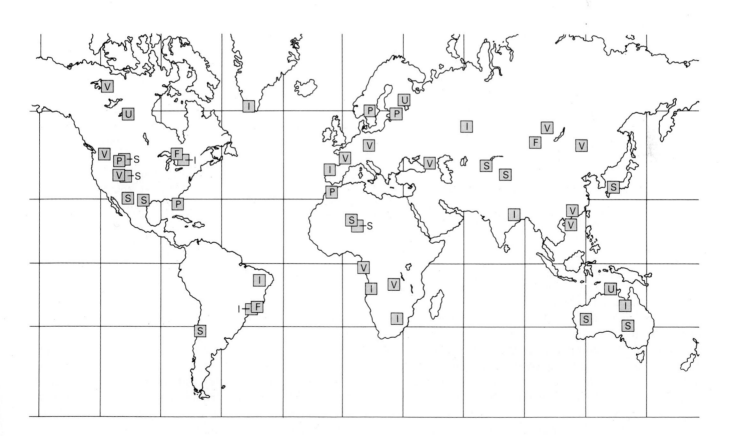

FIGURE 5-10. Major uranium deposits occur worldwide as shown on this map. The deposit types are V-veins; U-unconformity; S-sandstone; F-fossil placers; P-phosphate and black shale; I-igneous and metamorphic.

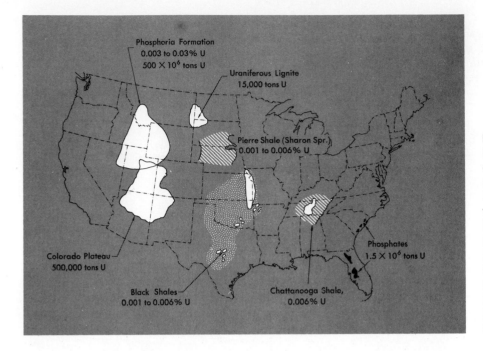

FIGURE 5-11. Long-term, but low-grade resources of uranium occur in phosphate deposits, lignites, and black shales. In the United States, richer deposits, for which reserve estimates can be made, occur mostly in and around the Colorado Plateau. (After M.K. Hubbert, Energy Resources, Publication 1000-D, Committee on Natural Resources, National Academy of Sciences— National Research Council, Washington, D.C., 1962.)

increasing uranium supply, as rising uranium prices would justify mining lower grades of ores. Others have put forward a less optimistic view that suggests that uranium reserves are not large enough to support future extensive use of power stations burning ^{235}U. If all the reserves and resources listed in Table 5.2 were used soley for their ^{235}U content and the conversion of heat energy to electricity was 40 percent efficient, the total energy produced would be only 8×10^{20} joules. On the other hand, an equally efficient fast-breeder reactor would be capable of extracting 1140×10^{20} joules, because it can utilize the much more abundant ^{238}U. Stockpiled ^{238}U and known reserves could supply energy through a fast-breeder reactor system for many hundreds of years.

The world's first commercial nuclear reactor at Calder Hall in Cumbria, England, started to supply electricity in 1956. Thirty years later, in 1986, more than 317 reactors in 25 countries were providing over 190,000 megawatts of the world's electricity. The global distribution of reactors shows the anticipated concentration of nuclear plants in the United States, Western Europe, and Japan. A breakdown of nuclear generating capacity in terms of reactor type illustrates both this point and the dominance of the light-water reactors that are so extensively employed in the United States. However, the nuclear generating capacity is often only a relatively small proportion of the total demand for electricity or that estimated until the end of the century. Also, in a number of countries (Sweden, for example), decisions have been taken to reduce or phase out nuclear power over the next few decades. Furthermore, the world is using less than half as much nuclear power as anticipated in 1970, and projections for future use have shrunk even more. The largest cutbacks have been in the United States, although most other countries have curtailed their programs. In 1983, *The Financial Times Energy Economist* reported that, "The day when nuclear power will be the world's leading electricity source now seems to have been postponed indefinitely." Although the unresolved problems surrounding safety, waste disposal, and nuclear weapons proliferation may have contributed to this lack of anticipated growth, the main reason is much simpler. In most countries, nuclear power is no longer economically attractive, both because of rising construction and operating costs and a much smaller growth in the demand for electricity than had been anticipated. Indeed many of the alternative energy sources to be discussed below are now becoming economically viable.

ALTERNATIVE ENERGY SOURCES

Solar Energy

The sun is essential to life and has been the major source of our energy throughout history (recall Fig. 5.1). This has been mainly through its role in biological growth and so in the formation of fuels such as wood, coal, and oil. These fuels (see Chapter 4) provide us with ways of indirectly harvesting energy from the sun. Other indirect ways of harvesting this energy come from the influence of the sun on the atmosphere and hydrosphere. It causes the wind and rain, ocean currents, and temperature differences in the oceans that are discussed

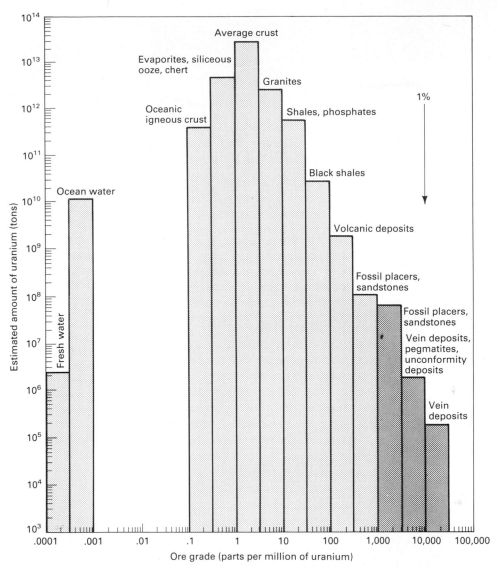

FIGURE 5-12. Diagram showing the distribution of uranium in the earth's crust as a log-log plot of estimated amount of uranium versus ore grade in parts per million of uranium. Bars represent various categories of uranium deposits or repositories of uranium in descending order of uranium content and define a log-normal global abundance curve. The three bars on the right represent deposits of the type now being mined specifically for uranium. The diagram shows that for approximately every ten-fold decrease in grade there is a 30-fold increase in the amount of recoverable uranium.

as sources of energy in later sections of this chapter. The relationships between direct and indirect energy from the sun are summarized in Fig. 5.14.

The term **solar energy** generally refers to the direct utilization of the sun's rays to generate energy in forms that can supply the needs of humankind. This energy can be best considered in two categories: **low-quality energy**—in which ordinary diffuse sunlight is used to produce low temperature forms of energy; and **high-quality energy**—which involves some form of so-

lar concentrator or a physical or chemical process that produces electricity or a fuel such as hydrogen.

The sun has a surface temperature of about 5500°C. From its distance of 1.5×10^8 kilometers, a total of approximately 4×10^{24} joules per year of energy reach the surface of the earth. This energy is mainly as infrared and visible light radiation with lesser amounts of ultraviolet radiation (Fig. 5.15). The amount of each type of radiation reaching the earth's surface depends on the distance that the sun's rays have to travel

FIGURE 5-13. A map to illustrate the worldwide utilization and anticipated future development of nuclear power (as of mid-1986). Countries involved in nuclear power generation are shown with the number of operating commercial nuclear reactors, reactors on order but not yet operating, and percentage of total electricity generated by nuclear energy.

through the atmosphere. This is because direct radiation from the sun is partly scattered and partly absorbed by molecules of various gases, water vapor, and dust in the air. Absorption at infrared wavelengths (>700 nanometers in Fig. 5.15) is due largely to water vapor and, to a lesser extent, carbon dioxide. Absorption at ultraviolet wavelengths (<300 nanometers) is principally due to ozone (O_3). At around noon on a clear day in midlatitudes, the direct radiation from the sun is reduced about 30 percent by these processes. Very cloudy conditions

may reduce direct radiation to less than 1 percent of the value above the atmosphere, but even under cloudy conditions there is appreciable diffuse radiation derived from scattered direct radiation.

Expressed in units of power, solar energy arrives at the surface of the earth at an average rate of 180 watts per square meter, but the range and distribution of the incident solar power in different parts of the globe varies greatly, primarily as a function of latitude (Fig. 5.16). This energy constitutes such a large potential en-

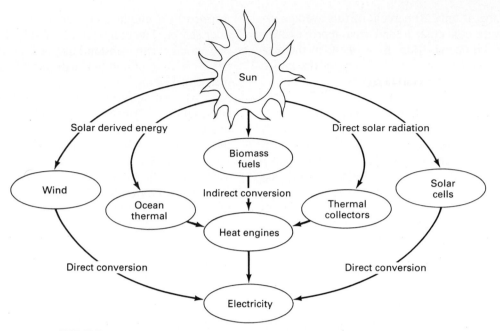

FIGURE 5-14. The ways in which electricity may be obtained from the energy of the sun, either directly or indirectly.

FIGURE 5-15. Energy from the sun (shown both in watts and in microcalories on the vertical scales) as a function of the wavelength of the sun's radiation expressed in both reciprocal centimeters (cm^{-1}, bottom scale) and in nanometers (nm, top scale). The dashed lined shows the total flux of solar energy incident *outside* the atmosphere of the earth (Johnson's solar constant); an amount of 178×10^{12} kilowatts continuous for the whole globe (or 1.5×10^{18} kilowatt-hours per year). The solid line represents the solar flux at *sea level* in direct sunshine for a solar attitude of 30°. The energy is depleted on passing through the atmosphere due to absorption by water vapor, carbon dioxide, oxygen, nitrogen, ozone, and dust particles (in some cases at very specific wavelengths). The average solar energy is reduced in this way to 2.16×10^{17} kilowatt-hours per year. (Data from Task Force Report—Solar Energy, U.S. Federal Energy Administration, 1974.)

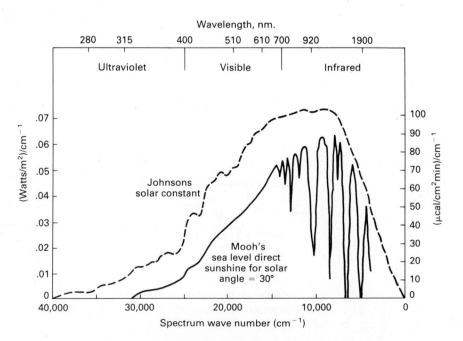

ergy resource, that if only 20 percent of this average incident power were collected, a land area approximately 7×10^4 square kilometers (less than one-fifth the size of California) would be sufficient to supply the entire energy requirements of the United States.

Low-Quality Solar Energy.   The simpler systems used for the direct collection of (unconcentrated) solar energy produce thermal energy of low quality in the sense that the temperatures produced are low (under 100°C) and the amounts of energy collected by any one system are small. In the United States, the thermal energy available for an average day varies from about 5400 kilocalories per square meter in southwestern states such as New Mexico to about 27 kilocalories per square meter in the Northeast and Great Lakes states. This low-quality thermal energy is well suited to many applications, particularly the heating of water and interior space where it is finding increasing use.

A south-facing window is the simplest possible type of solar collector. The sunlight that passes through the glass is absorbed by objects in the room and by the wall, from which it radiates, to warm the air of the room. Provided that good insulation reduces heat losses as much as possible, windows exposed to direct sunlight can maintain comfortable temperatures in a room even on a cold winter day. These simple principles are increasingly being used in the design of buildings—first, by arranging windows to capture sunlight and, second, by providing thermal storage facilities. Thermal storage is accomplished using massive objects, such as rocks, concrete, or containers filled with water, that are also warmed by sunlight and then slowly release their heat after sunset. The combination of solar heating and thermal storage can substantially reduce the heating fuel needs of a building but will rarely provide the sole means of heating.

All heating systems involve the transfer of heat energy, and it is important to recall that this can involve one or more of three mechanisms. Heat can be transferred (1) by **radiation,** in which waves (that may be visible light and infrared radiation) from a hot object such as the sun are absorbed by matter and reconverted into heat; (2) by **convection,** in which heat is carried by the motion of heat masses of matter (e.g., hot water circulating through pipes in a building); and (3) by **conduction,** in which heat is transferred by contact between particles of matter (e.g., from hot water to a metal pipe through which it passes). More elaborate systems for the heating of buildings and water involve purpose-built solar collectors, a heated transfer fluid such as air or water, and a heat storage system such as a large mass of rock or water. The collector is normally a large panel with a blackened collecting surface and with a pane of glass placed over the collecting surface to trap a layer of air above it and reduce heat loss by conduction. This air itself may be used as the heat transfer fluid, or water circulated through tubes that form part of the collecting surface may be used. An example of such a system is shown in Fig. 5.16. Here, water that is heated in the solar panels is circulated through a heat exchanger to transfer this energy (by conduction) to a storage water tank that directly provides the supply to space-heating radiators or to the supply of running water. Such a sys-

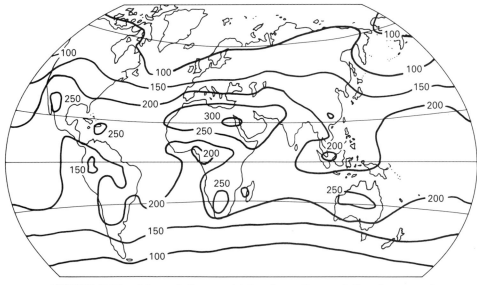

FIGURE 5-16.   Map of the world to show the variation in annual mean solar energy flux (on a horizontal plane). Contours are in watts per square meter.

tem is nearly always coupled with conventional heaters and is controlled by a system of thermostats, valves, and timers to permit the most efficient use of solar and conventional energy. Solar heating systems such as this are not technically complex, but, although operating costs are negligible, they tend to be costly to install. Also, the savings in conventional fuel costs may take many years to repay the investment in a system. Taking an average for the rate at which solar energy arrives at the earth's surface and assuming that the collector is about 50 percent efficient, its daily energy output per square meter will be roughly equivalent to burning one-tenth of a gallon of heating oil in a 70 percent efficient furnace.

One obvious problem in using solar energy for heating buildings is that the greatest needs occur when and where the available sunlight is least. This disadvantage does not apply to solar heating of water for domestic and commercial use, because it is needed throughout the year regardless of climate. A solar water heater of the type shown in Fig. 5.17 can be placed on top of flat-roofed buildings and provide domestic hot water needs throughout the year in a hot climate.

These few examples serve to illustrate the uses of low-quality solar energy. When it is considered that in countries such as those of North America and Europe, about one-third of all the energy consumed is used for space heating and water heating, the potential of this resource becomes clear. Also, the limitations of climate are not as great as may be imagined. Even in countries like Britain and Germany with cool temperate regimes

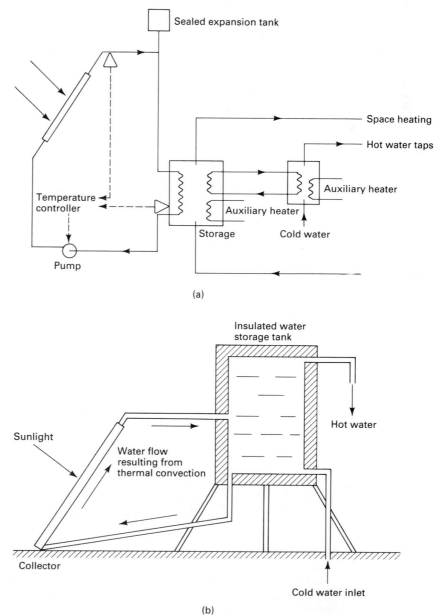

FIGURE 5-17. Domestic solar heating systems providing (a) both space heating and a supply of hot water, and (b) hot water only.

and considerable cloudiness, it would be possible to provide 50 percent of domestic heat by solar energy in most areas. Such systems are not more widely used because the conventional sources of energy are still readily and fairly cheaply available, and the initial cost of changing to any form of solar energy system is high. There is insufficient incentive to the individual house owner to invest in such a system, even though it is both very inexpensive to run and pollution free, but future rises in the cost of conventional resource fuels could likely bring about much more use of solar heating.

High-Quality Solar Energy. The generation of temperatures much above 100°C, or of the substantial amounts of energy required by many industrial operations, involves more sophisticated means of collecting solar energy than those described so far. Two main approaches may be used: the sun's rays may be concentrated using lenses or focusing mirrors, or, alternatively, the radiation may be allowed to fall on a material with which it can interact to produce a chemical reaction or an electric current.

The concentration of sunlight is based on the age-old principle of the burning glass in which a pocket lens can be used to burn a hole in paper by focusing the sun's rays on it. That this principle was known even to the ancients is shown by the story of Archimedes constructing a great burning mirror with which to set fire to the ships of the Roman fleet attacking Syracuse in 212 B.C. One form of system undergoing development today involves a central collecting receiver mounted on top of a high tower. As shown in Fig. 5.18, the sun's rays are reflected up to the receiver by a group of mirrors, called **heliostats,** which are programmed to automatically track the sun and keep its rays focused on the receiver. Temperatures of approximately 1000°C can be generated at the receiver. This receiver could simply be a boiler that generates steam to drive a turbine, or it could be a liquid metal such as sodium that is used to transfer the heat to a thermal storage system that in turn produces the steam for driving a turbine and generating electricity. Such a thermal storage facility, which might be tanks containing salts or hydrocarbon fluids, could maintain steam to drive the turbine during brief periods of cloud cover or extend the operating day for the plant. A prototype facility with 2000 mirrors, each about 20 square feet, has been constructed at Barstow, California, (Fig. 5.19) and can deliver 10^7 watts of electricity during daylight hours. Plants of this type convert the intercepted solar energy to electricity at about 20 percent efficiency. Full-scale plants would be 10 or more times the size of this one and would probably be located in desert regions where land costs are minimal and the quantity of available solar energy is higher than for other regions. The costs of constructing such plants are much more than for conventional fuel-burning power stations, large costs being involved in the mirrors and their control systems. However, as fossil fuel prices increase and design techniques for such large solar power stations improve, they become commercially more attractive.

Another type of solar energy concentrator gener-

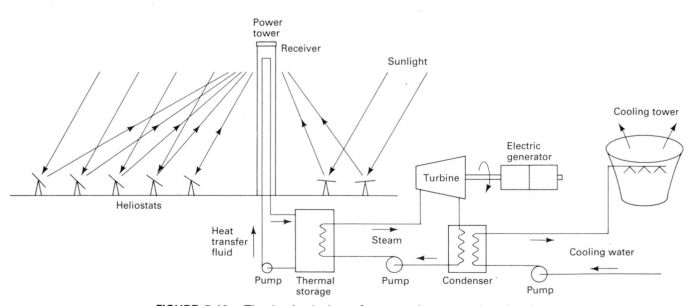

FIGURE 5-18. The basic design of a central tower solar electric power plant in which heliostats direct the sun's rays onto a central receiver. The heat generated is transferred via a fluid to some form of thermal storage facility and used to raise steam and drive turbines.

FIGURE 5-19. Solar One, on the desert floor near Barstow, California, is an array of 1818 heliostats, each with a surface area of 40 square meters (430 square feet). Computers aim the sun-tracking mirrors to reflect sunlight on the central receiver 100 meters above ground. The receiver absorbs solar heat that converts water to steam that drives a turbine to make electricity. (Courtesy of Southern California Edison Company.)

ally suitable for smaller power plants is the **parabolic reflector.** This employs a cylindrical reflector (Fig. 5.20) to focus the sunlight onto a small diameter collecting element, through which a heat-transporting medium such as hydrocarbon or liquid metal is passed. This medium may circulate to a heat storage facility from which heat exchangers extract the energy to make steam and drive turbines. Less complex movements are involved in tracking the sun, and the whole system can be constructed on a smaller scale suitable for a community-sized power generation system. Parabolic reflectors and other types of mirror systems have also been used to construct solar furnaces like the one in the French Pyrenees at Odeillo, where temperatures of up to 4000°C can be reached in a 50 square centimeter hot spot.

Solar energy can be converted directly into electrical energy by **photovoltaic cells.** In these devices, the light energy interacts directly with the electrons of a semiconductor to produce an electric current. These photovoltaic or **solar cells** are manufactured by pro-

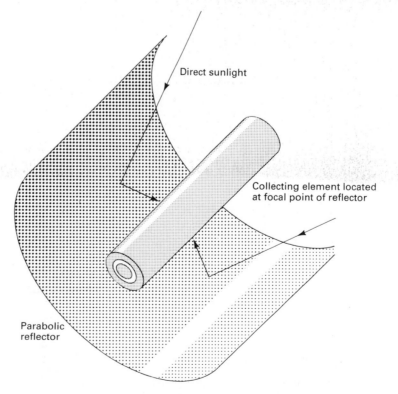

Direct sunlight

Collecting element located at focal point of reflector

Parabolic reflector

FIGURE 5-20. A focusing collector in which a parabolic reflector directs the sun's rays onto a heat transfer fluid located within an evacuated tube to minimize heat losses.

cesses similar to those used in making transistors. A variety of materials can be used, and a common one is silicon (see p. 194). The manufacture of solar cells is a fairly complex and costly business because the compositions of the materials must be carefully controlled, and very thin wafers of appreciable surface area (at least several square centimeters) must be fabricated.

The economics of large-scale power generation using photovoltaic cells is not very attractive at present. The conversion efficiencies of the cells are fairly low: 12–15 percent for single crystal silicon cells and 4–6 percent for the cheaper, but less reliable, cadmium sulfide/copper sulfide cells. Solar cells have the advantage of using the entire solar radiation, both direct and diffuse, and of converting solar energy directly to electricity. However, the direct current electricity produced has to be converted to alternating current, and so some form of storage system is required to provide a continuous source of power. A typical commercial silicon cell with a diameter of 7 centimeters would have an output of about 0.4 watts when operating in direct sunlight on a clear day. Obviously, very large numbers of these cells have to be mounted together in order to generate substantial output, and the cost of manufacture and installation is very great. Assuming an overall conversion efficiency of 10 percent for the complete collection-storage-conversion system, a 1000-megawatt power station in an area such as the southwest United States would require roughly 40 square kilometers of cell surface. Indeed for certain types of solar cells, the energy expended in its manufacture is comparable to that provided by the cell during its working lifetime of a few years. It is not surprising that these cells have mainly been employed as power sources in remote locations (Fig. 5.21) and in specialist applications such as solar-powered calculators. Perhaps the most spectacular success of the solar cell in energy generation has been in the powering of both manned and unmanned space vehicles. More widespread use in routine power generation will only come as new manufacturing methods, and designs reduce the cost by comparison with more conventional methods. Nevertheless, major advances in efficiency and reliability of photovoltaic cells have been made in the last decade, and costs have been falling dramatically along with greatly increased production.

The first major photovoltaic project in the third world was installed in Saudi Arabia in 1981 and generates 350×10^3 watts to meet the electricity needs of 3600 people in three villages. Indeed, it is in providing electricity for small isolated communities that this technology may make its greatest contribution. At the other end of the scale, work has begun on a 100×10^6 watts power plant (by far the world's largest) in Sacramento, California, due for completion in 1994. Judging from present and planned power schemes, total generating

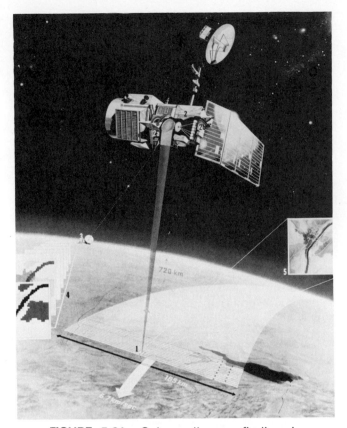

FIGURE 5-21. Solar cells are finding increasing use in remote locations on the earth and on communications satellites. The wings of the satellite shown above are arrays of solar power cells. (Courtesy of COMSAT.)

capacity the end of the century may be 500–10,000 megawatts, only a small fraction of the world's electricity. However, based on the evidence of present growth rates, some experts predict that photovoltaics may be providing 20–30 percent of the world's electricity by the middle of the twentyfirst century. One futuristic proposal for massive power generation involves earth satellites in stationary orbit with very large arrays of photovoltaic cells that collect solar energy that is then transmitted to earth by microwave beams (Fig. 5.22).

Certain chemical reactions, known as **photochemical reactions,** take place by utilizing light energy, just as many reactions only occur when energy is supplied in the form of heat. The energy used in these reactions may then be held within the products of the reaction as part of the bond energy and may be released later when, for example, these products are combusted as a fuel. The best known example of this is **photosynthesis,** the process in which carbon dioxide from the atmosphere and water are combined to form carbohydrates and more complex organic molecules with the liberation of oxygen. The resulting plant material, such as wood or the fossilized products of this vegetation (oil and coal), can be burned as fuels. Other ways in which biological ma-

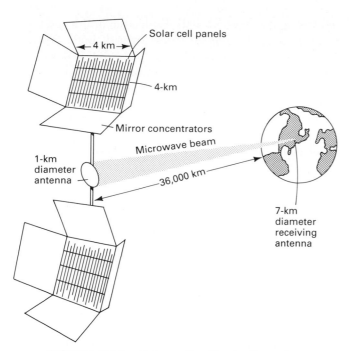

FIGURE 5-22. Schematic illustration of a satellite solar power station. Solar radiation is collected by large arrays of photovoltaic cells, and the electrical energy generated is transmitted to earth by a microwave beam.

terials may provide energy are discussed in a later section of this chapter. However, certain recent research work has concentrated on using energy from the sun to bring about chemical reactions in simpler systems and to synthesize fuels. The ideal reaction, if it could ever be made to work in this way, is the breakdown of water,

$$H_2O \text{ (liquid)} \longrightarrow H_2 \text{ (gas)} + 1/2O_2 \text{ (gas)} \qquad (5.4)$$

The hydrogen gas (H_2) produced would provide an excellent fuel for burning to generate electricity and, of course, the starting material is abundantly available! However, the heat energy required to breakdown water involves temperatures of 2500°C (which can be achieved in solar furnaces). Research workers have been looking for compounds that could be added to the water to cause the breakdown to occur simply by absorption of the sun's rays (i.e., to **catalyse** the reaction). Promising materials (such as a ruthenium complex resembling chlorophyll, the key compound in biological photosynthesis) have been found but require more development. Other researchers are attempting to reproduce photochemical reactions using molecules much more like those used by biological systems. Whether any of these methods will ever become commercially significant will depend not only on their workability but also on their efficiency and the complexity and cost of producing the necessary chemicals.

A potential method for the transformation of solar energy directly to electrical energy, and which involves photochemical processes, is **photoelectrochemical conversion.** This involves directing the sun's rays onto an electrochemical cell, rather like the wet battery cell used to store electrical energy in the modern automobile. Whereas in the normal electrochemical cell the electrical current is generated solely by chemical reactions, in the **photogalvanic** cell, a photochemical reaction is involved. It is also possible to use such a photogalvanic cell to bring about the breakdown of water and to produce hydrogen. All these cells are still the subject of research and development. That the problems are considerable is illustrated by the fact that the French chemist Becquerel, grandfather of the man who discovered radioactivity in 1895, first discovered the photovoltaic effect in 1839, but it has yet to find a significant technological application.

Hydroelectric, Wind, Wave, Ocean, and Tidal Power

Nature transforms the solar energy reaching the earth into several other forms of energy. About 23 percent of incoming solar radiation is consumed in evaporating the water that subsequently falls as rain and snow (Fig. 5.1). In effect, the sun acts as a great pump drawing water from the sea and dropping it onto the land, from where it runs downward to the sea. Flowing water is therefore a renewable resource. A further 46 percent of incoming solar energy is absorbed by the oceans, land, and atmosphere. This energy warms the seas and produces ocean currents, winds, and waves. At least some of this can be considered a renewable, potential energy resource.

Water and wind power have both been used in small ways such as water wheels and windmills for many thousands of years. Water wheels were known to the ancient Greeks, but their capacity was very small. Toward the end of the eighteenth century, the largest water wheels for industrial use did not exceed 10 horsepower. Nevertheless, they were a major source of power prior to development of the steam engine that heralded the start of the industrial revolution in Europe. However, it was only at the beginning of the twentieth century that large-scale damming of rivers commenced for generation of electricity.

Hydroelectric Power. **Hydroelectricity,** the electricity generated by the force of flowing water, is usually produced at large dams (see p. 312). Dams are constructed to increase the height from which the water drops (or the head of water) and to provide a constant flow of water through turbines that, in turn, drive electrical generators. Because falling water is a form of mechanical energy directly used to drive the turbines, the two-stage process involved is 80–90 percent efficient in converting that energy to electricity. In fuel-powered

generating stations, the heat produced by burning the fuel has first to be converted to mechanical energy by raising steam to drive turbines, which are then used to drive electrical generators. The efficiency of this three-stage process is much less (approximately 40 percent for fossil fuels and 30 percent for nuclear fuels). Where the construction of a dam is not always practical, water may be routed to turbines via canals or large pipes as in the power plant at Niagara Falls, New York. Hydroelectric power stations are generally very large, because large quantities of water are needed to produce even modest amounts of energy. For example, for an elevation change of 50 meters (approximately the height of Niagara Falls), 8 metric tons of water must flow through a turbine to produce 1 kilowatt of electricity.

If a reservoir is present as part of a hydroelectric system, the impounded water acts as a form of stored energy. Also, since hydroelectric systems can be started almost instantaneously, this energy can be made available as electricity at very short notice and serve as a very effective backup system for plants using other sources of energy. An extension of this idea, now used in a number of countries, is the **pumped-water storage system** (Fig. 5.23). When excess electricity is available within a linked network of power plants (often at night), water is pumped from a lower reservoir or storage area to a higher one and is then available to drive turbines and produce electricity when needed.

The installed hydroelectric generating capacity around the world has been steadily increasing throughout this century (Table 5.3). In certain countries, it accounts for a substantial proportion of the electrical energy produced. In the United States, 15 percent of electrical energy is produced from hydroelectric plants, and three times as much water flows daily through hydroelectric plants as is discharged by all rivers into the sea (because of pumped storage and the presence of more than one dam on many rivers). However, the percentage of this energy source currently developed worldwide is still very small. Evaluation of this resource involves an assessment of the amount of water flowing in streams and rivers and how far downhill it flows before reaching the sea. One estimate of the world's potential for generating electricity by water power is 29×10^{12} watts and the distribution of this worldwide is shown in Table 5.3. At present, less than 15 percent of this power has been developed, but if it were fully developed, the energy produced each year would be 0.9×10^{20} joule, about one-third of the total energy now consumed and larger than the world's presently installed electrical generating capacity.

Even if the world's community would accept the total damming of its great river systems, the dams have finite and, sometimes, rather short lifetimes. All rivers carry large masses of suspended sediment that is deposited as soon as the stream is dammed. Depending on the sediment load, many reservoirs will be completely filled by sediment in periods ranging from 50–200 years. For example, the Great Aswan High Dam on the Nile built in the 1960s will be at least half silted up by the year 2025. Hydroelectric power may be renewable, therefore, but the sites for its generation are nonrenewable. The second point, that is a favorable one, can be seen from Table 5.3. The world's largest undeveloped potential lies in South America and Africa. Inasmuch as these continents have small fossil fuel resources, it is fortunate that their water power should be plentiful. The long-term future for hydroelectric power in the Southern Hemisphere must be considered very promising.

Wind Power.   Wind has been tapped as an energy source for thousands of years, both through sails on ships and through windmills to lift waters and to grind grain. Among the largest windmills were those used in Holland (Fig. 5.24) and which have become the picturesque symbol of that country. Smaller windmills were extensively used throughout the United States for pumping water before electricity became available and

TABLE 5.3

International hydroelectric power generation

Area	Total runoff potential* watts $\times 10^{11}$	Exploited potential** watts $\times 10^{11}$	Potential exploited percent	Power generation in 1984*** kilowatt hours $\times 10^9$
Asia and Europe	10.8	1.7	16	675
Africa	7.8	0.2	3	65
South and Central America	5.8	0.3	5	251
North America	3.1	1.3	42	628
Oceania	1.1	0.1	9	323
TOTAL	28.6	3.6	13	1942

*From M.K. Hubbert, "Energy Resources, A Report to the Committee of Natural Resources," National Academy of Sciences–National Research Council, Publication 1000D, 1962.

**From World Energy Supplies as reprinted in Worldwatch Institute Paper No. 44, 1981.

***From Energy Information Administration, *Annual Energy Review 1985.*

FIGURE 5-23. Hydroelectric pump storage facilities such as this one in Bath County, Virginia, generate electricity when water falling through large tunnels in the dam turns turbines. At times of low electricity demand, excess electricity generated in other fossil fuel or nuclear power plants is used to pump water into the reservoir so that it is available to generate power at peak demand times. (Courtesy of Virginia Power.)

FIGURE 5-24. The traditional windmills of Holland have been used to harness wind energy for grinding grain and sawing wood since the middle of the thirteenth century. They also played an important role in shaping the Dutch landscape, because from 1414 to the present day they have been used to pump lakes dry and lower the water table to create the low-lying agricultural areas known as polders. (Courtesy of Royal Netherlands Embassy.)

FIGURE 5-25. Modern windmills or wind turbines for use in generation of electricity. In the foreground, the so-called Darrieus wind turbine is a vertical axis machine, whereas the propeller-type machine in the background is a more conventional design. (Courtesy of Southern California Edison Company.)

are still used in many parts of the world. However, the power output under optimal conditions of even the large Dutch-type windmills is considerably less than that produced by a small automobile engine.

In 1895, the first wind-electric system was built in Denmark. By 1910 several hundred small wind-powered generators (5000 to 25,000 watts) were in operation in that country. It was not until 1931, however, when the Soviet Union built a 100,000 watt unit near Yalta, that a really large wind turbine expressly designed for producing electricity was constructed. The United States built a two-bladed, 175-foot diameter, propeller-like turbine at Grandpa's Knob, Vermont, that produced 1.25×10^6 watts in a 30 miles per hour (13.4 meters per second) wind, a machine that was tested between 1941 and 1945. Since that time, a great variety of windmill designs have been proposed and some tested using models and prototypes. An example is a machine with a blade nearly 70 meters in diameter and rated at 2×10^6 watts (at 11.5 meters per second) that was built in North Carolina in 1979. An unexpected problem developed, however, when this unit generated a low frequency hum that kept many people in the nearby community awake at night. Efforts to stop the sound were never successful, and the windmill was shut and dismantled after a mechanical failure. A very different design, sometimes called the Darrieus wind turbine, is a

vertical axis machine (Fig. 5.25) that is less efficient but can be built to an even larger size. The United States, Canada, and many of the northern European countries have programs for the development and installation of larger machines. Indeed, in the United States, the wind Energy Systems Act of 1980 initiated an 8-year, $900 million program to develop wind power systems. A consequence of this has been the sudden growth in **wind farms**—clusters of turbines connected to the electric grid—in parts of the United States. Although the world's first commercial wind farm began generating power in New Hampshire in 1981, the major developments since then have been in California, a state blessed with mountain passes that provide ideal wind farm sites. With farms like the one at Altamont Pass (Fig. 5.26), where over 2000 machines generate up to 142×10^6 watts, the goal is to supply 8 percent of the state's electricity from wind power by the end of the century.

What then is the likely future of wind power for large-scale energy generation? There are certainly a number of problems with this technology. The most obvious is that winds blow intermittently and do not readily lend themselves to large-scale power schemes in many parts of the world. (Windmills typically operate between 35–60 percent of the time.) What makes this problem more acute is that a wind turbine has to be designed for maximum output at a particular sustained

FIGURE 5-26. The U.S. Department of Energy operates an experimental wind farm with more than 2000 windmills at Altamont Pass, near San Francisco. (Courtesy of U.S. Department of Energy.)

wind speed. A turbine designed for producing a maximum power output with a wind speed of 10 meters per second, for example, would have an output only one-eighth of this at half the wind speed (5 meters per second). Furthermore, above 10 meters per second wind speed the output would not be increased, the unit already being at maximum power, and at about double the optimum wind speed the blades are feathered and power generation cuts out altogether. Further problems are associated with the siting of windmills, both technical and environmental. Because of the problems of land costs in the more populated areas where electric power is required, problems with radio and television interference, noise generation, and general disruption of the environment by these large machines, it has been suggested that they might be erected at sea (as, for example, in one British plan to create offshore farms in the windy North Sea). The number of windmills required for a major power generation program would be very large. For example, the generation of 4×10^9 watts in California (8 percent of state requirements) will require the placing of between 10,000 and 100,000 machines occupying an estimated 615 square kilometers of land. Despite these problems, the future appears good for wind power, with experts predicting that wind farms will have an economic advantage over coal and nuclear power plants in many parts of the world by the 1990s. The smaller scale uses of wind power, as in transportation at sea, recreation, and farm use, have long had many applications, and experts also predict a resurgence of small-scale windmills and related devices in the future. We may see a rebirth of the large sailing ship in forms that use not only sails but wind turbines designed to drive propellers (Fig. 5.27). Indeed, a Japanese prototype cargo ship employs computer-controlled sails made of canvas on steel frames that can provide 58 percent of the power when the fully laden ship is travelling at 12 knots in a 30-knot wind.

Wave Power. Wave power is closely related to wind power because waves arise from winds blowing over the ocean. Waves contain much more energy than winds of equal velocity because the mass of water involved is more than 800 times that of the same volume of air. A single wave that is 1.8 meters high, moving in water 9 meters deep, generates approximately 10^4 watts for each meter of wavefront. Vast amounts of energy (estimated to be as much as 2.7×10^{12} kilowatt hours per year) are continuously being dissipated on the shorelines of the world. Although wave power has been used to ring bells and blow whistles for navigational aids for many years, large-scale energy recovery has only recently been considered. Over the past decade, many research groups have developed designs and tested small-scale prototypes that they have claimed could generate electricity at costs competitive with conventional power stations. One example is the Sea Energy Associates (SEA) Clam illustrated in Fig. 5.28 that consists of a series of flexible air bags mounted along a long hollow spine of reinforced concrete. Passing waves compress the bags and force the air into and out of the spine through a turbine. The self-rectifying turbine, which turns in the same direction whether the air is moving in or out, drives a conventional electric generator. Other devices involve floating rafts that transmit the mechanical energy of wave motion to hydraulic pumps that power a generator, and rigid concrete structures in which a column of air is trapped in such a way that the

FIGURE 5-27. The *Minilace,* shown above, is an experimental modern cargo ship that uses a sail as well as a conventional engine. The sail can increase speed and decrease fuel consumption and hence significantly increase efficiency. (Courtesy of the Wind Ship Development Company.)

volume changes as waves pass, forcing the air through a turbine.

There is no shortage of ideas on how to harness wave power for the generation of electricity. What at present seems not to be available are the funds to put these ideas into full-scale operation. It has been estimated, for example, that a 2×10^9 watts wave power SEA Clam system, comparable to a large conventional power station, would require 320 of these devices along 130 kilometers of coastline. The cost would be considerable, estimated at more than $5000 million at 1987 prices. Because of the cost and because the ultimate potential of wave power is still unclear, groups like the British Central Electricity Generating Board, having

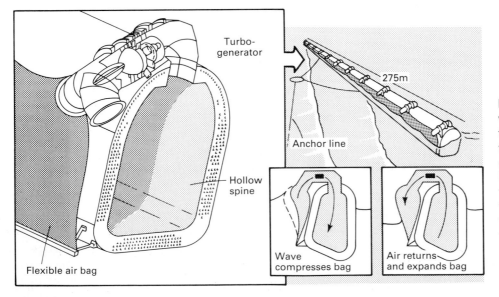

FIGURE 5-28. The SEAClam wave energy converter, one of the proposed systems designed to harness wave energy in power generation. The diagram shows how wave motion compresses a flexible bag and forces air through a small self-rectifying turbine into the hollow spine, air which then expands back out. As shown, large numbers of individual units would be assembled in line to form a generating station.

supported the relatively low cost, early development of wave power devices, have not yet provided the funds to build more costly prototypes.

Ocean Power.   The term *ocean power* usually refers to a system of **Ocean Thermal Energy Conversion** (OTEC). The sun warms the surface waters of the ocean, and this water, being less dense than the cold water at depth, remains near the surface. A temperature gradient is created as shown in Fig. 5.29, and if the water at the two temperatures can be brought together, we have the basis for a heat engine that can generate electricity. The difficulty is the relatively small temperature difference involved, only about 20°C from top to bottom even in the tropics. Although the thermal efficiencies would only be 2–3 percent, the very large reservoir of heat in the oceans should make such a plant feasible. Small pilot plants have been setup and operated earlier

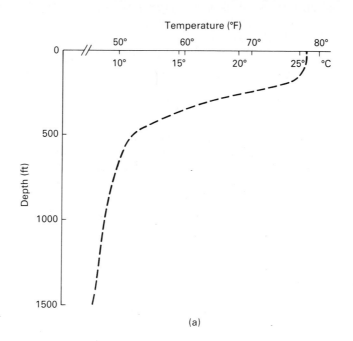

(a)

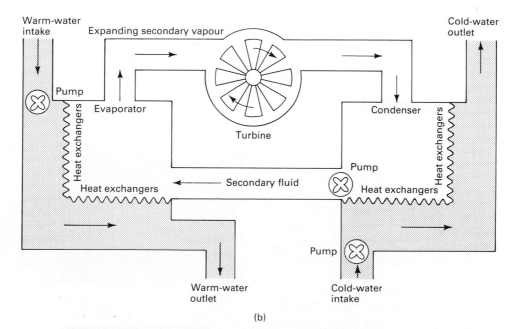

(b)

FIGURE 5-29.   The OTEC approach to energy generation. (a) Typical temperature variation with depth in the ocean in equatorial regions. This difference is used as the basis for a heat engine cycle of the type illustrated in (b).

this century in Cuba and on the west African coast and demonstrate that OTEC is possible in principle.

Most of the recent development efforts have centered on using a closed-cycle turbine employing a fluid such as ammonia that boils at a low temperature (25°C) but at a much higher pressure than water. As shown in Fig. 5.29, the warm surface water is used to heat the fluid and vaporize it so that it expands through the turbine. It is then condensed back to liquid by contact with cold water pumped from the ocean depths. A power plant would probably be enclosed in a submerged unit floating beneath the ocean surface. Electric power generated from the turbine could be transmitted ashore via submarine cables and possibly used at the site of the plant to produce hydrogen by the electrolysis of water, the hydrogen then being shipped away in tankers.

Whether large-scale schemes using OTEC are economic remains uncertain, and cost estimates vary widely. Unresolved problems include technical aspects of construction, corrosion and encrustation of the machinery with marine life, and the environmental impact of OTEC plants. Supporters say that bringing cold nutrient-rich water to the surface would increase fish catches in the area around a plant. Surface sea temperatures play a major role in the earth's climate, however, and the effects of a large network of OTEC's would need careful investigation. If all these problems were to be solved, a very large source of energy would be made available. Just how large is difficult to estimate because it depends on the efficiency of the generating plant. Even if it were less than 1 percent efficient, the ocean's thermal energy potential exceeds the potential from fossil fuels. Another novel use of the ocean's deep cold waters (approximately 4°C) does not involve electrical generation but makes use of the water's low temperatures as a refrigerant to preserve foods such as flour and corn and to serve as a tropical air-conditioning system.

Tidal Energy. Tidal energy differs from the other energy sources since it is not derived ultimately from the heat of the sun. The ocean's tides are the result of the gravitational pull of both the moon and sun on the earth and its oceans. The changes in ocean height resulting from the rhythmic rise and fall of tides can be used to drive a water turbine connected to an electric generator. However, only in certain parts of the world is the tidal rise and fall sufficient to justify constructing a power plant. The best areas, where tidal ranges exceed 10 meters, include the Bay of Fundy, the English Channel, the Patagonian coast of Argentina, the Murmansk coast (Barents Sea), and the coast of the Sea of Okhotsk (north of Japan). This is because the effect of ocean bottom shape and contours of the shorelines enhances tidal rise and fall; elsewhere, the range is generally much less.

The harnessing of tides is not a new idea, because for several centuries beginning in 1580, 6.5-meter diameter water wheels installed under London Bridge used the tidal rise and fall of the River Thames to pump water for London. At present, the only large-scale tidal power station in the world is at the Rance Estuary on the Britanny coast of France (Fig. 5.30). This site has a peak electricity generating capacity of 240×10^6 watts, but because of the rhythmic nature of tides, the average capacity is only 62×10^6 watts. The system involves isolating the estuary from the ocean by a barrage containing turbines and floodgates. At high tide a reservoir behind the barrage is allowed to fill; then the floodgates are closed as the tide goes out. At low tide the elevation of water in the reservoir exceeds that of the ocean by roughly the tidal range. The water can then be used to drive a water turbine and generate electricity in much the same way as a conventional hydroelectric plant. The reservoir level then drops to that of the ocean at low tide, and, if the turbine passages are closed as the tide comes in, the difference in elevation between the high ocean and lower reservoir water levels can also be used to generate power by opening the turbines to fill the reservoir. In this way, power is obtained at high and low tides roughly four times a day.

Tidal power is limited in the number of sites around the world that could be developed and in the total amount of energy potentially available. Development of all the suitable sites would only generate about 16×10^9 watts, or less than 1 percent of the world's present total usage of electric power.

The oceans do contain other sources of energy in the form of the great surface currents. The Gulf Stream, for example, has mechanical power from its flow equal

FIGURE 5-30. The dam built across the Rance estuary on the French coast is equipped with flood gates and turbines, visible at the right side. As the tides rise and fall, the flow of water in and out through the turbines generates electricity. (Photograph courtesy of Electricité de France.)

to 2.2 × 10^{14} watts (or 7 × 10^{21} joules) per year. Speculative proposals have been put forward for harnessing this vast renewable resource, such as the mooring of massive (170-meter diameter) turbines in the ocean off the coast of Florida (Fig. 5.31). The flexible turbine blades would rotate at one revolution per minute, and it is estimated that 230 such turbines could extract 1 × 10^{10} watts, enough to supply Florida's current electricity needs. Another, as yet totally unexploited source of energy in the oceans involves their salinity, or rather the salinity difference between fresh (river) and salt (ocean) water. The difference in **osmotic pressure** between these two natural waters can produce a positive flow through a suitable membrane that could be used to raise salt water that could then be discharged through a turbine to generate power.

Geothermal Energy

Except for the near-surface rocks where weather and ground water conditions exert major influences, temperatures increase with depth in the earth. The rate of temperature increase varies from place to place. Measurements made in deep drill holes around the world show **geothermal gradients** ranging from 15°C to 75°C (with an average of 25°C) per kilometer beneath the surface. Temperature increases are believed to level off at depths of about 100 kilometers with estimates of temperatures in the earth's mantle being around 1000°C and in the core around 5000°C or more. From this it is clear that a vast amount of heat energy is stored within the earth.

The slow but continuous outward flow of heat from the earth averages 6.3 × 10^{-6} joules per square centimeter per second, or 32.3 × 10^{12} joules per second (32.3 × 10^{12} watts) over the entire surface of the earth. The total amount is vast but very diffuse, and the quantity reaching the surface is equivalent to little more than one three-thousandth of the heat received from the sun. If all the heat escaping from 1 square meter could somehow be gathered and used to heat a cup of water, it would take 4 days and nights to bring it to the boil.

Despite the heat loss, the earth is not cooling; new heat is added continually. Several naturally radioactive isotopes, principally uranium -238, uranium -235, thorium -232, and potassium -40, occur in trace amounts throughout the earth. Each time a radioactive atom disintegrates, a very small amount of heat is released. For example, atoms in an average igneous rock in the continental crust release 9.4 × 10^{-8} calorie (3.93 × 10^{-7} joules) per gram per day. Although this is not much, summed over the whole earth it is enough to maintain a nearly constant average temperature distribution. The rate at which new heat is added is so low that we could never harness it, but the accumulated heat from millions of years can be used. However, if it is used at a faster rate than it is replenished, geothermal heat must be considered a nonrenewable resource.

How can geothermal energy be recovered? In certain special circumstances, especially along major tectonic plate boundaries, nature has already provided the answer to this question. In some areas, such as in the vicinity of active volcanoes, abnormally hot rocks are

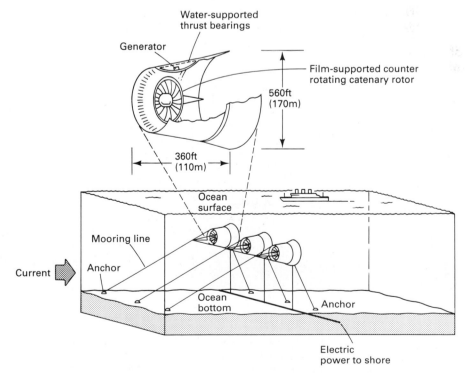

FIGURE 5-31. Proposed design and mooring arrangements of rim-driven turbines for use in generating electrical power from ocean currents.

found close to the surface. Ground water slowly seeping downward is heated and may reemerge as geysers or hot springs (Fig. 5.32 (a) and (b)). Regions where this occurs are known as **geothermal fields** and are of three types. The first is a field of low temperature water (≤85°C) that cannot be used efficiently in the generation of power but can be used for spaceheating in homes, industry, and greenhouses. Resorts specializing in hot baths, as in the famous spa towns that were popular in eighteenth and nineteenth century Europe, have long used geothermal hot springs. In Hungary and France, geothermal water is still used to heat homes, and in Reykjavik, Iceland, the entire city is heated by geothermal hot water. Although throughout the world more than 10^9 watts of low temperature thermal power is derived from geothermal wells, nearly half of this is in Iceland.

The geothermal energy that is used today as a source of power occurs in either **dry-steam** (vapor-dominated) or **wet-steam** (liquid-dominated) fields. Dry-steam fields occur in geothermal settings where the temperature is high and the water under little more than atmospheric pressure. The water boils underground, making steam that fills fractures and pores in the rock and that can be tapped directly by wells drilled into the field. Examples of major dry-steam fields are Larderello in northern Italy that has been producing power since 1904, and the Geysers field in California [about 145 kilometers (90 miles) north of San Francisco] where the first geothermal power plant in the United States was commissioned in 1960 (Fig. 5.33). By 1983, 17 power plants were providing over 1×10^9 watts capacity. In the more common wet-steam fields, the reservoir of hot water (in effect, a **brine**) is under high pressure and may reach temperatures approaching 400°C without boiling. The most famous wet-steam field is at Wairakei in New Zealand.

The use of geothermal fields in electricity generation is shown in Table 5.4. In 1983, more than 130 geothermal power plants were operating in over a dozen countries and producing in excess of 3×10^9 watts. Thus, the total amount of power generated in this way is very small compared to world needs, and the areas where geothermal power has been developed are those

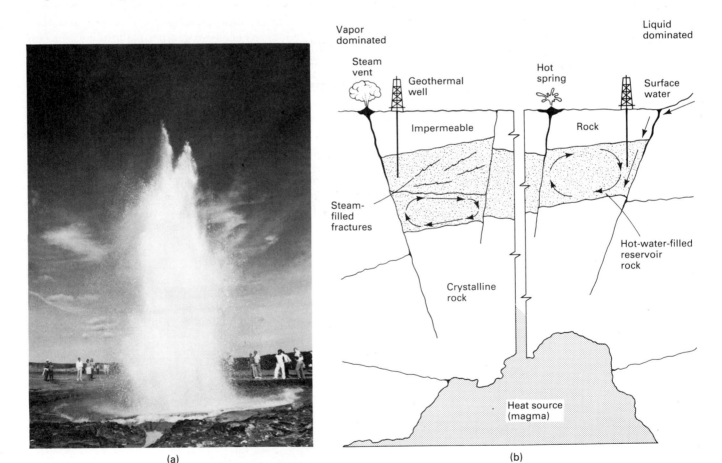

(a)   (b)

FIGURE 5-32. (a) Geothermal energy is locally evidenced by natural geysers such as those in Yellowstone Park, Wyoming. (Courtesy of J.D. Rimstidt.) (b) Schematic diagram to show the geological features of **dry-steam** and **wet-steam** geothermal fields.

FIGURE 5-33. The Geysers power plant north of San Francisco, California, is the largest complex of geothermal power plants in the world. The plant began operation in 1960 and generated more than two million kilowatts by 1980. The steam rising from stainless steel lined drill holes reaches the surface at more than 355°F and is used to spin turbines to generate electricity. (Courtesy of Pacific Gas and Electric Company.)

of volcanic activity; chiefly, ringing the Pacific, in Iceland, and in the central Mediterranean. No doubt, other sources will be developed, but they are likely to be localized in the areas of active volcanism.

A number of systems are being used or have been proposed for the conversion of geothermal energy into electricity. Four of them are illustrated in a simple way in Fig. 5.34. The first is a direct steam cycle of the type used at dry-steam fields such as Larderello and the Geysers. Steam brought out of the ground here is clean enough to go directly into the turbine after which it is condensed and may simply be returned to the ground. The flash steam approach is used in most of the wet-steam fields, and here the release of pressure in the flash chamber results in the spontaneous generation of the steam to drive the turbines, with the condensed steam again being returned to the ground. Two more advanced cycles have been developed for maximum efficiency at lower temperatures. In the flash binary system, the wet-

steam is flashed and vaporizes a working fluid (usually a hydrocarbon) that is expanded through the turbine in a closed circuit, maintaining a clean, long-life turbine. In the liquid-liquid binary system, the brines are not allowed to flash, and heat is transferred to a working fluid to drive the turbine. This reduces some of the problems caused by flashing the brine and also isolates the hydrogen sulfide (H_2S), commonly found in such brines, from the atmosphere. In both cases, the condensed brine is returned to the ground. The practice of simply discharging the condensed brine is a wasteful one that is gradually being replaced by the use of flash distillation to desalinate and produce usable freshwater, or even by the extraction of valuable salts and minerals from the brines.

Several other potential geothermal resources exist, but the technology to exploit them has yet to be developed. The first, sometimes called **geopressured zones,** involves pockets of hot water and methane trapped un-

---

TABLE 5.4

Geothermal power plants operating worldwide as of 1986.*

Country	Dry Steam units	Dry Steam megawatts	Flash and Binary Types units	Flash and Binary Types megawatts	Total megawatts
United States	26	1788	31	218	2006
Philippines	—	—	23	894	894
Mexico	2	10	12	635	645
Italy	41	500	4	5	505
Japan	1	22	8	193	215
New Zealand	—	—	10	167	167
El Salvador	—	—	3	95	95
Kenya	—	—	3	45	45
Iceland	—	—	5	39	39
Nicaragua	—	—	1	35	35
Indonesia	2	30	1	2	32
Other**	—	—	20	55	55
TOTALS	72	2350	118	2383	4733

*From R. DiPoppo, Geothermal Power Plants, Worldwide Status–1986, *Geothermal Resources Council Bulletin,* vol. 15, Nov. 1986, p. 3–14.
**Includes Turkey (21 mw), China (15 mw), Soviet Union (11 mw), France, Guadeloupe (4 mw), Portugal, Azores (3 mw), and Greece (2 mw).

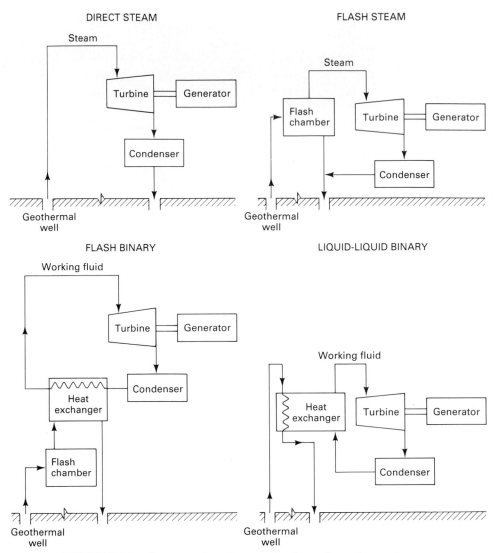

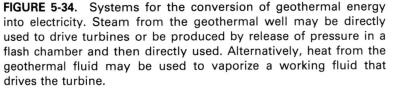

FIGURE 5-34. Systems for the conversion of geothermal energy into electricity. Steam from the geothermal well may be directly used to drive turbines or be produced by release of pressure in a flash chamber and then directly used. Alternatively, heat from the geothermal fluid may be used to vaporize a working fluid that drives the turbine.

der high pressure and at fairly high temperature (approximately 175°C) in deep sedimentary basins. Examples occur in the United States along the coasts of Louisiana and Texas at depths between 1200–8000 meters. It is hoped that energy could be extracted from this resource via three routes: the geothermal heat of the water, the hydraulic energy of the water under high pressure (approximately 2000 pounds per square inch at surface), and the gas dissolved in the water. However, test wells drilled in 1979–1981 proved disappointing in terms of water temperatures, gas content, and the extent of this resource. The second is usually called **hot dry rock,** and as the name implies, involves extracting the heat from dry rocks at depth. Unlike geopressured zones that

are limited in extent, the hot dry rock resource is potentially very large worldwide and does not require the rather exceptional geological conditions associated with geothermal fields.

Many parts of the earth's surface are underlain by rocks such as granite that generate more heat than the average because of the relatively greater amounts of radioactive atoms they contain or by igneous intrusions that still retain excess heat from the time of their emplacement. The most probable means of exploiting the heat energy involves drilling two boreholes into a mass of granite and then explosively or hydraulically fracturing the zone between the bottoms of the two holes. Water is then pumped down the first hole, passing though

the fractured rocks, taking heat from them, and returned up the second hole to be used for electricity generation in the usual way on reaching the surface (Fig. 5.35). This method of power generation is not as simple as it sounds. To reach regions with temperatures greater than 200°C generally requires wells around 5–7 kilometers deep that are expensive and difficult to drill. Furthermore the transmission of fluids between the input and output wells has been plagued with problems, and at the low steam temperatures involved, present turbines are only about 10 percent efficient. Nevertheless, the

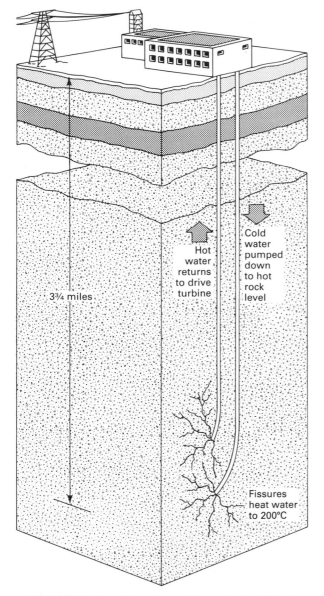

FIGURE 5-35. The generation of electricity using hot dry rock geothermal energy. Cold water is pumped down the well, heated in passing through fissures in the fractured hot rocks at depth, and then returns to the surfaces to be used to drive turbines.

technical problems can, in some cases, be overcome as shown by a full-depth pilot plant at Los Alamos that generated 6×10^4 watts from granite at 3000 meters. For the ultimate future of geothermal energy it is also possible to consider drilling into molten magma chambers or exploiting dry rocks at greater depths in areas of only average geothermal gradient.

The extraction of energy from geothermal fields is well established, but as we have seen, it is a resource that is limited geographically and probably also in terms of worldwide reserves. The U.S. Geological Survey estimates that down to a depth of 3 kilometers, which seems to be a limit for the occurrence of big geothermal fields, the worldwide reserves are 8×10^9 joules. Such a small amount suggests that this type of geothermal energy will be locally important, but globally insignificant. The total heat energy in the pools is, of course, much larger than 8×10^9 joules, but the estimate takes account of the low efficiency with which electricity can be generated from geothermal steam. Experience in Iceland, New Zealand, and Italy suggests that no more than 1 percent of the energy in a pool can be effectively recovered.

Reserves of energy in geothermal fields represent only a tiny fraction of all geothermal heat. Experts cannot agree how much of the remainder should be considered a potential resource. A map of the United States showing areas and types of potential geothermal resources suggests a very large amount (Fig. 5.36). However, the technological problems involved in exploiting even a very small fraction of this geothermal energy are likely to be considerable and the costs prohibitive. In the case of Britain, for example, it has been estimated that to meet between 1 and 2 percent of the national demand for electricity by the year 2000 would require 120 pairs of holes 6000 meters deep costing nearly $2 billion for drilling alone.

Energy from Biological Materials and Waste Products

The staple energy sources in many parts of the developing world are not the fossil fuels or nuclear power plants of the developed nations but are wood and animal dung. In the advanced societies, methods are being developed to convert organic wastes and otherwise useless plant materials into more usable forms for energy production. The name given to these wastes, which include manure, sewage, forms of urban refuse, and waste products from crop cultivation and forestry, is **biomass.** Considerable quantities of biomass wastes generated by technologically advanced societies are illustrated by the estimated annual figures for the United States shown in Table 5.5 (The methods of extracting energy from wastes other than biomass have already been discussed in Chapter 3.)

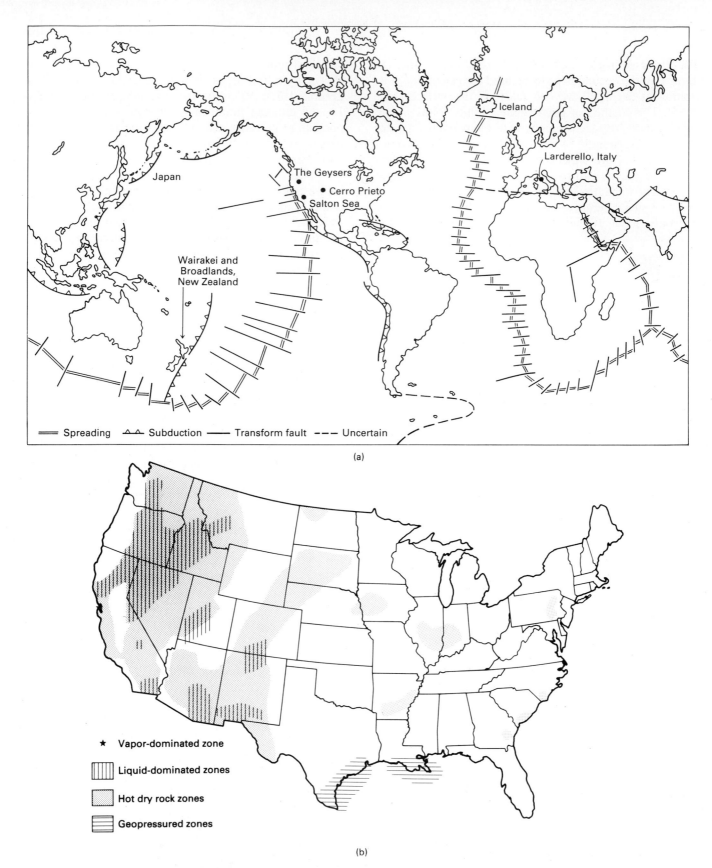

Spreading ‖ △△ Subduction ─── Transform fault ‒‒‒ Uncertain

(a)

★ Vapor-dominated zone

▮ Liquid-dominated zones

▒ Hot dry rock zones

▤ Geopressured zones

(b)

FIGURE 5-36. (a) The major geothermal areas of the world occur along the major lithospheric plate boundaries. (b) A map of the United States showing the location and types of geothermal resources.

TABLE 5-5

Approximate values of waste biomass collected in the United States

Sources	Millions Dry Tons/Yr
Municipal	170
Raw sewage	60
Forestry	120
Field crops/processing residues	64
Manure	174
TOTAL LAND BIOMASS	588

A variety of processes are being developed for the conversion of biomass into fuels, and Fig. 5.37 illustrates several of the basic routes. For example, a fermentation process known as **anaerobic digestion** can be used to convert biomass into methane that can be directly substituted for natural gas. The technology is now available to produce methane gas in this way at costs similar to those involved in the gasification of coal. It is also possible to produce liquid fuels such as alcohols from biomass by a process called **pyrolysis** that involves heating the organic material in an oxygen-deficient atmosphere. One use of this liquid fuel, much publicized in the United States, is as a partial substitute for gasoline in automobile engines. A mixture of roughly 10 percent ethyl alcohol derived from biomass and 90 percent unleaded gasoline produces a fuel named **gasohol.** Although the energy savings in using gasohol appear to be marginal, if any, precious resources of petroleum are conserved. This is particularly important for countries such as Brazil that have to import large amounts of oil and have, therefore, concentrated in recent years on alternative energy sources.

Brazil produces large amounts of anhydrous ethyl alcohol from sugar cane, sugar beet, cassava, and sorghum. This alcohol is blended with gasoline to produce a gasohol. The amount of alcohol added has been increased gradually up to the 20 percent maximum that can be burned in a conventional engine. Cars that run entirely on alcohol have also been developed, and by early 1983 a majority of new cars purchased in Brazil had alcohol fuel engines. One unfortunate side effect of the spread of alcohol pumps throughout garages in Brazil is that because the hydrous ethyl alcohol tastes a little like cachaca, the national spirit, some drivers have been drinking the fuel intended for their cars. The shift from gasoline to alcohol as a fuel has been particularly attractive in Brazil with its large bill for oil imports and vast sugar cane producing areas in the depressed northeastern part of the country. Through the efforts of the Brazilian government, alcohol production has risen from 1 million barrels per year in 1976 (providing 1 percent of fuel for automobiles) to 34 million barrels in 1983 (around 25 percent of automotive fuel needs).

The example of Brazil draws attention to the use of biomass as an energy source not just as a waste product of other activities, but also through the biological harvesting of energy. It has been proposed, for example, that single cell algae that are particularly

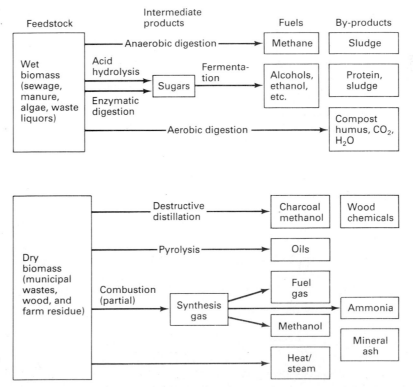

FIGURE 5-37. Block diagram to show how biomass can be converted into fuels, the processes involved, types of fuels produced, and by-products of the operation.

efficient in producing hydrocarbons by photosynthesis could be grown in ponds, harvested, and fermented in a digester to produce methane. This could either be used as a substitute for natural gas or used on site to generate electricity. In the latter case, the carbon dioxide produced from methane combustion could be returned to the growing pond to promote the growth of the algae. The Nobel prize winning scientist Melvin Calvin believes that a significant contribution to world energy requirements could be made by plants by the end of this century. He envisages the use of currently unproductive land (avoiding competition with food crops) to grow plants that would be mechanically harvested and dried. This material would be treated with chemical solvents to dissolve out sugars and other hydrocarbons; the sugars could be fermented to produce alcohol. Suitable plants for use as feedstock for such a "green factory" have been identified and include the gopher plant (*Euphorbia lathyris*). From 1000 metric tons of plant material, Calvin suggests it is possible to obtain 80 metric tons of hydrocarbons, 260 metric tons of sugar (that could yield 100 metric tons of alcohol on fermentation), and still have 200 metric tons of woody residue that itself can be used as a fuel. The important feature of the green factory is not its energy efficiency but the fact that it produces liquid fuels and other chemicals (such as feedstocks) that currently depend heavily on oil supplies. The principles involved in the green factory can be extended to a wide range of farming activities both on land and in the sea.

In countries such as the United States, cultivated plants and grains are unlikely to provide a major future source of energy. For example, to satisfy the current U.S. consumption of natural gas using methane derived from plants would require a land area roughly equivalent to the total presently under cultivation (1.1 million square miles or 2.85 million square kilometers). Nevertheless, recent decades have seen a major resurgence in the fuel that sustained the early development of America—wood. This is largely being used for heating homes and small industries and in the small-scale generation of steam and electricity. Some authorities have suggested that as much as 10 percent of U.S. energy requirements could be met using wood energy systems by the year 2000.

Nuclear Fusion—the Ultimate Energy Source?

The energy that is emitted by the sun and by other stars throughout the universe results mainly from the process of **nuclear fusion,** in which nuclei of light atoms combine to form heavier atoms. The most promising candidates to provide fusion energy on earth are heavy isotopes of hydrogen known as deuterium (^2_1H) and tritium

(^3_1H) that can be fused to produce the heavier element helium (He) as ^4_2He or ^3_2He. The fusion of two deuterium atoms can produce helium, a free neutron (n), and a great deal of energy:

$$^2_1H + ^2_1H \longrightarrow ^3_2He + n$$
$$+ \text{ energy (3.2 million electron volts).} \quad (5.5)$$

A related reaction results in the formation of tritium by fusion of deuterium atoms:

$$^2_1H + ^2_1H \longrightarrow ^3_1H + ^1_1H$$
$$+ \text{ energy (4 million electron volts).} \quad (5.6)$$

These two reactions are about equally probable when fusion of deuterium atoms occurs, but whereas in the first case a stable product is formed, in the second the tritium atom reacts with another deuterium atom:

$$^2_1H + ^3_1H \longrightarrow ^4_2He + n$$
$$+ \text{ energy (17.6 million electron volts).} \quad (5.7)$$

Therefore, the net result of these three reactions can be written as:

$$5^2_1H \longrightarrow ^4_2He + ^3_2He + ^1_1H + 2n$$
$$+ \text{ energy (24.8 million electron volts).} \quad (5.8)$$

and the energy released per deuterium atom in these fusion reactions is 4.92 million electron volts. The fusion of deutrium and tritium to produce helium and release very large amounts of energy has already been achieved by humans but only in the most uncontrolled and explosive manner imaginable. It is, in fact, the basis of the nuclear weapon known as the hydrogen (H) or thermonuclear bomb. In the H-bomb, the conditions needed for fusion are created by first detonating an atomic bomb. The problem of using nuclear fusion as an energy source for the benefit of humankind consists entirely in the *controlled* and sustained production of such fusion reactions.

The technical problems involved in producing controlled fusion reactions are so great that, despite several decades of research already undertaken, it is most unlikely that commercial fusion reactors could be in operation before the next century. In order to initiate a fusion reaction such as that involving two deuterium atoms, temperatures greater than 100 million degrees have to be reached. At such temperatures, a gas is so hot that its atoms have been torn apart by collisions into their component electrons and nuclei, and it is known as a **plasma.** This plasma has to be confined to allow collision and fusion, and one means of achieving this is to hold it within a magnetic field that is toroidal in shape (like a doughnut). The success of a Soviet toroidal magnetic confinement machine called *Tokamak* has been followed by further work along these lines in the United States and England (Fig. 5.38). An alternative to this

FIGURE 5-38. Fusion reactors such as the Tokamak reactor, shown in an artist's rendering above, generate power by fusion occurring in the central donut-shaped chamber. By mid-1986, plasma temperatures above 200 million degrees Kelvin had been generated in this chamber for short periods of time. (Courtesy of the Princeton Plasma Physics Laboratory.)

approach is called **inertial confinement** and involves firing a large amount of energy, which may be in the form of laser beams, electron beams, heavy ion beams, or even fragments of discrete matter, into a small blob of the mixture of hydrogen isotopes. Such beams, focussed from different directions, can create shock wave compression and heating effects and at the same time confine the plasma. This method aims at producing fusion as a series of small explosions, perhaps several a second, whereas in magnetic confinement systems, a more continuous reaction is the objective. The plasma would have to be heated to the temperature of ignition when, like putting a match to a flammable material to start a fire, the reaction would begin and the energy released maintain the temperature and hence, in turn, the reaction. Methods of heating the plasma, in addition to compression within an enormous magnetic field, have included shooting beams of neutral atoms into the plasma so as to collide with particles and raise the temperature, and the use of radio frequency heating that is the principle employed in the domestic microwave oven. Whichever system is used to confine and heat the plasma must be capable of controlling the three critical factors for fusion: temperature, plasma density, and time. A fusion reactor would, of course, generate energy as large amounts of heat that could be extracted using conventional systems, probably based on those used in fission reactors.

Assuming that the great technical problems involved in controlled fusion can be overcome, what will be the fuel for such power plants and its cost and availability? If a reactor were to be constructed that utilizes the deuterium-deuterium reaction, then seawater would provide a vast supply of this fuel. Seawater contains one deuterium atom for every 6500 atoms of hy-

drogen, so that 1 cubic meter of water contains 1.028×10^{25} atoms of deuterium that, if utilized in deuterium-deuterium fusion, has a potential fusion energy of 8.16×10^{12} joules. This is equivalent to the heat of combustion of 269 metric tons of coal or 1360 barrels of crude oil. If we extend this calculation to estimate the energy that would potentially be derived from 1 cubic kilometer of seawater, this would be the equivalent to 269 *billion* metric tons of coal or 1360 *billion* barrels of crude oil. The latter figure is of the same order as some estimates of ultimate world resources of crude oil. Therefore, deuterium-deuterium fusion holds the possibility of generating the same amount of energy from a cubic kilometer or so of seawater as would be provided by all of the world's remaining oil. Comparable estimates suggest that the world's remaining coal could be matched in energy by a few tens of cubic kilometers of seawater.

However, these calculations assume that the fusion reactor is based on the deuterium-deuterium reaction, whereas much current research is aimed at a controlled deuterium-tritium reaction (as in Eq. 5.7), which requires far less stringent experimental conditions. Tritium, however, is very much rarer than deuterium and has to be produced by neutron bombardment of another light element, lithium (Li):

$$^6_3\text{Li} + \text{n} \longrightarrow {}^4_2\text{He} + {}^3_1\text{H}$$
$$+ \text{energy (4.8 million electron volts)} \qquad (5.9)$$

and

$$^7_3\text{Li} + \text{n} \longrightarrow {}^4_2\text{He} + {}^3_1\text{H} + \text{n}$$
$$+ \text{energy (2.5 million electron volts).} \qquad (5.10)$$

This tritium would then combine with deuterium as in reaction 5.7, and the net result would be equivalent to

$$^6_3\text{Li} + {}^2_1\text{H} + \text{n} \longrightarrow 2{}^4_2\text{He} + \text{n} + \text{energy}$$
$$\text{(22.4 million electron volts).} \quad (5.11)$$

Unfortunately, lithium is not available in great abundance (in seawater, for example, it occurs as only one part in 10 million), and the isotope ^6Li constitutes only 7.4 percent of natural lithium. It is an element that can be extracted from certain brines and is mined in the form of the mineral spodumene ($\text{LiAlSi}_2\text{O}_6$) that occurs in pegmatite deposits. It is much more limited as a resource, and estimates suggest that if used as a major energy source, it may only last a few hundred years.

The ultimate fuel for fusion reactors would be hydrogen itself, the supply of which is virtually unlimited. It is hydrogen fusion that is chiefly responsible for energy production in the sun and stars, but it requires still greater temperatures. The technical problems involved in harnessing hydrogen fusion for energy generation are even greater than for the other fusion reactions.

Nuclear fusion can potentially provide humankind with an energy source that is almost limitless. A further advantage of nuclear fusion is that hazardous radioactive wastes are not produced as by-products of reactor operation; thus, there is neither the problem of transport or storage of dangerous fissionable materials. Neutron radiation is produced in fusion, however, as the above equations show, but some scientists believe that reactors could be developed employing reactions like that of deuterium and ^3He that, although requiring much higher temperatures than deuterium-deuterium or deuterium-tritium reactions (namely, about 300 million degrees), produce 10–50 times less neutron radiation. The potential of nuclear fusion as an energy source of the future is obvious, and its limitations lie not in the availability of fuel but in our ingenuity in developing the necessary technology.

THE FUTURE

There is not an energy shortage. Vast amounts of energy are available on the earth, more than we could ever use. Any energy crisis is of our making because we rely too heavily on relatively cheap and convenient fossil fuels. There are many alternatives to the fossil fuels as we have shown in this chapter, but each of the alternatives also has drawbacks.

Nuclear energy is still the most likely future energy source in many of the industrialized societies, if only because of the considerable amount of money already spent on research, development, and plant construction. Nuclear energy brings with it great problems, however. Wastes from nuclear power plants remain lethally radioactive for periods of thousands to tens of thousands of years, and there is still no consensus on how to safely dispose of these wastes. Furthermore, breeder reactors produce more and more fissionable materials that could be used for nuclear weapons.

The other forms of alternative energy discussed in this chapter range from well-established sources such as hydroelectric power to the highly speculative sources such as ocean power and nuclear fusion. Some have obviously limited potential, many are being actively developed on a small scale, and still others require a great deal of research and development before they could ever make a significant contribution.

Which of these alternative sources will replace the fossil fuels will depend on a whole range of economic, social, and political factors, some of which may be undreamed of as yet. Only two points about the future now seem to be certain. Energy needs will continue to rise for at least the near future, and energy sources will have to change. What is vital for many of the technologically advanced societies is to prepare for that change, because it will surely involve changes in the need for many other resources and in the life styles of future generations.

FURTHER READINGS

GRAY, T. J. and GASHUS, D. K., *Tidal Power*. New York: Plenum Press, 1972.

HUNT, S. E., *Fission, Fusion and the Energy Crisis*, 2nd ed. New York: Pergamon Press, 1980.

MERRICK, D., ed. *Energy, Present and Future Options*. New York: John Wiley and Sons, 1984.

National Academy of Sciences, *Energy in Transition. 1985–2010*. San Francisco: W. H. Freeman and Co., 1979.

RINEHART, J. S., *Geysers and Geothermal Energy*. New York: Springer-Verlag, 1980.

RUEDISILI, L. C., and FIREBAUGH, M. W., *Perspectives on Energy*, 2nd. ed. New York: Oxford University Press, 1978.

6

The bridge at Ironbridge, constructed between 1775 and 1779 on the Severn River in England, was one of the first major structures constructed of iron. It remains today as a monument to the Industrial Revolution. (Courtesy of the Ironbridge Gorge Museum Trust.)

ABUNDANT METALS

If we remove metals from the service of man, all methods of protecting and sustaining health and more carefully preserving the course of life are done away with. If there were no metals, men would pass a horrible and wretched existence in the midst of wild beasts; they would return to the acorns and fruits and berries of the forest. They would feed upon the herbs and roots which they plucked up with their nails. They would dig out caves in which to lie down at night and by day they would rove in the woods and plains at random like beasts, and inasmuch as this condition is utterly unworthy of humanity, with its splendid and glorious natural endowment, will anyone be so foolish or obstinate as not to allow that metals are necessary for food and clothing and that they tend to preserve life?

DE RE METALLICA, GEORGIUS AGRICOLA, 1556, FROM TRANSLATION BY HERBERT C. AND LOU H. HOOVER, 1912

METALS AND THEIR PROPERTIES

Metals are unique among the chemical elements in being opaque, tough, ductile, malleable, and fusible and in possessing high thermal and electrical conductivities. Approximately half of the chemical elements possess some metallic properties, but all true metals have two or more of the special metallic properties. Our early ancestors were drawn to the use of metals because they are tough (but not brittle like stone), malleable, and can be melted and cast. These same properties are important today, but we also rely heavily on the special electrical and magnetic properties of metals and their machineable characteristics. Without metals, technology as we know it could not have come into being, nor could it be continued.

Today, approximately 30 metallic elements are made commonly available through mining and processing of their ores. Although each metallic element is used in its pure form because of its unique properties, modern society commonly finds that chemical mixtures (**alloys**) of two or more metals, or metals and nonmetals, have superior characteristics. The alloys are also metallic but usually have properties of strength, durability, or corrosion resistance that exceed the properties in the component pure metals. Examples of common alloys are steel, brass, bronze, and solder. **Steel** is an alloy in which the main constituent, iron, is combined with other metallic elements such as nickel, vanadium, or molybdenum, or a nonmetallic element such as carbon. Steels are tougher, less brittle, and more resistant to wear than iron alone. Brass is an alloy of copper and zinc. It melts at a lower temperature than copper, the metal it most nearly resembles, and it is much easier to cast. Bronze was the first alloy used by our ancestors

and was developed about 3500 B.C. This alloy of copper and tin melts at a relatively low temperature, is very easily cast, is harder than pure copper, and is corrosion resistant. Common solder is an alloy of lead and tin that has an especially low melting temperature. The molten alloy has the property of melting or combining with certain other metals. This property allows a solder, when cooled and solidified, to effect a join between two pieces of the same metal, or in some cases, two fragments of different metals.

THE NATURE OF ORE DEPOSITS

Metals can be separated into groups, as discussed in Chapter 1, on the basis of their abundances in the earth's crust (Fig. 1.5). The abundant metals are those that individually makeup at least 0.1 weight percent of the earth's crust. There are only six such metals—silicon, aluminum, iron, magnesium, manganese, and titanium (Table 6.1). Silicon, though significantly different in physical properties from other metals, is included in the following discussion because of its importance in iron smelting. All other metals occur in much lower concentrations and are thus categorized as scarce metals. These are discussed in Chapter 7. Many kinds of common rocks contain significant quantities of several of the abundant metals and small amounts of the scarce metals, but few of these rocks can now, or ever be considered as resources or ores from which we will extract the metals. It is helpful to recall the discussion in Chapter 1 that defined ores (reserves) as deposits that can be worked profitably for *economic* or *strategic* reasons. Thus, there are important distinctions between average rocks, in which the concentrations of elements are too low to be profitably extracted, local concentrations

TABLE 6-1

The abundant metals

Element	Symbol	Atomic No.	Atomic Wt.	Crustal Abundance, (%)	Specific Gravity (gm/cc)	Melting Point (°C)
Magnesium	Mg	12	24.31	2.3	1.74	649
Aluminum	Al	13	26.98	8.2	2.70	660
Silicon	Si	14	28.09	28.2	2.33	1410
Titanium	Ti	22	47.90	0.57	4.50	1660
Manganese	Mn	25	54.94	0.095	7.20	1244
Iron	Fe	26	55.85	5.6	7.86	1535

that may be rich but too small for consideration, and **ore deposits,** that may be economically exploited.

Many factors determine whether or not a given rock is an ore, not only of the abundant metals but of any metals; these have been discussed at length in Chapter 3, but it is worthwhile to recall that the most important are:

1. mineralogy;
2. grade;
3. grain size and texture;
4. size of the deposit;
5. depth of the deposit;
6. geographic location;
7. possible by-products.

The mineralogy, or the form in which a metal is held, and the grade or proportion of metal content are the most important factors because they detemine the process and the energy that must be used to extract the metal and the value of the extracted product. Each of the abundant metals occurs in a wide variety of minerals, but it is only the few listed in Table 6.2 that serve as **ore minerals** for these metals. Iron is present in large quantities in minerals such as fayalite (Fe_2SiO_4) and pyrite (FeS_2), but neither is mined primarily as an iron ore because the large amounts of energy needed to extract the iron from the fayalite, and the pollution problems resulting in extraction of the iron from the pyrite make use of these minerals noneconomic. Similarly, aluminum is present in many silicate minerals, but the extraction is generally prohibitively expensive relative to that for the minerals listed.

The grain size and texture determine the methods of processing and extraction and may, in the case of very fine grain size, actually make rich ores unworkable. The size and depth of the deposit control the mining method and, hence, much of the cost. Geographic location influences accessibility, environmental conditions, and even the tax or royalty charges incurred in mining.

The recovery of by-products commonly helps

make the mining of mineral deposits profitable; in fact, some important metals (e.g., cadmium, gallium, germanium) are recovered almost only as by-products. The abundant metals are generally recovered from ores in which they are the only metal refined, but many ores of the scarce metals yield a variety of useful by-product metals. The by-products are not present in sufficient grades to warrant their being mined alone, but they are recovered at little or no additional cost when mining the major metal, and their sales help pay for the total mining operation. In many instances, the by-products (that may also include waste rock products such as sand or agricultural limestone as well as metals) have helped make mining operations profitable when major metal prices have fallen or when the grades of the major metals have been insufficient alone to keep a mine profitable.

Our attention in this chapter will be focussed on the **abundant metals,** which are used in great quantity in our society. In the following chapter, we shall consider the important **scarce metals.** The ore minerals of the abundant metals are listed in Table 6-2. Note that the minerals are all simple oxides, hydroxides, or cabonates. Even though silicate minerals are by far the most abundant in the earth's crust, they are rarely used as the sources for metals because they are difficult to handle and extremely expensive to smelt. However, it may be that the future will see many silicate minerals being used, but at present only two silicate minerals, kaolinite and anorthite, are viewed as potential ore minerals. Where geochemically scarce metals are concerned, silicate minerals are sometimes used under special circumstances. Examples are beryl ($Be_3Al_2Si_6O_{18}$) used as a source of beryllium because there are few other minerals containing this metal, and willemite (Zn_2SiO_4) that is mined for zinc only in localities where the high grade of the ore warrants its recovery.

IRON: THE BACKBONE OF INDUSTRY

Iron is the third most abundant metal in the crust, but historically it has been the workhorse of industry. Today

TABLE 6-2

The abundant metals and their principal ore minerals

Metal	Important Ore Minerals	Amount of Metal in the Ore Mineral
Silicon	Quartz (SiO_2)	46.7
Aluminum	Boehmite ($AlO \cdot OH$)	45.0
	Diaspore ($AlO \cdot OH$)	45.0
	Gibbsite ($Al(OH)_3$)	34.6
	Kaolinite ($Al_2Si_2O_5(OH)_4$)	20.9
	Anorthite ($CaAl_2Si_2O_8$)	19.4
Iron	Magnetite (Fe_3O_4)	72.4
	Hematite (Fe_2O_3)	70.0
	Goethite ($FeO \cdot OH$)	62.9
	Siderite ($FeCO_3$)	62.1
	Chamosite ($Fe_3(Si,Al)_2O_5(OH)_4$)	45.7
Magnesium	Magnesite ($MgCO_3$)	28.7
	Dolomite ($CaMg(CO_3)_2$)	13.1
Titanium	Rutile (TiO_2)	60.0
	Ilmenite ($FeTiO_3$)	31.6
Manganese	Pyrolusite (MnO_2)	63.2
	Psilomelane ($BaMn_9O_{18} \cdot 2H_2O$)	46.0
	Rhodochrosite ($MnCO_3$)	39.0

it accounts for more than 95 percent by weight of all metals consumed and a significant proportion of the remainder—most of the nickel, chromium, molybdenum, tungsten, vanadium, cobalt, and manganese—are mined principally for use in the steel industry. The reasons for iron's dominance are not hard to find: The first is the abundance and ready accessibility of rich iron ores; the second is the relative ease with which the smelting process can be carried out; the third, and most important, is the special property of iron and its alloys which allow it to be tempered, shaped, sharpened, and welded to give a product that is exceptionally strong and durable. No other metal enjoys the same range of versatile properties. Rudyard Kipling in his brief poem "Cold Iron," captured the versatility of iron in a striking way:

> Gold is for the mistress—silver for the maid
> Copper for the craftsman, cunning at his trade.
> Good'!' Said the Baron, sitting in his hall,
> but iron—cold iron—is master of them all.

Iron is the most extensively used metal in the world, and there is virtually no part of our society that does not make use of iron and steel products in some manner. In recent years, total world production of iron and steel has exceeded 1 million (10^9) metric tons, and in countries such as the United States more than 600 kilograms per capita are used. Although the end products of iron and steel are nearly countless, the major categories for use in industrialized societies today (and their approximate percentages of total use) are construction (30 percent), transportation (25 percent), and ma-

chinery (20 percent). Other important uses include grocery cans, home appliances, and oil, gas, and water drilling equipment. Today, we take for granted the ready availability of iron and steel in a large variety of forms. It was not always so, and we need to go back only about 250 years to recount the advances that have led iron and steel to their positions of prominence today.

Iron Minerals and Deposits

Iron, because of its crustal abundance and its chemical reactivity, occurs in hundreds of different mineral forms. However, like the other abundant metals, it is economically extracted from only a few minerals (Table 6.2). The iron oxides, **hematite** (Fe_2O_3) and **magnetite** (Fe_3O_4) are by far the most important ore minerals and will no doubt continue to be for many years. The other ore minerals were important in the past and are still locally significant today.

Iron deposits occur worldwide (Fig. 6.1) and have formed as a result of many different processes throughout geologic time. The behavior of iron in geologic processes, especially at the earth's surface, is strongly influenced by its ability to exist in more than one oxidation state. Under the reducing conditions that may exist beneath the earth's surface and in some deep relatively oxygen-free waters, iron may exist in the **ferrous** state, (Fe^{+2}). In this form iron is relatively soluble, and it may form ferrous minerals such as siderite ($FeCO_3$), chamosite ($Fe_3(Si,Al)_2O_5(OH)_4$), and mixed ferrous-ferric minerals such as magnetite. At the earth's surface and wherever oxygen is abundant, the iron oxidizes to its **ferric** state (Fe^{+3}), an extremely insoluble form, and

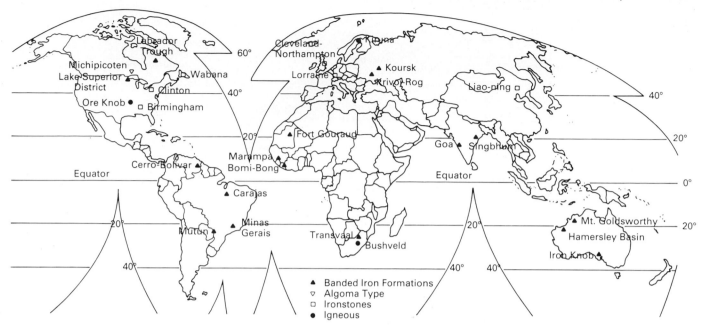

FIGURE 6-1. The locations of some of the major iron deposits in the world. The banded iron formations constitute the world's major iron reserves.

is deposited in ferric minerals such as hematite or **goethite** (FeO•OH). Iron deposits have formed by **igneous, metamorphic,** and **sedimentary** processes. There are many distinct types of deposits, but nearly all the major deposits mined today or in the recent past are of only a few types. These will likely continue to serve as our major sources of iron ore and are concisely described below.

Deposits Formed through Igneous Activity. Three major types of iron ores arise from igneous activity: (1) accumulation in large **mafic** intrusions, (2) contact metamorphic deposits, and (3) ores formed through submarine volcanism.

(1) Large mafic igneous intrusions, such as the Bushveld intrusion in the Republic of South Africa, commonly contain significant concentrations of magnetite. In these intrusions, much of the magnetite was precipitated in thick layers as it crystallized and settled out of the magma onto the floor of the chamber (see Fig. 7.6). The total amount of magnetite in the igneous rock may be only a few percent, but its occurrence in nearly pure layers makes its mining convenient. Although these accumulations in mafic igneous rocks are not presently mined for their iron content, in the Republic of South Africa they do serve as important ores of the vanadium that is concentrated in the magnetite.

(2) Contact metamorphic deposits form where iron-bearing fluids given off by igneous intrusions react with adjacent rocks, especially limestones (Figs. 6.2 and 6.3). The hot fluids given off by the cooling intrusions react with and sometimes completely replace the

wall rocks, leaving a mixture of coarse-grained iron oxides and a host of unusual metamorphic minerals. Most of these occurrences are too small to be economically recovered, but in the United States at localities such as Cornwall and Morgantown, Pennsylvania; Iron Springs, Utah; and Pilot Knob, Missouri, massive rock contact deposits were mined for many years.

(3) Sea floor volcanism is almost always accompanied by submarine hot springs that issue forth solutions rich in iron and silica. The rapid cooling and oxidation of the solutions as they mix with sea water results in the precipitation of iron oxide and silica known as **Algoma-type** deposits after the locality in the Canadian Shield where they were first recognized. A few of these deposits in Canada and elsewhere have proven rich enough to mine, but most are too small or too low in grade to be successfully worked.

Residual Deposits. These deposits of iron minerals are formed where the weathering process oxidizes ferrous iron in rocks and leaves behind concentrations of the insoluble ferric minerals. This process accounts for the brown, yellow, and red colors that are familiar in most soils. Locally, especially in tropical regions where the chemical reactions are more rapid because of higher temperatures and abundant rainfall, the weathering process removes the more soluble compounds and leaves concentrated residues of iron oxides and hydroxides. These types of deposits, known as **brown ores,** have been forming since Precambrian times and are widespread. Most of the deposits are small, however, and although locally important in the past are not considered

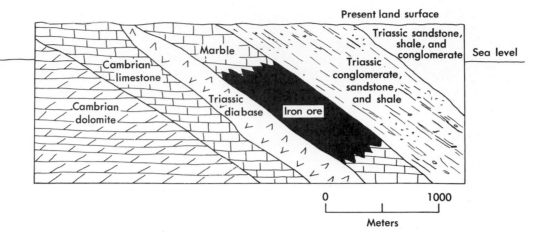

FIGURE 6-2. The Cornwall mine in Pennsylvania is an example of a contact metamorphic iron oxide deposit formed where iron-rich fluids from an intrusive Triassic diabase replaced part of a limestone bed with magnetite. The relationship of the ore to the limestone, converted to marble near the intrusion, is shown in the cross section.

FIGURE 6-3. A view of the open pit mine at Cornwall, Pennsylvania, in which the massive magnetite ore (dark zone in the base of the pit, shown in black in Fig. 6.2) is visible below the white marble formed by metamorphism of the original limestone. (Photograph courtesy of Bethlehem Steel Corporation.)

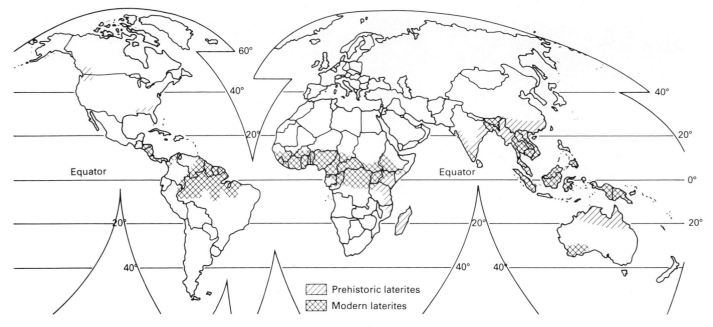

FIGURE 6-4. Laterites are hard, red, residual soils, rich in iron minerals, that are formed in tropical to subtropical regions. The shaded regions on the map above show where intense leaching has removed more soluble compounds and formed iron-rich lateritic soils.

economic in terms of today's large-scale mining operations.

In tropical regions the intensive leaching process has left large areas of hard red residual soils known as **laterites** (Fig. 6.4), a name derived from the Latin *latere* meaning *brick*. These soils are poor agriculturally and often become worse when they are used for farming because the exposure causes iron hydroxide, $Fe(OH)_3$, in the soil to irreversibly convert to $FeO \bullet OH$. This dehydration reaction is similar to that which occurs when clays are baked to form bricks and results in the soils becoming so hard that they do not absorb moisture and become unworkable. Where most intensely developed, laterites may contain 30 percent or more iron and may thus represent large future sources of iron. The tonnages of iron potentially available from the lateritic soils probably exceed those from all other sources by a factor of at least ten, but their mining would cause massive environmental problems.

Sedimentary Deposits. Three important types of iron ores have formed through sedimentary processes: **bog iron deposits, ironstones,** and **banded iron formations.**

The bog iron deposits are the smallest of these

types of sedimentary deposits and, although not mined today, provided ore for many early European operations and the first iron ore to the fledging American industries in the seventeenth and eighteenth centuries. These deposits form locally in glaciated regions and in coastal plain sediments where iron, originally put into solution by the reducing conditions created by decaying organic matter, is oxidized and precipitated as lenses and sedimentary cements (Fig. 6.5). The deposits are generally quite local in extent and are highly variable in grade.

Ironstones are iron-bearing formations that are much larger and more important than bog iron deposits. The ironstones are continuous sedimentary beds that may extend for tens or even hundreds of kilometers and are a few meters to tens of meters in thickness. In many respects they are similar to many other sedimentary rocks, containing cross-beds, abundant fossils, oolites, facies changes, and other sedimentary features. The main difference is that they contain significant amounts of goethite, hematite, siderite, or chamosite (a complex iron aluminum silicate) as coatings on mineral fragments, as oolites, and as replaced fossil fragments (Fig. 6.6).

The origins of the ironstones are not clear, but they appear to represent shallow, near-shore marine,

FIGURE 6-5. Bog iron ores form where reduced iron carried in ground water is oxidized and precipitates as insoluble ferric iron compounds.

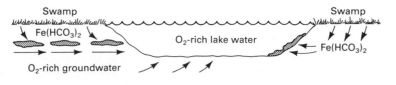

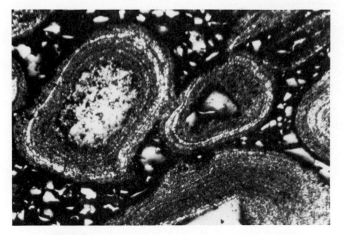

FIGURE 6-6. Ironstones consist of pellets, cements, oolites, and fossil fragments that have been infilled and replaced by iron hydroxides. This microscopic view is of an area 1mm across.

and rarely, freshwater sediments where the formation of the iron minerals occurred both as direct sedimentation and as a diagenetic replacement. The distribution of the individual iron minerals was controlled by the nearness to shore, water depth, and amount of oxygen in the water (Fig. 6.7). In the shallowest areas, the abundance of oxygen resulted in oxidation of the iron to the ferric state and the formation of goethite, whereas in the deeper areas, richer in CO_2 but poorer in oxygen, the iron precipitated in the form of siderite or chamosite.

In both instances, the iron must have been transported to the sites of deposition in the more soluble fer-

rous state, either as ground water or as deep basin fluids. The special conditions that led to the formation of the ironstones are believed to have resulted from generally warm and humid climates that permitted the generation of abundant organic matter. This resulted in significant amounts of organic acids and carbon dioxide in ground water solutions that then readily reduced and dissolved iron minerals in the soils and rocks. The leached iron moved slowly via the ground water system into lakes or shallow marine basins where iron accumulated. In some cases the iron minerals precipitated directly on the sea or lake floor; in others, the iron minerals replaced calcium carbonate minerals, fossils, and oolites, or were precipitated by diagenetic processes interstitially among the other minerals.

The ironstones have formed since the beginning of the Cambrian period, a time span inclusively called the Phanerozoic eon. Consequently, these ores have sometimes been referred to as the **Phanerozoic type.** Iron ores of this type have been very important in Europe where they are collectively referred to as the **Minette type** and where they supplied much of the ore for the iron and steel industries of the United Kingdom, France, Germany, and Belgium. In North America, where Appalachian examples of these ores are called the **Clinton (or Wabana) type,** they were important resources from the late eighteenth until the mid-twentieth century. Today, the importance of these ores is much diminished because the richest areas have been mined-out and because banded iron formations are more economical to work.

The largest concentrations of iron oxides are found

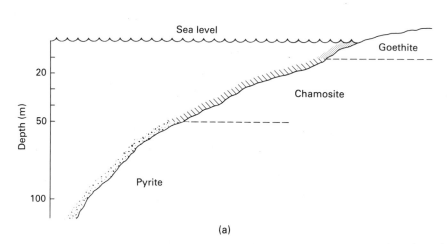

(a)

(b)

FIGURE 6-7. (a) Schematic diagram showing the relationship of water depth with different facies of iron minerals forming today. This is believed to be similar to the formation of ironstones. (b) Iron stones mined on the Yorkshire coast of eastern England were major sources of iron for the Industrial Revolution. Today, the old workings are visible along the rocky coast. (Photograph courtesy of F.M. Vokes.)

in banded iron formations (commonly called BIF's for short), which today supply most of the world's iron ores and constitute the bulk of the world's iron ore reserves (Table 6.3). They are also known as **Lake Superior-type** ores after the large deposits that are mined in the United States. Formations of this type occur in the Precambrian rocks of all continents and are mined extensively in the United States, Canada, Brazil, Venezuela, Australia, India, China, and the Soviet Union (see Fig. 6.1). A wide variety of terms has been applied to deposits of this type in different parts of the world. Commonly encountered names for silica-rich ores are **taconite** (in the United States), **itabirite** (in Brazil), or **banded jaspilite** (in Australia). They are from 30–700 meters in thickness and often extend over hundreds to thousands of square kilometers. Many of these deposits, including all in the United States and Canada, have been metamorphosed to some degree, so that they now consist of fine-grained magnetite and/or hematite in a matrix of quartz, iron silicates, and iron carbonate in a

very compact finely laminated rock (Fig. 6.8). The BIF's, like the ironstones, commonly display strong facies development indicating that at the same time differing conditions resulted in the formation of iron oxide-rich zones closest to shore, and iron carbonate or iron silicate zones farther out into the basin. The iron contents of the BIF's vary widely, but the presently mined deposits typically have 20–40 percent iron.

The banded iron formations have produced billions of tons of ore and now are the world's major source of iron; however, their modes of origin remain somewhat enigmatic. Banded iron formations, which are present on all continents, have several major characteristics in common. The most important is that most if not all of them formed during the period of 2.6–1.8 billion years ago. They all exhibit the typical banding visible in Fig. 6.8, and all are very low in aluminum content and are nearly free of common detrital sedimentary debris. They resemble the Algoma-type deposits in that they consist of fine layers of silica and iron oxide minerals

TABLE 6-3

World iron ore reserves and production in 1983; in 10^6 metric tons

Continent and Country	Crude Ore Reserves	Iron Content Reserves	Production in Fe Content in 1984
North America:			
United States	16,000	3360	37
Canada	11,900	4080	26
Mexico	400	180	8
Total	28,300	7620	71
South America:			
Brazil	15,900	9800	74
Venezuela	2000	1090	8
Other	900	450	10
Total	18,800	11,340	92
Europe:			
France	2200	820	5
Sweden	3000	1450	11
U.S.S.R.	60,000	22,700	148
Other	1900	730	16
Total	67,100	25,700	180
Africa:			
Liberia	900	450	10
South Africa	4100	2630	15
Other	1000	450	12
Total	6000	3530	37
Asia:			
China	9200	3170	40
India	7200	4350	29
Other	900	360	8
Total	17,300	7880	77
Oceania:			
Australia	15,200	9160	60
Other	500	270	3
Total	15,700	9430	63
WORLD TOTAL	153,200	65,500	520

(Source U.S. Bureau of Mines, 1985.)

FIGURE 6-8. Banded iron formations (BIF's) may have very regular layering or display irregular banding as shown above. The light-colored bands consist of nearly pure iron oxides (hematite and magnetite), whereas the darker zones are nearly pure silica.

but the BIF's are much broader in extent and do not show any apparent relationship to submarine volcanism. Detailed studies of the BIF's indicate that they were formed in broad sedimentary basins following prolonged periods of continental weathering and erosion and the inundation of the land surface by shallow seas. The erosion had previously removed most detrital debris so that deposition in the basins was largely that of chemical precipitates. The origins of the iron are not clear, but it is likely that it was derived from several different sources including weathering of continental rocks, leaching of marine sediments, and submarine hydrothermal systems that discharged iron-rich fluids onto the sea floor. Today it would be impossible to transport the huge quantities of iron from eroding land surfaces in rivers and streams or to disperse it widely from submarine vents, because it would be quickly precipitated in the insoluble ferric form. However, during the period of the Precambrian when the BIF's formed, there was probably little free oxygen in the earth's atmosphere or dissolved in surface waters. The carbon dioxide content of the atmosphere was probably much higher and gases such as methane could have been present. Under these conditions rain water, stream and lake waters, and ocean waters would have been slightly acidic and much less oxidizing, conditions that would have allowed for the ready transport of iron in solution in the soluble ferrous form. The iron accumulated in the broad shallow basins and gradually precipitated as iron oxides and hydroxides. The cause of the repetitive precipitation of layers of alternating iron oxides and silica has been a point of much debate with suggestions including annual

climate changes, cyclical periods of evaporation, the effects of microorganisms altering silica availability and releasing oxygen, episodic volcanism, and many others. Whatever our final understanding of the origins of these important deposits, their formation was apparently directly controlled by the nature of the Precambrian atmosphere. As the atmosphere changed, so did the capacity of the ocean to serve as a transporter of iron. When photosynthesis started contributing large quantities of free oxygen into the atmosphere, banded iron deposits no longer formed. Therefore, we have no analogous processes active in the world today.

Banded iron formations typically contain 20–40 percent iron, values that were long considered too low for economic recovery. In some areas, however, surficial chemical weathering has removed the associated siliceous or carbonate minerals and left enriched residual ores containing 55 percent or more iron. The initial mining efforts of the mid-to-late 1800s in the great Precambrian iron deposits of the world such as the Lake Superior district of the United States and in the 1950s and 1960s in the Labrador Trough in Canada, Cerro Bolivar in Venezuela, Minas Gerais in Brazil, the Hamersley Range in Australia, and Krivoi Rog in Russia were all for the enriched ores. In the early parts of this century there was concern, echoed by the words of the American steel industry pioneer, Andrew Carnegie, reproduced on p. 175, that these rich ores were nearing depletion in places such as the Lake Superior district. Initial efforts in the early 1900s to concentrate the lower grade ores, the taconites, were only moderately successful, but renewed interest in the 1940s led to the development of economic concentration techniques. This new technology opened the way for exploitation of billions of tons of ores previously considered waste and led to the present iron ore mining industry. Since that time the technology for processing the lean ores of the BIF's has spread worldwide, and these ores have become the world's dominant source of iron ore, a position they will certainly hold for many years to come.

Mining and Beneficiation

Iron ore mining on a small scale dates back several thousand years. The earliest operations obtained ores locally by digging in a wide variety of shallow pits and underground tunnels. However, as better means of transportation evolved, many smaller mines closed and iron mining became concentrated in larger, more efficient operations.

Today, about 85 percent of the world iron ore production is mined from open pit operations; in the United States and Canada open pits account for 97 percent of the total. Surface mining has become dominant because

the iron ore bodies have large lateral dimensions and many of them lie relatively close to the surface. Furthermore, open pit mines have larger production capacities, they are generally cheaper to operate per ton of ore, and easier and safer to maintain than underground mines. As a result, the underground iron mines have found their ability to compete with open pit mines continually reduced. This is evidenced by a drop in the number of underground iron mines in the United States from about 30 in 1951 to one in 1984. United States open pit mines operate at a disadvantage relative to many foreign mines, because they must mine 5–6 metric tons of rock, about 3 metric tons of ore, and 2–3 metric tons of overburden waste, for each metric ton of iron oxide product produced. In contrast, the large Brazilian and Australian mines only have to mine 1.5–2 metric tons for each ton of iron oxide produced.

The mining in open pit mines is done primarily with large power shovels and with trucks having capacities of 120–150 tons. The ore is removed in a series of steps, called **benches** (Fig. 6.9), by drilling 30–38 centimeters (12–15 inches) diameter blast holes that are charged with an explosive mixture of ammonium nitrate and fuel oil. Individual blasts can break up to 1.5 million metric tons of ore at a time.

The richest iron ores, those that consist almost entirely of the iron ore minerals listed in Table 6.2, are referred to as **direct shipping ores.** These usually contain more than 50 weight percent iron and can be effectively processed at the smelter after only being crushed. Un-

fortunately, such ores usually constitute only a portion (often a small one) of most iron ore deposits, and these areas are usually the ones that are mined first. Once these ores are exhausted the mines must close or adapt to the processing of lower grade materials. Thus, for example, the original mining of the ores in the Lake Superior district of the United States was based on the direct shipping ores, as mining and recovery methods had not yet been developed to handle the lower grade ores. Andrew Carnegie lamented that the depletion of the richer ores could spell disaster for the American iron mining industry. In his address to the Conference of Governors at the White House, May 13–15, 1908 he said:

> I have for many years been impressed with the steady depletion of our iron ore supply. It is staggering to learn that our once-supposed ample supply of rich ores can hardly outlast the generation now appearing, leaving only the leaner ores for the later years of the century. It is my judgment, as a practical man accustomed to dealing with those material factors on which our national prosperity is based, that it is time to take thought for the morrow.

The lower grade materials of the Lake Superior district and most other important iron ore districts are called **taconites** and consist of admixed, often banded, iron oxides and silicates. They commonly contain only 40 to 50 percent iron oxide and average only 25–35 percent

FIGURE 6-9. Open pit mining of taconite iron ore in the Lake Superior district. The ore is blasted out in a series of benches and is then transferred by large power shovels into trains or large trucks for transport to the processing plant. (Courtesy of U.S. Steel Corporation.)

iron. Fortunately, the technology to effectively process these ores has been developed, and Andrew Carnegie's fears for the exhaustion of iron ores are no longer relevant. In order to use these ores, they must be upgraded by **beneficiation,** which serves to concentrate the useful iron minerals and remove problem impurities such as minerals containing phosphorus and sulfur. The final product is powdery to fine sand-sized grains of iron oxides. The grains are difficult to handle and cannot be fed directly into blast furnaces without being blown out the top. Therefore, the iron oxide grains are formed into 1–2 centimeter pellets (Fig. 6.10) by adding a binder, usually bentonite, fine volcanic ash, or a clay and then fired so that they are strong enough to be transported and easily handled. These pellets have proven very useful to the iron and steel industries because they are easy to handle, have uniform compositions of 63–65 percent iron, and because their natural porosity allows them to react rapidly with the carbon monoxide gas in the blast furnace during the smelting process.

Iron and Steel Smelting

The very first iron objects were hammered pieces of iron meteorites that did not need smelting. Meteorites are rare, however, and the use of terrestrial iron ores, consisting of iron combined with other elements, required **smelting,** the technique of separating the pure metal by melting the ore. The origins of iron smelting are unknown but probably lay in the Middle East or Asia Minor more than 3000 years ago. The **Iron Age** is usually dated as beginning about 1200 B.C. when the use of iron tools spread rapidly across the Middle East and

FIGURE 6-10. After the iron ores have been mined, they are finely ground to liberate the iron oxides. The powdery oxides are then formed into the pellets shown here that are then charged into the blast furnaces. (Courtesy of U.S. Steel Corporation.)

across Asia to China. Iron making was subsequently spread throughout Europe by the Romans who learned the technique from the Greeks. European colonialization then disseminated iron smelting to other parts of the world, such as the Americas, where it was not yet known. The modern blast furnace had its basic origins in about 1340 A.D. and slowly evolved into its present form as shown in Fig. 6.11. It consists of a refractory-lined cylindrical shaft into the top of which the charge can be introduced and from the bottom of which the molten iron and slag can be drawn.

In order to produce 1 metric ton of iron, 1.6 metric ton of iron ore pellets must be mixed with 0.7 metric ton of coke and 0.2 metric ton of limestone. This is introduced into the blast furnace where it reacts with 3.6 metric tons of air at temperatures of about 1600°C

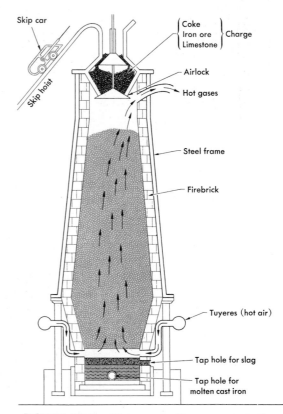

FIGURE 6-11. Diagrammatic representation of the interior of a blast furnace. The production of each metric ton of pig iron from an ore containing 60 percent iron requires approximately 250 kilograms of limestone as a flux and a metric ton of coking coal. Electrical and oxygen furnaces require different mixes and are noteworthy for being more efficient in their use of coke, but the same three ingredients are used. The production of iron illustrates how interdependent are the uses of the different metals. (From Skinner, 1986.)

(3000°F). The chemical reactions are complex, but the two principal reactions are the controlled combustion of the coke to produce carbon monoxide and then the reduction of the iron oxides to iron by the carbon monoxide which is simultaneously oxidized to carbon dioxide.

$$C + 1/2O_2 \longrightarrow CO$$
(coke)   (air)   (carbon monoxide gas)

$$3CO + Fe_2O_3 \longrightarrow$$
(carbon monoxide gas) (iron ore)
$$2Fe + 3CO_2$$
(free iron)   (carbon dioxide gas)

The limestone aids in the formation of a slag that absorbs undesirable elements from the charge. Molten iron, referred to as **pig iron,** is tapped from the bottom of the blast furnace into a transfer ladle that delivers it to the steel-making furnace (Fig. 6.12). The slag is tapped separately and either dumped or cooled and used for such things as concrete aggregate, railroad ballast, or soil conditioner.

Approximately two-thirds of all the pig iron produced is subsequently used in the manufacture of **steel,** an alloy of iron with one or more elements that give the resulting metal specifically desired properties. Carbon steel, the most easily produced and most widely used steel, is produced by adjusting the amount of carbon left after original smelting. Today, as shown in Table 6.4, a wide variety of different metals are added to iron to produce steels with different properties for specific uses. The actual steel production usually takes place in a separate furnace where the alloying elements are carefully admixed. After the steel is refined, it is cast, rolled, or otherwise shaped into the useful forms we see around us every day.

Iron and Steel Production

Since the Industrial Revolution, the quantity of iron ore mined and the amount of iron and steel produced have far surpassed the production of all other metals combined. Indeed, iron and steel production have sometimes served as a general measure of the economic well-being of a nation.

The iron ores that fed the fledgling European iron industry at the beginning of the Industrial Revolution in the 1700s were taken from large deposits in England, in the Alsace-Lorraine area along the French-German border, and in Sweden. The first European settlers in eastern North America had to import iron products from Europe. As they explored the Atlantic coastal plain, however, they discovered local accumulations of iron hydroxides, known as **bog irons** in the swamps and bogs. Such ores had been mined in earlier times in Europe but were used up by about 1700. As the American settlers moved westward, they found sedimentary iron-stones in the high ridges of the Appalachians from New York to Alabama. Although these formations contain significant quantities of iron oxide minerals wherever

FIGURE 6-12. Iron, melted in a blast furnace, here is transferred by a large ladle into a steel-making furnace where it will be converted to a specific steel alloy prior to processing into finished products. (Courtesy of U.S. Steel Corporation.)

TABLE 6-4

Elements added to iron to give desirable properties to steel

Element	Function in Steel
Aluminum	Remove oxygen; control grain size
Chromium	High temperature strength; corrosion resistance
Cobalt	High temperature hardness
Niobium	Strength
Copper	Corrosion resistance
Lead	Machinability
Manganese	Remove oxygen and sulfur; wear resistance
Molybdenum	High temperature hardness; brittleness control
Nickel	Low temperature toughness; corrosion resistance
Rare earths	Ductility; toughness
Silicon	Remove oxygen; electrical properties
Sulfur	Machinability
Tungsten	High temperature hardness
Vanadium	High temperature hardness; control grain size

they occur, iron concentrations only locally reached economic levels (40–50 percent Fe). The largest district was that near Birmingham, Alabama, which remains an iron and steel center today.

Westward expansion in the United States eventually resulted in the discovery of extremely large iron deposits near the western end of Lake Superior in 1845. Production from the vast deposits there gradually displaced that from all others. Furthermore, the discovery of similar deposits in many parts of the world and the development of techniques for bulk mining and processing these ores that in places have only 30–40 percent iron have resulted in the Lake Superior-type ores becoming the dominant source of iron in the world today, a position they are likely to retain for many years to come.

The modern steel industry traces its origins to the development of blast furnaces in central Europe in the fourteenth century. Growth was slow and production limited in quantity and quality until Abraham Darby found the way to use coke in iron smelting in 1709 in Shropshire, England. Europe, and England in particular, was the center of iron and steel production and technology until the mid-nineteenth century when the combined effects of the discovery of the Lake Superior ores, the development of the Bessemer smelting process (in England), and the rapidly expanding American economy shifted the focus across the Atlantic. Before the turn of the century, the United States had become the world's dominant steel producer, a position it held until the 1970s. The United States was well supplied with high-grade ores, abundant coal and limestone and an effective lake and rail transport system was developed to bring the ores to places such as Bethlehem and Pittsburgh, Pennsylvania, and Gary, Indiana, where the major iron and steel centers grew.

Iron and steel production surged worldwide in the first years of the twentieth century but then was reduced in continental Europe by the effects of World War I. Production began to expand in the 1920s, only to stagnate during the Great Depression of the early 1930s. By the late 1930s production once again began to increase as economies improved and as Germany and Japan began preparations for World War II. The war drastically reduced European and Japanese capacity for iron and steel production but left the United States with an intact industry and a large world market.

Thus, in 1950 the United States was the preeminent steel producer, supplying 47 percent of the world's total (Fig. 6.13). Since that time, there has been a very marked change in the industry as Japan and Western Europe were rebuilt and as larger and more effective means of transport were developed. Japan and the European countries that once bought American steel could make their own more efficiently and less expensively than the United States could because their plants were new and their operating costs less. Japan, in particular, benefitted from the new large low-cost ocean transport of raw materials and the opening of huge, low-cost deposits in Western Australia. In spite of having very limited reserves of iron ore, coal, or even limestone, Japanese industrial efficiency overcame difficulties arising from having to import all the raw materials and export most of the products. Their costs were lower than those of the countries in Europe or the United States that had abundant domestic supplies of all the materials. Consequently, as shown in Fig. 6.13, since 1950 world steel production has increased more than six-fold while that of the United States has declined so that the United States' total is now only 12 percent of the world's. The decline in total American iron and steel production, combined with cost-cutting efforts in order to try to re-

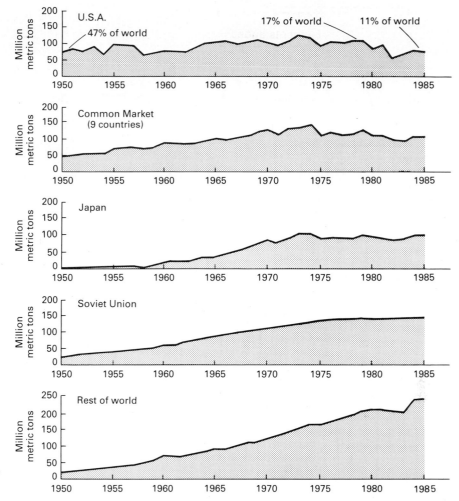

FIGURE 6-13. Raw steel production, 1950–1985 for the United States, the European Common Market, Japan, the Soviet Union, and the rest of the world. (Modified from the U.S. Bureau of Mines, *Mineral Facts and Problems,* 1980.)

main competitive, has resulted in a reduction in the number of jobs in the blast furnaces and steel mills from more than 470,000 from 1976–1979 to less than 300,000 in 1983–1985 (Fig. 6.14). There are no indications that this trend will change in the years ahead. The situation is very similar in a number of European countries, especially Great Britain, where the iron and steel industry has experienced a large loss of markets and jobs because it cannot compete effectively with Japan.

While the American and British iron and steel industries struggle, two other nations in particular are expanding theirs—the Soviet Union and South Korea. The Soviet Union has placed great emphasis on the production of more iron and steel from her own resources to meet her own growing domestic needs. In contrast, South Korea, resource limited like Japan, has developed an extremely modern and efficient industry that competes very effectively with Japan in terms of iron and steel exports.

Today, the problems for the American iron and steel industry are not those of resource adequacy but rather of economic competitiveness. Thus, mines and mills are operating far below capacity. Even so, the U.S. is now importing more and more iron and steel because it is cheaper than producing it domestically. Since 1980, iron ore imports have ranged from 19–37 percent of consumption and steel imports have ranged from 15–23 percent of consumption. Canada has been the largest foreign supplier of iron ore, whereas the European Economic Community and Japan have been the largest sources of imported steel (Fig. 6.15). This has resulted in the number of jobs in the American iron ore mining business decreasing from more than 20,000 in the mid-1970s to less than 10,000 in the mid-1980s. Unfortunately, there is no evidence that this situation will change in the foreseeable future.

Iron Ore Reserves and Resources

The world's reserves of iron ore today are both large and widespread as evidenced by Fig. 6.1 and the data in Table 6.3. Considering that annual world production is now about 800×10^6 metric tons, the known world reserves of about 153×10^9 metric tons will be sufficient

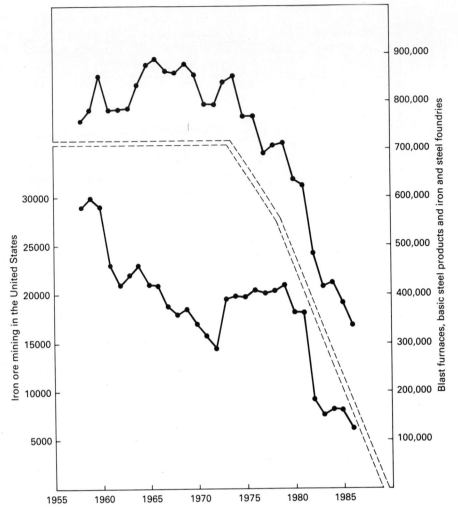

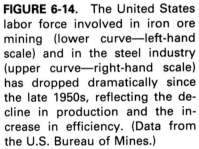

FIGURE 6-14. The United States labor force involved in iron ore mining (lower curve—left-hand scale) and in the steel industry (upper curve—right-hand scale) has dropped dramatically since the late 1950s, reflecting the decline in production and the increase in efficiency. (Data from the U.S. Bureau of Mines.)

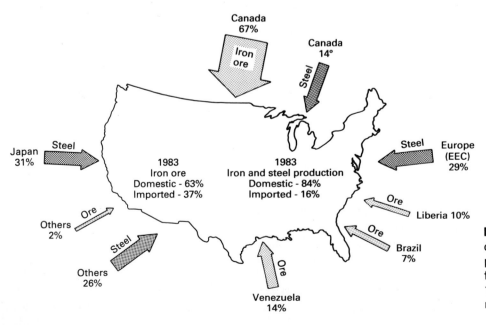

FIGURE 6-15. The United States domestic production and its importation of iron ore and steel from major foreign sources for 1980–1983. (Data from U.S. Bureau of Mines.)

to last for nearly 200 years. The reserve figures given are no doubt conservative, and some estimates place the amount of iron ore ultimately mineable at values of four to five times larger. It is apparent that sufficient iron ore is available to meet our needs far into the future.

MANGANESE

Manganese is a metal that is little known to the general public but which is very important to modern society, because it is essential for the production of iron and steel. Manganese, like iron, exists in nature in more than one oxidation state; these oxidation states (Mn^{2+}, Mn^{3+}, Mn^{4+}) control its geological behavior and distribution. Manganese tends to be concentrated by chemical sedimentary processes, and important manganese resources in the world are sedimentary rocks, mixed sedimentary and volcanic rocks, or residual deposits formed by leaching of primary deposits. Like iron, manganese is very soluble in acidic or reducing solutions that carry it as Mn^{+2}, but it is very insoluble, precipitating as minerals such as pyrolusite (MnO_2) or psilomelane ($BaMn_9O_{18} \bullet 2H_2O$), when it becomes oxidized. Manganese has little use on its own as a pure metal because of its brittleness and is little used even as an alloy in steels. However, there is no other substitute for its use as a scavenger of minor detrimental impurities such as

sulfur and oxygen during the smelting of iron. Although the distinctive purple colors of manganese compounds and strong oxidizing properties of manganese had been utilized for centuries, manganese was not isolated as an element until 1774, and it did not become important industrially until its importance in steel making was discovered in the middle 1800s. After that, it was soon found that the most useful form of manganese, and that still used today, is as **ferromanganese**, an alloy of iron and manganese containing 78–90 percent manganese. Up to 7 kilograms of manganese are necessary for the production of each metric ton of iron or steel. Although more than 90 percent of the world's manganese consumption is in the iron and steel industry, there are also important uses for manganese oxides in the chemical industry. Two of the best known uses are as potassium permanganate, a powerful oxidizing agent used for water treatment and purification, and as manganese dioxide, a necessary component in dry cell batteries.

Manganese ores usually consist of dark brown to black oxides, especially pyrolusite and psilomelane, that range from hard and compact to friable and earthy. Locally the carbonate, rhodochrosite ($MnCO_3$), or the silicate, braunite ($MnSiO_3$), are important ores. The largest and most important sedimentary deposits include Groote Eylandt on the north coast of Australia, the Molango District in Mexico, the Kalahari Field in the Republic of South Africa, and the Bol'shoy Tokmak,

TABLE 6-5

World manganese production, reserves and reserve base

Continent and Country	Production in 1983	Reserves	Reserve Base
North America:			
Mexico	133	3350	7800
South America:			
Brazil	907	18,960	62,600
Europe:			
U.S.S.R.	3129	331,100	507,900
Bulgaria	13	4100	4100
Africa:			
Gabon	857	99,800	172,300
Ghana	77	3600	6000
Morocco	39	540	1500
South Africa	1111	369,000	2,630,000
Asia:			
China	481	13,600	29,000
India	481	18,100	27,200
Oceania:			
Australia	672	68,000	153,000
Other	80	6000	101,400
WORLD TOTAL	7980	936,150	3,702,800
Seabed nodules as resources		16,300,000	

(U.S. Bureau of Mines, Mineral Facts and Problems, 1985.)
Data in thousands of metric tons of manganese content.

Chiatura, and Nikopol' deposits of the Soviet Union. Important residual deposits include the Sierra do Navio in Brazil, the Moanda in Gabon, and several deposits in India. At present, only deposits containing 35 percent or more manganese constitute reserves (Table 6.5). If deposits with manganese contents down to approximately 30 percent are also considered in the reserve base, the available manganese increases about four times. When world reserves are compared against total annual production, it is apparent that there will be sufficient manganese to meet people's needs for many years to come. However, despite the relative abundance of manganese on a global scale, the distribution is irregular, and the United States, Japan, and Western Europe are all lacking in economic deposits of this important metal. Relatively small deposits were mined in the United States as early as the 1830s. This continued until the end of World War II, but the most significant remaining domestic deposits have average grades of less than 20 percent. This has led to a concern about the adequacy of stable long-term supplies from foreign producers. For many years the Republic of South Africa has been a major U.S. supplier, but differences in political views have jeopardized this source. If South Africa were no longer a major source for manganese, it is probable that Brazil and several of the African countries would increase their production to fill the needs.

There is yet another potentially exploitable manganese resource—the deep ocean floor. The ship *Challenger*, sent around the world by the Royal Society of London between 1873–1876 in order to gather data about the waters, rocks, plants, and animals of the oceans, found that some parts of the deep ocean floor are covered by quantities of black nodules up to several centimeters in diameter (Fig. 6.16). Subsequent studies have found that these nodules, generally referred to as **ferromanganese nodules,** or just **manganese nodules,** are widespread on the oceans' floors and are complex mixtures of iron and manganese oxides and hydroxides with minor but potentially important amounts of other metals (Table 6.6). The nodules consist of onionlike concentric layers that have grown over a central nucleus of rock or shell material (Fig. 6.17). Growth appears to be very slow—on the order of 1 millimeter per 1000 years—and may well be influenced by bacterial activity. The manganese and other metals are probably derived both from the land, as terrestrial weathering and erosion slowly liberate metals and transport them to the oceans, and from submarine hydrothermal and volcanic vents that occur along midocean ridges. The total quantity of manganese recoverable in the form of nodules is not well known, but the U.S. Bureau of Mines conservatively estimates the figure for the richest deposits alone to be more than 16×10^9 metric tons, ap-

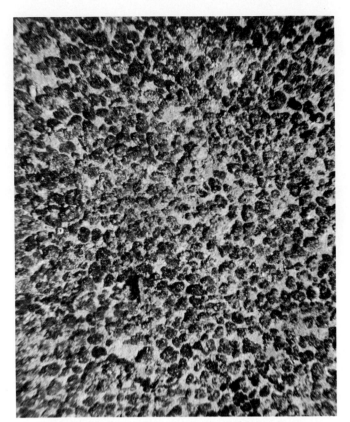

FIGURE 6-16. Manganese nodules such as those shown here are common on many parts of the deep ocean floor. These nodules in the Pacific Ocean are 5 to 10 centimeters in diameter. (Photograph by W.T. Allen, DeepSea Ventures.)

proximately 20 times the known terrestrial resources and more than 2000 years worth of production at present rates of use.

The ultimate exploitation of the sea floor nodules presents economic, technological, and legal challenges. American and Japanese companies have recovered nodules from the Pacific Ocean floor on a trial basis, but commercial processing appears to be many years away. Possible recovery methods, shown schematically in Fig. 6.18, make use of simple drag dredges, a continuous

TABLE 6-6

Average elemental compositions of ferromanganese nodules from the major oceans

Element	Atlantic	Indian	Pacific	Pacific*
Manganese	15.5	15.3	19.3	24.6
Iron	23.0	13.4	11.8	6.8
Nickel	0.3	0.5	0.9	1.1
Copper	0.1	0.3	0.7	1.1
Cobalt	0.2	0.3	0.3	0.2
Zinc	—	—	—	0.1

*A 230 km² area at 8°20'N and 153°W.

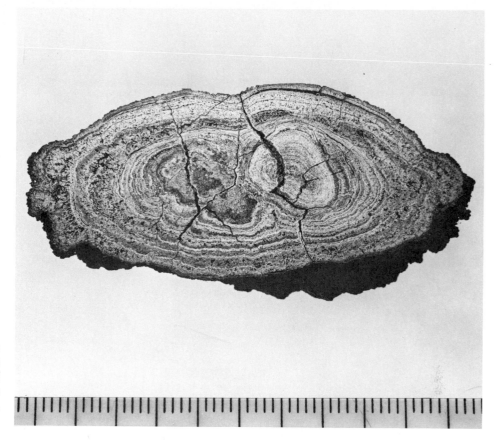

FIGURE 6-17. A cross section cut through a manganese nodule shows the concentric nature of the manganese and iron oxides within the manganese nodule. (Photograph by B.J. Skinner.)

bucket line, or a vacuum cleaner-like device in which air bubbles injected at the base provide the suction. Regardless of the technique employed, the recovery of nodules from depths of 4000 meters (12,000 feet) is difficult and expensive. The exploitation of nodules on the deep sea floor raises two additional questions. The first is, What are the possible environmental effects? Little is known of the deep-sea life forms and the extent, if any, to which they could be harmed by sediment disturbance caused by sea floor mining. The second question is, Who has the right to mine on the ocean floor? The international Law of the Sea conference of the United Nations worked for many years to try to define ownership of, and access to midocean resources. It resulted in the general recognition of exclusive economic zones covering the continental shelves but did not resolve the problems of mining manganese nodules and other deep ocean resources. Serious international problems remain, and a legal framework for the recovery of manganese nodules has still to be worked out and to be accepted by all countries. Despite the active participation by three previous American administrations in the drafting of the Law of the Sea Treaty, the Reagan administration refused to accept it. The actions of future administrations may play an important role in the access of the United States to the oceans' manganese resources.

ALUMINUM, THE METAL OF THE TWENTIETH CENTURY

Aluminum is the second most abundant metallic element (after silicon) in the earth's crust, where it occurs at an average concentration of 8.3 percent. However, it is so difficult to free the metal from its minerals that aluminum has been produced commercially for only about 100 years. Despite its relatively recent appearance on the industrial scene, aluminum has proven to be a remarkably useful metal. It weighs only about one-third as much as either iron or copper, it is malleable and ductile, easily machined and cast, it is corrosion resistant, and it is an excellent conductor of electricity. This versatility has resulted in such widespread use that today the only metal with a greater consumption worldwide is iron.

Rubies and sapphires have been valued since Biblical times, but it was not until the end of the eighteenth century that they and corundum were recognized as oxides of aluminum (Al_2O_3) and were collectively called *alumina*. From this, the metal was named *aluminum* in 1809, but it was not isolated in its free state until 1825. Because of the difficulty in producing the metal and its novelty, it was valued more highly than gold for a short time. Napoleon III, nephew of Napoleon Bonaparte and

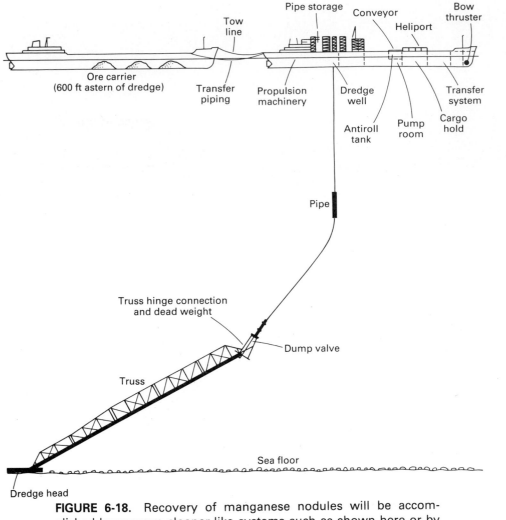

FIGURE 6-18. Recovery of manganese nodules will be accomplished by vacuum cleaner-like systems such as shown here or by bucket-line systems. The major problem is maintaining continuous and economic recovery in ocean depths of 3300 to 5000 meters (10,000 to 15,000 feet). (Courtesy of DeepSea Ventures.)

emperor of France from 1852 until 1871, even had a baby rattle for his infant son and his most prized eating utensils made of aluminum. The breakthrough that permitted commercial production, and hence the wide-scale use of aluminum, came in 1886 when chemists Charles Hall in the United States and Paul Heroult in France developed an electrolytic process to release the metal from the oxide. At about the same time, Karl Bayer, a chemist from Austria, developed a chemical process to produce alumina in large quantities from bauxite. The Hall-Heroult and Bayer processes laid the foundations of the modern aluminum industry. Commercial production began in 1888, and the processes continue to be used in only slightly modified forms today.

Aluminum Products and Usage

Because of its versatility, aluminum now finds a wide range of uses in our daily lives. The annual usage of alu-

minum metal in the United States reached more than 5 million metric tons by 1985 or about 22 kilograms (49 pounds) per person and is projected to increase by more than 3 percent per year to the end of the century. No other country uses so much aluminum in total, nor so much per person, as the United States, but its use is increasing significantly in nearly every country. In the United States the major uses are packaging and containers (35 percent), transportation (20 percent), and building (18 percent). Other important uses include electrical (9 percent) and consumer durable goods, such as refrigerators (8 percent). The principal packaging use is in aluminum beverage cans, 56.5 billion of which were produced in the United States in 1983. Transportation uses continue to be important because the light weight of aluminum affords more efficient use of fuels and because aluminum is so resistant to corrosion. Approximately 70 kilograms (150 pounds) of aluminum were used in the average U.S.-built car in 1985; the quantity

is projected to reach 90 kilograms (200 pounds) by 1990. Aluminum is widely used in construction because of its light weight and resistance to weathering, and it seems likely that there will be increased consumption in this area. Although copper is nearly always used for household wiring, it is aluminum that serves as virtually all the high power transmission lines that extend across the country. It is the light weight and relatively high strength-to-weight ratio of the aluminum that allow the construction of the long spans between towers.

Less visible than the uses of aluminum metal are the uses of aluminum compounds. The most important of these are alumina and aluminum hydroxide $(Al(OH)_3)$, which is also called activated bauxite. Both activated bauxite and alumina are widely employed in the petroleum industry as absorbents in oil and gas refining. Other important uses are as fire retardants and as fillers in plastics and paper. Alumina has long served as a major component in refractories for the steel industry because it has a very high melting point and is relatively unreactive. Alumina is an important grinding and polishing compound, but increasingly it has to compete with harder materials such as synthetic diamond and silicon carbide. A quantitatively small, but very important and growing use of alumina is in the production of synthetic rubies and sapphires used in the construction of lasers, as jewel bearings in precision mechanisms, and as synthetic gemstones.

Aluminum Ores

Aluminum, like iron, is such an abundant element that it is a constituent of many common minerals. The most important are feldspar, the most abundant mineral in the earth's crust, mica, and clay. To date, and probably for the near future, most aluminum production has been from **bauxite** (a name derived from the southern French village of Les Baux where it was first recognized in 1821), a heterogeneous material composed chiefly of the aluminum hydroxides gibbsite $(Al(OH)_3)$ and boehmite and diaspore (both $AlO \bullet OH$). These relatively uncommon minerals are formed by the breakdown of aluminum-bearing rocks under special conditions of lateritic weathering. The conditions occur most frequently in subtropical to tropical climates where there is abundant rainfall and the ground water is neither too acid nor too alkaline, where there are aluminous parent rocks and where there is subsurface drainage, but low relief so that mechanical erosion is slow relative to chemical leaching.

During the intense chemical weathering characteristic of lateritic conditions, the three least soluble components are silica (SiO_2), alumina (Al_2O_3), and ferric oxide (Fe_2O_3). After the more soluble constituents, such as sodium, potassium, magnesium, and calcium have been removed in solution, the residue is mainly iron hydroxide plus clays such as kaolinite $(Al_2Si_2O_5(OH)_4)$. Percolating waters, made slightly acid by the decay of organic debris, slowly dissolve the clays and carry off the silica and some of the iron. What remains are aluminum and iron hydroxides. Where the ratio of aluminum hydroxides to iron hydroxides is high, the resulting rock is an aluminum-rich laterite called **bauxite.** Successive solution and precipitation commonly results in a characteristic pisolitic texture of the type shown in Fig. 6.19.

Aluminum-rich rocks serve as the parent rock for some deposits, but bauxites can form from the weathering of any rock that is aluminum bearing. In fact, some important bauxites, those known as the terra rosa type, develop on limestones which contain very little aluminum. In these cases, the calcium carbonate of the limestones is relatively rapidly dissolved in the acid ground waters developed in tropical climates. This leaves a clay residue that can be altered to form discontinuous and localized, but rich, lenses of bauxite. Most major commercial bauxite deposits have formed during the past 60 million years, and all the largest have formed in the tropics over the past 25 million years. Deposits such as those in Arkansas or France, found in areas that are presently temperate, formed in earlier geologic times when the climates of those areas were tropical. No doubt, many additional bauxites have formed during the earth's history, but because they are surficial deposits, they have been destroyed by erosion. Bauxites are unknown in arctic regions because they would not form there today, and because any deposits formed in the geologic past would likely have been removed or covered up by glaciation.

Aluminum Smelting and Production

The conversion of raw bauxite into alumina or aluminum metal is a multistep process, as shown in Fig. 6.20. Bauxite mining is relatively easy and inexpensive because the deposits lie on or near the earth's surface and the ores are usually soft and easily removed. In contrast, the processing, and especially the production of metallic aluminum, is complex and extremely energy intensive. Unfortunately, the bauxite deposits that supply the raw material, the sources of abundant inexpensive energy needed to process the ore, and the markets for the end products tend to be widely separated. Most mining of bauxite takes place in tropical regions which have neither abundant cheap electricity nor large markets for the aluminum products. In order to maximize the efficiency of shipping to processing sites, the bauxite is first crushed, washed to remove impurities and then dried as shown in Fig. 6.20. The washed concentrate is then shipped to countries such as Norway, Canada, and

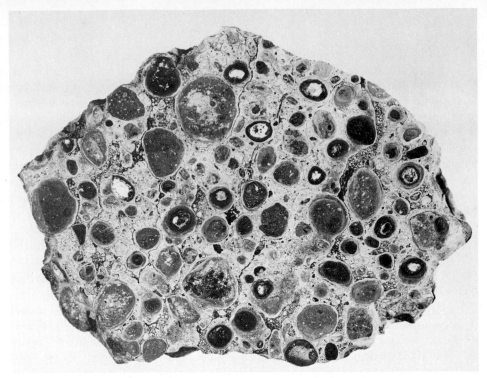

FIGURE 6-19. Bauxite, the ore of aluminum, commonly exhibits a characteristic pisolitic texture. (Photography by B.J. Skinner.)

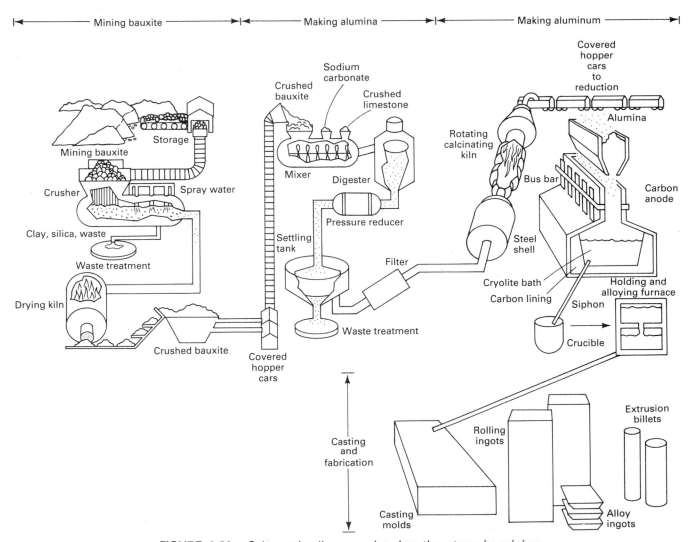

FIGURE 6-20. Schematic diagram showing the steps in mining, processing, and smelting of aluminum. (Courtesy of The Aluminum Association.)

the United States where there is now (or was when plants were established) abundant cheap electrical power. In each of these countries, the source of the power for processing is principally hydroelectric plants.

The production of aluminum metal is accomplished by the electrolytic reduction of alumina in a molten bath of natural or synthetic cryolite (Na_3AlF_6) that serves both as an electrolyte and a solvent. The actual metal production takes place in a series of large bathtublike vats called a **pot line** where hundreds of aluminum ingots, each weighing up to a metric ton, are produced simultaneously. The metal reduction process uses very large amounts of electricity, because the temperatures must be maintained at 950°C or more, and because the electrical currents and voltages must reach as much as 150,000 amperes and 1000 volts, respectively. In the United States the growth of the aluminum industry in the first half of the twentieth century coincided with the development of regional power networks and the building of major hydroelectric facilities. The availability of the large amounts of cheap electricity generated in the Columbia River basin and the Tennessee Valley led to the construction of major aluminum smelters in these areas. This situation worked well because the aluminum companies, while getting the cheap power they needed, provided a use for the surplus electricity generated by the hydroelectric dams. Consequently, United States' aluminum metal production rose rapidly from the beginning of the century until 1973 when it exceeded 4100 million kilograms (Fig. 6.21). At that time, the oil embargo raised energy prices and ended the period of growth of the American aluminum industry. As a result of rising energy costs, American production levelled off between 1973 and 1985 and is expected to gradually decrease through to the year 2000. Other countries, that were dependent on expensive imported energy, sharply curtailed, or in the case of Japan, terminated primary aluminum production, deciding that it was more economic to import aluminum metal than to refine it. This underscores what is generally recognized as the major problem of aluminum refining—it is energy intensive.

The amount of energy needed to refine aluminum relative to that for iron and titanium is shown in Fig. 6.22. It is apparent that the energy required to extract a ton of aluminum from typical bauxites is much greater than that required per ton of iron extracted from taconites. It is also apparent that the energy that would be required if we were to refine aluminum from other common aluminum-bearing minerals such as clay or feldspar is even greater than that for refining bauxite.

A concern for aluminum resources and the energy intensive extraction of the metal has led to a great deal of recycling of aluminum. In 1984, 830,000 metric tons of scrap were recycled, and this constituted about 18 percent of American aluminum production. This quantity was second only to iron in terms of recycled metal. It consisted of new scrap, which is waste material generated in the production of new aluminum products, and old scrap, which consisted of old aluminum products which have been discarded (cans, foil, engine parts, wire, etc.). In 1970, 3 billion (3×10^9) aluminum beverage cans were recycled in the United States; in 1983, that had risen to 26.5 billion (26.5×10^9) cans. As noted in Chapter 3, recycling of these cans, and all aluminum scrap, is important because it represents not just a saving of resource, but also a large saving of energy. This is so because the remelting and forming of a new aluminum can from an old one requires only 5 percent of the energy needed to make the can from bauxite in the first place. Thus, the recycling of aluminum represents a 95 percent energy saving. When Japan announced the closing of its primary aluminum production facilities in 1985, the country decided, instead, to step up the importation of aluminum scrap for reprocessing because it is economically more efficient and saves the large costs and problems involved in the importation of the fossil fuels and bauxite needed for primary production. In a very real sense, the importing of the aluminum scrap represents the importing of energy, the energy that some other country had supplied to initially refine the metal.

Bauxite Reserves

The specification of bauxite reserves is complicated because the quality of deposits is not judged solely on the accessibility and aluminum content, but also on other chemical properties, such as iron and silica content, on local factors such as energy costs, and proximity of markets. Typical bauxites mined in Jamaica contain 49 percent Al_2O_3 (on a dry basis), and high-grade ores from South America, Guinea, and Australia contain 50–60 percent Al_2O_3, whereas mineable reserves in Arkansas and Western Australia have only 40 percent Al_2O_3. Most European bauxites have 45–65 percent Al_2O_3.

World bauxite reserves (Table 6.7) are concentrated in tropical and semitropical regions (Fig. 6.23). Exploration over the past 40 years has greatly expanded reserves from 1×10^9 metric tons in 1945, to 3×10^9 metric tons in 1955, to 6×10^9 metric tons in 1965, to 21×10^9 metric tons in 1985. Guinea and Australia together have about one-half of world reserves; more than 25 percent occurs in the Western Hemisphere in Brazil, Jamaica, Guyana, and Surinam. The principal U.S. deposits are about 36 million metric tons in central Arkan-

FIGURE 6-21. World bauxite production (a) increased rapidly in this century, especially between 1950 and 1975. Aluminum production in the United States (b) in the twentieth century parallels the world bauxite production. (a) from U.S. Geological Survey Professional Paper 1076-B; (b) based on data from the U.S. Bureau of Mines.

188

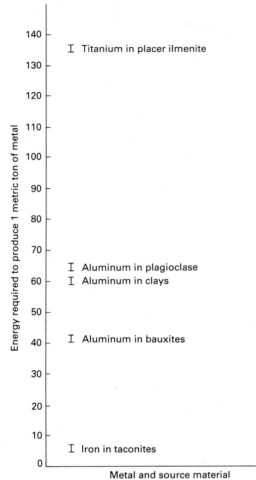

FIGURE 6-22. Energy requirements for the recovery of iron, titanium, and aluminum from different types of ores.

sas plus 2–3 million tons that occur in Alabama and Georgia. At the present world mining rate of approximately 80 million metric tons of bauxite annually, the reserves presently identified would last nearly 350 years. Estimates of total world bauxite resources that may one day be mineable are 40 to 50 × 10^9 metric tons and would allow for bauxite mining for a much longer period of time. From this, a quantity of 9 to 11 × 10^9 metric tons of aluminum metal can be extracted. This quantity is indeed large, but very much smaller than the amount of iron that will ultimately be recoverable.

Concerns over the sufficiency of bauxite as the source of aluminum, especially in countries like the United States which have limited bauxite reserves, have led to the consideration of other types of materials as potential sources of aluminum. The Soviet Union currently produces alumina from nepheline (($Na,K)AlSiO_4$) and alunite ($KAl_3(SO_4)_2(OH)_7$). In addition to nepheline and alunite, particular interest has been focused on clays (especially kaolinite), oil shales (the aluminum-rich waste after processing for oil), and anorthosite (composed primarily of the **plagioclase feldspar** anorthite, $CaAl_2Si_2O_8$). The potential resources of clays and anorthite are large and widespread. Unfortunately, as is evident in Fig. 6.22, the processing of these materials for aluminum requires even more energy than needed to process bauxite. The potential use of oil shales would also be dependent on the economic extraction of the oil, something that seems unlikely in the foreseeable future.

In summary, the total bauxite reserves appear to be adequate for many years, but several other mineral commodities will continue to be investigated as possible

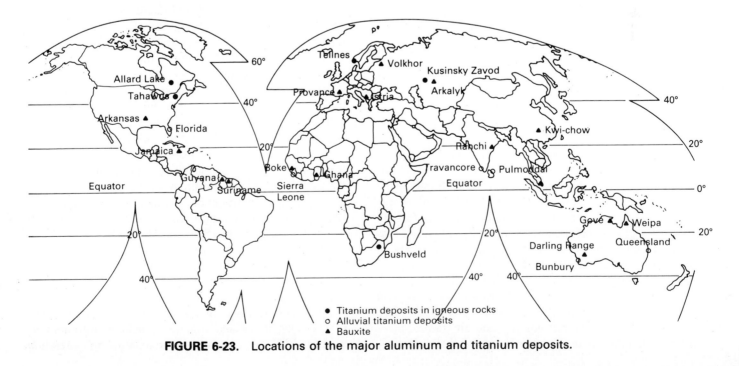

FIGURE 6-23. Locations of the major aluminum and titanium deposits.

TABLE 6-7

World bauxite resources and production; in 10^6 metric tons

Continent and Country	Reserves		1984 Production
	Bauxite	Recoverable Al-content	Bauxite
North America and Caribbean Islands:			
United States	38	10	0.9
Jamaica	2000	450	6.9
Other	40	9	—
Europe:			
Greece	600	136	3.2
Hungary	300	68	2.9
U.S.S.R.	300	60	4.6
Other	442	98	—
South America:			
Brazil	2250	540	7.5
Guyana	700	182	1.9
Suriname	575	153	1.7
Venezuela	235	47	—
Africa:			
Guinea	5600	1298	12.0
Cameroon	680	136	—
Other	594	119	—
Asia:			
India	1000	229	1.9
Indonesia	750	161	0.9
Other	210	42	—
Oceania:			
Australia	4440	998	25.0
Other	200	40	9.4
WORLD TOTAL	20,954	4766	78.8

(U.S. Bureau of Mines, Mineral Commodity Summaries 1985 and Mineral Facts and Problems, 1985.)

aluminum sources. This arises from the hope that their processing costs can be made competitive with that of bauxite and from the desire of many industrial nations to be less dependent on foreign sources for the aluminum raw materials.

TITANIUM

Titanium, one of the lesser of the abundant metals, comprises only at 0.56 percent of the earth's crust. Like several other of the abundant metals, it has found application only in the modern world. Although titanium was recognized as a chemical element in 1790, more than 100 years passed before any commercial potential was realized, and it has only been used on a large scale in the past 50 years. Today it has two major applications. The first is in a variety of alloys where it imparts a high strength-to-weight ratio, a high melting point, and great resistance to corrosion. These properties have led to its widespread use in aircraft engines and air frames, electricity generating plants, welding rods, and a wide variety of chemical processing and handling equipment, and to its designation as a strategic metal. The second use, that accounts for approximately 95 percent of the world's consumption of titanium minerals, is the preparation of white titanium oxide pigment. Because of its whiteness, opaqueness, permanence of color, and low toxicity, it is now the principal white pigment used in paint, paper, plastic, rubber, and many other materials (see also Chapter 9). Formerly, white lead oxide had been widely used, but this resulted in numerous cases of lead poisoning. In addition, white lead is more susceptible to changes in coloration when subject to air pollution. The use of titanium is relatively inconspicuous; nevertheless, the amounts used every year are very large. For example, in 1984, the United States produced approximately 21 million metric tons of titanium metal worth about $180 million and about 720 million metric tons of titanium dioxide pigment valued at approximately $1 billion.

Titanium occurs in minor amounts in most types of rocks as the oxide minerals **rutile** (TiO_2) and **ilmenite** ($FeTiO_3$). Locally, **leucoxene**, an alteration

product of ilmenite, is also present. Generally, these minerals are widely dispersed in igneous and metamorphic rocks as accessory minerals. Locally, however, the igneous processes involved in the formation of **mafic** rocks (**gabbro** to **anorthosite**) have concentrated large amounts of iron and titanium oxides, especially ilmenite, into lenses or thick layers. When the iron oxide present is magnetite (Fe_3O_4), separation of the titanium minerals into a relatively pure concentrate is usually possible, because the minerals are coarse grained and because the magnetite is magnetic. In contrast, mixtures of ilmenite with hematite are usually very fine-grained intergrowths as shown in Fig. 6.24(a) and are nearly impossible to separate into pure concentrates by mechanical means. The only way to thoroughly separate the titanium from these ores is by expensive chemical processes in which the ores are dissolved.

Most sedimentary rocks contain minor amounts of titanium oxide minerals derived from igneous or metamorphic rocks by weathering and erosion. The ilmenite and rutile are hard (5–6.5 on the **Moh's scale**) and resistant to solution or chemical attack, and thus survive the weathering and erosional processes intact [Fig. 6.24(b)]. Because their specific gravities (rutile = 4.25; ilmenite = 4.8) are higher than those of common constituents of river and beach sands (quartz = 2.65; feldspar = 2.6–2.7), the titanium minerals may be selectively concentrated into specific zones or sedimentary horizons (known as **placer deposits**). The gold panner makes use of the same properties as he concentrates black sand and gold in his pan; in fact, the

black sand is often largely ilmenite and rutile. The TiO_2 content of the ilmenite in placer deposits varies as a function of the initial composition of the ilmenite and the degree of weathering, because the slow alteration can result in preferential leaching of iron. Thus, placer ilmenite concentrates from South Africa average only 48 percent TiO_2, whereas those from Florida and New Jersey have 61–65 percent TiO_2. Rutile concentrates are usually 93–96 percent TiO_2, and leucoxene concentrates contain up to 90 percent TiO_2. Even though the grade of the titanium may not be so rich as that in igneous deposits, the unconsolidated nature of the sediments makes processing both simple and economic.

Titanium minerals are mined today from both deposits in igneous rocks (*hard rock* mines) and from placer sand occurrences. Until about 1942, nearly all commercial ilmenite and rutile production came from placer deposits. Today, rutile production still comes only from placers, but nearly 40 percent of the ilmenite comes from hard rock mines. Worldwide production of titanium metal and titanium oxide in 1983 are shown in Fig. 6.25 and reveal that ilmenite is the dominant source for both products.

Titanium, like silicon, aluminum, and magnesium, requires large amounts of energy for processing from its source mineral forms to produce either pigment or metal. The energy required to produce titanium metal from ilmenite and rutile is shown relative to iron and aluminum in Fig. 6.22. Most titanium is used to produce pigment and does not require so much energy for its production. Comparison of the amounts of energy

(a)

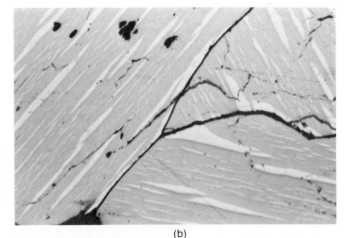

(b)

FIGURE 6-24. The two principal mineralogical sources of titanium are rutile (TiO_2) and ilmenite ($FeTiO_3$). (a) Placer rutile grains concentrated from beach sands; (b) microscopic view of intimate lamellar intergrowth of ilmenite (dark grey) with hematite (white) in the hard rock ores at Tahawus, New York. (Photographs by J.R. Craig.)

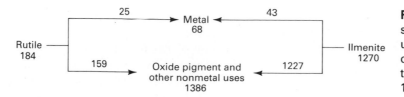

FIGURE 6-25. The worldwide sources and use of titanium products given in terms of thousands of metric tons of titanium content. (From U.S. Bureau of Mines, 1985.)

needed to form oxides and metals of aluminum and titanium is shown in Table 6.8.

Titanium occurs in small amounts in all types of rocks worldwide, but economically viable deposits are much less common; the major reserves are summarized in Table 6.9. The most important hard rock ilmenite reserves are those at Allard Lake, Quebec; Tahawus, New York; Tellnes, Norway; and Otanmaki, Finland. Important placer deposits are worked in Australia, India, the Republic of South Africa, the Soviet Union, Sri Lanka, and Sierra Leone. It is apparent from Table 6.9 that known reserves are adequate for many years of production at present rates. Furthermore, recent investigations of the detrital deposits of the continental shelves have revealed the presence of very much larger potential resources of placer titanium minerals that could be exploited if those on land are exhausted.

The mining of titanium minerals does not create any unusual environmental problems, but the processing of ilmenite to produce pigment generates up to 3.5 metric tons of toxic sulfate and sulfuric acid waste per ton of product. Previous methods of disposing of such wastes into streams and the ocean have now been replaced by acid neutralization plants. Unfortunately, the runoff of sulfates from the waste sites of older plants has seriously polluted streams and continues to cause problems locally.

MAGNESIUM

Magnesium, the eighth most abundant element in the earth's crust, is the lightest of the abundant metals. Like most of the other abundant metals, its common occurrence and its important uses are generally little realized by most people. It finds its largest use not as the metal but as the oxide MgO (called **magnesia**) and as the silicate mineral, **forsterite** (Mg_2SiO_4), both of which are used as **refractories** (see also Chapter 9) in the steel and some base metal industries. As a metal, magnesium is commonly mixed with aluminum to produce lightweight corrosion-resistant alloys that are widely used in beverage cans, automobiles, aircraft, and machinery. In addition, magnesium compounds are used in such varied materials as cement, rubber, fertilizers, animal feed, paper, insulation, and pharmaceuticals.

Magnesium-bearing raw materials are abundant and geographically widespread. They consist of several minerals, brines, and seawater (Fig. 6.26). The first magnesium resources exploited, in the mid-eighteenth century, were **magnesite** ($MgCO_3$) deposits in Czechoslovakia, Austria, and Greece. Similar deposits were subsequently discovered in California, and mining began there in 1886. During World War I, a process was developed whereby magnesium-bearing refractory materials could be extracted from dolomite ($CaMg(CO_3)_2$), a very common sedimentary rock, by intense baking (called **calcining**) to drive off the CO_2 (Fig. 6.27).

Magnesium is unique in being the only metal to be extracted directly from brines and from seawater. The recovery of magnesium metal from deep-well brines that contain several thousand parts per million magnesium, began in Michigan in 1916. There, brines are trapped in the thick sequence of evaporite minerals that underlie the Michigan Basin (see Fig. 8.8). Recovery of magnesium from seawater, in which it is the third most plentiful dissolved element (1350 parts per million), began in 1940. The extraction process, shown schemati-

TABLE 6-8

Energy requirements to produce aluminum and titanium oxides and metals (per metric ton) in btu

	Aluminum	Titanium
Mining	1.1–3.3	5.1
Shipping	0.5–3.3	0.5–3.6
Production of alumina (per ton)	52.8	—
Production of TiO$_2$ pigment (per ton)	—	75–112
Production of aluminum metal (per ton)	70.7–102.0	—
Production of titanium metal (per ton)	—	453–522
Total energy requirement in btu	125–161	534–643

(Data from the U.S. Bureau of Mines, 1985.)

TABLE 6-9

World titanium production in 1983 and titanium reserves (in 1000 metric tons of titanium content)

Country	Ilmenite	Rutile	Total	Production 1983*
United States	7200	200	7400	590
Canada	16,300	—	16,300	310
Brazil	1000	33,600**	34,600	35
Norway	19,000	—	19,000	150
U.S.S.R.	3600	1500	5100	240
Republic of South Africa	22,700	2200	24,900	240
China	18,100	—	18,100	50
India	18,100	2600	20,700	75
Australia	13,600	5200	18,800	460
Others	3200	1700	4900	800
WORLD TOTAL	122,800	47,000	169,800	2950

(Data from U.S. Bureau of Mines, 1985.)

*Estimated

**In Brazil, this is mostly anatase, another form of TiO_2

TABLE 6-10

Production and reserves of magnesium compounds*

Continent and Country	Production 1984 (in thousands of metric tons of magnesium content)		
	Mg metal	Mg compounds	Magnesite
North America:			
United States	118	567	9100
Canada	8	—	27,000
South America:			
Brazil	—	—	136,000
Europe:			
Austria	—	314	13,600
France	9	—	—
Italy	8	—	—
Norway	36	—	—
Yugoslavia	4	89	4500
U.S.S.R.	83	628	653,000
Asia:			
China	7	566	744,000
Japan	6	—	—
North Korea	—	533	444,000
Other	—	2303	508,800
WORLD TOTAL	279	5000	2,540,000

(Data from U.S. Bureau of Mines.)

*Does not include magnesium in seawater or brines.

cally in Fig. 6.27, is relatively simple chemically but requires large quantities of electricity. In 1984, magnesium metal was being produced in the United States from seawater at Freeport, Texas, and from the brines of the Great Salt Lake in Utah. In addition, magnesium oxide was being produced from seawater in California, Delaware, Florida, and Texas, the Great Salt Lake in Utah, and brines in Michigan.

Resources from which magnesium metal and its compounds can be recovered are globally widespread, and estimates range from very large to virtually unlimited. The reserves of the highest quality raw materials such as magnesite (Table 6.10) exist in quantities sufficient to meet people's needs for a very long time. Furthermore, the amounts of magnesium available in the form of dolomite, and in seawater and brines are so large that they could never be exhausted.

SILICON

Silicon is the second most abundant element in the earth's crust and is an essential constituent of all the common silicate minerals that comprise many of the common rocks. Because of its very strong affinity for oxygen, with which it is combined in quartz (SiO_2) and all silicate minerals, free silicon only occurs in nature under the most unusual circumstances. The only confirmed occurrence is at a place in Michigan where an

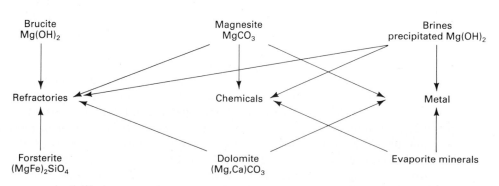

FIGURE 6-26. The uses of the principal raw materials of magnesium. (From U.S. Geological Survey Professional Paper 820, 1973.)

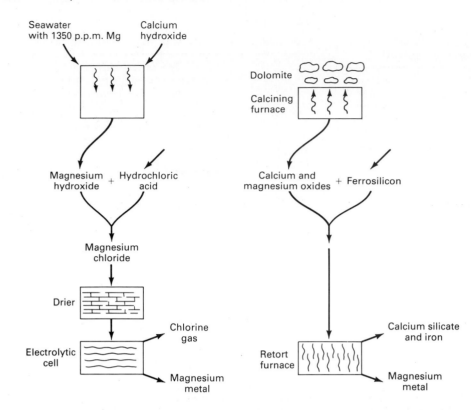

FIGURE 6-27. Magnesium metal is prepared from seawater by reaction with calcium hydroxide and hydrochloric acid followed by electrolytic refining or by reacting calcined dolomite with ferrosilicon in a high-temperature or retort furnace.

intense lightning strike fused some glacial debris, producing temperatures of about 2000°C and reducing some quartz to native silicon.

In spite of its abundance in oxide forms all around us and its importance in modern technological applications, silicon metal is relatively unfamiliar to most people. Pure silicon is a lightweight, silvery substance that has a lustrous semimetallic appearance. Although the use of silicates such as clay minerals dates from prehistoric times, and the use of glass made from silicates began at least 12,000 years ago, free silicon was not prepared until 1824. In the late 1800s, the use of silicon as a deoxidizing (oxygen removing) agent for steels was discovered, and this led to a large demand in the growing steel industry. Today, silicon (or an iron-silicon alloy called **ferrosilicon**) is prepared by melting clean quartz, usually coarse vein quartz or well-cemented quartzite [Fig. 6.28(a)], with iron or steel scrap and coal, coke or charcoal (as a reductant) in a large electric arc furnace. These furnaces, up to 13 meters in diameter and 13 meters high, can prepare 150–200 metric tons per day. Periodically, the furnaces are tapped and the molten silicon or ferrosilicon is cast into elongate bars called ingots. The ferrosilicon is mixed with the molten iron or steel to remove oxygen and to serve as an alloying agent. The addition of up to 17 percent silicon in cast iron reduces scaling and corrosion at high temperatures. Silicon is also added into aluminum and copper alloys in amounts up to 25 percent because it improves the casting properties, adds strength, and reduces corrosion.

In recent years, silicon has found many additional uses outside of metallurgy. The best known of these began in 1949 when E.I. du Pont de Nemours and Co. produced the first silicon pure enough for use in transistors and other semiconductors. Today, the **silicon chip** [Fig. 6.28(b)] is the basis for many electrical devices in computers, calculators, and communications equipment. The chips are prepared by first producing ultrapure single crystals of silicon and then by introducing into these crystals specific amounts of certain chemical elements in order to produce desired electrical properties. Another important use is as photovoltaic devices, commonly called **photocells** or **solar cells** (Fig. 6.29), in which thin layers of silicon, either as single crystals or as amorphous films, with other compounds convert sunlight into electrical energy. Today, photovoltaic cells are in broad use from pocket calculators to earth circling satellites, and their application will probably continue to expand rapidly.

Silicon is also used to produce compounds such as **silanes** (silicon hydrogen compounds, for example, SiH_4) that are used in the manufacture of numerous kinds of silicone resins, rubbers, lubricants, adhesives, antifoaming agents, and water-repellent compounds. In 1891, E.G. Acheson failed in his attempts to synthesize diamonds, but he accidentally discovered silicon carbide (SiC), also known as carborundum. This substance, with a Moh's hardness of 9.5 (compared with 9 for

(a)

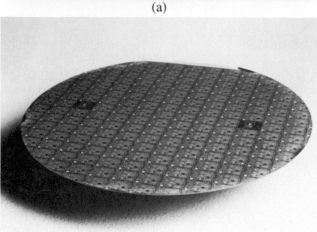

(b)

FIGURE 6-28. Quartz in the form of (a) sand, quartzite and crystals serves as the source of silicon that now finds broad application as (b) chips in many modern technological applications. (Photograph of silica chip courtesy of ITT; photograph of silicon sources by S. Llyn Sharp.)

FIGURE 6-29. Modern solar cells as shown here produce electricity for an increasing variety of applications. These contain layers of crystalline or amorphous silicon in which the incident solar radiation directly produces electricity. (Photograph courtesy of Solarex Corporation.)

TABLE 6-11

World production of silicon

Country	1984 Production in 1000's of metric tons of Si content
United States	400
Brazil	136
Canada	90
France	154
Italy	54
Japan	118
Norway	345
South Africa	100
Spain	63
Yugoslavia	100
U.S.S.R.	500
Other	617
WORLD TOTAL	2677

(Data from U.S. Bureau of Mines, 1985.)

corundum and 10 for diamond), is now one of the most widely used commercial abrasives and is commonly found in hardware stores on some of the better grades of sandpaper.

The world's resources of silicon in the form of silica in quartz and other silicates is virtually unlimited. The constraints on the production of silicon or ferrosilicon are those of purity, which are reasonably met by quartz from many **quartzites,** pegmatite masses, and gravel deposits, and the availability of electrical power. Silicon is produced in many countries (Table 6.11), but the large increases in electrical power costs in recent years has seen a shift in silicon production from countries such as Japan and the United Kingdom to countries with lower power costs. Consequently, Norway, with abundant hydroelectric power and only a small domestic steel industry, has become the world's largest exporter

of ferrosilicon. The growth in demand for silicon will be nearly totally dependent on the world's steel industries, because they account for most of the consumption. Semiconductor usage will likely continue to rise but accounts for less than 1 percent of the total.

ABUNDANT METALS IN THE FUTURE

It is now apparent that the earth's crust contains vast quantities of the abundant metals in concentrations and forms that will be exploitable by current technologies. Their geochemical abundance coupled with increasingly diverse uses ensures that they will remain the principal metals of society in the foreseeable future. Iron will no doubt remain the dominant metal because of its low cost, availability, and broad range of uses. Manganese will be needed because it is essential to the production of the steels made from iron. Aluminum, magnesium, titanium, and silicon will no doubt find expanded use, especially in construction and transportation where they permit weight and energy savings. However, because these latter metals are energy intensive in terms of their extraction, their usage could be affected by the availability and costs of energy. We now turn our attention to the scarce metals, which though constituting only trace proportions of the earth's crust, serve modern society in a wide range of important roles.

FURTHER READINGS

DIXON, C. J., *Atlas of Economic Mineral Deposits*. New York: Cornell University Press, 1979.

EDWARDS, R., and ATKINSON, K., *Ore Deposit Geology*. London: Chapman and Hall, 1986, 466 p.

GUILBERT, J. M. and PARK, C. F., *The Geology of Ore Deposits*. New York: W.H. Freeman and Co., 1986, 985 p.

HUTCHISON, C. S., *Economic Deposits and Their Tectonic Setting*. New York: John Wiley and Sons, 1983, 365 p.

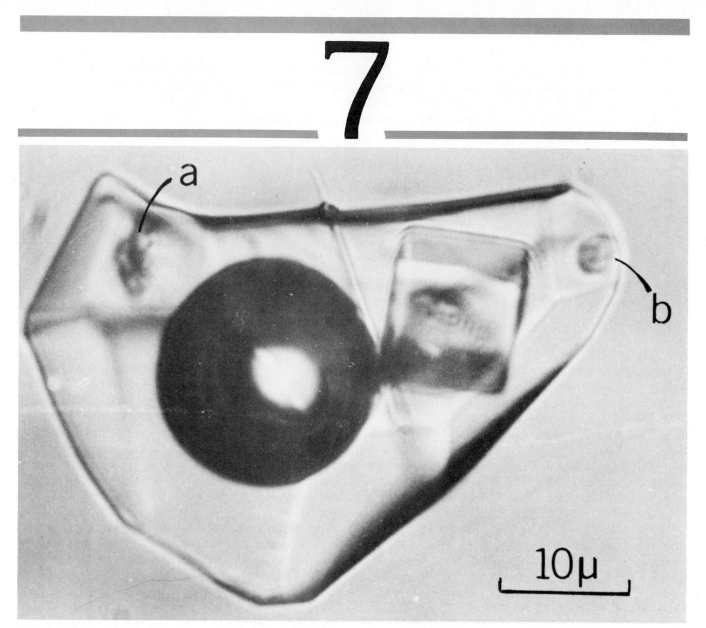

Fluid inclusions are droplets of the ore-forming solutions that were trapped at the time the ores were deposited. This inclusion from the Laramesta tin and tungsten deposit in Bolivia contains a round vapor bubble that formed on cooling from its formation temperature at 430°C. The large halite crystal and two smaller salt crystals, at a and b, crystallized from the saline solution as it cooled. (Reproduced from W. C. Kelly and F. C. Turneaure, Economic Geology, vol. 65, no. 651, (1970). Used with permission.)

THE GEOCHEMICALLY SCARCE METALS

The total volume of workable mineral deposits is an insignificant fraction of the earth's crust, and each deposit represents some geological accident in the remote past. Deposits must be mined where they occur—often far from centers of consumption. Each deposit has its limits; if worked . . . it must sooner or later be exhausted. No second crop will materialize. Rich mineral deposits are a nation's most valuable but ephemeral material possession—its quick assets.

T.S. LOVERING, 1969, "MINERAL RESOURCES FROM THE LAND," P. 109 - 134 IN RESOURCES AND MAN, EDITED BY P. CLOUD, PUBLISHED BY W. H. FREEMAN & CO., SAN FRANCISCO, 259 P.

PRODUCTION OF THE GEOCHEMICALLY SCARCE METALS

The backbone of industry is built from the geochemically abundant metals. It is the geochemically scarce metals, however, that keep industry efficient, effective, and healthy. It is the scarce metals, used in small amounts, that control the properties of alloys of the abundant metals, carry electric currents, and allow automobiles to run and planes to fly. Consider iron, which is so widely used that it accounts for about 95 percent by weight of all metals used. The properties of pure iron are so limited that iron alone could not possibly satisfy all the requirements of modern industry. For some uses iron must be hardened, for others it must be made more flexible or more ductile, tougher to abrasion, or more resistant to rust. All such changes can be accomplished by the addition of small amounts of geochemically scarce metals as alloying agents. Consequently, several of the geochemically scarce metals—nickel, chromium, molybdenum, tungsten, vanadium, and cobalt—are mined and used principally as alloying components for special steels.

The **geochemically scarce metals** (Table 7.1) are those that are present in the earth's crust in such trace amounts that none exceeds 0.1 percent of the crust by weight. Indeed, some metals are so geochemically scarce that they make up 1 millionth of a percent or less of the mass of the crust. Examples are gold, which has a crustal abundance of 0.0000004 percent by weight, and ruthenium, which only has a crustal abundance of 0.00000001 percent! Despite their extreme geochemical scarcities, both gold and ruthenium have special properties that make them important, or even essential, commodities for industry. Approximately 35 geochemically scarce metals are now mined and used for special industrial purposes. No other group of natural resources fills such a wide and varied range of needs helping things to happen more rapidly, more efficiently, and more effectively. In a sense, the geochemically scarce metals are like the enzymes that make our bodies work effectively, enabling them to carry out the complex chemical processes needed to keep us healthy. The geochemically scarce metals are, in a sense, the enzymes of industry. It is their special properties that have led to such technological marvels as the generation and distribution of electricity, the telephone, radio and television, automobiles, aircraft, and rockets. Yet it is in this same group of metals that many experts believe shortages and restrictions of natural resources might first appear. When shortages do appear, it is not entirely clear whether or not they will affect the way we use all the technological innovations of the past, but it is almost certain that shortages will retard future technological developments.

There are many differences between the geochemically scarce and geochemically abundant metals in addition to the ways in which they are used. Where the world's annual production of iron has, for many years, been 100 million tons or more, only four of the geochemically scarce metals—chromium, copper, lead, and zinc—have ever been produced at rates that exceed 1 million tons a year. The production rate of many scarce metals is still less than 1 thousand tons per year (Table 7.1). One might well ask how it could be, with such small annual rates of production, that material shortages could possibly develop? The answer lies in the way the geochemically scarce metals are distributed through the crust, in the difficulty of finding new ore deposits, and in the difficulty of extracting these metals from the host minerals.

DISTRIBUTION OF SCARCE METALS IN THE CRUST

Approximately ninety different chemical elements have been identified in the earth's crust. The average concentrations of individual elements range from as low as

TABLE 7-1

Geochemically scarce metals. Abundances for the continental crust*

Metal	Chemical Symbol	Crustal Abundance (wt%)	World Production (m.t./yr.)	Major Producers
Antimony	Sb	0.00002	53.4×10^3	China, Bolivia, U.S.S.R., South Africa
Arsenic	As	0.0002	$32.7 \times 10^{3\dagger}$	U.S.S.R., U.S.A.
Beryllium	Be	0.0002	351	U.S.A., U.S.S.R., Brazil
Bismuth	Bi	0.000004	3.9×10^3	Australia, Mexico, Japan, Peru
Cadmium	Cd	0.000018	17.7×10^3	U.S.S.R., Japan, U.S.A., Canada
Cesium	Cs	0.00016	$25^{\dagger\dagger}$	Canada
Chromium	Cr	0.0096	9.5×10^6	South Africa, U.S.S.R., Albania, Turkey
Cobalt	Co	0.0028	32.3×10^3	Zaire, U.S.S.R., Zambia, Canada
Copper	Cu	0.0058	7.8×10^6	Chile, U.S.A., Canada, U.S.S.R., Zaire
Gallium	Ga	0.0017	$30^{\dagger\dagger}$	U.S.A., France, Hungary
Germanium	Ge	0.00013	$115^{\dagger\dagger}$	U.S.A., Belgium, France, Japan
Gold	Au	0.0000002	1432	South Africa, U.S.S.R., Canada, U.S.A., China
Hafnium	Hf	0.0004	670×10^3	Australia, South Africa, U.S.A., U.S.S.R.
Indium	In	0.00002	$29^{\dagger\dagger}$	U.S.A., Belgium, France, U.K.
Iridium	Ir	0.00000002	13.2	U.S.S.R., South Africa, Canada
Lead	Pb	0.0010	3.2×10^6	Australia, U.S.S.R., U.S.A., Canada
Mercury	Hg	0.000002	6.0×10^3	U.S.S.R., Spain, China, U.S.A.
Molybdenum	Mo	0.00012	95.7×10^3	U.S.A., Chile, U.S.S.R., Canada
Nickel	Ni	0.0072	743×10^3	Brazil, Canada, U.S.S.R., South Africa, Canada
Niobium	Nb	0.0020	12.7×10^3	Brazil, Canada, U.S.S.R., South Africa, Canada
Palladium	Pd	0.0000003	87.7	U.S.S.R., South Africa, Canada
Platinum	Pt	0.0000005	87.7	U.S.S.R., South Africa, Canada
Rare Earth Elements§		~0.002	$40 \times 10^{3\dagger\dagger}$	U.S.A., Australia, Brazil, India
Rhenium	Re	0.00000004	20	U.S.A., Canada, Chile, U.S.S.R.
Rhodium	Rh	0.00000001	19.7	U.S.S.R., South Africa, Canada
Ruthenium	Ru	0.00000001	8.8	U.S.S.R., South Africa, Canada
Silver	Ag	0.000008	12.4×10^3	Mexico, Peru, U.S.S.R., U.S.A.
Tantalum	Ta	0.00024	318	Thailand, Brazil, Australia
Tin	Sn	0.00015	207.8×10^3	Malaysia, U.S.S.R., Thailand, Bolivia
Tungsten	W	0.00010	44.9×10^3	China, U.S.S.R., Canada, Korea
Vanadium	V	0.017	31.1×10^3	South Africa, U.S.S.R., U.S.A., Finland
Zinc	Zn	0.0082	6.42×10^6	Canada, U.S.S.R., Australia, Peru
Zirconium	Zr	0.014	670×10^3	Australia, South Africa, U.S.A., U.S.S.R.

* Production figures for 1984. Producers listed in order of importance.
† Reported as As_2O_3.
†† Estimated production. Data incomplete.
§ The rare earth elements are: cerium (Ce), dysprosium (Dy), erbium (Er), europium (Eu), gadolinium (Gd), holmium (Ho), lanthanum (La), lutetium (Le), neodymium (Nd), praseodymium (Pr), samarium (Sm), terbium (Tb), thulium (Tu), ytterbium (Yb), yttrium (Y). Individual production figures are not available.

10^{-8} percent to as high as 45 percent by weight, but only nine major elements account for 99 percent of the mass of the crust (Table 7.2). The combined total of the remaining 79 elements accounts for only 1 percent of the mass of the crust. Most of the 79 minor elements fulfill the definition of geochemical scarcity in that their individual abundances are less than 0.1 percent by weight.

The nine major elements are the ones that form the common minerals found in all common rocks. Only the most common of the geochemically scarce metals—copper, zinc, and chromium—form minerals that can be found in common rocks, and even those minerals are of very limited occurrence. Nevertheless, careful analyses reveal that essentially all naturally occurring chemical elements are present in trace amounts in all common

TABLE 7-2

The most abundant chemical elements in the continental crust

Element	Weight Percent
Oxygen	45.2
Silicon	27.2
Aluminum	8.0
Iron	5.8
Calcium	5.1
Magnesium	2.8
Sodium	2.3
Potassium	1.7
Titanium	0.9
TOTAL	99.0%

rocks. However, most rocks contain, at most, three or four major minerals plus an equal number of minor ones. Both the major and minor minerals are generally compounds of two to five of the nine major chemical elements. There is a simple explanation for the seemingly contradictory statement that all common rocks consist of minerals that contain the nine major elements, but that the same rocks also contain trace amounts of all the geochemically scarce elements. The explanation is that the geochemically scarce elements are all present in the common minerals by **atomic substitution** or, as it is sometimes called, **solid solution**. Atoms of nickel, for example, can substitute for atoms of magnesium in the magnesium silicate mineral olivine (Mg_2SiO_4), and atoms of lead substitute for atoms of potassium in orthoclase feldspar ($KAlSi_3O_8$). The properties that con-

trol solid solutions are like those that control liquid solutions. Hence, when the saturation limit of a liquid solution is exceeded, crystals of the solute start to grow. So too, when a solid solution becomes saturated, a new mineral must form. When the limit is exceeded for substitution of Pb for K in orthoclase feldspar, a lead mineral must form. The reason that minerals of geochemically scarce metals do not occur in common rocks—or do so only in rare circumstances—is that the amounts of the scarce metals present in the crust do not exceed the conditions of saturation of the solid solutions in common minerals.

There is no single rule concerning the concentration levels at which geochemically scarce metals form separate minerals because of the differences between the properties of the various metals. However, a rough rule of thumb is that at concentrations above about 0.1 percent a mineral will form. Below that level, scarce metals occur only in solid solution. The rule is approximately correct for many metals including copper, lead, and zinc, but it is too low for a few metals such as gallium and germanium, and it is too high for a few others such as gold, molybdenum, and uranium.

Suppose we were to attempt to mine **granite**, a common igneous rock, and after crushing the rock to a powder, we attempted to break down the solid solutions in order to recover the most valuable of the geochemically scarce metals. The result, as shown in Table 7.3, would be economically ludicrous. It costs about $10 a metric ton just to mine and crush granite to a fine powder that is suitable to start the necessary chemical treatments. The final cost of extraction would be hundreds of dollars a ton. Rather than attempting to mine metals

TABLE 7-3

Calculated value of geochemically scarce metals in solid solution in a metric ton of average granite

Element	Concentration in Average Granite* (%)	Price of Metal (1985)[†] ($US/kg)	Value of Metal in a Metric Ton ($US)
Thorium	0.002	160	3.20
Beryllium	0.0002	800	1.60
Lithium	0.003	40	1.20
Niobium	0.002	45	0.90
Tantalum	0.0002	120	0.24
Uranium	0.0005	28	0.14
Zinc	0.005	0.95	0.05
Tungsten	0.0002	14	0.03
Gold	0.0000002	12,710	0.03
Copper	0.0024	1.4	0.03
Lead	0.0039	0.56	0.02
Molybdenum	0.001	9.7	0.01
Silver	0.0000036	195	0.01
			$7.46

* After Wedepohl (1978).
[†] Some values estimated because not quoted as metal.

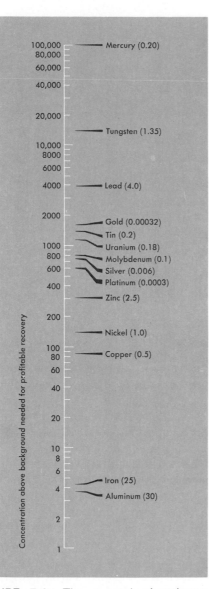

FIGURE 7-1. The crustal abundances of geochemically scarce metals are so low that large concentrations above background average are needed before deposits can be profitably mined. The abundant metals require lower concentration factors to produce rich ores. The bracketed percentages are the minimum metal contents an ore must have before it can be mined under the most favorable circumstances with present-day technology. Note that as the price of a metal goes up or down, its position will move on the diagram. Between 1969 and 1982, for example, the concentration factor needed for a viable gold deposit dropped from about 4000 to 1600, largely as a result of the rising price of gold. (From Skinner, 1986.)

from common rocks, therefore, society has always sought ore deposits, those localized geological circumstances in which are found ore minerals that carry unusually high contents of a desired scarce metal, and that can be mined at a profit.

As described in Chapters 3 and 6, many factors determine whether or not a local concentration of such minerals can be considered an ore deposit. Presuming all factors such as grade, size, depth, and so forth are favorable, the minimum grade that a scarce metal ore deposit must reach is shown in Fig. 7.1. The ratio of that minimum grade, over the grade of that metal in average, common rocks, is the concentration factor that must be attained by geological processes. Some of the concentration factors are enormous. Mercury, for example, must reach a local concentration 100,000 times greater than the crustal average in order for an ore deposit to be economic. The circumstances required for this happen very rarely indeed. Not surprisingly, ore deposits of geochemically scarce metals tend to be small and rare by comparison with ore deposits of geochemically abundant metals. The minimum concentration factors can change as the prices of metals change or as technological developments occur. Over the last 200 years, the minimum concentrations have tended to decline because great advances have occurred in mining and metallurgical technologies. It is not known how low concentration factors can be pushed, but if copper can be taken as an example, it is possible that an end to declining grades has already been reached (Fig. 7.2).

ORE MINERALS OF THE SCARCE METALS

Between 99.90 and 99.99 percent of the total amount of any given scarce metal is present in the crust in atomic substitution in common silicate minerals. Therefore, only a tiny fraction—between 0.01 and 0.1 percent—of a given metal occurs in ore minerals. Fortunately, the ore minerals tend to be found in localized concentrations rather than being scattered and disseminated. Fortunately, too, the geochemically scarce metals tend to form ore minerals that are sulfide or oxide compounds, or in a few cases, native metals, and it is relatively easy to separate these ores from the associated and valueless silicate gangue minerals. The most important geochemically scarce metals and the classes of ore minerals they form are listed in Table 7.4.

CLASSIFICATION OF GEOCHEMICALLY SCARCE METALS BY USAGE

All the important geochemically scarce metals can be divided into four major groups based on their properties or the way they are used. The first group of metals is

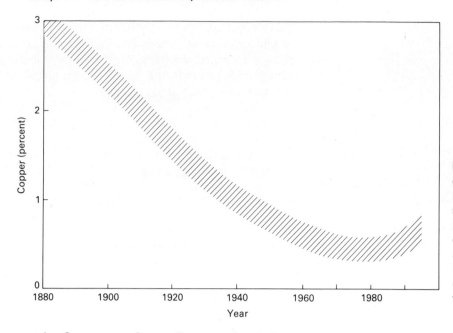

FIGURE 7-2. The minimum grade of copper that could be mined profitably dropped steadily from about 1880 to 1970 largely as a result of increased efficiencies in mining practices and the low cost of energy. Lower metal prices and higher energy costs caused the curve to flatten after 1970 and to start rising after 1980.

known as the **ferrous** or **ferro-alloy metals.** It is a group of metals that are mined and used principally for their alloying properties, especially in the preparation of specialty steels. Examples of the ferrous metals are chromium, vanadium, nickel, and molybdenum.

The second group of metals are variously called **nonferrous metals** or **base metals.** The term *base*

TABLE 7-4

Kinds of ore minerals formed by the geochemically scarce metals

Sulfide Minerals	Examples of Ore Minerals
Metal:	
Copper	Chalcocite (Cu_2S), chalcopyrite ($CuFeS_2$)
Lead	Galena (PbS)
Zinc	Sphalerite (ZnS)
Mercury	Cinnabar (HgS)
Silver	Argentite (Ag_2S)
Cobalt	Linnaeite (Co_3S_4), Co-pyrite$((Fe,Co)S_2)$
Molybdenum	Molybdenite (MoS_2)
Nickel	Pentlandite $((Ni,Fe)_9S_8)$
Oxide Minerals:	
Beryllium	Beryl ($Be_3Al_2Si_6O_{18}$)
Chromium	Chromite ($FeCr_2O_4$)
Niobium	Columbite ($FeNb_2O_6$)
Tantalum	Tantalite ($FeTa_2O_6$)
Tin	Cassiterite (SnO_2)
Tungsten	Wolframite ($FeWO_4$), scheelite ($CaWO_4$)
Vanadium	V in solid solution in magnetite (Fe_3O_4)
Native Metal:	
Gold	Native gold
Silver	Native silver
Platinum	Platinum-palladium alloy
Palladium	Platinum-palladium alloy
Iridium	Osmium-iridium alloy
Rhodium	Solid solution in osmium-iridium alloy
Ruthenium	Solid solution in osmium-iridium alloy
Osmium	Osmium-iridium alloy

metal is an old name that arose in the middle ages, during the days of **alchemy.** Metals such as copper, lead, zinc, tin, and mercury were less valuable than the precious metals and less desirable—and hence base—so the ancient alchemists tried to convert them into gold and silver (Fig. 7.3). The ancients were not successful in their efforts, and it is possible that today we might well argue that copper, zinc, and tin are actually more important than gold and silver because of their importance in industry and technology. Nevertheless, the terms *precious* and *base* remain with us. There is, however, an alternate designation for base metals. Because the principal uses of the base metals are for purposes other than alloying agents with iron, base metals are also known by the term *nonferrous metals.* Neither base nor nonferrous is a completely correct description, but both terms are nevertheless widely used.

The third group, but almost certainly the first group of scarce metals to be used by our ancestors, is the **precious metals** (Table 7.5). The precious metals of antiquity, gold and silver, were called **noble metals** because they are not readily altered or debased by forming compounds with other chemical elements, and hence little subject to corrosion. In more recent times, platinum, palladium, osmium, iridium, rhodium, and ruthenium (the so-called platinum group elements) have also come to be called precious or noble metals because they too exhibit nonreactive properties.

The fourth and final group, the **special metals,** does not fit into the previous three categories; however, these metals have unusual properties that make them important for industry. Tantalum, for example, is widely used for electronic purposes because of its desirable electrical properties. Beryllium, on the other hand, is a very useful metal in nuclear technology and high-speed aircraft. Production and use of the special metals

FIGURE 7-3. An alchemist (right) and his assistant testing formulas for the transmutation of base metals to gold. Even though the search for a successful transmutation was futile, many chemical processes were successfully developed by alchemists. (From a woodcut by Hans Weiditz, 1520.)

are recent and most have only come into use in the twentieth century. It is not surprising that the special metals do not readily fit into the traditional grouping of precious, base, and ferrous metals, because the uses to which they are put have only been developed as a result of twentieth century technology.

THE FERRO-ALLOY METALS

The ferro-alloy metals are major components of twentieth century technology. Although the individual chemical elements were all known and had been separated into their elemental forms well before the dawn of the twentieth century, their widespread use as alloying metals for special steels only started in this century.

TABLE 7-5

Classification of the geochemically scarce metals by property or use

Name	Alternate Name	Examples
Precious metal	Noble metal	Gold, silver, platinum, palladium, rhodium, iridium, osmium, ruthenium
Base metal	Nonferrous metal	Copper, lead, zinc, tin, mercury, cadmium
Ferro-alloy metal	Ferrous metal	Chromium, vanadium, cobalt, nickel, molybdenum, tungsten, niobium
Special metal	—	Beryllium, bismuth, cesium, gallium, germanium, indium, tantalum, zirconium

Chromium

Chromium was first discovered in 1765 through analysis of a chromate mineral found in Siberia. The metal was first separated as a pure chemical element in 1797. Chromate compounds have long been used in the tanning industry and in the manufacture of pigments for textiles, and they are still used for these purposes today. The properties of chromium as a valuable alloying metal were discovered as early as 1820, but the widespread use of chromium alloys only started in 1899 when ferrochromium [an iron-chromium mixture produced by chemically reducing the mineral chromite ($FeCr_2O_4$)] was first produced in an electric furnace. Ferrochrome is still the way chromium is added to a batch of molten iron in order to make a chromium steel.

Chromium is one of the most visible yet least recognized metals in our modern industrial society. Chromium plating on steel and chromium-containing alloys, such as **stainless steel,** are the shiny, noncorroding metal surfaces we find on automobiles, kitchens, on faucets, and in the cutlery we use. Chromium is also one of the so-called strategic metals, which means it is a metal considered to be vital to national defense and the continued operation of industry. This designation results from the widespread use of chromium-steel alloys in aircraft engines, military vehicles, weapons, and the chemical industry.

Chromium finds important uses today in three broad fields: metallurgy, chemistry, and refractories. As discussed above, metallurgy is an essential usage because of chromium's unique alloying properties. A steel containing between 12 percent and 36 percent chromium by weight has much less tendency to react with oxygen and water—that is, a chromium-bearing

steel corrodes very slowly. Chromium is also added to the steel used to make various machine tools because it increases hardness and resistance to wear.

The principal use of chromium as a chemical continues to lie in the production of pigments. Chromium pigments range in color from deep green and intense yellow, to bright orange. Such pigments are widely used in paints, inks, roofing materials, and textile dyes. A lesser known, but still very important chemical use of chromium compounds, is in the tanning of animal skins. The lightweight leathers used for furniture, clothing, shoes, wallets, and similar objects are produced by bathing raw hides in solutions of chromium sulfate under controlled conditions of temperature and acidity. Chromium in solution forms chemical bonds with the amino acids in the leather, and this stabilizes the organic material by reducing its tendency for biological decay, and at the same time increasing its resistance to heat.

In the refractory industry, the ore mineral **chromite** has proven to be ideal for making the bricks used to line very high temperature smelter, blast, and gas furnaces. Chromite is a member of the spinel family of minerals for which the general formula $A^{+2}B_2^{+3}O_4^{-2}$ can be written: A designates any of the divalent ions Fe^{+2}, Mg^{+2}, and Mn^{+2}, while B designates the trivalent ions Fe^{+3}, Al^{+3}, and Cr^{+3}. Chromite thus has the formula $(Fe,Mg)(Cr,Al,Fe)_2O_4$. Chromites preferred for the production of ferrochrome have high contents of Cr^{+3} and Fe^{+2}, whereas chromites preferred for refractory bricks contain more Mg^{+2} and a little Al^{+3} as well as Cr^{+3}. Chromites of suitable composition are usually mixed with MgO in order to impart strength and to increase the resistance of refractory bricks to thermal and chemical attack.

Geological Occurrence. Chromium is present in small amounts in all **mafic** and **ultramafic** rocks—that is, rocks rich in iron and magnesium but poor in silica. Chromite is the major ore mineral of chromium, and its occurrence is essentially restricted to ultramafic rocks. It occurs in two major types of ore bodies, **podiform** and **stratiform.** The podiform deposits appear as irregular pods or lenses that may range in mass from a few kilograms to several million tons and that occur nearly always in highly faulted and deformed portions of tectonically active zones. A common feature of these deposits is the appearance of the chromite as rounded or eyelike granules (Fig. 7.4). The pods are enclosed in deformed masses of **dunites, serpentinites,** and related ultramafic rocks that are believed to be solid fragments from the upper mantle that were squeezed up during tectonic collisions between continents. Typical podiform deposits occur in the Ural Mountains of the Soviet Union, the Appalachian and Pacific Coast ranges of the United States, Cuba, the Philippines, and the countries

FIGURE 7-4. Pelletal grains of chromite in a podiform deposit from Greece. (Photograph by S. Llyn Sharp.)

around the eastern end of the Mediterranean. The bodies, though small, contain chromites with very desirable compositions.

Stratiform chromite deposits are, as the name indicates, discrete, sharply bounded strata of essentially pure chromite that occur in large, mafic intrusions where the layering developed as an artifact of the processes of cooling and crystallization (Fig. 7.5). Individual monomineralic layers of chromite are known to range up to several meters in thickness in the largest layered intrusions, but such thick layers are very rare. More commonly, chromite layers are a meter or less in thickness. Whether thick or thin, however, the chromite layers may extend laterally up to tens of kilometers, and in the largest known layered intrusion, the Bushveld Igneous Complex in South Africa, up to hundreds of kilometers. Stratiform chromite layers contain most of the world's known chromite resources, although in many cases the compositions of the stratiform chromites are not as desirable for metallurgical or refractory purposes as the chromites from podiform deposits.

The origin of stratiform layers of chromite remains in question. For many years, geologists accepted the idea that the layers formed when dense chromite grains crystallized from cooling bodies of **magma,** then settled to the floor of the magma chamber to form the monomineralic layers we see today. A dense mineral such as chromite was presumed to sink rapidly, while a less dense mineral such as pyroxene would sink more slowly, and as a result a separation would be effected. Recently, this simple picture based on crystal settling has been questioned and found wanting. The textures of the chromite grains, and indeed the sequence of miner-

FIGURE 7-5. Stratiform layers of chromitite, a rock comprised almost entirely of chromite, exposed along banks of the Dwaars River, South Africa. The chromitite is interlayered with anorthositic norite (white) in the lower portion of the Bushveld Igneous Complex. (Photograph by B.J. Skinner.)

als in the layers, suggest that the minerals actually grew on the bottom of the magma chamber and that little or no settling was involved. The thick, economic layers of chromite formed during long periods of time when chromite was the only mineral crystallizing from the magma. We now believe that the periods of chromite formation were brought about by relatively large scale, but temporary, changes in the composition of the crystallizing magma as a result of contamination by overlying or underlying rocks. Such contamination would have altered the chemistry of the magma just enough so that, for a period, only chromite crystallized. After that period, the normal sequence of igneous minerals would again crystallize.

By far, the most important stratiform deposits of chromite in the world occur in the Bushveld Igneous Complex of South Africa. This enormous complex of layered intrusions covers 66,000 square kilometers, is 12 kilometers thick in places, and is also host to the world's largest known resource of vanadium and the platinum group metals.

Production and Reserves. The production and reserves of chromite are dominated by the Republic of South Africa which holds more than 70 percent of the world's reserves and is the largest producer (Table 7.6). The United States and all Europe, except Finland and Greece, are without economically viable chromite deposits. The United States does have large, low-grade stratiform deposits in the Stillwater Complex, Montana, but the chromite has a composition that is difficult to process and expensive to use. As a result, the industrial countries of the world depend for their supplies on strat-

iform deposits in South Africa and Zimbabwe, and podiform deposits in the Soviet Union.

Because of the strategic importance of chromium, there is continuing concern about the potential for supplies being cut off from the major sources either due to civil unrest or from political considerations. The data in Table 7.6 indicate that the known world reserves of chromite are certainly adequate to meet needs for many years to come. Furthermore, it seems likely that the Bushveld Igneous Complex probably has additional large resources, not included in the reserve number in Table 7.6, that can also be exploited in the future. Chromium is thus one of the important commodities where future availability may well be far more dependent on political and social issues than on the physical limits of resources.

TABLE 7-6

Production and reserves of chromite*

Country	Production, 1984 (m.t.)	Reserves (m.t.)
Republic of South Africa	3,005,000	825,000,000
U.S.S.R.	2,993,000	15,000,000
Albania	870,700	1,800,000
Turkey	607,700	4,500,000
Zimbabwe	453,500	17,000,000
Brazil	281,200	8,100,000
Philippines	272,100	21,000,000
Others	1,011,300	38,000,000
WORLD TOTAL	9,494,500	971,000,000

*Data are reported for the mineral chromite that contains between 28% and 33% chromium, depending on the exact composition of the mineral.

Vanadium

Vanadium was identified as a chemical element in 1830, and like chromium, its salts soon found uses in the tanning of leather and in preparation of colored pigments for textiles, pottery, and ceramics. The use of vanadium as an alloy came much later. In 1896, French scientists found that vanadium so toughened steel that it could withstand the impact of bullets and hence could be used to make armor plate. It was soon discovered that vanadium steel also toughened the cutting edges of knives, improved swords, and greatly increased the strength of certain constructional steels. This later discovery led the U.S. automobile industry to start using vanadium steel, and by 1908 its use was advertized as a special feature of Ford motor vehicles.

Vanadium steels continue to be very widely used in automobiles and in industry in general because the incorporation of as little as 0.2 percent vanadium in an ordinary carbon steel greatly increases its strength, high temperature abrasion resistance, ductility, and even the ease with which steels can be welded. The use of high strength vanadium steel allows a minimum weight of steel to be used in an automobile, and this, in turn, leads to increased efficiency and to a reduction in the amount of fuel needed to run an automobile.

The ease and reliability with which vanadium steel can be welded has led to its widespread use in gas and oil transmission pipelines. The 1288-kilometer Alaskan pipeline that brings oil from the Prudhoe Bay to the port of Valdez incorporates 650 tons of vanadium.

Geological Occurrence. Despite a crustal abundance of 0.017 percent, which makes vanadium one of the most common of the geochemically scarce elements, vanadium ore deposits are rare. The reason deposits are rare is that vanadium readily substitutes for ferric iron (Fe^{+3}), and hence readily enters into solid solution in common minerals such as magnetite (Fe_3O_4). The solid solution of vanadium is so extensive that the limits are rarely exceeded, and hence local concentrations of vanadium minerals are rare. The most important ore deposits of vanadium are thus vanadium-rich magnetites (containing approximately 2 percent V_2O_5). These are found as monomineralic stratiform layers of magnetite in certain layered intrusions of mafic igneous rock. By far, the most important vanadiferous magnetite deposits discovered so far are in the Bushveld Igneous Complex in South Africa. The stratiform layers of vanadiferous magnetite, of which there are about ten, are near the top of the Bushveld Igneous Complex, while the stratiform chromite layers which they closely resemble are near the base (Fig. 7.6). The vanadium magnetite layers, like the chromite layers, appear to have formed as a result of monomineralic crystal growth on the floor of the magma chamber.

When separate deposits of vanadium minerals do occur, they apparently form as a result of weathering. When igneous rocks that contain vanadium-bearing magnetites or other vanadium-bearing minerals are weathered in arid climates, the vanadium is oxidized from the trivalent V^{+3} state to the more soluble pentavalent V^{+5} state. Pentavalent vanadium can be transported long distances in solution. Precipitation of vanadium minerals can occur through evaporation or, as in the Colorado Plateau region of the United States, through contact with organic matter, which serves as a reducing agent that causes the vanadium in solution to be converted to the less soluble V^{+3} state. Uranium and copper also have more than one valency state, and exhibit a behavior similar to vanadium. Uranium and vanadium are sometimes found concentrated together as a result. The region of Colorado, Wyoming, Utah, and New Mexico where deposits of this kind are found is known as the **Uravan district** because of the co-occurrence of uranium and vanadium. For many years in the early part of the present century, deposits in the Uravan district were worked for vanadium. From the time of World War II and the development of atom bombs and nuclear power, attention in the region has been focused almost entirely on uranium.

Vanadium tends to be concentrated, at least to a small degree, whenever concentrations of organic matter occur. The vanadium content of coal averages about 0.02 percent, while that of crude oil is about 0.005 percent. Certain very heavy oils (tars) have much higher vanadium contents. The tar in the Athabasca Tar Sands of Canada contains up to 0.025 percent vanadium, while that from the Orinoco Tar Sands of Venezuela contains 0.05 percent. In Peru and Argentina, veins of solid bitumen, believed to have formed by distillation of petroleum, contain 0.1 percent and 0.85 percent vanadium, respectively.

The role of vanadium in fossil fuels is not well understood. It is clear that much of the vanadium must enter the deposits after sedimentation because the vanadium contents of living plants and animals are not high. The vanadium appears to enter during degradation of the original organic matter in the sedimentary pile, perhaps brought in by ground water, and to be locked up in compounds called **porphyrins.** The atomic structures of the vanadium porphyrins found in crude oils resemble cages, with the vanadium atoms at the center. The cages are nearly identical to the structures of the chlorophylls (magnesium-centered porphyrins) of green plants, and the hemoglobins (iron-centered porphyrins) of blood. Vanadium probably exchanges places in the structures with magnesium and iron during **diagenesis.**

FIGURE 7-6. Dark-colored stratiform layer of magnetite in the upper portion of the Bushveld Igneous Complex, South Africa. The layers are almost entirely comprised of magnetite and have the same origin as the chromitite layers shown in Fig. 7-5. The magnetite contains vanadium in solid solution and is one of the world's major sources of this valuable alloy metal. (Photograph by Craig Schiffries.)

Production and Reserves. The bulk of the vanadium produced today (78 percent) comes from the vanadiferous magnetite deposits of South Africa, the Soviet Union, and China (Table 7.7). Lesser amounts are recovered as by-products from the slags of iron smelters and smelters producing elemental phosphorous. In the western United States, the ores of the Uravan District of the Colorado Plateau are mined for uranium, and vanadium is recovered as a by-product. Hence, the economic viability of the deposits is primarily dependent on the price of uranium. The decline in the demand and price of uranium, as a result of the Three Mile Island nuclear accident, has severely curtailed production of vanadium from the major American deposits.

The recovery of vanadium by-products from the ash of burned fuel oils during petroleum refining and from spent catalytic converters used in oil refining now accounts for 1510 metric tons of metal, or about 5 percent of the world's annual production. In the United States, this type of recovery accounts for more than 26 percent of total production.

It is apparent that known world reserves of vanadium will last for at least another hundred years. Furthermore, it has been estimated that if the price of crude oil does rise sufficiently to permit mining of the rich tar sands of the world, those in the Athabasca region of Alberta alone could supply well over 2 million tons of vanadium, sufficient for an exceedingly long time into the future.

Nickel

Nickel has been used for millenia. Small amounts of nickel are present in some of the ancient copper coins dug up in the Middle East. It is probable that the use of nickel in this case was accidental and that it came about because nickel was present in small amounts as an unrecognized contaminant in the copper ore used to make the coins. Nickel really entered the cognizance of the Western world when it was encountered during the seventeenth and eighteenth centuries by copper miners in

Saxony, a part of what is now East Germany. Certain nickel minerals so resemble copper minerals in their color, and in other properties, that the Saxon miners attempted to smelt the ore to recover copper. What they obtained were specks of a shiny white metal that could not be worked into useful objects, so they named the material *kupfernickel*, or "Old Nick's" copper. They believed that the devil, Old Nick, and his mischievous gnomes had bewitched the copper ore. The frustrations of those old miners lives on in the name nickel. Early in the eighteenth century, a Swedish chemist, Axel Cronstedt, showed that nickel is actually a separate chemical element, but it was not until 1781 that pure, metallic nickel was prepared.

The first practical use of metallic nickel was in a nickel-silver alloy, the so-called German silver, that is used for trays, teapots, and other household utensils. Extensive demand for nickel arose as a result of discoveries by the English scientist, Michael Faraday, who developed the process of **electroplating.** This is a process by which metal is dissolved into solution from a metal plate connected to one terminal of a battery and then deposited on another metal object connected to the other terminal. Nickel dissolves when connected to the anode (the positive terminal of the battery), moves as a result of the electrical current, and then is deposited as a thin layer on the metal object connected to the cathode (the negative terminal). Because nickel resists corrosion and can be polished to a high luster, nickel plating soon became very popular, and by 1844 a plating industry was firmly established in England. Soon thereafter, nickel was added to copper coins in order to harden them. Belgium did so in 1860, and the United States followed in 1865. Use of the term *nickel* for the five-cent piece in the United States and Canada soon followed.

The use of nickel as an alloying agent with iron came about in the twentieth century. Nickel and chromium steels do not corrode or rust; hence, they are stainless. Used alone, or in combination with chromium and other alloying agents, nickel-bearing steels find many uses in the manufacture of aircraft, trucks, railroad cars, and other structures where great reliability and high strength are required. It is probably not an overstatement to say that nickel has proved to be the most versatile of all the ferro-alloying metals.

Nickel is still widely used as a plating metal, is still used in coinage, and is still used to harden copper and make versatile alloys with metals other than iron. The major use of nickel today, however, accounting for about half of the world's total production, is as an alloying agent with iron.

Geological Occurrence. All the important nickel deposits in the world are found in, or adjacent to, mafic and ultramafic igneous rocks. Nickel is one of the chemical elements that is depleted in the crust but en-

TABLE 7-7

Production and reserves of vanadium

Country	Production, 1984 (m.t.)	Reserves (m.t.)
Republic of South Africa	12,510	862,000
U.S.S.R.	9520	2,630,000
China	4540	608,000
Finland	3060	32,000
United States	1470	168,000
Others	—	63,000
WORLD TOTAL	31,100	4,363,000

Plate 1 Strip mining for coal can cause total destruction of arable farmland, but careful reclamations can restore the original productivity. The devastation of unreclaimed spoil piles is plainly visible at this coal mine in northern Texas, but when the spoil heaps are leveled and topsoil is replaced, as in the foreground, a verdant pasture grows within 12 months. (Photograph by B.J. Skinner.)

Plate 2 Every scrap of arable land must be cultivated in order to feed the growing population of Nepal. When hill slopes are steep, terraces must be built to prevent topsoil from washing away, to reduce the possibility of landslides, and to increase the efficiency of irrigation systems. (Photograph by Howard Massey.)

Plate 3 Remains of engine-houses and shaft-towers of the Botallock Mine cling to the rugged cliffs of Cornwall, England. From such mines, some of which extended far out under the ocean, a rich stream of tin, copper, lead, and other metals flowed for over 2000 years. In the nineteenth century, the Cornish production was so great that England was a major world producer. (Photograph by J.R. Craig.)

Plate 4 Production of gold ore at the Bessi Mine, Japan, during the fourteenth century. When the miner had broken enough ore to fill a basket, his assistant would carry it to the surface for processing by climbing a system of ladders made by notching tree trunks. (Photograph by W. Sacco.)

Plate 5 Acid waters seeping from the base of a pile of waste rock left after coal mining in southwest Pennsylvania. When iron sulfide minerals in the coal are exposed to the air as a consequence of mining, they become oxidized and produce soluble sulfates that cause the acidity. The yellow crust arises from sulfate compounds that precipitate from the seeping drainage water. (Photograph by J.R. Craig.)

Plate 6 A colorful but dangerous oil slick on the surface of the sea off the coast of California. The oil leaked from a shallow reservoir during drilling operations in the Santa Barbara channel in 1973. Oil from such slicks can clog the wings of sea birds and the fur, eyes, and noses of aquatic mammals. Prolonged exposure leads to death. The field of view is 2 meters across. (Photograph by B.J. Skinner.)

Plate 7 Sedimentary strata, originally horizontal but now folded into a dome-shaped anticline, have been exposed by erosion at Sheep Mountain, Wyoming. The crest of the anticline plunges downward toward the northwest (right-hand side of photograph). Anticlinal structures are important petroleum traps. (Photograph by Brendan Caulfield.)

(a)

(b)

Plate 8 Modern peat swamps that are precursors of future coal seams. (a) The north side of the island of Sumatra, Indonesia, seen here in a satellite image, is low-lying, swampy, and densely vegetated by a tropical rain forest. Swamp vegetation appears dark red in this false color image. The light pink areas are agricultural regions. (b) Ground view of a Sumatran peat swamp on the east side of the Siak River, near the center of image (a). Note the dense tropical vegetation and the profusion of both large and small plants. (Photograph by C. Blain Cecil.)

Plate 9 The Rossing Mine, Namibia (S.W. Africa), is one of the world's largest and most mechanized uranium mines. A truck load of ore has just passed under a radioactive scanning device that measures the richness of the ore and sends the information ahead to the processing mill in order to recover the uranium as efficiently as possible. (Photograph by B.J. Skinner.)

Plate 10 A forest of windmills at Altamont Pass Windmill Farm, California. The windmills convert the kinetic energy of flowing air (wind) into electrical energy. The amount of electricity produced by each mill is small, but the total from all mills on the farm is large. (Courtesy of U.S. Department of Energy.)

Plate 11 Finely banded layers of cherty silica (white) and hematite (red) in a specimen of a banded iron formation known as the Negaunee Formation, Marquette District, Michigan. Banded iron formations are ancient chemical sediments. They are known on every continent, and they contain the largest resources of mineable iron in the world. (Photograph by H.L. James, *Economic Geology*)

Plate 12 Nodular bauxite, the preferred ore of aluminum. This rich ore is the highest grade product mined at Weipa, in Queensland, Australia. Weipa contains one of the world's largest resources of bauxite. (Photograph by H. Murray.)

Plate 13 The M-Vein, Casapalca, Peru, is a rich mass of sulfide minerals containing silver, lead, copper, zinc, and other minerals. The ore minerals were deposited by a hydrothermal solution that flowed through a pre-existing fracture in volcanic rocks. (Photograph by B.J. Skinner.)

Plate 14 The Main Reef Leader, one of the rich, gold-bearing conglomerates mined in the Witwatersrand Basin, near Johannesburg, South Africa. The rounded quartz pebbles are set in a matrix of sand grains and rounded pyrite (FeS_2) grains, here seen as gold-colored particles. Gold is present but too fine grained to be seen. (Photograph by Carlos Pais; courtesy of Geological Society of South Africa.)

Plate 15 A giant dragline scoops up rich phosphate ore in Florida. The ore is then pumped via slurry pipeline to the processing plant. The very fine-grained waste material that remains after processing is allowed to settle and dry in huge settling ponds such as the one visible in the upper left-hand corner of the photograph. (Photograph courtesy of IMC Corporation.)

Plate 16 A line of fumaroles along a fault at Alae, on the southwest flank of Kilauea volcano, Hawaii. At the time this photograph was taken, volcanic vapors were depositing sulfur crystals in the fumarolic vents and laying down a yellow blanket of fine-grained sulfur on the countryside. (Photograph by B.J. Skinner.)

Plate 17 Cutting blocks of granite at a modern quarry, Corbelli, Italy. Explosives are rarely used when rock that is being quarried is to be used as cut stone. Instead, blocks are drilled and chiseled out in order to minimize the risk of fracture. (Courtesy of the Industrial Diamond Review.)

Plate 18 The Taj Mahal, Agra, India, is a breathtaking example of a building constructed with cut stone. The principal building stone is marble, but it is adorned with intricate insets of semiprecious stones, many in the form of passages from the Koran. The Taj Mahal is a mausoleum, completed about 1650 A.D. by Shah Jahan following the death of his favorite wife, Mumtaz Mahal. The Shah and his wife are both buried in the Taj Mahal. (Photograph courtesy of the Government of India Tourist Office.)

Plate 19 An intricate pattern of intersecting circles produced by a spray irrigation system used in the midwestern states of the United States. The sprinkler system rotates around the water supply at the center of the circle. (Photograph courtesy of Valmont Industries.)

Plate 20 The Central Arizona Project, a giant system of canals and pump stations, is designed to bring water from the sparsely populated drainage basin of the Colorado River system in northern Arizona to the heavily populated cities and irrigated farmlands of southern Arizona. (Photograph courtesy of U.S. Bureau of Reclamation.)

Plate 21 Two soil profiles. (a) Layering visible in the highly weathered soils such as those that underlie the stable land surface of the upper coastal plain of North Carolina. Technically, such soils are called plinthic paleudults. Iron has been leached from the upper layers, leaving them bleached and light colored. The leached iron is deposited about a meter below the surface in a pronounced reddish-color layer. (b) The soil profile at Poor Mountain, Virginia, formed above a base of sandstone and sandstone colluvium (brown). The uppermost, or A zone, is an organic-rich, forest soil. Below it lies a thin, very dark Bh zone, rich in both iron and humus, and below that lies a bleached and leached E zone, where organic chelates have removed the iron oxides in solution. (Photographs by James C. Baker.)

(a) (b)

Plate 22 Deflation near Meningie, South Australia. Grazing sheep removed much of the vegetation, leaving the sandy soil vulnerable to wind erosion. A large tussock, not touched by the sheep, stabilized a remnant of the original surface. Wind erosion has lowered the surface as much as 1.5 meters in places. (Photograph by B.J. Skinner.)

Plate 23 Miners swarm over the working face of the fabulously rich gold deposit at Serra Pelada, Brazil. The Brazilian government did not allow mechanized mining operations, instead letting the small-time miner have a chance to make a fortune. This photograph was taken in 1985. (Photograph by Glenn Allcott.)

Plate 24 The earth, seen here from space, will be the only source of mineral resources for many years to come. The blue ocean stands in marked color contrast to the brown landmass of Africa and the wispy, white cloud systems. The northeast corner of South America is visible and the Mediterranean Sea and Europe can be seen above Africa. (Photograph courtesy of European Space Agency.)

riched in the **mantle.** Thus, mafic and ultramafic igneous rocks derived from magmas generated in the mantle tend to have high nickel contents. Whereas the average nickel concentration in the continental crust is only 0.0072 percent by weight, many mafic and ultramafic igneous rocks contain as much as 0.1 percent nickel. The nickel is present in mafic igneous rocks in solid solution in **pyroxenes** and **olivines,** where it substitutes in the structures for magnesium and iron.

Ordinary mafic and ultramafic igneous rocks are not sufficiently enriched in nickel to be considered ores. Concentrations occur in two entirely different ways. The first is a form of magmatic segregation involving **liquid immiscibility.** When a magma cools and starts to crystallize, minerals such as olivine and pyroxene form and grow in the liquid. The growth of crystals of pyroxene in the magma indicates that the liquid has become saturated in pyroxene. Suppose, however, that the cooling magma becomes saturated in a compound but that the temperature is still above the melting temperature of that compound. That is what sometimes happens in the case of the iron sulfide mineral **pyrrhotite.** Instead of a crystal of pyrrhotite forming in the cooling magma, tiny drops of a molten iron sulfide liquid form. The silicate magma and the iron sulfide liquid do not mix and are said to be immiscible, like oil and water [Fig. 7.7(a)]. The immiscible liquid is not pure iron sulfide but tends to scavenge atoms of nickel, copper, platinum, and certain other chemical elements in the magma, so it is really an iron-nickel-copper-sulfide liquid. The immiscible sulfide drops are more dense than the silicate magma, so they tend to sink and form sulfide-rich zones near the base of the magma chamber. When the sulfide liquid eventually crystallizes, the main mineral that forms is pyrrhotite ($Fe_{1-x}S$), but intergrown with the pyrrhotite are grains of the only important sulfide ore mineral of nickel, pentlandite ($(Ni,Fe)_9S_8$) [Fig. 7.7(b)], together with chalcopyrite ($CuFeS_2$), and tiny grains of metallic platinum and other platinum group minerals. By the processes of concentration through liquid immiscibility and magmatic segregation, nickel contents as high as 3 or 4 percent can be reached.

The world's richest and most important nickel ore bodies are sulfide ores that formed as a result of magmatic segregation. The most famous nickel ore deposits are at Sudbury, Ontario, where intrusive, mafic igneous rocks form an elliptical ring, 56 kilometers on the long axis and 26 kilometers on the short axis. Around the outer edge of the basin, near the base of the intrusion, a number of large, rich deposits occur (Fig. 7.8). One of the strange features about Sudbury is that the intrusion has the shape of a cone rather than a flat sheet as is usual for most dikes and sills. The probable reason for the conical shape was realized in the 1960s as a result of investigations associated with space research. Many features on the surface of the moon and other bodies in the

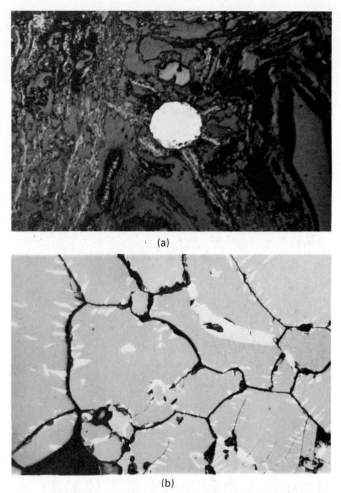

(a)

(b)

FIGURE 7-7. (a) Droplet of iron and nickel sulfides in basalt from mid-ocean ridge. (Photograph by J.R. Craig.) (b) Pentlandite exsolved from pyrrhotite due to cooling. (Photograph by D. J. Vaughan.)

solar system result from large meteorite impacts. As the properties and characteristics of impact structures on the earth were studied, it became apparent that the Sudbury ring might be an ancient (1.9 billion year) impact structure, and that the magma carrying the immiscible sulfide droplets probably rose from the mantle along fractures created by the impact event. Other rich and important sulfide ores of nickel are found in Canada in the Thompson Lake district of Manitoba, at Kambalda in Western Australia and in Botswana, Zimbabwe, and the Soviet Union.

The second important way that nickel can be concentrated in a mafic or ultramafic rock is through weathering. When mafic igneous rocks are subject to chemical weathering under tropical or semitropical conditions, the silicate minerals (pyroxene, olivine, and plagioclase) break down to form hydrous compounds, and iron is oxidized to the ferric state. The small amount of nickel present in solid solution in the olivines and pyroxenes is released in the process, and it either

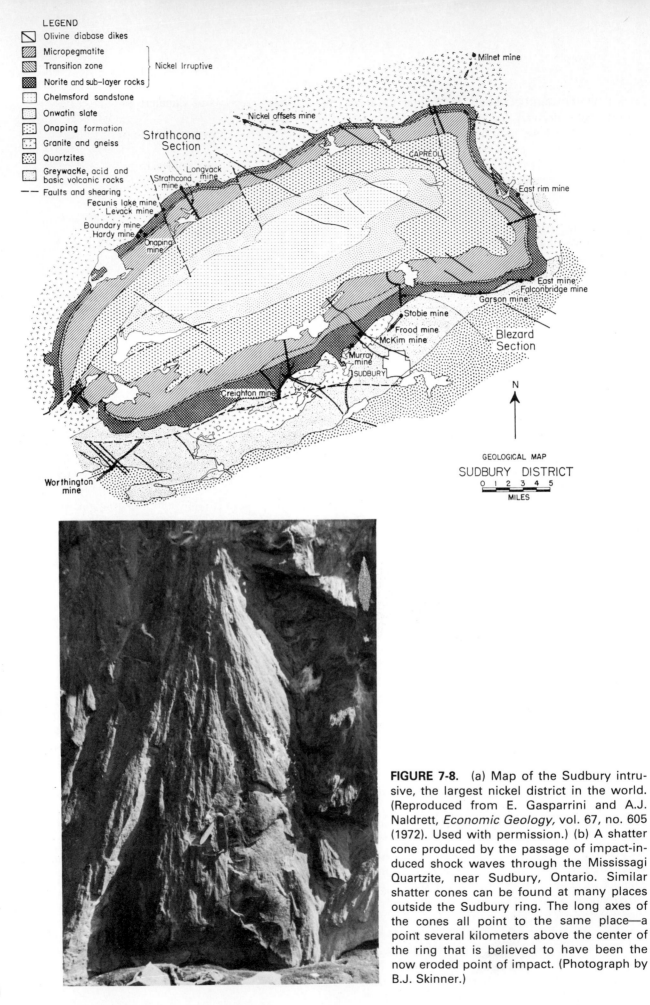

LEGEND

▨ Olivine diabase dikes
▨ Micropegmatite ⎫
▨ Transition zone ⎬ Nickel Irruptive
▨ Norite and sub-layer rocks ⎭
▨ Chelmsford sandstone
▨ Onwatin slate
▨ Onaping formation
▨ Granite and gneiss
▨ Quartzites
▨ Greywacke, acid and basic volcanic rocks
-- Faults and shearing

Milnet mine

Nickel offsets mine

Strathcona Section

CAPREOL

East rim mine

Longvack mine

Strathcona mine

Fecunis lake mine
Levack mine

Boundary mine
Hardy mine

Onaping mine

East mine
Falconbridge mine

Garson mine

Blezard Section

Stobie mine

Frood mine
McKim mine

Murray mine

SUDBURY

Creighton mine

Worthington mine

N

GEOLOGICAL MAP
SUDBURY DISTRICT
0 1 2 3 4 5
MILES

FIGURE 7-8. (a) Map of the Sudbury intrusive, the largest nickel district in the world. (Reproduced from E. Gasparrini and A.J. Naldrett, *Economic Geology,* vol. 67, no. 605 (1972). Used with permission.) (b) A shatter cone produced by the passage of impact-induced shock waves through the Mississagi Quartzite, near Sudbury, Ontario. Similar shatter cones can be found at many places outside the Sudbury ring. The long axes of the cones all point to the same place—a point several kilometers above the center of the ring that is believed to have been the now eroded point of impact. (Photograph by B.J. Skinner.)

210

forms nickel silicate minerals, or it is incorporated into the structure of other minerals formed during weathering. The weathering minerals, such as chlorite and serpentine, sometimes contain 1 percent or 2 percent of nickel. Under certain circumstances the nickel silicate minerals, collectively called **garnierite,** may form and produce ores as rich as 4 percent or 5 percent. Residual weathering ores are referred to as **laterite ores.** The most famous laterite ore is in New Caledonia, where French interests have been mining garnierite-rich bodies for most of this century. There, a nickeliferous **peridotite** has weathered to form lateritic garnierite ore (Fig. 7.9).

Rich garnierite deposits are rare, but lateritic weathering of mafic igneous rocks is widespread around the world. As a result, there are a great many low-grade lateritic deposits. Such ores are difficult to process, but some are worked today in Cuba, the Dominican Republic, the Philippines, and Indonesia.

Production and Reserves. Nickel is one of the strategic minerals for which the United States has very limited resources of high-grade deposits. It does have very large, low-grade deposits, however. These sulfide ores are in the Duluth Gabbro, Minnesota, and average about 0.21 percent nickel.

A large fraction of the world's nickel has, for many years come from the Sudbury and Thompson Lake districts of Canada. A steady increase in the mining of nickel from the Norils'k deposits in the Soviet Union has now brought the production there to the same level as Canada (Table 7.8). Important production of sulfide ore also comes from Australia, Botswana, Finland, the Republic of South Africa, and Zimbabwe, while mining of lateritic ore is carried out in Cuba, the Dominican Republic, Greece, Indonesia, New Caledonia, the Philippines, and the United States.

Molybdenum

Molybdenum is a versatile and important member of the ferro-alloy family of metals, but it is relatively unknown outside of metallurgical circles. This is because molybdenum, like several other metals, is scarcely ever used in its pure elemental form. Nevertheless, it is an extremely versatile metal that is used in a wide assortment of products.

The name molybdenum comes for the Latin word *molybdaena* and from the older Greek word *molybdos*, that actually refers to the lead mineral galena and metallic lead, respectively. There are a number of soft, easily deformed, gray minerals that look like lead and galena. Among those confusing minerals are graphite (C) and the mineral we now call **molybdenite** (MoS_2). From the time of the Greeks and Romans, all the leadlike minerals were called *molybdos*. The confusion was only resolved in 1778, when molybdenite was identified as a sulfide compound of a new chemical element; in 1782, the element was separated as a metal. The chemistry required to prepare the metal is difficult, and it was not until 1893 that the pure metal was produced.

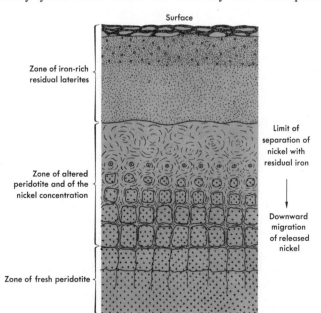

FIGURE 7-9. Chemical weathering of nickeliferous rocks, such as peridotite, release nickel trapped in the olivine; the olivine is then redeposited in the form of minerals such as garnierite. Residual ores of this kind are worked in New Caledonia and Cuba. (After E. de Chétalat, *Bull. Soc. Geol. France,* Sér. 63, XVII, 129, Fig. 4, 1967.)

TABLE 7-8

Production and estimated resources of nickel

Country	Production, 1984 (m.t.)	Reserves (m.t.)
Sulfide Ores:		
Canada	174,000	8,200,000
U.S.S.R.	174,000	7,300,000
Australia	75,000	4,700,000
Republic of South Africa	25,000	800,000
Botswana	17,500	360,000
Zimbabwe	10,000	180,000
Lateritic Ores:		
Indonesia	62,500	2,100,000
New Caledonia	41,000	12,700,000
Cuba	31,800	2,900,000
Dominican Republic	24,200	900,000
Philippines	16,500	5,000,000
United States	13,100	2,200,000
Others	92,100	4,700,000
WORLD TOTAL	743,600	52,040,000

(Data from U.S. Bureau of Mines and U.S. Geological Survey.)

As soon as pure molybdenum was available, its alloying properties were tested by French scientists. It proved to make a very tough and resilient steel that was ideal for armor plating. By 1898, molybdenum tool steel had also been developed. However, neither of these uses created much demand. A few small mines were opened in the latter years of the nineteenth century, but those in the United States had ceased to operate by 1906. Production in those days was satisfied by molybdenum ores worked in Norway, Australia, and Canada.

Molybdenum finally found a market in World War I when it was discovered that molybdenum steels could be substituted for the widely used tungsten steels in high-speed cutting tools and armaments. As a result, large deposits were opened at Climax, Colorado, and Questa, New Mexico. When World War I ended, military demand for molybdenum slumped and production at Climax and Questa was stopped. Starting about 1920, new uses were found for molybdenum steels, and in the electrical industry, it was found that molybdenum alloys made desirable heating elements. These new markets led to a resumption of full-scale mining by 1924.

About 90 percent of the molybdenum mined today is still used as an alloying element in steels, cast irons, and **superalloys** where it imparts hardness, toughness, resistance to corrosion and abrasion, and adds strength at high temperatures. Its content in steel ranges from 0.1–10 percent by weight, and it is usually employed in combination with other of the ferro-alloy elements. The steels produced are now used in all segments of industry but find special demand in cutting tools, transportation, and oil and gas production equipment. The anticorrosion properties imparted by molybdenum have led to the increasing application of its steels in severe chemical environments and seawater.

Nonmetallic applications for molybdenum include lubricants, catalysts, and pigments. Molybdenum disulfide (MoS_2) has a well-defined layer structure, somewhat like mica (see p. 345), it is exceedingly soft and slippery to the touch, and the compound resists breakdown even at high temperature and pressure. Consequently, it is widely used as an additive to oils and greases where it helps significantly to reduce friction and wear in automobile engines. Molybdenum catalysts are also used in the production of petroleum-based chemicals and alcohols. Molybdenum orange (MoO_2) is an important pigment in paints, dyes, and inks.

Geological Occurrence. Nearly all the known molybdenum ores consist of molybdenite, a lead-gray metallic mineral that occurs in **porphyry-type** igneous intrusions of the type described under copper. The large porphyry-type deposits, closely related to subduction zones at the edges of continental plate boundaries (Fig. 7.19), and commonly rich in copper minerals, usually contain minor amounts of molybdenite as well. A significant fraction of molybdenum production comes as a by-product from porphyry copper mining. A few large deposits such as those at Climax and Urad, Colorado, and Questa, New Mexico, contain molybdenite plus minor tin and tungsten minerals, almost to the exclusion of copper sulfides. The molybdenite occurs as disseminations and thin coating in cross-cutting fractures in the igneous intrusions and surrounding rocks. It was deposited along with large amounts of quartz by **hydrothermal** solutions that were episodically released from the crystallizing magma.

Molybdenite also occurs in much lesser, and usually uneconomic, quantities in **contact metamorphic** zones adjacent to silica-rich igneous rocks, in quartz vein deposits, and in pegmatites. Molybdenite is usually recovered as a by-product from these deposits.

Production and Reserves. The United States dominated the world molybdenum market for many years with the bulk of production coming from the large deposits at Climax, Colorado, and Questa, New Mexico. In recent years, however, production has increased in the Soviet Union, Chile, Canada, Mexico, and Peru. The decline in the United States steel industry, long the principal market for American production, combined with increasing competition from other Western Hemisphere producers, has resulted in at least temporary closing of the Questa mine in 1986 and major cutbacks in the mining at Climax and Urad, Colorado. Many of the porphyry copper mines that produce by-product molybdenum in the western United States were also shut down or cut back, primarily because of lagging sales of copper.

The known reserves of molybdenum (Table 7.9) are clearly adequate for many years to come. It does appear, however, that there will be a continuing shift in

TABLE 7-9

Production and reserves of molybdenum

Country	Production, 1984 (m.t.)	Reserves (m.t.)
United States	47,000	2,727,000
Chile	16,800	1,136,000
U.S.S.R.	12,500	455,000
Canada	10,900	455,000
Peru	3100	136,000
Mexico	2100	91,000
China	2000	455,000
Others	1300	5000
WORLD TOTAL	95,700	5,460,000

(Data from U.S. Bureau of Mines.)

production away from the United States as the dominant world source to Chile, China, Mexico, and Peru.

Cobalt

The earliest uses of cobalt, as a brilliant blue coloring agent, date from antiquity. Egyptian and Babylonian potters used cobalt oxide, known as cobalt blue, to color glass and ceramics. Chinese craftsmen extensively developed the art of cobalt coloring during the Ming Dynasty (fourteenth to seventeenth centuries), and in Europe, Venetian artisans of the fifteenth and later centuries were renowned for their cobalt-colored glassware.

The name *cobalt,* like that of nickel, has an association with old German miners. During the sixteenth century, arsenic-bearing silver-cobalt ores were mined in the Harz Mountains (now mostly in East Germany). The roasting of these ores released poisonous arsenical fumes that caused ulcers on the bodies of the miners tending the furnaces. The miners believed the source to be silver-stealing goblins called *Kobolds*, who replaced good silver minerals with useless cobalt arsenides that look somewhat like silver.

Cobalt was shown to be a separate chemical element in 1780, and the modern history of cobalt dates from this time. The principal uses of cobalt continued to be in coloring agents and chemical compounds used in various industrial processes. In 1910, the use of cobalt as an alloying compound was finally demonstrated by an American, Elwood Haynes, who showed that the addition of about 5 percent cobalt to a steel-containing chromium and tungsten greatly improved its qualities as a tool-steel. This alloy and other chromium-cobalt alloys were the forerunners of today's **superalloys** that retain their mechanical strength at high temperature and are resistant to the corrosion of hot gases. The recognition of the importance of cobalt and its marked increase in superalloys employed in jet engines, rocket nozzles, and gas turbines after World War II has led to cobalt being designated a strategic metal. Cobalt alloys also have remarkable magnetic properties—the magnetism is very strong and it is retained forever. The magnets used in the loudspeakers of high fidelity sound systems are almost all cobalt-based magnets.

Geological Occurrence. Most of the world's cobalt is produced as a by-product from the mining and metallurgical treatment of the ores of copper, nickel, and silver. The most important cobalt ores are **stratiform** copper sulfide ores, as are found in the "copperbelt" in Zaire in central Africa. This type of deposit consists of copper sulfide minerals, such as chalcopyrite ($CuFeS_2$), together with cobalt sulfide minerals such as linnaeite (Co_3S_4) and cobaltiferous pyrite (Fe,Co)S_2 enclosed in fine-grained **clastic** strata. The origin of the deposits is problematic, but the sulfide minerals appear to have been introduced into the sedimentary strata soon after deposition by warm saline solutions circulating in subsurface aquifers.

Cobalt also tends to be concentrated wherever nickel is concentrated. Thus, cobalt is an important by-product from the exploitation of both magmatic segregation nickel sulfide ores and lateritic nickel ores.

Production and Reserves. One country, Zaire, produces almost as much cobalt as all the other countries of the world combined (Table 7.10). Zaire is the only country where mines are worked principally for cobalt. Elsewhere, cobalt is simply a by-product.

The reserves and even the resources of cobalt are unknown because insufficient work has been done to make accurate estimates. In 1973, scientists at the U.S. Geological Survey considered the known data and estimated that *at least* 4,500,000 metric tons of cobalt existed in identified resources. The largest resources were in Cuba in the nickel-laterite ores. Large resources were also identified in Zaire, and in the United States, principally associated with the low-grade nickel deposits of the Duluth Gabbro in Minnesota. Further very large deposits are believed to lie on the ocean floor, where some of the ferromanganese nodules, described in Chapter 6, contain up to 1 percent cobalt (Table 6.6). Thus, even though definite reserve figures cannot be quoted for cobalt, the long-term future for the metal appears to be assured.

Tungsten

Tungsten is a grayish-white colored metal that has many alloying properties similar to those of chromium and molybdenum. It has the distinction of being the metal

TABLE 7-10
Production and reserves of cobalt

Country	Production, 1984 (m.t.)	Reserves (m.t.)
Zaire	17,000	1,360,000
U.S.S.R.	2600	136,000
Zambia	4600	363,000
Canada	2000	45,000
Cuba	1500	180,000
Finland	900	23,000
New Caledonia	250	204,000
Philippines	100	122,000
Australia	1300	23,000
Others	2050	260,000
WORLD TOTAL	32,300	2,716,000

(Data from U.S. Bureau of Mines.)

with the highest melting temperature (3400°C) and the further distinction of being the metal with the highest tensile strength. Alloys of tungsten are therefore extremely hard and extremely stable at high temperatures.

Metallic tungsten and the ore minerals of tungsten are very dense. The name *tungsten* recognizes this property and comes from two Swedish words, *tung,* meaning heavy, and *sten,* stone. Until the middle of the eighteenth century, the mineral we know today as scheelite ($CaWO_4$), but then called tungsten, was thought to be an ore mineral of tin. In 1781, the Swedish chemist K.W. Scheele showed that tin was not present, and that a new chemical element was probably involved. Two years later, two Spanish chemists, the brothers d'Ellhuyar, prepared metallic tungsten for the first time. The name *tungsten* was thereafter reserved for the element, and the mineral was named *scheelite* in honor of Scheele. The first use of tungsten as an additive to steel occurred in France in 1855. Within a few years, the toughness of tungsten steels came to be appreciated, and by 1868 small amounts of tungsten were added to train rails made in France. Today tungsten steels are used in many circumstances where toughness, durability, and resistance to impact are needed.

The single most important use of tungsten is not for its alloying properties—although these uses are certainly very important—but for the manufacture of tungsten carbide (WC), a compound with a hardness approaching that of diamond. Tungsten carbide can be sintered into intricate shapes, and it is widely used in the preparation of tungsten carbide tools, drill bits, cutting edges, and even armor-piercing projectiles.

The high melting temperature of tungsten facilitates its use as the filaments of electric light bulbs, the distributor points of automobiles, and various heating elements. When the overall uses of tungsten are considered, approximately 45 percent of the annual production is used to make tungsten carbide, 25 percent for ferroalloys, 18 percent for tungsten metal and alloys in which tungsten is the major metal, and 11 percent for nonferrous alloys. All other uses total only 1 percent.

Geological Occurrence. Tungsten has a geochemical abundance of 0.001 percent by weight and is therefore one of the scarcest of the geochemically scarce metals. It forms only two minerals of economic importance, scheelite ($CaWO_4$) and wolframite (($Fe, Mn)WO_4$). The most important deposits were formed by hydrothermal solutions. These fluids are widespread in the earth's crust, and indeed, more ore deposits are formed through their agency than any other deposit-forming agency. The origin and chemistry of hydrothermal solutions are discussed more fully in the section on copper. Such solutions deposit small amounts of wol-

framite or scheelite, together with tin minerals, in quartz-rich **veins** that are usually closely related to intrusive igneous rocks that are felsic in character. Much of the world's tungsten production comes from quartz veins and closely spaced quartz stringers called **stockworks.** A small amount of production arises as a by-product of gold, tin, or copper mining. Tungsten deposits also occur where igneous rocks that have been intruded into limestones or marbles forming **contact metamorphic** deposits (also sometimes called **skarn ores**). The ore mineral in these deposits is usually scheelite, and the deposits, although often rich, are generally small. Several deposits of this kind are worked in the United States in Nevada, Utah, and California.

Production and Reserves. By far, the largest producers of tungsten in the world are China and the Soviet Union. Most Chinese ores are quartz vein deposits, and resources are believed to be huge, although they are not completely explored and tested. Significant production also comes from Korea, Burma, and Thailand (Table 7.11), three countries adjacent to China, and each is endowed with mineralization similar to that in China.

Reserves of tungsten are not adequately measured. Estimates shown in Table 7.11 are possibly too low for China and Australia. So far as resources are concerned, estimates are practically meaningless because so little information is available.

THE BASE METALS

A **base metal** is commonly defined as a metal or alloy of comparatively low value and one that is relatively inferior in certain properties such as corrosion. Such a definition seems to suggest that the base metals are second-class citizens in the family of metals. Nothing could be further from the truth, for the base metals are endowed with many important and unique properties. It was the base metals that our distant ancestors first

TABLE 7-11
Production and reserves of tungsten

Country	Production, 1984 (m.t.)	Reserves (m.t.)
China	13,500	1,200,000
U.S.S.R.	9100	280,000
Canada	3690	480,000
Republic of Korea	2703	58,000
Bolivia	2100	45,000
Australia	1843	130,000
Others	12,003	607,000
WORLD TOTAL	44,939	2,800,000

learned to shape into useful objects. We still recognize those achievements in the terms *Copper Age* and *Bronze Age*. The Copper Age designates that first great step humankind took when it advanced from the Stone Age by learning to work and employ metals. The next step, into the Bronze Age, took humankind into the field of alloy metallurgy. Bronze is an alloy of two or more metals but is principally copper plus tin. From the time our ancestors first learned how to work copper into needles, axes, arrowheads, and other useful objects (Fig. 7.10), the practical uses found for the base metals have expanded continually. When the first indoor plumbing was installed by the Romans, they used lead pipes. When

FIGURE 7-10. A 20-centimeters-high, copper figurine of Gudea of Lagash, made approximately 4200 years ago. The inscription in Sumerian reads "For Bau, the good lady, the daughter of An, the lady of the holy city. His lady, Gudea governor of Lagash the man who built the temple E-Ninnu of the god Ningirsu, built her wall of the holy city." (Specimen from the Yale Babylonian Collections. Photograph by W. Sacco.)

the ordinary working person wanted something better than leather or wooden plates to eat from, it was pewter, an alloy of base metals, that came into common use. When it was shown to be possible to transmit and use electricity in the nineteenth century, it was a base metal, copper, that electricians turned to in order to carry electricity from generating plants to people's houses. Is it possible to imagine how today's world of 5 billion people could operate without the widespread use of electricity? Nothing has changed our lives so much as this one great technological advance, and it is a base metal that has been the workhorse.

The base metals of antiquity were copper, lead, tin, and mercury. Several hundred years ago, zinc was added to the list. Zinc was actually used by the Chinese and Romans over 2000 years ago, because it is found in bronze dating from those times. The Chinese and Romans apparently could not smelt and prepare zinc metal, however, so the presence of the zinc in the alloy probably means that it was added as a sulfide or oxide mineral during smelting of the copper ore. The last of the base metals, cadmium, has properties similar to those of zinc. Like the ferro-alloy metals, use of cadmium is a product of twentieth century technology.

Copper

Nobody knows whether use of gold preceded that of copper or whether both were first used at about the same time. Wherever and whenever the first use of metallic copper occurred, it is so far back in time that we will probably never find out who used it or for what purpose. It is not surprising that the use of copper should go so far back in time because copper, like gold, sometimes occurs as a native metal, so our ancestors did not have to first learn how to smelt ores in order to obtain the metal. What they had to learn was how to hammer native copper, rather than grind or chip it as they had been used to doing with stones in order to make useful shapes. They had obviously learned to do so by 6000 years ago, because excavations of the remains of civilizations that existed at that time yield finely wrought copper artifacts (Fig. 7.10). The use of copper probably goes even further back in time, because the smelting of copper ores seems to have started between 5500–6000 years ago, and it is reasonable to think that the use of native copper metal started much earlier.

The earliest underground mining activities, remains of which can still be seen today in several places in Europe, go back to the Stone Age and seem to have been for flints. The earliest underground mining for metal seems to have been for copper and to have been carried out at least 6000 years ago.

The value of copper, from antiquity until the later years of the nineteenth century, was related to its **mal-**

leability and the ease with which both copper and its alloys can be worked and cast. Copper metal and the main copper alloys, bronze and brass, are attractive to look at, durable, and relatively corrosion resistant. Copper and its alloys found innumerable uses in weapons, utensils, tools, jewelry, statuary, pipes, building, and architectural features.

The nineteenth century brought a great expansion in the use of copper because one of copper's most desirable properties is its high electrical conductivity. Not only can copper transmit electricity with a minimum loss of power, but the transmission wires are flexible and malleable, and they can be easily joined and soldered. The spectacular growth of the electrical power industry, plus all the industries using electricity, would certainly have been hampered without copper. Not surprisingly, the production of copper rose rapidly during the nineteenth century. In the early decades of the nineteenth century, average world annual production was less than 10,000 metric tons. We now produce more than double that amount each day! By the 1850s, production had risen to about 50,000 metric tons a year, and by the 1890s when electric power and telegraph needs started growing rapidly, production reached about 370,000 tons. In 1984, the world's copper production was 7,838,000 metric tons!

Geological Occurrence. The geochemical abundance of copper is high—among the highest of the geochemically scarce metals. Its average content in the continental crust is 0.0058 percent, and in the oceanic crust it is still higher. Not surprisingly for a metal that has been used for so long and in such large quantities, literally hundreds of thousands of copper deposits, large and small, have been discovered around the world. A great deal is known about copper deposits as a result, but even so, many questions remain to be answered.

All the important copper ore minerals mined today are sulfides. They are: chalcopyrite ($CuFeS_2$), digenite (Cu_9S_5), chalcocite (Cu_2S), bornite (Cu_5FeS_4), enargite (Cu_3AsS_4), and tetrahedrite ($Cu_{12}Sb_4S_{13}$). In addition, there are many other less important minerals. Historically, ores containing native copper, the two carbonate minerals, azurite ($Cu_3(CO_3)_2(OH)_2$) and malachite ($Cu_2(CO_3)(OH)_2$), and the two copper oxide minerals, tenorite (CuO) and cuprite (Cu_2O) were also important. Native copper deposits, such as the famous ores of the Keweenaw District on Michigan's northern peninsula are infrequent, and none is currently a large producer on the world scene. The oxide and carbonate minerals of copper form as a result of weathering interactions between the atmosphere and ground water and a sulfide ore body. They are found in secondary, oxidized cappings above primary sulfide ores. Beneath the oxidized

cappings there is sometimes a blanket of very high-grade sulfide ore in a zone of secondary enrichment (Fig. 7.11). Oxidized cappings and secondary enrichment zones are often very rich, and sometimes they contain spectacular mineral specimens (Fig. 7.12). When found, such zones are soon mined, leaving a once rich mine to face a future dependent on the lower-grade primary sulfide ores. Historically, the rich surface ores often provided a means to repay the initial costs of finding and opening an ore body. By the time the leaner sulfide ores were reached, it was possible to mine them because the cost of the initial investment had been repaid. Many of the famous ore bodies in the western Americas, both north and south, were developed in this fashion. Today, however, they all mine primary sulfide ores.

Copper sulfide deposits can be conveniently separated into three classes: magmatic segregation deposits, hydrothermal deposits, and sediment-hosted stratiform deposits. Each of the deposit classes deserves separate discussion.

Magmatic Segregation Deposits: The least important class of copper deposit so far as current production is concerned is the magmatic segregation class. Such deposits have the same origin as the ores of nickel formed by magmatic segregation of immiscible sulfide liquids. The ore bodies are therefore associated with large bodies of mafic or ultramafic igneous rocks. Sudbury, Ontario, discussed under nickel, is an example. Indeed, nearly all the magmatic segregation ores that are

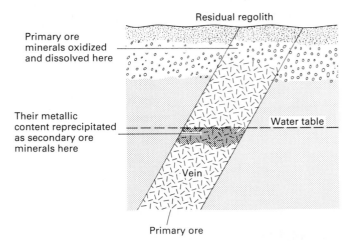

FIGURE 7-11. Descending ground water oxidizes and impoverishes copper ore above the water table, forming an acid solution that removes soluble copper compounds and leaves a residue of limonite. The descending acid solution deposits copper at and below the water table, producing secondary enrichment below.

FIGURE 7-12. Gossans, the oxidized cappings that form above sulfide ore deposits as a result of weathering, often contain spectacular mineral specimens. These crystals of cerussite ($PbSO_4$) formed in the limonite gossan above the ore at the Flagstaff Mine, Utah. The specimen is 16 centimeters across. (Photograph by W. Sacco.)

mined for nickel also produce important amounts of copper.

Hydrothermal Deposits: Copper deposits (and deposits of many other metals, too), that are formed through the actions of **hydrothermal solutions**—hot aqueous solutions circulating through the crust—are numerous. Most common are small veins, usually found close to bodies of intrusive igneous rock but also found in metamorphic and sedimentary rocks far removed from known igneous intrusions. Such veins are usually quartz-rich, and they almost always are secondary features formed long after the host rocks became lithified. They are confined in what were once open fractures through which the hydrothermal fluids flowed. Most vein deposits are small, containing only a few tons of ore, and hence not of much economic interest. When they are large and rich, as were the great veins that surrounded the granitic intrusions in Cornwall, England

(Fig. 7.13), and at Butte, Montana, they constitute some of the richest and most profitable deposits ever found. Such rich bonanza veins were very important historically, but today, many of the richest veins have been worked out, and they are of less importance than they once were. Nevertheless, investigations of vein deposits have been particularly informative in unraveling the complex questions that surround hydrothermal solutions.

Hydrothermal solutions are, as their name indicates, hot, water-based solutions. The water can come from two quite separate sources. First, the water may start as rainwater or seawater at the earth's surface. Such water trickles down the innumerable openings and fractures in surface rocks; below the water table, every opening is filled. At sufficient depth—a few thousand meters—the surrounding rocks are hot enough so that the buried waters become effective solvents. Small amounts of material are dissolved from the enclosing rocks, and the hot water becomes a solution containing such constituents as $NaCl$, $MgCl_2$, $CaSO_4$, SiO_2, and sometimes small amounts of one or more of the geochemically scarce metals (Table 7.12).

The second way a hydrothermal solution can arise is from a cooling magma. When rock melts and a magma forms deep in the crust or upper mantle, the magma assimilates any water that is present. Magmas formed in the crust, such as granites and diorites, generally have several weight percent water in them. When such magmas cool and crystallize, much of the dissolved water is released as a hot, aqueous solution that carries with it the same soluble constituents that deeply buried rainwater and seawater pick up.

TABLE 7-12

Analyses of hydrothermal solutions

Chemical Element	(1)	(2)	(3)	(4)
Chlorine	15.50	15.70	15.82	4.65
Sodium	5.04	7.61	5.95	1.97
Calcium	2.80	1.97	3.64	0.750
Potassium	1.75	0.041	0.054	0.370
Strontium	0.40	0.064	0.111	—
Magnesium	0.054	0.308	0.173	0.057
Bromine	0.12	0.053	0.087	—
Sulfur*	0.005	0.031	0.031	0.160
Iron	0.229	0.0014	0.030	—
Zinc	0.054	0.0003	0.030	0.133
Lead	0.010	0.0009	0.008	—
Copper	0.0008	0.00014	—	0.014

* Sulfur analyzed as $(SO_4)^{-2}$

(1) Salton Sea Geothermal brine (Muffler and White, 1969).
(2) Cheleken geothermal brine (Lebedev and Nikitina, 1968).
(3) Oil field brine, Gaddis Farms D-1 well, Lower Rodessa reservoirs, central Mississippi, 11,000 ft (Carpenter et al., 1974).
(4) Fluid inclusion in sphalerites, OH vein, Creede, Colorado (Skinner and Barton, 1973).

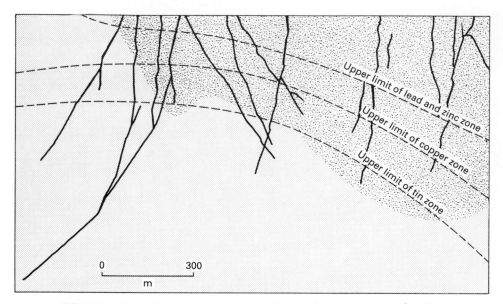

FIGURE 7-13. Mineral zoning developed in a system of veins formed around a granitic stock in Cornwall, England. Each of the veins is mineralized and contains the tin mineral cassiterite (SnO_2), copper minerals of which chalcopyrite ($CuFeS_2$) is the most important, and the zinc and lead minerals sphalerite (ZnS) and galena (PbS). The zonation is believed to arise from a drop in temperature of the hydrothermal solutions as they flowed through the vein fractures.

FIGURE 7-14. A hot spring and geyser, Yellowstone National Park, Wyoming. Such hot springs are believed to be the surface expressions of large, deeply circulating hydrothermal systems of the kind that formed the veins in Cornwall (Fig. 7-13) and Casapalca (Plate 13). (Courtesy J. Donald Rimstidt.)

Because hydrothermal solutions from the two different sources are so similar in chemical composition, it is exceedingly difficult to say what the origin of a given fluid is. The problem is complicated still further because the major driving force that causes hydrothermal solutions to flow is heat. When heated, a solution expands and rises convectively, thereby creating fluid flow. The principal heat sources in the crust that cause convective flow are shallow bodies of cooling magma and piles of hot lava, the very bodies that release magmatic hydrothermal solutions. But the rocks into which magmas are intruded also contain rainwater- and seawater-generated hydrothermal solutions in the pore spaces. A magmatic heat source will start these solutions flowing too. Once flow starts, both kinds of hydrothermal fluids became inextricably mixed. Hot springs in areas of active magmatic activity, such as those in Yellowstone National Park (Fig. 7.14), are the tops of convectively driven hydrothermal systems. At Yellowstone, scientists have been able to show that more than 90 percent of the hot water started as rainfall.

When a hydrothermal solution starts to rise upward, a number of things can happen: the solution may start to cool; because such a solution tends to be slightly acidic, it will react with rocks such as limestone; the pressure will drop; and boiling may occur. Each of these changes, or more likely a combination of them, can cause the solution to reach saturation and start precipitating the dissolved constituents. If it is the sulfide minerals of the geochemically scarce metals that precipitate, usually with associated quartz, an ore deposit may result (Fig. 7.15). A rising hydrothermal solution tends to change progressively as the dissolved ore and gangue

minerals precipitate. As a result, a sequential or zonal pattern of mineral precipitation may develop as shown in Fig. 7.13.

The major kind of hydrothermal copper deposit being worked today is closely related to vein deposits. Known as **porphyry copper deposits** because the intrusive igneous rocks with which they are always associated have porphyritic textures, the deposits consist of innumerable tiny fractures, usually no more than a millimeter or so thick, spaced every few centimeters through a body of intensely fractured rock (Fig. 7.16). The geological setting of porphyry copper deposits, and the rocks with which they are associated, indicate that they represent subsurface conduits and chambers that once lay beneath volcanoes. The formation process began with the intrusion of a magma. As nonhydrous minerals such as feldspars began to crystallize around the outer edges of the intrusion, the water content of the remaining magma increased until the pressure was so great that steam explosions shattered the crystallized rock. The escaping hydrothermal solutions, carrying silica, potassium and sodium salts, and dissolved metal sulfides, moved outward, precipitating minerals and sealing the fractures. As cooling continued, this process was repeated several times, leaving many generations of small fractures, several of which contain small but significant amounts of copper ore minerals. When the volume of shattered rock is large, a porphyry copper deposit can also be very large—over 1 billion (10^9) tons of ore in some of the largest. The deposits have distinctive zonal patterns that can be related to the fluid circulation system (Fig. 7.17).

When porphyry copper deposits are mined, it is

FIGURE 7-15. Photograph of W-vein at Panasqueira, Portugal, showing large quartz crystals (on lower side), dark wolframite crystals and arsenopyrite. (Photograph by A. Arribas.)

FIGURE 7-16. Specimen from the porphyry copper deposit at Butte, Montana. The sample, which has been slightly oxidized by weathering, consists of a network of tiny veins filled with pyrite and chalcopyrite, cutting through a highly altered igneous rock. The alteration was caused by the hydrothermal solutions that deposited the network of sulfide veins. The specimen is 15 centimeters wide. (Photograph by B.J. Skinner.)

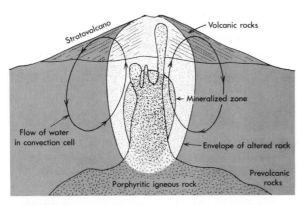

FIGURE 7-17. Idealized section through a stratovolcano showing convection cells of hydrothermal solution, the limits of hydrothermally altered rocks, and the location of a mineralized zone in which a porphyry copper deposit is forming. (Adapted after Sillitoe, 1973. From Skinner, 1986.)

impractical to dig out the individual tiny veinlets. Instead, the entire body of shattered rock is mined. As a result, porphyry copper deposits tend to have lower grades, ranging from 0.25 to 2 percent copper plus small amounts of molybdenum and gold, than the richer bonanza vein deposits. What makes these porphyry-type deposits profitable at such low grades is their very large size and shape. Most are relatively near-surface, approximately cylindrical bodies of mineralized rock that lend themselves to very large mining schemes. Indeed, it was at the porphyry copper deposit at Bingham Canyon, Utah (see Fig. 3.1), where the American mining engineers, D.C. Jackling and R.C. Gemmell, first proposed and demonstrated that large-scale bulk mining is more profitable than small-scale, labor intensive, selective mining. They made their proposal in 1899. By 1907, they had installed an open-pit mining scheme capable of producing 6000 metric tons of low-grade copper ore per day. The daily capacity of Bingham Canyon in recent times was well above 100,000 metric tons, and once achieved a maximum 24-hour production of 400,000 tons (360,000 metric tons).

Literally hundreds of porphyry copper deposits have been found, and today they account for more than half of the world's copper production. The deposits are concentrated around the rim of the Pacific Ocean basin, where they have formed as a result of volcanism associated with the subduction of oceanic crust (Fig. 7.18). The porphyry copper deposits around the Pacific are geologically young and related to the present phase of plate tectonics. Older deposits are known, and in all cases they seem to be related to ancient plate edges where subduction once occurred.

Two other kinds of hydrothermal copper deposits also deserve discussion because each is a significant producer of copper. The first is a **contact metamorphic** or **skarn** class of deposit. When granitic magma intrudes a pile of rock that contains limestone or marble, the acid solutions released by the cooling magma react with the $CaCO_3$ in the limestone. The reactions cause rapid precipitation of copper minerals and lead to very rich ores. Commonly, skarn ores form rich pockets associated with larger masses of porphyry-type ore. Examples are the Gaspé Copper deposit in Quebec, and the Yerington deposit in Nevada.

The final class of hydrothermal copper deposit is known as **volcanogenic massive sulfide** deposits. The enclosing rocks are invariably volcanic in origin, and invariably the volcanic rocks have features suggesting that they were erupted under the sea. The ore minerals are always sulfides, and the term *massive* reflects the fact that very little volcanic debris or silicate gangue minerals are present to dilute the sulfides. Unfortunately, pyrite (FeS_2) is usually the most abundant sulfide mineral, but generally chalcopyrite ($CuFeS_2$), sphalerite

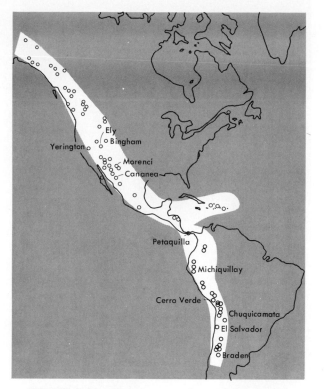

FIGURE 7-18. Porphyry copper deposits in the Americas define a remarkable metallogenic province that parallels the western continental boundary. Another belt of porphyry coppers is now being exposed by prospecting in the Pacific Islands. (From Skinner, 1986.)

(ZnS), and other useful sulfide minerals are present in small amounts too.

Volcanogenic massive sulfide deposits are known in rocks as old as 3 billion years, and such deposits can be observed forming on the sea floor today. They are among the most common of all hydrothermal ore deposits, but most are too small to be of economic interest.

Deep diving submarines have, in recent years, discovered submarine hot springs along the volcanic rifts that mark the mid-ocean ridges. The springs are places where hot seawater erupts after it has been heated at depth in the piles of volcanic rock that make up the upper layers of the oceanic crust. The hot circulating seawater is apparently heated by the magma chambers that underlie the mid-ocean ridge. It reacts with and alters the basaltic lavas it passes through, and by the time it rises again to the ocean floor it is a rapidly flowing jet of brine as hot as 350°C. When such a jet erupts into cold ocean water, it is quickly cooled; as a result, its dissolved load precipitates, sometimes as very fine sootlike sulfide minerals (thus giving the name *black smokers* to some vents) (Fig. 7.19) and sometimes forming a blanket of massive sulfide ore around the vent. Only one of

the modern deposits so far discovered, in the Red Sea, is large enough to be of potential interest for mining. More than a hundred others have been found in the eastern Pacific and mid-Atlantic, but all are small. Furthermore, the known deposits are all at 1500 meters or greater depths of water.

It may well be that other large, rich, modern massive sulfide deposits may someday be found on the ocean floor. For the present, the only massive sulfide deposits that are being mined are in ancient fragments of oceanic crust found on the continents. Such massive sulfide deposits have been mined since ancient times as on Cyprus, and the word *copper* comes, in fact, from the old Greek word *cyprus*.

Sediment-hosted Stratiform Deposits: The final group of copper deposits share distinctive and puzzling features. They are always in **clastic,** marine sedimentary rocks, usually shales, that contain a certain amount of organic matter and calcium carbonate, and they are usually stratiform, which means the mineralization occurs in stratalike layers. The ore minerals are either native copper or, much more commonly, sulfide minerals. Because neither copper metal nor sulfide minerals are known to precipitate directly from modern seawater, and it is not likely that ancient seawater had the composition for this to happen either, a puzzle surrounds the origin of such ores.

One group of theories concerning the origin of stratiform deposits suggests that the deposits are related to volcanogenic massive sulfide deposits, and that the sulfide minerals were precipitated from submarine hot springs. The trouble with such theories is that hot springs usually produce massive ores, but the sediment-hosted stratiform ores always contain very large proportions of clastic silicate mineral grains. A second group of theories, which the authors of this volume prefer, ascribes the origin to hydrothermal solutions that circulated in coarse, clastic sedimentary layers beneath the now mineralized shales. Such theories ascribe the origin of the ores to reactions between the solutions and mineral constituents in the shales. The reactions seem to have occurred soon after the sediments were deposited and, in certain cases, before they were consolidated to solid rock. The most famous of the sediment-hosted stratiform copper deposits are enclosed in the **Kupferschiefer,** a Permian-aged shale found through much of northern Europe (Fig. 7.20). The Kupferschiefer deposits, which average only about 20 centimeters in thickness but extend laterally over more than 6000 square kilometers, have been mined continually since the fourteenth century. Larger and richer stratiform deposits, discovered in the twentieth century, are now worked in Zambia and Zaire in central Africa (Fig.

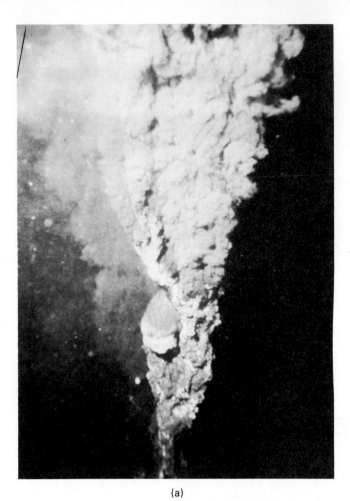

(a)

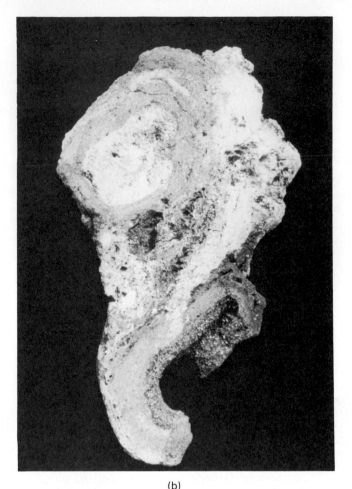

(b)

FIGURE 7-19. (a) A chimneylike structure of sulfide minerals built up around the vent from which a hydrothermal solution (350°C) is emitted into the sea above the East Pacific Rise. The solution is colorless, but when it mixes with cold seawater a dense black cloud of exceedingly fine-grained sulfide minerals is precipitated. Such structures and precipitates are colloquially referred to as chimneys and black smokers. (Photograph by R. Ballard.) (b) Section of a chimney recovered by a deep-diving submarine from a depth of 2500 meters at 20°N latitude on the East Pacific Rise. The principal sulfide mineral present is pyrite. Small amounts of chalcopyrite and sphalerite are also present. The specimen is 22 centimeters across. (Photograph by B.J. Skinner.)

7.21). In the United States, there are deposits at White River, Michigan, and at Creta, Oklahoma, that are of this class.

Production and Reserves. About 60 percent of the world's copper production comes from porphyry copper and associated skarn deposits. An estimated 20 percent comes from sediment-hosted stratiform deposits, and about 12 percent comes from volcanic-hosted massive sulfide deposits. The remainder comes as a by-product from the mining of nickel, lead, and zinc ores, and from chemical leaching of old mine dumps. Copper is so widely produced around the world that, in 1984, 60 countries reported production. Not surprisingly for

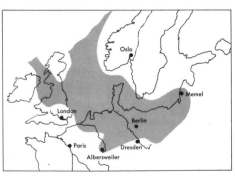

FIGURE 7-20. Extent of the shallow Zechstein Sea, in which the thin sedimentary bed now known as the Kupferschiefer was laid down during the Permian period. (After R. Brinckmann, 1960. From Skinner, 1986.)

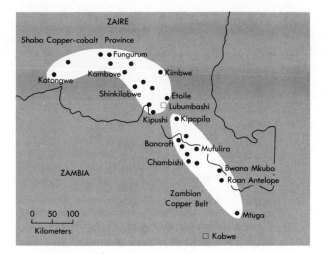

FIGURE 7-21. The Zambian Copper Belt and adjacent Shaba Copper-Cobalt province in Zaire contain a remarkable series of stratabound copper deposits. Deposits in the Zambian Copper Belt are contained in sediments laid down along an ancient Precambrian shoreline. Those in Zaire are similar in age but are not shoreline sediments. (From Skinner, 1986.)

such a widely used and widely exploited metal, both the reserves and resources of copper are very large (Table 7.13).

Resources of copper in large deposits that are below today's mining grades are very large—several times larger than the reserves. In the United States, large quantities of copper exist in magmatic segregation deposits in the Duluth Gabbro, Minnesota. Very large stratiform resources also exist in the late Proterozoic-aged Belt Series rocks of Montana. But the largest copper resources of all do not belong to any country. They are in the ferromanganese nodules that lie on the deep sea floor. In areas of slow sedimentation, such as the central Pacific Ocean, ferromanganese nodules average

more than 1 percent copper (Table 6.6), and many are known to contain as much as 2 percent. The same nodules also carry important amounts of nickel and cobalt. Some estimates put the total copper resource in recoverable manganese nodules in excess of a billion (10^9) tons of copper. This suggests, therefore, that the sea floor resources of copper are about the same size as the on-land resources. Despite the fact that copper is mined at such a high annual rate, the world's reserves and resources appear adequate for a century or more. The big question to be answered in the future concerns the cost of working presently uneconomic resources.

Lead and Zinc

Lead and zinc are discussed together because their ore minerals so commonly occur together. Their uses as metals are rather different, however. Lead is another metal with a history that stretches back to antiquity. It rarely occurs in the native state, so the use of lead metal only commenced when our ancestors learned how to smelt lead ores. Lead was used in weights, sheet metal, solders, ceramic glazes, and glassware by the ancient Egyptians, the Phoenicians, Greeks and Romans. The Phoenicians worked lead mines in Cyprus, Sardinia, and Spain and traded the metal around the Mediterranean. The famed mines at Laurium in Greece produced both silver and lead and supplied the ancient Greeks with much revenue. The great quantities of silver that enriched Rome and paid for so many of its conquests, and much of its high living, were derived from lead smelting and from refining operations carried out in Spain, Sardinia, and Britain.

An unusual combination of properties has given lead a wide range of industrial uses. The metal is soft and easily worked, it is very dense, it has a low melting temperature, and it possesses very desirable alloying properties, it resists corrosion, and it is an excellent

TABLE 7-13

Production and reserves of copper

Country	Production, 1984 (m.t.)	Main Kinds of Deposits	Reserves (m.t.)
Chile	1,290,000	Porphyry	97,000,000
United States	1,091,000	Porphyry and skarn	90,000,000
Canada	712,400	Porphyry and massive	32,000,000
U.S.S.R.	590,000	Porphyry and stratiform	36,000,000
Zambia	541,000	Stratiform	34,000,000
Zaire	540,000	Stratiform	30,000,000
Peru	364,000	Porphyry	32,000,000
Poland	360,000	Stratiform	13,000,000
Others	2,349,600		147,000,000
WORLD TOTAL	7,838,000		511,000,000

(Data from U.S. Bureau of Mines.)

shield against harmful radiations. The principal uses of lead today are for automobile storage batteries, for tetraethyl lead that is an antiknock additive used in gasoline, for cable coverings, in paint pigments, for flashings in building construction, in ammunition, in various alloys (especially solder), in bearings, and in printer's type. Lead also has unpleasant properties, however. It is toxic, and this has led to a reduction in its use in situations where humans might ingest lead or lead compounds. Thus, the use of lead in paints and gasoline has been drastically curtailed. For a number of years now, all new automobiles sold in North America have been designed to use unleaded gasoline. Presumably, leaded gasoline will eventually cease to be sold.

Zinc is a relatively soft, bluish-white colored metal. It is more difficult to produce zinc metal by standard smelting practice than it is to produce copper or lead. Therefore, zinc was a relatively late addition to the family of base metals used by humankind. The first commercial production of the metal is claimed to have been in China some 600 years ago, but details are poorly recorded. The first reliable record of zinc smelting was from Bristol, England, in 1740. As demand grew, other smelters were opened in Belgium, Germany, Russia, and in 1860 in the United States.

The largest part of the world's zinc production is used in galvanizing, a process by which protective coatings are put on steel and iron, mainly by a hot-dipping process in which the object to be coated is dipped into a bath of molten zinc. Because zinc resists corrosion and does not rust, even a thin coating prevents rust from forming on iron and steel. Zinc also has desirable alloying properties, and many die-cast objects that are not subject to abrasive wear are made from zinc-based alloys. Zinc is a constituent of brass and in its oxide form (ZnO), it is used in paint pigments, ointments, lotions, and creams to prevent sunburn. Zinc became more prominent, if not more conspicuous, to Americans when the copper penny was replaced in 1982 by a zinc penny that is copper coated.

Geological Occurrence. Lead and zinc minerals are formed in deposits that resemble copper deposits in many ways. There are four important kinds of deposits, and in all of them the same two minerals occur, galena (PbS) and sphalerite (ZnS).

The first kind of deposit is a hydrothermal vein type. As with copper, lead and zinc minerals are very common in veins, but also as with copper, most of the veins are too small to be of much interest. Nevertheless, in many countries, including Peru and the United States, vein deposits still contribute to the production total.

Volcanogenic massive sulfide deposits, the second kind of deposit, are often rich in zinc, or in zinc plus lead. The famous Kuroko deposits of northern Honshu, Japan, are of this type, and they have a long production history of both lead and zinc. In New Brunswick, Canada, large massive sulfide ores have been known for many years. Many of the New Brunswick ores are so fine grained that it is not possible to separate the galena and sphalerite in order to prepare concentrates suitable for smelting, so even though the deposits are large and easily mined, they cannot be exploited profitably.

The third and most important class of hydrothermal lead-zinc deposit is known as the **Mississippi Valley type** (MVT), after the remarkable metallogenic province stretching from Oklahoma and Missouri, to Kentucky and Wisconsin, a region that includes most of the drainage basin of the Mississippi River [Fig. 7.22(a)]. Deposits with similar affinities have been discovered in Canada, northern Africa, Australia, the Soviet Union, and Europe. MVT deposits always occur in limestones where the ore minerals have either replaced the limestone beds or have been precipitated in between fragments of limestone **breccia.** The solutions that form the MVT deposits develop in sedimentary basins and flow laterally outward until they come in contact with limestones around the margins of the basins [Fig. 7.22(b)]. There, the solutions may dissolve the limestone and precipitate the galena and/or sphalerite. The rich zinc deposits in Tennessee have formed where ground waters had first dissolved much limestone, leaving a well-developed cave system. The ore-bearing solutions then deposited the ore minerals, sometimes as large spectacular crystals, in between **breccia** blocks that developed either from cave collapse or tectonic fracturing (Fig. 7.23). Other important deposits of this kind are the lead deposits in southeast Missouri and the great zinc deposits of Pine Point in Canada.

An increasingly large production of lead and zinc now comes from deposits of the fourth kind, sediment-hosted stratiform deposits. As with stratiform copper deposits, the origin of these deposits is problematic. The clearest example is the Kupferschiefer, where a zonal pattern of lead and zinc mineralization occurs around the copper deposits. The origin of the ores is, most likely, deposition in the Kupferschiefer by hydrothermal solutions that circulated in coarse, clastic sediments below the shale.

Most of the large, stratiform lead-zinc deposits are Precambrian in age. One very large and very rich deposit, the Sullivan body, occurs at Kimberley in British Columbia. The largest bodies of this kind, however, have been found in Australia. One, at Broken Hill in New South Wales, is one of the richest ore bodies ever found. The second, at Mount Isa in Queensland, is also very large, and besides lead and zinc has large copper reserves, too. The deposits at Broken Hill, Mount Isa,

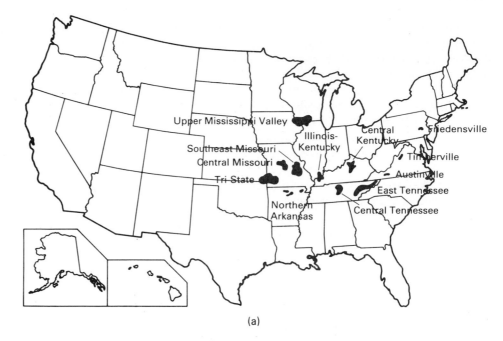

(a)

FIGURE 7-22. (a) Map showing the principal Mississippi Valley-type (carbonate-hosted) lead-zinc deposits in the United States. (b) Cross section of a large sedimentary basin showing expulsion of metal-bearing fluids from shales with subsequent deposition in the limestones on the flanks of the basin.

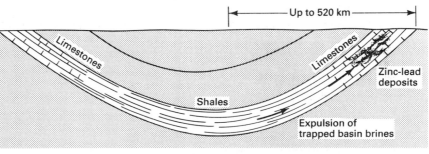

(b)

(a)

(b)

FIGURE 7-23. (a) Typical example of Mississippi Valley-type breccia ore from east Tennessee. The sphalerite was precipitated around the edges of the irregular and disoriented limestone and dolomite blocks, and the white is a late stage white dolomite. (Photograph by J.R. Craig.) (b) Example of well-developed crystals of sphalerite, fluorite, and barite from a cavity in the Central Tennessee zinc deposits. (Photograph by S. Llyn Sharp.)

and Sullivan are so rich that the ores contain combined values of lead plus zinc in excess of 20 percent. In fact, the ores are so rich, they closely resemble massive sulfide deposits.

Production and Reserves. The world's production of lead and zinc is dominated by six countries (Table 7.14), but significant lead production is reported from 50 countries, and zinc production from 52 countries.

Reserves are large, but not so large as to encourage complacency. Probably mineral exploration will discover new lead-zinc ore bodies in the future, but it is strange that very few occurrences of large, low-grade deposits have ever been found. In the case of zinc, low-grade deposits have been identified in shales associated with salt domes. Additionally, certain shales rich in organic matter have unusual zinc contents. No such low-grade resources have been identified for lead. Therefore, while the immediate future is assured for both lead and zinc, the long-term future can be considered reasonable for zinc, but uncertain for lead.

Tin

Tin shares the distinction with copper and lead of having been used by people for more than 5000 years. Where and when tin was first used is not known, but it was probably either in the Middle East or in southeast Asia. Most likely, the earliest use was as an alloying agent. Two tin-bearing alloys have been used since very ancient times. The first is bronze, a copper-based alloy in which tin serves as a hardening agent for the copper. Bronze is tougher and more durable than pure copper, and thus bronze tools last longer and are more efficient than copper tools. The discovery of bronze was one of the great milestones in the technological history of the human race. The second alloy of antiquity is pewter. Tin itself is too soft to be worked into spoons, knives, plates, and similar utensils, but when lead is added to tin, an inexpensive, harder, and very useful alloy is the

result—pewter. By the addition of small amounts of antimony or copper, pewter can be made even stronger and more durable than a straight tin plus lead pewter.

Tin is a soft, white metal with a low melting temperature. It does not corrode or rust, and so is an effective coating agent to cover metals that do corrode. The method for plating tin on copper was developed at least 2000 years ago, and tin-plated iron was first manufactured in the sixteenth century. Although the use of steel, aluminum, and plastic cans is rising rapidly and supplanting tin-plated cans, tin-plating is still an important process.

The low melting temperature of tin and alloys of tin and lead make tin the prime constituent of solders. The principal use of tin today is in solders, consuming approximately 35 percent of all tin mined. Bronze is used in certain soft-metal bearings, in ornamentation, automobiles, and aircraft.

Geological Occurrence. There are many tin minerals, but almost all production comes from cassiterite (SnO_2). A small amount of tin is produced as a by-product from the mining of other base metals, and in such cases, tin is usually present in the ore as the sulfide mineral stannite (Cu_2FeSnS_4).

Cassiterite is sometimes found in **pegmatites** associated with granitic rocks, but more commonly, it is found in hydrothermal deposits related to andesitic or rhyolitic volcanism. The hydrothermal deposits may be veins, disseminations in altered rocks, or even **skarns.**

Cassiterite is a dense, chemically stable mineral that does not alter or dissolve in stream waters. As a result, cassiterite is readily concentrated in **placers,** and worldwide, more tin is produced from placers than from hard-rock mines because placer mining is inexpensive compared to hard-rock mining.

Production and Reserves. Seven countries dominate the tin market (Table 7.15). Tin produced in Malaysia, Thailand, and Indonesia, three of the world's largest producers, comes almost entirely from placers.

TABLE 7-14

Production and reserves of lead and zinc

Country	Lead		Zinc	
	Production, 1984 (m.t.)	Reserves (m.t.)	Production, 1984 (m.t.)	Reserves (m.t.)
Australia	460,000	23,000,000	634,000	24,000,000
U.S.S.R.	440,000	Not reported	810,000	Not reported
United States	333,200	25,000,000	277,500	51,000,000
Canada	259,400	22,000,000	1,213,000	62,000,000
Peru	196,000	4,000,000	558,400	7,000,000
Mexico	195,000	5,000,000	289,400	3,000,000
WORLD TOTAL	3,190,400	146,000,000	6,418,000	243,000,000

(Data from U.S. Bureau of Mines.)

TABLE 7-15

Production and reserves of tin

Country	Production, 1984 (m.t.)	Reserves (m.t.)
Malaysia	41,300	600,000
U.S.S.R.	36,000	200,000
Thailand	21,900	217,000
Indonesia	21,500	500,000
Bolivia	21,100	485,000
Brazil	16,000	300,000
China	15,000	500,000
27 other countries	35,000	848,000
WORLD TOTAL	207,800	3,650,000

(Data from U.S. Bureau of Mines and U.S. Geological Survey.)

The remaining countries report both placer production and hard-rock production.

The reserves of tin are reasonably large—more than ten times the annual production rate—and resources are even larger. The U.S. Geological Survey has estimated that tin resources might be as high as 30 million metric tons. Whether or not all the tin in the estimated resources can actually be found and mined is an open question. Even if it can all be found, present-day production rates would, if maintained, see tin in short supply little more than a century ahead.

Mercury

Mercury is the only metal that is a liquid at room temperature. It combines readily with other metals to form alloys—in the case of mercury, such alloys are called amalgams. One common use for a silver-mercury amalgam is filling cavities in teeth.

There is only one important ore mineral of mercury, cinnabar (HgS). It is a soft, blood-red colored mineral found in hydrothermal vein deposits at a few places around the world. Small quantities of metallic mercury are often found with cinnabar. Mercury is produced both by primary mining and as a by-product from zinc and copper mining. The principal producing countries, in order of importance, are the Soviet Union, Spain, China, and the United States (Fig. 7-24). Between them, they produce 82 percent of the world's production. Reserves and resources are both small. Mercury is one of the metals for which it is likely that production will be unable to meet the demand within a few decades. The principal use of mercury is in batteries (55 percent). Other important, though lesser uses, are in chemicals (23 percent) and scientific measuring devices (5 percent).

Cadmium

Cadmium is a soft, malleable, silver-white metal that was discovered and first separated as a pure metal in 1817 by a German scientist who was investigating impurities in zinc minerals. Cadmium minerals are rare, but cadmium itself is widespread in trace amounts in the principal zinc ore mineral sphalerite (ZnS). Cadmium replaces zinc by atomic substitution, and in the smelting of zinc, the cadmium can be recovered. All cadmium production now comes as a by-product of zinc mining.

FIGURE 7-24. The mercury collection system used at Almadén in Spain for more than 200 years, from 1720–1928. The cinnabar-bearing ore was roasted in the chambers at the left, and the mercury vapor condensed as it passed through the terra cotta pipes. A hole in the pipe at the low point allowed the liquid mercury to drip into a channel and flow to a collection site at the far end. Modern systems operate in the same manner but are enclosed to prevent exposure to the mercury vapor. (Photograph by J.R. Craig.)

For about 60 years after discovery of the chemical element cadmium, its only use was in chemical compounds as pigments for paints. Cadmium compounds have very bright and intense colors—yellows, reds, blues, and greens. By the 1830s, they were being used by French artists and, in the 1840s, by English watercolor painters. Starting about 1890, cadmium found new uses as a metal in low-melting alloys and in chemical reagents. In 1919, a cadmium-electroplating process was developed. Cadmium plating is similar to zinc plating, and this accounts for the bulk of the cadmium used today. Other uses are in batteries, pigments, and alloys.

Because cadmium is produced as a by-product of smelting zinc ores, it is the large zinc smelting countries, the Soviet Union, Japan, and the United States, that are the main producers. In 1984, the world's total production of cadmium was 17,700 metric tons. It is somewhat meaningless to talk about cadmium reserves because the production of cadmium is dependent on the mining of zinc.

THE PRECIOUS METALS

The **precious metals** owe their name to their high values. Two of them, gold and silver, have been known and prized since antiquity. The other precious metals, the six platinum group metals, joined the select list in more recent times. The metals are precious (and expensive) for several reasons, but two are paramount. First,

they are all rare and costly to find and recover. Second, to varying degrees, the precious metals resist corrosion and have great lasting qualities. Their resistance to chemical reaction is said to be due to their nobleness, hence their alternate name—**noble metals.**

Gold

Metallic gold is soft and malleable, but also extremely resistant to chemical attack, and it is corrosion-free. Indeed, gold is so stable and has so little tendency for corrosion that most of the gold that has ever been mined is still in use. The gold that was present in the bracelets that adorned Cleopatra's arms could possibly now be residing in someone's teeth, a wedding ring, or a gold coin. Once gold has been recovered from the ground, it can be melted down repeatedly and used again and again.

Gold was possibly the first metal used by our ancestors; in all likelihood, the first uses were for ornamentation. Gold's rarity and imperishability soon made it a medium of exchange, and eventually it became an accepted measure of value around the world (Fig. 7.25). To a certain extent, it still fills this role, although few countries still back their issue of paper currency with gold. In addition, as the use of gold for monetary purposes has declined, its use for industrial purposes has grown so large that more than half of the world's annual production is now used in electronic products, aerospace applications, special alloys, and dentistry.

FIGURE 7-25. Stacks of gold bullion bars in the Federal Reserve Bank vault. Gold has often served as a monetary standard and remains a measure of wealth. (Photograph courtesy of the Federal Reserve Bank of New York.)

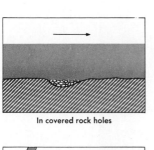

Behind covered bars

In covered rock holes

In potholes below waterfalls

On the inside of meander loops

Downstream from the
mouth of a tributary

In the ocean behind bars against
the prevailing current

(a)

(b)

FIGURE 7-26. (a) Typical sites of placer accumulations where obstructing or deflecting barriers allow faster-moving waters to carry away the suspended load of light and fine-grained material while trapping denser and coarser particles that are moving along the bottom by rolling or partial suspension. Placers can form wherever there is moving water, although they are most commonly associated with streams. (b) Grains of placer gold from California. By continual pounding in fast-moving streams, malleable gold is freed from brittle quartz and other valueless minerals. The tiny, but dense gold grains accumulate in placers. It was gold such as this that the "forty-niners" mined in the streams of California. The grains are 1–2 millimeters in diameter. (Photograph by W. Sacco.)

Geological Occurrence. Gold deposits are formed by hydrothermal solutions. By far, the most important mineral in such deposits is native gold, but in a few instances the telluride minerals, calaverite (Au Te$_2$) and sylvanite ((Au,Ag)Te$_2$), are also important. Hydrothermal gold deposits are commonly veins, in which the associated gangue mineral is generally quartz. Disseminated deposits of gold are also known, particularly in the western United States, where the Carlin and Cortez deposits in Nevada are examples, but production from them is a small fraction of the production from vein deposits.

Gold is a dense, indestructible mineral. It is therefore readily concentrated in streams where the action of flowing water washes away the less dense sand grains and leaves the gold concentrated behind barriers, and

near the base of the stream channel (Fig. 7.26). Alluvial **placers,** as these deposits are called, were almost certainly the first deposits to have been worked by our ancestors, and they are still important producers. Many of the great gold rushes were started when prospectors discovered alluvial gold. Not only was the gold in the alluvial deposits worth recovering, but there was always the hope that prospecting upstream would lead to the mother lode from which the gold was derived. The great gold rush to California in 1849 is an example [Fig. 7.27(a)], and from that rush, many interesting things follow. The great mother lode of California was discovered, but other parts of American heritage grew from the gold rush, too. Few readers will remember that it was James Marshall who found the first California gold at Sutter's Mill in 1848, but most will be familiar with

(a)   (b)

FIGURE 7-27. (a) Hydraulic placer mining in California in the 1860s. (b) Levi Strauss—the most famous name from the California Gold Rush—did not pan for gold. (Photograph courtesy of Levi Strauss & Co.)

the name Levi Strauss [Fig. 7.27(b)]. Strauss, though not a miner, left his impact by producing the tough, durable canvas pants that the miners needed in their demanding labors. These were the first Levis, the blue canvas jeans now worn around the world.

The greatest gold deposits that have ever been discovered, the Witwatersrand deposits in the Republic of South Africa, are ancient placers. These famous deposits were discovered in 1886, and they soon became the main gold producers in the world, a position they continue to fill today. The extreme mining depths now being reached and the rapidly escalating costs of mining suggest, however, that these famous deposits may not see a second century of production.

The Witwatersrand deposits are ancient conglomerates that were laid in a shallow marine basin (Fig. 7.28). Into the basin ran ancient rivers, and at the mouth of each river a delta slowly built up. The gold

and other heavy minerals are found in the coarse clastic sediments—the **conglomerates**—that make up the deltas (Fig. 7.29), and they are presumed to have been brought into the basin as clastic particles by the same streams that brought the pebbles into the conglomerates. There are many unusual and still unexplained features of the Witwatersrand ores. The deposits are very old, between 2.3 and 2.8 billion years of age. They are enormous—more than 20 times larger than any other single gold district in the world. The source of the gold and how it came to be in the ancient conglomerates has been the subject of fierce debate for a century. Because the deposits are so much larger than any other kind of deposit, what could the source of the gold possibly be? Is it possible that geologists have misread the evidence, and the deposits are not really placers? The issues are still unresolved. Also unresolved is the question of whether or not other Witwatersrands exist. Similar de-

FIGURE 7-28. The place where the fabulous Witwatersrand gold conglomerates were discovered by two prospectors, George Harrison and George Walker, in 1886. The conglomerate is somewhat weathered due to oxidation of pyrite (compare Plate 14). The man in the photograph is Dr. Desmond Pretorius, one of the greatest living authorities on the geology of this remarkable deposit.

posits occur in the Elliot Lake region of Canada and the Jacobina region of Brazil, but none has been found to be as rich as South Africa's basin.

The gold mines of South Africa are the world's deepest. At the end of 1986, the deepest mining activity was being carried out 3600 meters (11,800 feet) below ground level. Plans are being laid to carry mining activities even deeper, to 4500 meters (14,700 feet). Whether it will be possible to mine safely and profitably at these extreme depths remains to be seen, but on that question rides South Africa's hope of continuing as the world's major producer of gold.

Gold is present in at least small amounts in a great many hydrothermal deposits of copper. The amount is rarely sufficient to warrant mining for gold alone, but when copper is being mined, gold can be recovered during smelting. Gold is one of the major by-products of porphyry copper mining and also from the mining of volcanogenic massive sulfide deposits.

Production and Reserves. There are two widely used units in the production of precious metals—the Troy ounce and the gram. One ounce (Troy) is equal to 31.104 grams. The total world production for 1984 was 46,035,098 ounces (Troy). This is equal to 1,431,875,600 grams, or 1431.87 metric tons of gold! The total amount of gold ever produced is estimated at approximately 110,000 metric tons (which would make

a cube approximately 18 meters on a side) with more than 70 percent of that produced since 1900.

Gold is so widely produced that 62 countries reported production in 1984. Almost certainly, there were small productions in other countries, too, but they were not reported. Despite the wide extent of gold mining around the world, production is dominated by seven countries (Table 7.16). The largest by far, producing 47.6 percent of the world's gold in 1984, is South Africa. Indeed, one huge mine in South Africa, the Vaal Reefs Mine, is said to produce more gold each year than the total productions of Australia, Canada, and the United States combined. As is apparent in Fig. 7.30,

TABLE 7-16

Production and reserves of gold

Country	Production, 1984 (m.t.)	Reserves (m.t.)
Republic of South Africa	681.30	23,640
U.S.S.R.	269.05	6220
Canada	81.32	1306
United States	64.04	2490
China	59.10	467
Brazil	54.43	715
Australia	37.32	715
55 other countries	185.31	4255
WORLD TOTAL	1431.87	39,808

(Data from U.S. Bureau of Mines.)

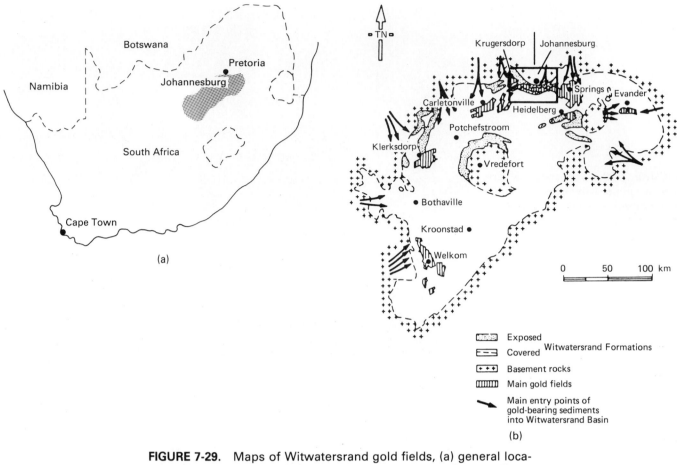

FIGURE 7-29. Maps of Witwatersrand gold fields, (a) general location in South Africa and (b) the basin showing the major gold fields and with arrows indicating the directions of transport of the conglomerates into the basin. (Courtesy of the Geological Society of South Africa.)

the production of gold around the world throughout this century has been dominated by South Africa. The world's total production curve is very nearly parallel to South Africa's production curve, and except for the depression years of the 1930s, South Africa has produced more than half of the world's annual production for most of the twentieth century. That dominance now seems to be slipping. Since 1980, the South African production has remained constant, but the world's total production has climbed steadily. The difference arises from the increasing amount of gold mined in the Soviet Union and other countries around the world. The increased production has come in response to higher gold prices. There is a lesson to be learned from the curves in Fig. 7.30 besides the lesson of the influence of metal price on production. The lesson concerns exhaustion. No matter how large, how rich, or how carefully a deposit is mined, every ore body has a finite lifetime. South Africa's gold mining days are far from finished,

but the flat production curve at a time of high gold prices is an early warning that the end must come someday.

What are the world's reserves and resources of gold? Reserves are not reported by all countries, so an accurate report is not possible. Both the U.S. Bureau of Mines and the U.S. Geological Survey made combined reserve and resource estimates in the 1970s. The numbers ranged between 350 million and 1 billion ounces of recoverable gold. These seem to be large numbers, but they are really quite small because the annual production is about 45 million ounces. If the low estimate were correct, mining should have ceased several years ago. Since the time when the estimates were made, about 500 million ounces of gold have been mined. Estimates of today's combined resource and reserve numbers of recoverable gold are still between 350 million and 1 billion ounces. The apparent discrepancy reflects the success of prospecting plus the reevaluation of known de-

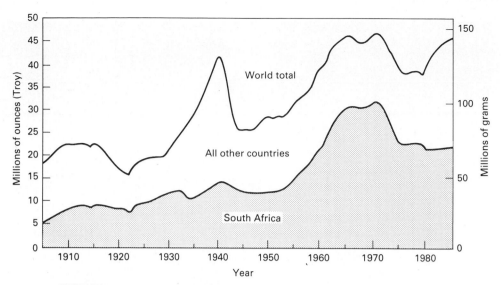

FIGURE 7-30. Annual world production of gold from 1905 to 1986. For most of this period, South Africa accounted for about half of the production. Note the big increase in world production during the depression years of the 1930s. Labor was cheap, and very low-grade gold deposits were worked. Note, too, that from about 1970 the South African production has declined and that up to 1986 it had not risen significantly in response to the rising price of gold. Intensive prospecting around the world accounts for the rise in the total world production from 1977 onward.

posits as a result of high gold prices in recent years. Can the trend continue? Certainly not forever, but probably it can for a century or so.

Silver

Silver, like gold, was one of the earliest known metals. It was probably first used for simple ornaments and utensils in the Middle East where silver objects more than 5000 years old have been excavated. Like gold, silver occurs as a native metal. Unlike gold, the native metal is not the most common mineral form. Much more common are silver-bearing sulfide minerals.

Silver was in wide use before the emergence of the Greek city-states, but it was one of those city-states, Athens, that showed the value of a good silver mine. The most famous of the ancient silver mines at Laurium belonged to Athens, and with the wealth it produced Themistocles built the fleet of ships that defeated Xerxes and saved Europe from Persian domination. Athens then grew to leadership among the city-states, and the Athenians became famous for their wealth and life-style. The mines at Laurium were worked for several centuries and are estimated to have produced over 250 million ounces (7.5 billion grams or 7500 metric tons) of silver.

The Greeks, Phoenicians, and other people from the countries bordering the Mediterranean used silver in their coinage, but it was the Romans who really brought it into wide usage. They made silver the basis of their monetary system (Fig. 7.31) and expanded their empire in order to control sources of silver and other metals. When the power of Rome weakened, and the empire finally fell, the mines of Europe closed. The Dark Ages descended on Europe. The metals, particularly silver, that had formerly been mined in Europe and sent east to the Asian and Middle Eastern countries slowed to a trickle and finally ceased. For 500 years, there was little or no mining. When Charlemagne came to power near the end of the eighth century, he opened once again the old mines of central Europe in order to build his revenue. Discoveries of new deposits followed in Germany, Bohemia, the Tyrol, and the Harz Mountains. Most significantly, the very rich silver deposits of Rammelsberg and Frieberg were found in Germany in 920 and in 1170 A.D., respectively, at Joachimsthal in Czeckoslovakia in 1200, and at Schneeburg in Germany in 1460. From these deposits, the flow of precious metals restored Europe's wealth and helped its emergence from the Dark Ages. Trade routes were reopened and new ones established. The land routes through the Middle East were particularly troublesome because of the taxes extracted by the Saracens and others on all materials passing through. This led Spanish and Portuguese sailors to seek sea routes. Vasco da Gama opened the routes around Africa, and Columbus sailed west and found the Americas.

The discovery of South and Central America with their enormous mineral wealth probably saved Europe

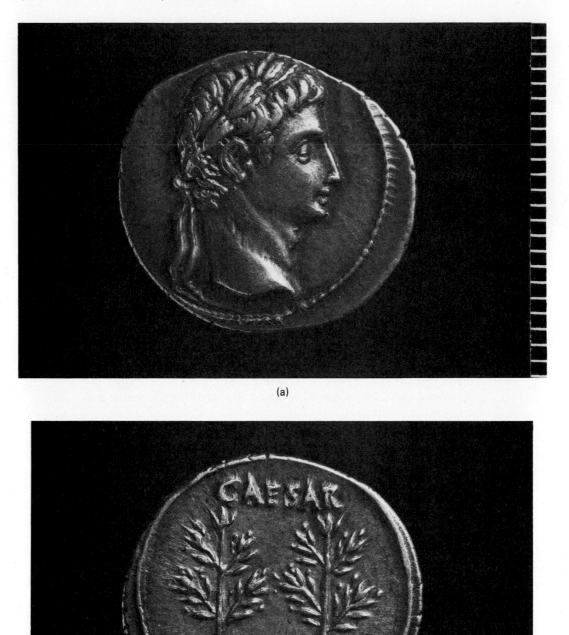

(a)

(b)

FIGURE 7-31. Silver denarius from Rome, in the time of Augustus (27 B.C. to 14 A.D.). (a) The head of Augustus appears on the front; (b) Augustus' title (Caesar) and name, together with two laurel trees, appear on the back. (From the Numismatic Collections, Yale University. Photography by W. Sacco.)

from a new dark age. The mines of Europe were unable to cover the debts of the crowned heads and ambitious bankers. The vast flood of silver and gold from Mexico, Peru, Bolivia, Ecuador, and Brazil filled Europe's coffers again. The greatest production came from Bolivia, where the fabulous deposits of Potosi gave forth a flow of silver that seemed to never end. Spanish treasury records show that between 1503 and 1650, nearly 17 billion (10^9) grams (> 540 million ounces) of silver had been shipped from the New World to Spain. By 1700, Bolivia alone had produced over 1 billion ounces of silver. The countries of South America were the main producers of silver until the 1870s, when the great deposits of Nevada, Utah, and the other western states pushed the United States into leadership (Fig. 7.32). The United States held that position until 1900, when Mexico took over. Mexico continues as the world's leading producer of silver to the present day.

Silver has many technical and industrial uses, but two of its properties account for about 75 percent of the consumption. The first property is its high electrical conductivity. Silver metal has the least resistance to electricity (the highest conductivity) of all metals. As a result, it is widely used in electrical contacts and conductors where the highest reliability is necessary. About 25 percent of all silver used in industrial countries is consumed in this manner. The second important property of silver, or rather of silver in certain compounds such as silver iodide, is that it is light sensitive. This is the property used in photography, and as a result, half of all silver consumed is used in photography. Other uses are in coins, sterling ware such as eating utensils and trays, jewelry, solders, and batteries. Silver was long used in American 10-, 25-, and 50-cent coins but was withdrawn after 1965.

Geological Occurrence. Silver is a chemical element that resembles copper in many ways. As a result, silver can readily proxy for copper, by atomic substitution, in most copper minerals. Not surprisingly, perhaps, much of the silver now mined comes as a by-product from copper mining. Silver also has an affinity for lead, and a great deal of the world's silver is also produced as a by-product of lead mining. Today, more than 75 percent of all the silver produced is by-product silver. Inasmuch as both copper and lead deposits are largely of hydrothermal origin, the by-product silver is also of hydrothermal origin.

A number of deposits around the world are still worked principally for silver. The minerals recovered are mainly argentite (Ag_2S) and tetrahedrite (($Cu,Ag)_{12}Sb_4S_{13}$), but a number of other silver minerals are also recovered. The deposits in which all these minerals are found are hydrothermal veins, and the geological settings in which the veins are located are principally volcanic rocks of andesitic and rhyolitic affinity. Because the great mountain chain that runs down the western edge of the Americas is made up of andesitic and rhyolitic volcanoes, it is from here that most of the world's silver has been won. More than three-quarters of all the silver that has ever been produced has been mined in the Americas.

Production and Reserves. Silver resembles gold in that a large number of countries (58 in 1984) report production. Unlike gold, no single country dominates silver production the way South Africa dominates gold production, but six countries do produce about 70 percent of the new silver each year (Table 7.17).

It is apparent from Table 7.17 that the annual world production of silver vastly exceeds the world's production of gold. There is, nevertheless, a real problem concerning silver. The present-day consumption of silver exceeds the production of silver. Because silver is subject to a certain amount of corrosion, and in many of the uses to which it is put it is not recoverable, there is a small but steady loss of silver. To make up the difference between the silver consumed and that produced, silver is withdrawn from inventory, from coinage, and from private hoards. Eventually, if consumption continues to exceed production, the hoards of silver will be depleted. The production of silver is not likely to rise very much, however, because so much of the production is a by-product. If copper and lead productions rise, silver production does, too. If copper and lead productions fall, silver production falls. Because the amount of copper in porphyry copper and in volcanogenic massive sulfide deposits is very large, silver production will not cease, but someday it may well decline. A drop would produce a rise in prices, and this, in turn, would make some of the use to which silver is put too expensive. Reduced consumption would then follow.

TABLE 7-17

Production and reserves of silver

Country	Production, 1984 (m.t.)	Reserves (m.t.)
Mexico	2109	32,966
Peru	1758	18,971
U.S.S.R.	1474	49,761
United States	1383	46,961
Canada	1168	49,761
Australia	995	31,722
52 other countries	3509	31,878
WORLD TOTAL	12,396	262,020

(Data from U.S. Bureau of Mines.)

FIGURE 7-32. The rich silver ores discovered at Eureka, Nevada, were one of the many rich deposits that made the United States the world's leading silver producer during the second half of the nineteenth century. The KC Mine as it looked in 1873 was one of several operating mines at Eureka. The entrance to the mine was a horizontal tunnel covered by the shed in the center of the photograph. Mined ore was tipped down the covered chutes to the processing plant just visible to the lower right. (Photographer not known. From the collections of Beinecke Library, Yale University.)

Platinum Group Metals

The six platinum group metals, platinum, palladium, rhodium, iridium, ruthenium, and osmium, always occur together. They occur in the same geological setting, and to a certain degree they can substitute for each other in minerals by atomic substitution. Many of their chemical and physical properties are similar, too, so it is convenient to discuss these metals as a group rather than individually.

The group takes its name from its most abundant member, platinum. Each of the metals is silvery white in color, and although the metals are all malleable to a certain degree, both platinum and palladium are sufficiently malleable that they can sometimes be mistaken for silver. Indeed, the first uses of platinum probably occurred as a result of such a misidentification. Platinum metal occurs in the native form in placers. Grains of platinum, intermixed with silver grains, were used by ancient Egyptian artisans in certain works of ornamentation. The artisans must have realized platinum was more difficult to work than silver, but because it can be soldered they probably regarded the platinum as just an impure form of silver.

When the Spanish conquistadors conquered South America they discovered finely-wrought objects of a strange, white metal among the Indian treasures they looted. The Indian metalsmiths had learned to shape, solder, and even alloy platinum. The Spaniards lacked these skills and did not attempt to learn from the Indians. They considered platinum to be valueless because they could not work it as they could silver. Consequently, they called the metal *platina,* a degrading term meaning "little silver." Furthermore, the importation of platinum into Europe from the New World was banned so that it would not degrade gold and silver, and much platinum was thrown into rivers and the sea.

The first precise separation of platinum as a chemical element and the first clear statement of its properties arose from the work of an English scientist, William Lewis. He published the results of his studies in 1763, and soon thereafter, other chemists in Germany and France learned how to purify the metal. As a result, they discovered many of platinum's alloying properties. During the purification of platinum it was discovered that other platinumlike metals were also present in many of the ores. In 1803, the English scientist, Wollaston, separated and identified palladium. In 1804, Wollaston described rhodium, while his countryman, Tennant, isolated and named osmium and iridium. Forty years were to pass until a German named Claus, working in Russia, discovered the last of the platinum group metals. He named it *ruthenium* in honor of his adopted country. *Ruthenia* is the latinized name for Russia.

All the platinum group metals are resistant to corrosion, each has a high melting temperature, and each has interesting properties as a **catalyst,** a substance that speeds chemical reactions. Speeding chemical reactions through catalysis, plus the use of the metals in highly corrosive environments, and in very high-temperature situations, accounts for the main uses of all the platinum group metals.

Geological Occurrence. The platinum group metals are found as native metals and as sulfide and arsenide minerals. There are only two important geological settings in which these minerals are found in economic quantities. The first is in mafic and ultramafic rocks where the platinum group metals are concentrated in both chromite horizons and sulfide-rich layers in layered intrusions. As a result, production of platinum group metals comes from the same deposits, such as Sudbury, Ontario, and the Bushveld Igneous Complex in South Africa that produce nickel, copper, and chromium from magmatic segregation ores.

The second geological environment in which the platinum group metals are concentrated is in placers. Like gold, the metals are dense and very resistant to corrosion. They concentrate readily in alluvial sediments. Commonly, the source of the metals in placers is ultramafic rocks such as serpentinites and peridotites. The great placer deposits of the Soviet Union have this origin. Serpentine in the Ural Mountains contains small amounts of platinum group metals, so that streams that carry debris from weathering of serpentine from the Urals have valuable placers associated with them.

Production and Reserves. Separate production figures are not reported for all the platinum group metals, but it is possible to estimate the approximate percentages from the amounts of metals consumed. Platinum and palladium each account for about 40 percent of the production. Rhodium accounts for 9 percent, iridium 6 percent, ruthenium 4 percent, and osmium 1 percent.

The world's production of platinum group metals is overwhelmingly dominated by two countries, the Soviet Union and the Republic of South Africa (Table 7.18). Between them, they produced 94 percent of all the platinum group metals mined in 1984. Between them, too, they own most of the world's reserves. Of particular importance are two horizons within the Bushveld Complex in South Africa. One horizon is the 0.5-meter thick Merensky Reef that has served as the major source for platinum for many years and that contains reserves estimated at 500–600 million troy ounces ($15 - 19 \times 10^9$ gram). The other horizon, known as the UG-2, lies below the Merensky Reef and

TABLE 7-18
Production and reserves of the platinum group metals

Country	Production, 1984 (m.t.)	Reserves (m.t.)
U.S.S.R.	115.08	6220
Republic of South Africa	90.20	30,170
Canada	10.82	280
8 other countries	3.28	650
WORLD TOTAL	219.38	37,320

(Data from U.S. Bureau of Mines.)

is estimated to contain reserves of 800–1350 million troy ounces (25—41 × 10^9 gram). In the United States, large resources of platinum group metals are present in the Stillwater Complex, Montana. These deposits occur in a Merensky Reef-like layer in a layered intrusion that is smaller, but that resembles the Bushveld Complex. The deposits have not yet been mined.

THE SPECIAL METALS

The special metals earned their name because of their unique properties and the special roles they fill in our twentieth century technology. None of them is mined in large quantities, but each fills one or more special roles that make their continued availability of vital importance to society.

Niobium and Tantalum

Niobium and tantalum have similar properties and commonly occur together in nature. They were identified as separate chemical elements in 1801, but for more than 125 years no use was found for them. Eventually, in the 1920s, tantalum came to be used in the chemical and electrical industries, but it was only at the time of World War II that it found uses in electrical capacitors and in alloys for armaments. Niobium was first used about 1930 when it was added to steel to make very high-temperature alloys.

Niobium is still used for high-strength alloys needed in such demanding environments as gas turbines and the engines of jet aircraft. It is also used to make superconducting magnets. Most of the tantalum used is still employed in the electronics industry for capacitors and rectifiers. Other applications included tantalum carbide for high-temperature cutting tools, and because it is corrosion resistant, insertion of tantalum mesh and pins in the human body during surgical repairs.

The main minerals that contain niobium and tantalum are columbite ($(Fe,Mn)Nb_2O_6$) and tantalite ($(Fe,Mn)Ta_2O_6$). Columbite always contains some tantalum in solid solution, and tantalite always contains niobium, so the two metals are always produced together.

Tantalum and niobium minerals are found in several kinds of igneous rock. The first is an alkali-rich rock called a **nepheline syenite.** Such rocks are rarely rich enough to be mined, but in the Kola Peninsula of the Soviet Union, they do reach mineable grade and are being exploited. The second kind of igneous rock is a **carbonatite.** This rare and unusual rock consists largely of calcium carbonate, and it is known both as an intrusive and extrusive igneous rock. Carbonatites have been worked for their niobium and tantalum contents at Oka in Quebec and at Axana in Brazil.

The third type of igneous rock that often contains interesting amounts of niobium and tantalum is the pegmatite. One of the major sources of tantalum in North America is the Bernic Lake pegmatite in Manitoba.

Both columbite and tantalite are chemically stable, hard, and dense. Therefore, the minerals tend to become concentrated in placers. Such deposits have been worked in Brazil, Western Australia, and West Africa.

The total world production of niobium in 1984 was 12,690 metric tons and of tantalum, 320 metric tons. The major producing countries were Canada, Australia, and Brazil.

Arsenic, Antimony, and Bismuth

The three elements arsenic, antimony, and bismuth have similar properties and tend to occur in the same kinds of geological environments. Arsenic is little used in its elemental form. It is a brittle, grayish-colored substance that lacks the malleability usually associated with metals. For this reason, arsenic is often called a semimetal. The main use for arsenic is in chemical compounds, mainly as arsenates used in wood preservation, fungicides, insecticides, and pesticides. All the arsenic produced comes as a by-product from base metal mining. The world's production in 1984 was 32,674 metric tons of arsenic trioxide (As_2O_3). The main producers were the United States, the Soviet Union, France, and Mexico.

Antimony, like arsenic, is really a semimetal, but it has useful alloying properties, so much of the production finds a use in the metallic form. Antimony metal is added to the lead plates in batteries in order to toughen the lead. It is also used as an alloying agent with other base metals besides lead in order to harden alloys and make them more resistant to corrosion. Antimony compounds find uses as pigments in paints and plastics, as fire-retarding agents, as stabilizers in glasses, and in many other circumstances. The world's production of antimony, stated as the metal, was 53,500 metric tons in 1984. The major producers, in order of importance, were China, Bolivia, the Soviet Union, and the Republic of South Africa.

Bismuth, the heaviest of the trio of semimetals, is also the most metallic in its properties. Most people know bismuth in its various chemical compounds used for medicinal purposes. The well-known antacid Pepto-Bismol is a proprietary form of a medicinal bismuth compound. The two largest uses of bismuth are medicinal and cosmetic compounds. The third major use of bismuth is as an additive to low-melting alloys. The world's annual production of bismuth is small. In 1984, the total production was only 4000 metric tons.

Arsenic, antimony, and bismuth are produced as by-products of smelting processes for more abundant metals such as lead, zinc, and copper, although antimony, the element used in the largest amount, is also produced directly at the Murchison Mine in South Africa. All the producing deposits, whether direct or by-product, are hydrothermal, and all the ore minerals are sulfides.

Germanium, Gallium, and Indium

Germanium, gallium, and indium are very much metals of the twentieth century. In each case, the major production is a by-product from the processing of major metals, principally aluminum and zinc, but to a lesser extent, lead and copper. In 1984, the first deposit to be mined principally for germanium and gallium, the Apex Mine, was opened in Utah.

The total quantity of the three metals produced is small, but the uses to which they are put are wide ranging. Germanium has a high electrical conductivity, and it is the material from which some of the semiconductors in computers are made. Gallium has the unusual property of expanding on crystallizing, and this leads to some most unusual alloying effects. Indium has a very low-melting temperature and is very soft and highly malleable, so it too has very interesting, although highly specialized, alloy properties. The principal uses for all three metals are in the electronics industry.

The world's annual production of the three metals is not known because the uses to which they are put are very sensitive; hence, most countries will not supply production figures. It is apparent, however, that if limitations to supply exist, they arise from the difficulty of separating and purifying the metals, not from supplies of raw materials. This trio of metals is widespread in small amounts and should not be considered limited in abundance for the distant future.

Beryllium

Beryllium metal is produced by a relatively young industry because many of its uses have arisen as a result of the nuclear and space industries. A beryllium compound has been known and used since antiquity, however. The two gemstones emerald and aquamarine are species of the beryllium mineral, beryl (Fig. 7.33).

The chemical element beryllium was first identified in 1797, but only in 1828 was the metal itself produced. It is a very light metal, reddish in color, very strong and rigid, and it has a very high-melting temperature. Mixed with copper, beryllium produces a very hard and elastic alloy. The low atomic weight of beryllium makes it almost transparent to X-rays and thermal neutrons, so the metal is widely used for the windows in X-ray tubes.

There are two major sources of beryllium. The first is the mineral beryl that is found in many pegmatites around the world. Unfortunately, none of the deposits is particularly large or rich. The second important mineral is bertrandite ($Be_4Si_2O_7(OH)_2$), which occurs in certain hydrothermal deposits associated with rhyolitic volcanic rocks. The deposits at Spor Mountain, Utah, are the largest known deposits of this kind.

The world's annual production of beryllium, reported as beryl, was only 8800 metric tons in 1984. Production has been a little larger at times, but at no time has beryllium ever been produced in very large quantities. The restriction on production is two-fold. First, deposits are small and very expensive to work. Second, the separation of beryllium from its ores is a very expensive and exacting process.

Rare-earth Elements

The **rare-earth elements (REE)** really do not deserve their name because they are much more abundant than many other geochemically scarce metals. There are 15 REE (Table 7.19), starting with lanthanum (atomic number 57) and ending with lutetium (atomic number 71). They differ only in the number of electrons in their inner electron shells, hence they all have very similar chemical properties. When first discovered, the REE were known only in their oxide forms, and because they resembled the oxides of the alkaline earths (CaO, BaO, etc.), and did not seem to form common minerals, they were labeled *rare earths*.

The REE are the basis of a small industry that started more than a century ago. The oxides are stable at high temperatures, and they were added to the thorium oxide mantles used in gas lamps by our great-grandparents. In more recent times, they have found uses in such diverse applications as petroleum-cracking catalysts, opacifiers, and coloring agents in the glass and ceramics industry, inhibitors of radiation in television tubes, lasers, and special optical glasses.

The REE are produced mainly from two minerals, monazite ($CeYPO_4$) and bastnaesite ($CeFCO_3$). Although the formulae of both minerals are written for cerium compounds, all the REE substitute for cerium in the structures by atomic substitution.

FIGURE 7-33. Beryl crystal from a pegmatite at Portland, Connecticut. Note the hexagonal shape of the crystal. The specimen is 4 centimeters in diameter. (Photograph by W. Sacco.)

REE minerals are found in small amounts in many igneous rocks, but principally in pegmatites, carbonatites, and granites. Some of these deposits are mined, as at Mountain Pass in California, but the main production comes from monazite concentrated in placers. It is recovered as a by-product from the mining of rutile, ilmenite, cassiterite, and other placer minerals.

The world's production of REE, reported as monazite, was 26,500 metric tons in 1984. The figure is somewhat misleading, though. Production in the United States, which is believed to be large, was not reported for proprietary reasons. Nor was any production from the Soviet Union or other eastern countries reported. Australia, Brazil, and India, in that order, are the most important countries among those that do report production.

DISTRIBUTION OF DEPOSITS OF THE SCARCE METALS

There are literally hundreds of thousands of mineral deposits, large and small, that have been discovered, tested, and sometimes mined. As a result, geologists have long realized that certain kinds of deposits occur more commonly in some kinds of rocks than in others. For example, the association between mafic igneous rocks and nickel deposits, or the similar association with chromium deposits, has long been recognized. Despite such associations, it was only during the 1970s, when the consequences of plate tectonics and continental drift were being considered, that the possibility of a larger

TABLE 7-19

The rare-earth elements. The relative amount of each REE produced is in proportion to its geochemical abundance in the crust

Name	Chemical Symbol		Atomic Number	Geochemical Abundance (wt %)
Yttrium*	Y		39	0.0035
Lanthanum	La		57	0.005
Cerium	Ce		58	0.0083
Praseodymium	Pr		59	0.013
Neodymium	Nd	The light REE	60	0.0044
Promethium	Pm		61	Human-made
Samarium	Sm		62	0.00077
Europium	Eu		63	0.00022
Gadolinium	Gd		64	0.00063
Terbium	Tb		65	0.0001
Dysprosium	Dy		66	0.00085
Holmium	Ho	The heavy REE	67	0.00016
Erbium	Er		68	0.00036
Thulium	Tm		69	0.000052
Ytterbium	Yb		70	0.00034
Lutetium	Lu		71	0.00008

*Yttrium is commonly classed with the REE because its properties are so similar.

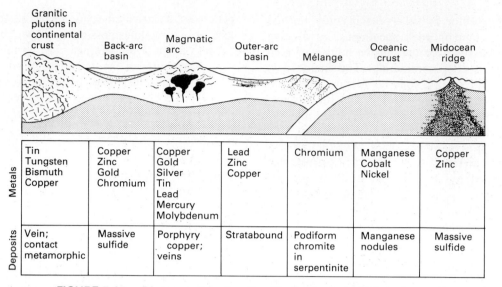

FIGURE 7-34. Diagram showing the kinds of mineral deposits and the most important metals concentrated in relation to tectonic plates.

underlying pattern was realized. A great deal remains to be deciphered, but it is now apparent that many classes of ore deposits formed where and when they did as a consequence of plate tectonic motions.

Most volcanism around the world is associated either with plate spreading edges (mid-ocean ridges) or with plate subduction edges (deep-sea trenches). The kinds of volcanism differ at the two edges, but each serves as a heat source to drive hydrothermal systems and to bring metal-rich magma up from the mantle or lower crust (Fig. 7.34). Most of the young, active hydrothermal systems that have been discovered around the world can be shown to be directly related to the modern plate edges. We must conclude, therefore, that hydrothermal mineral deposits formed as a result of volcanism arose as a direct consequence of plate tectonics, and that present and past plate motions must control their distribution.

The origins of sediment-hosted stratiform deposits and even Mississippi Valley-type deposits can also be re-lated to plate motions. Most stratiform deposits are located in grabens, which are sediment basins formed by blocks of crust dropped downward along normal faults (Fig. 7.35). Grabens arise as a result of tensional forces, and those tensional forces are a consequence of plate tectonics. Mississippi Valley-type deposits form in sediments deposited on the shelves of large sedimentary basins. The basins form as a consequence of plate motions, so these deposits also appear to be distributed in a way that suggests a plate tectonic control. We may eventually be able to understand and decipher the underlying controls on all mineral deposits, but at present, only the broadest outline is visible.

PROSPECTING FOR DEPOSITS OF THE SCARCE METALS

Most of us have an overly romanticized image of the grizzled old prospector going about his work. The image usually includes a mule and a faithful dog who ac-

FIGURE 7-35. One way that stratiform orebodies are believed to form in sediments is through hydrothermal solutions rising up faults and spreading laterally through a porous aquifer. If the sediment above the aquifer reacts with the solution, sulfide minerals such as chalcopyrite, sphalerite, or galena may precipitate.

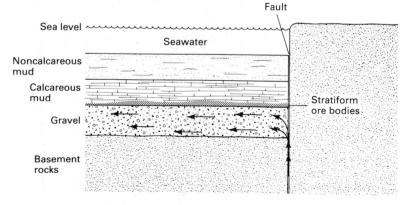

company the prospector as he works his way up and down hill slopes, tapping rock specimens, or digging shallow holes, searching for the elusive nugget of gold or rich showing of copper minerals. The image may once have been correct, but it is no longer. The rich, easily discovered deposits that crop out at the surface, just waiting for some knowledgeable prospector to come along, have mostly been discovered. In some well prospected areas, it is many centuries since the last outcropping deposit was found. In that part of Europe that was once controlled by the Romans, for example, no new deposits of base or precious metals have been discovered since the Roman empire fell. Deeper extensions of known mineral districts have indeed been located, but prospectors have not found any entirely new mineral districts. Much more sophisticated techniques are now needed to find new mines.

The pattern of discovery just described for Roman Europe can also be discerned in other well-prospected parts of the world. The New England States for example—Connecticut, Massachusetts, Rhode Island, Vermont, New Hampshire, and Maine—were active mining states and were producers of important quantities of scarce metals at some time in their histories. With the exception of Maine, those days are long gone, and prospectors have not turned up deposits of interest for many, many years.

Eventually, each country will have been thoroughly prospected by traditional means. That does not mean that all deposits will have been found, however. More than half of the earth's surface is covered so deeply by soil and sediment that it is not possible to see the rock below. To prospect in such terrains, it is necessary to use indirect means. Three such means are employed. The first is geological interpretation. By knowing the kinds of rocks and geological settings in which ore deposits might be found, geologists can locate drill holes more carefully and get samples from as deep as 5000 meters. Such testing is expensive, though, and the ore deposit targets being sought are small. Even a large massive sulfide deposit is only a few hundred meters in diameter. What chance does a driller have of hitting such a body when it is 2 or 3 thousand meters deep? The chances are poor, unfortunately. To increase the opportunity of making a hit, two additional methods are called into play. The first is geochemistry. Ground water in contact with a buried ore deposit can sometimes produce a dispersed halo of trace elements around the ore. By carefully sampling water, soil, and even sediments in streams, faint imprints of trace elements such as mercury, zinc, or copper can sometimes be detected. The second method employs geophysics. Some ore bodies contain magnetic minerals, and others contain minerals that conduct electricity. By making very sensitive mag-

netic and electrical measurements on the ground surface, it is sometimes possible to detect buried ore bodies beneath as much as 500 meters of barren rock.

The future of prospecting depends not on the old prospector and his mule, but rather on the sciences of geology, geochemistry, and geophysics. On them, too, depends the future supplies of scarce metals that society will need.

THE LONG-TERM FUTURE FOR THE SCARCE METALS

The geochemically scarce metals are distributed in two ways in the earth's crust. More than 99.9 percent of the total amount of any given scarce metal is distributed by atomic substitution in common silicate minerals. The remaining tiny fraction is distributed in ore minerals. Let us consider the problem of recovering metals from ores versus recovering metals from common rocks, and let us use copper as an example.

The energy used in mining a sulfide ore is a function of the grade of the ore and the difficulty of smelting the concentrate. It takes less energy to mine and produce a concentrate of sulfide minerals from a high-grade ore than from a low-grade one. As shown in Fig. 7.36,

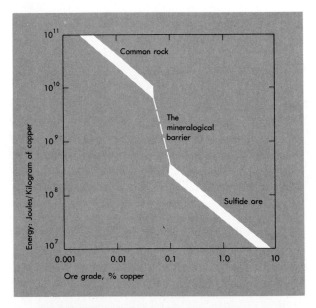

FIGURE 7-36. Energy used to extract metallic copper from ores containing sulfide minerals and from solid solution in silicate minerals of common rocks. The two curves are parallel but do not overlap. The gap represents a mineralogical barrier to the trend to mine increasingly lower grade ores. All geochemically scarce metals seem to display this relationship. (From Skinner, 1986.)

a plot of grade versus energy rises steeply toward lower grades. Now consider the case of an ordinary rock. The energy used to mine a ton of rock is the same as that used to mine a ton of high-grade ore. In the case of the rock, however, the copper is present in solid solution, so it is not possible to make a rich concentrate to send to the smelter. Instead, the entire rock must be smelted and processed, and that is a very energy intensive process. The recovery curve for getting copper out of common rocks is on the left-hand side of Fig. 7.36.

Note that the two curves on Fig. 7.36 do not meet or overlap. This is so because there is a lowest grade for sulfide ores, and below that grade, all copper is in solid solution. Similarly, there is a highest grade for copper in solid solution in the minerals of common rocks. If the day should ever be reached when all the sulfide ores of copper had been mined, we would have to find a way, technically, to overcome the mineralogical barrier and start mining common rocks. The cost in energy to produce copper from the highest grade common rocks will

be 10 times as much as the energy cost of mining the lowest grade sulfide ores. Whether society might wish to pursue this source is a decision for the future.

When might the mineralogical barrier be reached? Obviously, if prospecting beneath cover rocks is successful and efficient mining practices are conducted, there is a great deal of scarce metal ore still to be mined. A century or more ahead, however, the day will be reached when both the exposed and buried rocks have been prospected, and common rocks may have to be considered as sources. It may well be that those who follow us, and who have to face this prospect, will choose not to mine common rocks for scarce metals but rather will work to develop a technology based on the abundant metals such as iron, aluminum, and magnesium for which there are no forseeable supply limitations. What that society will be, and how the technology of the day will cope with material demands, is a question that only can be answered in the future.

FURTHER READINGS

BROBST, D. A. and PRATT, W. P., eds., United States Mineral Resources. U.S. Geological Survey Professional Paper 820, 1973, 722 p.

EDWARDS, R. and ATKINSON, K., *Ore Deposit Geology: And Its Influence on Mineral Exploration.* London: Chapman and Hall, 1986, 465 p.

SAWKINS, F. J., *Metal Deposits in Relation to Plate Tectonics.* Berlin: Springer-Verlag, 1984, 325 p.

SKINNER, B. J., *Earth Resources, 3rd ed.* Englewood Cliffs, New Jersey: Prentice-Hall, Inc., 1986, 184 p.

The Staff, Minerals Yearbook, *Metals and Minerals,* vol. 1, U.S. Bureau of Mines, published annually, 1985.

8

The guano deposits of the Chincha Islands of Peru, shown above while being mined in the 1860s, accumulated from the droppings of millions of birds feeding in the rich waters of the Humboldt Current. Between 1840 and 1880, these deposits were the world's principal source of fertilizer with more than 4 million metric tons being shipped to Britain alone. (Courtesy of Department Library Services, American Museum of Natural History. Neg. #311830.)

FERTILIZER AND CHEMICAL MINERALS

Man can live without gold but not without salt.

FLAVIUS MAGNUS CASSIODORUS, A ROMAN POLITICIAN OF THE FIFTH CENTURY A.D.

INTRODUCTION

The importance of the mineral resources used in our fertilizer and chemical industries often goes unrealized because the general public usually only sees the products of their use, not the minerals themselves. These mineral groups are two of the major types referred to as **nonmetallic minerals**—a general term used to describe earth resources that are not processed for the metal they contain and that are not used as fuels. Instead, they are mined and processed either for the nonmetallic elements within them or for the physical or chemical characteristics they exhibit. Nearly everyone is familiar with fertilizers because they are widely used on home gardens and lawns as well as large commercial farms. In contrast, many of the chemical minerals are little known because it is the end products of their use, rather than the minerals themselves, that we see (e.g., we see the steel or iron but not the fluorite that served as a flux in their smelting and we use soaps daily but never see the boron minerals from which they are made). The large number of minerals used in chemical processes and the very specialized uses of many precludes a comprehensive discussion. The following account gives an overview and shows the diversity of the important chemical minerals.

MINERALS FOR FERTILIZERS

The constant increase in world population requires that there be a constant expansion in the production of food crops. The growth of these crops requires the availability of 10 chemical elements: hydrogen, oxygen, carbon, nitrogen, phosphorus, potassium, sulfur, calcium, iron, and magnesium. The first three of these, which constitute 98 percent of the bulk of a living plant, are supplied as water drawn up from the soil and as carbon dioxide absorbed from the atmosphere. The other elements, although constituting only 2 percent of the plant matter, are vital to the growth processes. These elements are extracted by the plants directly from mineral or organic matter in the soil or ground waters. It is not so much the absolute concentration of these elements in the soil that is important, but rather the concentrations that are available in a water-soluble form that the plant can absorb. Natural soil-forming processes, discussed in greater detail in Chapter 11, slowly decompose many of the primary rock-forming minerals into clays, oxides, and sol-

uble salts from which the plants can extract these necessary elements. Long before our ancestors understood soil formation or knew anything of chemistry, they had found that many kinds of organic wastes, such as animal dung and fish heads, were helpful in increasing the yields of crops. Before considering the resources we now use for fertilizers, it is informative to consider the progression of events leading to our present state of understanding.

HISTORICAL OVERVIEW OF FERTILIZERS

Our food supply depends on three types of resources: **soil, water,** and **fertilizer.** Our earliest hunter-gatherer ancestors needed water directly for survival, but they gave little thought to soils and had no concept of fertilizers. However, when they became agriculturalists, planting and tending crops, they noted that the yields in different areas were not equal but were dependent on the availability of water and some unseen characteristics of the soils.

We shall never know who first had the idea to fertilize crops or when, but it is apparent that the earliest fertilizers were manures—animal and possibly human. Our ancestors did not know that these manures contain the three most important elements for plant growth—**nitrogen, phosphorus,** and **potassium**—but they did recognize the increased growth and yield that the applications of manure brought about for their crops. By Greek and Roman times, manures were classified according to their richness, with that of birds and fowl being rated the best. About 400 B.C., Xenophon noted "The estate has gone to ruin [because] someone did not know it was well to manure the land." Perhaps he gave the greatest compliment to this so often unappreciated product when he wrote, "There is nothing so good as manure."

Written records are sparse, but it is evident that the use of natural waste organic materials as fertilizers became a worldwide practice, nearly always on a local scale. An exception was the exploitation of the large Peruvian coastal **guano** deposits that developed into a major element of commerce between Peru and Europe from 1808 until after 1880. These deposits, that had accumulated on coastal islands where there was nearly no rainfall, were easily accessible and very inexpensive to mine. The Indians had exploited them for hundreds of

years but had been careful not to disturb or dislodge the large bird colonies that generated the deposits. England, seeking fertilizer for the newly introduced and important turnip crop, was thus a ready market for English merchants who rapidly took advantage of the decline of Spanish influence in the region. Shipments were sent to Germany and England before 1810, but significant commercial development did not occur until 1840. From 1840 until 1880 more than 4,350,000 metric tons of guano were shipped to England with a peak of 274,000 metric tons in 1858; in the decade 1855–1864 the value of the Peruvian guano cargoes to Britain exceeded £20,000,000. A Peruvian exporter of that period, who first believed that there could be no viable trade of guano, later noted, "The base manure could well be transformed into the purest gold."

The demise of the great guano trade came in the period 1878–1885 as two other fertilizer industries— nitrates in South America and phosphates in Europe— were rapidly expanding. The nitrates and nitrate compounds, commonly referred to as **saltpeter** or **niter** and consisting of potassium nitrate (KNO_3), sodium nitrate ($NaNO_3$), and calcium nitrate ($Ca(NO_3)_2$), occur in the very dryest parts of the coastal regions of southern Peru, what was then western Columbia, and northern Chile. They were mined on a small scale as early as 1810, and major shipments to Europe began about 1830. The nitrate exports rose to 21,300 metric tons in 1850, 106,000 metric tons in 1867, 535,000 metric tons in 1883, and peaked at 3,100,000 metric tons in 1928. The

total production of the area from 1830 has been estimated at 23.4 million metric tons of contained nitrogen from about 140 million metric tons of raw ore. The natural nitrates, all controlled by Chile after the War of the Pacific from 1879–1883, met with competition from ammonia produced by a coal coking process beginning in 1892, and with nitrates prepared by the fixation of atmospheric nitrogen beginning about 1900. The rise in world nitrate demand and the rapid expansion of the by-product nitrate industries quickly relegated the natural Chilean nitrate to a minor role in world production: It was 67 percent of the world's nitrogen production in 1900, 22 percent in 1929, and had dropped to 0.14 percent in 1980.

The earliest uses of **phosphates** parallel those of nitrates because many of the earliest fertilizer compounds used contained both elements (Table 8.1). The earliest uses of distinctly phosphatic mineral substances was in about 1650, when English farmers applied ground bones to their fields. Usage gradually expanded, but it was not until 1835 that the phosphate in the bones was recognized as the valuable component. In attempts to make bones more soluble, in 1840 the German chemist Justus von Liebig dissolved some in sulfuric acid. His experiment provided the basis for modern phosphate fertilizer, but he fused the phosphate with lime and produced a water insoluble product that appeared to be of no value. Within two years, an English chemist, John Lawes, put Liebig's ideas to use and mixed sulfuric acid with bones and natural phosphate rock and produced what he called

TABLE 8-1

Compositions of fertilizer materials

	(%)		
	Nitrogen (N)	Phosphate (P_2O_5)	Potash (K_2O)
Natural Materials			
Saltpeter ($NaNO_3$)	15.6–16	—	—
Fish scrap	8	5–8	—
Sewage sludge	5–7	2–3.5	—
Urea	46	—	—
Bones	3.5	20–25	—
Kainite	—	—	12–14
Seaweed ash	—	—	Up to 30
Carnallite	—	—	8–10
Wood ashes	—	2	Up to 6
Peruvian guano	13	12.5	2.5
Synthetic Materials			
Superphosphate ($CaH_4(PO_4)_2 \cdot H_2O$)	—	16–22	—
Triple superphosphate ($3CaH_4(PO_4)_2 \cdot H_2O$)	—	44–52	—
Ammonium nitrate (NH_4NO_3)	33–35	—	—
Ammonium phosphate ($(NH_4)_3PO_4$)	11	60	—
Diammonium phosphate ($NH_4H_2PO_4$)	21	53	—
Potassium chloride (KCl)	—	—	48–62
10-10-10	10	10	10

superphospate, a name still used today. The value of this new fertilizer led to phosphate rock mining in France in 1846, England in 1847, Canada in 1863, and the United States in 1867.

Recognition of the value of potassium as a fertilizer component developed in the early 1800s and was finally confirmed by John Lawes and his coworker J.H. Gilbert in 1855. Prior to this, many farmers had found that the application of wood ash, a material that can contain significant amounts of potassium, was beneficial to their crops. Although this **potash,** consisting of a mixture of potassium-sodium carbonates and hydroxides served as a fertilizer, it was primarily valued for its use in making soaps and glass. Significant world production of potassium salts began with the discovery of **evaporite** deposits at Strassfurt in what is now East Germany in 1857 and in France in the early 1900s. These sources provided the relatively small world needs until World War I when the major German supplies were cut off. This stimulated exploration for alternative sources and led to potassium production commencing in the United States in 1917 from subsurface brines at Searles Lake in California and to the discovery of large bedded deposits near Carlsbad, New Mexico, in the 1930s. During the 1920s and early 1930s, discoveries were also made and production begun in Poland, Palestine, Spain, and the Soviet Union. Rich deposits were found in Saskatchewan, Canada, in the late 1940s, but commercial production did not begin until 1958.

Today, the world's fertilizer industry is focused on the extraction, manufacture, and distribution of the nitrogen, phosphorus, and potassium either in bags for home use or in bulk liquid or solid forms for commercial farming. The numbers such as 5–10–10 or 5–10–20, seen on fertilizer bags refer to the percentages of nitrogen as nitrate (NO_3) or ammonia (NH_3), of phosphorus as phosphate (P_2O_5) and of potassium as potash (K_2O) present in the fertilizer. The remaining 65–75 percent is mostly inert material such as clay, although 1 or 2 percent of sulfur, calcium, and magnesium are also commonly present. The total percentage of major fertilizer components may seem low—only 25–35 percent—but greater concentrations could lead to damage of the delicate growth hairs on plant roots or upset the delicate levels of dissolved substances in plant fluids. The demand for fertilizers has been climbing rapidly (Fig. 8.1) so that the total world consumption is doubling on about a 14-year cycle. Unfortunately, the effectiveness of increased fertilizer usage appears to be diminishing. The **Global 2000 Report to the President** notes that a 200,000,000 ton increase in grain production in the early 1960s was associated with a 20,000,000 ton increase in fertilizer consumption suggesting a 10:1 ratio. The growth from the early 1960s through the early 1970s appears to have been at a ratio of 8.5:1; this

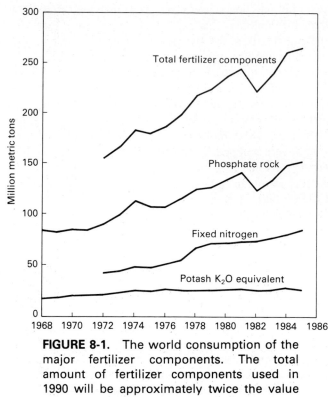

FIGURE 8-1. The world consumption of the major fertilizer components. The total amount of fertilizer components used in 1990 will be approximately twice the value used in 1970. Potassium and nitrogen fertilizers are listed in terms of their K_2O and elemental nitrogen contents, respectively, because they are produced in a variety of forms. (Data from U.S. Bureau of Mines.)

grain production to fertilizer ratio deteriorated to roughly 7:1 by 1985 and projects to 5.5:1 by the year 2000. Clearly, world demand for fertilizers will continue to rise because they will be needed in the production of foodstuffs to feed the increasing world population. Fortunately, reserves are large. Except for nitrogen, however, the reserves suffer from the same problems that beset many of the scarce metals—they are geographically restricted and we have already used the richest and most accessible deposits.

NITROGEN

Nitrogen is vital to plant growth because it is an essential part of all proteins, more than 100 different amino acids, and is an integral part of the chlorophyll molecule responsible for **photosynthesis,** the food making process in green plants. Most rocks and soils contain little or no nitrogen as discrete minerals, but many kinds of plants provide organic nitrogen, as ammonia or nitrate, into soils where it can be readily bound to the surfaces of clay particles.

The earliest nitrate fertilizers were the animal wastes that our ancestors spread on fields to stimulate plant growth. Locally derived farm manures were a sufficient source of nitrogen for crops until about the middle of the nineteenth century. At that time, the expansion of agriculture outpaced these local sources, and Europe turned to the importing of guano from Peru to provide its nitrogen fertilizer needs. The guano deposits accumulated on very arid coastal islands over countless years from huge colonies of nesting seabirds. The local Indians had long made use of the guano (which is rich in both nitrogen and phosphate, Table 8.1), but it did not become known to Europeans until reports of it were brought back by the German naturalist and geographer, Baron von Humboldt, after his visits there in 1802. Some small shipments were made by 1810, but the major trade did not develop until 1840, after which it flourished for 40 years, then being displaced by the production of nitrate minerals from what is now northern Chile.

Today the guano trade from western South America has nearly ceased. The world's only significant guano industry remaining is that on the island nation of Nauru in the South Pacific where annual production still averages about 2,000,000 metric tons. It is mined for its phosphate and nitrogen contents and is shipped primarily to Australia and New Zealand.

Natural nitrate mineral deposits occur only rarely because nearly all nitrate compounds are very soluble and hence are easily washed away by rains or percolating ground waters. They generally occur as efflorescences or crusts resulting from the oxidation of nitrogen-bearing substances in the presence of other salts. Potassium nitrate is the most widespread of these minerals. It occurs as crusts on the walls and in the soils of some caves, such as those in Kentucky and Virginia, where it has apparently accumulated as a result of the evaporation of ground waters that dissolved nitrogen compounds derived from organic matter in the overlying soils. In the 1700s and 1800s the demand for saltpeter as an ingredient in gunpowder led to the development of saltpeter plantations, or nitriaries, in France and Germany. In these plantations, the natural conditions of saltpeter formation were simulated by exposing heaps of decaying organic matter mixed with potash or lime to the atmosphere; the crusts of saltpeter were episodically gathered and processed. Calcium nitrate was also produced in the saltpeter plantations when lime was added to the organic matter. In addition, it commonly appeared as a crust on the walls of stables where it formed from reaction of the nitrogen compounds in horse wastes with lime that was used to reduce odors and insects.

Sodium nitrate, or ordinary niter, though much more restricted geographically than the potassium or calcium forms, has been much more important as a source of nitrogen. This mineral occurs in very large deposits in the northern part of the Atacama desert in what are now the two northernmost provinces of Chile (Figs. 8.2 and 8.3). This is one of the dryest places on earth, with no precipitation at all for many years at a time and an annual average rainfall of less than 2.5 centimeters. The nitrates are believed to have their origin in sea spray that precipitates in the soils from frequent fogs. The rare rain dissolves the very soluble nitrates and concentrates them as cements, or **caliches,** in the soils before evaporating. Mining of the nitrate deposits began near the beginning of the nineteenth century and by 1912 there were at least seven operations in which the caliches were boiled in water to dissolve the nitrates. The saltpeter settled out as the liquids were cooked. By the 1830s the increased use of chemical fertilizers in European agriculture made the nitrates a useful return cargo for ships sailing to Europe. Although the mines were in the Tarapaca district of Peru and the Antofagasta district of Bolivia, the labor and the investment was dominantly Chilean. In response to Peruvian attempts to expropriate the mines and to increased Bolivian taxation, Chile took the two provinces with a small army and with naval forces in the War of the Pacific. This crippled the Peruvian economy and made Bolivia a landlocked nation, but left Chile with a near monopoly on world nitrate production.

Chilean nitrates continued as the world's principal source of nitrogen until about 1915 when nitrogen from coking ovens and atmospheric fixation processes became dominant. In 1892, a new type of coal coking oven, that trapped the expelled gases, was introduced. The ammonia, one of the most abundant gases, immediately found use in the fertilizer and chemical industries. About 1900 it was also discovered that ammonia could be prepared from atmospheric nitrogen. This developed into the **Haber-Bosch process,** used in only a slightly modified form today. Fritz Haber, a famed German chemist, found that controlled combustion of a fossil fuel, coke, or gas with steam would yield carbon monoxide and hydrogen and that with the aid of a catalyst he could react the hydrogen with atmospheric nitrogen to form ammonia. (Today, the hydrogen is usually supplied by natural gas.) The ammonia could be used directly to make fertilizers or could be oxidized to make explosives such as glyceryl trinitrate (formerly known as nitroglycerin) and trinitrotoluene (or TNT). Haber's discoveries were thus very important to the German military, cut off from Chilean nitrate supplies during World War I.

Today, the synthetic nitrate industry produces more than 99.8 percent of world nitrogen needs. Chile still mines nitrates at rates of more than 500,000 metric tons per year, but they constitute only about 0.14 percent of world usage, and even the total Chilean nitrogen

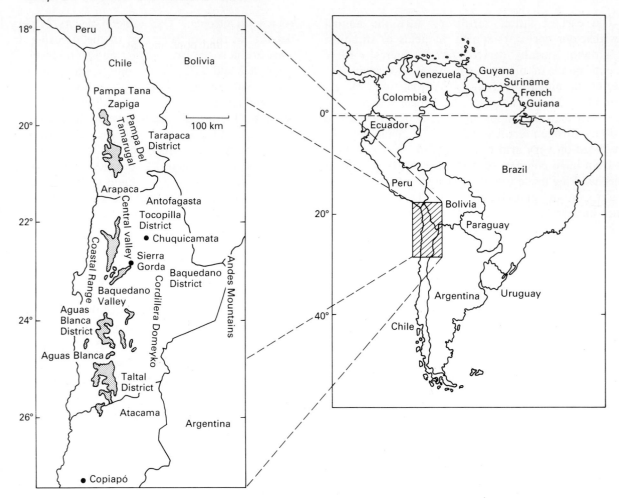

FIGURE 8-2. The world's largest natural nitrate deposits, shown shaded, lie in the Tarapaca and Antofagasta provinces in what is now northern Chile. The extreme aridity of this area that allows for the preservation of these deposits results from the cold Humboldt Current that flows northward along the western coast of South America. Tarapaca and Antofagasta were parts of Peru and Bolivia before Chile annexed them in the War of the Pacific, 1878–1883.

FIGURE 8-3. The nitrate deposits of northern Chile, shown here being drilled for processing and shipping as fertilizers to North America and Europe in the 1930s, occurred as thick cemented portions of the desert soils.

reserves of 2.5×10^9 metric tons (containing more than 7 percent sodium nitrate, $NaNO_3$) would not equal one-half of the world's present yearly consumption.

Nitrogen remains primarily a fertilizer component, with more than 75 percent of world production for that use. The United States was for many years the world's primary fixed nitrogen producer but has been surpassed since 1980 by the Soviet Union and China (Table 8.2). Nitrogen compounds have a variety of other important uses: plastics, fibers, resins, refrigerants, detonating agents for explosives, and nitric acid that is widely used in the chemical industry.

The availability of nitrogen from the earth's atmosphere for the production of fixed nitrogen (ammonia, NH_3) is unlimited. The hydrogen is most commonly derived from natural gas; hence, there is a strong price dependence of fixed nitrogen on the cost of fossil fuels. The natural Chilean nitrate reserves, containing more than 7 percent $NaNO_3$, are estimated at 2.5×10^9 metric tons. The probable resources at grades less than 7 percent are thought to be more than 22×10^9 metric tons.

PHOSPHORUS

Phosphorus is indispensable for all forms of life because it plays a vital role in **deoxyribonucleic acid** (DNA), in **ribonucleic acid** (RNA), and in the ADP and ATP that function in the energy cycle of cells. In natural ecosystems, it is usually the availability of phosphorus that is life limiting.

The earth's crust contains about 0.23 percent phosphate (phosphorus is nearly always referred to in its oxide form, P_2O_5), most of which is present as the mineral apatite, $Ca_5(PO_4)_3(F,Cl,OH)$. Apatite is a disseminated accessory mineral in many types of rocks, but may occur in mineable concentrations in igneous rocks or in marine sedimentary rocks. Phosphorus is also present in the guano deposits left by birds or bats that were described in the previous discussion of nitrogen.

Another natural occurrence of apatite phosphate, and the first used as a fertilizer, is bone. As early as the

TABLE 8-2
Production of fixed nitrogen (ammonia), 1984 (in metric tons of nitrogen content)

U.S.S.R.	15,000
China	14,000
United States	12,000
India	3800
Rumania	2650
Canada	2500
WORLD TOTAL	81,800

(Data from U.S. Bureau of Mines.)

mid-1600s, English farmers had observed that applications of ground bone increased crop yield, and the Pilgrims learned from the Indians that buried fish carcasses and bones would help corn grow. Although some nitrogen compounds are also present, it is primarily the effect of the phosphorus that promotes growth. By the middle of the nineteenth century, European countries were importing bones, possibly some human, from every available source. The problem of apatite insolubility was solved in 1842, when John Lawes dissolved bone in sulfuric acid and formed a more soluble compound that he called **superphosphate.** As a result of his success, there were 14 fertilizer plants in Great Britain by 1853, and production had reached 100 metric tons a day by 1862. Lawes' techniques found use rapidly with the development of phosphate-rock mining in France and England by 1850. In the United States, the first phosphate mining took place in South Carolina in 1867, but the major development of the industry dates from 1888 when the great deposits in Florida were discovered. Today, deposits are known in several states (Fig. 8.4), but nearly 90 percent of American production comes from the large deposits in Florida and North Carolina.

The techniques used today to convert natural phosphate minerals into usable fertilizer forms are still based on Lawes' experiments. The apatite in natural ores is reacted with sulfuric acid to make superphosphate $(Ca_3(H_2PO_4)_2)$. Much is used in this form, but some is used as liquid fertilizers and some is transformed into triple superphosphates that have much higher P_2O_5 contents. Historically, the sedimentary phosphorites have been the world's dominant sources, but igneous bodies that contain large concentrations of apatite are slowly increasing in production, especially in the Soviet Union. The guano deposits of Chile and Peru, once major producers, have diminished in importance but still find demand among organic gardeners.

Phosphate rocks are found in many parts of the world (Fig. 8.5), and major reserves are held and mined by many nations (Table 8.3). It is apparent, however, from this table that the major world suppliers of phosphate are the United States, Soviet Union, and Morocco. The marine phosphorites, which constitute the principal reserves, presently supply approximately 80 percent of the world phosphate rock production and 100 percent of United States production. Although minor amounts of phosphate occur in nearly all marine sediments, major accumulations appear to have developed only where upwelling cool phosphate-saturated sea water moved across shallow platforms and into near-coastal environments (Fig. 8.8). Here the phosphate was precipitated, probably by complex microbiological processes, as microcrystalline muds, nodules, and hard crusts. In some areas there were also vast accumulations of fish

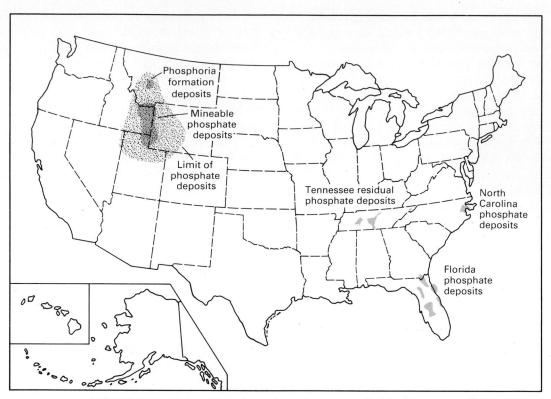

FIGURE 8-4. Major phosphate deposits are worked in four areas of the United States. The beds of the Phosphoria Formation and those in North Carolina and part of Florida are primary marine sediments. The deposits in Tennessee and parts of Florida are residual accumulations resulting from weathering. Although nearly 90 percent of present production comes from Florida and North Carolina, the largest recoverable phosphate resources occur in the Phosphoria Formation. (After U.S. Geological Survey Circular 888, 1984.)

bones and teeth (Fig. 8.6) that further contribute phosphate. Partial replacement of some calcite shells by apatite suggests that phosphate-bearing solutions also percolated through the sediments after deposition.

The largest of the marine phosphorite deposits occur in the Miocene sediments of the North Carolina and Florida coastal plains of the United States and in Morocco. These phosphorites are relatively thin (2–10 meter) beds that extend over broad areas (more than 2500 square kilometers in Florida and at least 1200 square kilometers in North Carolina). The sediments are mostly unconsolidated and are thus easily mined by using large drag lines and dredges as shown in Fig. 8.7. The North American deposits, that are now the world's major producers, will continue to be major sources of phosphate rock but are the object of increasing environmental concerns. The main problems are the vast amounts of ground water that are pumped out of the mines and underlying formations to permit mining at greater depths, the release of trace amounts of radioactive elements from the ores, and the generation of mountains of very fine-grained gypsum as a by-product of the sulfuric acid treatment.

Another particularly large, and apparently unique, deposit of this type was formed during Permian times in a shallow marine basin covering what are now parts of Idaho, Nevada, Utah, Colorado, Wyoming, and Montana in the United States. The phosphate-rich sediments, called the Phosphoria Formation, cover more than 160,000 square kilometers and reach thicknesses of as

TABLE 8-3

Production and reserves of phosphorous, 1985

Country	Production (in 10^6 m.t.)	Reserves (in 10^6 m.t.)
U.S.A.	51.0	1300
U.S.S.R.	33.0	6500
Morocco	21.2	2100
West Sahara	—	850
South Africa	2.6	1800
Jordan	6.3	530
Australia	0.01	350
WORLD TOTAL	150.0	14,000

(Data from U.S. Bureau of Mines are expressed in terms of phosphorous rather than phosphate rock.)

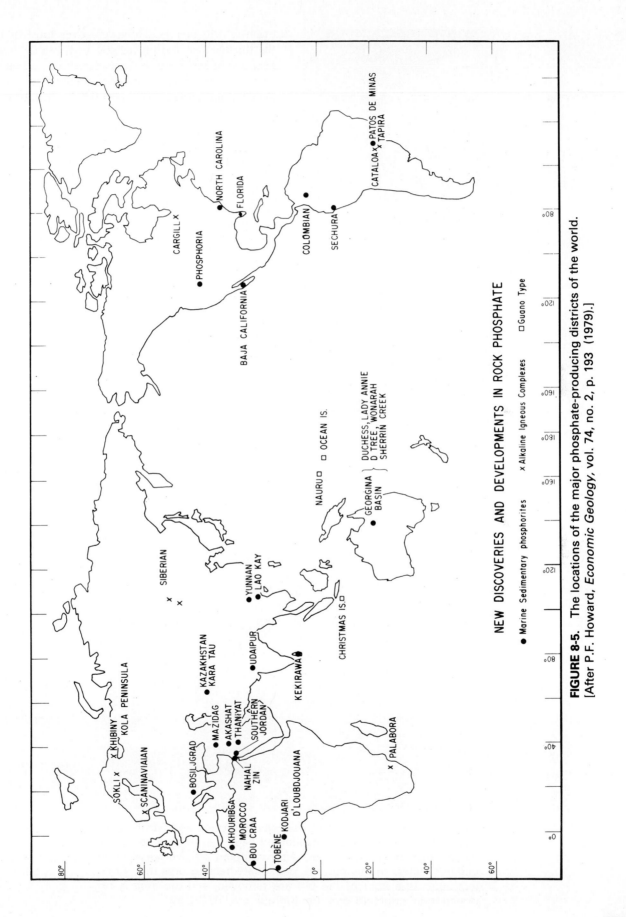

NEW DISCOVERIES AND DEVELOPMENTS IN ROCK PHOSPHATE

● Marine Sedimentary phosphorites   × Alkaline Igneous Complexes   □ Guano Type

FIGURE 8-5. The locations of the major phosphate-producing districts of the world. [After P.F. Howard, *Economic Geology*, vol. 74, no. 2, p. 193 (1979).]

FIGURE 8-6. The marine sedimentary phosphate deposits of North Carolina and Florida consist of unconsolidated pebbles and granules and contain abundant remains of fish, reptile, and mammal bones.

much as 140 meters. However, over most of the area the thickness of the phosphatic bed is only 1 meter or less, and at best it can be considered only a potential resource. The tonnage, however, is enormous and is estimated at more than 2,000,000,000 metric tons.

There is no substitute for phosphate fertilizers; hence, the need for phosphate rock will continue to grow for at least the next 100 years in response to the need for food to feed the increasing world population. The world's phosphate reserves are large and, with the likelihood of new discoveries and the technological advances to permit mining of lower grade deposits, probably adequate for the next century. There will, however, be considerable change in world supply patterns because the relatively rapid depletion of the United States' richest mines will force the United States, now a major exporter, to become an importer shortly after the year 2000. Unless there are major discoveries, phosphate production in Florida, the United States' principal producer, will begin dropping rapidly after 2000 A.D. North Carolina will continue to produce significant amounts of phosphate rock, and minor production will be available from the western states.

Potential resources of phosphorus are large. Prospecting for phosphate deposits has not been thorough enough to be certain that very large deposits still remain undiscovered. In part, this is a recognition of the economic difficulties entailed in opening new deposits in competition with existing mines. However, it also stems from the difficulty of recognizing a phosphorus-rich rock. Even to an expert, many phosphate rocks

FIGURE 8-7. The phosphate deposits of Florida and North Carolina occur in flat-lying unconsolidated beds that are mined by the use of large mobile drag lines. After stripping the overburden (the upper 3 meters in this pit), the phosphate-bearing ores (the 4 meters above the floor of the pit) are removed, and the area is returned to its original form. (Photograph by J.R. Craig.)

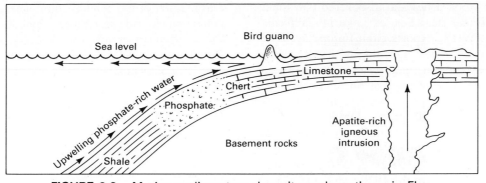

FIGURE 8-8. Marine sedimentary deposits such as those in Florida, North Carolina, and those in the Phosphoria Formation were deposited along continental margins where there was upwelling of phosphate-bearing ocean waters. The other major types of occurrences have formed from phosphate-rich igneous intrusions and from the accumulation of phosphate-rich bird guano on arid coastal islands.

look like ordinary shales and limestones. We can, therefore, probably anticipate discoveries of new, large deposits in the future.

One large potential resource has already been discovered. The U.S. Geological Survey recently announced the finding of phosphatic crusts and nodules in the off-shore continental shelf extension of the rich phosphate beds in Florida. Unfortunately, the deposits are lower grade than their landward equivalents, but the tonnages are large, probably as large as the present reserves. We must therefore conclude that the availability of phosphorus, like nitrogen and potassium, will not soon become a limitation to food production.

POTASSIUM

Potassium, the third of the important fertilizer elements, is the eighth most abundant element in the rocks of the earth's crust. Potassium occurs in nearly all rocks and soils, although its quantity varies widely. It occurs in igneous and metamorphic rocks primarily as potassium feldspar ($KAlSi_3O_8$). Weathering releases the potassium which is then incorporated in clay minerals such as illite ($KAl_2(Al, Si)_4O_{10}(OH)_2$). The K^+ ion of the clay minerals is exchanged with plants by substitution of a hydrogen ion. Unlike nitrogen and phosphorus, the potassium does not form an integral part of plant components, but it is vital as a catalytic agent in numerous plant functions such as nitrogen metabolism, the synthesis of proteins, activation of enzymes, and maintenance of water content.

Although potassium occurs in most rocks, the only occurrences that can be economically extracted and processed into fertilizers are those in evaporite sequences. The formation of these special accumulations by the evaporation of large amounts of seawater in broad basins is described in detail in the discussion of halite that follows on page 264. Nearly complete evaporation results in the deposition of large amounts of halite (NaCl) and smaller amounts of a variety of potassium and potassium-magnesium salts among which the most important are sylvite (KCl), langbeinite ($2MgSO_4 \bullet K_2SO_4$), kainite ($KCl \bullet MgSO_4 \bullet 3H_2O$), and carnallite ($KCl \bullet MgCl_2 \bullet 6H_2O$).

Because the potassium salts are very soluble, they are only preserved in very arid regions or in salt beds that are buried below meteoric or ground water zones. The evaporites generally occur as flat-lying beds that are now mined by rubber-tired diesel or electric mining machines. The salts are blasted or cut from walls in the mining areas and then brought to a surface refining facility where the ores are crushed and then separated into different minerals by a complex flotation system. The concentrates of potash minerals are then processed into a wide variety of solid and liquid fertilizers.

Potassium, in the form of carbonates and hydroxides in wood ashes, was used as a fertilizer long before it was recognized in the 1840s as an element vital for plant growth. The first important mining of potash minerals (the name *potash* was derived from the custom of leaching wood ashes and then boiling the solutions in large iron pots to crystallize the soluble potassium salts that were then used in soaps and in glass making) began in 1857 when potassium choride-bearing evaporite deposits were found at Strassfurt in Germany. These, and additional deposits found in the Alsace-Lorraine area, were controlled by a German cartel that had a virtual monopoly over the international trade in potash until 1915. In January 1915, Germany imposed an embargo on potash exports, and prices in the United States rose from their preembargo level of about $45 per ton to more than $480 per ton in 1916. Spurred by the shortage and the high prices, the United States stepped-up

production from wood ashes and discovered potassium-rich subsurface brines near Searles Lake in California. Following World War I, exports from Europe again became available, but the shortages during the war period had stimulated exploration and resulted in significant discoveries in Poland, Palestine, Spain, and the Soviet Union. In 1925, potash deposits were found near Carlsbad, New Mexico, by oil prospectors. Mines were opened in the 1930s and soon not only supplied the United States but became major exporters. High-grade deposits of potash were discovered in the Canadian Province of Saskatchewan in the 1940s while drilling for oil. These were not brought into production until 1958, but now constitute the western world's major supplies and reserves.

The American deposits are part of a broad evaporite sequence that underlies parts of New Mexico, Texas, Oklahoma, and Kansas where, in Permian times, a large, shallow sea deposited thick beds of evaporite salts over an area of at least 160,000 square kilometers. In a 4800-square kilometer portion of the basin, near Carlsbad, New Mexico, the sequence contains potassium salts in beds that reach 4 meters in thickness. These deposits, which are among the richest in the world but are small in total volume by comparison with several others, have indicated reserves of potassium of nearly 100,000,000 metric tons.

North America has two other large potassium reserves (Fig. 8.9, Table 8.4). The Paradox basin of Pennsylvanian (Carboniferous) age in southeastern Utah and southwestern Colorado contains an estimated 12,600 square kilometers (3000 square miles) of potassium-rich salts, although much of it is too deep to warrant present recovery. In Saskatchewan, Canada, a huge and as yet incompletely explored resource of potassium salts has been found in the Williston basin (Devonian period). Estimates of as much as 14,000,000,000 metric tons of K_2O that are accessible by today's mining standards have been published. Large reserves also exist in the

Perm region of the Soviet Union where beds containing potassium chloride reach more than 30 meters (100 feet) thick, extend over an area of 1000 square kilometers (386 square miles) and contain at least 3,000,000 metric tons of potassium salts. The existence of such large quantities of potash-bearing evaporites, plus the very large quantities dissolved in the oceans, ensure that we should not have any problem of regarding potash reserves in the near future.

SULFUR

Sulfur, one of the first nonmetallic chemical elements known, is important because of its diverse uses. It is the fourth major fertilizer element, and the U.S. Bureau of Mines notes that "most products produced by industry require sulfur in one form or another during some stage of their manufacture."

Sulfur is abundant on the earth's surface as native sulfur, metal sulfides (especially pyrite, FeS_2), mineral sulfates (primarily **gypsum**, $CaSO_4 \cdot 2H_2O$), sulfate dissolved in the oceans, hydrogen sulfide (sour gas) in natural gas, and organic sulfur in petroleum and coal.

Sulfur was known in the ancient world as **brimstone**, "the stone that burns," and has been used for thousands of years as a fumigant, medicine, bleaching agent, and as an incense in exotic religious ceremonies. During the Peloponnesian War between the Greek city-states of Athens and Sparta in the fifth century B.C., mixtures of burning sulfur and pitch (oil residue) were used to produce suffocating gases to incapacitate soldiers. The Romans advanced the use of sulfur in warfare by combining brimstone with pitch and other combustible materials to produce the first incendiary weapons. A thousand years later, in the tenth century, the Chinese developed gunpowder in which sulfur is a necessary ingredient. The subsequent introduction of gunpowder into European warfare in the fourteenth century made sulfur an important mineral commodity for the first time.

It was, however, the development of chemistry in the 1700s and the growth of the chemical industries in the 1800s that brought sulfur to its position of prominence in the modern world. Early chemists found that sulfuric acid was simple and inexpensive to prepare and that it was the most versatile of the mineral acids. Prior to the mid-1800s, world demand for sulfur was satisfied primarily by the native sulfur deposits in Sicily. The rise in demand and a large price increase controlled by the Sicilian monopoly resulted in a shift to pyrite as a major sulfur source. The pyrite, when roasted in air, yields sulfur oxide gases that readily react with water to form sulfuric acid. In 1894, the **Frasch process** for mining

TABLE 8-4
World production and reserves of potash, 1985

Country	Production (in 10^6 m.t. of K_2O)	Reserves (in 10^6 m.t. of K_2O)
U.S.A.	1.3	95
U.S.S.R.	9.6	3000
Canada	7.5	4400
East Germany	3.5	800
West Germany	2.3	500
Spain	0.7	30
Israel	1.1	200
England	0.4	60
WORLD TOTAL	28.6	9100

(Data from U.S. Bureau of Mines.)

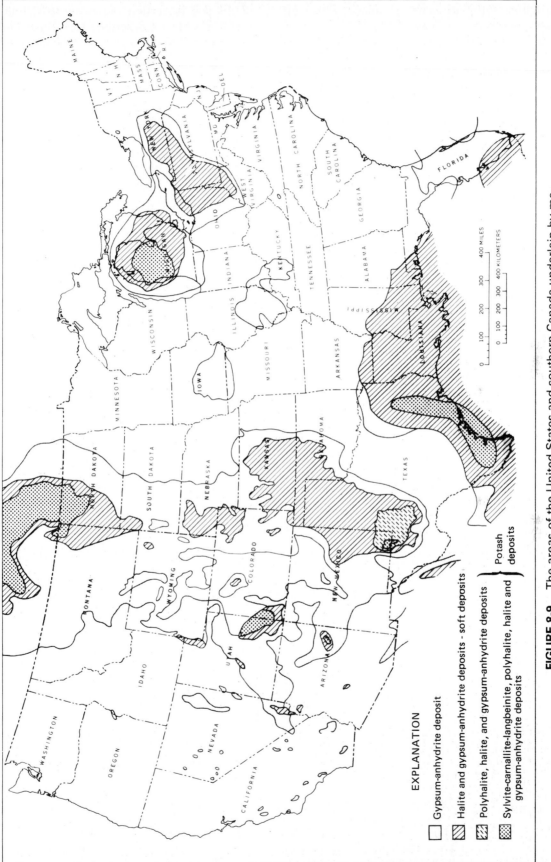

FIGURE 8-9. The areas of the United States and southern Canada underlain by major marine evaporite deposits of gypsum and anhydrite, halite, and potassium salts. (After U.S. Geological Survey Bulletin 1019-J and U.S. Geological Survey Professional Paper 820, 1973.)

EXPLANATION

☐ Gypsum-anhydrite deposit

▨ Halite and gypsum-anhydrite deposits - soft deposits

▨ Polyhalite, halite, and gypsum-anhydrite deposits

⸬ Sylvite-carnallite-langbeinite, polyhalite, halite and gypsum-anhydrite deposits

} Potash deposits

subsurface native sulfur deposits associated with Gulf Coast salt domes was introduced. This process (Fig. 8.10) employs hot water to melt the sulfur from the host limestones and gypsum and to transport it to the surface. A series of concentric pipes are emplaced in a 25-centimeter hole drilled into the sulfur-bearing rock. Hot water is passed down the outer pipe at 140°C to melt the sulfur. Once molten, the sulfur is forced up the intermediate pipe by hot air forced down the inner pipe. The Frasch process remains an important method of sulfur recovery.

The native sulfur recovered by the Frasch process occurs with **anhydrite** ($CaSO_4$) or gypsum on top of salt domes and in certain evaporite beds. Salt domes, the origin of which is described later, occur in many parts of the world but are especially abundant along the Gulf Coast of the United States from Alabama to Mexico (Fig. 8.11). When the gypsum and anhydrite, which commonly form a cap on the salt domes, are brought into a near-surface environment, they are attacked by certain anaerobic bacteria. These derive their oxygen from gypsum and their food from organic matter (commonly petroleum) and convert the gypsum into calcite ($CaCO_3$) and free sulfur. Only a small proportion of salt domes contain commercial quantities of native sulfur, but these have proven to be very rich and account for

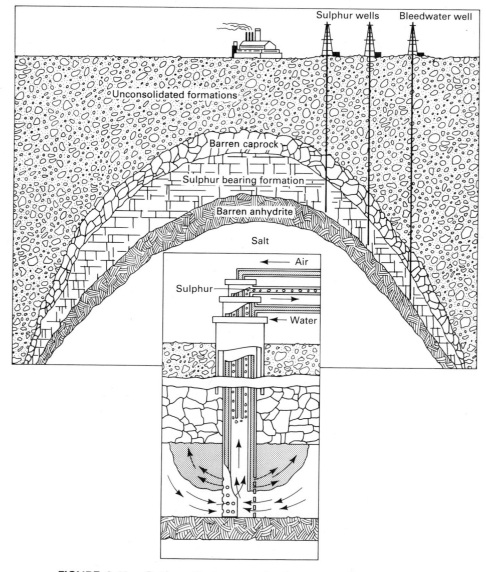

FIGURE 8-10. Sulfur often occurs in the cap rock overlying salt domes. The sulfur is extracted by the Frasch process, shown enlarged in the insert, whereby superheated water is forced down the outer shells of concentric pipes. The melted sulfur is then drawn up a center pipe and pumped to chemical plants for processing. (After a diagram courtesy of Freeport McMoRan Inc.)

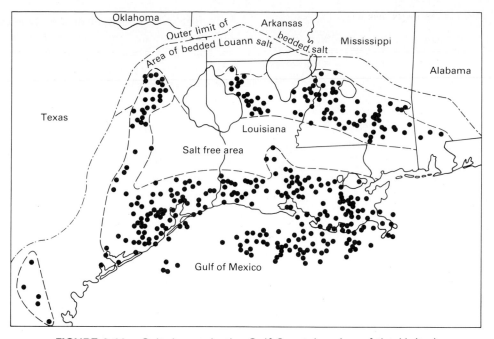

FIGURE 8-11. Salt domes in the Gulf Coastal region of the United States. The individual domes may be 100 meters to more than 2 kilometers across and have risen through as much as 12 kilometers of overlying marine sediments. The domes lie in distinct zones where the surface is underlain by the Louann Salt bed that was deposited in an evaporite basin in Permian time. (Figure courtesy of Gulf Coast Geological Society).

more than 50 percent of America's, and more than 25 percent of world production. If circulating subsurface waters locally dissolve gypsum beds in sequences of evaporite rocks, petroleum and bacteria can enter the resulting voids and thus lead to the formation of rich localized zones of sulfur. This has happened on a large scale in west Texas, where more than 50,000,000 metric tons of recoverable sulfur have been found in one oil field alone.

Since the 1940s, by-product sulfur recovered from petroleum during refining and from natural gas during treatment has become increasingly important. Sulfur was originally removed from oil and gas merely to produce cleaner petroleum products and odorless gas, but the sulfur has proven to be useful and valuable itself, and in the United States alone, more than 5,000,000 metric tons of sulfur were derived in this manner in 1983. This accounted for more than 50 percent of domestic production. Production of sulfur in the United States and other major suppliers is summarized in Table 8.5.

Today, sulfur is used in a broad range of industrial applications and in a wide variety of chemical compounds. More than 80 percent of American domestic sulfur used is as sulfuric acid. The principal use of the acid is to convert very insoluble natural phosphates into superphosphates that are more soluble and hence more useful for agricultural applications. Sulfuric acid or sul-

fur is also used in products such as soaps, rubber, plastics, acetate, cellophane, rayon, explosives, bleaches to make white paper and white titanium oxide paint pigment, leachates for copper and uranium ores, and the **pickling** or cleaning agent used on the surface of steel products prior to further processing (Fig. 8.12). New uses still in the developmental stage include sulfur-asphalt paving for highways and sulfur concretes for use in acid and brine-rich environments where salt attack leads to significant deterioration of conventional materials.

The world reserves of native sulfur shown in Table 8.5 certainly represent only minimum values of the total sulfur we can extract. These figures do not include much of the sulfur ultimately available in natural gas and petroleum, that extractable from the processing of metal sulfides, the at least 600×10^9 metric tons contained in coal, oil shale, and shales rich in organic matter, and the almost limitless amounts of sulfur contained in gypsum and anhydrite. The sulfur in these sources is not yet available because we lack the low cost methods to extract it.

MINERALS FOR CHEMICALS

A large number of nonmetallic minerals serve as important raw material sources of elements or compounds

TABLE 8-5

World production and reserves of sulfur, 1985

Country	Production (in 10^6 m.t.)	Reserves (in 10^6 m.t.)
U.S.A.:	11.4	
Frasch process —6.4		155
Recovered		
from oil, coal—4.3		
Other —1.5		
Canada	6.8	150
France	1.8	15
Mexico	2.0	80
West Germany	1.6	20
Spain	1.3	20
U.S.S.R.	—	350
Poland	5.1	130
Iraq	0.3	155
WORLD TOTAL	54.0	1290

(Data from U.S. Bureau of Mines.)

used in the chemical industry. Many of these are little known to the public, because the chemical products often bear no resemblance to the original source mineral or because the minerals are only used in the processing and are not incorporated into the final product. The total list of chemical minerals is very long indeed, and includes the fertilizer minerals already discussed. Table 8.6 lists several of the important chemical minerals and summarizes their uses; a few of the most important are discussed below.

Halite (NaCl)

Halite, or common salt, is a basic industrial raw material that serves as a source of sodium, chlorine, soda ash (Na_2CO_3), hydrochloric acid (HCl), caustic soda (NaOH), and other compounds indispensable in the manufacture of hundreds of other products and chemical reagents. Salt itself is important in food production and preservation, water softening, and snow and ice removal. It is essential to our diets, but only small amounts of total production are used for human consumption. The recent recognition that excessive salt usage is associated with hypertension is leading to a reduction of salt levels in many foods. Much of the table salt used today contains about 0.01 percent potassium iodide as an additive to provide the iodine needed by the body.

NaCl occurs naturally in solution in seawater, saline seas, and lakes (e.g., the Dead Sea in Israel; Salton Sea in California; Great Salt Lake in Utah), and as thick sequences of marine evaporites (Fig. 8.13). Evaporite deposits have formed throughout geologic time as a result of the evaporation of ocean or, more rarely, lake waters in large basins.

The most abundant of the chemical elements dissolved in seawater are shown in Fig. 8.14 and are listed in Table 8.7. They can be recast into the constituents that actually precipitate from seawater by balancing the positively charged cations, such as sodium (Na^+) against negatively charged anions, such as chloride (Cl^-), so as to preserve electrical neutrality (Table 8.7). Sodium chloride, halite, is by far the most abundant constituent. This is followed by magnesium chloride and magnesium sulfate, calcium sulfate, and potassium chloride. Evaporation of seawater, which normally contains about 3.5 percent total dissolved salts, will cause the precipitation of each salt when the brine becomes saturated in that salt.

The succession of compounds to precipitate during progressive evaporation is shown in Fig. 8.14. Calcium carbonate is the first substance to precipitate, but the quantity is very small. Once the volume of seawater has been reduced to only 19 percent of the starting amount, $CaSO_4$ (or $CaSO_4 \bullet 2H_2O$ depending on temperature) begins to precipitate. Halite begins to first precipitate when the volume reaches about 9.5 percent of the original. When the volume is finally reduced to 4 percent, a complex magnesium and potassium salt called **polyhalite** ($K_2SO_4 \bullet MgSO_4 \bullet 2CaSO_4 \bullet 2H_2O$) begins to crystallize. The amount of NaCl in solution is large to begin with, and considerably more than half of it will be precipitated during the reduction in solution volume from 9.5–4 percent, so the thickest layer formed during a single evaporation cycle will be the NaCl layer. The sequence of minerals separating from the final 4 percent of the brine (called the **bitterns**) is complex and variable, depending on such factors as the temperature and whether or not the final liquid remains in contact with, and hence can react with, the earlier-formed crystals. Two of the precipitates in the last stage, sylvite (KCl) and carnallite ($KCl \bullet MgCl_2 \bullet 6H_2O$), constitute the world's principal sources of soluble potassium used for fertilizers.

The complete evaporation of an isolated body of seawater should produce the sequence and volume of salts shown in Fig. 8.14. However, the examination of natural marine evaporite sequences nearly always reveals greater amounts of calcite, gypsum, and halite and only rare presence of potassium and magnesium salts. Furthermore, complete evaporation of a body of seawater even as deep as the Mediterranean Sea, which averages about 1370 meters, would produce only 24 meters of halite and a layer of gypsum only 1.4 meters thick. However, beds of gypsum and halite several hundreds to more than 1000 meters thick are known from numerous localities, and many of these contain fossil and textural evidence of having formed in shallow water. It is thus apparent that these thick marine evaporite sequences did not form as a result of a single evaporative

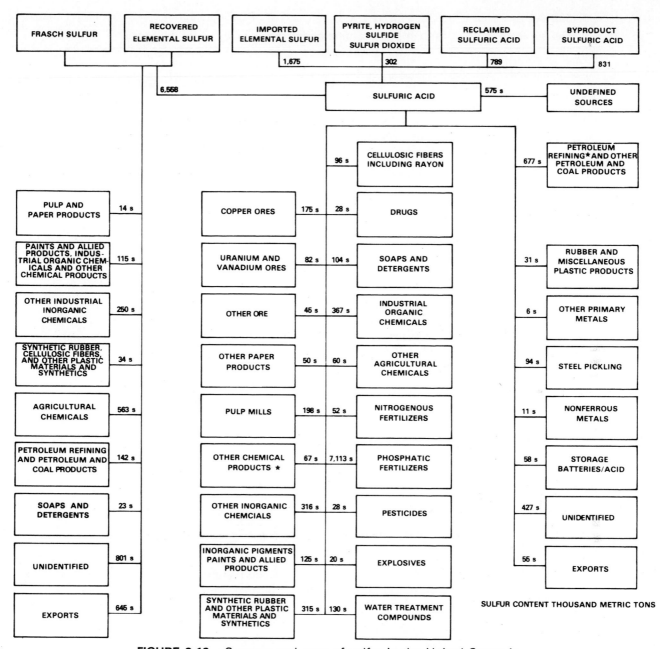

FIGURE 8-12. Sources and uses of sulfur in the United States in 1983. Sulfur, as indicated by the complexity of this diagram, is one of the most important and widely used industrial chemicals. Note that the largest single use, by far, is for the preparation of phosphatic fertilizers. The numbers are thousands of metric tons of sulfur per year. (Data from U.S. Bureau of Mines, 1985.)

episode in very deep totally isolated basins, but rather through the continuous evaporation of water from a partially isolated basin that was episodically fed with seawater for thousands of years or longer. The circumstances were probably similar to those depicted in Fig. 8.15. Water flows into the basin over a shallow barrier bar. As the water evaporates, the remaining brine becomes more concentrated and heavier and sinks to the bottom of the basin where it is trapped. Depending on the rate of influx of additional seawater and the rate of evaporation, the brine in the basin may precipitate only calcite, or calcite and gypsum, or these and halite. The distribution of evaporite sequences shown in Fig. 8.9 reveals that only in a few places has evaporative concentration

TABLE 8-6

A brief survey of some of the important mineral-derived chemicals and their uses*

Principal Element or Compound	Mineral Source	Chemical Products and Uses
Antimony	Stibnite (Sb_2S_3) Tetrahedrite ($Cu_{12}Sb_4S_{13}$)	Flame retardants, batteries, glass, ceramics
Arsenic	Tennantite ($Cu_{12}As_4S_{13}$) Arsenopyrite (FeAsS) Realgar (AsS)	Wood preservatives, agricultural herbicides and desiccants, semiconductors
Bismuth	Bismuthite (Bi_2S_3)	Pharmaceuticals
Boron	Borax ($Na_2B_4O_7 \cdot 10H_2O$) Kernite ($Na_2B_4O_7 \cdot 4H_2O$) Brines	Glass products, detergents, fibers
Bromine	Brines	Gasoline additives, flame retardants
Cadmium	Minor component of sphalerite ((Zn,Fe)S)	Batteries, pigments, plastics
Chlorine	Halite (NaCl) Brines	Plastics, water treatment, paper manufacture
Fluorine	Fluorite (CaF_2)	Steel and aluminum flux, welding rods, enamels, water fluoridation
Gallium	Minor component of sphalerite ((Zn,Fe)S)	Semiconductors, light-emitting diodes, lasers
Germanium	Minor component of sphalerite ((Zn,Fe)S)	Semiconductors, infrared optics, catalysts, phosphors
Indium	Residues from base metal refining	Alloys, nuclear reactor control rods, glass coating for liquid crystal displays
Iodine	Brines	Colorant in dyes, antibiotics, iodized salt
Lead	Galena (PbS)	Glass, paints, ceramics
Lime	Limestone ($CaCO_3$)	Agriculture, refractory
Lithium	Brine Lepidolite ($K(Li,Al)_3(Si,Al)_4O_{10}(F,OH)_2$)	Glass, ceramics, greases, batteries, Al-production
Mercury	Mercury (Hg) Cinnabar (HgS)	Paints, fungicides, chlorine gas production
Nitrogen	Atmospheric (N_2) Nitre ($NaNO_3$)	Ammonia for fertilizers and chemical reagent, plastics, fibers, explosives (see text discussion)
Phosphorus	Apatite ($Ca_5(PO_4)_3(F,OH,Cl)$)	Phosphate fertilizers (see text discussion)
Potassium	Sylvite (KCl)	Potash fertilizers (see text discussion)
Rhenium	By-product of molybdenite (MoS_2)	Catalysts in gasoline production, thermocouples, flash bulbs
Rubidium	Minor element in lepidolite ($K(Li,Al)_3(Si,Al)_4O_{10}(F,OH)_2$)	Photochemical applications, medicines
Salt	Salt (NaCl) Brines	Basis for many chemicals including chlorine, caustic soda, soda ash (see text discussion); food products, de-icing, water treatment, aluminum and steel manufacture, many other uses
Selenium	By-product of copper refining	Photoelectric copiers, semiconductors, glasses, pigments, rubber compounds
Silver	Argentite (Ag_2S) Tetrahedrite (($Cu,Ag)_{12}Sb_4S_{13}$)	Black and white photographic film
Sodium	Halite (NaCl) Soda ash ($NaCO_3$) Mirabilite ($Na_2SO_4 \cdot 10H_2O$)	Detergents, glasses, pulp and paper manufacture
Sulfur	Sulfur (S) By-product of oil refining	Sulfuric acid for phosphate fertilizer production (see Fig. 8.12)
Zinc	Sphalerite (ZnS)	Alloys, paints, medical compounds

*Materials used primarily for alloys or building materials are omitted.

FIGURE 8-13. Salt mining from the evaporite beds that underlie the city of Cleveland, Ohio. Note the layering that probably represents annual cycles of salt deposition. The thicker white beds formed during the summer when there was more rapid evaporation. The thinner beds represent periods of slower evaporation in winter and are dark because of the presence of minor amounts of weathered organic matter. (Photograph by Burke and Smith Studios, Inc.; courtesy of International Salt Company.)

TABLE 8-7
Major constituents of seawater

Constituent	Total Dissolved Solids (%)
NaCl	78.04
MgCl$_2$	9.21
MgSO$_4$	6.53
CaSO$_4$	3.48
KCl	2.11
CaCO$_3$	0.33
MgBr$_2$	0.25
SrSO$_4$	0.05

FIGURE 8-14. Schematic presentation of the sequence of minerals precipitated by the evaporation of seawater. When evaporation reduces the volume to 19 percent of the original, gypsum begins to precipitate; at 9.5 percent, salt starts to precipitate; and at 4 percent potassium and magnesium salts begin to precipitate. (After B.J. Skinner, *Earth Resources, 3rd ed.,* Englewood Cliffs, N.J.: Prentice Hall, 1986.)

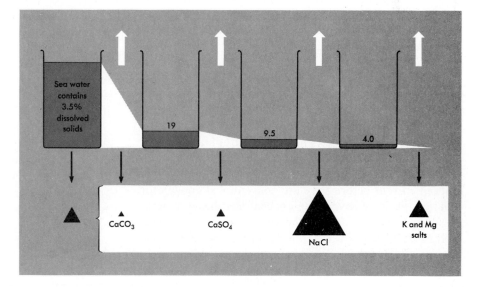

FIGURE 8-15. Cross section of a basin in which evaporite salts accumulate. Seawater containing approximately 3.5 percent dissolved salts flows into the basin through a shallow inlet and is concentrated by evaporation. The concentrated brine is heavier than the seawater and sinks below fresh inflowing seawater. When the brine reaches a sufficiently high salinity (as shown in the previous figure), salts precipitate and accumulate on the floor of the basin.

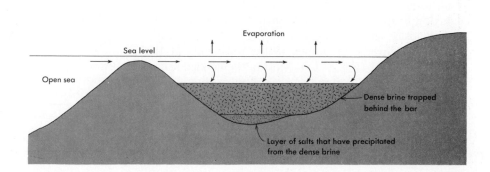

been sufficient to result in the precipitation of potassium and magnesium salts as well as halite, calcite, and gypsum.

Evaporite deposits are widespread in the geologic record both in time and space. High temperatures are important but not necessary for the evaporative concentration of salts. Indeed, the largest evaporites forming today are within 30° of the equator, but there are several small lakes in which salts are depositing in Antarctica. Most of these lakes, which owe their evaporative concentration to high winds and very low humidities, are rich in sodium chloride. One small Antarctic lake, named Don Juan Pond, is well known for being rich in calcium chloride and being the only place on earth where the evaporite mineral antarcticite ($CaCl_2 \bullet 6H_2O$) exists.

There are no modern evaporite basins comparable with the major ones found preserved in the geologic record. The largest evaporite area today is the 18,000 square kilometers Kara-Bogaz-Gol at the eastern edge of the Caspian Sea. At this site, the waters spilling into the basin are evaporatively concentrated so that sodium sulfate is precipitating on large flats. Numerous small flats, where halite is forming, exist along the shores of the Red Sea, and salt pans are well known adjacent to landlocked lakes such as Great Salt Lake and the Dead Sea.

The Mediterranean Sea, with its narrow inlet at Gibraltar and its location in a relatively arid region, is almost an evaporite basin. Here, evaporation increases the salt content and the density of the surface waters so that they begin to sink. The Straits of Gibraltar, however, are deep enough to permit these heavier waters to escape out of the Mediterranean as a westward-flowing bottom current before they are concentrated enough for salt deposition. Above these concentrated heavy waters, less salty and less dense seawater flows into the Mediterranean as an eastward-moving surface current. If the channel at Gibraltar were shallower, the evaporatively concentrated water would not escape but would become further concentrated until salts precipitated.

Evaporite sequences containing halite occur worldwide. The problem is not availability of this resource but one of mining and shipping. Furthermore, the world's oceans contain essentially inexhaustible quantities. In the United States salt is mined (Fig. 8.13) from flat-lying evaporite sequences, such as those in Michigan, Kansas, and New Mexico (Fig. 8.9), and from large remobilized salt domes in the sediments of the Gulf coastal area (Fig. 8.11). Most of the bedded salt in the Gulf coastal region is too deep to mine, but in hundreds of places the salt has risen upward through the weak sediments as great columns. This occurs because

the salt has a slightly lower density than the overlying rocks and has slowly risen buoyantly toward the surface. The salt domes range from 100 meters (330 feet) to more than 2 kilometers (1.25 miles) across and have risen upward through the sediments by as much as 12 kilometers (7 miles).

Salt domes are known in many areas of the world: Europe, South America, the Middle East, and the Soviet Union. They are particularly abundant in the area on the north side of the Gulf of Mexico as shown in Fig. 8.11. Although the domes serve as an obvious site for salt mining, they also serve as major sources of sulfur extracted from the overlying cap rock by the Frasch method (described above) and as major sources of petroleum that may occur trapped in upturned beds adjacent to the dome. The extraction of both oil and salt from the same dome has led to problems. In 1980, an oil drill operating from a barge in Lake Peigneur, Louisiana, a lake that lies directly above a buried salt dome, penetrated a salt mine some 430 meters (1410 feet) below. The entire lake drained into the salt mine, carrying with it the drill rig, several barges, many holly trees from a shoreline garden, and a tug boat. Fortunately, all drillers and miners escaped unharmed, but the well and the salt mine were lost.

Salt production occurs in many parts of the world; the major producers are shown in Table 8.8. The mining of salt in beds or salt domes is carried out by modern diesel equipment as shown in Fig. 8.13. In arid regions, including the southwest coastal areas of the United States, salt is harvested by evaporating seawater or brines in large fields or terraced ponds as shown in Fig. 8.16. Approximately 60 percent of salt is used in the chemical industry for the manufacture of chlorine gas

TABLE 8-8

World production of salt, 1985

Country	Production (in 10^6 m.t.)
U.S.A.	39.7
West Germany	12.3
Canada	11.5
U.S.S.R.	18.5
China	18.0
Mexico	6.5
England	7.1
India	8.3
France	7.8
WORLD TOTAL	186.0

(Data from U.S. Bureau of Mines.)

(a)

(b)

FIGURE 8-16. Simple solar evaporation of brines and seawater has served as a source of salt for thousands of years. (a) Terraced evaporation ponds in the mountains of Peru. (Photograph courtesy of V. Benavides, Geological Society of America Special Paper, 88, 1968.) (b) Salt being harvested in a broad evaporation pond in Colombia. (Photograph courtesy of the Colombian Government Tourist Office.)

and sodium hydroxide, and approximately 15 percent of the salt is used for de-icing. Although the most visible use of salt for most people is in their salt shakers, the consumption of salt in all food products represents only less than 6 percent of total usage. Few data are available on actual reserves, but all producing countries are well endowed. Because of the vast quantities of bedded evaporites, the enormous amounts of salt dissolved in the oceans, and the simplicity of salt extraction, the world's supply of salt is inexhaustible. A greater concern than the availability of salt is the environmental impact of salty waters released from chemical processing, or as runoff into rivers and lakes when salt is used for highway de-icing.

Soda Ash (Na_2CO_3) and Sodium Sulfate (Na_2SO_4)

Sodium carbonate (trona) and sodium sulfate (thenardite) are chemical minerals widely used in the manufacture of glass, soaps, dyes, detergents, insecticides, paper, and water treatment. Sodium bicarbonate ($NaHCO_3$) is the common household baking soda. Natu-

ral **soda ash,** as the carbonate is commonly called, was probably first derived from mineral crusts around alkaline lakes in southern Egypt in Biblical times. The early Egyptians and Romans used it to make glass, as a medicine, and in bread making. Until the eighteenth century, it was primarily obtained by leaching the ashes of burned seaweed, but in 1791 a process was developed to prepare it from halite and sulfuric acid. In the 1860s a more efficient process was developed to prepare soda ash from salt, coke, limestone, and ammonia. This process became a major source of soda ash for many years, but the discovery of large deposits in the western United States made the recovery of natural materials cheaper than synthesis. Sodium carbonate and sodium sulfate are evaporite minerals that form in some arid region lakes where the weathering of rocks releases abundant sodium and, sometimes, sulfur. Modern examples of such areas include the Searles, Owens, and Mono Lakes of California, and Lake Magadi in Kenya. The lakes supply some of these sodium salts, but the bulk of production comes from bedded deposits formed from preexisting lakes. There are more than 60 identified sodium carbonate deposits in the world, the largest of which is in southwestern Wyoming. One unit in the Green River

Formation, Wyoming contains 42 beds of trona, 25 of which have a thickness of 1 meter or more. Eleven of these beds are more than 2 meters thick and underlie an area of more than 2850 square kilometers. These beds alone contain more than 52×10^9 metric tons of soda ash of which more than 22×10^9 metric tons are reserves. These reserves are enough to meet the United States' needs for more than 700 years. The American reserves are much larger than those of other parts of the world, but several alkaline lakes in eastern Africa contain large quantities of soda ash. These deposits and many others known, but insufficiently evaluated, in South America and Asia will likely supply the world's needs for many years.

The world's reserves of sodium sulfate are much smaller than those of sodium carbonate but are also sufficient to meet the world's needs for at least 600 years. Commercial sources in the United States include shallow subsurface brines in west Texas, Searles Lake in California, and Great Salt Lake in Utah.

Boron

Natural boron minerals are very restricted in their geologic occurrence. Nevertheless, we find boron compounds in glass products, insulation, laundry detergents, food preservatives, fire retardants, and ceramic glazes and enamels. The trade in boron compounds dates from the thirteenth century when Marco Polo brought borax ($Na_2B_2O_4$) crystals from Tibet to Europe. The discovery of natural boric acid (H_3BO_3, the mineral sassolite) in the hot springs of Tuscany, Italy, in 1771 led to the development of an industry that supplied most of the world markets from the 1820s into the 1870s. This market was superceded by Chilean production in the latter part of the nineteenth century. Borax crystals were found in springs north of San Francisco, California, in 1864, but the modern U.S. boron industry is based on large deposits subsequently discovered in Nevada and southern

California. Deposits developed in Death Valley, California, between 1881 and 1889 had their borax minerals transported by the celebrated 20-mule teams (Fig. 8.17).

Although limited to a few deposits where volcanically derived fluids have concentrated and formed boron-bearing minerals, there are economic deposits in the United States, the Soviet Union, China, Turkey, Chile, Peru, and India with reserves of more than 350 million metric tons of boron oxide content. This will be sufficient to meet the world's needs far into the twenty-first century (Table 8.9). The United States leads in both reserves and production.

Fluorine

Fluorine compounds are of vital importance to the production of most steel and aluminum and are used in the production of the uranium fuel in nuclear power plants. Fluorine compounds are also used in such forms as ceramics, water fluoridation agents to reduce dental cavities, teflon to line cooking pans, and an experimental artificial blood substitute for humans. Nearly all fluorine is derived from the mineral **fluorite** (CaF_2) that occurs in minor amounts in many hydrothermal ore deposits and in relatively rich limestone-hosted deposits. These were formed by low temperature, high salinity brines that were squeezed out of sedimentary basins. The fluorite in these latter deposits is commonly associated with lead and zinc mineralization and with barite ($BaSO_4$). World fluorite reserves are widespread and total about 300 million metric tons, enough to last well into the twenty-first century. The United States, though processing large fluorite resources, has very limited reserves and currently relies heavily on Mexico, the western world's largest producer (Table 8.9).

Fertilizer and Chemical Minerals in the Future

The demand for the fertilizer minerals will surely increase for the next 100 years or more because they will be needed to grow the food to feed the expanding world population. It is also likely that the use of minerals in the chemical industry will continue to increase and diversify. Worldwide reserves of the mineral resources are large and certainly appear adequate to meet these needs for at least 100 years. It is likely, however, that production patterns will change as less-developed countries increase production and become competitors for the advanced countries. Among the nonmetallic resources, the fertilizer and chemical minerals are the most vital, but their use is small when compared with that of the construction and industrial minerals to which we now turn.

TABLE 8-9
World production and reserves of fluorspar in 1985

Country	Production (in 10^3 m.t.)	Reserves (in 10^3 m.t.)
Mexico	680	34,500
Mongolia	700	10,000
U.S.S.R.	545	20,000
South Africa	345	106,000
China	635	7300
Spain	245	9100
France	225	12,700
Other	1350	100,400
WORLD TOTAL	4725	300,000

(Data in terms of ore with 35% CaF_2 from U.S. Bureau of Mines.)

FIGURE 8-17. The celebrated 20-mule team drawn wagons carried boron minerals from the deposits in Death Valley, California, in the 1880s. (Photograph courtesy of United States Borax & Chemical Corporation.)

FURTHER READINGS

BLAKEY, A. C., *The Florida Phosphate Industry*. Cambridge, Massachusetts: Harvard University Press, 1973, 199 p.

Economic Geology, an issue devoted to phosphate, potash and sulfur, March–April 1979, vol. 74, no. 2.

ERICKSEN, G. E., "The Chilean nitrate deposits." In *American Scientist*, 71, 366–374, 1983.

TISDALE, S. L. and NELSON, W. L., *Soil Fertility and Fertiliz-ers*, 3rd ed. New York: Macmillan Publishing Co., Inc., 644 p., 1975.

U.S. Bureau of Mines, *Mineral Facts and Problems*, published annually.

WINES, R. A., *Fertilizer in America*. Philadelphia, Pennsylvania: Temple University Press, 1985, 247 p.

9

The Sphinx and the great pyramids attest to abilities of the early builders and to the durability of natural stone as a building material. (Courtesy of the Egyptian Tourist Authority.)

BUILDING MATERIALS AND OTHER INDUSTRIAL MINERALS

> *Stones make a wall, walls make a house, houses make streets, and streets make a city. A city is stones and a city is people; but it is not a heap of stones, and it is not just a jostle of people.*
>
> JACOB BRONOWSKI, THE ASCENT OF MAN (1973)

INTRODUCTION

Building materials are the largest volume mineral commodity that we extract from the earth. They rank second only to the fossil fuels in value. Almost every known rock type and mineral has contributed in some way to the construction of buildings, roads, bridges, dams, or similar structures.

Most building materials, unlike metals, fuels, or fertilizers and chemical minerals, have little intrinsic value. They are both abundant and widely distributed, and it is only after removal from the earth and processing to more useful forms that their value increases, often by many times. Thus, for example, the limestone and shale used to make cement may have values of $4 per metric ton or less in the ground, but after mining, crushing, firing, and conversion to a high-quality cement, the product is worth $50 or more per ton. As Fig. 9.1 shows, the processing of building stone or of the clays used in ceramic products adds even more to their value.

Because building materials are widely distributed and of little intrinsic value, the factors controlling their

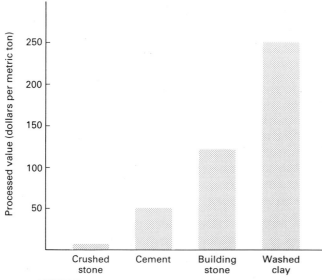

FIGURE 9-1. Processing of building materials adds greatly to their value. (After B.J. Skinner, Earth Resources, *3rd ed.*, Englewood Cliffs, N.J.: Prentice Hall, 1986.)

exploitation and marketing are very different from those for such relatively expensive commodities as fuels or metals. Normally, mining operations are undertaken to satisfy a local demand since the cost of transportation for any great distance is rarely justified. For many of the materials discussed in this chapter, the volume of the trade is large, but it is conducted only at a national or more local level. Only in the case of special building stones is the expense of distant transport justified. Therefore, discussion of the contributions made by particular nations is not relevant, since demand is commonly satisfied internally. Reserves also tend to be large and potential resources even larger. Commodities such as building stone are so abundant that it is pointless to even attempt putting numbers on reserves. The wide distribution of such building materials also means there is little point in detailed discussion of the geology of particular deposits. This is not true, however, of a few of the more specialized building materials such as vermiculite and perlite, or of some of the major industrial minerals.

In this chapter, major types of building material are discussed, emphasizing the character of the raw materials, problems of their extraction and processing, the uses to which they are put, and their limitations. As explained below, the building materials are separated for discussion into two groups—*untreated* and *treated* rock products. Also discussed in this chapter are other major industrial minerals that do not readily fall into the categories of fertilizers and chemical minerals dealt with in the previous chapter. These include minerals valued because of particular properties they possess, such as great hardness, resistance to high temperatures, inertness, distinctive color, or high density.

UNTREATED ROCK PRODUCTS

In discussing building materials, it is convenient to distinguish between those materials that have simply been quarried or mined and either used directly or cut or crushed to a suitable size, and those that have been subjected to more complex treatments that change the finished product into something very different from the raw material. The former we shall call *untreated* rock

products and discuss first. Treated rock products are discussed in detail later in this chapter. The two major categories of untreated rock products are the various types of **building stone** and the **aggregates**, which include **crushed rock, sand** and **gravel,** and **lightweight aggregates** (although the last of these commonly are subjected to heat treatment). Aggregates are used mainly in concrete, as highway or railroad base or ballast materials, or graded fill on construction sites.

Building Stone

Natural stone is one of the oldest building materials known to humans (Fig. 9.2). Historically, it has had the advantages of being widespread, available, durable, easy to maintain, and pleasing in appearance. However, throughout the twentieth century, its use has been declining in the face of competition from processed materials. In the United States, for example, at the turn of the century more than half of the stone produced was so-called **dimension stone,** stone that was quarried, cut, and finished to a predetermined size. By 1981, dimension stone accounted for only 0.2 percent of the stone that was quarried. Before considering the types of rock that are commonly used, the various categories of building stone will be outlined.

FIGURE 9-2. Natural stone was the principal construction material used by the Romans. The durability of a structure built using carefully cut shaped blocks is evident in this amphitheater constructed in Nimes in France by the Romans in the first century. (Courtesy of the French Government Tourist Office.)

Rubble and rough construction stone refer to large blocks of rough-hewn rock used in sea walls, bridge work, etc., and which must be very resistant, and to smaller blocks used as wall-facing material.

Rip-Rap is the name given to large, irregularly shaped stones (generally from around 7–70 kilograms in weight) used in river and harbor work and to protect highway embankments from erosion.

Ashlar consists of rectangular pieces of stone of nonuniform size that are set randomly in a wall. Ashlar blocks are generally 10 centimeters or more thick and up to a square meter or more in area and may have rough-hewn or smooth faces (Fig. 9.3).

Cut stone includes all building stone that is cut to precise dimensions on all sides, the surfaces being textured, smoothed, or polished. Most cut stone is used as a facing on exterior or interior walls of buildings and therefore applied in thin slabs as a veneer.

Monumental stone is employed in gravestones, statues, mausoleums, or more elaborate monuments.

Flagstones, curbing, and paving blocks, as the names suggest, are used in paving pedestrian areas in town and cities.

Roofing slate and mill-stock slate; the former term is self-evident, and the latter refers to smooth-finished slabs of slate used in electric switchboards, billiard tables, laboratory bench tops, blackboards, etc.

Terrazzo is sized material, usually marble or limestone, that is mixed with cement for pouring floors, and which is then smoothed to expose the chips after the floor has hardened.

Almost every kind of rock has been used at some time or another as building stone. The important factors governing the suitability of any particular rock for use in building are its physical properties and whether or not it is pleasing to the eye. The names used for rock types by those in the building industry, although comparable to those used by professional petrologists, are nevertheless applied much more loosely. The most important rock types are as follows:

Granite is used commercially to include not only those coarsely crystalline igneous rocks made dominantly of **feldspars** and **quartz** (true **granite** and **granodiorite**), but also coarsely crystalline igneous rocks containing feldspars but devoid of quartz (**syenite**) and containing appreciable **ferromagnesian minerals (diorite)**, or even very high concentrations of these minerals (**gabbro, norite**) when they are called black granites. Granites in this very broad (and unscientific) use of the term may be ideal building stones for rough construction as they break easily along joints, are commonly used for curbstones as they resist abrasion and weathering, and often are very attractive materials for use as cut stone and monumental stone. The scientific classification of the most important igneous rocks is shown in Table 9.1.

FIGURE 9-3. Ashlar, as shown here on the campus of the Virginia Polytechnic Institute and State University, is commonly used as a building facing. It consists of randomly set rectangular pieces of building stone. (Photography by J.R. Craig.)

Sandstone is defined in commercial terms as a consolidated sand in which the grains are chiefly of quartz and feldspar cemented by various materials that may include silica, iron oxides, **calcite,** or clay. A conspicuous feature of these clastic sedimentary rocks is their bedding or stratification. Bedding planes are commonly planes along which the rock splits easily; when these planes are regular and evenly spaced, the rock may be a natural flagstone. Sandstones are also widely used for cut stone, ashlar, and rubble. A notable example is brownstone, a red sandstone of Triassic age used in the eastern United States as a building material.

Limestone is the other sedimentary rock that is most widely used in building. In commercial terms, it is a "rock of sedimentary origin composed principally of calcium carbonate or the double carbonate of calcium and magnesium" and therefore includes true limestones and **dolostones.** Like sandstone, it is a well-known building material used for ashlar and cut stone and may also form a natural flagstone. It has been widely used

TABLE 9-1

Classification of some of the most important igneous rocks

	Abundance of quartz and/or light colored (felsic) minerals			Abundance of dark-colored (mafic) minerals, especially ferromagnesian minerals (olivine, pyroxene)		
	FELSIC	INTERMEDIATE		MAFIC	ULTRAMAFIC	
	Mainly potash feldspar ($KAlSi_3O_8$)		Mainly plagioclase feldspar ($(Na,Ca)(Al,Si)Si_2O_8$)		No feldspar	
	with quartz	little or no quartz	with biotite and/or hornblende	with pyroxene and/or olivine	without olivine	with olivine
Coarse grained (plutonic)	GRANITE (granodiorite has dominant Na-plagioclase)	SYENITE	DIORITE	GABBRO (also norite)	PYROXENITE	PERIDOTITE
		MONZONITE				
Medium grained (hypabyssal)	MICRO-GRANITE	MICRO-SYENITE	MICRO-DIORITE	DIABASE (dolerite)		
Fine grained (volcanic)	RHYOLITE	TRACHYTE	ANDESITE	BASALT		

FIGURE 9-4. The Radcliffe Camera with All Souls College. Many of the university buildings at Oxford are built from limestones of Jurassic age quarried in central England. (Photograph by D.J. Vaughan.)

throughout Europe in the construction of large public buildings, cathedrals, and mansions. Many of the colleges of the Universities of Oxford and Cambridge were constructed from limestones of Jurassic age quarried from central England (Fig. 9.4).

Marble, which in scientific usage refers to a limestone (or magnesian limestone or dolostone) that has been thoroughly recrystallized during metamorphism, also has a broader use as a commercial term. Commercial marble includes not only true marbles but also certain crystalline limestones and even highly altered ultramafic igneous rocks that are almost entirely made of the hydrated magnesium silicate minerals known as **serpentines** (and therefore called serpentinites). All these marbles are materials that can easily be cut, carved, or shaped, and take a good polish (Fig. 9.5). They are the best known of all monumental stones and are greatly prized as facing materials for exterior and interior use (Fig. 9.6).

Slate is a very fine-grained rock produced when clay-rich sediments have been compressed during metamorphism. As well as hardening the rock, this process imparts the cleavage whereby the rock is very readily split into thin parallel sheets. The dominant minerals are quartz with fine **micas** and other platy minerals that align with the cleavage planes. The best known use of slate is as a roofing material, and it is still regarded by many people as the highest quality and most permanent form of roof covering. However, as with the other building stones, its use has largely been superceded by less expensive processed materials, and the great slate

FIGURE 9-5. High quality marble for use in construction may be mined in open quarries or in underground mines as shown here in Vermont. The marble is cut into rough blocks in the mine and then shaped and polished for its final usage. (Courtesy of the Vermont Marble Corporation.)

quarries, like those in North Wales which once supplied most of England and Wales, have been abandoned (Fig. 9.7).

Crushed Rock

Crushed rock constitutes the largest volume mineral commodity used in the United States and many other countries. Its principal use is as the base for the construction of roads, but very large quantities are also used in the foundations of buildings and as the aggregate

FIGURE 9-6. The "Pietà" of Michelangelo is a classic example of sculpture making use of a white marble quarried at Carrara, Italy. (Courtesy of the Italian State Tourist Office (E.N.I.T.) London.)

FIGURE 9-7. Slate, widely used in the past as a roofing material and for a variety of other uses, was mined in regionally metamorphosed terrains such as North Wales in the United Kingdom. The large Bethesda Quarry is typical of slate-producing operation. (Photograph by Brian Skinner.)

used in concrete. Lesser amounts find a wide range of other uses in fertilizers, glass making, refractories, fillers, and terrazzo surfaces. Many of these uses are discussed in detail elsewhere in the book.

The best rocks for use as aggregate should be hard and inert but still easy to mine and crush. Specifications for crushed rock to be used for various purposes are usually established by national organizations and include properties such as resistance to abrasion, ability to withstand freeze-thaw conditions, size distributions of fragments, and absence of material that may react with the alkali substances in the cement matrix of a concrete. Depending on the specifications, the crushed rock may be used for concrete, coarse or fine bituminous (asphaltic) concrete, **macadam** (the common black top) or other surfacing for roads, road base, railroad ballast, fill, and a variety of other uses.

Many rock types meet the basic requirements for use as aggregate. In the United States, limestone and dolostone make up more than two-thirds of the stone quarried for this purpose because they are widely available, easy to mine and crush, and strong in use (Fig. 9.8). Second in importance, making up about one-seventh of the stone quarried, is granite and related light-colored igneous rocks. The only other rock types that

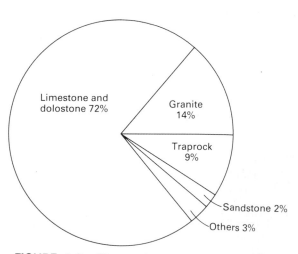

FIGURE 9-8. The rock types most widely used in the preparation of crushed stone in the United States. (After U.S. Bureau of Mines.)

make any significant contribution to the U.S. production are fine-grained, dark-colored igneous rocks such as basalt, known collectively in the trade as traprocks, and sandstones or quartzites.

In most countries, surface exposures of rock suitable for aggregate are commonplace. Extraction in large quantities by blasting and quarrying in an open pit followed by crushing at the site of mining operations can be combined with a location close to the user to lower transport costs. For these reasons, crushed stone is one of the lowest unit cost items of commerce, averaging less than $4 per metric ton in the United States, a country that produced 950 million tons of this commodity in 1984. The growth of this industry can be gauged by the fact that it is little more than a century since Eli Whitney Blake invented the modern rock crusher in 1858. This was to provide crushed rock for the then ambitious project of a 2-mile long macadam road from New Haven to Westville, Connecticut. Before this, all rock crushing was done by hand, even for the construction of roads using the methods pioneered by the Scottish inventor John McAdam in 1819.

Sand and Gravel

Sand and gravel mining constitute the second largest nonfuel industry in the United States and in many other parts of the world. In 1985, approximately 800 million metric tons were mined in the United States in operations at over 5000 locations, involving more than 3500 producers and with a total product value of $2.4 billion. The principal uses were as aggregates for concrete and as the rock matter added to bituminous mixtures to make macadam road surface. Sand is classified as having particle sizes less than 2 millimeters in diameter;

particles of gravel are larger and may range up to approximately 9 centimeters. In the United States, where the construction industry consumes more than 95 percent of the sand and gravel produced, the tonnage of gravel used is about twice that of sand.

Commercially, sand and gravel are obtained from rock units of many types, but the main sources are present-day or ancient river channels, their flood plains, or **alluvial fans.** Here, rounded pebbles are produced by the action of transport downstream, and often only the harder and more stable rock fragments survive. There is also some separation of different sized particles, with finer grains being washed further downstream or out to sea. The deposits that result may have properties desirable for use in concrete aggregate (rounded, hard, and stable particles) as well as being readily accessible and easily mined. The deposits of sand and gravel that were left behind following the retreat of the great ice sheets that once covered much of northern Europe, Canada, and the northern United States are also commercially important (Fig. 9.9); so are some beach deposits.

As with crushed rock, sand and gravel are resources that are exploited in areas as close to the consumer as possible to reduce transport costs. However, in some regions, local resources are limited or have largely been consumed, as in the densely populated areas of Europe and North America. In these northern latitudes, extensive sand and gravel deposits occur beneath the sea on the **continental shelves,** having been deposited there by glaciers during the height of the geologically recent Ice Age. These submarine deposits are now being exploited by dredging off the west coast of Europe on a substantial scale, and in a smaller way, off the shores of New Jersey, New York, and the New England states. Gravel deposits are sparse or absent off many tropical

FIGURE 9-9. Sand and gravel are the products of natural geological weathering processes, and exploitable deposits occur worldwide. Glacial outwash deposits, such as that shown here near Trondheim, Norway, can provide excellent sources of naturally washed and sorted gravels and are very easily worked. (Photograph by J.R. Craig.)

coasts, and in these areas there may also be little surface exposure of rocks suitable for crushing. In the Gulf of Mexico, for example, although sands can be found in river deltas, gravels are almost unknown. The only available coarse-grade building materials are old shell beds and coral reefs, and when such supplies are used up, it will be necessary to import gravel or crushed stone into areas like southern Texas, Louisiana, and Florida.

Deposits of sand and gravel are generally simple to mine using power shovels, bulldozers, and draglines in dry pits, or through dredging in rivers, offshore, and in natural or artificial lakes. The processing may involve no more than washing and screening to separate the different size fractions. There may be crushing operations or even some form of separation process to remove unwanted impurities such as particles of shale.

The crushed stone industry and the sand and gravel industries are both increasingly subject to land-use and environmental problems. These problems result primarily from the necessity of locating the quarries and pits near consumers, which are for the most part in areas of rapidly expanding urban growth.

Vermiculite, Perlite, and Other Lightweight Aggregates

Lightweight aggregates include a variety of materials used chiefly in making boards, plaster, concrete, and insulation. Use of these materials is increasing because they are much more easily handled in construction work, and because the trapped air that they contain makes them good insulators and valuable in energy conservation. Examples include such natural materials as volcanic cinders and **pumice** which are simply crushed and sized after quarrying. There are also similar synthetic materials that are by-products of industrial operations such as processed slag. Other lightweight aggregates involve treatment, usually by heating, of some product of mining operations. In some instances, clay or shale is sintered or roasted in kilns which drives off water and causes them to expand. Two particularly interesting natural substances that expand on heating are **vermiculite** and **perlite.** For both, the expansion is so great that the end product is an *ultra*-lightweight aggregate.

Vermiculite is a mineral with a layer structure like micas and clays. Although the composition is variable, it is basically a hydrous magnesium-iron aluminum silicate. When it is heated rapidly to above 230°C, the layers separate as water between the layers is converted to steam and **exfoliation** occurs. The increase in volume that results averages eight to twelve times, although individual flakes may expand as much as 30 times to form wormlike pieces (the name vermiculite comes from the

Latin *vermiculare*, to breed worms) (Fig. 9.10). Vermiculite occurs in many places throughout the world, although important deposits are found in the United States (Montana and South Carolina) and South Africa (Palabora, N.E. Transvaal). The Montana deposit is a large altered **stock** of mafic igneous rock **(pyroxenite),** and at Palabora it is also part of an altered igneous rock **(carbonatite)** complex. Mining of the brown or greenish flakes of vermiculite is by open-pit methods, and the total world production in 1983 was about 450,000 metric tons. Of this, an estimated 256,000 tons were produced in the United States. The exfoliation plants are usually sited close to the final markets (in 1981 there were 47 plants in some 30 states in the United States) as this reduces transport costs. The U.S. Bureau of Mines estimates the total world reserves (excluding the Soviet Union and China) at 180 million metric tons of which 90 million metric tons are in the United States and 72 million metric tons in South Africa. Total world resources are estimated as up to three times the reserves.

FIGURE 9-10. Vermiculite exhibits the unusual characteristic of swelling when heated. The effect is shown here in the contrast of the vermiculite as mined (on the left) and that which has been heated (on the right). (Sample courtesy of The Virginia Vermiculite Corporation; photograph by S. Llyn Sharp.)

Perlite is a glassy volcanic rock that contains a small amount of combined water that vaporizes on rapid heating so that it also expands—to between four and 20 times its original volume. The resulting material is a solid filled with bubbles and pores and having a characteristic white color. Perlite ore is found in belts of volcanic rock in many parts of the world, but the major producers are Greece, Hungary, Italy, the Soviet Union, and the United States. As with vermiculite, deposits are mined by open-pit methods and the ore crushed, dried, and screened before shipment to expanding plants near the final markets. Annual world production was estimated at 1,600,000 metric tons in 1983 from estimated world reserves of 1700 million metric tons.

TREATED ROCK PRODUCTS

Treated rock products are materials that must be chemically processed, fired, melted, or otherwise altered after mining and before use so that they can be molded and set into new forms. Important examples include the raw materials for the manufacture of cement and of plaster, clay, and other materials needed in the production of bricks and a wide range of other ceramic products, and the raw materials for the glass industry.

Cement

Cement, a chemical binder made chiefly from limestone, is one of the most important construction materials of the twentieth century. It is generally mixed with sand to produce mortar, the binding agent for brick, block or other masonry, or with sand and gravel to make concrete (a sort of instant rock). The first use of cement and mortar was by the ancient Greeks and Romans. They added water to a mixture of quicklime [lime (CaO), made by heating or calcining limestone], sand, and a finely ground glassy volcanic ash. Because the volcanic ash came from the town of Pozzuoli, near Naples, it is known as **pozzolan cement.** The addition of water to this mixture causes a series of chemical reactions leading to recrystallization and hardening of the cement when it dries. The end product is then stable in air and water, as we can judge from the fact that pozzolan cement was used to build the Roman Pantheon and the Colosseum, still standing after more than 2000 years. However, the "art" of making such cements, although further developed by these ancient civilizations, was forgotten during the middle ages and was only rediscovered in 1756 when a British engineer named John Smeaton was commissioned to rebuild the famous Eddy-

stone Lighthouse off the coast of Cornwall. He searched for a hydraulic cementing material that would set and remain stable under water, and he is said to have found the formula when examining an ancient Latin document. Smeaton found that clay must also be present to produce hydraulic cement and that this could be introduced by calcining a limestone naturally rich in clay (and hence known as **cement rock**). Such **natural cements** were further developed during the eighteenth century, but because the compositions of cement rocks vary widely, the cement was not uniform in strength or setting times. In an effort to improve the uniformity of cement, an Englishman, Joseph Aspidin, in 1824 patented a formula for **portland cement,** so called because of a fancied resemblance to Portland Stone, a limestone widely used in British buildings. It soon supplanted all other cements, and today is the basis of modern cements and concretes—the most common construction material in the world with twice as much concrete being used as all the other structural material combined.

The raw materials needed for portland cement manufacture are a source of lime (CaO) which is generally from $CaCO_3$ in a limestone, a source of alumina (Al_2O_3) which is commonly a shale or clay, and a source of silica (SiO_2) which may also come from clay and shale or from sand. Because limestone is the major ingredient, outweighing the others by roughly a factor of ten to one, cement works are usually located near limestone quarrying operations. Sometimes, a natural limestone contains clay or shale impurities of the desired composition and is therefore a cement rock. Small amounts of iron-containing materials (iron ores or waste products from iron works) are also used, and gypsum or anhydrite are added later to control setting times. The winning of the major raw materials involves the same kinds of open-pit mining as for other forms of crushed rock.

The steps involved in the manufacture of portland cement require crushing and grinding of the raw materials, and blending together either as dry powders or as slurries mixed with water (Fig. 9.11). The blend is then fed into a long rotating kiln in which temperatures of about 1500°C are reached. This drives off the carbon dioxide and water and partly melts some of the material to a glass. The resulting clinker is ground to a powder with the addition of gypsum (approximately 5 percent of the bulk) and is then ready for use. Portland cements are, in fact, largely mixtures of complex silicates and aluminates of calcium that react chemically when water is added. The new compounds that form grow as a hard mass of interlocking crystals.

The raw materials needed for cement manufacture are widely available throughout the world, and well over 100 countries produce significant amounts of cement.

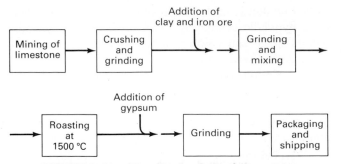

FIGURE 9-11. The conversion of limestone into cement involves a large number of steps as illustrated in this schematic diagram. (Courtesy of the Portland Cement Association.)

The Soviet Union leads the world in cement production, followed by the United States and Japan (Table 9.2).

Plaster

Plaster is made by heating or **calcining** gypsum, the hydrated form of calcium sulfate ($CaSO_4 \bullet 2H_2O$). When gypsum is calcined at 177°C, the result is to drive off 75 percent of the water and form the new compound $CaSO_4 \bullet \frac{1}{2}H_2O$. This is commonly called **plaster of Paris** after the famous gypsum quarries in the Montmartre district of that city from which a plaster of particularly high quality has long been produced. When plaster of Paris is mixed with water, it solidifies by rehydrating and reverting to a finely interlocked mass of tiny gypsum crystals. The earliest known use of gypsum and the plaster made from it was by the Egyptian civilization some 5000 years ago, and the early Greek writer Theophrastus described the burning of gypsum to prepare plaster in a manner that remains little changed today. Plaster of Paris was used in England as early as the

TABLE 9-2

Producers of cement, 1985

Country	Production (m.t. × 10⁶)	Total (%)
China	142	13.4
U.S.S.R.	131	13.4
U.S.A.	72	7.4
Japan	72	7.4
West Germany	29	3.0
Italy	40	4.1
France	23	2.4
Other market economy countries	330	34.0
All other	132	13.6
WORLD TOTAL	972	

(After U.S. Bureau of Mines.)

Over 100 countries produced 20,000 metric tons or more cement in 1985 with the seven industrial countries above accounting for 41.5% of total world production.

thirteenth century, but the first British manufacture of plaster dates from the late seventeenth century.

However, the use of plaster remained limited until about 1870 because of its very rapid setting time. Then the use of organic additives such as glue and starch to retard setting was discovered. This revolutionized the industry and permitted the first large-scale use of plaster in construction. Most early construction use was as hand-applied wet plaster that was spread over a wire screen or wooden laths to cover walls and ceilings. The development of prefabricated wall board in 1918 provided a way to greatly reduce labor costs while still using plaster. Today, **plasterboard** is by far the most widely used indoor wall covering in North America and Europe. It is prepared by feeding a slurry of plaster onto a rapidly moving, continuous roll of heavy paper. A second sheet of paper is fed onto the slurry in order to sandwich it. As the sandwich of paper and plaster travel several hundred meters on a conveyer system, the plaster sets sufficiently for the continuous slab to be cut into standard-sized sheets. These sheets are then sent slowly through a long kiln so that the plaster slurry hardens into solid gypsum, and the boards are ready for use.

Gypsum occurs in marine evaporite sequences, the formation and distribution of which was discussed in Chapter 8. It has now been recognized that calcium sulfate deposits can buildup on hot saline tidal flats without the development of thick salt accumulations. In fact, calcium sulfate occurs in evaporites not only as gypsum but also as anhydrite ($CaSO_4$), so called because it does not contain any water of crystallization. Which of the two forms of calcium sulfate originally precipitates depends on the temperature, with anhydrite being favored by higher temperatures and more commonly produced under the hot climatic conditions in which most evaporites initially form. However, this anhydrite is often converted to gypsum by subsequently taking water from rainfall percolating through the deposits. Because of this relationship between the two minerals, most large deposits contain a mixture of gypsum and anhydrite. Anhydrite cannot be used to produce plaster of Paris; hence, materials from deposits rich in anhydrite are finely ground and soaked in water so that gypsum is formed prior to further processing into plaster of Paris. Some anhydrite is used directly, however, in the cement industry or as a soil conditioner or mineral filler (see p. 277 and 287).

The United States, which possesses gypsum-producing areas that are widely distributed (Fig. 9.12), is the world's largest producer and consumer of gypsum and anhydrite. In fact, as much as 10 percent of the land area in the United States is underlain by gypsiferous rock, indicating that U.S. potential resources are so large (over 20 billion tons) as to be superabundant. The U.S. Bureau of Mines has, in fact, stated that reserves

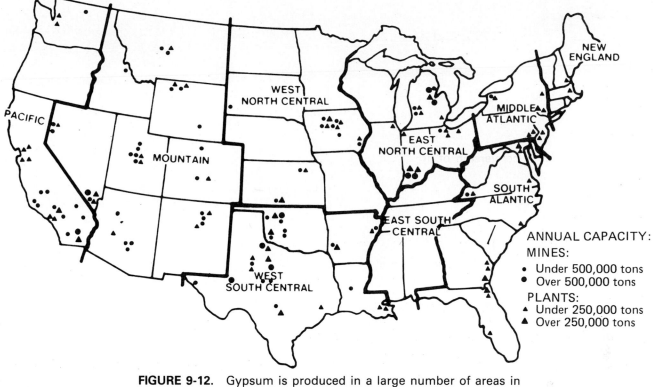

FIGURE 9-12. Gypsum is produced in a large number of areas in the United States as shown above. (Map after U.S. Bureau of Mines.)

are sufficient for 2000 years at projected rates of production. The size of some deposits is impressive. For example, gypsum deposits in Texas and Oklahoma extend for more than 320 kilometers over a width of 32-80 kilometers with a thickness of up to 7 meters. Culberson County, Texas, is underlain by a gypsum bed covering more than 1500 square kilometers and up to 20 meters thick. Undoubtedly the most picturesque gypsum deposits are the 700 square kilometers of snow white dunes at White Sands National Monument in New Mexico (Fig. 9.13). The widespread geologic occurrence and extensive use of gypsum is shown by the fact that it is produced in over 60 countries, with the major producers being (in addition to the United States) Canada, Germany, France, the Soviet Union, Great Britain, Spain, and Italy. With deposits being so widespread and transportation costs high relative to the value of the commodity, there is only limited world trade in gypsum. The price of gypsum in 1986 was $7–$8 per metric ton in the United States and around £5–£7 per metric ton in Britain. In spite of the United States being the world's largest producer, it is also the world's largest importer, most of the imports coming from Canada. Gypsum is mined using both open pit and underground methods, and apart from crushing and grinding, there is little processing of the ore prior to calcining.

Brick and Ceramic Products

A very large range of raw materials and a vast range of finished products are the province of the ceramics industry. Most of these products are chiefly made from clays that can be molded into the desired shapes before firing to hardness. Structural ceramics such as bricks, tiles, sewer pipes, and related products are a major part of that industry. In this chapter, we can do no more than mention a few examples of the raw materials used in this field, their availability, and their utilization.

Ceramic products require materials to make up the bulk of the product (skeleton formers or fillers), bonding agents that may be glass formers, fluxes that help during the firing, and various materials to give special properties to the product (color, durability, etc.). Clays are the usual skeleton formers and so make up the major raw material used in the industry. Fluxes, pigments, and glasses are discussed later in this chapter, as are the clays used in the making of refractories. The term **clay** is used to refer to a group of very fine-grained minerals with hydrated layer structures at the atomic level (see also p. 345). The ability of many clays to become plastic by the taking up of further water enables them to be molded. Firing at high temperatures in a kiln drives off the water and melts some of the particles which then

FIGURE 9-13. The great sand dunes at White Sands National Monument in New Mexico are composed of gypsum that has weathered out of the nearby mountains and accumulated by the action of wind. (Courtesy of White Sands National Monument, National Park Service.)

welds the material together. As further explained in Chapter 11 on soils, rocks largely or wholly made up of clay minerals (and also called clays) are mostly formed by weathering at the earth's surface of those rocks (granites, basalts, gneisses) rich in alumino-silicate minerals such as feldspar and mica. They may accumulate as residual deposits, as discussed in the section on aluminum in Chapter 6, or may be transported and deposited as sediments in lakes, seas, or oceans. Clays soon transform to other solid rocks when they are dehydrated and heated by burial, so they are found only near the earth's surface, not deeper in the crust. Like many of the other building materials, they are usually recovered by large quarrying operations in surficial deposits, with the quarries located as close as possible to the manufacturers and markets. Some of the most important clay minerals are listed in Table 9-3 along with information on their compositions, properties, and geologic occurrence.

The clays used in the manufacture of bricks and tiles are very widespread, and reserves are so large that few countries make attempts to estimate them. Those of the United States, for example, are said by the U.S. Bureau of Mines to be more than sufficient for another century of production at anticipated rates of growth. Potential resources are even larger. These structural ceramic products are normally manufactured by extruding the stiff plastic mass, formed by mixing the mined clay with water (10–15 percent), through a die of appropriate shape, drying under conditions of controlled humidity, and then firing in a kiln. The dehydration and vitrification on firing results in a resistant material made of high silica glass, **mullite** ($3Al_2O_3 \bullet 2SiO_2$), pure silica, and other compounds welded together.

There are also a number of special types of clays used in ceramics, deposits of which are more restricted. **China clay** or **kaolinite** is a particularly pure hydrated aluminum silicate much used originally for high quality porcelain. This is now a relatively minor use compared to its importance as a filler. The occurrence and utilization of china clay is further discussed on p. 288. **Ball clay** is also largely made up of kaolinite and is used in the manufacture of electrical porcelain, floor and wall tiles, dinnerware, etc. Deposits occur in the United States (Tennessee and Kentucky), Great Britain (Devonshire), and India. In the manufacture of whiteware (tableware, sanitaryware, etc.), ball clay is used to impart plasticity and dry strength and china clay to impart a whiter color. Also mixed with these clays are very finely ground silica called potters flint to decrease the

TABLE 9-3

The names, compositions, structures, and some information regarding properties, occurrence, and uses of some identically important clay minerals. Note that most mined clays are mixtures of several clay minerals.

Name	Composition	Structure (see Fig. 9.11)	Properties, Occurrence, and Uses
Kaolinite (The Kaolinite Group or "Kandites" includes kaolinite, dickite, nacrite, and halloysite—see below.)	$Al_4[Si_4O_{10}](OH)_8$	One layer on linked SiO_4 tetrahedra bonded to a layer with Al in octahedral coordination (1 : 1).	Kaolinite can form the white high purity material prized for porcelain making, as a filler in paper manufacture, and a wide range of other industries. May be of hydrothermal, residual or sedimentary origin. Many refractory fire clays are essentially of kaolinite.
Halloysite	$Al_4[Si_4O_{10}](OH)_8 \cdot 8H_2O$	As above but with a single layer of water molecules between the (1 : 1) sheets	Halloysite occurs in residual and hydrothermal deposits. Used for a variety of purposes including catalysis in the oil industry.
Illite (The Illite Group includes illite, hydro-micas, phengite, and glauconite.)	$K_{1-1.5}Al_4[Si_{7-6.5}Al_{1-1.5}O_{20}](OH)_4$	A sheet of octahedrally coordinated Al atoms sandwiched between two tetrahedral $(Si,Al)O_4$ sheets (2 : 1). K between these (2 : 1) sheets	Deposits are generally sedimentary in origin and contain other clay minerals. Used in common structural clay products such as bricks and tiles.
Montmorillonite (The Montmorillonite Group or "Smectites" includes montmorillonite, notronite, saponite, and hectorite—see below.)	$Na_{0.7}(Al_{3.3}Mg_{0.7})[Si_8O_{20}](OH)_4 \cdot nH_2O$	Again a (2 : 1) sheet with interlayer Na and H_2O	Montmorillonites are the essential clays in the "bentonites" produced by alteration of volcanic rocks. These are used in foundry clays and drilling muds. A moderate amount of montmorillonite is important in structural clay products to give plasticity. Also used in bleaching clays and adsorbents.
Hectorite	$(Ca,Na)_{0.66}Mg_{5.3}Li_{0.7}[Si_8O_{20}](OH)_4 \cdot nH_2O$	As above but with Mg and some Li instead of Al.	Results from alteration of volcanic rocks. One use is in drilling muds.
Chlorite (The Chlorite Group includes "chamosite" and clinochlore.)	$(Mg,Al,Fe)_{12}[(Si,Al)_8O_{20}](OH)_{16}$	A (2 : 1) sheets with a further sheet of octahedrally coordinated Al,Fe,Mg. Hence a (2 : 1 : 1) sheet.	Chlorite occurs as a component in many clays and shales mined for use in structural clay products.
Attapulgite (Member of a miscellaneous group that includes sepiolite and palygorskite.)	$Mg_5Si_8O_{20}(OH)_2 \cdot 4H_2O$	A chain-type structure. Double silica chains linked together by octahedral groups of oxygens and hydroxyls containing Al and Mg atoms.	Deposits of sedimentary origin occur. Attapulgite is in the clays called fullers earth (fulling is removal of grease from wool) valued for adsorbing properties.

shrinkage that occurs during drying and firing, and feldspar $((Na,K,Ca)Al_{1-2}Si_{3-2}O_8)$ as a flux to lower the firing temperature.

Glass

The glass industry uses substantial amounts of many industrial minerals to make its products. Glass is actually made by melting together certain rocks and minerals that can be cooled in such a way that crystallization does not occur. Consequently, glasses are made of atoms bonded together rather as in the liquid state (i.e., without the repetitive ordering characteristic of crystals; see Fig. 9.14).

By far, the most important and common glass-forming material is silica which is usually obtained from the quartz in sandstones. However, its high melting point (1713°C) and high viscosity in the liquid state make it difficult to melt and work, so that fused silica products are only used when their special properties (high softening point, low thermal expansion, resistance to corrosion, etc.) are essential. To lower the melting temperature of silica (sometimes to as low as 500°C), soda (Na_2O) is added. Since the resulting product (referred to as **water glass)** has no chemical durability and is soluble even in water, lime (CaO or CaO + MgO) is also added as a stabilizing agent. The first of these ingredients comes from sodium carbonate or sodium nitrate (see Chapter 8) or from the processing of **rocksalt** and **limestone,** and the second comes from crushed limestone or dolostone. A few percent of alumina is also

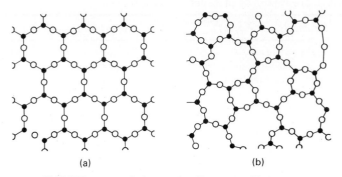

FIGURE 9-14. Schematic diagrams illustrating the differences between a crystalline solid on the left and a glass on the right. The crystalline material has a regular repeated atomic pattern, whereas the glass exhibits a more variable random pattern.

often incorporated into the glass to further improve chemical resistance. Feldspars from **pegmatites** and **aplites** are a common source of this ingredient. The resulting product is the basic soda-lime-silica glass that is used for the bulk of common glass articles (bottles, window glass, etc.).

Other minerals are used in smaller amounts in glass manufacture to give particularly desired properties or provide glass for more specialized applications. Borosilicate glass contains approximately 10–14 percent boron oxide (B_2O_3) derived from the mining of **borax** (see Chapter 8). The borosilicate glasses are both resistant to corrosion and withstand heating and cooling, so they are used in oven and tableware and for industrial glassware (such as the commercial product "Pyrex"). High alumina glasses (15–30 percent Al_2O_3) are used in the manufacture of fibers and certain cooking utensils. As noted above, alumina for the glass industry is obtained from the mining of feldspar-rich rocks such as pegmatites, aplites, and also **nepheline syenite,** an igneous rock made largely of feldspar and **feldspathoid** minerals. Lead crystal glass may contain as much as 37 percent lead oxide (PbO) for which red lead is the basic raw material, generally obtained as a by-product of base metal mining (see Chapter 7). This is the glass used for high quality tableware and certain optic uses.

Small amounts of a wide range of substances are used to color glass. Commonly, these are the oxides of metals such as chromium, cobalt, nickel, copper, iron, vanadium, manganese, and uranium. On the other hand, in producing high-quality colorless glass, iron oxide impurity in the sand and limestone raw materials may be a problem. This is overcome by using a decolorizing agent, most commonly made up of selenium and cobalt oxide or certain oxides of the rare earth elements. These additives have the effect of absorbing light of spectral colors not absorbed by the iron oxides and

hence cancelling their effect to the observer. The decolorizing agents are among the most expensive materials used in the glass industry. Small amounts of chemicals such as sodium sulfate (Na_2SO_4) and arsenic oxide (As_2O_3), and mineral products such as fluorite and rocksalt are also used as refining agents. The two basic raw materials used to make glass—sand and limestone—are abundant and widely distributed in the earth's crust and have low initial cost. Soda (Na_2O) is the most expensive of the major raw materials used to make the common types of glass and accounts for over 50 percent of the raw material cost per ton.

Glass production involves batch mixing of the raw materials and their melting together in pots and crucibles or large tanks, usually heated by burning oil or gas. After forming, it is slowly cooled or **annealed** to reduce internal stresses, and during this stage it may be rolled out to form plate glass or subjected to a wide variety of manufacturing processes that range from injecting the molten glass into molds to make bottles or glasses to the traditional mouth blowing and hand shaping of art glass.

OTHER MAJOR INDUSTRIAL MINERALS

All the substances discussed in this chapter and in Chapter 8 on fertilizers and chemical minerals would normally be classed as **industrial minerals** (and rocks). This class of materials normally excludes metallic ores, mineral fuels, and gemstones (but included here on pg. 294–297) but includes many other substances not previously described. It would be impossible to discuss them all here, but a number of the more important examples will be chosen. As we have already noted, these will include minerals and rocks valued because of particular properties they possess. **Asbestos** minerals are fibrous materials that are strong, flexible, inert, and heat resistant. A whole range of rocks and minerals are capable of withstanding great heat and are used to make refractory products, whereas others serve as **fluxes** by lowering melting temperatures. Another large group of minerals and rocks are used simply as **fillers** or bulking agents in a wide range of products because they are inert and physically and chemically harmless. More specialized minerals are required for **pigments** or coloring agents, whereas a mineral such as **barite** finds industrial applications because of its high density combined with inertness, **diamond** because of its hardness, or the **zeolites** because of their unusual crystal structures.

Asbestos

Asbestos is not a single mineral; the term refers to a number of silicate minerals that occur as fibrous crystals (Fig. 9.15). Hence, the definition of asbestos is complicated because the term is based on mineral habit. The

FIGURE 9-15. Chrysotile asbestos, shown above, has found many uses because it forms as strong, flexible fibers. (Sample from Thetford, Ontario; photograph by S. Llyn Sharp.)

U.S. Bureau of Mines, summarizing the definition given by the American Society for Testing and Materials in 1984, says: "Asbestos is a term applied to six naturally occurring minerals exploited commercially for their desirable physical properties, which are in part derived from their asbestiform [fibrous] habit. The six minerals are the serpentine mineral chrysotile and the amphibole minerals grunerite asbestos (also referred to as amosite), riebeckite asbestos (also referred to as crocidolite), anthophyllite asbestos, tremolite asbestos, and actinolite asbestos. Individual mineral particles, however processed and regardless of their mineral name, are not demonstrated to be asbestos if the length-to-width ratio is less than 20:1." The six types of asbestos, their chemical formulae and properties, are listed in Table 9.4. The remarkable properties of asbestos minerals are chiefly the result of their crystal structures. For example, chrysotile (a sample of which is shown in Fig. 9.15) has a structure in which silica and magnesium hydroxide atomic layers are rolled up to form "scrolls," several such scrolls making an individual fiber (Fig. 9.16).

Asbestos is valuable because the fibers, which are strong and flexible, can be separated, spun, and woven like organic fibers such as cotton and wool. They also make flexible materials when just embedded in a suitable matrix. Unlike organic fibers, these products are fire and heat resistant, stable in many corrosive environments, and good electrical and thermal insulators. They are also wear resistant and strong as the tensile strength shows. (See Table 9.4 and compare these values with the tensile strength of steel piano wire which is 100,000 pounds per square inch.) Only some asbestos is suitable in length and flexibility for spinning; chrysotile has the best spinnability, amosite and crocidolite are fair, and the others are poor. The length and flexibility of fibers will also vary within and between particular asbestos deposits. Asbestos is classified commercially on the basis of length of fiber and the degree of openness (or separation) of the fibers.

Asbestos is used in a wide range of products. Some of the well-known uses are in the motor industry—for brake linings, clutch plates, and other friction materials—and in asbestos textiles used in the electrical industry. The single greatest use is in asbestos cement products where the large volume of short fibers unusable for spinning are bound in portland cement to make

TABLE 9-4

Types of asbestos fibers and their properties

Type	Formula	Color	Tensile Strength (p.s.i.)	Resistance to: Acids, etc.*	Heat**
Chrysotile	$Mg_6(Si_2O_5(OH)_4)_2$	White, grey, green, yellowish	80,000–100,000	Poor	Good
Crocidolite ("Blue asbestos")	$Na_2Fe_5(Si_4O_{11}(OH))_2$	Blue	100,000–300,000	Good	Poor
Amosite	$(Mg,Fe)_7(Si_4O_{11}(OH))_2$	Ash grey, brown	16,000–90,000	Good	Poor
Anthophyllite	$(Mg,Fe)_7(Si_4O_{11}(OH))_2$	Grey-white, brown, green	4000	Very good	Very good
Tremolite	$Ca_2(Mg,Fe)_5$-$(Si_4O_{11}(OH))_2$	Grey-white greenish, yellow blue	1000–8000	Good	Fair to good
Actinolite	$Ca_2(Mg,Fe)_5$-$(Si_4O_{11}(OH))_2$	Greenish	1000	Fair	—

*Refers to resistance to dissolution in 25% HCl, CH_3COOH, H_3PO_4, and H_2SO_4 (and also NaOH) at room temperature for long periods and boiling temperature for short periods.
**Refers to weight loss on heating at temperatures between ~200–1000°C for 2 hours due to loss of OH.

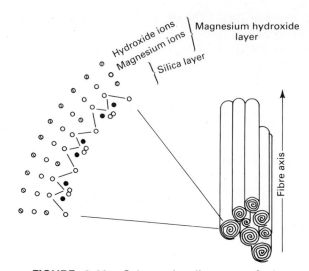

FIGURE 9-16. Schematic diagram of the structure of a fiber of chrysotile asbestos. Each crystal is in the form of a scroll made from a closely connected double layer with magnesium hydroxide units on its external face and silica units on its inner face. The details of a small section of the scroll show the structure of the double layer. Each fiber is made of several such rolls. (Reproduced from A.A. Hodgson, "Chemistry and physics of asbestos," in L. Michaels and S.S. Chissick, Asbestos, vol. 1, Wiley & Sons, Ltd., 1979. Used with permission.)

pipes, jackets, shingles, sheets, or corrugated and flat boards. The addition of asbestos increases the strength or flexibility of the product. It is also added to some papers, millboards, paints, putties, and plastics to provide desirable properties.

Chrysotile asbestos, which makes up the great majority of world production, is formed during the alteration of magnesium-rich (ultramafic) rocks such as **peridotite** and **dunite.** This alteration by hydrous solutions produces the serpentine minerals antigorite, lizardite, and chrysotile (which may or may not be asbestiform), which are all hydrated magnesium silicates. Many ultramafic rocks have undergone this process of **serpentinization,** but few contain workable deposits of chrysotile asbestos. Formation of such deposits requires an unusual combination of faulting, shearing, folding, serpentinization, and metamorphism of the host rocks. Many mountain belts around the world contain bodies of ultramafic rock that have been serpentinized. Commonly, these rocks are parts of **ophiolite complexes,** a name given to masses of mafic and ultramafic rocks with associated volcanic rocks that were originally formed as part of the earth's crust beneath the oceans, and then thrust up onto the continents during mountain building episodes.

Because only a very small fraction of serpentine bodies contain commercially exploitable asbestos, the availability of this commodity is similar to that of scarce metals. World production is dominated by the Soviet Union and Canada which contribute about three-quarters of the total tonnage (Table 9.5). The Republic of South Africa is a major producer of chrysotile, and the only large producer of crocidolite and amosite. Total world reserves are estimated to be in excess of 100 million tons and will likely be adequate for the foreseeable future. Canadian production of chrysotile comes mainly from the eastern townships of Quebec where the deposits lie in a serpentine belt that extends from Newfoundland down into Vermont where there is small-scale U.S. production. The deposits of the eastern townships are a good example of the location of asbestos ore within the serpentinized rocks of an ophiolite suite. Other Canadian deposits occur in Ontario and within the Rocky Mountains in British Columbia and the Yukon. Major producing areas for chrysotile in the Soviet Union occur in the Ural Mountains (Bajenova District). Crocidolite and amosite are mined in South Africa where they occur in banded ironstones. Anthophyllite is mined in Finland, and there are small deposits worked for tremolite in Italy. Most of the mining of asbestos is by open pit methods, with some underground mining of deeper deposits of those of unsuitable shape for surface exploitation. The ore is crushed and milled as a dry process with screening to separate impurities.

Asbestos has apparently been known and used in small quantities for thousands of years, but it was not until the late nineteenth century that it became important as an industrial mineral. The modern industry grew from the processing in England and Italy of asbestos mined in Quebec, Canada. In 1900, the total production was 200–300 thousand metric tons, and it has been estimated that the cumulative world total production to 1930 was about 5 million metric tons. After that time, the use of asbestos accelerated so rapidly that in 1979

TABLE 9-5

Producers of asbestos, 1985

Country	Production (m.t. × 10³)
Canada	742
Centrally planned economies	2548
Other market economies	599
Republic of South Africa	165
U.S.A.	57
WORLD TOTAL	4111

(After U.S. Bureau of Mines.)

The largest producing countries own the largest reserves. The world has 200×10^6 tons of identified resources.

alone world production was just about 5 million metric tons. However, the health hazards associated with asbestos have had a profound effect on its use in the United States where consumption dropped from a high of 803 thousand metric tons in 1973 to only slightly over 100 thousand metric tons in 1986, the lowest level of American usage since 1938. Consumption in the world reached a peak in 1977 and, although declining, remained above 4 million metric tons per year (Fig. 9.17, Table 9.5) in 1986.

Although the relationship between asbestos and various diseases has received the most attention in the last 20 years, health problems associated with asbestos were evident before 1900 and within 20 years of the first factory production. Between 1890–1895, 16 of 17 workers in a French asbestos weaving factory had died. Asbestosis, a disease resulting from the inhalation of very fine particles of asbestos dust, was first recognized in 1906 and completely described in 1927. The deposition of the asbestos fibers in the lungs causes the formation of scar tissue (fibrosis) and results in fatigue and breathlessness after some years. Other diseases associated with asbestos exposure include lung cancer (which develops in about 50 percent of asbestosis sufferers and which is also promoted by smoking) and mesothelioma, a rare cancer only associated with the presence of crocidolite.

In most applications, asbestos fibers are totally encapsulated in various matrix materials, cannot be inhaled, and do not pose a health risk. However, when as-bestos fibers are free during mining and processing, during drilling and sawing, or during deterioration of the matrix (e.g., breakdown and peeling of old asbestos-bearing paints), they constitute a major health hazard. The recognition that exposure to asbestos can have such deadly consequences has led to increasingly stringent rules concerning its use. In 1985, the U.S. Environmental Protection Agency (EPA) proposed banning the use of many asbestos-containing products (pipes, flooring, tiles) and phasing out the remaining uses of asbestos over a 10-year period. Although these regulations have not been enforced, they reflect the grave concerns about exposure to asbestos and suggest that consumption will probably continue to decline. However, the health hazards of asbestos create a dilemma for some parts of the mineral industry, since no other natural or synthetic material has been found that exhibits the qualities of strength, chemical inertness, and durability of asbestos and at such low cost.

It is also true, as pointed out by Dr. M. Ross of the United States Geological Survey, that crocidolite and amosite have been shown to be far more dangerous than the chrysotile asbestos which accounts for about 90 percent of total usage. Careful thought must be given to the costs of removal of asbestos-containing materials and of the imposition of rigorous safety standards; for example, there is no evidence that ingestion of asbestos in drinking water causes disease. Furthermore, it is now apparent that the removal processes often liberate more asbestos dust than was present from its original applications.

Refractories, Foundry Sand, and Fluxes

Refractories are materials that can withstand high temperatures without cracking, spalling, or reacting despite contact with molten metals, slags, or other substances. Not only do refractories have to withstand such temperatures, but they also may be subjected to abrasion, impact, sudden temperature change, chemical attack, and high loads under these extreme conditions. They provide linings for the furnaces used in the smelting and refining of metals and the production of alloys, for the furnaces or kilns used in the ceramic industry, in glass and cement manufacture, and for coke ovens or boilers used in gas or electricity generation plants. There are a host of other uses ranging from the linings of incinerators to the manufacture of spark plugs for automobiles. This wide variety of applications means that many different raw materials with different refractory properties are used.

The industrial minerals now used in the greatest quantities to make refractories are clays that have traditionally been called **fire clays.** These are generally of

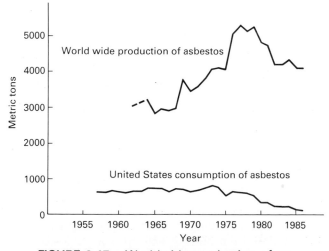

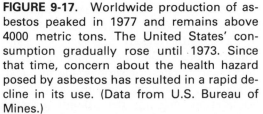

FIGURE 9-17. Worldwide production of asbestos peaked in 1977 and remains above 4000 metric tons. The United States' consumption gradually rose until 1973. Since that time, concern about the health hazard posed by asbestos has resulted in a rapid decline in its use. (Data from U.S. Bureau of Mines.)

sedimentary origin and are often found beneath coal seams in a sequence of sedimentary rocks. The dominant clay mineral present is kaolinite with various impurities that affect such properties as the plasticity of the clay. Fire clays have the advantages that they can be molded and shaped to make bricks, tiles, or more elaborately shaped products before being fired. The heat resistance of such products ranges from 1500°C–1650°C, and they have a wide range of applications as furnace and boiler linings. Fire clays are also used in the manufacture of refractory cements. Important sources of these clays are found in England, Germany, and parts of the United States such as Pennsylvania, Georgia, and Alabama. The U.S. production of fire clay is approximately 3 million metric tons, and there are very large reserves of this material worldwide.

Silica in its various widely occurring natural forms is commonly used to manufacture refractories. Some sandstones are directly cut into bricks; alternatively, quartzite or quartz itself may be crushed and bonded with lime to make silica bricks. Such bricks do not soften much below their melting point (approximately 1700°C) and are used in many metallurgical processes. Other refractories are high in alumina and are made using bauxite (see p. 185) and other forms of natural alumina such as **diaspore** ($Al_2O_3 \bullet H_2O$). The aluminosilicate minerals (**sillimanite, andalusite, kyanite** which are all **polymorphs** of Al_2SiO_5) are also used to make high-alumina refractories. These minerals are common in metamorphic rocks, and concentrations mined as commercial deposits occur in South Africa (andalusite), Sweden (kyanite), and Australia (sillimanite) as well as in the United States (in Virginia, California, and Nevada). High-alumina refractories can withstand temperatures up to 1800°C–2000°C. Magnesia (MgO), produced from magnesium in seawater and from quarried magnesite and dolomite, is an important component in refractories used in the steel industry. Some of the best raw materials for high-temperature refractories are chromite (see below), the nature and origin of which is discussed on p. 204, and **zircon** ($ZrSiO_4$). Chrome refractories are widely used in steel mills, whereas zirconia (ZrO_2), which will withstand temperatures of 2500°C, is used for refining precious metals. Zircon, providing the raw materials for these refractories, comes from beach sands in India, Brazil, Australia, and Florida.

Foundry sand is used to make the molds in which molten metals are cast. The most widely used foundry sand is known in the industry as **greensand** and is a mixture of silica, clay, and water. In some cases, the silica is a clay-free sand dredged from lakes or taken from dunes and then washed, graded, and dried. To this is added clay (commonly **bentonite),** water, and some cellulose to provide the necessary binding properties.

There are also natural moulding sands that contain sufficient clay to be used directly in the foundry. Other minerals that are sometimes used instead of silica for foundry sands include the silicates **olivine** (($Fe,Mg)_2 SiO_4$) and zircon and the oxide chromite (($Fe,Mg)(Cr,Al,Fe)_2 O_4$). The refractory properties of chromite vary with its exact composition (Fe/Mg, Cr/Al, and Cr/Fe ratios). The particular type of "sand" used will depend on the nature of the casting operation. In general, raw materials for producing foundry sands are widespread and not in short supply. Annual production in the United States, for example, is about 30 million metric tons.

In contrast to the refractories and foundry sands that are valuable because they resist high temperatures and can be used to contain molten metals, **fluxes** are substances that help in the melting of material during smelting or in operations like **soldering, brazing,** and welding. The fluxes used in smelting are aimed at efficiently separating the waste products from the metal in the form of a **slag.** The slag must have a relatively low formation and melting temperature, must be fluid at smelting temperatures, must have an appreciably lower specific gravity than the metal, and must not dissolve appreciable amounts of the metal being smelted. The more common fluxing materials are limestone, silica, and **fluorspar.** Limestone is a "basic" flux used in ferrous and nonferrous metallurgy. The calcium oxide formed when limestone decomposes produces slags of low specific gravity and low fusion temperatures when used in the smelting of copper and lead ores. As discussed on p. 177, it is also used in iron and steel making. Silica, an "acid" flux, is also used in steel making, whereas fluorspar is a widely used "neutral" flux used to make slags more fusible and fluid. Limestones, quartzites, and sandstones suitable for use as fluxing agents are relatively widespread throughout the world. Fluorspar deposits, which have precipitated from relatively low temperature **hydrothermal fluids,** are widespread but often small and impure.

Soldering and **brazing** are metallurgical joining operations in which a joint is formed using a filler metal of different composition and lower melting point to the joined pieces. Fluxes act to aid the spread of the solder or braze and mop up impurities (such as oxide coatings) that may hinder forming a successful joint. In soldering, which differs from brazing only in being a lower temperature operation (< 425°C), fluxes employed may contain various chlorides of zinc, ammonia, sodium, and tin along with various organic compounds and acids. Brazing fluxes commonly contain borax (see p. 266) and various borates, or various fluorides and chlorides of sodium, potassium, lithium, and zinc. Fluxes are also used in welding, the joining of metals by

heating to high temperatures with or without a filler metal being present. In this case, the compounds used in the fluxes include silica and oxides of manganese, titanium, aluminum, calcium, and zirconium. All industries using metals for construction and fabrication (for example, automobiles, ships, aircraft, household appliances, etc.) make use of these metal joining techniques, especially welding.

Fillers and Pigments

Mineral fillers are fine particle, inert and cheap mineral substances that are added to a great range of manufactured products to provide bulk or to modify the properties of the product by giving weight, toughness, opacity, or some other characteristic. A list of the more important mineral fillers is given in Table 9.6 with information on their compositions, useful properties, and applications. As can be seen, these materials range from the hydrated magnesium silicate **talc,** a very soft mineral best known for its use in cosmetics, through a variety of clays, to rocks such as limestone or pumice. Some major industries that use fillers are the manufacturers of paper, paint, plastics, rubber, pesticides, detergents, and fertilizers. Many of the mineral substances listed have other uses and are discussed elsewhere in the book, so their nature, occurrence, and exploitation need not be considered again here.

TABLE 9-6
The more important mineral fillers

Substance	Composition	Useful Properties/Major Applications
Asbestos*	See pg. 283	Fibrous and strong; building materials, tiles, plastics, etc.
Barite*	$BaSO_4$	Dense and inert; rubber, paint
Bentonite	Clayrock, a mixture of clay minerals (montmorillonite dominant)	Pesticides and detergents
Diatomite	Sedimentary rock, dominantly SiO_2 from shells of small organisms (diatoms)	Porous and light; absorptive; paints, paper, plastics, pesticides
Fuller's earth	Clayrock, a mixture of clay minerals (dominant montmorillonite and attapulgite)	Absorptive; pesticides, greases, paper
Gypsum*	$CaSO_4 \cdot 2H_2O$	Low cost; paints, paper, cotton goods, pesticides
Kaolin* (China clay)	A pure clay mineral $(Al_4Si_4O_{10}(OH)_8)$	White color, low cost; paper, paint, adhesives, plastics, rubber, ink, pesticides
Limestone*	Rock, dominantly $CaCO_3$	Soft particles, soluble in acids, abundant and cheap; asphalt, fertilizers, insecticides, paints, rubber, plastic
Mica (muscovite)	Layer silicate $(KAl_2(AlSi_3)O_{10}(OH)_2)$	Layer structure and electrical insulation properties; roofing material, paint, rubber, wallpaper
Perlite*	See section pg. 276	Lightweight; fines used in paint, drilling muds, plastic
Portland cement*	See section pg. 277	
Pumice*	Vesicular volcanic rock	Stuccos, plasters, paint
Pyrophyllite	$Al_2Si_4O_{10}(OH)_2$	Soft platey structure; asphalt roofing, paint, rubber battery boxes
Rock dusts	Variable; commonly carbonates	Low cost, strong; asphalts and cheap fillers
Quartz (+ other silica)	SiO_2	Low cost, hard, inert; quartz paints, bitumens
Slate*	Rock comprised of silica and micaceous minerals	Low cost, inert, compatible with bitumens; roofing, sealing compounds, paints, hard rubber
Talc	$Mg_3Si_4O_{10}(OH)_2$	Soft platey structure, good adhesion; paints, rubber, roofing, insecticides, asphalt, paper, cosmetics, textiles
Vermiculite*	See section pg. 276	Fines used; fertilizers, pesticides

*Discussed in detail elsewhere in the book. See index for relevant sections.

Several of the clay minerals (or clay rocks) provide useful fillers, being already of fine particle size. Kaolin or china clay, although originally used in the manufacture of fine porcelain, is now used in large amounts by the paper industry. The best quality clays, which are of high purity and whiteness, are used to coat high-gloss papers. The United States and Great Britain are the world's principal producers of kaolin clays. The U.S. deposits occur as clay sediments and kaolinitic sands of late Cretaceous-early Tertiary age in Georgia and South Carolina. The kaolin was probably derived from deeply weathered bedrock and deposited by a system of rivers. The mined material is 90 percent kaolinite with quartz as the main impurity. The British deposits are in Cornwall and Devon and come from the **hydrothermal alteration** of feldspars in granite bodies (Fig. 9.18).

Clays such as **fuller's earth** and **bentonite** occur in sedimentary sequences, although they probably come from the breakdown and alteration of volcanic ash deposited within those sequences. Bentonite is chiefly made of **smectite** group clay minerals such as **montmorillonite, saponite,** and **hectorite** (see Table 9.3). Most bentonites appear to have formed from volcanic ash that was transported considerable distances in the atmosphere and then deposited into the sea or lakes where it broke down to form the constituent clay minerals. Com-

monly, the parent volcanic material is thought to have been a **rhyolite** or **andesite** (see Table 9.1) Some bentonites appear to have formed by hydrothermal activity and occur as irregular bodies in rocks showing other evidence of hydrothermal alteration. Some hectorite deposits in California are thought to have formed by alteration of volcanic ash or **tuff** as a result of hot-spring activity in alkaline lakes. Most fuller's earth deposits are, in fact, bentonites, although there are also some consisting largely of the minerals **palygorskite (attapulgite)** and **sepiolite** (see Table 9.3). These may not have formed from alteration of volcanic materials, possibly having been precipitated from seawater evaporating in a tidal-flat environment. The distribution of bentonite and fuller's earth districts in the United States is shown in Fig. 9.16. The name *fuller's earth* comes from the process of **fulling** that is removing the grease from wool or other organic fibers. Such clays, as well as being used as fillers, therefore have important applications because of their absorptive properties and are used as filters and purifiers of oils, fats, and various chemicals. **Diatomite,** a sedimentary rock made up of the siliceous skeletons of microscopic organisms called **diatoms,** also has important applications in purification and filtration (Fig. 9.19). The United States is the world's leading producer from beds in California, Washington, and Oregon.

FIGURE 9-18. Clay pits such as that shown above in Cornwall southwest England, provide a raw material used chiefly in the paper industry and also in the manufacture of fine China and ceramics. (Photograph courtesy of English China Clays Ltd.)

CELITE 512
500X

100 microns

FIGURE 9-19. Diatomite consists of the accumulated remains of siliceous shells of marine diatoms as shown in this photomicrograph from Lompoc, California. (Courtesy of the Manville Sales Corporation.)

The addition of fillers will commonly modify the color of materials, whereas pigments are mineral-derived powders added solely to give color. From the cave paintings of primitive humans to the modern production of paints for industrial and domestic use, mineral pigments have been employed to provide long-lasting color. Some pigments are the untreated natural minerals, others are made by burning or subliming natural minerals, and a third group is chemically manufactured. Natural pigments include the ochers, umbers, and siennas that come from iron oxides and hydroxides (**hematite, limonite**) sometimes mixed with clays and manganese oxides and which provide permanent reds, yellows, and oranges. Roasting of some of these mixtures gives the brown colors of burnt umber or burnt sienna. Green colors are provided by silicates rich in iron and magnesium and white by gypsum, barite, and white clays. Chemical paints were formerly made using lead compounds, now little used because of their toxicity. Zinc oxide, barium sulfate, and titanium dioxide are used in white paint manufacture and consume substantial amounts of these commodities. Natural pigments like the ochers, umbers, and siennas generally form as residual surface deposits through the alteration of ores and rocks. Certain areas are noted for particular pigments: yellow ocher from France and the United States, sienna from Italy, umber from Cyprus, and red oxides from Spain are examples.

Diamond and Other Abrasives

Abrasives, of which **diamond** is the most important, are the materials that are used to cut, shape, grind, and polish all the modern alloys and ceramics. Diamond—the most dense form of carbon—is the hardest natural or synthetic substance known. This hardness makes it essential for some uses and much more efficient than other abrasives for many other uses. We think of diamonds most often as beautiful cut gemstones (see p. 295). However, most natural diamonds are small, poorly shaped and contain imperfections, and thus are unsuitable for use as gems. In fact, only about 20 percent of natural diamonds are suitable as gemstones. The remaining 80 percent are used in industry. The diamonds are classified using such terms as die stones, tool stones, dresser stones, drilling stones, bort, diamond dust, and powder. Their principal uses are in diamond saws, drilling bits, wire drawing bits, glass cutters, grinding wheels, and bonded and loose abrasives for lapping and polishing.

Diamond requires high pressures for its formation, pressures reached only at depths of 150 kilometers or more in the earth. Diamond-bearing rocks called **kimberlites** originate in the **mantle** of the earth and reach the surface in narrow pipelike vents, often no more than 50 meters in diameter (see Fig. 9.20). The reasons for the formation and location of the pipes remain a geologic puzzle. Not only are kimberlites rare, few kimberlite pipes actually contain diamond. Of the several hundred kimberlite pipes found in Africa to date, only 29 are known to contain diamond, and only 17 of these are rich enough to warrant mining. Even the richest kimberlites contain no more than 0.2 grams (1 carat) for every 3 metric tons of rock (0.000007 percent). Because diamonds are so hard and resistant to weathering, they also accumulate in placer deposits. In fact, about 40 percent of diamonds mined today come from placers. The African deposits have been the world's largest producers since their discovery in the 1860s, first in South Africa from kimberlite pipes rich in gem material, and more recently in Zaire and Ghana (Fig. 9.21). Recent finds in northern Siberia account for a growing Soviet production. As indicated in Table 9.7, the world's principal suppliers of industrial diamonds in 1984 were Zaire (14.1 million carats), Botswana (7.1 million), the Soviet Union (6.4 million carats), and South Africa (5.7 million carats). Mining operations being developed in Australia are soon expected to produce 10–20 million carats a year from a reserve of 500 million carats and were already producing 2.8 million carats in 1984.

In 1955, the General Electric Company in the United States announced the development of a process for the synthesis of industrial diamonds. This, the first commercially viable process for the manufacture of diamonds, was the culmination of many years of research. It involved subjecting graphite to pressures greater than 1 million pounds per square inch (70,300 kilograms per square centimeter) and temperatures up to 2000°C in a sealed reaction vessel. The problem of promoting the transformation of graphite to diamond was solved by using molten nickel to dissolve the graphite and recrystallize the carbon as diamond. This process spawned an industry that by 1986 was producing about 80 million carats a year, far in excess of world production of natural industrial diamonds (about 39 million carats in 1985, Table 9.7). Thus, more than two-thirds of all abrasive diamond grit used is now manmade, with production taking place not only in the United States, but also in Sweden, South Africa, Ireland, Japan, and the Soviet Union. Although other diamond synthesis techniques have been developed, including some using explosive charges to generate very high pressures for very short times as a shock wave, most methods result in diamonds of small size (Fig. 9.22). Larger gem quality crystals have been made since about 1970 by using processes employing seed crystals. However, these processes are difficult and costly since growth must take place slowly to produce a quality, flaw-free crystal. The natural diamond is still preferred as a gemstone.

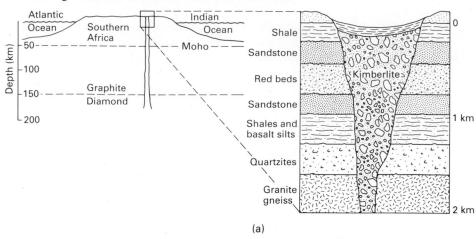

(a)

(b)

FIGURE 9-20. (a) Kimberlite pipes, shown schematically in cross section above, are the only primary sources of diamonds. The pipes formed as violent gas-rich volcanic explosions carried mixtures of volcanic rocks and fragments of the surrounding rocks upward. Diamond-bearing pipes must have originated at depths of 150 kilometers or more because diamonds do not form at the pressure conditions encountered at shallower depths (see also Fig. 2.14). (b) Kimberlites consist of breccias with a wide variety of fragments representative of all rock types through which the pipe has intruded. Diamonds are recovered by crushing and carefully processing the kimberlite. (Photograph by B.J. Skinner.)

FIGURE 9-21. Diamond-bearing kimberlites occur in all continents, but the greatest number of pipes and the largest production come from central and southern Africa. The size of the circles shows, in a relative sense, the size of the deposits.

Gem diamonds are priced arbitrarily according to people's desires and range from hundreds to thousands of dollars per carat depending on size, color, and clarity. In contrast, the prices of the industrial stones reveals the value (1986—about $1.20 per carat) of the diamond (bort) relative to the competing abrasive materials. Larger stones needed for special cutting dies are, of course, more expensive and may range up to $80 per carat.

Other important natural abrasives include **corundum, emery,** and **garnet.** Corundum, hexagonal aluminum oxide, is the second hardest natural substance. It is used almost exclusively as a finely crushed and sized material for lapping and polishing optical glass and metals. As with diamond, methods have been developed for the synthesis of corundum, most particularly by heating bauxite in an electric arc furnace with small amounts of coke that chemically reduces impurities, especially iron with which the other impurities can then combine and sink to the bottom of the furnace.

TABLE 9-7

The principal producers of industrial diamonds in 1985

Country	Production (millions of carats)
Zaire	14.1
Botswana	7.1
Soviet Union	6.4
South Africa	5.7
Australia	2.8*
Brazil	0.8
All others	2.3
World	39.2

(Data from the U.S. Bureau of Mines.)

*Australian production is projected to rise to 14.6 million carats per year by 1987.

TABLE 9-8

Important zeolite minerals

Name	Formula
Analcime	$NaAlSi_2O_6 \cdot H_2O$
Chabazite	$(Ca,Na)_2Al_2Si_4O_{12} \cdot 6H_2O$
Clinoptilolite	$(Na_2K_2Ca)_3Al_6Si_{30}O_{72} \cdot 24H_2O$
Erionite	$(Na_2K_2Ca)_{4.5}Al_9Si_{27}O_{72} \cdot 27H_2O$
Faujasite	$(Na_2Ca)_{1.75}Al_{3.5}Si_{8.5}O_{24} \cdot 16H_2O$
Ferrierite	$(K,Na)_2(Mg,Ca)_2Al_6Si_{30}O_{72} \cdot 18H_2O$
Heulandite	$(Ca,Na_2)Al_8Si_{28}O_{72} \cdot 24H_2O$
Laumontite	$Ca_4Al_8S_{16}O_{48} \cdot 16H_2O$
Mordenite	$(Na_2K_2Ca)Al_2Si_{10}O_{24} \cdot 7H_2O$
Phillipsite	$(K_2Na_2Ca)_2Al_4Si_{12}O_{32} \cdot 12H_2O$

FIGURE 9-22. Synthetic diamonds such as those shown above now constitute the world's major source of diamond used as an abrasive. Despite the crystalline shape of these diamonds, no economic method for synthesizing gem-sized stones has yet been devised. (Courtesy of General Electric Company, Specialty Materials Department.)

FIGURE 9-23. Garnet is a common mineral in many metamorphic rocks. It serves as an important abrasive material because it develops and retains sharp cutting edges when it is broken. Only rarely, however, are the crystals abundant or large enough to be economically exploitable. This crystal is from Gore Mountain, New York, where crystals as large as 20 centimeters or more in diameter were long mined for use in abrasives. (Photograph by R.J. Tracy.)

Corundum could be completely replaced by other abrasives but retains some usage because it has the tendency to cut with a chisellike edge rather than scratching. The United States has no reserves of corundum, and the small amounts used are imported primarily from South Africa. Emery is a gray to black granular mixture of variable amounts of corundum, magnetite, spinel, hematite, garnet, and other minerals. It has been widely replaced by synthetic abrasives because of its variability but is still used in coated abrasive sheets, nonskid pavements, and in stair treads. Garnet remains a popular sheet abrasive for dressing wood and soft metals. Much more garnet is used as a sandblasting medium and as a grit and powder for optical grinding and polishing. Garnet is almost exclusively an American abrasive, with the United States contributing more than 95 percent of world production and more than 80 percent of use. This cubic silicate mineral that has no cleavage is extracted from metamorphic rocks, especially the very coarsely crystalline gneisses at North Creek, New York, where individual garnet crystals are often 10–20 centimeters or more in diameter (Fig. 9.23).

The development of synthetic abrasives, such as α- and β-alumina, and various carbides and nitrides (materials of uniform quality, superior hardness, and comparable price to many natural abrasives), threatens the economic future of the natural abrasive industry.

Barite (BaSO₄)

The consumption of **barite** reflects the state of the world economy because barite is almost entirely used by the petroleum industry. Approximately 90 percent of

world barite production is finely ground for use in drilling mud, the circulation of which lubricates the drill stem, cools the drill bit, and seals off the walls of the hole. Barite is also well suited for oil and gas drilling, because its high density helps prevent blowouts that can occur when pressures are met at depth. World barite production has soared this century, especially since the 1940s, as oil demand and hence oil drilling have rapidly increased (Fig. 9.24). Barite occurs worldwide in vein and cavity-filling deposits, in weathered residual surface deposits, and in bedded accumulations. The origin of these deposits is not entirely clear, but most barite appears to have been deposited from hydrothermal solutions as fracture fillings or as chemical precipitates on the sea floor near volcanic vents. The world's principal producers are China (an estimated 1 million metric tons in 1983) and the United States (684,000 metric tons in 1983) along with the Soviet Union, India, Mexico, Chile, and Morocco. The United States is the world's major consumer (around 2 million metric tons in 1983). Present world reserves should be adequate into the next century.

Zeolites

The **zeolites** are a group of hydrous aluminum silicates of sodium, calcium, potassium and, to a lesser extent, barium and magnesium. They have crystal structures in which silicon and aluminum tetrahedral clusters (SiO₄

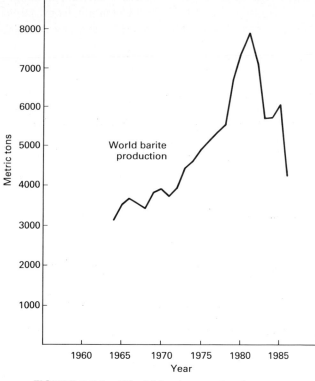

FIGURE 9-24. World barite production rose rapidly through the 1960s, and especially in the 1970s, as the world demand and price of oil rose. The reduction in the consumption of oil in the early 1980s was followed by a sharp drop in the demand for barite. (Based on data from U.S. Bureau of Mines.)

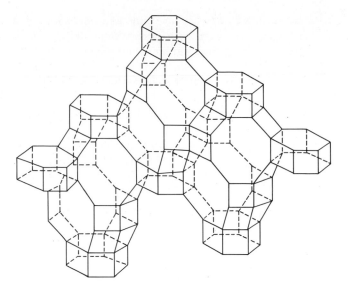

FIGURE 9-25. Schematic representation of the crystal structure of the zeolite mineral chabazite. The framework outlined consists of silicon and aluminum tetrahedra. Each framework unit contains a cavity connected to adjacent cavities by channels. [After Breck and Smith, Scientific American, vol. 200, p. 881 (1959).]

and AlO_4) of atoms are joined together to form frameworks within which are large cavities containing water molecules (Fig. 9.25). The cavities may be interconnected in one, two, or three directions, and when zeolites are dehydrated by heating to approximately 350°C, this leaves a crystal permeated with channel systems in up to three directions. The sizes of these channels (apertures are generally approximately $2.5\text{-}7.5 \times 10^{-8}$ centimeters) are such that they will allow certain smaller molecules to pass through them but not the larger molecules. Hence, zeolites have great commercial importance as molecular sieves.

Zeolitic tuffs, formed by the alteration of volcanic ash deposits, have been used for more than 2000 years as lightweight building materials and in pozzolan cement. However, it has only been since the 1950s that the zeolite minerals themselves have been extracted to make use of their unique **ion exchange** and adsorption properties. Early applications were as water softening agents to extract calcium and magnesium from drinking water and replace it with sodium. Subsequently, applications have greatly increased and include the selective extraction of radioactive elements such as cesium-137 from contaminated water, the extraction of poisonous

ammonium ions from sewage and agricultural effluent, the extraction of sulfur and nitrogen oxides from stack gases, and of CO_2 and H_2S from natural gas.

Far more important today than the natural zeolites are the hundreds of thousands of kilograms of synthetic zeolites prepared from solutions of sodium hydroxide, sodium silicate, and sodium aluminates. The synthetic zeolites have larger structural cavities and may be prepared with structural sites that allow them to be used to breakdown large organic molecules in the refining of oil. As a result, these synthetic zeolites now serve as the catalysts in the catalytic cracking units at every major oil refinery. The use of zeolites is more efficient than using simple thermal cracking (merely heating the oil to cause its breakup into smaller hydrocarbon units) and may be used to add hydrogen to the oil. This process, known as hydrogenation, results in an increased yield of gasoline from every barrel of oil.

Zeolites, the most important of which are listed in Table 9.8, occur in a wide variety of rock types, although prior to about 1950 most examples described came from fractures or cavities (known as **vesicles**) in igneous rocks. In these environments zeolites form good crystals, readily identifiable, and of the kind sought after by museums and collectors but not occurring in the quantities necessary for economic recovery. In recent years, zeolites have been recognized as important constituents in a variety of sedimentary rocks and in metamorphic rocks of low grade (i.e., formed by metamorphism under conditions of relatively low tem-

perature and pressure). Clay minerals, feldspars, and feldspathoids can react with pore waters during metamorphism or in buried sediments to form zeolites. In sediments, the breakdown and reaction of **volcanic glass** appears to have often been the way in which zeolites formed, although they may also form by processes related to weathering or to alteration by hydrothermal solutions.

Commercial interest centers on the bedded, near-surface sedimentary zeolite deposits. These include deposits formed from volcanic material in saline lakes which, although only a few centimeters to a few meters thick, commonly contain nearly monomineralic chabazite and erionite. Deposits formed in marine environments or from ground water systems may be several hundred meters thick and are characterized by clinoptilolite and mordenite. Zeolites are mined in the United States, Japan, Italy, Hungary, Yugoslavia, Bulgaria, Mexico, and Germany. The use of natural zeolites will continue to increase in the future as new applications are developed, but there will be increasing competition from synthetic zeolites that can often be tailored for special purposes.

Bituminous Materials

Bitumen is the general name for a group of materials made up of mixtures of hydrocarbons and includes petroleum, asphalts, asphaltites, pyrobitumens, and mineral waxes. Petroleum is discussed at length in Chapter 4 as a fossil fuel, although it is worth emphasizing here its importance as the source of a wide range of organic products including plastics and other polymers widely used in industry, often in conjunction with many of the mineral products discussed in this chapter. **Asphalt** is a solid (or near solid) hydrocarbon found in native form in fissures and pore spaces in rocks and as lakes. It probably formed by slow natural fractionation of crude petroleum at or near the earth's surface. Because of its resistant and waterproof characteristics, it is widely used in road construction, flooring, roofing, and more specialized waterproofing compounds. Although most asphalt is refined from crude petroleum, rock asphalts (bituminous sandstones and limestones) are mined in parts of the United States (Kentucky, Texas, Oklahoma, Louisiana) and certain European countries (France, Germany, Italy, and Switzerland) where they are used for local industries. Bitumen content is generally 3–15 percent. The best known of the much richer lake deposits is on Trinidad (West Indies) where the lake covers 114 acres and reaches 285 feet deep.

Asphaltites, pyrobitumens, and mineral waxes are the other natural bitumens. The first two are dark solids mostly found in veins and fissures. Mineral waxes are

softer as the name suggests. These relatively uncommon materials have a variety of uses ranging from paints, inks, and varnishes to rubber and plastic manufacturing.

GEM STONES

The first uses of gems date from very ancient times. The wearing of gems for personal adornment is even thought by some to have preceded the wearing of clothes. The designation "gem stone" is generally accepted to refer to materials appropriate for personal adornment. Gems are a unique type of resource because very small amounts can have extremely high value. Hence, gems are the most valuable of earth resources per unit size or unit weight. A flawless diamond no more than a centimeter across can cost many tens of thousands of dollars, while a beautiful emerald can be even more expensive.

The most important properties of gem materials are color, luster, transparency, durability, and rarity. Size alone is not of great importance; thus, a perfect small stone is commonly worth far more than a large imperfect, or poorly cut stone.

Of the 3000 or so known mineral species, only about 100 have attributes that allow them to be considered gems. The most important gem stones are listed in Table 9.9. Gems are commonly designated as precious

TABLE 9-9

Principal types of precious and semiprecious gems

Name	Composition
Amber	Hydrocarbon (fossil resin)
Beryl:	$Be_3Al_2Si_6O_{18}$
Aquamarine	"
Emerald	"
Chrysoberyl:	$BeAl_2O_4$
Catseye	"
Corundum:	Al_2O_3
Ruby	" (with trace of Cr)
Sapphire	" (with trace of Ti)
Diamond	C
Feldspar:	$KAlSi_3O_8$
Amazonstone	"
Garnet	$(Ca,Mg,Fe)_3(Al,Fe,Cr)_2(SiO_4)_3$
Jadeite	$Na(Al,Fe)Si_2O_6$
Peridot	Mg_2SiO_4
Opal	Hydrous silica
Pearl	$CaCO_3$
Quartz:	SiO_2
Agate	"
Amethyst	"
Jasper	"
Onyx	"
Spinel	$MgAl_2O_4$
Topaz	$Al_2SiO_4(F,OH)_2$
Turquoise	$CuAl_6(PO_4)_4(OH)_8 \cdot 5H_2O$

(diamond, ruby, sapphire, emerald, and pearl) or semi-precious (all others) on the basis of market price, but all species exhibit wide variations in quality. Long used in jewelry because of their beauty, gems have also been viewed as endowing their wearers with mystical powers. Diamond, with a hardness greater than any other substance, thus was considered a symbol of strength. Sapphire has been viewed as a symbol of heavenly bliss and faithfulness and as a protection for its owner against poverty and snake bites. Ruby was believed to bring peace, love, and happiness to its possessor, and emerald was thought to confer riches, fame, and wisdom to its wearer. In contrast to these positive attributes, some well-known kinds of gem stones have associated stories of curses that befall those who own or wear them.

Gems are generally measured by weight, and the unit of weight employed by jewelers is the carat; each carat is 0.2 grams. Small stones are also commonly measured in points, each point being $\frac{1}{100}$ of a carat. The size of gems range from the smallest of chips that can be incorporated into jewelry up to crystals measured in hundreds of carats. The largest cut gem known is the Brazilian Princess, a 21,327-carat (about $9\frac{1}{2}$ pounds), light blue topaz found in eastern Brazil in the 1960s. Many large and beautiful diamonds have been found, but among the most famous are the Hope Diamond (a blue, 44-carat stone from India now in the Smithsonian Institution's Museum of Natural History) and the Cullinan or Star of Africa (a colorless, 530-carat stone from South Africa) that is held in The Crown Jewels in London.

For many thousands of years, gems were used as they were found without cutting or polishing; however, from about 4000 B.C. onward, gem stones have been engraved, drilled, and cut. Until the late middle ages, most gems were cut as flat slabs or rounded into a low dome shape called a *cabachon*. In the fifteenth century, the cutting power of diamond was discovered by gem workers in France and the Netherlands, and modern cutting and polishing techniques, employing diamond abrasive, were developed. Today, virtually all crystalline gems are cut and polished in order to provide the most effective display of light and color. Thus, diamonds are transformed from fragments and roughly equal crystals [Fig 9.26(a)] into lustrous and striking cut stones [Fig. 9.26(b)]. The form into which a gem is cut depends on its original size, shape, and impurities. The most common of these cuts are shown in Figure 9.27. The most favored cut for diamond is the "brilliant" cut with 58 facets. It was developed in Venice about 1700 and promotes the internal reflection of light so as to enhance the appearance of the diamond.

Since about 1900, techniques for the synthesis of several types of precious and semiprecious gems have been developed. Examples are sapphire, ruby, emerald,

(a)

(b)

FIGURE 9-26. (a) Uncut gem diamonds as recovered from diamond mines in South Africa. Many of the crystals exhibit a crude octahedral shape. (b) "Brilliant" and "marquise" cut diamonds ready for mounting in jewelry. The diamonds are cut to take advantage of their ability to reflect light internally and hence to increase their sparkle. (Photographs courtesy of De Beers Consolidated Mines Limited.)

and spinel. Millions of carats of diamonds are now synthesized for industrial purposes, but no procedures have yet proven economic for the production of gem-quality stones. Although several techniques for gem synthesis are now available, the most commonly used, particularly for sapphire and ruby, are fusion processes in which a carrot-shaped single crystal, known as a boule, is grown up to several centimeters across and 10 or more centimeters long. Many modern gem stones, both natural and synthetic, are treated to enhance their appearance. The processes include bleaching, staining, heat treatments, and radiation treatments. Other means

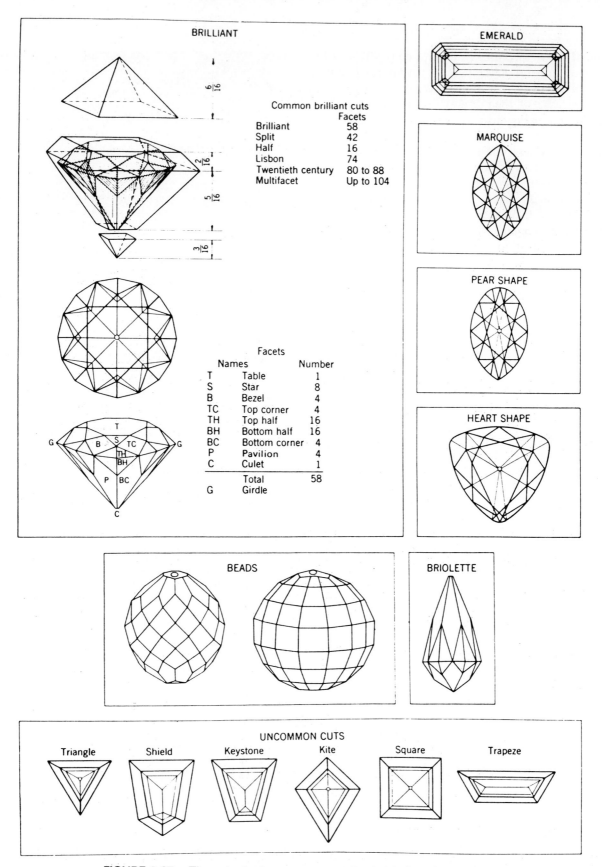

FIGURE 9-27. The principal gem stone cuts used in jewelry today. The most popular cut for diamonds is the "brilliant" shown in the upper left. (From U.S. Bureau of Mines, *Mineral Facts and Problems,* 1985.)

of enhancement include the use of foils or dyes on the backs, gluing stones together, and using gels to fill in cracks and pits.

Gem stones occur in many parts of the world and have formed in such diverse environments as the mantle of the earth (diamond), oysters along many beaches (pearls), and trees (amber). So far as commerce is concerned, diamonds are by far the most important of gems, and South Africa has been the most important source of gem diamonds since discovery there in the 1860's. The original discoveries were of placer diamonds weathered out of diamond pipes, volcanic vents that have brought up material from the earth's mantle. Placer diamonds are still being recovered, but the major mines today are the diamond pipes themselves, such as that at Kimberley (Fig. 2.14). In recent years, however, Botswana, Zaire, the Soviet Union, and Australia have become major and growing producers (Table 9.10). Dia-

monds were discovered in western Australia in 1967 and production began in 1981. By 1984, it had become the fifth largest producer in the world. There is no commercial diamond production in the United States; however, the Crater of Diamonds State Park near Murfreesboro, Arkansas, is open to the public and yields several gem-quality stones to visitors every year. Few data exist on the world's reserves of gem stones, but production has grown larger throughout the twentieth century.

THE FUTURE FOR BUILDING MATERIALS AND INDUSTRIAL MINERALS

The mineral commodities discussed in this chapter are essential, directly or indirectly, to nearly all modern industries. The construction of roads, bridges, dams, and all kinds of buildings, the extraction of fossil and nuclear fuels and metals, and the manufacture of chemicals, plastics, ceramics, glass, paper, and processed foodstuffs require them. They are essential to the complex system of dependencies on which modern industrial societies are built.

The reserves of most of the minerals and rocks discussed in this chapter are large, and the potential resources are even larger. Commodities such as building stone are so abundant that it is pointless even to attempt an estimate of the reserves. Because of this abundance, some experts have suggested that society should try to find ways of using these nonmetallic minerals to replace commodities that are in short supply such as the scarce metals. Such a solution requires the innovation of new technologies and calls for the undertaking of appropriate research programs.

TABLE 9-10

International production of gem diamond in 1984

Country	1984 Production (in Thousands of Carats)
Botswana	5810
Zaire	5170
South Africa	4520
U.S.S.R.	4300
Australia	3410
Namibia	880
Angola	750
All others	1320
TOTAL	26,160

FURTHER READINGS

BATES, R. L. and JACKSON, J. A., *Our Modern Stone Age*. Los Altos, California: Wm. Kaufmann, Inc., 1982.

BRUTON, E., *Diamonds*. London: NAG. Press, 1978.

HARBEN, P. W. and BATES, R. L., *Geology of the Nonmetallics*. Cornwall, U.K.: Robert Hartnoll Ltd., 1984.

LEFOND, S. J., editor, *Industrial Rocks and Minerals*, 5th ed. New York: Society of Mining Engineers of the American In-

stitute of Mining, Metallurgical and Petroleum Engineers, 1983, two volumes.

MICHAELS, L. and CHISSICK, S. S., *Asbestos: Volume I, Properties, Applications, and Hazards*. New York: Wiley Interscience, 1979.

O'NEIL, P., *Gemstones*. Alexandria, Virginia: Time-Life Books, 1983.

10

Three major components of the earth's hydrologic cycle are the oceans, which contain the vast majority of all water, glaciers, and ice caps, which contain most of the fresh water, and the atmosphere, which serves as a conduit to transport water. These are all visible in this photograph of the Muir glacier on the coast of Alaska. (Courtesy of Andrew Maslowski.)

WATER RESOURCES

A nation that fails to plan intelligently for the development and protection of its precious waters will be condemned to wither because of its shortsightedness. The hard lessons of history are clear, written on the deserted sands and ruins of once proud civilizations.

PRESIDENT LYNDON B. JOHNSON, 1968

INTRODUCTION

The earth has been described as the "water planet" because the dominant scene of the earth from outer space is water in the form of blue oceans and white clouds (Fig. 10.1). Indeed, no resource is more abundant or more necessary to us than the water that covers nearly three-quarters of the earth's surface and moves constantly about us in visible and invisible forms. From earliest times the oceans, rivers, lakes, and springs have served us in many ways: as gathering points, routes of transportation, and either the means of, or barriers to, our migrations. Indeed, the availability of clean water is as important for the development and maintenance of our modern technological societies as it was for the most primitive of early societies. In spite of the vast global abundance of water, its very uneven distribution constantly creates problems of there being too much or too little of it to satisfy our needs. These problems are often compounded by our desire to use ever increasing amounts of water, our modification of natural water systems, and our contamination of surface and ground waters. These factors highlight our need for a thorough knowledge of the distribution of water, an understanding of the effects of our activities on water availability and purity, and for long-range planning of water requirements.

THE GLOBAL DISTRIBUTION OF WATER

The total amount of water available in the earth's hydrosphere is approximately 1.36×10^{10} cubic kilometers or 1.36×10^{21} liters distributed in a variety of forms and locations (Fig. 10.2). The overwhelming proportion of the water, 97.2 percent, lies in the oceans; an additional 2.15 percent is held in polar icecaps and glaciers. Because the oceans are saline and not directly usable for most human needs, and because the glacial and polar ice is inaccessible, the vast majority of our requirements must be met by the remaining 0.65 percent. The distribution of this small proportion of the earth's water at any given time is a function of the hydrologic cycle and the natural storage capacity of the rocks and surface land forms. Thus, the problems of water supply are more complex than mere total abundance, they also include local distribution patterns, the rates of recharge and natural loss, and, increasingly, the cleanliness. The availability of **potable water** (i.e., water suitable for drinking), more than any other factor in the future, will determine the number of people who can live in any geographic province as well as their use of natural resources and their overall life style.

The Hydrologic Cycle

The free water on the earth's surface, though essentially unchanging in quantity, is constantly in motion in the hydrologic cycle (Fig. 10.3). The earth's atmosphere is a great solar-powered heat engine that draws up water by evaporation, transports water as a vapor and clouds,

FIGURE 10-1. Earth, "the water planet," as seen from the Apollo 17 spacecraft. The abundance of water in the oceans, clouds, and icecaps gives the earth an appearance that is unique among the planets. (Photograph from NASA.)

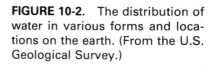

	Location	Water volume (liters)	Percentage of total water
Surface water			
	Fresh-water lakes	125×10^{15}	.009
	Saline lakes and inland seas	104×10^{15}	.008
	Average in stream channels	1×10^{15}	.0001
Subsurface water			
	Vadose water (includes soil moisture)	67×10^{15}	.005
	Ground water within depth of half a mile	$4,170 \times 10^{15}$	.31
	Ground water—deep lying	$4,170 \times 10^{15}$	.31
Other water locations			
	Icecaps and glaciers	$29,000 \times 10^{15}$	2.15
	Atmosphere	13×10^{15}	.001
	World ocean	$1,320,000 \times 10^{15}$	97.2

FIGURE 10-2. The distribution of water in various forms and locations on the earth. (From the U.S. Geological Survey.)

and discharges water after condensation as rain and snow. The precipitated water may complete its cycle by flowing via the rivers and streams and ground water systems back to the oceans or may be short-circuited back into the atmosphere by evaporation from the land surface or by transpiration from plants. Each region of the world has a natural water budget in terms of precipitation, **evapotranspiration**, and runoff. The effects of people's alteration of the budgets in many areas are discussed later in this chapter.

Water has the highest heat capacity—or ability to absorb and hold heat with minimal temperature change—of any substance known. Consequently, the movement of massive amounts of water in the atmosphere and in ocean currents also represents movement of large quantities of thermal energy that play very direct roles in the control of the world's climates. This effect is probably best seen in the North Atlantic Ocean where the Gulf Stream, warmed by the sun in the Caribbean, flows northeastward as the North Atlantic Current, giving heat to provide the mild climate of northern Europe. Without the Gulf Stream to transport this heat, England and Scandinavia would likely be as cold as northern Canada or Siberia that lie at the same latitude.

The evaporation of water from any wetted surface requires the input of 540 calories for every gram of water that is changed from a liquid to a vapor state. Since this heat comes from the surrounding environment (e.g., remaining water, soil, air, etc.), there is a tremendous cooling effect. The melting of ice to water requires less energy—80 calories per gram—and hence is also effective for cooling. The condensation of water vapor to liquid water reverses this process and liberates 540 calories per gram of liquid water produced.

Precipitation and Evaporation Patterns

Precipitation around the world is very unevenly distributed (Fig. 10.4). The highest precipitation zone is the equatorial belt where annual precipitation generally exceeds 100 centimeters (40 inches) and commonly exceeds 200 centimeters (80 inches). This zone is flanked by two zones, at approximately 25–30 north and south latitude, that contain many of the world's major deserts and in which precipitation is commonly less than 25 centimeters (10 inches). Precipitation generally increases in the temperate regions of 35–60 north and south latitude and then decreases to less than 20 centimeters in the polar regions. These zones result from

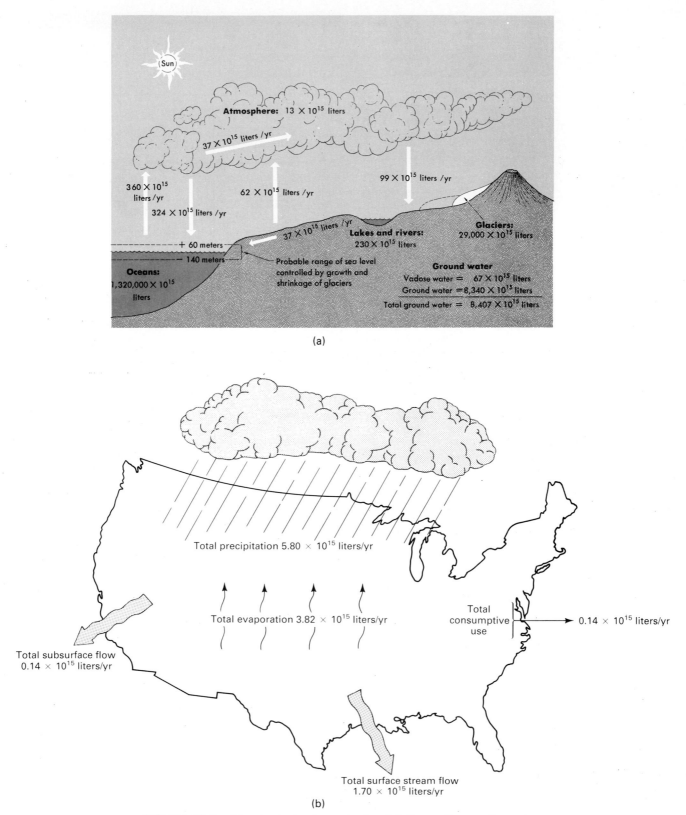

(a)

(b)

FIGURE 10-3. The hydrologic cycle for (a) the entire earth and (b) the continental United States. [(a) After A.L. Bloom, *The Surface of The Earth,* Englewood Cliffs: Prentice Hall, 1969; (b) from *The Nation's Water Resources 1975–2000,* The Water Resources Council, 1968.]

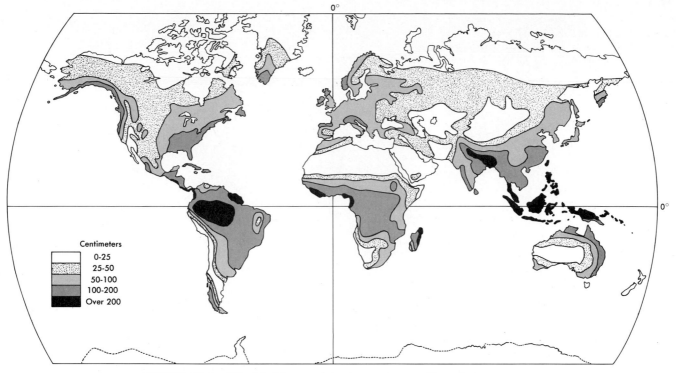

FIGURE 10-4. Worldwide precipitation patterns. Note that a zone of high rainfall lies along the equator and that more arid zones lie along belts that are 25 to 30 degrees north and south of the equator. (From B.J. Skinner, *Earth Resources,* 3rd edition, Englewood Cliffs: Prentice Hall, 1986.)

the earth's reception of solar energy and the movement of the major atmospheric cells (Hadley cells). They may be significantly affected by major ocean currents (e.g., Humboldt Current that results in the extension of desert conditions up the west coast of South America) and by major mountain chains (e.g., the desert regions of the western United States that lie on the eastern flank of the Rocky Mountains).

The United States is, in general, an example of a relatively rich country in terms of water resources because it receives an average of about 75 centimeters (30 inches) of rainfall per year. This rainfall is, however, quite irregularly distributed with annual values ranging from more than 250 centimeters (100 inches) in some mountainous areas of Washington, Oregon, and North Carolina, to less than 10 centimeters (4 inches) in some desert regions of the southwest [Fig. 10.5(a)]. The actual amounts of precipitation vary significantly with the highest percentage variations occurring in the areas of lowest average precipitation. The eastern United States, thanks largely to the Gulf of Mexico, enjoys an abundant supply of water and receives 65 percent of the total precipitation in the continental states whereas the western part of the country, due largely to high mountains, is subject to a deficiency of water. This geographic variation is compounded by temporal variations tied to long-term weather fluctuations. Thus, although water is a re-

newable resource, the rate of renewal is neither uniform nor totally predictable. Accordingly, the long term availability of water to satisfy national needs requires both efficient storage systems and effective distribution systems.

Water is returned to the atmosphere from land or standing water by evaporation and by **transpiration**—the loss of water by plants directly to the atmosphere. The average annual evaporation rate for a site is calculable on the basis of weather conditions, is readily tested by simple experiments, and is hence well established for many areas [Fig 10.5(b)]. The rates are highest where solar insolation (radiation) and winds are greatest and especially where humidity is least, and are lowest where temperatures are lowest. Transpiration is a function of the type of plants involved as well as weather conditions and can vary markedly, depending on the vegetation cover of an area. Nevertheless, the effects of both processes are to return water into the atmosphere, cool the surface where they occur, and reduce the availability of free water for agriculture, domestic, or industrial use. For the world, the combined evapotranspiration rate is about 62 percent (see Fig. 10.3) and for the United States it is about 70 percent. The percentages are much greater in areas of low rainfall and high temperature and much lower in areas of high rainfall and cooler climate. In arid countries, such as Australia, the fraction of water

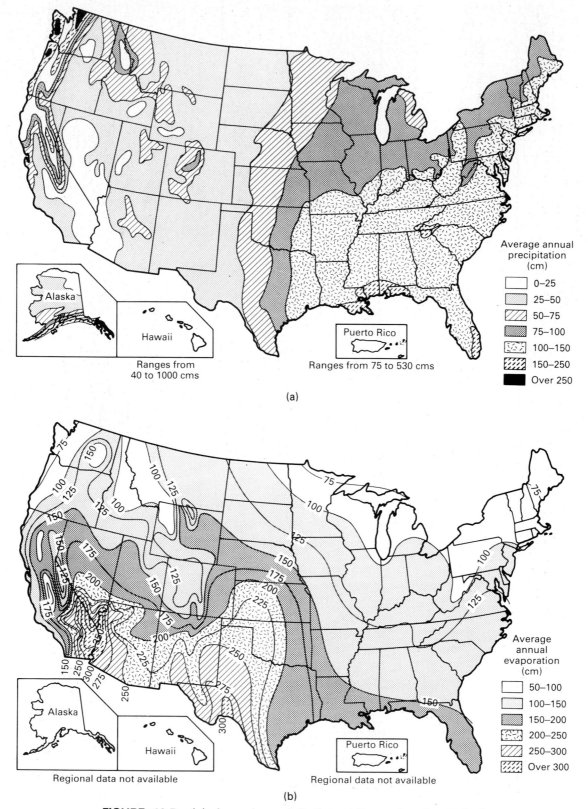

FIGURE 10-5. (a) Annual precipitation patterns for the United States. (b) Annual pan evaporation pattern for the United States. (c) Annual runoff patterns for the United States. (d) General water surplus-deficiency relationship in the United States. From *The Nation's Water Resources, 1975–2000,* The Water Resources Council, 1968.

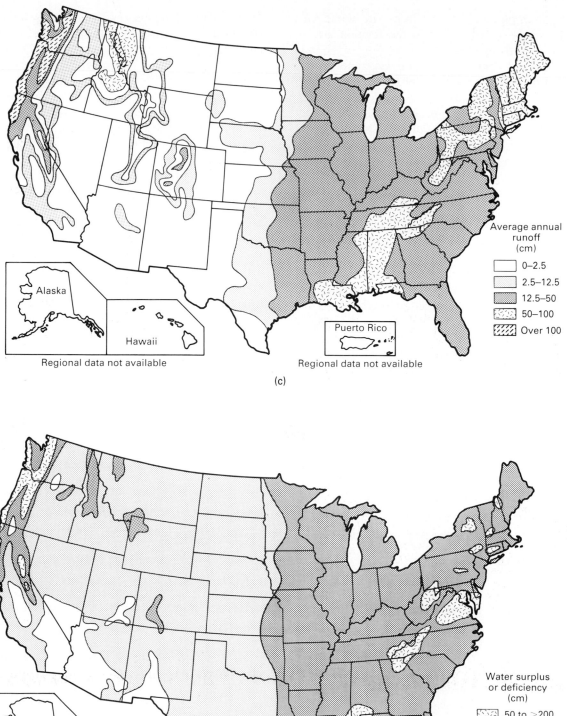

(c)

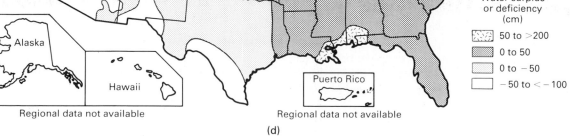

(d)

FIGURE 10-5. (*cont.*)

lost to evapotranspiration is very large. In humid climates such as that in Great Britain the fraction lost to this process is relatively small.

The type and density of natural vegetation commonly reflect the availability of water in a region. In areas of low rainfall, plant cover will develop to a point where all precipitation is used in evapotranspiration and none is left for stream flow. Additional plant growth can only occur if there is ground water to support it. Ephemeral (or temporary) streams may, of course, flow during periods of high rainfall. In several parts of the southwestern United States pest plants, such as mesquite, have become such major consumers of both surface and ground water that they threaten the meager supplies available and are the objects of major eradication programs.

Evapotranspiration is a significant contributor to problems of surface water and soil quality in many arid parts of the world, including the desert southwest of the United States. There, the very high evaporation rates, exceeding 250 centimeters (100 inches) over large areas, result in the loss of very large quantities of water in reservoirs created by dams. These losses reduce the availability of water for any use and the capacity to generate hydroelectric power. In addition, the evaporation from rivers and reservoirs leads to a deterioration of the water quality because of the residual concentration of salts (see p. 333). The buildup of salts on the surface of irrigated fields in areas of high evapotranspiration has resulted worldwide in the deterioration or loss of millions of acres of previously productive crop land (see p. 334).

Surface Water—Rivers and Lakes

The presence of rivers and lakes is an indication that the precipitation in an area exceeds the losses of water to evapotranspiration and ground water seepage. In a very general sense the annual runoff pattern for the United States [Fig. 10.5(c)], therefore, reflects the combined effects of precipitation [Fig. 10.5(a)] and evaporation [Fig. 10.5(b)]. Thus, the areas of high rainfall are areas of high runoff and large areas of low rainfall such as parts of the western states have essentially no runoff at all. It is, of course, important to remember that many areas in which the average annual evaporation exceeds average annual precipitation still have significant stream flow, at least for part of the year. This occurs because neither rainfall nor evaporation are constant during all seasons of the year or all times of the day. Precipitation may be seasonal but usually can occur at all hours of the day, whereas evaporation increases sharply during summer months and during afternoon hours. Furthermore, in periods of high rainfall much of the water may flow out of an area before there is time for it to evaporate.

The Water Resources Council has found, on the basis of available surface water and water demand, that the eastern portion of the United States constitutes an area of water surplus whereas the western (and geographically larger) region is generally an area of water deficiency [Fig. 10.5(d)]. This pattern of water availability has played, and will continue to play, an important role in population distribution and in the manner of land use and resource exploitation. In order to permit accurate assessment of the regional water supply and demand, the continental United States has been subdivided into 18 Water Resources Regions by the U.S. Water Resources Council, primarily on the basis of major surface water drainage systems (Fig. 10.6).

The 30 percent of precipitated water shown as flowing in rivers and streams into the oceans in Fig. 10.3 is a bit misleading because it does not show that considerable water, ultimately lost to evapotranspiration, actually first travels long distances as stream flow. Much of this water has, in fact, already been used in domestic water supplies and in industry before it returns to the atmosphere.

Ground Water

The earth's near-surface rocks and soils serve as the storage site for quantities of water estimated to be 3000 times larger than the volume of water in all rivers at any given time and 35 times larger than the volume of all inland lakes and seas. Although this water represents, by far, the largest quantity of accessible fresh water, it often represents a nonrenewable resource because the natural rates of recharge are so slow relative to the rapid rates at which we withdraw it. Deep ground water often consists of water trapped and isolated in sediments some time in the geologic past. In contrast, shallow ground water supplies are often intimately related to surface water as shown in Fig. 10.7. Depending on the land surface slope, vegetation, soil depth, and rock-type, widely varying amounts of precipitation and runoff may percolate into the intergranular pore spaces and fractures. In most areas, the water percolates downward until it reaches the **water table**, the surface below which the pores and fractures are water filled. The water table is not flat but usually has a shape that is similar to, but smoother than, the topography of the land surface.

Above the water table is an unsaturated or **vadose** region of the soil. The upper part of this zone fills with water when it rains but then drains relatively quickly except for water adhering to mineral surfaces. However, even this small amount of water is very important because it is the principal water supply for most plants. During periods of drought this upper soil zone can also lose much water directly to evaporation. Under these conditions some moisture actually moves upward by

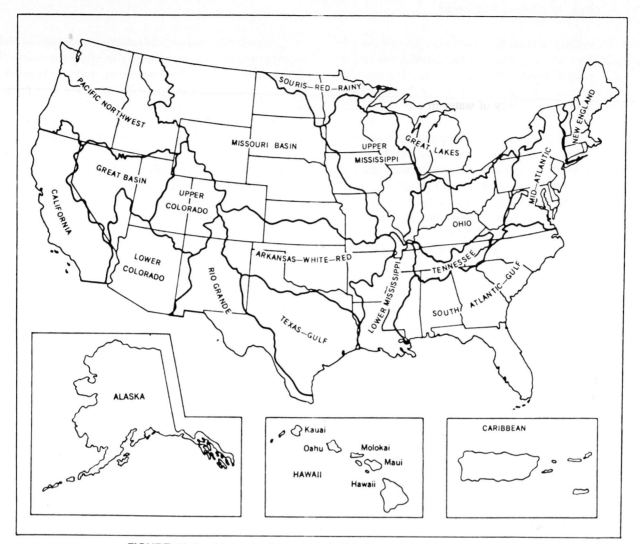

FIGURE 10-6. Major hydrologic subdivisions of the United States; these are named for geographic area or major rivers in the areas. (From *The Nation's Water Resources, 1975–2000,* U.S. Water Resources Council, 1968.)

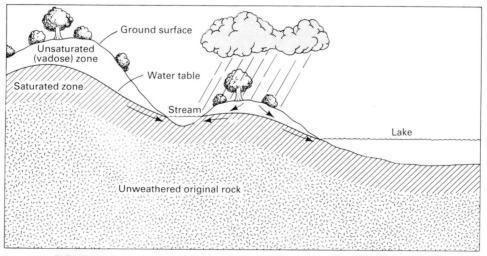

FIGURE 10-7. Cross section of a typical soil zone showing the relationship of the water table to the ground surface, streams, and lakes.

means of capillary action. Somewhat deeper is a zone in which the flow of water through the unsaturated soil or rock is downward toward the water table. The soil and vadose water zones do not constitute direct resources of water but are essential for the replenishing of the ground water zones.

It is important to recognize that most streams and lakes in equilibrium with their surroundings represent the intersection of the ground water table with the surface topography. It is the slow lateral seepage of ground water that provides the water for stream flow when there is no surface runoff. In humid areas, streams will continue to flow, although with reduced volumes, even in long periods of drought. In arid regions, where the ground water table may lie far below the land surface, streams will often flow after rainstorms only until the water has either evaporated or percolated into the subsurface. In these areas, the high rates of evapotranspiration commonly result in the return of most water to the atmosphere. The shallow penetration of the rainfall before being evaporated often allows the water to pick up dissolved salts that are then left as a near-surface soil cement (referred to as **caliche** or hard pan) that makes the soil less permeable and reduces the value of the soil for agriculture (see Chapter 11).

Aquifers, geologic formations that possess sufficient porosity and permeability to allow for movement of the water contained within them, underlie large areas of the United States (Fig. 10.8). In many arid parts of the world, aquifers constitute the only significant source of water. Even in more humid parts of the world where surface water is present, aquifers are commonly utilized as major water sources because they provide a relatively constant flow of good quality water.

The major problems in the utilization of ground water are rate of water flow, rate of recharge, and water quality. The surfaces of many parts of the continents are underlain by metamorphic or igneous rocks in which the only available ground water is the meager quantities that lie in the fractures of joint systems or along faults. Interconnectedness of the joints allows ready movement of the water, but the quantities are often very limited. Even in many areas underlain by sedimentary rocks, porosity or permeability is too low to allow for a worthwhile rate of water flow. If an aquifer is to have a sustained yield, there must be a constant replenishment from surface water through the generally slow process of percolation. It has been estimated that 150 years would be required to totally recharge all the ground water in the United States to a depth of 750 meters (2460 feet) if

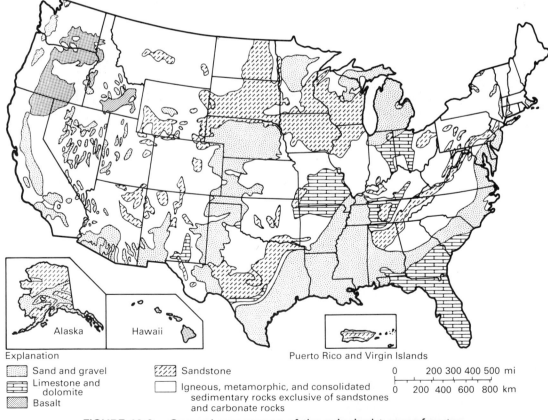

Explanation

▨ Sand and gravel   ▨ Sandstone

▤ Limestone and dolomite   ☐ Igneous, metamorphic, and consolidated sedimentary rocks exclusive of sandstones and carbonate rocks

▨ Basalt

Puerto Rico and Virgin Islands

0   200 300 400 500 mi

0   200 400 600 800 km

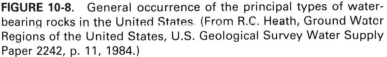

FIGURE 10-8. General occurrence of the principal types of water-bearing rocks in the United States. (From R.C. Heath, Ground Water Regions of the United States, U.S. Geological Survey Water Supply Paper 2242, p. 11, 1984.)

it were all removed. The problem of the slow recharge of aquifers is becoming evident in several parts of the world, including the western United States where withdrawal rates up to 100 times those of the recharge rates are rapidly lowering the water table (see p. 327). In these areas, the water is considered as being "mined" in that it is being extracted just as any other nonrenewable mineral commodity. The effect of the loss of water on land value is being recognized, so that the farmers who own the land are permitted to depreciate the land as the water table falls. Even in humid regions where there is abundant rainfall, the withdrawal of water from aquifers at rates exceeding those of recharge creates problems such as the draining of wells by depression of the water table and the movement of salt water into previously fresh water beds. The third problem of aquifers is water quality. As ground water moves through the rocks it dissolves the more soluble constituents. The problem varies with rock-type and flow rate and has been greatly aggravated in recent years by the introduction of contaminants from agricultural, domestic, and industrial sources. In general, water with less than 0.05 percent (500 parts per million) total dissolved solids is considered suitable for human consumption (specific requirements for potable water are listed in Table 10.1). However, water with up to 1 percent dissolved solids can be used for some purposes. Bacteria present within the soil may cleanse slow moving water of harmful natural biological contaminants. Unfortunately, complex synthetic chemical contaminants have seriously limited the usefulness of some aquifers, particularly where there is a rapid rate of water movement that spreads them much more rapidly than they can be filtered or decomposed by bacteria.

Another problem resulting from the withdrawal of water from aquifers is land subsidence. This is a local, but increasingly observed, phenomenon that can have serious consequences. This is discussed in greater detail on p. 328.

Icecaps and Glaciers

More than 70 percent of the world's nonsaline water is held in icecaps and glaciers. This water is primarily contained within the icecap and glaciers of Antarctica and is unavailable for virtually all practical purposes (Fig. 10.9). Proposals to tow large icebergs to water-deficient areas such as the Middle East have been discussed episodically but have not yet resulted in any significant financial backing or serious efforts. In the short term, the amount of water held in glaciers and icecaps may be considered constant, but in the not-too-distant geologic past—the Pleistocene or Ice Ages—the amount of water held as ice in these regions was as much as 50 percent greater than at present. During the major glacial advances, more of the snowfall over polar and cold temperate land masses built up and persisted with the result that glaciers advanced and sea level dropped as much as 100 meters (330 feet) below its present level.

Surface Runoff, Floods, and Flood Control

Most rainfall produces some **surface runoff**, that is, water which flows off the land surface in streams and rivers. The amount of this runoff is a function of the amount of rainfall, the slope and length of the drainage basin, the rock and soil type of the drainage basin, the vegetation cover, and the extent of any impermeable areas in the basin. The runoff may range from zero to more than 90 percent of total rainfall in a given basin. The remainder evapotranspires back into the atmosphere, percolates into the ground water system, or is held back in storage facilities.

Surface runoff may be characterized in terms of a **hydrograph** or **lag-time diagram** [Fig. 10.10(a)]. This depicts both the quantity and time of rainfall and the subsequent runoff from a drainage basin. Small drainage basins may have lag times measureable in minutes or hours, whereas large ones may have lag times of hours to days. Once the runoff characteristics have been determined for a basin, it is possible to predict water flow levels and to estimate potential flood conditions.

Activities, such as mining, timbering, farming, and construction, frequently promote an increase in the amount and rate of surface runoff as shown in Fig. 10.10(b). Consider, for example, the effects of urbanization of a previously tree or grass covered area. Construction of a typical suburban community makes 10–30 percent of the area impermeable (streets, driveways, houses, sidewalks, etc.) and construction of a city environment or large shopping center may make 50–100 percent of an area impermeable. Most of the water from the impermeable area runs off onto permeable areas, thereby subjecting the permeable sections to water conditions equivalent to added rainfall. The result of natural rainfall plus the effect of the added water is then the **equivalent rainfall**. Much of the added runoff water does not actually drain onto adjacent land but is carried by storm drains into streams or rivers. Nevertheless, that extra water will appear in some part of a drainage basin. Unfortunately, as more water runs off more rapidly, less of it is able to percolate into the soil to be added to the ground water system. Assuming uniform rain distribution in a basin and 100 percent runoff of water from impermeable areas (this is never true but suffices for the demonstration here), converting 25 percent of a basin to an impermeable condition results in a 33 percent increase in equivalent rainfall for the permeable portion, conversion of 33 percent to impermeable condition raises equivalent rainfall by 50 percent, and 50 percent impermeability raises equivalent rainfall by

TABLE 10-1

National drinking-water regulations*

Constituent	Maximum Concentration, p.p.m.
Arsenic	0.05
Barium	1
Cadmium	0.010
Chromium	0.05
Lead	0.05
Mercury	0.002
Nitrate (as N)	10
Selenium	0.01
Silver	0.05
Fluoride	1.4–2.4
Turbidity	1–5 turbidity units
Coliform bacteria	1/100 mL (mean)
Endrin	0.0002
Lindane	0.004
Methoxychlor	0.1
Toxaphene	0.005
2,4-D	0.1
2,4,5-TP Silvex	0.01
Total trihalomethanes [the sum of the concentrations bromodichloromethane, dibromochloromethane, tribromomethane (bromoform) and trichloromethane (chloroform)]	0.10
Radionuclides: (for units, see p. 36)	
Radium 226 and 228 (combined)	5 pCi/L
Gross alpha particle activity	15 pCi/L
Gross beta particle activity	4 mrem/yr

Constituent	Maximum Level, p.p.m.
Chloride	250
Color	15 color units
Copper	1
Dissolved solids	500
Foaming agents	0.5
Iron	0.3
Manganese	0.05
Odor	3 (threshold odor number)
pH	6.5–8.5
Sulfate	250
Zinc	5

Data from U.S. Environmental Protection Agency, 1982.

*The U.S. Environmental Protection Agency's National Interim Primary Drinking-Water Regulations and National Secondary Drinking-Water Regulations are summarized here. The primary regulations, which specify the maximum permissible level of a contaminant in water at the tap, are health related and are legally enforceable. If these concentrations are exceeded or if required monitoring is not performed, the public must be notified. The secondary drinking-water regulations control contaminants in drinking water that affect the esthetic qualities related to public acceptance of drinking water. These secondary regulations are intended to be guidelines for the States and are not federally enforceable.

100 percent. Of course, even in rather permeable soils, there can be some runoff during very heavy rainfall; thus, the actual increase in runoff resulting from pavement or construction also depends on the intensity and duration of the rainfall.

The increase in runoff that will inevitably result from increases in impermeable area due to urbanization can either be permitted to contribute to normal stream flow or can be controlled. An example of such control is found on Long Island, New York, where the runoff from impermeable areas is diverted into shallow catchment basins from which the water seeps downward enriching the ground water supply.

Flooding occurs when surface runoff exceeds a normal stream channel's capacity and the water spreads out onto the flood plain or beyond. Flooding is a natural

FIGURE 10-9. The world's icecaps and glaciers such as these in Victoria Land Antarctica contain most of the world's non-saline water. (Photograph by J.R. Craig.)

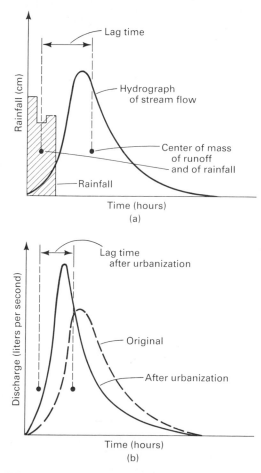

FIGURE 10-10. Hydrographs showing the relationships of rainfall, lag time, and runoff in an area (a) prior to, and (b) after urbanization. Note that after urbanization, the lag time is decreased and the rate of discharge is, for a while, greater than before urbanization. (From U.S. Geological Survey Circular 554.)

phenomenon brought on by intense or prolonged rainfall or rapid melting of snow cover. It is of little or no consequence in undeveloped areas, but our tendency to build homes, businesses, and factories on flood plains has brought us into conflict with nature and often into peril. Although the extent to which our activities actually cause flooding is not completely understood, it is evident from the previous discussion that the removal of vegetation from large parts of the drainage basins and the subsequent expansion of impermeable surfaces increases runoff and contributes to the potential for flooding. Once hydrographs (Fig. 10.10) have been defined they can serve as valuable aids in predicting floods and the time of their rise, crest, and fall.

In an effort to reduce the vast amounts of damage and the scores of deaths and injuries that occur annually as a result of flooding, two procedures are now widely used—the construction of dams and the channelization of rivers (Figs. 10.11 and 10.12, respectively). These processes operate on different principles but attempt to achieve the same result. **Dams** serve as temporary water barriers to hold back high flow before it reaches an area and hence prevent it from causing a flood. **Channelization**, in contrast, provides an efficient means by which water may be carried out of an area so quickly that it does not rise to flood levels.

Dams, of course, serve many other purposes, such as water storage for irrigation, electric power generation, recreation, and livestock watering, but in the United States a significant proportion of the more than 58,000 dams are used at least in part for flood control. The dams range from earthen barriers used for farm ponds, to the 250 meters (770 feet) high Oroville Dam in California, and to the 23 kilometer (14.5 mile) long Watkins Dam in Utah. Dams have been effective in the reduction of flooding and have provided the added benefit of generating very large amounts of electricity. They have also provided many new lakes for recreational purposes. Unfortunately, the water requirements for these activities are often incompatible. Flood control calls for the emptying of reservoirs, at least before anticipated heavy precipitation, so there is ample storage capacity for the runoff; power generation calls for a steady water flow or one cycled to match electricity demand; and recreation calls for lakes to remain at a constant high level. A contribution frequently overlooked is enrichment in the quantity of ground water around dam sites. As dams fill, ground water tables generally rise as more water percolates into the subsurface.

Against the advantages of dam construction must be weighed some disadvantages, such as sediment catchment, increased evaporation, loss of inundated land, interruption of river transport and fish migration, and environmental alteration. Construction of the Aswan High Dam in Egypt on the Nile River in the 1960s ended the

FIGURE 10-11. Dams such as the Tennessee Valley Authority's Fontana Dam in western North Carolina have been used for flood control, recreation, and hydroelectrical power generation. (Photograph courtesy of Tennessee Valley Authority.)

annual flooding of the Nile Valley and has provided electricity generation facilities, but the reservoir that formed is now filling with the sediment that for thousands of years served as natural fertilizer for the agriculture in the lower Nile Valley. This has markedly reduced soil fertility along the lower Nile and is rapidly leading to **eutrophication** of the reservoir behind the dam. In all arid regions, the damming of rivers provides water for many uses but at the same time promotes evaporative water loss and the buildup of salts in the remaining waters. The construction of nearly every new dam meets with opposition from those whose land will be inundated and from those who do not want to see further change of the natural environment. In the 1970s the concern for endangered species of both fish and plants in the United States nearly prevented the completion of massive dams in Tennessee and Maine. The discovery

of the snail darter, a 3-inch minnowlike fish found only in the area to be flooded by the $116 million Tellico Dam in Tennessee, provided the basis for halting construction for more than 1 year until it was determined that these fish could and do live in other rivers of the area. The finding of the Furbish lousewart, a wild snapdragonlike plant that was thought to be extinct, in the valley to be flooded by the $600 million Dickey-Lincoln Dam in Maine, provided grounds to delay the construction for many months until it was determined that additional colonies of the plants existed.

Channelization has provided an expedient means of flood control in many areas. The principle, illustrated in Fig. 10.12, is straightforward. Replacement of a natural sinuous channel by a shorter and straighter one allows for more rapid water flow out of a flood-prone area, thereby reducing the likelihood of a flood. The

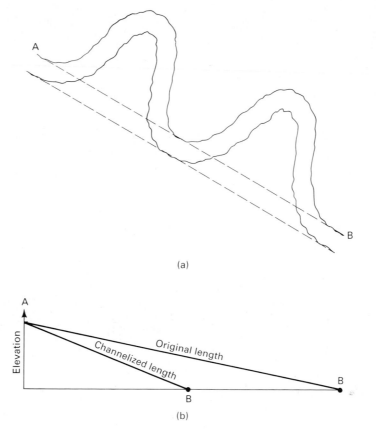

(a)

(b)

FIGURE 10-12. Channelization has frequently been used as a way to reduce flooding. (a) A plan view schematically shows the change from the original meandering channel (curved solid lines) to a reworked straight channel (dashed lines) to allow for more rapid water movement. (b) A profile shows that the straightening and shortening of the channel results in a steeper gradient and hence a more rapid flow of the water.

rate of water flow is increased because the straighter channel offers less resistance and because the gradient of the new shorter channel is steeper. Frequent secondary effects have included the lowering of the water table and drainage of swamp lands adjacent to the river. Such land then usually has considerable real estate value.

Although often effective and carried out in hundreds of areas, channelization has also been found to have significant drawbacks, such as increased erosion, transfer of flooding, reduced natural filtering of ground water, and the loss of wetlands habitat. Unless the channelization extends to a flood control reservoir or to the ocean, the rapid transport of water through one part of a river basin, only to dump it back into its original channel further downstream, merely transfers the problem of flooding downstream. An example of this in the United States is the Blackwater River in Johnson County, Missouri, where channelization did reduce local flooding but created extra flooding in adjacent counties downstream. The decrease in channel length from 53.6 to 29 kilometers (33.5 to 18 miles) nearly doubled the gradient and increased the water velocity that, in turn, increased stream channel erosion. The original channel was 15–30 meters (45–90 feet) wide, but erosion broadened the channel up to 70 meters (200 feet) and resulted

in the collapse of several bridges. The much greater rate of water flow tended to scour the channel and reduced the total amount of **biomass** production (fish, plants, algae, insects, etc.) in the river by about 80 percent.

In the 1960s, the Kissimmee River in central Florida (Fig. 10.13) was converted from its original 163-kilometer (102-mile) meandering bed into a 93 kilometer (58 mile) long canal with six small dams to control flooding. By the mid-1970s the state had realized that the channelization that had also drained thousands of acres of natural marshlands along the river had dramatically altered the delicate ecology of central Florida. The wetlands had served as an extremely important water filter to remove nitrogen and phosphorous from sewage and played a key role in supplying much of the water that evapotranspired into the atmosphere to provide frequent rainstorms. With the absence of the wetlands, rainfall decreased, water levels fell, water purity decreased, the water flow in the Kissimmee dropped, and water fowl and fish populations were essentially eliminated. In 1976, the state authorized restoration of the Kissimmee River to its original state. There is doubt whether this can ever be accomplished because land prices soared from the approximate $400 per acre value for the original marsh land to more than $4000 per acre for the drained land. The minimum cost of restoration

FIGURE 10-13. Photograph of the Kissimmee River in central Florida showing the difference between the original meandering course in the foreground and the straightened channel in the background. (Photograph courtesy of South Florida Water Management District.)

now exceeds $100 million. If carried out, more than $130 million will have been spent simply to restore the land to its original condition.

Dams and channelization remain two possible means of flood control; however, we have learned that both can have undesirable side effects that need to be evaluated before construction takes place.

OUR USE OF WATER

Water Usage and Consumption

Water is more widely used and more essential than any other resource. The amount used per capita, however, has varied widely as a function of each society's life style and standard of living. In discussing water usage, it is important to distinguish between **withdrawal** (sometimes called usage), which is the water physically extracted from its source, and **consumption**, which is the withdrawn water that is no longer available because it has been evaporated, transpired, incorporated into products or crops, consumed by humans or livestock, or otherwise held from returning to its source.

Withdrawal uses of water are generally subdivided into: (1) public supply (for domestic, commercial, and industrial use); (2) rural supply (domestic and livestock); (3) irrigation; and (4) self supplied industrial (including thermoelectric). Hydroelectric power generation, in which water is actually withdrawn only to the extent that it is diverted through turbines to generate electricity, is considered a special category. The distribution of the water withdrawn varies according to the type of society and the climatic conditions in an area [Fig. 10.14(a)]. In the United States, public supplies account for approximately 7 percent of water withdrawal—about 110×10^9 liters (29×10^9 gallons) per day total or 636 liters (168 gallons) per day per capita. About 36 percent of this figure is transport loss and public use, such as fire fighting and public swimming pools. Some idea of the large quantities of water required to support our modern western life style may be gained from the data presented in Table 10.2. Most of the water withdrawn for public supply is returned to its source after use, hence consumption [Fig. 10.14(b)] is relatively small.

Rural water withdrawn from private wells constitutes only about 1 percent of U.S. water usage, but in many sparsely populated areas this represents the dominant water supply. The use at any one site varies from the small amounts withdrawn for a single house to very large quantities used to supply large herds of livestock. In many lesser developed parts of the world the rural water supply commonly constitutes the major water source for large segments of the population (Fig. 10.15). Because rural water is used for many agricultural purposes as well as for household needs, a somewhat larger proportion of the rural water is consumed.

Supplying Our Cities

The growth of cities has always required the availability of continuous supplies of freshwater. Hence, virtually all ancient, and most modern, cities were established

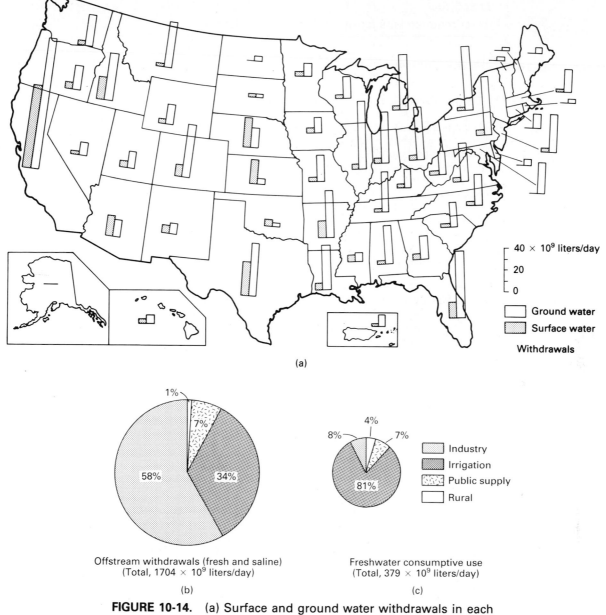

40 × 10⁹ liters/day

20

0

☐ Ground water

▨ Surface water

Withdrawals

(a)

1%

7%

58%

34%

☐ Industry

▨ Irrigation

▨ Public supply

☐ Rural

4%

8%   7%

81%

Offstream withdrawals (fresh and saline)
(Total, 1704 × 10⁹ liters/day)

(b)

Freshwater consumptive use
(Total, 379 × 10⁹ liters/day)

(c)

FIGURE 10-14. (a) Surface and ground water withdrawals in each of the United States. The total withdrawal of water (b) from streams and rivers and the total consumptive use (c) of water in the United States for industry, irrigation, public supply, and rural use. (From U.S. Geological Survey Circular 1001.)

along rivers or where there were ample springs. As cities grew, so did their need for water. When these needs exceeded local supplies, it became necessary to find additional water and to develop means to transport it to urban distribution centers.

The earliest human-made water transportation systems, or **aqueducts**, were probably stream channels that were altered or extended so that they flowed into more accessible areas. Biblical Jerusalem was served by an aqueduct consisting of limestone blocks through which a

38-centimeter hole had been drilled by hand. The Greeks bored tunnels, up to 1280 meters long at Athens, and built masonry structures to carry water. The ancient masters of the construction of aqueducts were, however, the Romans who built nine major aqueducts that brought 322 million liters (85 million gallons) of water a day to Rome in 97 A.D. All told, the Romans constructed aqueducts (Fig. 10.16) to service nearly 200 of their cities and some of their mining efforts throughout their empire. Few additional aqueducts were built until the late

TABLE 10-2

Water requirements for modern western society

Activity or Product	Water Required (liters)	(gallons)
Home use:		
Shower (per minute)	19	5
Bath	114	30
Toilet flush	15	4
Automatic washing machine	114	30
Hose flow per hour of lawn watering or car washing	1136	300
Food production:		
Sugar per ton	946,000	250,000
Corn per ton	946,000	250,000
Rice per ton	9,460,000	2,500,000
Milk per gallon	61,000	16,000
Beef per pound	14,000	3700
Nitrate fertilizer per ton	568,000	150,000
Industrial:		
Paper	23,700	62,500
Bricks per ton	950–1900	250–500
Oil refining per 42-gal barrel	1770	468
Synthetic rubber per ton	2,500,000	660,000
Aluminum per ton	1,325,000	350,000
Iron per ton	113,600	30,000
Human survival:		
70 kg (154 lb) person per year	720	190

(Data from: *Scientific American,* September 1963, World Book Encyclopedia, and U.S.G.S. pamphlet Water & Industry)

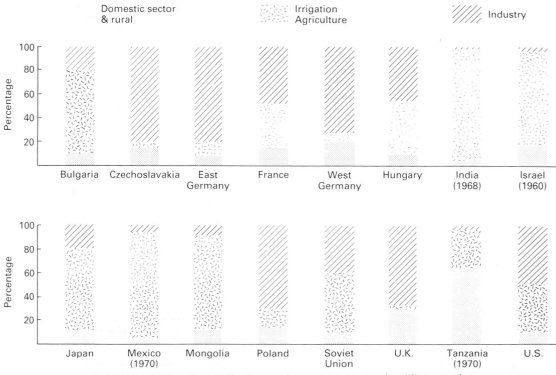

FIGURE 10-15. The differences in water usage in 16 countries reflect their different types of economies. [From The Global Report 2000 (1980).]

FIGURE 10-16. Supplying water to cities has been a major concern since the Romans built aqueducts, such as the Pont du Gard at Nimes, France, to transport water to nearly 200 cities. This was built in the first century A.D. and carried water from two springs to Nimes and is one of the best preserved of Roman structures. (Photograph courtesy of the French Government Tourist Office.)

1500s when Sir Francis Drake, then mayor, constructed one that was 39 kilometers (24 miles) long for Plymouth, England. In 1609 a 61-kilometer (38-mile) aqueduct called the New River was built to bring water to London.

In the era of modern cities, even though the demand for water has increased, the large scenic aqueducts of the past have been nearly completely replaced by buried steel pipes and pumping stations. A prime example is New York City where a complex system of aqueducts links 15 major reservoirs containing more than 1860×10^9 liters (approximately 490×10^9 gallons), some of which are as much as 200 kilometers (125 miles) from the city (Fig. 10.17). In spite of the vastness of the system used to supply New York City, there is little problem because the abundance of rainfall in the northeastern United States provides more than adequate water for all other users as well as those in New York. Another major modern aqueduct system is that which extends more than 1100 kilometers (685 miles) in California to bring water from many parts of the state to Los Angeles. It is discussed later in this chapter under "Water for Drinking—The Los Angeles Aqueduct System."

Irrigation

Irrigation has become an essential requirement for farming in large areas of the world where soils are sufficiently fertile, but rainfall is too low or too irregular to support the types of crops being grown. Water demand for this purpose has been rising rapidly and is now approximately 30 percent of total U.S. usage and as much as 80–90 percent of usage in India and Mexico (Fig. 10.15). In the United States as in many countries, the withdrawal of water for irrigation takes place on a very irregular geographic distribution pattern depending on rainfall. Thus, the eastern part of the United States uses only approximately 5 percent of its water withdrawal for irrigation, whereas the western United States uses 90 percent of its water for this purpose. Irrigation systems range from simple siphons (Fig. 10.18) in which gravity carries water from a main water course into the furrows, to large mechanized walking systems [Fig. 10.19(a)] that may systematically distribute water from a central well in a circular pattern up to 1.6 kilometers (1 mile) in diameter [Fig. 10.19(b)]. Depending on the weather conditions and the crops raised, irrigation may consume very large quantities of water. For example, whereas irrigation constituted only 34 percent of total U.S. water used in 1975, it accounted for 83 percent of water consumed. The demand for irrigation water has resulted in the building of elaborate surface water catchment and transport systems as seen in the lower Colorado River region (p. 324) and in areas where severe drainage of ground water from parts of some aquifers, such as the Ogallala where 150,000 wells now draw water (p. 330) for farms along the eastern flank of the Rocky Mountains.

Water for Industry and Hydroelectricity

Self-supplied industrial water (i.e., water drawn from rivers or wells) is the dominant form of water usage in the United States and in many parts of the industrial world. The vast proportion of this water, more than 80 percent, is used by thermoelectric plants (i.e., coal, oil, gas, or nuclear power plants) to generate steam to turn turbines. Only a small proportion of the industrially used water is actually consumed within products or lost to evaporative cooling, hence most of it is returned to its source. Thus about 99 percent of the total water with-

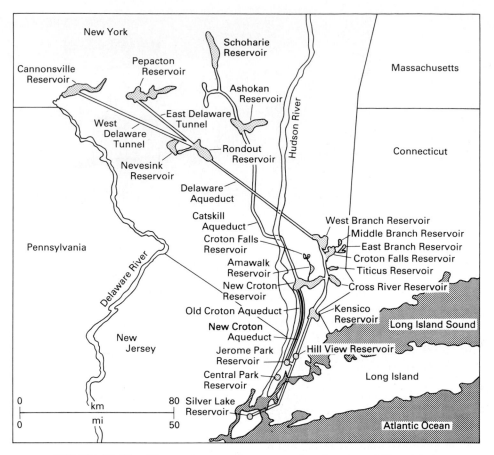

FIGURE 10-17. The water supply system for the city of New York links 15 major reservoirs, some as much as 200 kilometers away, to meet the needs of approximately 10 million people. (After a map courtesy of the City of New York Department of Water Resources.)

drawn by thermoelectric plants is used for condensing spent steam from generators. The principal concerns for industrial water are therefore not that it is consumed but rather that it may be contaminated by industrial chemicals and, to a lesser degree, its elevated temperatures.

The problems associated with availability and quality of water make it likely that, in the future, increasing numbers of industries will turn to recirculating water systems to reduce withdrawals and that thermoelectric power plants will turn to the use of seawater for cooling.

By the late 1970s, it was estimated that hydroelectric power generation (see Fig. 10.11) in the United States was using 2.75 times as much water as runs off the country in its rivers and streams. This apparent impossibility results from the repeated reuse of water within pumped-storage power plants (where excess electricity generation capacity is used to pump back into a reservoir so that it can be used another time), from the repeated reuse that occurs in successive hydroelectric plants along the same river and from the use of some

water before it is evaporated or consumed in irrigation. The process of hydroelectric power generation itself consumes very little water, but the ponding of large reservoirs behind power dams, especially in arid regions, does result in the evaporative loss of significant quantities of water.

The potential for hydroelectric power generation in a country like the United States has been largely developed. Although the potential generating capacity for the world is approximately seven times that presently generated, the development of additional hydroelectric capacity will be hampered by the remoteness of suitable areas from population centers (see also Chapter 5).

The United States is a relatively water-rich nation but because of its size and variable climate it has an irregularly distributed water supply. The differences in supply and consumption of the various water regions are considerable (Table 10.3), but it is apparent that by the late 1970s the nation was withdrawing only about one-third of available runoff and consuming only about one-third of that withdrawn. In spite of the remaining large

FIGURE 10-18. Simple gravity siphon irrigation system in which the water flows from a feed canal into furrows across the field. (Courtesy of B.B. Ross.)

capacity for development, local supply problems are becoming increasingly apparent and careful decisions will be needed in future years to insure a constant high quality supply.

The **Global 2000 Report to the President** (1978) has summarized the world water supply situation and notes that there will apparently be adequate water available on the earth to satisfy aggregate totals of projected water withdrawals in the year 2000. However, because of the regional and temporal nature of water resources, and the local demands that do not always correspond to the abundances, shortages will probably be more frequent and more severe than those experienced today.

Water Composition and Quality

The waters of the earth range widely in composition and suitability for human usage. The most pure spring or rain waters may have as little as 30 parts per million (0.003 percent) dissolved materials, whereas the most saline waters, such as found in the Dead Sea or Great Salt Lake, may have nearly 300,000 parts per million

(30 percent) dissolved substances (Table 10.4). Seawater, which constitutes more than 97 percent of the earth's water, is remarkably homogeneous, with about 35,000 parts per million (3.5 percent) dissolved salts. In general, waters with more than 500 parts per million (0.05 percent) dissolved salts are considered unsuitable for human consumption and those with more than 2000 parts per million (0.2 percent) are unsuitable for most other human uses. The dissolved constituents in surface and ground water are derived from the atmosphere and from the soils and rocks with which they come in contact (see Chapter 11). Rain water and snow generally contain a predominance of bicarbonate (from the solution of atmospheric carbon dioxide) but only a few parts per million of salts, dominantly sodium chloride carried in the winds from ocean spray. Other natural sources of atmospheric salts are volcanic eruptions that can release significant amounts of sulfates and chlorides into the atmosphere, wind blown dust from continental areas, and organic aerosols released by vegetation. In recent years there has been a growing concern about the effects on the quality of rain waters of both gases and particulate matter released by industrial processing and as a result of fossil fuel combustion. Numerous studies have

(a)

(b)

FIGURE 10-19. (a) Walking irrigation system used to disperse water over large fields. (b) Aerial view of a large center-well walking irrigation system in which a central well supplies water sprinklers that continuously proceed in circular paths up to 1 mile (1.6 kilometers) in diameter. (Photographs courtesy of Valmont Industries, Inc.)

TABLE 10-3

United States water supply and consumption (billions of liters per day, bld)

	Average Runoff				Dependable Supply (bld)	Withdrawals		Freshwater Consumption or Export (bld)	Evaporation (bld)
	Area (×10³ sq km)	cms per yr	bld	Annual Flow Exceeded in 90% of yr (bld)		Surface (bld)	Ground-water (bld)		
1. New England	186	58	298	185	83	19	2.4	1.8	0
2. Mid-Atlantic	272	41	306	257	136	69	10.1	7.0	0
3. South Atlantic-Gulf	717	46	880	488	284	93	20.6	18.4	0
4. Great Lakes	295	36	274	204	261	162	4.6	9.8	0
5. Ohio	922	48	526	284	182	132	7.0	6.8	0
6. Tennessee	106	53	154	106	53	28	1.0	1.2	0
7. Upper Mississippi	492	20	288	136	117	47	9.0	4.4	0.2
8. Lower Mississippi	269	38	284*	144	95	55	18.3	15.3	0
9. Souris-Red Rainy	153	3	23	8	11	1	0.3	0.4	0.1
10. Missouri Basin	1323	8	216	110	114	144	39.4	58.7	18.6
11. Arkansas-White-Red	642	15	247	136	76	49	33.5	30.5	9.9
12. Texas-Gulf	469	10	128	42	64	64	27.3	42.6	6.5
13. Rio Grande	344	2.5	18	8	11	24	8.9	16.1	2.8
14. Upper Colorado	293	8	47	333	30	26	0.5	12.3	2.7
15. Lower Colorado	365	1	23**	4	8	34	19.0	17.4	4.5
16. Great Basin	368	3	22	11	11	30	5.4	14.3	1.2
17. Pacific Northwest	717	51	1009	560	265	142	27.8	45.1	7.6
18. California	458	20	272	114	106	150	72.5	100.6	2.5
CONTERMINOUS UNITED STATES	7891	23	5015	3130	1907	1269	307.6	402.7	56.6

*Does not include the inflow from the Upper Mississippi.

**Virtually all water flow in the Lower Colorado Basin is the result of inflow from the Upper Colorado. More than 95 percent of precipitation evapotranspirates before becoming stream flow.

From *The Nation's Water Resources 1975–2000,* U.S. Water Resources Council, 1978.

TABLE 10-4

Compositions of some typical river waters in the United States and ocean water

Substance (ppm)	Kootenai River, Roxford, MO	Mississippi River, Cape Graidean, MO	Arkansas River, Derby, KS	Chicorrea Creek, Hebron, NM	Colorado River, Hoover Dam, AZ	Delaware River, Philadelphia, PA	Ocean Water
Silica (SiO_2)	6.9	6.8	13	11	8.7	45	—
Iron (Fe^{2+})	0.06	0.18	—	—	0.01	—	—
Calcium (Ca^{2+})	46	47	107	225	92	18	413
Magnesium (Mg^{2+})	14	14	26	129	30	5.0	1288
Sodium (Na^+)	3.8	11	355	3.2	106	13	10,717
Potassium (K^+)	1.0	4.0	13		5.3	2.1	385
Bicarbonate (HCO_3^-)	160	138	249	380	159	28	—
Carbonate (CO_3^{2-})	0	0	0	0	0	0	—
Sulfate (SO_4^{2-})	45	64	217	1300	322	39	2863
Chloride (Cl^-)	2.0	12	505	48	104	19	19,275
Fluoride (F^-)	1.2	0.4	1.0	0.6	0.4	0.2	—
Nitrate (NO_3^-)	0	7.9	9.3	17	2.0	13	—
Total Dissolved Solids	215	254	1375	2220	763	128	35,000
pH	7.9	7.5	8.0	7.4	8.0	7.3	8.1

(Data from Quality of Surface Waters of the U.S., Geological Survey Water Supply Paper 2141-2150, 1969.)

demonstrated an increase in the acidity of rainfall in certain areas (so called **acid rain**), which has been found to be harmful to vegetation, fish, and many terrestrial organisms and which promotes the weathering of building materials and natural rocks. In recent years, the pH of rainfall has dropped to 4.5–4.2 over large parts of southern Norway, southern Sweden, and the eastern United States. The most extreme case was a rainfall of pH 2.4, equivalent to the acidity of vinegar, in Scotland in 1974. Two primary causes of acid rain appear to be sulfur dioxide (SO_2) and nitrogen oxides (NO_X) generated by the burning of fossil fuels in power plants, industries, and motor vehicles.

Most of the dissolved substances in terrestrial waters are derived from the associated rocks, but the degree of concentration varies not only with rock-type but also with the duration of contact and the amount of evaporative concentration. Compositions of waters in several American rivers that are typical of waters worldwide are listed in Table 10.4. The differences demonstrate the effects of evaporative concentration (higher salt levels in rivers from Kansas, Arizona, and New Mexico) that occur in arid parts of the world. The partial dissolution of limestone leads to higher concentrations of calcium, magnesium, and bicarbonate. Evaporation leads to higher concentrations of all substances, especially sodium chloride. Most surface waters are usable directly for most purposes, but the evaporative concentration has caused significant deterioration in some

waters in arid regions. An example is the problem of the high salinity of the Colorado River as it passes from the United States into Mexico (see p. 324).

The U.S. Public Health Service and World Health Organization have established recommended maximum limits for the concentrations of many mineral, organic, and synthetic substances in public water supplies (Table 10.1). Of particular concern is the accidental introduction of synthetic organic chemicals into water supplies because many have toxic effects even in extremely low concentrations. The maximum total dissolved solids should not exceed 500 parts per million, but numerous public and private supplies, especially in arid regions and many developing countries, yield waters that are above this limit (usually excess sodium chloride), because better water is not available or because costs to purify the water to meet these standards are prohibitive. There will be increased difficulty, both in maintaining old and in developing new clean water supplies in future years as population pressures mount and the number and complexity of possible chemical contaminants grows.

Water Ownership

The ownership of most mineral resources is relatively straightforward because they are static materials lying on or below the land surface in some relatively easily definable form. In most areas of private land ownership, the resources are considered a part of the land and may

be exploited at the discretion of the owner, subject to state and local zoning regulations. Frequently, however, mineral rights have been separated from land ownership or have been sold or leased by the land owners to companies. The companies may exercise these rights to extract mineral resources if they comply with state and local laws regarding disturbance to overlying or adjacent properties.

The ownership of water, in its constant movement in visible surface waterways and invisible subsurface aquifers, has commonly been much less well defined. The present rules of ownership and use differ from one country to another, but the complexities are perhaps best shown by considering the example of the United States where the existence of a relatively water-rich East and a relatively water-poor West has resulted in the enactment of different types of laws. It is impossible to briefly and thoroughly discuss the complexities of water law; hence, the following is intended to serve as an overview and to demonstrate the basis of modern American water laws.

Riparian Rights in the Eastern United States. Basic **riparian** law may be summarized as the right of every landowner to make reasonable use of a lake or stream that flows through, or borders on, his or her property as long as this use does not damage the similar rights of other landowners. Although now locally much modified by regulatory statutes to provide for cities or public utilities, the riparian principal still basically governs the use of surface water in most of the eastern states. It has generally functioned in a proportional manner with the understanding that when water is plentiful, all have plenty, and when water is scarce, all share the hardship. The major exception to this is that municipal water supplies are now usually given protection of the right of eminent domain; hence, in times of shortage, cities get their quantities of water first, and riparians share what remains. The sale of riparian rights to those who do not border on streams has been allowed in some states but is not common. Because the eastern United States generally has large and continuous water supplies, the riparian system has worked well.

Prior Appropriation in the Western United States. The law of **prior appropriation** grew out of the California gold rush when the forty-niners staked claims for placer gold and for the water to wash the gold from the gravel. The rights to both the gold and the water were, "First come, first served." This concept grew into the formalized laws that allowed the settlers in an area to make an appropriation of a specific quantity of water for any beneficial use, and that protected the appropriations on the basis of the oldest are honored first and newer appropriations are honored as long as there is sufficient water. Thus, in times of shortage the more recent appropriations would be denied water, whereas the earliest appropriations would always have some water unless there was none at all. In contrast to the riparian rights that are generally held only by the landowner adjacent to a stream, appropriation rights have generally been available for sale to anyone who would pay, even if he were long distances from the stream. The consequences of this are seen in California where cities such as Los Angeles were very far-sighted in the early 1900s and bought up water rights in areas hundreds of miles away in anticipation of their needs decades later. Today, Los Angeles exercises its appropriation right to secure water that is transported by a complex series of aqueducts. Protests over the removal of water from the source regions such as the Owens Valley east of San Francisco to Los Angeles have led to numerous law suits, small pitched battles, and even bombings of the aqueducts. Nevertheless, Los Angeles bought the water appropriations and will have the rights to use them until or unless the courts rule otherwise.

Just as many riparian principles have been altered, appropriation rights have now been modified or overlaid by various compacts, agreements, or legislature decrees in many areas to allow for either more equitable or more economical use to be made of the water. Nevertheless, the original stamp of the appropriative right is still clearly visible in the water laws of many western states.

Ground Water

However difficult or arbitrary have been decisions on surface water rights, the decisions on ground water rights have been even more difficult, because its source, its quantities, and its movements have generally been unknown. Most courts in the past, and some still today, follow the "English rule of absolute ownership" that states that ground water, like the rocks, belongs to the property and thus is the possession of the owner of the surface who can extract as much as he desires for any purpose. As long as wells were widely spaced and pumping relatively limited, there were few problems; however, the advent of modern high capacity pumps and the turning of many large cities to ground water for portions of their water supplies has resulted in the drying up of many shallow wells. This led to widespread application of the "American rule of reasonable use" that permits unlimited extraction of ground water for use on a plot of overlying land but not the removal of water to distant places for sale (e.g., to cities) without compensating farmers whose wells go dry as a result. In the western United States, many states have simply applied the law of prior appropriation to both ground water and surface water. However, increasingly the western states

have placed ground water usage under the control of water commissions so that this valuable resource is not subject to excessive nor wasteful withdrawals. Fortunately, in recent years, courts have increasingly considered our growing knowledge of the limits of ground water resources and the manner in which ground water moves rather than solely relying on previous rulings that assumed the presence of unlimited quantities.

POTENTIAL WATER PROBLEMS

Water, like most other mineral resources, is irregularly distributed over the earth's surface. Unfortunately, this distribution often does not correspond to our needs or desires for water at a given place and time. These inconsistencies have frequently led to problems of supply and quality and clearly suggest that such problems will increase in years to come. In general, humid regions with more than about 75 centimeters (30 inches) of annual precipitation have sufficient surface water available in the forms of lakes, rivers, and permanent streams to meet water needs. However, in areas of intense population concentration, especially those without neighboring large rivers, the local demand can easily exceed supplies. Arid regions are constantly plagued with inadequate surface water supplies, with the deterioration of water quality due to the evaporative concentration of salts, and in some areas, with dwindling ground water supplies.

It is not possible to chronicle here examples of all current and potential water problems, but the following pages do attempt to discuss some of the major problems with which we must contend in the near future.

Limited Surface Water Supplies— The Colorado River Project

Deserts, by virtue of the absence of life-sustaining water, have always been some of the most inhospitable areas of the world for humankind. We have partly overcome the aridity of the desert by diverting rivers into it and by pumping up ground water that occurs in underlying aquifers. Ancient irrigation systems brought about the spread of civilization from the Fertile Crescent—the valleys of the Tigris and the Euphrates in what is now Iraq—across Iran, Afghanistan, Pakistan, and India. More modern systems have allowed the spread of agriculture through arid regions of many lands and have converted parts of deserts in Israel and in California into some of the most productive regions in the world. The introduction of additional water supplies has allowed for the development of large population centers where naturally available surface water would not have permitted it.

The low latitude desert regions of the world have offered good sites for large scale agriculture and development because many of them permit year-round growth of crops. The extensive agricultural development of these areas does, however, call for the consumption of very large quantities of water. The high evaporation rates mean that the water becomes a nonrenewable resource because there can be little recycling, and there must be a constant influx of the water to maintain these activities. The sources of the massive amounts of water needed to develop and sustain our activities in arid regions have been twofold: water imported from rivers in more humid adjacent areas, and ground water. Water provision schemes for arid regions have met with considerable success as evidenced by the creation of millions of hectares of agriculturally productive land. Unfortunately, even some of the largest and most carefully planned projects have the potential for major problems. An example is the well-known Colorado River Project that supplies water to seven western states and Mexico [Fig. 10.20(a)]. Since the late 1800s, farmers have tapped the Colorado for its water. By the 1920s, it became apparent that the water of the Colorado was too valuable a resource to allow uncontrolled exploitation. Therefore, in 1922 the Colorado River Compact, signed by the states in its drainage basin, decreed that the upper basin states of Wyoming, Colorado, New Mexico, and Utah should forever get 7.5 million acre feet (= 9.2×10^{12} liters; 1 **acre foot** of water is equivalent to about 1.2×10^6 liters or 3.26×10^5 gallons) of water annually. The lower basin states of Arizona, California, and Nevada would draw an equal amount. In 1944, a treaty guaranteed Mexico 1.5 million acre feet (1.8×10^{12} liters) of water annually. Although the original treaty did not specify the quality of the water reaching Mexico, a subsequent agreement established that it should not contain more than about 900 parts per million dissolved solids. The problem that has arisen is threefold. The Colorado River does not generally carry as much as 16.5 million acre feet of water [Fig. 10.20(b)]; the water reaching Mexico has contained as much as 1500 parts per million of salt; and the Navajo Indian reservation, never considered in allotment schemes, has proposed a project that would claim a significant part of the Colorado River to irrigate its crops.

The original allocations of water between the upper and lower basin states were based on water flow estimates from 1896 until 1922. Unfortunately, these estimates were made during a particularly wet period during which the average annual flow was about 16.8×10^6 acre feet (20.6×10^{12} liters). Since 1931, however, the flow has only averaged about 13.1×10^6 acre feet (16.1×10^{12} liters), and in 1934 the flow was only 5.6×10^6 acre feet (6.9×10^{12} liters).

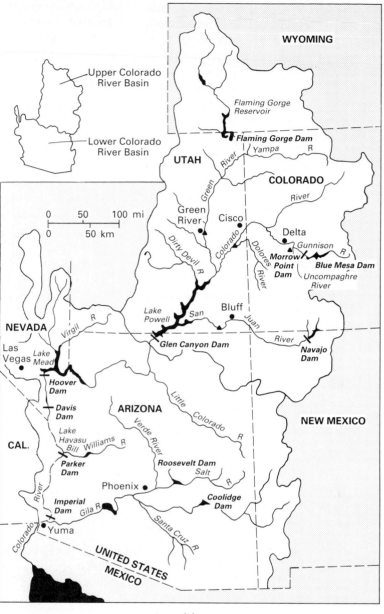

(a)

FIGURE 10-20. (a) The Colorado River basin showing the location of the major dams and lakes and the areas of the upper and lower basins. (b) The annual discharge of water in the Colorado River at Yuma, Arizona, from 1905 until 1964. The sharp decline from 1934 to 1938 represents the filling of Lake Mead behind Hoover Dam. The remainder of the decline resulted from increasing diversion of water for irrigation and municipal water supplies. (From U.S. Geological Survey Water Supply Paper 2275, 1985.)

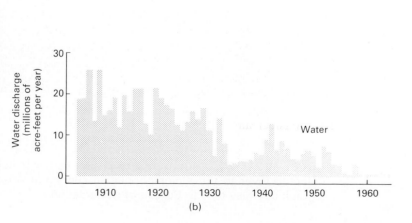

(b)

In order to smooth annual and seasonal fluctuations and to retain waters, an elaborate scheme has been built for trapping and tapping the Colorado River as is shown in Fig. 10.20(a). The dams store water for usage but also bring about an increase in the salinity by allowing extra evaporation. The problem of supply has not yet been fully felt because some states have not yet demanded their total allocation and the Navajo Indians have not pressed their demands. However, the completion of the Central Arizona Project (Fig. 10.21) in the 1980s results in Arizona's using its allocation and California having to give up the extra million acre feet over its allocation that it has been taking to satisfy the water needs of San Diego and Los Angeles. Furthermore, projections for future water demand for agriculture and for processing of energy resources (coal, oil, and perhaps oil shale) in the Colorado basin exceed the river's flow.

The solution to the problem of the quality of water being passed on to Mexico has been the construction of a large desalinization plant at Yuma, Arizona. This $350 million facility operating by **reverse osmosis**, will deliver 1.5 million acre feet (1.8×10^{12} liters) of water with only about 800 parts per million impurities to Mexico for its irrigation needs. The saline byproduct water from the plant, with about 8200 parts per million dissolved salts, will be channelled in a diversionary canal into the Gulf of California. The cost of the desalinated water to be delivered to Mexico to meet treaty obligations has been estimated at 30 times the cost of irrigation water in California.

Additional conflicts have arisen along the Colorado River basin over the function of the dams that hold back the large reservoirs. The dams have eliminated the problems of flooding that had previously occurred periodically along the lower Colorado; however, the dams are now often so filled with water being held for irrigation that they no longer have the excess capacity necessary to stop flood waters. Furthermore, the flood plains below the dams are now heavily populated. This limits the rapid release of water, sometimes needed to create the excess capacity for flood control. Compounding

FIGURE 10-21. The Central Arizona project carries water from the Colorado River to the major population centers in Arizona. (Photograph courtesy of U.S. Bureau of Reclamation.)

these problems is the need to be able to generate hydroelectric power to meet the increasing energy demands to pump water to the various areas served by the basin.

Ground Water Depletion and the Problem of the High Plains Aquifer

Under normal conditions, the quantity of ground water and the level of the water table exist in a long-term equilibrium in which the recharge is balanced by the discharge. If pumping begins, the equilibrium is disrupted and, in general, the ground water levels fall. If pumping is only of small quantities, the decline may be local, as a **cone-of-depression** around a single well. On the other hand, if pumping is of large quantities from many wells, the fall may be very widespread. Pumping may also bring about decreases in the natural discharge to streams, the sea, or in the rates of evapotranspiration.

A safe or a sustained yield is the amount of ground water withdrawal that may be pumped for long periods of time without a continuing drop in the water table. Withdrawals in excess of that quantity result in *water mining* and a progressive drop of the water table and, at some point, a decrease in the rate at which water can be pumped. Water mining is thus much like the mining of any other mineral resource except that there is often at least some replenishing of supplies by natural recharge.

The pumping of ground water has increased rapidly in this century in response to larger populations, increased industrial demands, the expansion of irrigation into semiarid regions, and the development of high capacity pumps. An example of this increase in the United States since 1950 is shown in Fig. 10.22. The present rate of pumping ($> 90 \times 10^9$ gallons per day; 340×10^9 liters per day) approaches 10 percent of the estimated 10^{12} gallons per day (3.8×10^{12} liters per day) of water estimated to be passing through the aquifers. Unfortunately, the demand for ground water is very unevenly distributed and often does not correspond to the rates of recharge. Hence, ground water mining with a resultant fall in the water table has indeed occurred in many parts of the United States as shown in Figs. 10.23 and 10.24.

The aquifers of the Atlantic and Gulf coastal plains are recharged by relatively high rainfalls (> 92 centimeters; 40 inches per year), but the heavy demands of dense population and industry have resulted in areas where there has been a fall in the water table in every coastal plain state. An example of this decline is the area near Houston, Texas, where the water table dropped nearly 100 meters from 1940 until 1970. Ground water levels in the upper Midwest and the western part of the United States display marked declines in

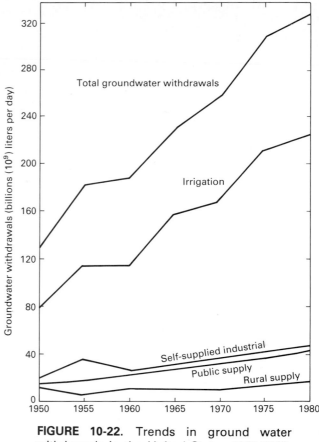

FIGURE 10-22. Trends in ground water withdrawals in the United States 1950-1980. (From U.S. Geological Survey Water Supply Paper 2250, p. 37, 1984.)

many areas because the lower rates of precipitation have been unable to recharge the aquifers as rapidly as pumping for irrigation withdraws water. This problem is especially prevalent in California, the nation's principal user of ground water. The California Department of Water Resources has determined that large drops in the ground water are occurring in 11 basins, eight of which are in the San Joaquin Valley, where agricultural irrigation is greatest. In the mid-1980s the water table was declining as much as 2 meters (6 feet) per year and averaged about 0.8 meters (2.5 feet) per year. The coastal basins, serving cities as well as irrigation schemes, experienced water table drops of as much as 65 meters (200 feet) from 1950–1983. Another prime example of water table decline is in Arizona, southeast of Phoenix, where water has been withdrawn for agricultural and municipal use since 1930. The average drop annually is now about 2.7 meters (8 feet) per year, and the total fall is nearly 130 meters (400 feet).

The southern high plains of the United States although commonly dry, hot, and windswept on the surface is the location of one of the major ground water accumulations in the United States—The Ogallala aquifer

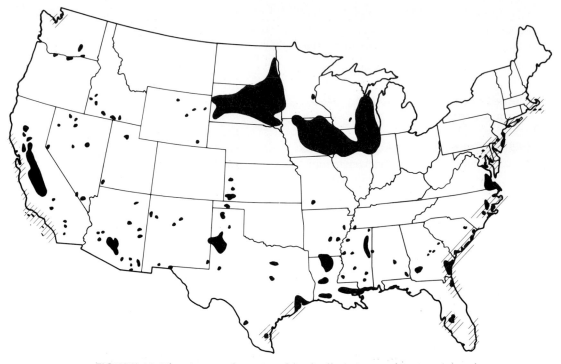

FIGURE 10-23. Areas of water table decline or artesian water-level decline in excess of 12 meters (40 feet) in at least one aquifer since predevelopment are shown in black. Areas of salt water intrusion into aquifers along coastal margins are shown by the striping. (From U.S. Geological Survey Water Supply Paper 2250, p. 40, 1984.)

(Fig. 10.25). This Miocene deposit contains more than 24,000 cubic kilometers of gravel much of which is saturated with high-quality ground water. The southern high plains, with an annual rainfall of 50–75 centimeters (20-30 inches) and an evaporation rate of 150–250 centimeters (60–100 inches) was the site of poor dry land farming until the water of the Ogallala was discovered in the 1930s. Since that time, some 150,000 wells have penetrated the aquifer to draw out millions of acre feet per year for use in irrigation. By the late 1960s, it became apparent that the water table in several parts of the aquifer was being depressed at rates as great as 1.5–2 meters per year. A few parts of the aquifer have actually registered a rise in the water table due to the addition of irrigation water, but large areas in the Texas Panhandle and in western Kansas have seen a drop in the water table of 30 meters or more in a span of less than 50 years. The mining of this water at present rates, in an area where recharge is effectively nil, will leave many parts of the Ogallala dry by the year 2000. At stake are some 5 million acres in six great plains states, an area as large as the state of Massachusetts, which have been major agricultural producers. The inevitability of the draining of the Ogallala and the nearly valueless nature of the land when there is no more water has even led the Internal Revenue Service to grant Texas high plains farmers a depreciation on their land as the water table drops.

The examples of ground water depletion discussed here are representative of a problem that is growing in magnitude both in the United States and worldwide. We shall either have to find ways to live with the amounts of continuously available water in each area or be willing to pay for massive water transport systems. We shall never find a way to live without water.

Land Subsidence Due to Ground Water Withdrawal

The removal of large quantities of ground water in some areas has resulted not only in the lowering of water tables but also in the local and significant subsidence of the land surface as shown in Fig. 10.26. Extraction of ground water from most aquifers has little or no effect on the land surface because the water is only interstitial to the grains of the rock that support the entire rock column. However, in some confined or semiconfined aquifers containing fine-grained sediments, the trapped water actually partially supports the rocks. Hence, when the water is pumped out there is a slow and generally irreversible subsidence of the land surface.

Although subsidence rates are rarely dramatic, the effects and damages can be considerable and include: (1) damage to well casings; (2) structural damage to buildings, roads, and bridges; (3) damage to buried cables,

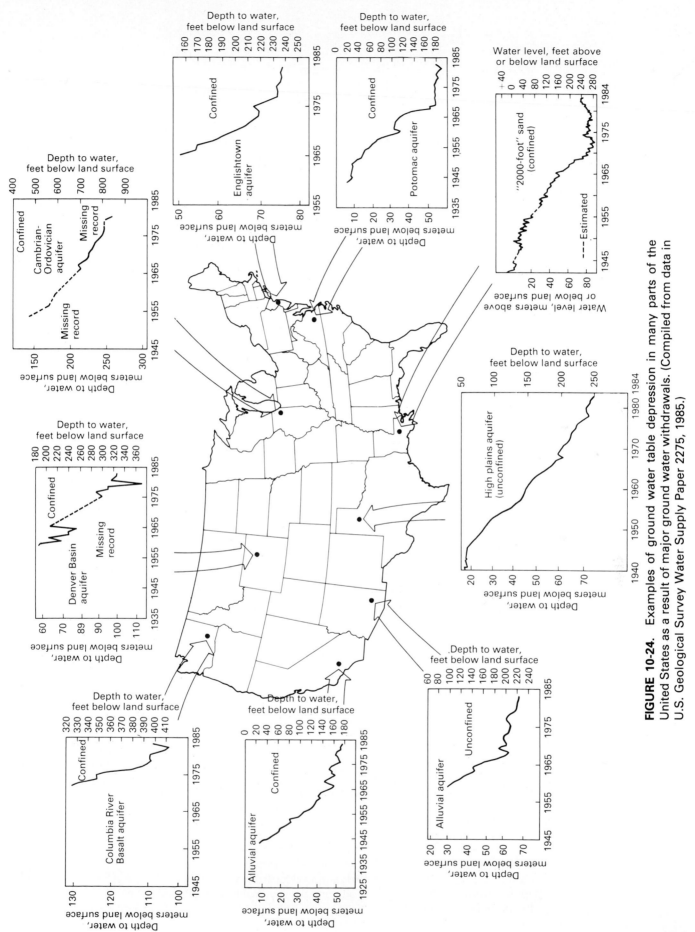

FIGURE 10-24. Examples of ground water table depression in many parts of the United States as a result of major ground water withdrawals. (Compiled from data in U.S. Geological Survey Water Supply Paper 2275, 1985.)

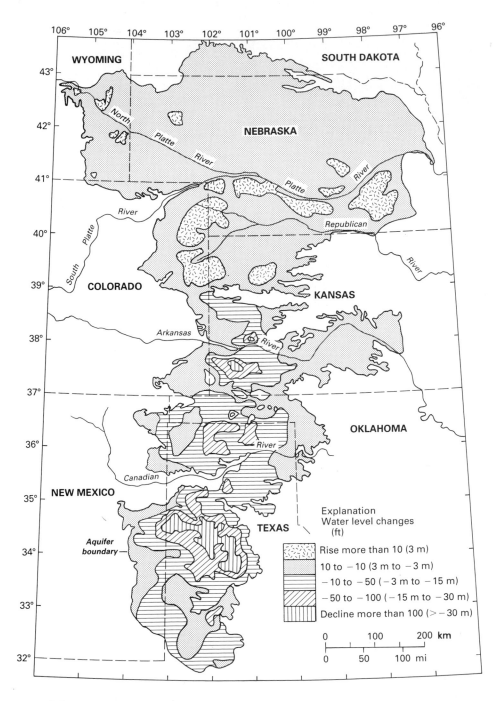

FIGURE 10-25. Ground water level changes in the High Plains aquifer, the Ogallala formation, from predevelopment to 1980. Note the maximum depression in excess of 30 meters (100 feet) in the Texas panhandle and southwestern Kansas. In contrast, the water table has been raised by more than 3 meters (10 feet) in parts of southern Nebraska, southern Colorado, and northwestern Kansas as a result of the infiltration of irrigation water from the Platte and Republican rivers. (From U.S. Geological Survey Professional Paper 1400-B, 1985.)

FIGURE 10-26. Areas of significant land surface subsidence caused by the withdrawal of ground water. (From U.S. Geological Survey Water Supply Paper 2250, p. 66, 1985.)

pipes, and sewers; (4) changes in the grades and efficiencies of canal and irrigation systems; and (5) increased susceptibility of flooding in low-lying coastal areas. Subsidence in the Santa Clara Valley of California has lowered the land surface below sea level with resulting costs estimated at more than $30 million. In the Central Valley of California, subsidence began in the 1920s as ground water was utilized for irrigation. By 1964, annual ground water withdrawals had exceeded 20 million acre feet (24 × 10⁶ liters) and subsidence had affected about 13,500 square kilometers (5200 square miles). By 1970, the water table had dropped as much as 110 meters (350 feet) and the land surface had subsided as much as about 8 meters (26 feet) (Fig. 10.27). The combined effect even reversed the direction of water flow in the aquifer.

The extraction of ground water to meet the growing needs of the Houston-Galveston area since 1915 has resulted in subsidence of 2.5 meters (8 feet) in the Brownwood subdivision of Baytown. As a consequence, most of the 450 houses of this coastal subdivision have become permanently inundated by seawater.

Saltwater Intrusion to Aquifers

Under normal conditions, the slow but steady percolation of ground water in response to the pull of gravity is sufficient along most coastal areas to keep marine saline waters from seeping inland into the aquifers. The location of the boundary—the freshwater-saltwater interface—varies from one shoreline to another depending on the rainfall and the permeability of the rocks and sediments and changes slightly in any given area as a function of annual or longer term climatic conditions.

Since the 1960s, it has become apparent that the extraction of large quantities of water from many aquifers to serve growing metropolitan areas has altered the natural hydrologic balance. The consequence of removing vast quantities of water that previously held back the saline waters is the landward movement of the freshwater-saltwater interface, resulting in **saltwater intrusion** into the previously freshwater aquifers. This phenomenon has been observed in many places but is especially well documented along the coastal areas of the United States (Fig. 10.23). Thus, freshwater wells have

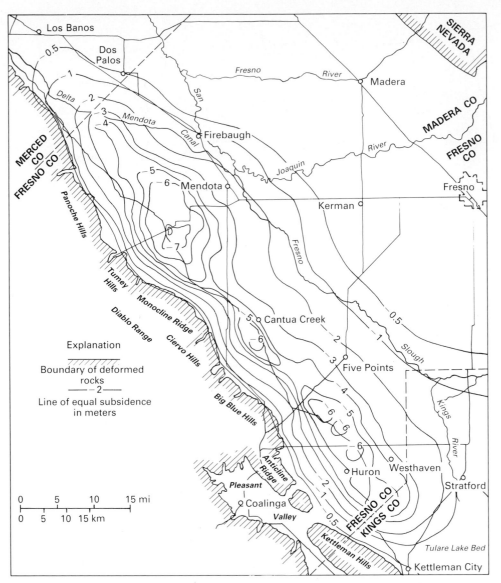

FIGURE 10-27. An example of land surface subsidence as much as 8 meters (26 feet) in the Los Banos-Kettleman City area of California between 1920 and 1966 as a result of ground water withdrawal. Further subsidence has been prevented by reinjection of ground water and the use of alternative sources. (From U.S. Geological Survey Professional Paper 437-F, 1970.)

been abandoned near Savannah, Georgia, New York City, and Los Angeles, and increases in salinity threaten usable water supplies near many rapidly growing sites. One example of the problem, as shown in Fig. 10.28, results from the effects of heavy pumping of freshwater from an aquifer near New York City. The increase in salinity resulting from saltwater intrusion into the aquifer parallels the increase in pumping activity.

Although saltwater intrusion occurs primarily in coastal areas, similar problems may occur in other areas. Thus, in the Central Valley of California an exten-

sive body of saline water containing up to 60,000 parts per million dissolved solids lies below the freshwater aquifers. There is considerable concern about the potential upward movement of this saline water into the aquifers. In Mississippi, the reinjection of saline waste water from oil production has led to the contamination of normally freshwater wells in areas far removed from the coasts. The saline water was reinjected in order not to pollute surface waters. Unfortunately, the directions of movement of underground waters, especially those under increased pressure, is not well known.

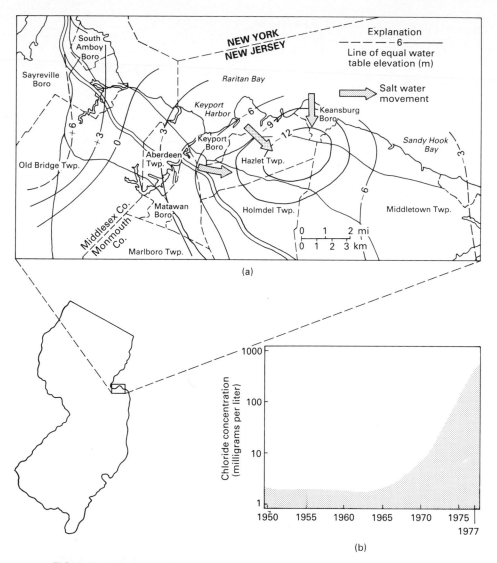

FIGURE 10-28. (a) Ground water table depression in Monmouth County, New Jersey, as a result of increased pumping to meet the needs of a growing population. (b) The rise in chloride concentrations in water samples from the Union Beach Borough well field from 1950–1977 has forced abandonment of the wells. (From U.S. Geological Survey Water Supply Paper 2184, 1984.)

It is apparent that the movement of saline water, especially when promoted by our activities, poses a threat to many important water supplies. Our increasing demands on ground water supplies are likely to intensify the problems and hence require careful consideration of the most efficient uses of this valuable resource.

Soil Deterioration Due to Water Logging, Salinization, Alkalinization

Irrigation in arid regions, although intended to bring unused or low productivity land into full agricultural pro-

duction, has unfortunately also caused the deterioration or loss to production of an estimated 125,000 hectares of land every year. The problems arise in arid regions where irrigation systems supply water to soils faster than drainage can remove it. The excess water raises the water table to near the soil surface, causing **water logging**, and permits evaporation to concentrate dissolved salts. Water logging is a problem by itself because most crop plants are not able to survive if their roots are under water; rice is the major exception. The buildup of mineral crusts (Fig. 10.29) of halite (**salinization**) or alkali salts (**alkalinization**) impairs plant growth. Furthermore,

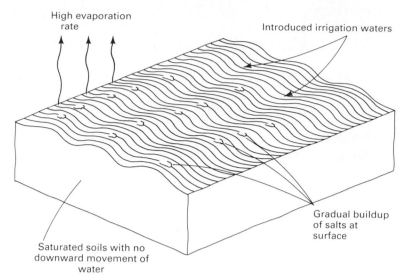

FIGURE 10-29. Salts may build up in soils as a result of evaporation of water brought in for irrigation. Ultimately, the soils may become so salt rich that they can no longer be used to grow food stuffs.

High evaporation rate

Introduced irrigation waters

Gradual buildup of salts at surface

Saturated soils with no downward movement of water

runoff of salt-laden waters into streams reduces the usefulness of that water for irrigation elsewhere. The deterioration of soils by salt buildup as early as 2400–1700 B.C. is believed to have caused the collapse of ancient civilizations in Mesopotamia and in the upper Nile Valley in Egypt. In 1959, it was estimated that 60 percent of Iraq's agricultural land was seriously affected by salinity. In the 1960s, the same problem arose in the Sind, one of Pakistan's major provinces, when 49 percent of all agricultural land was waterlogged. Furthermore, 50 percent of the irrigated land of the Sind was highly saline, and 25 percent was moderately saline. Argentina has 2 million hectares of irrigated land affected in this way, Peru has 300,000 hectares, and the United States potentially faces the same problem in more than 1 million hectares of the rich San Joaquin Valley in California.

The land can be reclaimed by the installation of expensive subsurface drainage systems that allow the irrigation water to percolate downward through the soil. This downward movement is similar to the water movement in soils in humid areas and eliminates the buildup of the soluble salts at the soil surface. Such reclamation, however, has only been carried out in local areas because it is very expensive to install the drainage systems, because it requires even larger amounts of water to flush out the salt-rich soils, and because the salts that have been washed out may reach ground water supplies or merely be deposited in downstream areas.

Desertification is a relatively recently used term to describe the deterioration of previously useful land adjacent to desert regions, at least partly in response to human activities such as farming and grazing. It frequently occurs in semiarid regions in response to changes in precipitation patterns but remains primarily a problem of soil usage and hence is discussed in greater detail in Chapter 11.

LARGE SCALE TRANSPORTATION AND DIVERSION SYSTEMS

Although we live on a planet 70 percent covered by water, we continually find that, in many areas, either the quantity or the quality of water is not sufficient for our needs. Consequently, we have deepened, dammed, and diverted rivers and streams so that they deliver the water in more useful places or so that they provide better avenues for transportation. Schemes that alter or divert the flow of rivers have, in this time of environmental awareness, also become emotional issues that commonly bring those who desire to keep the status quo into opposition with those who see benefit from change. Because water, as a measurable and often limited resource, is considered in terms of municipal service, industrial production, power generation, or crop growth, its availability has broad economic implications.

It is, of course, not possible to begin to evaluate all the types of water transportation and diversion schemes that have been constructed. The following discussion treats only three major examples.

Water for Transportation— The Tennessee-Tombigbee Waterway

When we think of water as a resource, we generally consider only that which is actually used or consumed in daily life, in industry, or in irrigation. Water is no less an important resource when it serves as an avenue for transportation. Thus the oceans and the world's rivers have served as trade routes since before recorded history. In Italy, coastal rivers and estuaries were modified into canals for commerce and, as in England, a wide-reaching canal system was built to facilitate transport of the coal and iron ore needed to fuel the Industrial Revolution. In the United States, the famed Erie Canal and

many others like it were built to provide efficient and inexpensive means of large-volume transport. In a similar manner, the great St. Lawrence Seaway, a channel with a series of locks, was constructed to permit the direct movement of commodities from the Great Lakes to the Atlantic along an otherwise non-navigable river.

Perhaps the two most famous water transport systems are the Suez and the Panama canals. The Suez, opened in 1869, provided a short sea route to the Far East from southern European ports. The Panama Canal, completed in 1914, reduced the length of the route from American Atlantic to Pacific ports by more than 15000 kilometers (9400 miles).

Within the United States the construction of canals, dams, and diversions has, in this century, commonly been referred to as "pork barrel" politics and has been the purview of the U.S. Army Corps of Engineers. The latest, largest, most expensive, and most controversial of these projects has been the Tennessee-Tombigbee Waterway (Fig. 10.30). First discussed in the early 1800s, a plan was formulated in 1874 and finally authorized by Congress in 1946. Construction began in 1971. In January 1985 the 433-kilometer (234-mile) waterway with 10 locks that can lift ships 104 meters (341 feet) was opened to traffic at a cost of nearly $2 billion. The Tennessee-Tombigbee, as it is called, greatly reduces the distance and time of river transport from the Ohio Valley to the Gulf Coast and has been heralded as one of the nation's great achievements. It has also been considered an environmental disaster and an economic dilemma. The great canals noted above have had both political and economic impact; the effects of the Tennessee-Tombigbee remain to be seen.

Water for Drinking—The Los Angeles Aqueduct System

Out of the desert with its rocks, heaven-hued and awe inspiring, its cactus-like sentinels of solitude, rose this Los Angeles—your city and mine. The magic touch of water quickened the desert into its flowering life—our city. And lest our city shrivel and die, we must have more water, we must build a great new aqueduct to the Colorado.

This statement by William Mulholland, the long-time water czar for Los Angeles, succinctly summarized the recurring plight of that city, this time in 1925, when it was realized that further growth could not occur without additional water supplies. Similar statements have, no doubt, been made in many other cities with various responses. The response in Los Angeles has been the construction of one of the world's largest, most com-plex—and controversial—aqueduct systems (Figs. 10.31 and 10.32).

When Los Angeles was founded as a pueblo on a small river in 1781, no one envisioned that it would one day grow into a major city, covering more than 1165 square kilometers (450 square miles) with an overall population of over 7 million. The river served as an adequate source for 120 years, but by 1904 the city began to search for additional supplies to accommodate anticipated growth. Surface and ground waters in adjacent areas were already in use, so city officials turned their attention to the Owens Valley on the eastern flank of the Sierra Nevada Mountains 250 miles to the east. Land and water rights were acquired, sometimes by subterfuge, and construction began. By 1913 the $25,000,000 aqueduct was completed and Owens Valley water flowed into Los Angeles.

By 1923 the growth of the population to more than one-half million brought the realization that yet more water was needed. This time the Colorado River aqueduct system reached east and began to tap water dammed in Lake Havasu. The project was completed in 1941. Because Arizona did not use its full share of water as authorized by the Colorado River Compact (see p. 324), Los Angeles was allowed to temporarily take Arizona's unused portion. With continued growth, more water was needed, and a second Owens Valley aqueduct was added in 1970.

Two circumstances have forced Los Angeles, in the 1980s, to again look for more water, this time to the north where there are plans for a $5 billion Peripheral Canal that would take water from the Sacramento River and pass it south via the California Aqueduct. First, population has continued to grow and to require increased amounts of water. Second, in 1985, Arizona completed the first part of the Central Arizona Project to supply Colorado River water from Lake Havasu to Phoenix and Tucson. Consequently, Arizona is reclaiming the Colorado River water it had allowed Los Angeles to use since 1941. Its right to do so was upheld in the Supreme Court.

The water supply system for Los Angeles has some similarities with that for New York City (described on p. 317), but the legal and emotional ramifications of the former are far greater. Because of the abundance of water in the northeastern United States, New York's use of water has negligible impact on the availability of water for others. In contrast, Los Angeles' needs and claims on water supercede the availability of water for many others, including those who live where the surface waters originate. This has resulted in scores of law suits, bombing of aqueducts, and, in recent years, concern about severe environmental effects. The continued growth of major cities such as Los Angeles in relatively

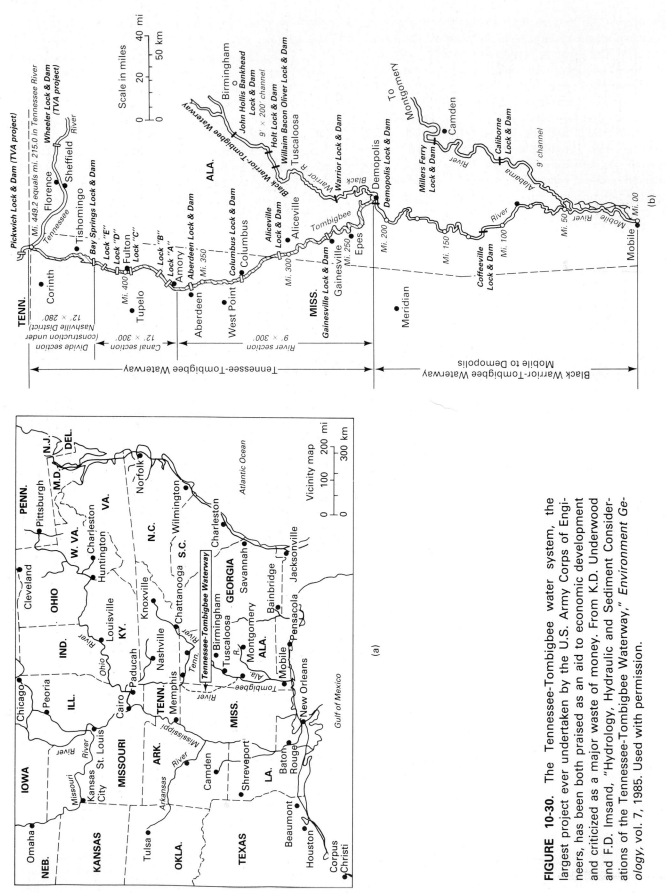

FIGURE 10-30. The Tennessee–Tombigbee water system, the largest project ever undertaken by the U.S. Army Corps of Engineers, has been both praised as an aid to economic development and criticized as a major waste of money. From K.D. Underwood and F.D. Imsand, "Hydrology, Hydraulic and Sediment Considerations of the Tennessee-Tombigbee Waterway," *Environment Geology,* vol. 7, 1985. Used with permission.

FIGURE 10-31. The water supply system of southern California involves the transport of water by aqueducts from various parts of the state. From the Los Angeles Department of Water and Power.

FIGURE 10-32. Aqueducts such as this one transport water from the well-watered mountains of California to the agricultural and urban areas of southern parts of the state where needs far exceed the local supply. (Courtesy of the Los Angeles Department of Water and Power.)

water-poor areas are going to place greater demands on scarce or distant water supplies in the years ahead.

Water for Irrigation—The Russian Water Diversion Scheme

The steppes of central Asia are similar to the Great Plains of North America in that they represent a great agricultural belt that in large areas receives insufficient water to produce to their full potential. This, coupled with constantly falling water levels and increasing salinities in the Caspian and Aral seas, has led to renewed consideration of a Soviet water diversion scheme that would be the largest engineering project of all time. The diversion would reverse the flow of a dozen or more rivers that now flow north into the Arctic Ocean and deliver approximately 38 billion cubic kilometers of water to south European Russia and 60 billion cubic kilometers to southern Siberia. Such a plan (Fig. 10.33) would require at least 50 years to complete and would displace tens of thousands of people from farms and towns along flooded valleys. The environmental effects of diverting so much water into arid areas and away from the Arctic Ocean are not known and are strongly debated.

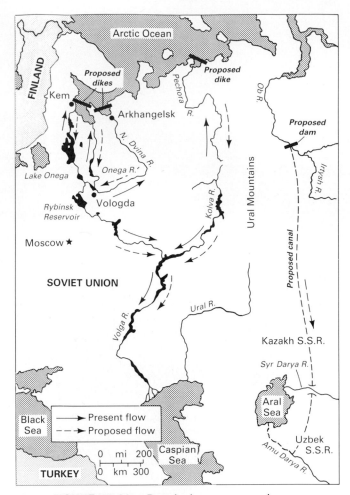

FIGURE 10-33. Russia has proposed a major water diversion scheme that would reverse the direction of flow of water in rivers now flowing into the Arctic Ocean and take it into the drier steppe region and the Caspian Sea.

FURTHER READINGS

AMBROGGI, R. P., "Water." *Scientific American* 243 (1980) p. 101–115.

FETH, J. H., "Water Facts and Figures for Planners and Managers." *U.S. Geological Survey Circular* 601–1 (1973) 30 p.

PEIXOTO, J. P. and KETTANI, M. A., "The control of the water cycle." *Scientific American* 228 (1973) p. 46–61.

SOLLEY, W. B., CHASE, E. B., and MANN, W. B., "Estimated Use of Water in the United States in 1980." *U.S. Geological Survey Circular* 1001 (1980) 56 p.

UNITED STATES GEOLOGICAL SURVEY, 1985, "National Water Summary 1983—Hydrologic Events and Issues." U.S. Geological Survey Water-Supply Paper 2250, 243 p.

UNITED STATES GEOLOGICAL SURVEY, 1985, "National Water Summary 1984—Hydrologic Events, Selected Water-quality Trends, and Ground-water Resources." U.S. Geological Survey Water-Supply Paper 2275, 467 p.

11

The fragile nature of the soils on which we depend for food supplies is illustrated by the severe wind erosion and deposition that occurred during the "Dust Bowl" days in the central and western United States during the 1930s. This photograph, taken in Gregory County, South Dakota, in 1936, shows a buried car and farm machinery on a previously prosperous farm. (Courtesy of Soil Conservation Service, U.S. Department of Agriculture.)

SOIL AS A RESOURCE

We abuse land because we regard it as a commodity belonging to us.
When we see land as a community to which we belong, we may begin
to use it with love and respect.

ALDO LEOPOLD, A SAND COUNTY ALMANAC

INTRODUCTION

Most of the land surface of the earth is covered by a continuous layer of **soil** that is commonly less than 2 meters thick. The term *soil*, as used in soil science, refers to a naturally formed earth surface-layer containing living matter and capable of supporting the growth of rooted plants. Soil results from the weathering of underlying rocks by physical and chemical processes involving the **hydrosphere** and **atmosphere,** but a key role in soil formation and development is also played by living organisms of the **biosphere.** Where underlying rocks are covered by broken, unconsolidated materials devoid of living matter (as on the surface of the moon, for example), the surface material is not a soil as the term is used here. Such a surface covering is described by the more general term **regolith.** Soil is made of inorganic material (mineral) matter and both living and dead organic matter. It is, therefore, a complex geological *and* biological system and there are many different types of soil. Although soils only makeup a minute fraction of the material of the whole earth, they are essential to life and are literally a *vital* resource. Because soils support the growth of rooted plants, they are at the base of the life support system on which humans depend. They are the earth resource that we exploit through agriculture and are renewable in the sense that they can be preserved through careful use of fertilizers and by crop rotation. Although soils can be made agriculturally productive through irrigation and fertilization, however, they can also be destroyed or irreparably damaged by natural agencies or careless human intervention. In the natural cycle of weathering, soil formation, and soil erosion, to which humans have introduced the utilization of soil for agriculture, there is a balance that is easily disturbed. It is much easier for people to damage or destroy soils than to create them.

In this chapter, the formation of salts, their chemistry, characteristics, classification, and distribution are reviewed; then their utilization and conservation are considered. Certain types of soils are exploited as sources of metals (e.g., aluminum is derived from bauxites), but these soils are really ores and are discussed elsewhere in the book (see Chapter 6).

SOIL FORMATION AND DISTRIBUTION

In order to understand the types of soil and their distribution, it is necessary to consider how soils form and the factors that lead to all the diverse soil types.

Formation—The Major Factors

The type of soil that is found at any given place results from the action of many processes on many different materials. However, five major factors can be identified in soil formation. These are as follows:

1. the parent material (the underlying rock or rock debris transported to the area);
2. the climate;
3. the vegetation;
4. the slope of the ground (which determines how quickly rain water will drain away and how deeply it will penetrate the ground); and
5. the time (in the sense of the extent to which the various processes have progressed and the maturity of the soil).

In view of these factors, it is not surprising that soils exhibit great diversity and considerable variation both laterally and vertically.

Formation Processes

Most rocks exposed at the earth's surface are not chemically stable and are constantly undergoing the process of breakdown known as **weathering,** a process that involves both mechanical disintegration (physical weathering) and chemical decomposition (chemical weathering). Weathering is the first stage in soil formation.

In physical weathering, rocks are broken down to smaller and smaller pieces by various natural agencies, the importance of which will depend on the type of rock being weathered and the climate under which weathering occurs. Wind, rain, frost action, and the differential expansion and contraction during rapid heating and cooling all contribute to the breaking down of rocks.

340

Most rocks already contain planes of weakness or planes along which fracturing has occurred. The release of the confining pressure of overlying rocks, when material originally formed at depth is exposed at the surface, causes expansion, fracturing, and the formation of joints. Joint planes are also formed when an igneous rock cools. Bedding planes (original sedimentary layers) in sedimentary rocks, or fracture planes introduced into rocks when major earth movements (**tectonism**) or minor movements (such as landslips) occur, are other examples of planes of weakness. In the broad temperate belts, frost wedging is probably the most important physical weathering agent. When water, trapped in fractures or pore space in rocks at the surface, freezes, its volume increases by about 9 percent. The maximum pressure force that can be generated when confined water freezes is about 2100 tons per square foot (about 40 times greater than the force needed to break an average granite). Although such maximum forces do not occur, because ice itself is not strong enough to seal water into a rock crack, frost wedging does produce stresses capable of disintegrating the hardest rocks. Plants and animals can also contribute significantly to physical weathering through the wedging action of plant and tree roots and the activities of burrowing animals.

Chemical weathering involves the breakdown of the *primary* minerals in the rock to new *secondary* minerals that are more stable in the surface environment or to material that may be carried away in solution. The extent to which the breakdown has occurred may be given as the **index of weathering,** usually expressed as the ratio of a common element like aluminum or iron present in the secondary mineral compared to the total present in the soil. Water is the essential agent in chemical weathering, either reacting with the minerals directly or carrying dissolved species which themselves react with the minerals. The reactions involved are many and complex, but they can be grouped into major categories as follows:

Hydrolysis is decomposition and reaction with water and is common in the major rock-forming silicate minerals, e.g.,

$$Mg_2SiO_4 + 4H^+ + 4OH^- \longrightarrow$$
$$2Mg^{2+} + 4OH^- + H_4SiO_4. \quad (11.1)$$

(olivine mineral + 4 ionized water molecules $\longrightarrow$

magnesium and hydroxyl in solution

$+$ silicic acid in solution).

Hydration is addition of the entire water molecule to the mineral structure and commonly occurs in clay minerals, sometimes causing them to swell.

Carbonation is the reaction with carbonic acid, which forms when carbon dioxide from the atmosphere dissolves in rain water:

$$CO_2 + H_2O \longrightarrow H_2CO_3 \quad (11.2)$$

(carbon dioxide gas + water $\longrightarrow$ carbonic acid).

Carbonic acid reacts with minerals, in particular the carbonate minerals (calcite, dolomite) that are the principal components of limestones, e.g.,

$$CaCO_3 + H_2CO_3 \longrightarrow Ca^{2+} + 2HCO_3^- \quad (11.3)$$

(calcite mineral + carbonic acid $\longrightarrow$

dissolved calcium + dissolved bicarbonate ions).

Oxidation is the bonding of oxygen, abundantly available dissolved in surface water, to the metallic elements (potassium, calcium, magnesium, and iron) of the primary minerals. A common example is the formation of the rusty brown and orange oxides of iron on the surfaces of iron-containing rocks. Thus in the case of the olivine mineral, fayalite, iron released by hydrolysis undergoes oxidation to ferric oxide:

$$Fe_2SiO_4 + 2H_2CO_3 + 2H_2O \longrightarrow$$
$$2Fe^{2+} + 2OH^- + H_4SiO_4 + 2HCO_3^- \quad (11.4)$$

(olivine mineral + carbonic acid + water $\longrightarrow$

iron hydroxyl ions in solution + silicic acid in solution

$+$ bicarbonate ions in solution),

$$2Fe^{2+} + 4HCO_3^- + \tfrac{1}{2}O_2 + 2H_2O \longrightarrow$$
$$Fe_2O_3 + 4H_2CO_3 \quad (11.5)$$

(iron and bicarbonate in solution + gaseous oxygen

$+$ water $\longrightarrow$ ferric oxide mineral

$+$ carbonic acid).

Ion-exchange involves the transfer of charged atoms (**ions**) of calcium, magnesium, sodium, and potassium between waters rich in one of the ions and a mineral rich in another. It is particularly important in the alteration of one clay mineral to another (e.g., illite, the K-rich clay mineral may lose potassium into solution and take up Mg^{2+} to form montmorillonite).

Chelation is the taking of metal atoms or ions into hydrocarbon molecules and relates to the biological processes that take place in soil formation.

Common secondary minerals produced on weathering of major rock-forming silicate minerals are shown in Fig. 11.1. This figure also emphasizes the fact that the different primary minerals weather at different rates, i.e., their **weatherability** as shown in the figure, is highly variable. Although variable, it is systematic and the re-

sistance to weathering of the primary silicates can be rationalized in terms of their crystal structures. For example, olivine, a mineral that contains SiO_4 tetrahedra linked by Mg or Fe ions, is much less resistant than quartz which is made up of SiO_4 tetrahedra linked by their corners to form a complete framework of these stable units. Thus, quartz (SiO_2) has a very low solubility. Because it is also hard, resists abrasion, and is a common primary mineral in many rocks, it is a common constituent of soils.

As Fig. 11.1 clearly shows, the secondary minerals that result from weathering processes depend directly on the nature of the primary minerals and hence the type of underlying bedrock. Therefore, rock-type (parent material) exercises a major control over the kind of soil that forms. The typical weathering products of a granite are given in Table 11.1 and show that in chemical weathering, many reactions are taking place simultaneously. It is also important to note that many of the rocks exposed at the surface of the earth are sediments that are already made largely of the secondary minerals in Fig. 11.1, redeposited after one (or more) weathering cycles.

Climate is second only in importance to parent material as a controlling factor in soil formation. The climate controls weathering and soil formation directly, through the amount of precipitation and the temperature, and indirectly through the kinds of vegetation that can cover the land. The importance of climate can be illustrated by considering four contrasting examples:

Humid tropical climates lead to intense chemical weathering that produces soils largely made of insoluble residues—iron oxides (laterites) and aluminum oxides (bauxites). The process of removal of metal atoms in forming bauxite from an original igneous rock may follow a sequence of the type shown below for the breakdown of the potash feldspar present:

$$4KAlSi_3O_8 + 4H^+ + 18H_2O \longrightarrow$$
$$Al_4Si_4O_{10}(OH)_8 + 8H_4SiO_4 + 4K^+ \quad (11.6)$$

(feldspar + H ions in solution + water $\longrightarrow$

kaolinite + silicic acid in solution

+ K ions in solution)

$$Al_4Si_4O_{10}(OH)_8 + 7H_2O \longrightarrow$$
$$2Al_2O_3 \bullet 3H_2O + 4H_4SiO_4 \quad (11.7)$$

(kaolinite + water $\longrightarrow$

gibbsite (bauxites) + dissolved silica)

Humid midlatitude climates with seasonal freezing allow much greater accumulation of vegetational debris—a **humus** layer—and dissolved species may not be removed but recombine to form stable clay minerals.

Hot arid climates allow for the growth of little vegetation and provide too little water to permit much chemical weathering. Consequently, such regions often do not develop true soils. Instead, salts may be left at or near the surface from the evaporation of the little available water, or a variety of rocklike crusts may form such as the calcium carbonate-rich calcrete (or caliche). Weathering involves rapid mechanical and chemical break-

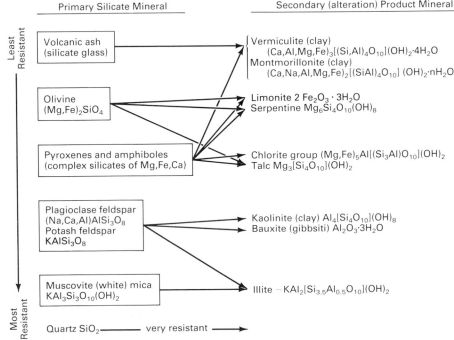

FIGURE 11-1. Weatherability of the major (primary) silicate minerals and their common (secondary) alteration products.

TABLE 11-1

Products of weathering of a granite (idealized)

Mineral Component	Chemical Composition (idealized)	Products of Weathering	
		Soluble	Insoluble
Orthoclase feldspar	$KAlSi_3O_8$	K^+ (minor), Soluble silica	Clay with K^+
Plagioclase feldspar	$(Na, Ca) Al_2Si_2O_8$	Na^+, Ca^{2+}, Soluble silica	Clay with some Na^+, Ca^{2+}
Biotite	$K_2(Mg, Fe)_6(Si, Al)_4O_{10}$	K^+ (minor), Mg^{2+}, Soluble silica	Clay minerals, hematite (Fe_2O_3) and/or limonite (FeO, OH)
Quartz	SiO_2	None	Quartz grains

down of the less resistant silicates. Clays may be blown away to leave only sands made up largely of quartz. *Cold climates* may also be very dry because all the water has turned into the solid form (snow, ice, frost) and is useless for chemical weathering. The biological activity of plants and microorganisms is also much reduced, although the slow rate of decay of organic material can lead to its accumulation forming peat bogs and the thick peat accumulations found in Canada and known as **muskeg.** Mechanical breakdown (by frost wedging) is the major weathering process.

The degree to which biological processes, chiefly involving vegetation and microorganisms, contribute to soil formation is dependent on the temperature and available moisture. Living plants take up certain elements (as essential **nutrients**), and these are returned to the surface soil when the plant sheds its leaves or dies. Plants also control the moisture content of the soil by transpiring water and serve to protect soils from erosion. Animals living in (or burrowing into) the soil may also play an important role, for example, earthworms rework the soil by burrowing and passing the soil through their intestinal tracts. These biological processes are, in turn, influenced by climate and by the parent rock material from which the soil forms, since these control the development of vegetation which, in turn, may permit animals to flourish. A soil is, therefore, a complex and constantly changing (or dynamic system) in which many interacting physical, chemical, and biological processes are going on at the same time.

Soil Chemistry

Soils are both complex mixtures of chemical compounds and complicated systems within which chemical reactions are constantly taking place. The reactions are made possible chiefly by the water that is present, and by the air present in pore spaces that provides gases (oxygen, nitrogen, carbon dioxide) that dissolve in the water and play an important role in reactions. The water in soils contains a large number of dissolved atoms, usually in the form of positively charged **cations,** such as Al^{3+} (aluminum), Ca^{2+} (calcium), K^+ (potassium),

Mg^{2+} (magnesium), Na^+ (sodium), Fe^{2+} or Fe^{3+} (iron), NH_4^+ (ammonium), H^+ (hydrogen) and negatively charged **anions,** such as Cl^- (chlorine), SO_4^{2-} (sulfate), HCO_3^- (bicarbonate), OH^- (hydroxide), NO_3^- (nitrate).

Soil temperature exerts an important control over both the chemical and biological processes occurring in soils. Below 0°C there is essentially no biological activity, and chemical processes are virtually inoperative. Between 0°C and 5°C (41°F), root growth of most plants and germination of most seeds is impossible, but water can move through the soil and chemical reactions can occur. Biological activity increases at higher temperatures, although the germination of seeds of many low-latitude plants requires a soil temperature of over 24°C (75°F). Temperatures vary both through diurnal and annual cycles and as a function of depth beneath the surface, and lead to the recognition of various **soil temperature regimes** that are described by the mean annual soil temperature and average seasonal fluctuations from that mean (Table 11.2). As noted above, water also plays a key role in soil chemistry and biochemistry, and the amount of water generally available in the soil also leads to the recognition of **soil-water regimes.** The five soil-water regimes in the most modern classification are also given in Table 11.2. Both soil-temperature regime and soil-water regime are important factors when overall soil classification is considered.

Chemical processes in soils are particularly influenced by the clay minerals that are present. These minerals have crystal structures in which the atoms form layers (Fig. 11.2), and the forces bonding the layers together are much weaker than those within each individual layer. This enables water molecules and various other ions dissolved in the water to penetrate between layers and become loosely bonded into the structure. Ions may also be attached in a similar fashion to the surface of the clay particles. Ions and molecules bound to clay particles in this way may be replaced by other ions and molecules in a process of **exchange.** Most commonly, this involves **cation exchange** with the commonly occurring cations selectively replacing the others in a sequence that has aluminum (Al^{3+}) replacing calcium (Ca^{2+}) then, in turn, magnesium (Mg^{2+}), potas-

TABLE 11-2
Soil-temperature and soil-water regime

Name of Soil-temperature Regime	Mean Annual Soil Temperature (T°C)	Difference between Mean Temperature of Warm and Cold Seasons
Pergelic	T < 0° (32°F)	—
Cryic	0° < T < 8° (47°F)	—
Frigid	T < 8°	>5°C
Mesic	8° < T < 15° (59°F)	>5°C
Thermic	15° < T < 22° (72°F)	>5°C
Hyperthermic	T < 22°	>5°C

Name of Soil-water Regime	Definition	Prefix Used in Classifications
Aquic	Soil saturated with water most of the time (e.g., bogs, marshes, swamps).	Aqu-
Udic	Soil is not dry for as long as 90 days in a year and there is little or no water deficiency (found in moist climates).	Ud-
Ustic	Soil has a moderate amount of stored water when needed for plant growth and is not frozen, but is dry for 90 or more cumulative days most years. Found in semiarid or tropical wet-dry climates.	Ust-
Aridic	Soil is never moist for as long as 90 consecutive days. Found in semidesert and desert climates.	Aridi-
Xeric	Found in Mediterranean-type climates where summer is long and dry, and winter is rainy. Soil is dry for 45 days or more in summer, moist for 45 or more (consecutive) days in winter.	Xer-

sium (K^+), and sodium (Na^+). The capacity of a soil to hold and exchange cations in this way is its cation exchange capacity. The clay minerals formed in the early stages of weathering or by less intense weathering (e.g., **montmorillonite** and **vermiculite**) generally have high cation **exchange capacities,** whereas those of clays formed in advanced stages and by intense weathering (e.g., kaolinite) are much lower. Soils with a high cation exchange capacity can usually function well in storing plant nutrients and are generally more fertile than those with low exchange capacity.

Another important factor in soil fertility is the acidity or alkalinity of the soil. This property is really a consequence of the concentration of hydrogen ions (H^+) in the soil and is quantified in terms of the pH of the soil. Certain cations in addition to H^+, especially Al^{3+} and $Al(OH)^{2+}$, promote acid conditions in the soil and are said to be acid-generating. Others promote alkalinity, and these base cations include Ca^{2+}, Mg^{2+}, K^+, and Na^+. Both types of cations must be present in the soil water or sufficiently loosely held in the clays to readily enter the soil water, otherwise they will have no effect on soil chemistry. Certain crops require near-neutral values of pH (i.e., pH = 7 and soil neither acid nor al-

kaline), but other plants may show considerable preference for either acid or alkaline soils, a factor that strongly influences the distribution of plant types. Soils with pH less than 6 require the addition of **lime** (calcium oxide or calcium carbonate in this usage of the term) to bring the pH closer to neutral if most farm crops are to be successfully cultivated. Acid soils are also commonly deficient in other nutrients and may require the addition of fertilizers as well as limestones to raise the pH. Table 11.3 shows the relationship between the pH scale, the qualitative description of soils as acid or alkaline, the lime requirements for cultivation, and the sort of environment in which such soils are found.

Soil Characteristics

Before considering the difference between soil types, it is useful to emphasize some of the most important properties and characteristics of soils that might form the basis for a classification scheme.

Color. An obvious property that can be described using quantitative scales. Sometimes, it directly arises from the parent matter that weathers to form the

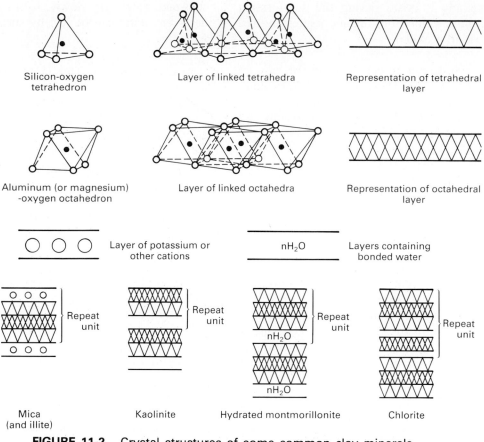

Silicon-oxygen tetrahedron

Layer of linked tetrahedra

Representation of tetrahedral layer

Aluminum (or magnesium) -oxygen octahedron

Layer of linked octahedra

Representation of octahedral layer

○ ○ ○ Layer of potassium or other cations

nH_2O Layers containing bonded water

Mica (and illite)

Kaolinite

Hydrated montmorillonite

Chlorite

FIGURE 11-2. Crystal structures of some common clay minerals. The basic building blocks are sheets of silica tetrahedra and alumina (or magnesia) octahedra between which may be layers of potassium, sodium or other cations, or bonded water. Different layer sequences occur in the different clay minerals as shown schematically.

TABLE 11-3

Soil acidity and alkalinity

pH Range	Acidity/Alkalinity	Lime Requirements	Cause and Occurrence
3.5	Extremely acid	Lime needed except for crops needing acid soil	Mine spoil; coast marsh clays with acid sulfates. Excess Al^{3+} may make soil toxic to plants (rare)
4.5	Highly acid	Lime needed except for crops needing acid soild	Mine spoil; salt marsh clays with sulfides; organic matter (frequent)
4.5–5.8	Moderately acid	Lime needed for all but acid-tolerant crops	Mineral-rich soils (very common in cultivated soils in humid climates)
5.8–6.5	Slightly acid	Lime generally not needed	Soil partly saturated with base cations (common in subhumid and arid climates)
6.5–8.0	Neutral to weakly alkaline	No lime needed	Soil fully saturated with base cations, some $CaCO_3$ may be present (common in subhumid and arid climates)
8.0–8.5	Alkaline	No lime needed	Exchangeable Ca^{2+}, Mg^{2+}. Free $CaCO_3$ is present (common in all subhumid and arid climates)
8.5–8.10	Strongly alkaline	No lime needed	Large amounts of soluble salts present (limited areas in deserts)
10	Extremely alkaline	No lime needed	Soil saturated with sodium and may be toxic to many plants (limited areas in deserts)

soil, but commonly it arises during the soil-forming process (e.g., black color from organic matter and red color from ferric iron oxide).

Texture. Soils can be classified on the basis of texture, following a U.S. Department of Agriculture scheme, by defining the percentages of sand, silt, and clay present in the soil. The three components are defined in terms of particle size:

Sand—particle size, 2.0–0.05 millimeter diameter

Silt—particle size, 0.05–0.002 millimeter diameter

Clay—particle size, less than 0.002 millimeter diameter

The boundaries are drawn somewhat differently than those used by geologists classifying sedimentary rocks when sand per silt is at 0.06 millimeter (1/16 millimeter) and silt per clay at 0.004 millimeter (1/256 millimeter). It is also important to note that the term *clay* is used purely to describe particle size and not mineralogy. A mixture in which all three size range materials occur in substantial amounts is called a **loam.** The complete soil texture classification is shown in Fig. 11.3. Texture is important because it largely determines the extent to which water is retained or passes through the soil. Pure clay holds the most water and pure sand the least; hence, sandy soil requires more frequent watering. Clay-rich

soils take water very slowly, so if irrigation is being undertaken, water can be lost by surface runoff if care is not taken.

Consistence. This is a property that relates to the stickiness of wet soil or plasticity of moist soil. Some soil horizons may become cemented through the accumulation of minerals such as silica, iron oxides, or calcium carbonate.

Soil Structure. This refers to the presence and nature of lumps made from clusters of individual soil particles. Such a natural lump is called a **ped,** as distinct from a **clod** that is produced during plowing. Soil structure is described in terms of the shape, size, and durability of the peds and is a property of considerable importance in agriculture, affecting ease of cultivation, susceptibility to erosion, and ease of water penetration into the dry soil. There are four basic types of soil structure: platy, prismatic, blocky, and spheroidal. These are shown in Fig. 11.4.

Soil Horizons. These are the distinctive horizontal layers (exposed in a vertical **soil profile**) that differ in their chemical composition and structure (see Fig. 11.5). The two major classes of soil horizons are *horizons of organic matter and mineral horizons of differing compositions.* The former (labelled with a letter O) is made of plant and animal debris and commonly has an

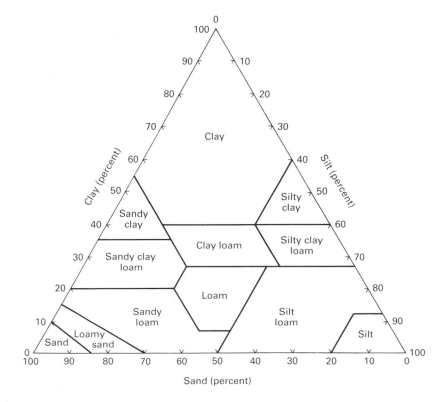

FIGURE 11-3. A triangular diagram illustrating the textural classification of soils (note that in this classification the terms "clay" and "sand" refer only to the sizes of particles and not their compositions).

(a)

(b)

(c)

(d)

FIGURE 11-4. An illustration of the four basic soil structures: (a) blocky (angular) soil from a B horizon in western New York; (b) granular (spheroidal) soil from an A horizon in southwestern Kansas; (c) platy soil from an A horizon in central Iowa; and (d) prismatic soil from a B horizon in central South Dakota. The scales are all in inches. (Photographs courtesy of Roy W. Simonson, Soil Conservation Service, U.S. Department of Agriculture.)

upper horizon (O1) of recognizable plant material underlain by decomposed material (humus) comprising the O2 horizon. Mineral horizons consist of detrital particles of sand and silt-size mineral fragments and of clay minerals and other similar weathering products and are labelled with the letters A and B (various subdivisions being indicated by adding numbers or, in some cases, other abbreviations). The A horizon overlies the B horizon and typically contains more organic matter, the latter containing more mineral matter and being generally less friable. Underlying the B horizon may be a C horizon of weathered parent material and the bedrock that is labelled the R horizon. An example of a hypothetical soil profile is shown in Fig. 11.5. In detail, the variations found in soil profiles are extensive, and the system of labelling them is suitably complex.

Soil Classification

Older systems of soil classification emphasized factors such as climate, relief, and parent material that control soil formation. A widely used scheme of this type was developed by the U.S. Department of Agriculture in 1938 with its recognition of three orders of soils: **zonal soils** formed under conditions of good drainage with marked involvement of climate and vegetation; **intra-zonal soils** formed under conditions of poor drainage (e.g., bogs), and **azonal soils** formed under conditions that do not enable any real development of a soil profile (as on steep slopes and in certain deserts). Further division into a number of suborders was followed in this classification by the recognition of great soil groups. The names of some of these groups reflect the important

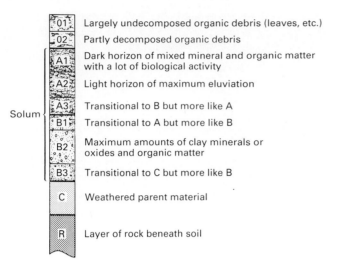

FIGURE 11-5. The designation of horizons for a hypothetical soil profile that could represent a forest soil in a cool, moist climate.

influence of Soviet scientists in this field (e.g., podzol and chernozem), and others reflect American contributions (e.g., prairie soils and chestnut soils). However, by the latter half of the twentieth century, it became increasingly clear to soil scientists that classification schemes of this type are inadequate, both in being insufficiently comprehensive and in being based on unsupported and often untestable assumptions about the mode of soil formation (e.g., the role of climate). New approaches were adopted, and they led to the presentation of a **Comprehensive Soil Classification System** (CSCS) at the Seventh International Congress of Soil Science in 1960 (hence sometimes known as the "Seventh Approximation"). The system relies on the characteristics of the soils (morphology and composition) with every attempt being made to quantitatively define these characteristics and to use readily observable features. The CSCS is based on a hierarchy with six levels named as follows: Orders—10 in all, Suborders—47 in all, Great groups—185 in all, Subgroups—over 1000, Families—over 5000, Series—over 10,000. The smallest distinctive division of the soil of a given geographical area is termed the **polypedon,** and every polypedon falls within only one of the 10 **soil orders.** A variety of criteria are used to uniquely define each of the orders, and these may include gross composition (e.g., percent clay, percent organic matter); degree of development of soil horizons and presence or absence of certain diagnostic horizons; and degree of weathering of the soil minerals (possibly expressed by cation exchange capacity). The names and major characteristics of the 10 soil orders are listed below.

Entisols lack any developed horizons and include desert sands that can support plants, alluvial deposits, and frozen ground.

Inceptisols show only weakly developed horizons and include soils in areas of tundra climate, soils formed from new volcanic deposits, and from recently accumulated flood plain sediments.

Histosols have a large proportion of organic matter, often as a thick upper layer, and include peat and other bog soils.

Oxisols are old and intensely weathered, nearly horizonless soils that occur in tropical and subtropical latitudes and have an oxic horizon as in the iron oxide-rich laterites or aluminum oxide-rich bauxites.

Ultisols are deeply weathered clay-rich soils, often red or yellow in color and developed on old land surfaces in humid temperate to tropical latitudes.

Vertisols are also clay-rich soils that hydrate and swell when wet and crack on drying and occur in subtropical and tropical zones.

Alfisols are young soils in humid and subhumid climates that have a clay-rich B horizon and are commonly developed under deciduous forests.

Spodosols have an iron- or organic-rich B horizon and often an ashy-grey leached A horizon, commonly found as the soils in humid forests.

Millisols show a thick, dark, organic-rich surface layer and are the soils of temperate grasslands.

Aridisols are the soils of dry climates that may show accumulations of salt, gypsum, or carbonates.

The suborders within each soil order may be as few as two or as many as seven, and a variety of criteria are used to define them (e.g., soil-water regime, organic or mineral content of the soil, etc.). It is inappropriate to detail all the various suborders here, but the five suborders of the important order of Alfisols can be given as one example of how this is done (here soil-water and soil-temperature regimes, as illustrated in Table 11.2, are the basis of division):

Aqualfs are alfisols of wet areas.

Boralfs are the alfisols of boreal forests.

Udalfs are from the udic (humid) soil-water regimes.

Ustalfs are from the ustic (dry) soil-water regimes.

Xeralfs are from the xeric regime of Mediterranean climates.

The brief account above illustrates the approach now adopted to the complex problem of producing a comprehensive classification of world soils.

Soil Distribution

The processes of formation and problems of classification of soils are topics that naturally lead to considering the distribution of soils. The factors influencing soil distribution are well illustrated in Fig. 11.6 by the simplified cross-section from the southwest to northeast of the North American continent. In Fig. 11.7, a map of the world is presented with soils indicated in terms mainly of the 10 soil orders discussed above. The map is oversimplified, but it does show the correlations to be expected between soil types and climate as, for example, the aridisols being located in the world's greatest deserts and the oxisols in the great tropical zones. This overall pattern of soil distribution must be kept in mind as we now consider the utilization, management, and conservation of soils.

SOIL TYPE AND LAND USE

The soil classification systems we have talked about provide the basis for discussing soil use in agriculture on a global or regional scale. The potential use of a soil depends on its particular properties. However, suitable soils are not the only factors governing successful utilization of the land for agriculture—there are other factors of which the most important is certainly the water supply. The practical exploitation of soils through agriculture may be one of several forms of utilization of the land in a particular area. The conflicts that result are problems of land management and may involve individual landowners, communities, companies, or local and national governments.

Soils and Agriculture

We commonly refer to soils that can be used to grow crops as fertile, a word meaning that the soil is rich enough in the nutrients needed for the sustained growth of plants and trees useful to humans. The actual capacity of the soil to support such growth is called its productivity, and this depends on the soil being fertile and having a structure and consistence that makes it easily tilled. Tilling aerates the soil, allows passage of water, and promotes the spreading of plant roots. Despite adequate rainfall, some soil is unproductive because it drains too quickly, that is, it is too **permeable**, whereas other soils may be barren because they are **impermeable** to moisture.

The soils that are productive belong only to certain categories we have named in the (CSCS) classification outlined earlier. In general terms, soils of mountainous areas and deserts (entisols and aridisols) are nonproductive, whereas the most productive of soils include the mollisols, alfisols, and spodosols of temperate and more humid areas of the globe. The oxisols and many utisols of the subtropical and tropical areas are also chiefly unsuited to agricultural use because the essential nutrients have been removed, leaving an infertile soil that may be hard and bricklike, as are many laterites and bauxites. The inceptisols of tundra areas will not support agriculture because of the frozen ground conditions, and the organic-rich histosols of many bog land areas are too acid for utilization.

Examination of Fig. 11.7 emphasizes the obvious point that productive soils, like many other types of resources, are very unevenly distributed over the surface of the earth. For example, whereas desert soils are estimated to cover about 17 percent of the land surface of the earth, the continent of Australia is about 44 percent desert, and Africa is 37 percent, whereas Eurasia is only 15 percent desert. A question that immediately arises

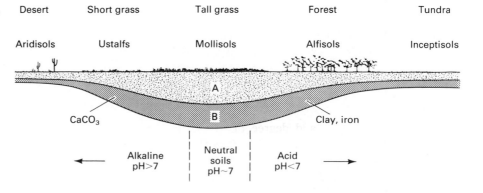

FIGURE 11-6. Idealized soil profile from the southwest to northeast of the North American continent. Note that the thickest and richest soils occur in the midwest. Soils in the desert Southwest, where it is arid, and in the subarctic Northeast, where it is cool, are much thinner.

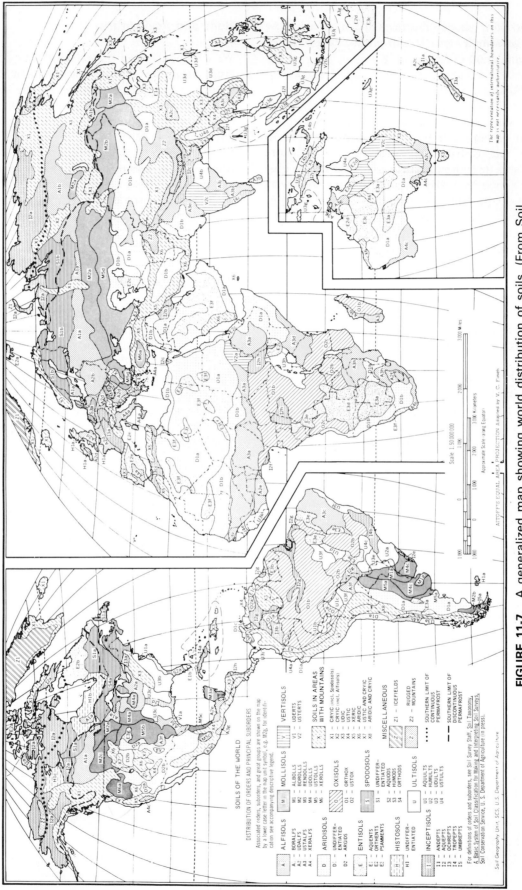

FIGURE 11-7. A generalized map showing world distribution of soils. (From Soil Conservation Service, U.S. Department of Agriculture.)

here is, Need all these desert areas be unproductive? In theory, the answer to this question is no. Deserts include some potentially very fertile and productive areas, and the main thing that prevents their utilization is lack of water. The question then becomes one of cost, because water is precisely the resource that is least available in desert areas, and it would be required in enormous volume to counter losses through evaporation. In the examples where the irrigation of desert areas takes place on a large scale, nature has generally provided a water supply in the form of a great river or underground aquifer. Perhaps the most outstanding example of this is the Nile River in Egypt, around which formed one of the world's first agriculturally-based societies.

Land areas that are unproductive for reasons other than lack of water supply may, in theory, be made productive. Problems concerning the permeability of the ground or the absence of essential nutrients may be remedied by farming methods and the use of chemicals and fertilizers (see also Chapter 9). Seven chemical elements are needed in substantial amounts for plant growth. These are: hydrogen, oxygen, nitrogen, and carbon (originally from the air and water), phosphorus, potassium, and calcium (originally from minerals in the soil). Another nine elements are needed in minor or trace amounts: magnesium, sulfur, boron, copper, iron, manganese, zinc, molybdenum, and chlorine. The elements that are generally added as fertilizers in substantial amounts are nitrogen, phosphorus, and potassium. Nitrogen deficiency is commonly corrected by addition of ammonia compounds [such as NH_4NO_3 or $(NH_4)_2SO_4$] or various nitrates (NO_3^-). In the eastern and central United States, the nitrogen content of the soil to a depth of 100 centimeters (40 inches) is estimated at 5000–17,000 kilograms per hectare (approximately 11000–37000 pounds per acre), making up on average about 0.2 percent of the soil by weight. Phosphorus makes up roughly 0.025–0.075 percent of the ploughed layer of farmed land in the United States, and its deficiency is remedied by the addition of phosphate fertilizers. Potassium is commonly present in the surface layers of the soil in much greater amounts than nitrogen or phosphorus (averaging perhaps 2 percent in productive soils), although much of this may be held in mineral structures and be unavailable for immediate uptake by plants. Deficiency in readily available potassium can be countered by addition of potassium chloride (KCl or the mineral sylvite). The elements needed in only minor trace amounts can be readily supplied by spraying with appropriate additive compounds or by addition to the major fertilizers. It has been noted already that extreme acidity or alkalinity of soils has a very adverse effect on fertility, since nutrients may be destroyed or removed under such conditions. Acid ground is, of course,

treated with lime in order to increase the pH to nearer neutral values (see Table 11.3).

Previously unproductive land may therefore be converted to agricultural land. The limiting factors are the cost of the process, the return on an investment of this kind, and the alternative uses for the land. These are questions of land management that we will now consider.

Land Management

Land, and therefore soil, is an unusual resource because it can be put to a range of different uses, many of which are mutually exclusive. Land prices, tax laws, and life styles ranging from that of the nomadic tribesman of parts of Africa and Asia to the traditional village communities of old Europe and the urban sprawl of many U.S. cities, all influence the ways in which land is managed. If we consider the example of the United States, the total land area of the country is approximately 930×10^6 hectares (2300×10^6 acres) of which slightly more than half is devoted to raising crops and livestock (57 percent) and the remainder to a variety of other uses including forestry (23 percent), urban and transport systems (3 percent), and mining (0.3 percent). A more complete breakdown is given in Fig. 11.8. It must also be remembered that the overall pattern of land use is constantly changing. Considering again the example of the United States, the total land area used for raising crops is approximately 190,000,000 hectares (470,000,000 acres). In an average year during the last decade, roughly 142,000 hectares (350,000 acres) were lost to make way for urban development and a staggering 770,000 hectares (1,900,000 acres) lost to make way for roads, airports, or flood control or recreational projects. Balanced against these figures, roughly

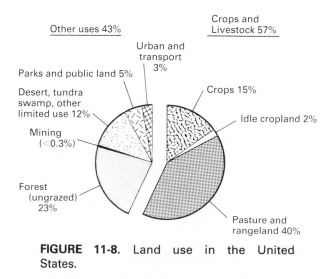

FIGURE 11-8. Land use in the United States.

890,000 hectares (2,200,000 acres) of land was transformed to crop-producing areas each year through irrigation and fertilization, processes that may cost $2500 or more for every new hectare added ($1000 per acre). Much of this new cropland has also been added at the expense of former pasture or range land.

There are also cases where new agricultural land has been created by reclamation from the sea. The most famous example is the extensive network of dikes in the Netherlands, a system commenced over 300 years ago and enabling the Dutch to reclaim 20 percent of the land area of their country from coastal submergence (Fig. 11.9). The danger of storm damage to the dikes and consequent flooding of the type that occurred in 1953 when 1800 people were drowned and 47,000 buildings lost has been averted by closing large estuaries with vast

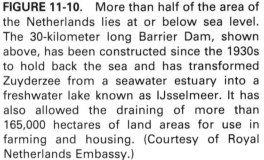

FIGURE 11-10. More than half of the area of the Netherlands lies at or below sea level. The 30-kilometer long Barrier Dam, shown above, has been constructed since the 1930s to hold back the sea and has transformed Zuyderzee from a seawater estuary into a freshwater lake known as IJsselmeer. It has also allowed the draining of more than 165,000 hectares of land areas for use in farming and housing. (Courtesy of Royal Netherlands Embassy.)

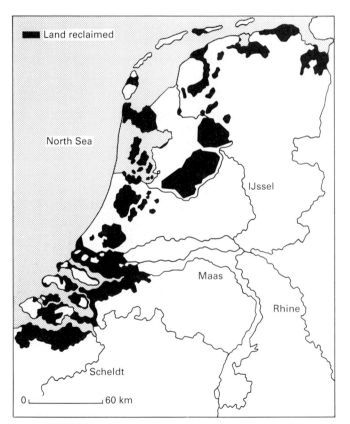

FIGURE 11-9. The areas shown in dark are the more than 20 percent of the land area of the Netherlands that has been reclaimed from the sea by the construction of dikes and by the pumping of water to dry the land. Dikes were built as early as 1000 A.D., and windmills were used to pump water from the reclaimed areas in the early 1400s. (Courtesy of Royal Netherlands Embassy.)

dams to put the dikes out of reach of storm tides (Fig. 11.10).

The utilization of soil as an agricultural resource must inevitably come into conflict with the alternative uses for that particular area of land. A good illustration of this problem is provided by considering the large areas of the central United States that have underlying coal at shallow depth that could be removed by strip mining. Many such areas are largely or partly the croplands responsible for much of the United States' wheat and corn production, as clearly shown in Fig. 11.11.

The encroachment of alternative forms of land utilization, whether urban development, road construction, or mining operation, pose an obvious threat to the soil resource and food production chain dependent on it. However, another, and many would say much more serious threat, is that posed by the degradation and deterioration of soils by natural agencies, human intervention, or both.

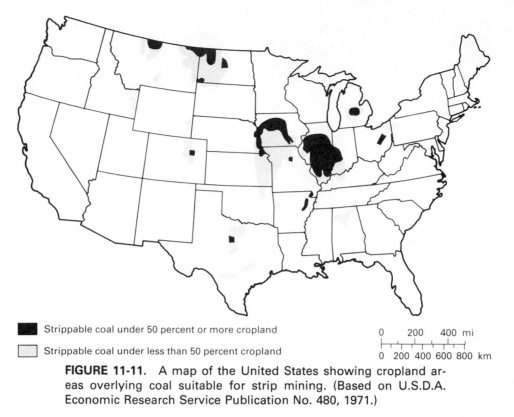

Strippable coal under 50 percent or more cropland

Strippable coal under less than 50 percent cropland

0   200   400 mi

0 200 400 600 800 km

FIGURE 11-11.   A map of the United States showing cropland areas overlying coal suitable for strip mining. (Based on U.S.D.A. Economic Research Service Publication No. 480, 1971.)

EROSION AND DETERIORATION OF SOILS

Soil Erosion

The beginning of this chapter explained that soils form through the weathering and breakdown of bedrock material. Without the binding and stabilizing effect of the organic matter and vegetation, which combine with the mineral fragments to make up the soil, this material would soon be swept away by wind and rain into rivers and the sea. In fact, such erosion is the ultimate fate of nearly all soils, and part of the continuous process of recycling of the material that makes up the surface of the earth. The questions that concern us are the rate at which this process is taking place, the extent to which human intervention is affecting that rate, and whether or not the soil resource is being depleted by erosion more rapidly than it is being regenerated by chemical weathering.

The rate of natural erosion will clearly vary from one area to another and is dependent on local geology, climate, and topography. Estimates have been made for a number of areas. For example, the Amazon River drainage basin is being lowered at a rate of 4.7 centimeters per 1000 years with the removal of 780 million metric tons of material a year. For the Congo River basin, the figures estimated are 2.0 centimeters per 1000 years and 133 million metric tons of material. Neither of these

basins have been significantly affected by human activities. However, studies of this kind on a global scale have led to the estimate that, before people appeared, the rivers of the world annually carried 9.3×10^9 metric tons of material into the oceans. After humans intervened by carrying out extensive cultivation, this figure rose to 24×10^9 metric tons, roughly two and a half times the original rate. A detailed study of one area near Washington, D.C., illustrates the effects of different human activities on erosion rates. The area was originally forest (before the year 1800), and erosion was estimated to be reducing the ground level by 0.2 centimeters per 1000 years. Throughout the nineteenth century, forests were cleared and the land developed for farming during which time the erosion rate rose to 10 centimeters per 1000 years. A partial return to forest and grazing land in the early to middle 1900s reduced the rate to about 5 centimeters per 1000 years until a period of construction in the 1960s caused a very rapid erosion rate of 1000 centimeters per 1000 years. The consequent urbanization has now brought the rate back to about 1 centimeter per 1000 years. Figure 11.12 shows this sequence of erosion rates as a graph with tonnages of soil removed (per square kilometer) over the time since 1780. This study illustrates very well the pronounced effect that human activities can have on the destruction of soil by erosion.

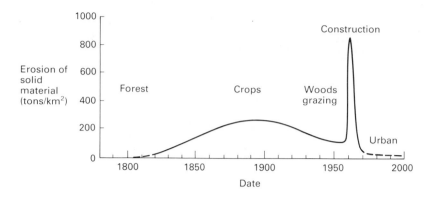

FIGURE 11-12. Variation in rate of soil erosion as a function of land usage in an area near Washington, D.C., U.S.A., since 1800. From Judson, "The Erosion of the Land," *American Scientist,* vol. 56, p. 356. Reprinted by permission.

Soil Depletion, Deterioration, and Poisoning

In areas of natural vegetation where there is no human intervention in the chemical and biological cycles involving the soil, organic and inorganic nutrients are returned to the soil when plants shed their leaves or die. There is no loss of such nutrients unless, for climatic reasons, excess leaching occurs. However, many farmed crops are totally removed from the ground, leaving no possibility of replenishing the soil. If action is not taken to counteract this depletion, yields will fall and crops will become dwarfed, deformed, or diseased, and ultimately the soil will become barren.

Soils may also be unable to support most or all plant growth because of the presence of certain toxic substances in relatively large amounts. An excessive amount of a substance necessary for plant growth may also prove toxic. For example, flowering plants and trees will not grow where the soil water contains more than a small amount of sodium chloride (common salt). Toxic substances may be naturally present in the soils but may also be introduced by humans as a by-product

of various extraction and production industries (see Chapter 3). For example, destruction of vegetation has occurred in the vicinity of many mining areas due to sulfurous fumes from smelting operations. The heavily eroded wastelands that have resulted are a stark reminder of the consequences of such abuse of the environment (Fig. 11.13).

Desertification

Desertification is a term used in recent years to describe the transformation of once productive agricultural land into desert (or other forms of wasteland). Although prolonged drought may appear the obvious cause of desertification, recent studies have shown that people are the chief culprit. Desertification may be caused by overgrazing, excessive woodcutting, land abuse, improper soil and water management, and land disturbance. It may be anything from slight to severe in extent and results in reduced productivity of land and environmental degradation, which in extreme cases is catastrophic for the local people. It is not a new prob-

FIGURE 11-13. Severe erosion as shown here in the Ducktown, Tennessee, mining district resulted initially from the cutting of trees to provide wood to roast the copper ores. The open roasting of the sulfide ores released large amounts of sulfur oxides, much of which was converted into sulfuric acid that killed the remaining vegetation. By the 1960s and 1970s, the entire Copper Basin, shown here beyond the old Burra Burra Mine open cut, was denuded, and erosion had removed nearly all of the upper soil horizons. (Photograph by J.R. Craig.)

lem. The Greek philosopher Plato wrote 2000 years ago that Grecian Attica was "a mere relic of the original country . . . . All of the rich soft soil has moulted away leaving a country of skin and bones." The deplorable conditions in Attica were the result of tree cutting and overgrazing, with subsequent water erosion.

The best known modern examples of desertification center on the Sahel region of central Africa, a region that lies along the southern edge of the Sahara Desert and includes parts of Mauritania, Senegal, Gambia, Mali, Upper Volta, Niger, Chad, Ethiopia, and The Sudan. A severe drought from 1969–1973, which first focussed world attention of the plight of the peoples of the Sahel, put the region's agricultural resources under severe strain. Had resource management been good, little or no permanent damage need have been done, but this was not the case. Overcultivation and overgrazing, in response both to drought conditions and growing populations, led to the depletion and erosion of fertile soils. In turn, atmospheric moisture is reduced because there are fewer plants to transpire water in the air,

drought conditions become more prevalent, populations are forced to rely on still smaller land areas for food, and the process of desertification accelerates. At present, desert areas in the Sahel are expanding at rates of up to 6 million hectares (14 million acres) per year, and the harrowing sight of thousands of starving people has become all too familiar from television and newspaper reports across the world. Although the human suffering caused by desertification has been greatest in Africa, it is by no means the only area affected. The problem is worldwide as can be seen from Fig. 11.14.

CONSERVATION—THE KEYWORD FOR SOIL SCIENCE

Soils are a resource on which the ever-increasing population of the world must rely, but an unusual resource because we need to increase rather than diminish the availability of good agricultural soil along with continued use. The problem is therefore one of conservation

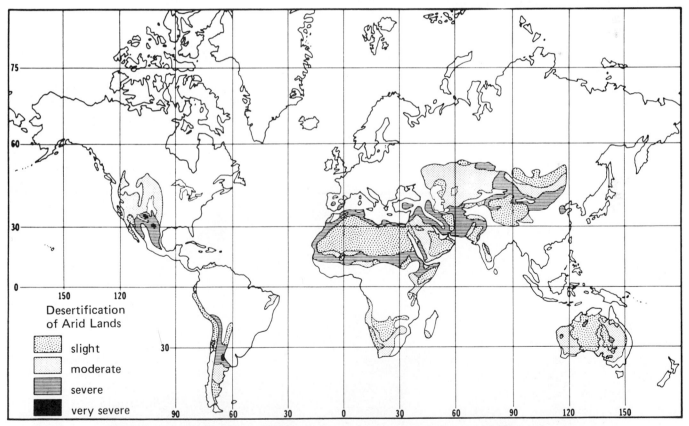

FIGURE 11-14. The desertification of arid lands around the world. The term *very severe* indicates land essentially denuded of vegetation and crop yields reduced by more than 90 percent, *severe* indicates poor range conditions and crop yields reduced by 50–90 percent, *moderate* indicates fair range conditions and crop yields reduced by 10–50 percent, and *slight* indicates good range conditions and crop yields reduced by less than 10 percent. (From H.E. Dregne, *Desertification of Arid Lands,* Harwood Academic Publisher, p. 6, 1983. Used with permission.)

and soil buildup, and it is a very serious problem indeed. On every continent, precious agricultural land is being lost because conservation measures are not being taken.

Conservation is concerned with minimizing soil erosion, minimizing the loss of nutrients through leaching, preventing the buildup of excess salts or alkalis through control of drainage (see Fig. 10.29), and restoring nutrients to the soil that are removed during cultivation through the use of fertilizers. Certain conservation practices are well known, such as crop rotation that involves planting a succession of different crops on the same piece of ground. The principle involved is that where a cultivated crop (e.g., potatoes, turnips) exposes the ground to maximum erosion, small grain crops cause less exposure, and grasses protect the ground against erosion. Hence, in the northeast United States, a common combination of rotated crops involves oats, red clover, and potatoes. Another common practice is contour plowing where surface runoff is checked by the furrows (Fig. 11.15). Sloping ground can also be terraced to reduce runoff and prevent gullys forming, and natural

channels can be controlled by damming and ditch building. Farmed land can be protected from erosion by hedges, wood areas, and grassy areas, and the removal of such protection can prove disastrous since the plowed soil is very vulnerable to removal by wind and rain. In many areas, conventional plowing is giving way to seed drilling in which seeds are buried at the appropriate depth as a hole is punched or drilled. This procedure reduces the amount of energy consumed because only one pass of a tractor is needed instead of two or three, and it greatly reduces the amount of erosion. One added cost, however, that must be weighed against the benefits is the need for additional herbicides to control the weeds that are normally eliminated by being turned under by plowing.

Despite the vital importance of soil conservation, the threat to this resource is considerable. The United Nations recently reported that not only is more than one-third of the earth's land surface now desert or semi-desert, but another 19 percent of the land surface spread among 150 countries is threatened. As we have already emphasized, the chief cause of this threat is people—

FIGURE 11-15. Contour plowing and strip farming, as shown here in Carrol County, Maryland, in 1983, are effective ways to minimize the loss of soil by erosion. (Courtesy of Soil Conservation Service, U.S. Department of Agriculture.)

stripping land of trees and other cover, overplanting, overgrazing, and ignoring proper fertilization, irrigation, and crop rotation, as well as selling good agricultural land for urban development. A special study prepared for the United Nations recently concluded that,

"As a result of the unsound use of land, deserts are creeping outward in Africa, Asia, Australia, and the Americas. Worse, the productive capacity of vast dry regions in both rich and poor countries is falling."

FURTHER READINGS

BUOL, S. W., HOLE, F. D., and McCRACKEN, R. J., *Soil Genesis and Classification,* 2nd ed. Ames, Iowa: The Iowa State University, 1980.

DREGNE, H. E., *Desertification of Arid Lands*. New York: Harwood Academic Publishers, 1983, 235 p.

DUCHAUFOUR, P., *Ecological Atlas of Soils of the World*. Translated by G. R. Mehuys, C. R. Dekimpe, and Y. A. Martel. New York: Masson Publishing Co., 1978.

LOCKERETZ, W.,"The lessons of the Dust Bowl." In *American Scientist,* vol. 66, 560–569, 1978.

REVELLE, R.,"The world supply of agricultural land." In *The Resourceful Earth,* edited by J. L. Simon and H. Kahn. New York: B. Blackwell Publishers, 1984, p. 184–201.

TROEH, F. R., HOBBS, J. A., and DONAHUE, R. L., *Soil and Water Conservation*. Englewood Cliffs, New Jersey: Prentice-Hall, Inc., 1980, 718 p.

12

The search for resources is being carried out under more and more difficult conditions. Drilling for oil from a humanmade ice island anchored to the floor of the Arctic Ocean off Alaska. The island was constructed to prevent the drill rig from being damaged by floating ice. (Photograph courtesy of Exxon Corp.)

FUTURE RESOURCES

You must love the crust of the earth on which you dwell more than the sweet crust of any bread or cake. You must be able to extract nutriment out of a sand heap. You must have so good an appetite as this, else you will live in vain.

HENRY DAVID THOREAU, JANUARY 25, 1858

INTRODUCTION

We have seen that the uses of natural resources are intimately intertwined whether they are renewable or nonrenewable. We have also seen that both a desire for rising standards of living and a growing population are causing more resources to be used all the time. For soil and water, the resource answer is quite clear—we must learn to live with what we have. For other resources, and especially metallic ores, the case is not so clear. The ways we now use resources have developed through a combination of technological advances, economic opportunity, and social acceptance. Undoubtedly, changes will occur in the future in response to new technological and economic possibilities or to social pressures. Because we cannot predict these changes, neither can we predict exactly how use patterns of resources will change. Some mineral resources may become very expensive, and others may become abundant and inexpensive. The best we can do, therefore, is to look for trends and see if something in the trends suggests future directions.

The first trend that is obvious concerns geochemically scarce metals and has been mentioned in Chapter 2 and illustrated in Fig. 2.11 which shows that the production of mineral commodities goes through a cycle. Those countries in Europe that have been industrialized for several centuries are no longer producers of most scarce metals. Their mines are closed or closing because the known ores have been depleted. The pattern observed for Europe can be seen in all parts of the world—except that many countries, such as Australia and Brazil, are still in the period of active exploration for mineral deposits that are exposed at the surface or are buried by only a shallow soil cover. European countries, and increasingly the United States and Japan, have responded to a shortage of materials from their own mines by importing the balance from countries where ore deposits are still being discovered. For the next 20 years or more, it is probable that this pattern will continue, because there are still large areas of the continental crust that have not been intensively prospected. The day will come, however, when all the accessible deposits will have been found. Where will we turn then?

The challenge will probably be met in several ways, some of which may seem unlikely or even unreasonable by present-day standards. For example, one thing that is likely to happen is that lands, such as Antarctica, previously considered off limits will be tested and no doubt found to contain mineral resources. Exploration for, and exploitation of minerals and fuels are already being carried out in Greenland and in the Arctic islands of Canada, at latitudes north of the Arctic Circle, and under conditions of extreme difficulty (Fig. 12.1). It would be a relatively small step to use similar techniques in Antarctica. Another step will surely be intensive exploration of the ocean floor. We already know that manganese nodules are widely distributed on the deep sea floor and that certain types of metal deposits form along the mid-ocean ridges at water depths in excess of 1500 meters. The deposits found so far are mostly small and mainly of scientific interest. Within the geological record, however, there are other kinds of deposits that seem to have formed through the same submarine processes. It is thus very likely that continuing exploration of the sea floor will turn up some of these deposits, and that they and the manganese nodules will some day be mined. In a sense, we can think of the sea floor as another continent to explore for minerals, just as Antarctica is another continent to be explored. Both the sea floor and Antarctica are very difficult places to work, however, and it is hardly reasonable to think we will turn to such inhospitable places for all our needs—we are likely to seek only the richest and largest ore bodies in such environments.

A more likely place in which to seek ores of the future is the deeper portions of the continents. Excluding digging or drilling an actual test hole, even the most sophisticated techniques used today cannot locate ore deposits beneath 500 meters of barren rock. We believe that more deposits are there to be discovered because a few have been discovered by accident or brilliant deduction, and because many deposits extend down several thousand meters in depth and are only exposed at the surface because a happenstance of erosion has uncovered them. Unfortunately, that knowledge provides little help in finding deeply buried deposits (Fig. 12.2). Here, obviously, is a circumstance where technological devel-

FIGURE 12-1. Mining under difficult conditions. The Black Angel Mine in Greenland is covered by a glacier. The mine openings are high up on the cliff of a fjord. All people and materials must be moved by cable. The only water available for use in the mine is seawater, so special corrosion resistant equipment has had to be designed. (Photograph by F.M. Vokes.)

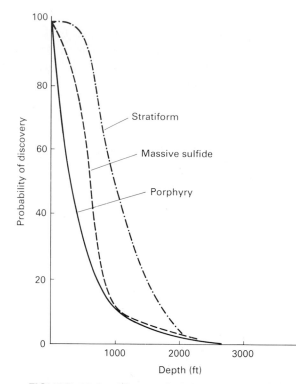

FIGURE 12-2. The probability that an ore deposit can be found declines with depth. A probability of 100, for ore deposits outcropping at the surface, means certain discovery. A probability of 50 means half of the deposits can be found. A stratiform deposit, because of its shape, is more likely to be found at depth than a porphyry copper deposit of the same size.

opments might be expected to play a role. Already, several countries–the Soviet Union, United States, Canada, and France among them—have programs of varying intensity aimed at developing a three-dimensional picture of the crust through new seismic techniques and special drilling programs (Fig. 12.3). These special programs are only the beginning of what someday will probably be full-scale attempts to map details of the earth's crust down to 10,000 meters or more. When that has been done, a new frontier larger than the surface of all continents explored to date will have been opened. We can hypothesize that a mineral production curve for a coun-

try such as the United States might, as a result, look like that in Fig. 12.4. No one can say when, or if, we will be able to explore and mine the crust at great depths, but it is our suspicion that we not only will be able to do so, but that we might start doing so within the next 20–30 years. We suspect, too, the places where the first deep discoveries might be made are the countries of Europe, North America, and Australia, where deep mapping is being carried out.

The time will eventually come when deposits of geochemically scarce metals of the kind we mine today are all gone, or are so expensive to find and mine, that other alternatives will be sought. Waiting in the wings are low-grade deposits that today are not of interest to miners because the mining costs are too great to produce metals economically. Examples of large low-grade deposits are certain black shales that are not only rich in organic matter but that also have anomalously high contents of metals such as copper, uranium, cobalt, and zinc. Other examples are certain very large igneous intrusions, such as the Duluth Gabbro in Minnesota, that

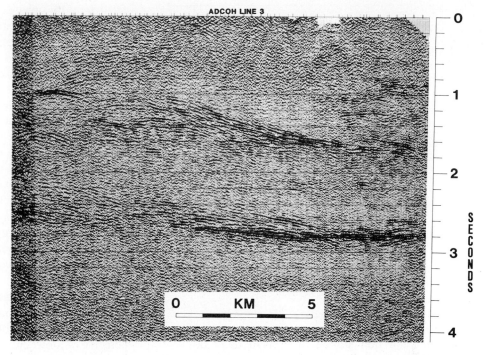

ADCOH LINE 3

0 KM 5

FIGURE 12-3. Deep seismic section across a portion of the Blue Ridge province of the Appalachians in northwestern South Carolina showing two major thrust faults (the areas of intense reflection) and indicating that the crystalline rocks of the Blue Ridge have been thrust northwest (to the left) over the lower Paleozoic sediments of the Valley and Ridge Province. (Courtesy of C. Coruh and J.K. Costain.)

contain very large tonnages of very low-grade nickel and copper deposits. As far as we can tell, the large, low-grade deposits are like most other mineral deposits and are just small, chemically anomalous volumes of the earth's crust. This means the day must come when a huge population will cause these deposits, too, to be depleted. Beyond identifiable mineral deposits, whether of high or low grade, we face the situation discussed in Chapter 7, where the great bulk of the geochemically

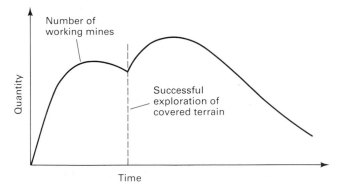

FIGURE 12-4. A Hewett curve depicting the number of working mines in a country versus time. If a new technological discovery allows deeper, formerly inaccessible terrain to be prospected, a new Hewett curve commences, rising to a new peak as the number of working mines increases. Unless another technological advance is made, the curve will eventually decline to zero when the last mine is worked out.

scarce metals in the crust are hidden in common silicate minerals by solid solution. In short, we reach the mineralogical barrier (Fig. 7–37). If we are to transgress that barrier, we will probably have to pay a high price. An example of the way copper production might develop in the future is given in Fig. 12.5. The pattern shown is conjectural, of course, but even if wrong in detail, it highlights an important factor—recovery of scarce metals will inevitably be more difficult and more expensive in the future. There is little doubt that we will continue to use the range of metallic resources we use today. What will change is the relative balance of the different metals. The per capita consumption of geochemically scarce metals will, by the year 2100 A.D., probably decline to small fractions of today's values, due partly to their increased costs and partly to their replacement by substitutes (e.g., copper wires by glass fiber optics). By contrast, we can anticipate that the per capita consumptions of geochemically abundant metals will have remained high and on a global basis, have risen. The metals of the future will be aluminum, magnesium, titanium, and probably iron, plus a number of nonmetallic substances like glass and ceramics, made from abundant materials.

The sources of the abundant materials in the future will no doubt be common rocks. Aluminum will be derived from clays, shales, or other aluminous rocks, iron from the astronomically large sedimentary rock units called banded iron formations, and magnesium from the common rock called dolostone. The materials used for building—crushed stone, ingredients for ce-

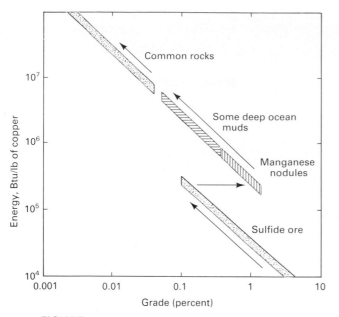

FIGURE 12-5. A hypothetical depiction of copper production in the centuries ahead. When the rich sulfide ores have been depleted, manganese nodules may be exploited. Some nodules contain more copper than certain sulfide ores, but the cost of recovery is higher from nodules. As nodules are mined, copper-rich deep-sea muds may be worked, and finally common rocks such as basalt may have to be used.

ment, clays for brick making, glass, and so forth, are derived from very common rocks. There are no real possibilities of shortages developing for these materials in the future except on a very local basis. What then of the critical chemical and fertilizer materials? This group of resources bears many resemblances to deposits of geochemically scarce metals in that the raw materials are won from special mineral deposits—marine and lake evaporite deposits, for example, or marine phosphorite deposits. Deposits of most of these compounds are very large. Furthermore, because most of the desired compounds are soluble to some extent, they are also present in seawater, saline lakes, or saline ground waters. These saline waters will probably be the future sources of a great many nonmetallic chemical resources and even now are producing compounds in many places (Fig. 12.6).

There are some important exceptions to the possibility that future production of nonmetallic compounds will be from brines. These are compounds that are not very soluble and hence are not present to any great extent in brines. Examples are fluorite (CaF_2), barite ($BaSO_4$), and apatite ($Ca_5(PO_4)_3(F,OH)$). Of the three, the most important by far is apatite, the main ingredient of phosphorite and the principal source of phosphatic

fertilizers. Phosphates are an essential fertilizer ingredient—there is no substitute. Renewable sources of phosphate, such as the bones of animals, the bodies of fish, and the manure from certain animals, are too small to be of any use. The only sources beyond today's rich ores (Chapter 8) that we know of are off-shore marine deposits, certain shales, and limestones that contain low concentrations of phosphates. No adequate assessment has been made of the low-grade deposits, but two things seem clear—first, the low-grade deposits are in the same areas as the present high-grade ores, and second, the magnitude of the low-grade ores seems astronomically large. We must conclude, therefore, that nonmetallic mineral resources may present problems in their local distributions, but that the total magnitude of the resources does not appear to be a problem. Resources of the future, in other words, will be extensions of today's resources.

In Chapters 4 and 5 we examined the sources from which we now draw our supplementary energy and from which we will probably draw energy in the future. We perceive a slow change from nonrenewable resources like oil, gas, and coal toward a mix of nuclear and renewable sources such as solar and ocean power. Even though we do not know by which techniques we will convert solar power to electricity, we suspect that the sun will eventually become our main energy source because it has few environmental problems, that nuclear power will be the second major source, and that electricity will be the way the user receives and uses the energy.

Eventually, we suspect there will emerge a society that is not limited or threatened by overall supply constraints. How the global society will reach this point, however, we cannot foresee. The reason we cannot foresee how the pattern will change is that, as we saw in Chapter 1, the world's population will probably grow to a number in excess of 11 billion people during the next 100 years. Somehow, society will have to respond to the needs and aspirations of this astronomically large population more rapidly than technologies can be invented to solve the problems. In short, the needs will have to be met to a great extent through technologies already developed and through use of resources already identified. To do this, however, will require maximum, efficient, and innovative use of our resources. An elegant example of such use is the invention of the charcoal briquet that we use for barbeques. It resulted from the application of a simple, existing technology to a common, but incompletely used resource, by one of America's most innovative geniuses, Henry Ford.

In the years prior to 1920, Ford operated a sawmill in the hardwood forests around Iron Mountain, Michigan, to make wooden parts for his then successful

FIGURE 12-6. The large brine recovery plant at the Great Salt Lake with brine evaporation ponds visible in the background. (Courtesy of Great Salt Lake Minerals and Chemicals Corp.)

Model T automobile. Ford watched the growing piles of wood scraps with distaste and sought a way to use them. Most charcoal available up to that time was made in lumps. It was not uniform in size or heat output and was used primarily as an industrial fuel or for home cooking in wood-burning stoves. Ford's idea was to chip the wood into small pieces and then, after the wood was turned into charcoal, to grind it into a powder, add a binder, and compress the mix into the now familiar pillow shape of the charcoal briquet. He called on his friend, inventor Thomas Alva Edison (Fig. 12.7), to de-

sign the plant. By early 1921, Ford's plant was in full operation. It was a complete operation, using every bit of the wood scrap pile, including the smoke.

Power came from a Ford-built-and-owned dam and hydroelectric facility nearby, and the wood byproducts drawn off during the charring process were run through a condenser to make ketones for paints for Ford's cars and methanol for anti-freeze. The briquets were sold to industry and later to the public through his automobile agencies. E.G. Kingsford, a relative who owned one of Ford's earliest automobile sales agencies,

FIGURE 12-7. Henry Ford and his associates who were responsible for producing the first charcoal briquets. From the left, Ford's close friend Harvey Firestone, Henry Ford, Thomas Alva Edison, who designed the briquetting plant, and E.G. Kingsford, first manager of the briquetting plant. (Courtesy the Kingsford Products Company, a subsidiary of the Clorox Company.)

was named manager of the briquet operation. A company town was built nearby and named Kingsford. This is the origin of the name Kingsford on one of the present-day popular brands of briquets.

We have seen that the resources are there and, as the charcoal briquet story demonstrates, the needed inventive genius is also available. We must be cautious, however, because the consequences of resource use can often lead to severe disruption of our living space. We have much more to learn about that. The challenge posed by the needs and aspirations of a population of 11 billion or more people, the uneven distribution of the natural resources required to meet the needs, and the pressures on the environment as the resources are produced and used will make the next 100 years the most crucial and difficult years the human race has ever faced. Every detail of our societal fabric will be examined and reexamined in the process.

FURTHER READINGS

CAMERON, E. N., *At the Crossroads: The Mineral Position of the United States*. New York: John Wiley and Sons, 1986.

WOLFE, J. A., *Mineral Resources*. New York: Chapman and Hall, 1984.

APPENDIX 1

UNITS AND CONVERSIONS

TABLE A1.1

Multiples and submultiples

	Name	Common Prefixes
$10^{12} = 1,000,000,000,000$	trillion	tera
$10^9 = 1,000,000,000$	billion	giga
$10^6 = 1,000,000$	million	mega
$10^3 = 1000$	thousand	kilo
$10^2 = 100$	hundred	hecto
$10^1 = 10$	ten	deka
$10^{-1} = 0.1$	tenth	deci
$10^{-2} = 0.01$	hundredth	centi
$10^{-3} = 0.001$	thousandth	milli
$10^{-6} = 0.000001$	millionth	micro
$10^{-9} = 0.000000001$	billionth	nano
$10^{-12} = 0.000000000001$	trillionth	pico

TABLE A1.2

Conversions between common units of measure

Linear, Area, and Volume Measures

1 kilometer	= 0.6214 mile
1 meter	= 3.281 feet
1 centimeter	= 0.3937 inch
1 square kilometer	= 0.386 square mile
1 square meter	= 10.764 square feet
1 hectare	= 10,000 square meters
	= 2.471 acres
1 square centimeter	= 0.155 square inch
1 cubic kilometer	= 0.240 cubic mile
1 cubic meter	= 35.32 cubic feet
	= 264.2 gallons (U.S.)
1 liter	= 0.264 gallons (U.S.)
1 barrel (oil)	= 42 gallons (U.S.)

Table A1.2 (cont.)

Weight and Mass Measures

1 long ton	= 1.016 metric tons
	= 2240 pounds
1 short ton	= 0.9072 metric tons
	= 2000 pounds
1 metric ton	= 1000 kilogram
	= 0.984 long ton
	= 1.102 short tons
1 kilogram	= 2.205 pounds
1 troy ounce	= 31.10 gram
	= 1.097 Adup. ounce

Energy and Power Measures

1 joule	= 0.239 gram-calorie
1 calorie	= 3.9685×10^{-3} British thermal units (btu)
1 kilowatt hour	= 10^3 watt hours
	= 3.6×10^6 joules
	= 3,413 btu
1 watt	= 3.4129 btu per hour
	= 1.341×10^{-3} horsepower
	= 1 joule per second
1 watt per min.	= 14.34 calories per minute

Average equivalents (as used in this book)

1 barrel oil weighs approximately 136.4 kilograms
1 barrel oil is equivalent to approximately 0.22 metric ton coal
1 barrel oil yields approximately 6.0×10^9 joules of energy
1 metric ton of coal yields approximately 27.2×10^9 joules of energy
1 barrel of cement weighs 170.5 kilograms

APPENDIX 2

GEOCHEMICAL ABUNDANCES OF SELECTED ELEMENTS IN THE EARTH'S CRUST
(parts per million)

Element	Symbol	Atomic Number	Atomic Weight*	Average Continental Crust	Seawater
Aluminum	Al	13	26.98	82,300	0.01
Antimony	Sb	51	121.75	0.2	5×10^{-4}
Arsenic	As	33	74.92	1.8	0.003
Barium	Ba	56	137.34	425	0.03
Beryllium	Be	4	9.01	2.8	6×10^{-7}
Bismuth	Bi	83	208.98	0.17	2×10^{-5}
Boron	B	5	10.81	10	4.6
Bromine	Br	35	79.91	2.5	65
Cadmium	Cd	48	112.40	0.2	1×10^{-4}
Calcium	Ca	20	40.08	41,000	400
Carbon	C	6	12.01	200	28
Chlorine	Cl	17	35.45	130	19,000
Chromium	Cr	24	52.00	100	5×10^{-5}
Cobalt	Co	27	58.93	25	1×10^{-4}
Copper	Cu	29	63.54	55	0.003
Fluorine	F	9	19.00	625	1.3
Gallium	Ga	31	69.72	15	3×10^{-5}
Germanium	Ge	32	72.59	1.5	6×10^{-5}
Gold	Au	79	196.97	0.004	$<1 \times 10^{-5}$
Hydrogen	H	1	1.008	1400	108,000
Iodine	I	53	126.90	0.5	0.06
Iron	Fe	26	55.85	56,000	0.01
Lead	Pb	82	207.19	12.5	3×10^{-5}
Lithium	Li	3	6.94	20	0.17
Magnesium	Mg	12	24.31	23,000	1350
Manganese	Mn	25	54.94	950	0.002
Mercury	Hg	80	200.59	0.08	3×10^{-5}
Molybdenum	Mo	42	95.94	1.5	0.01
Nickel	Ni	28	58.71	75	0.002
Nitrogen	N	7	14.01	20	0.5
Oxygen	O	8	16.00	464,000	857,000

TABLE (cont.)

Element	Symbol	Atomic Number	Atomic Weight*	Average Continental Crust	Seawater
Palladium	Pd	46	106.4	0.01	$<1 \times 10^{-5}$
Phosphorus	P	15	30.97	1050	0.07
Platinum	Pt	78	195.09	0.005	$<1 \times 10^{-5}$
Potassium	K	19	39.10	21,000	380
Rubidium	Rb	37	85.47	90	0.12
Selenium	Se	34	78.96	0.05	4×10^{-4}
Silicon	Si	14	28.09	282,000	3.0
Silver	Ag	47	107.87	0.07	4×10^{-5}
Sodium	Na	11	22.99	24,000	10,500
Sulfur	S	16	32.06	260	885
Thorium	Th	90	232.04	9.6	5×10^{-5}
Tin	Sn	50	118.69	2.0	8×10^{-4}
Titanium	Ti	22	47.90	5700	0.001
Tungsten	W	74	183.85	1.5	1×10^{-4}
Uranium	U	92	238.03	2.7	0.003
Vanadium	V	23	50.94	135	0.002
Zinc	Zn	30	65.37	70	0.01

*Source of atomic weights: International Union of Pure and Applied Chemistry, *Compte. Rendu.,* XXIII Conf., pp. 177–178, 1965. Based on atomic mass of $C^{12} = 12$; rounded to two decimal places.

APPENDIX 3

EARTH STATISTICS

TABLE A3.1

Earth Dimensions and Mass

Earth radius—equatorial	6378 km	3963 mi
—polar	6357 km	3950 mi
—average sphere	6371 km	3959 mi
Crustal thickness—continents	25–30 km	16–9 mi
—oceans	10–15 km	6–9 mi
Mantle thickness	2900 km	1802 mi
Outer core thickness	2420 km	1504 mi
Inner core thickness	1050 km	652 mi
Mass of the earth	5.98×10^{21} metric tons	
Mass of ice	$25–30 \times 10^{15}$ metric tons	
Mass of oceans	1.4×10^{18} metric tons	
Mass of crust	2.5×10^{19} metric tons	
Mass of mantle	4.05×10^{21} metric tons	
Mass of core	1.9×10^{21} metric tons	

TABLE A3.2

Areas of the major continents and oceans

Continents

Asia	44,120,650 km²	17,035,000 mi²
Africa	30,134,650 km²	11,635,000 mi²
North America	24,436,650 km²	9,435,000 mi²
South America	17,767,400 km²	6,860,000 mi²
Antarctica	13,209,000 km²	5,100,000 mi²
Europe	9,971,500 km²	3,850,000 mi²
Australia	7,705,300 km²	2,975,000 mi²
Greenland	2,175,600 km²	840,000 mi²
Total major continents	149,520,700 km²	57,730,000 mi²

Some Selected Countries

Soviet Union	22,403,500 km²	8,650,000 mi²
Canada	9,976,700 km²	3,852,000 mi²
United States	9,520,800 km²	3,676,000 mi²
South Africa	1,224,000 km²	472,600 mi²
United Kingdom	244,000 km²	94,200 mi²

TABLE A3.2 (cont.)

Major Oceans and Seas

Pacific Ocean	165,721,000 km²	63,985,000 mi²
Atlantic Ocean	81,660,000 km²	31,529,000 mi²
Indian Ocean	73,445,000 km²	28,357,000 mi²
Arctic Ocean	14,351,000 km²	5,541,000 mi²
Mediterranean Sea	2,966,000 km²	1,145,000 mi²
South China Sea	2,318,000 km²	895,000 mi²
Bering Sea	2,274,000 km²	878,000 mi²
Caribbean Sea	1,943,000 km²	750,000 mi²
Gulf of Mexico	1,813,000 km²	700,000 mi²

APPENDIX 4
GEOLOGIC TIME SCALE

Left column (Major Geologic Intervals)

Millions of Years

Millions of Years	Deposit	Major Geologic Intervals

Major Geologic Intervals

CENOZOIC
MESOZOIC
PALEOZOIC
PROTEROZOIC
ARCHEAN

- 500
- 1000 — Zambian Copper Belt
- 1500 — Sullivan, B.C. (Pb-Zn)
- Broken Hill, N.S.W. (Pb-Zn)
- Sudbury, Ont., (Ni)
- 2000 — Lake Superior-type banded iron formations
- Great Dike, Zimbabwe
- 2500 — Witwatersrand gold deposits
- Earliest known volcanogenic massive sulfide deposits
- 3000 (ARCHEAN)
- 3500
- Oldest known rocks
- 4000
- 4500

Formation of Earth's crust, about 4600 million years ago

Right column

Periods	Millions of Years Ago (Approx.)	Deposits
Recent and Pleistocene Pliocene	1.6	New Caledonia (Ni)
	5.3	
Miocene	23.7	Climax, Colo. (Mo)
Oliogocene	36.6	Bingham, Utah (Cu)
Eocene		Green River oil shales
Paleocene	57.8	Chiatura and Nikopol, USSR (Manganese)
	66.4	
		Major bauxite deposits
Cretaceous	144	
Jurassic		Major porphyry coppers
	208	
Triassic	245	
Permian	286	Carlsbad (USA) and Stassfurt (Germany) potash / Kupferschiefer
Carboniferous — Pennsylvanian	320	
Mississippian	360	Earliest economic coal measures
		Elk Point - Williston Basin (Potash)
Devonian	408	Emergence of land plants
Silurian	438	
Ordovician	505	
Cambrian	570	

GLOSSARY

Abundant metals Metals with an earth crustal geochemical abundance of at least 0.1 percent.

Acid mine drainage Waters issuing from an active or abandoned mine that are made strongly acid by the decomposition of sulfide minerals, usually pyrite, FeS_2.

Acid rain Rainfall that is abnormally acid; generally attributed to the presence of nitrous and sulfur oxide pollutants in the atmosphere.

Acre foot The volume of water required to cover 1 acre to a depth of 1 foot; 325,900 gallons; 1,233,500 liters.

Adit A horizontal tunnel serving as an entrance into a mine.

Age-sex pyramids Diagrams that display the distribution of population in terms of age and sex.

Aggregate Any hard inert construction material (e.g., sand, gravel, crushed stone) used in the preparation of concrete or as a road bed.

Alchemy The medieval science of chemistry, one objective of which was to transform base metals into gold; another was to discover a universal cure for disease and a means of indefinitely prolonging life.

Algoma-type A type of banded iron formation whose formation can be attributed to submarine volcanic exhalation.

Alkali feldspars A series of silicate minerals involving solid solution from $KAlSi_3O_8$ (potash feldspar, orthoclase) to $NaAlSi_3O_8$ (albite).

Alkalinization The buildup of salts of calcium, sodium, and potassium in soils due to evaporation.

Alloy A substance composed of two or more metals or a metal and certain nonmetals.

Alluvial fan A low, gently sloping, conelike accumulation of sediment that has been deposited where a stream issues from a mountain valley onto a plain.

Alpha particle A subatomic particle, having an atomic weight of 4 and a $+2$ charge (equivalent to a helium nucleus) released during radioactive disintegration.

Amphibole A group of silicate minerals of general formula $A_2B_5(Si, Al)_8O_{22}(OH, F)_2$ where $A = Na, Ca, K, B = Mg$, Fe, Ti, Al, Li, Mn.

Anaerobic digestion The breakdown of organic material by microorganisms in the absence of oxygen.

Andalusite A mineral, composition Al_2SiO_5; widely used in the manufacture of ceramics and glasses.

Andesite A fine-grained igneous rock composed primarily of intermediate plagioclase feldspar with one or more mafic minerals.

Anhydrite A mineral, composition $CaSO_4$; an evaporite mineral.

Anion A negatively charged atom.

Annealing The process of holding materials at high temperatures, but below their melting points, in order to change their physical properties such as brittleness and machinability by causing changes in the sizes and shapes of individual grains.

Anorthosite An igneous rock composed almost entirely of the mineral plagioclase feldspar.

Aplite A light-colored, fine-grained igneous rock consisting largely of quartz and potassium feldspar.

Aqueduct A conduit or channel built to convey water from one place to another.

Aquifer A rock formation that is water bearing.

Asbestos A general term applied to any of a group of fibrous silicate minerals that are widely used for industrial purposes because they are incombustible, nonconducting, and chemically resistant.

Asphalt A black to brown viscous liquid that consists of hydrocarbons; natural asphalts form by the evaporation of the volatile fractions of petroleum.

Asphaltine A solid, noncrystalline black hydrocarbon residual of crude oils or other bitumen.

Atmosphere The mixture of gases that surrounds the earth; composed approximately of 78 percent nitrogen, 21 percent

371

oxygen, 1 percent argon, and 0.03 percent carbon dioxide and variable amounts of water vapor.

Atmospheric inversion The abnormal condition in which a layer of warmer air overlies a layer of cooler air.

Atomic substitution The substitution of one element for another on the lattice sites in a crystalline solid.

Attapulgite (= palygorskite); a clay mineral of composition $(Mg,Al)_2Si_4O_{10}OH\bullet4H_2O$.

Azonal soil In U.S. classification systems, one of the three soil orders that lack well-developed horizons and that resemble the parent materials.

Backfill Rock debris, usually derived from mining or mineral processing, that is placed in mined-out areas of a mine.

Ball clay A light-colored, highly plastic organic containing refractory clay used in making ceramics; so named because of the early English practice of rolling the clay into balls approximately 35 centimeters in diameter for storage and shipping.

Banded iron formations The largest iron deposits. Sedimentary rocks consisting of alternating bands of iron oxide minerals, iron silicates, and silica also called banded jaspilite and itabirite.

Banded jaspilite A synonym for banded iron formations.

Barite A mineral, composition $BaSO_4$; a heavy soft mineral widely used in oil drilling muds and as a filler in paints, papers, and textiles.

Basalt A dark, fine-grained igneous rock composed chiefly of plagioclase, feldspar, pyroxene, and olivine.

Base cation Cations such as Ca^{2+}, Mg^{2+}, K^+, Na^+.

Base metal Generally any nonprecious metal, but used today to refer to the metals such as copper, lead, zinc, mercury, and tin that are neither precious nor used as ferroalloy metals.

Bauxite The principal ore of aluminum; a mixture of amorphous and crystalline hydrous aluminum oxides and hydroxides.

Benches Level, shelflike, areas in open-pit mines, where ore and waste rocks are extracted.

Beneficiation The process of producing a concentrate of valuable ore minerals through the removal of valueless gangue minerals.

Bentonite A soft, plastic, porous, light-colored rock consisting of colloidal silica and clay and that has the possibility of absorbing large quantities of water; forms as a result of the weathering of volcanic ash.

Beta particle A high energy electron released during radioactive decay.

Biochemical Oxygen Demand (BOD) The amount of oxygen required by microorganisms in natural waters of a river, stream, or lake.

Biodegradation The natural process by which biological activities breakdown and decompose organic matter.

Biogenic gas Gas formed as a result of bacterial action on organic matter.

Biomass The total amount of living organisms in a particular area, expressed in terms of weight or volume.

Biosphere The living sphere, encompassing all living species from the highest points on mountains to the deepest parts of the ocean.

Biotite Dark mica of composition $K(Mg,Fe)_3[(Al,Fe)Si_3O_{10}](OH,F)_2$.

Bitumen A general term applied to dark-colored liquid to plastic hydrocarbons such as petroleum and asphalts.

Bittern A solution, such as seawater, that has been concentrated by evaporation until salt, sodium chloride, has begun to crystallize; bitterns typically contain high magnesium contents.

Blowout An oil or gas well in which very high pressures encountered during drilling were sufficient to force the drill out the top of the drill hole; this usually results in the fountaining of oil, gas, and water as a gusher.

Boghead coal A coal composed primarily of algal debris.

Bog iron deposits Accumulations of soft, spongy hydrous iron oxides that form in bogs, swamps, shallow lakes, and soil zones.

Borax A mineral, composition $Na_2B_4O_7\bullet10H_2O$; a light-colored compound formed during the evaporation of alkaline lakes; widely used in the preparation of soaps, glasses, ceramics, and other materials.

Brazing The joining of metals by flowing a thin layer of metal between them. The term brazing is used at temperatures above 425°C, soldering at lower temperatures.

Breccia A coarse-grained clastic sedimentary rock composed of angular rock fragments set in a finer grained matrix; also said of any type of rock that has been highly fractured by igneous or tectonic processes.

Brimstone A common and commercial name for sulfur.

Brine Seawater that, due to evaporation or freezing, contains more than the usual 3.5 percent dissolved salts.

British thermal unit See BTU.

Bronze Age The period in the development of a people or region when bronze replaced stone as the material to make tools and weapons.

Brown ores Brown colored iron ores consisting of a mixture of amorphous and crystalline iron hydroxides.

BTU British thermal unit, the energy required to raise 1 pound of water 1°F.

Building stone A general term applied to any massive dense rock suitable for use in construction.

Cable-tool drill A method of drilling in which the cutting bit is attached to a long steel cable. Cutting is accomplished by the bit being raised and dropped again and again.

Calcining The roasting of limestone to drive off CO_2 to make lime, CaO.

Calcite $CaCO_3$; a common mineral and the principal constituent of limestone.

Caliche A layer of calcite that forms in soils in arid and semiarid regions as a result of the evaporation of calcium-bearing ground waters.

Calorie A unit of energy defined as the energy required to raise the temperature of 1 gram of water 1°C.

Cannel coal   A compact sapropelic coal consisting primarily of spores accumulated in stagnant water.

Capture   In nuclear processes, the absorption of a neutron, proton, or electron by an atom. This results in a change in atomic or isotopic identity.

Carat   A common term with two meanings. First, a standard unit, 200 milligrams, for weighing precious stones; second, a term used to define the purity or fineness of gold and meaning 1/24. Pure gold is 24 carat.

Carbon cycle   The cyclical movement of carbon compounds between the biosphere, lithosphere, atmosphere, and hydrosphere.

Carbonation   A chemical weathering process in which carbon dioxide dissolved in water converts oxides of calcium, magnesium, and iron into carbonates.

Carbonatite   A carbonate rock of apparent magmatic origin; commonly a host for rare-earth elements.

Cassiterite   A mineral, composition SnO_2; the most important ore of tin.

Catagenesis   Physical and chemical changes intermediate between near-surface diagenesis and deep burial metagenesis; used especially in reference to organic matter.

Catalysis   Acceleration of a chemical reaction by an element or compound that is not incorporated in the reaction products.

Catalyst   A substance that accelerates a chemical reaction without remaining in the reaction products.

Catalytic cracking   The use of catalysts to break heavier hydrocarbons into lighter ones.

Cation   A positively charged atom.

Cation exchange   The exchange of one cation for another, especially by clay minerals.

Cement   A binding material; see Portland cement.

Cement rock   A limestone with a sufficient clay content that it becomes cement upon calcining.

Chain reaction   Where one reaction leads on to further reactions; a controlled chain reaction (see Fig. 5.3) occurs in a nuclear reactor, an uncontrolled chain reaction in a nuclear weapon.

Channelization   The straightening, and sometimes deepening and lining, of a stream or river channel so that the water flows more rapidly; commonly used to alleviate flooding.

Chelation   The retention of a metallic ion by two atoms of a single organic molecule.

Chemical flooding   The injection of chemicals into an oil well to promote the release of oil trapped in the rocks.

Chemical weathering   The process of weathering by which chemical reactions convert the original minerals into new mineral phases.

China clay   A commercial term for kaolin used in the manufacture of chinaware.

Chlorofluoromethane   Compounds such as $CFCl_3$, used as propellants in aerosol cans, and which can damage the ozone layer in the earth's upper atmosphere.

Chromite   A mineral, composition $FeCr_2O_4$; the principal ore mineral of chromium.

Clastic   An adjective describing rocks or sediments composed of fragments derived from preexisting rocks.

Clay   A term with two common meanings. First, a natural rock fragment smaller in diameter than 1/256 millimeter; second, any of a group of hydrous sheet structure silicate minerals.

Cleavage   The general tendency of a mineral or rock to split along natural directions of weakness.

Clinton type   A fossiliferous sedimentary iron ore rich in hematite and goethite of the Clinton or correlative formations in the Silurian sandstones of the eastern United States.

Clod   A lump of soil produced by artificial breakage such as plowing. See ped.

Coal   A combustible rock containing more than 50 percent by weight and more than 70 percent by volume of carbonaceous matter derived from accumulated plant remains.

Coalification   The process by which plant material is converted into coal.

Col   An old British term for coal.

Cold-working   Shaping of metals at room temperature by hammering or rolling; a process that hardens and strengthens the metal.

Comminution   The process of crushing and grinding ores in order to break ore minerals loose from the valueless gangue minerals.

Comprehensive Soil Classification System   An extensive system of soil nomenclature based on physical and chemical characteristics.

Concentrate   Ground and beneficiated product that consists of one or more ore minerals that have been selectively removed from the original mixture of ore and gangue minerals.

Conduction (of heat)   The process by which heat is transferred by molecular impact without transfer of matter itself. The principal manner by which heat is transmitted through solids.

Cone-of-depression   The depression in the water table that develops around a well from which water is being pumped.

Conglomerate   A coarse-grained clastic rock comprised of coarse rounded fragments set in a finer matrix.

Consumption (of water)   The use of water such that it is not returned to the ground water or surface water source from which it was drawn.

Contact metamorphism   The thermal, and sometimes introduced chemical, effects occurring in a rock resulting from the intrusion of an adjacent igneous body.

Continental shelf   That portion of the continental margin that lies between the shoreline and the continental slope.

Convection   The movement of material, gaseous or liquid, wherein the hotter portion rises and cooler portions descend as a consequence of differences in density.

Convert (metallurgical)   The process of passing oxygen through a molten mass of sulfides in order to convert iron sulfides into iron oxides so that the iron may be more readily separated into the slag.

Corundum   A mineral, composition Al_2O_3; the second hard-

est mineral after diamond. In clear, colored crystals it is known as sapphire or ruby if blue or red, respectively.

Cracking The process by which heavier hydrocarbons are broken into lighter ones.

Critical(ity) (in a nuclear reactor) The condition at which a nuclear reactor is maintained in order to sustain a chain reaction.

Critical mass (in a nuclear reaction) The amount of uranium required to maintain a chain reaction in a nuclear reactor.

Crosscut Passageway of a mine that are cut perpendicular to the long dimension of the deposit.

Crushed rock Any rock material that has been crushed for use as fill, for road beds, or for construction aggregate.

Crushing (of rock) The process of breaking rock into smaller fragments to facilitate the separation of the ore minerals from the gangue.

Cupellation The process of freeing silver or gold from base metals by using a small bone ash cup, called a cupel, and lead.

Dam A barrier built across a river or stream to hold back water.

Decay (radioactive) Spontaneous, radioactive transformation of one nuclide to another.

Deoxyribonucleic acid DNA, the substance within the chromosomes of living cells that carries hereditary instructions and directs the production of proteins.

Desertification The expansion of desertlike conditions as a result of natural climatic changes or human-induced activities such as overgrazing or farming.

Deuterium An isotope of hydrogen containing one proton and one neutron in its nucleus.

Diagenesis Physical and chemical changes that occur in a sediment after deposition, and during and after lithification, but not including weathering or metamorphism.

Diamond A cubic form of carbon; the hardest mineral, widely used in jewelry and as an industrial abrasive.

Diaspore A mineral, composition $AlO(OH)$; a light-colored compound that occurs in bauxite.

Diatomite A rock or unconsolidated earthy material composed of accumulated siliceous tests of diatoms, single-celled marine or freshwater plants.

Diatoms Free-floating, single-celled marine organisms; the accumulation and thermal alteration of diatoms is believed to result in the formation of petroleum.

Dimension stone Building stone that is quarried and shaped into blocks according to specifications.

Diorite Igneous rocks generally composed of amphibole, plagioclase, pyroxene, and sometimes minor amounts of quartz.

Direct shipping ore Ore of sufficiently high grade that it can be profitably shipped to a smelter without first requiring beneficiation.

Distillation (or fractionation) The process of separating crude oil into various liquids and gases of different chemical and physical properties.

Dolomite A mineral, composition $CaMg(CO_3)_2$; a common sedimentary carbonate mineral; also commonly, but incorrectly, used to refer to a rock composed of dolomite.

Dolostone A rock composed of dolomite.

Doping The process of introducing trace amounts of an element into another element or compound to produce desirable electrical or other properties.

Dredging The excavation of ore-bearing or waste materials by a floating barge or raft equipped to bring up and process, or transport, the materials.

Drifts The passageways of a mine that are cut parallel to the long dimension of a deposit.

Dry steam Natural geothermal systems dominated by water vapor (steam) with little or no liquid in the system.

Dunite A rock composed nearly entirely of olivine.

Electroplating A process by which the passage of an electric current through a metal-bearing solution results in the plating out of that metal on an electrode.

Emery A granular mixture of corundum and varying amounts of iron oxides (magnetite or hematite); used as an abrasive.

Energy The capacity to do work.

Equivalent rainfall The amount of water, including rainfall and runoff, to which an area of land is subjected.

Eutrophication The process by which waters become deficient in oxygen due to an increased abundance of dissolved nutrients and decaying plant matter.

Evaporite Sedimentary rocks that form as a result of the evaporation of saline solutions.

Evapotranspiration The transfer of water in the ground to water vapor in the atmosphere through the combined processes of evaporation and transpiration.

Exchange The process by which a mineral, especially a clay, gives up one cation bound to its lattice for another cation in solution.

Exchange capacity The quantitative ability of a mineral to exchange ions with a solution.

Exfoliation The process by which thin concentric shells or flat layers of a rock or mineral are successively broken from the outer surface of a larger rock.

Face The wall in a mine where ore is being extracted. To remove the ore, holes are drilled into the face; these are filled with explosives and detonated to break the rock so that it can be removed.

Fast breeder reactor A nuclear reactor in which fuel is made or "bred" in a blanket of ^{238}U wrapped around the core.

Fast reactors Nuclear reactors that use high velocity neutrons to maintain chain reactions.

Fault A surface or zone of rock fracture along which there has been displacement.

Feldspar A group of abundant rock-forming minerals of the general formula $MAl(Al,Si)_3O_8$ where M is K, Na, Ca, Ba, Rb, Sr.

Feldspathoid A group of uncommon aluminosilicate minerals of sodium, potassium, or calcium and having too little silica to form feldspar.

Ferric Referring to the oxidized form of iron, Fe^{3+}.

Ferro-alloy metal Any metal that can be alloyed with iron to produce a metal with special properties.

Ferromagnesian mineral Iron and magnesium containing minerals.

Ferromanganese An alloy of iron and manganese used in iron smelting.

Ferro-manganese nodules Rounded, concentrically laminated masses of iron and manganese oxides and hydroxides that form on the floors of oceans and some lakes.

Ferrosilicon A synthetic phase FeSi used in the steel industry as a means of removing oxygen from iron and steel during smelting.

Ferrous Referring to the reduced form of iron, Fe^{2+}.

Fertilizer Natural or synthetic substances used to promote plant growth.

Filler A mineral substance added to a product to increase the bulk or weight, to dilute expensive materials, or to improve the product.

Fire clay A siliceous clay rich in hydrous aluminum silicates, capable of withstanding high temperatures without deforming; hence used in the manufacture of refractory cements.

Fission (nuclear) The process by which a heavy nuclide is split into two or more lighter nuclides by the addition of a neutron to the nucleus.

Fissure A surface or fracture in rock along which there has been distinct separation.

Flint A dense fine-grained form of silica, SiO_2, that was commonly used in the making of stone tools and weapons.

Fluorite A mineral, composition CaF_2; a common and variably-colored substance widely used in the preparation of glasses, the manufacture of hydrofluoric acid, and the smelting of aluminum.

Fluorspar An alternate name for fluorite.

Flux Any substance that serves to promote a chemical reaction; also, the number of radioactive particles in a given volume of space multiplied by their mean velocity.

Fly ash Fine particulates that are formed during the burning of fossil fuels, especially coal.

Forsterite A mineral, composition Mg_2SiO_4; a member of the olivine series of minerals.

Fossil fuel A general term for any hydrocarbon deposit that may be used for fuel—petroleum, natural gas, coal, tar, or oil shale.

Fractionation See distillation.

Frasch process A method of sulfur mining in which superheated water is forced down a well to melt sulfur that is then pumped to the surface for recovery.

Fuel element (or fuel rod) The long rodlike assemblies that contain the U_3O_8 pellets used as fuel in a nuclear fission reactor.

Fuel rods The long rodlike assemblies that contain enriched uranium and serve as fuel in nuclear power plants.

Fuller's earth A fine-grained earthy substance (usually a clay) possessing a high absorptive capacity; originally used in fulling woolen fabrics, the shrinking and thickening by application of moisture.

Fulling The process of thickening a cloth by moistening, heating, and pressing.

Fusion (nuclear) The combination of two light nuclei to form a heavier nucleus; a reaction accompanied by the release of large amounts of energy.

Gabbro A dark-colored, coarse-grained igneous rock composed primarily of plagioclase feldspar, and pyroxene.

Gangue A general term for the nonuseful minerals and rocks intermixed with valuable ore minerals.

Garnet A group of minerals of general formula $A_3B_2(SiO_4)_3$ where $A = Ca, Mg, Fe^{2+}$, and Mn^{2+} and $B = Al, Fe^{3+}, Mn^{3+}$, and Cr.

Garnierite A general term for hydrous nickel silicates with the approximate composition $(Ni,Mg)_3Si_2O_5(OH)_4$; an ore mineral of nickel.

Gasohol A mixture of gasoline and alcohol used as a fuel for automobiles.

Geochemical balance The distribution of chemical elements and chemical compounds among various types of rocks, waters, and the atmosphere.

Geochemical cycling The cyclical movement of chemical elements through the earth's lithosphere, hydrosphere, and atmosphere.

Geochemically scarce metals Metals with a natural geochemical abundance of less than 0.1 percent.

Geopressured zone A rock unit in which the fluid pressure is greater than that of normal hydrostatic pressure.

Geothermal energy Useful heat energy that can be extracted from naturally-occurring steam, or hot rocks or waters.

Geothermal field An area where there is the development, or potential development, of geothermal energy.

Geothermal gradient The rate of increase in temperature in the earth as a function of depth; the average is 25°C per kilometer.

Global 2000 Report to the President A large report on the status of the world's resources, population, and environment from 1975–2000 A.D. prepared for President Carter in 1980.

Gneiss A coarse-grained, layered, metamorphic rock.

Goethite The hydrated ferric oxide mineral, FeO•OH.

Grade The content of a metal or a mineral in a rock; usually expressed as a percentage by weight for most ores.

Granite A coarse-grained igneous rock consisting mainly of quartz and potassium feldspar, usually accompanied by mica, either muscovite or biotite.

Granodiorite A coarse-grained igneous rock consisting mainly of quartz, potassium feldspar, plagioclase, and biotite.

Graphite A mineral, composition C; a soft, black compound with a pronounced cleavage, widely used as a lubricant.

Gravel A general term for both naturally-occurring and artificially ground rock particles in the size range 2–20 millimeters in diameter.

Greenhouse effect The warming of the earth's atmosphere brought about by an increase in the CO_2 content.

Greensand An unconsolidated marine sediment consisting largely of dark, greenish grains of glauconite, a complex potassium-iron aluminosilicate; also used for a foundry sand composed of silica and clay.

Guano Accumulated bird or bat excrement; mined locally as a source of fertilizer.

Gusher An oil or gas well in which the high pressures encountered during drilling are sufficient to cause fountaining of the oil, gas, and accompanying water at the surface.

Gypsum A mineral, composition $CaSO_4 \bullet 2H_2O$; formed by evaporation of seawater and used to make plaster-of-Paris.

Haber-Bosch process A process perfected in Germany in the early 1900s by which nitrogen from the earth's atmosphere is fixed into ammonia so that it can be used in fertilizers and chemicals.

Half-life (of an isotope) The time required for half of the quantity of a naturally radioactive isotope to decay to a daughter product.

Hectorite A lithium-rich clay mineral closely related to montmorillonite.

Heliostat An assemblage of mirrors that is programmed to automatically track the sun in order to constantly focus the sun on a central receiver.

Hematite A mineral, composition Fe_2O_3; an important ore mineral used as a source of iron, as a polishing powder, and a cosmetic (rouge).

High level wastes Highly reactive nuclear wastes consisting primarily of spent uranium fuel rods.

High quality energy Solar generated, thermal energy with temperatures greater than 100°C.

Homogeneous reactor A nuclear reactor in which the fuel and moderator are intimately mixed.

Homogeneous system Fission reactors in which the nuclear fuel and the moderator are intimately mixed.

Horsepower A unit for measuring power originally derived from the pulling power of a horse. The rate at which energy must be expended in order to raise 55 pounds at a rate of 1 foot per second.

Hot dry rock Geothermal energy systems that involve the extraction of heat from dry rocks at depth.

Humic coals Coal derived from peat by the breakdown of plant matter by organic acids.

Humus The generally dark, more or less stable part of the organic matter of the soil so well decomposed that the original sources cannot be identified.

Hydration The process by which water is chemically bound in a chemical compound.

Hydraulic mining The use of high-pressure jets of water to dislodge unconsolidated rock or sediment so that it can be processed.

Hydroelectricity Electricity generated by water-driven turbines.

Hydrogenation A chemical process in which hydrogen is added to complex hydrocarbons to yield less complex molecules that have higher H to C ratios.

Hydrograph A diagram recording the relationship between time and the quantity of water leaving a drainage basin.

Hydrolysis A chemical process by which a compound incorporates water into its structure.

Hydro-mulching The application of a soil covering to prevent evaporation and erosion by means of a high-pressure hose.

Hydro-seeding The application of seed to barren soil surfaces by means of a high-pressure hose.

Hydrosphere The waters of the earth.

Hydrothermal alteration Mineralogic changes in rocks resulting from interactions with hydrothermal solutions.

Hydrothermal fluids Hot aqueous fluids, commonly rich in dissolved salts and frequently responsible for the deposition of metal-bearing veins.

Hydrothermal solutions Hot, aqueous solutions, some of which transport and deposit ore minerals.

Igneous A term applied to a rock or mineral that has solidified from magma.

Ilmenite A mineral, composition $FeTiO_3$; a principal ore mineral of titanium.

Impermeable Referring to a rock, sediment, or soil that does not permit the passage of fluids.

In situ leaching The extraction of metals or salts by passing solutions through rocks that have been fractured but not excavated.

Inclines (in mines) Drifts or shafts in mines that are at an angle to the horizontal.

Index of weathering A measure of the weathering characteristics of minerals.

Industrial mineral Any rock or mineral, of economic value, exclusive of metallic ores, mineral fuels, and gem stones.

Inertial confinement A nuclear fusion process in which large amounts of energy are fired into mixtures of hydrogen isotopes.

Ingot A mass of cast metal as it comes from a mold or a crucible.

Intermediate-level waste Radioactive waste with intermediate levels of activity; usually components from reactors and transport flasks and liquids from reactors.

Intrazonal soil One of the soil orders. All soils with more or less well-developed soil characteristics reflecting the dominant influence of relief, parent rock, or age over that of climate.

Ion Any charged atom.

Ion exchange The reversible replacement of certain ions by others, without change in the crystal structure.

Iron Age The period that began about 1100 B.C. with the widespread use of iron for tools and weapons. It followed the Bronze Age and, in a sense, continues today.

Ironstones Sedimentary rocks of large lateral extent that contain significant amounts of iron oxides, hydroxides, and silicates as coatings on, and replacements of, sedimentary mineral fragments and fossils.

Isotopes Species of the same chemical element having the same number of protons but differing numbers of neutrons in the nucleus.

Itabirite A metamorphosed banded iron formation consisting of thin bands of hematite and silica.

Joule A unit of energy equal to 0.24 calorie, or the flow of 1 ampere of electrical energy for 1 second at a potential of 1 volt.

Kaolinite A mineral, composition $Al_2Si_2O_5(OH)_4$; a common, light-colored clay mineral.

Kerogen Fossilized, insoluble organic material found in sedimentary rocks. Can be converted by distillation to petroleum products.

Kimberlite The rock type of which diamonds occur; a porphyritic alkalic peridotite containing olivine, mica, and chromium-garnet.

Kupferschiefer A copper-bearing, Permian shale present throughout much of northern Europe.

Kyanite A mineral, composition Al_2SiO_5; a compound found in certain metamorphic rocks and used in the manufacture of ceramics and glass.

Lag-time diagram A diagram that illustrates the relationship between rainfall and surface runoff of a drainage basin in terms of time.

Lake Superior type Precambrian banded iron formations of the type present in the Lake Superior District of North America.

Laterite A highly leached soil zone in tropical regions that is rich in iron oxides.

Leucoxene A general term for fine-grained alteration products of ilmenite, $FeTiO_3$.

Level (in a mine) A main underground passageway leading out from a shaft that provides access to mine working.

Liberation (of minerals) The freeing of valuable mineral particles from valueless gangue.

Lightweight aggregate Aggregate of appreciably lower specific gravity than normal rock or aggregate; prepared by using very lightweight clays or porous materials.

Lime The compound CaO; usually prepared by calcining limestone.

Limestone A bedded sedimentary rock comprised largely of the mineral calcite, $CaCO_3$.

Limonite A general term for amorphous brown, naturally-occurring hydrous ferric oxides with a general composition of approximately $2Fe_2O_3 \bullet 3H_2O$.

Lipids Fats or fatty oils.

Liquid immiscibility The inability of two liquids to mix and form a single, homogeneous liquid. Oil and water are immiscible.

Lithosphere The rocks forming the surface of the earth to a depth of about 60 kilometers and which behave as rigid "plates."

Loam A rich, permeable soil composed of a friable mixture of roughly equal proportions of clay, silt, and sand and naturally containing organic matter.

Low quality energy Solar generated, thermal energy with temperatures less than 100°C.

Macadam A road made by the addition of successive layers of finer and finer pulverized rock. Named for the developer of the process, John McAdam of Scotland.

Macerals The organic components of coal. Macerals are to coal what minerals are to a rock.

Mafic A term applied to igneous rocks composed primarily of one or more ferromagnesian minerals (most mafic rocks are also basic, i.e., having SiO_2 contents less than 54 percent).

Magma Molten rock beneath the surface of the earth.

Magmatic differentiation The changes that occur in the composition of a magma during processes of crystallization.

Magnesia The compound MgO; the rare mineral periclase has this composition. MgO is widely used in refractories.

Magnesite A mineral, composition $MgCO_3$; an ore mineral of magnesium and of the raw material used to produce MgO.

Magnetite A mineral, composition Fe_3O_4; an important ore of iron.

Malleability The property of a metal that allows it to be plastically deformed under compressive stress, such as hammering.

Manganese nodules See ferro-manganese nodules.

Mantle That zone of the earth that lies below the crust and above the core (from approximately 10–30 kilometers to 3480 kilometers).

Marble A coarse-grained rock composed of calcite; usually formed by metamorphism of a limestone.

Marginal reserve That part of the reserve base of a mineral resource that borders on being economically producible.

Marsh gas See swamp gas.

Matte A mixture of metal sulfides and oxides produced by melting ore mineral concentrates.

Metagenesis Physical and chemical changes that occur in response to the high temperatures and pressures of deep burial; used especially in reference to organic material.

Metasomatism Change in the character of a rock as in metamorphism, but when chemical constituents are added or removed in the process.

Metal An element or alloy possessing high electrical and/or thermal conductivity that is malleable and ductile.

Metamorphic Pertaining to rocks in which the minerals have undergone chemical and structural changes due to changes in temperature and pressure.

Metamorphism The mineralogical and structural changes of solid rocks in response to the changes in temperature and pressure resulting from burial or adjacent igneous intrusion.

Methane A colorless, odorless, flammable gas, CH_4. The principal constituent of natural gas.

Mica A group of sheet silicate minerals with a general formula of $(K,Na,Ca)(Mg,Fe,Li,Al)_{2-3}(Al,Si)_4O_{10}(OH,F)_2$.

Milling The crushing and grinding of ores so that the useful materials may be separated from gangue materials.

Mineral resource The sum of a group of valuable minerals in a given volume of crust.

Minette type A variety of sedimentary iron ore. The European equivalent of the North American Clinton type ores.

Mining The process of extracting mineral substances from the earth, usually by digging holes or shafts.

Mississippi Valley type The term applied to a class of mineral deposits that is widespread in the drainage basin of the Mississippi River. Zinc and/or lead sulfide ores that occur in carbonate rocks.

Moderator (in a nuclear reactor) The medium, such as graphite, that moderates the flux of neutrons produced during radioactive decay.

Moh's scale A standard of 10 minerals by which the relative hardness of a mineral may be rated. From softest to hardest, they are: talc, gypsum, calcite, fluorite, apatite, orthoclase, quartz, topaz, corundum, and diamond.

Molybdenite A mineral, composition MoS_2; the principal ore mineral of molybdenum.

Montmorillonite A common clay mineral with the general formula, $R_{0.33}Al_2Si_4O_{10}(OH)_2 \bullet nH_2O$ where R is Na^+, K^+, Mg^{2+}, Ca^{2+}.

Monazite A rare-earth phosphate mineral, $(Ce,La,Nd,Th)(PO_4)$.

Mullite $Al_6Si_2O_{13}$; a rare mineral, but common synthetic material in ceramic products.

Muscovite mica White mica of composition $KAl_2(AlSi_3)O_{10}(OH)_2$.

Muskeg A bog with deep accumulations of organic material forming in poorly drained areas in northern temperate or arctic regions.

Natural cement A limestone-rich rock of such composition that it can be directly used as cement after calcining.

Nepheline syenite An igneous rock composed essentially of plagioclase feldspar and the feldspathoid mineral nepheline, $(Na,K)AlSiO_4$.

Niter Naturally-occurring potassium nitrate; saltpeter.

Nitrogen Chemical element number 7; 78 percent of the earth's atmosphere and one of the most important fertilizer elements.

Noble metal A metal with marked resistance to chemical reaction; a term often applied to gold, silver, mercury, and the platinum metal group; synonymous with precious metal.

Nonferrous metal A general term referring to metals that are not normally alloyed with iron.

Nonmetallic minerals A broadly used term for minerals that are extracted other than for use of the metals they contain or for use as fuel.

Nonpoint sources Sources of pollution that are dispersed such as farm fields, road surfaces.

Nonrenewable resources Resources that are fixed in total quantity in the earth's crust.

Norite A coarse-grained igneous rock composed of plagioclase and an orthopyroxene.

Nuclear fission The breakdown of large nucleus (e.g., of uranium) to smaller nuclei with the emission of large amounts of energy.

Nuclear fuel cycle The complete sequence of processes involved in the mining, processing, enrichment, utilization, and disposal of uranium that is used to generate nuclear power.

Nuclear fusion The joining together of the nuclei of very light elements (hydrogen, lithium) to form heavier elements with the release of large amounts of energy.

Nuclear reactor The vessel in which nuclear fuels are reacted to generate heat, in turn used to raise steam and drive turbines.

Obsidian Volcanic glass; usually black, but also red, green, or brown.

Ocean Thermal Energy Referring to a system that makes use of warm ocean surface waters and cold deep ocean waters to evaporate and condense a substance thus driving turbines and generating energy.

Oil mining The process of mining oil-bearing rock so that it can be processed to extract the oil.

Oil shale A fine-grained sedimentary rock containing much bituminous organic matter incorporated when the sediment was deposited.

Olivine A mineral, composition $(Fe,Mg)_2SiO_4$; an igneous mineral used in making refractories.

Open pit mining Mining from open excavations.

Ophiolite complex A sequence of mafic and ultramafic igneous rocks including metamorphic rocks, whose origin is associated with the early phases of ocean floor rifting.

Ore Resources of metals that can now be economically and legally extracted.

Ore deposit Equals "reserve" when referring to metal-bearing concentrations.

Ore mineral Broadly used to include any mineral from which metals can be extracted.

Osmotic pressure The pressure resulting from the movement of molecules or ions in a fluid through a semipermeable membrane as they seek to establish the same concentrations on both sides of the membrane.

Overburden The valueless rock that must be removed above a near-surface ore deposit to permit open-pit mining.

Oxidant A compound or element that brings about oxidation.

Oxidation Combination with oxygen; more generally, any reaction in which there is an increase in valence resulting from a loss of electrons.

Palygorskite A mineral, composition $(Mg,Al)_2Si_4O_{10}OH \bullet 4H_2O$; a variety of clay that is sometimes fibrous and used as asbestos.

Parabolic reflector A concave reflector so shaped that the impinging sun's rays are focused by reflection onto a central tube that becomes heated; as a result, the tube contains a fluid that transports the heat for use elsewhere.

Peat An unconsolidated deposit of semicarbonized plant remains accumulated in a water-saturated environment such as a swamp or bog. The early stage of coal formation.

Ped A naturally formed granule, block, crumb, or aggregate of a soil. See clod.

Pegmatite An exceptionally coarse-grained igneous rock; sometimes contains rich accumulations of rare elements such

as lithium, boron, fluorine, niobium, tantalum, uranium, and rare earths.

Peridotite A coarse-grained igneous rock composed chiefly of olivine and pyroxene.

Perlite A volcanic glass with a rhyolitic composition, a high water content, and a characteristic cracked pattern.

Permeable A rock, sediment, or soil with the capacity of transmitting a fluid.

Petroleum A naturally-occurring complex liquid hydrocarbon that after distillation yields a range of combustible fuels, petrochemicals, and lubricants.

pH A measure of acidity expressed numerically from 0–14; neutral is 7, with lower values representing more acid conditions. Specifically, the negative logarithm of the H^+ concentration.

Phanerozoic type Ironstone deposits formed during the Phanerozoic.

Phosphate(s) Compounds, including some minerals, containing phosphorus in the form of the phosphate (PO_4^{3+}) anion.

Phosphorus Chemical element number 15; one of the most important fertilizer elements.

Photocell A layered chemical cell that produces electricity directly from light energy.

Photochemical conversion A chemical conversion that proceeds by the addition of energy in the form of electromagnetic radiation.

Photochemical reaction A chemical reaction promoted by the presence of electromagnetic radiation.

Photochemical smog A general term for visible atmospheric pollution that results from solar radiation-induced chemical reactions.

Photoelectrochemical conversion The chemical process active in a photogalvanic cell.

Photogalvanic A term used for a chemical reaction in which solar energy is converted directly into electrical energy.

Photosynthesis The process by which green plants use the radiant energy from the sun to create hydrocarbons and release oxygen.

Photovoltaic cell See photocell.

Pickling (of metals) The use of an acid bath to cleanse the surface of metal castings, sheet metal, etc.

Pig iron The raw iron produced during the smelting of iron ore.

Pigment A coloring agent.

Pitchblende A massive, brown to black, fine-grained variety of uraninite, UO_2; a term commonly applied to any black uranium ore.

Placer deposits A surficial mineral deposit formed by mechanical concentration of mineral particles from weathered debris.

Plagioclase feldspars A series of silicate minerals involving a solid solution from $CaAl_2Si_2O_8$ (anorthite) to $NaAlSi_3O_8$ (albite).

Plasma A fourth state of matter (solid, liquid, gas, plasma) capable of conducting magnetic force, usually generated by application of extremely high temperatures.

Plasterboard A common building material consisting of gypsum encased in cardboard in the form of 4×8 ft sheets.

Plaster-of-Paris Partially dehydrated gypsum, $CaSO_4 \bullet \frac{1}{2}H_2O$.

Podiform Referring to ore bodies with an elongate lenticular shape; especially some chromite ores.

Point source A single point, such as a smoke stack or pipe, from which pollution emanates.

Pollution The presence of abnormal substances or abnormally high concentrations of normal substances in the natural environment.

Polyhalite A mineral, composition $K_2MgCa_2(SO_4)_4 \cdot 2H_2O$; a principal ore mineral of potassium.

Polypedon A three-dimensional body of soil consisting of more than one recognizable soil type.

Polymorph One form of a mineral that is known to exist in more than one crystallographic form; e.g., graphite and diamond are polymorphs of carbon.

Porphyrin A large, complex, organic ring compound, e.g., chlorophyll and hemoglobin.

Porphyry copper deposit A low-grade copper deposit in which the copper minerals occur in disseminated grains or veinlets and which is closely related to an intermediate composition porphyritic intrusive igneous rock.

Porphyry-type An igneous rock that contains large crystals embedded in a fine-grained groundmass.

Portland cement A calcium aluminosilicate produced by calcining limestone and clay. This finely ground product will recrystallize and set when water is added.

Potable water Water that is safe for human use.

Potash A term locally used for potassium oxide or potassium hydroxide or to define the potassium oxide content of minerals.

Potassium Chemical element number 19; one of the most important fertilizer elements.

Pot line A series of large potlike electric furnaces in which bauxite is smelted to aluminum.

Power The measure of energy produced or used as a function of time. See horsepower.

Pozzolan cement A cement formed by grinding together hydrated lime and a pozzolana, a natural volcanic glass capable of reacting with the lime at ordinary temperatures to form cement compounds.

Precious metal The scarce metals that have high value—traditionally, gold, silver, and the platinum group metals.

Primary mineral A mineral formed at the same time as the rock enclosing it by igneous or hydrothermal processes.

Primary recovery Petroleum production that occurs as a result of natural flow or pumping.

Prior appropriation (of water) The law that permits the buying and selling of specified amounts of water from a stream for "beneficial use." The appropriations are honored in order of the oldest first.

Pumice A light-colored, vesicular, glassy rock formed by the eruption of gas-rich lava from a volcano.

Pumped-water storage system Hydroelectric power sys-

tems in which excess electricity at low demand times is used to pump water into a storage dam so that it can subsequently be used to generate electricity.

Pyrolysis   Chemical decomposition by the action of heat.

Pyrometallurgy   The metallurgical process involved in separating and refining metals where heat is used, as in roasting and smelting.

Pyroxene   A group of silicate minerals of general formula $WSiO_3$ (or $XYSi_2O_6$) where $W = Mg, Fe$; $XY = Mg, Ca, Fe, Na, Li$, etc.

Pyroxenite   A rock composed primarily of pyroxene.

Pyrrhotite   A mineral, composition $Fe_{1-x}S$; a common iron sulfide compound.

Quarry   An open surface working usually dug for the extraction of building stone.

Quartz   A mineral, composition SiO_2; a very common compound that is hard, lacks cleavage, and does not weather rapidly.

Quartzite   A metamorphic rock derived from sandstone and composed primarily of quartz.

Radiation   The process by which energy (or the energy itself) is emitted from molecules and atoms due to internal changes.

Radioactivity   See decay (radioactive).

Raise (in a mine)   A vertical opening connecting two levels of a mine.

Rank   A coal classification based upon physical, chemical, and thermal properties.

Rare-earth elements   The 15 elements from atomic numbers 57 to 71, including, for example, lanthanum (La), cerium (Ce), neodymium (Nd), europium (Eu).

Recycling   The reuse of metals or other materials.

Refining   Metallurgically—the process of extracting pure metals from their mineralogical forms; petroleum—the process of distilling and cracking crude oil in order to produce a wide variety of separate hydrocarbon liquids and gases.

Refractory   A term used for unreactive materials with high melting points used to line the furnaces in which metals are smelted or fuels burned.

Regolith   A general term for the surface layer of loose material that forms as a result of the weathering of rock.

Renewable resources   Resources that are naturally replenished by processes active in or on the earth's crust.

Reserve (of minerals)   Mineral resources that can now be economically and legally extracted.

Reserve base   That part of an identified resource that meets certain minimum physical and chemical criteria to present economic potential and that has a reasonable potential for becoming economic within planning horizons.

Reservoir rock   Any rock with adequate porosity and that contains liquid or gaseous hydrocarbons.

Resource   Naturally-occurring concentrations of liquids, gases, or solids in or on the earth's crust in such form and amount that economic extraction of a commodity is currently or potentially feasible.

Retort   A furnacelike chamber used to distill volatile materi-

als or to carry out the destructive distillation of coal or oil shale. Heat is usually applied externally, and the decomposition products are collected by cooling the gases so that different compounds condense at different temperatures.

Reverse osmosis   A process by which salt-free water is forced through a semipermeable membrane from a saline solution.

Rhyolite   A fine-grained extrusive igneous rock consisting largely of quartz and potassium feldspar.

Ribonucleic acid   RNA, a substance similar to DNA. It carries out DNA's instructions for making proteins.

Richter Scale   A scale used in the quantitative evaluation of the energy released by earthquakes.

Riparian   Pertaining to the shoreline areas of a body of water. Riparian law allows land owners to draw from a lake or stream adjacent to their property if their use does not harm other users.

Roasting   Heating of an ore to bring about some change, usually oxidation, of the sulfide or other minerals.

Rocksalt   Coarsely crystalline halite, naturally occurring or synthetically prepared.

Rotary drills   The commonest method of drilling. A hydraulic process in which a hard-toothed drill bit is attached to a rotating drill pipe. As the pipe turns, the bit grinds into the rock; the loose pieces are carried to the surface by fluid circulated down the center of the pipe.

Rutile   A mineral, composition TiO_2. The principal ore of titanium; used as a white paint pigment.

Salinization   The buildup of salts, usually $NaCl$, in soils as a result of evaporation.

Salt water intrusion   The movement of salt water into an aquifer, usually as a result of excessive extraction of freshwater near coastal areas.

Saltpeter   Naturally-occurring potassium nitrate; niter.

Sand   Detrital rock fragments 1/16 to 2 millimeters in diameter; natural sands are composed almost entirely of quartz.

Sandstone   A medium-grained, clastic sedimentary rock composed of sandsized particles (commonly largely quartz).

Saponite   A mineral, composition $(Ca/2,Na)_{0.33}(Mg,Fe)_3(Si_{3.67},Al_{0.33})O_{10}(OH)_2 \bullet 4H_2O$; a soft, soapy light-colored clay.

Sapropelic coal   Coal derived from organic residues (finely divided plant debris, spores, and algae) in stagnant or standing bodies of water.

Scarce metals   Metals whose average crustal abundance is less than 0.1 percent.

Secondary mineral   A mineral formed later than the rock enclosing it and usually at the expense of earlier primary minerals.

Secondary recovery   Oil production resulting from procedures, such as the injection of water, steam, or chemical compounds into a reservoir in order to increase oil production beyond primary production.

Sedimentary   Pertaining to rocks formed from the accumulation of fragments weathered from preexisting rocks, or by precipitation of materials in solution in lake or seawater.

Seismograph An instrument that records vibrations of the earth, especially those from earthquakes.

Sepiolite A mineral, composition $Mg_4(Si_2O_5)_3(OH)_2 \bullet 6H_2O$; a common clay that is widely used for ornamental carvings; also known as meerschaum.

Serpentine A group of minerals, general composition $(Mg,Fe)_3Si_2O_5(OH)_4$; widely formed in metamorphism with varieties including gems (jade) and asbestos (chrysotile).

Serpentinite A rock composed primarily of serpentine group minerals and formed through the alteration of preexisting ferromagnesian minerals such as olivine and pyroxene.

Serpentinization A process in which hydrothermal fluids cause the conversion of magnesium-rich silicates into serpentine minerals.

Shaft (of a mine) A vertical entrance into a mine.

Shale A fine-grained, indurated, detrital sedimentary rock formed by the compaction of clay, silt, or mud and with a partially developed rock cleavage.

Silanes Hydrogen silicon gases that serve as intermediate reaction products in the preparation of ultrapure silicon used in semiconductors.

Silicon chip A chip of silicon metal to which trace amounts of other elements has been added in order to affect the electrical properties.

Sillimanite A mineral, composition Al_2SiO_5; a compound found in metamorphic rocks and used in the manufacture of ceramics and glass.

Skarn An assemblage of lime-bearing silicates derived from limestones and dolomites by the introduction of silicon, iron, and magnesium, usually adjacent to an igneous intrusion.

Slag The nonmetallic top layer that separates during the smelting of ores; it is usually rich in silica, alumina, lime, and any other materials used to flux the smelting.

Slate A compact, fine-grained metamorphic rock formed from shale; it possesses the property of rock cleavage whereby it can be readily parted along parallel planes.

Smectite A term applied to the montmorillonite group of clay minerals.

Smelting The chemical reduction of a metal from its ore usually by melting to separate the metal from a slag.

Soda ash Sodium carbonate.

Soil The unconsolidated earthy material that overlies bedrock and that is a complex mixture of inorganic and organic compounds; the natural medium to support the growth of plants.

Soil order One of ten major subdivisions in the "Comprehensive Soil Classification System."

Soil profile A vertical section through a soil that reveals the different physical and chemical zones that are present.

Soil temperature regime The changes in temperature experienced by a soil in a normal annual cycle.

Soil water regime The changes in the amounts of water present in a soil during a normal annual cycle.

Solar cells A layered chemical cell that converts solar energy directly into electricity.

Solar energy The total energy in the sun's radiation.

Soldering The use of a metal or metal alloy to join metallic surfaces.

Solid solution A solid crystalline phase in which the composition may vary by one or more elements replacing others, e.g., Fe replacing Mg in the olivine minerals Mg_2SiO_4–Fe_2SiO_4.

Solution mining The extraction of resources by solutions instead of conventional mining procedures.

Soot A black substance consisting mainly of carbon from the smoke of wood or coal.

Source rocks Sedimentary rocks containing the organic matter that under heat, pressure, and time is transformed into liquid or gaseous hydrocarbons.

Special metal Metals such as tantalum and beryllium that are used increasingly because of unusual properties important to industry.

Spinel A mineral, composition $MgAl_2O_4$; a common accessory mineral in many rocks; also refers to a crystal structure, common to some ore minerals, in which the external shape of an octahedron is often seen.

Spot market The buying and selling of commodities for immediate delivery at a price agreed upon at the time of sale.

Stainless steel An iron-based alloy containing enough chromium to confer a superior corrosion resistance.

Stannite A mineral, composition Cu_2FeSnS_4; an ore of tin.

Steam flooding The injection of superheated steam down an oil well in order to promote the release of oil trapped in the rocks.

Steel An iron-based alloy; other metals or substances are alloyed with the iron to impart specific properties such has hardness or strength.

Stock An igneous intrusion that is less than 40 square miles in surface exposure.

Stockworks A mineral deposit in the form of a network of veinlets.

Stone Age The period in human culture when stone was used for the making of tools. It began with the first humans and ended at various times in different places (e.g., about 3000 B.C. in Egypt and Mesopotamia) when bronze was used to make tools.

Stope The roomlike area in a mine where ores are extracted.

Stratification The layerlike nature of a sedimentary rock.

Stratiform Referring to an ore deposit that is layered and parallel to the enclosing strata.

Stratigraphic traps Sedimentary units such as sandstone lenses into which oil migrates and is prevented from further movement by surrounding impermeable layers.

Strip mining The removal of coal or other commodity by surface mining methods in which extraction is carried out in successive strips of land.

Structural traps Folded or faulted rocks into which oil migrates and from which farther migration is prevented.

Subeconomic reserves That part of identified resources that do not meet the economic criteria of reserves or marginal reserves.

Subsidence The natural- or artificially-induced dropping of the land surface resulting from the removal of the underlying rocks either by mining or ground water solution.

Superalloys Alloys that retain great mechanical strength or are very corrosion resistant at high temperatures.

Superphosphate A soluble mixture of calcium phosphates produced by reaction of phosphate rock with sulfuric acid; used as fertilizer.

Surface runoff The water that flows directly off the land surface and the water that, after infiltrating into the ground, is discharged onto the surface.

Swamp gas Methane, CH_4, produced during the decay of organic matter in stagnant water.

Syenite An igneous rock comprised largely of potassium feldspar, any of the feldspathoid minerals, and an amphibole. Quartz is rare or absent.

SYNROC A synthetic rock prepared to incorporate and hold radioactive waste products.

Tactite An alternate name for skarn.

Taconite A term used in the Lake Superior district for laminated iron ores consisting of iron oxides and silica or iron silicates.

Tailings The valueless materials discarded from mining operations.

Talc A mineral, composition $Mg_3Si_4O_{10}(OH)_2$; it is extremely soft, making it a valuable lubricant and cosmetic ingredient.

Tectonism A general term referring to movements of the earth's crust.

Thermal cracking The application of heat to break heavier hydrocarbons into lighter ones.

Thermal maturation The progressive change in organic matter in sedimentary rocks resulting from increasing temperature as the depth of burial increases.

Thermal pollution Abnormal heating of the environment, usually rivers, caused by the combustion of fossil fuels, by nuclear power generation, or industrial processing.

Thermogenic gas Gas formed as a result of the thermal breakdown of organic matter.

Tidal energy Energy derived from the movement of water during the rise and fall of the tides.

Transpiration The release of water vapor by plants during their normal respiration.

Traps Rock structures or beds in which oil accumulates and is prevented from further migration.

Tuff A compacted deposit of volcanic ash.

Ultramafic Said of igneous rocks composed chiefly of one ferromagnesian mineral (most ultramafic rocks are also ultrabasic, i.e., having SiO_2 contents less than about 44 percent).

Uravan district A uranium and vanadium mining district in eastern Utah and western Colorado.

Vadose Referring to water in the uppermost soil, the zone in which most intergranular interstices are air filled.

Vein A sheetlike infilling of a fracture by hydrothermally deposited minerals often containing ore minerals.

Vermiculite A group of clay minerals that are characterized by the tendency to undergo extreme expansion when heated above 150°C; widely used as an insulator and as a component in lightweight construction materials.

Vesicles Cavities in a lava formed by the evolution of gas during the rapid cooling of a molten lava.

Vitrification The formation of a glassy or noncrystalline substance.

Volcanic glass A natural glass produced by the rapid cooling of lava.

Volcanogenic massive sulfide Copper-, zinc-, and lead-bearing sulfide deposits formed in volcanic terrains as a result of hydrothermal fluids issuing onto the seafloor.

Water flooding The injection of water into an oil well to promote the release of oil trapped in the rock.

Water glass An aqueous solution of sodium silicate.

Water logging The process by which water accumulates in soils and results in the drowning of plants.

Water table The surface in a soil or rock below which all the voids are water filled.

Watt A unit of power equal to work done at a rate of 1 joule per second; approximately equal to 1/746 horsepower.

Weatherability The rate at which weathering affects the physical and chemical nature of a rock or mineral.

Weathering The progressive breakdown of rocks, physically and chemically, in response to exposure at or near the earth's surface.

Wet steam Natural geothermal systems dominated by hot waters with associated steam.

Wind farms Clusters of windmills constructed with the potential of producing commercial amounts of electricity.

Winze A vertical opening connecting two levels of a mine. The same as a raise.

Withdrawal The extraction of water from a surface or ground water source.

Work Usually the result of applied force, defined as the product of the force and the displacement. Usually expressed in foot-pounds, joules, or kilowatt-hours.

Yellowcake A general term for yellow oxidized uranium oxide arising from concentration in the mining and processing of uranium ore.

Zeolite A group of hydrous aluminosilicate minerals characterized by their easy exchange of water and cations; used as catalysts in oil refining.

Zircon A mineral, composition $ZrSiO_4$; a common accessory mineral in many rocks; the main source of zirconium.

Zonal soil One of the soil orders that have well-developed characteristics that reflect the agents of soil genesis, especially climate and the action of organisms.

INDEX